MW00830722

"The ministry of John MacArthur has had a worldwide impact. The book clearly unfolds the doctrines that are at the heart of this ministry, which has touched so many. Here we see a ministry built on truth—the truth of God's Word and the truth of the gospel. A wonderful resource for students, pastors, and professors."

Thomas R. Schreiner, James Buchanan Harrison Professor of New Testament Interpretation, The Southern Baptist Theological Seminary

"This book comes from a lifetime of studying and from the garnered wisdom of centuries. In combining devotion to Scripture with commitment to biblical doctrine, it addresses a great contemporary need. Strong beliefs make strong churches. One does not have to agree with the esteemed author on every subject to be thankful for a volume of rich and enduring importance."

Iain H. Murray, author, *Jonathan Edwards: A New Biography* and *Evangelical Holiness*; Founding Trustee, Banner of Truth Trust

"It is a delight to wholeheartedly recommend *Essential Christian Doctrine.* It will be celebrated for the clarity of its outline and description of the Bible's doctrines. It is just too good to miss."

Walter C. Kaiser Jr., President Emeritus and Colman M. Mockler Distinguished Professor Emeritus of Old Testament, Gordon-Conwell Theological Seminary

"The emphasis of John MacArthur's ministry has always been preaching—unleashing God's truth by preaching God's Word. All the while, his ministry has been undergirded by doctrine—doctrine drawn carefully, consistently from the Bible. His thousands of expository sermons stand as proof of his faithfulness to the work of the preacher; *Essential Christian Doctrine* stands as proof of faithfulness to the work of the theologian. May both be used to encourage a new generation of preacher-theologians to commit their lives to the high calling of teaching and equipping Christ's church."

Tim Challies, blogger, Challies.com

"Clarity ought to be an essential requirement of books on systematic theology. And this one offers just that! A comprehensive summary of all that a Christian needs to know—sounds like something every Christian should have available, doesn't it? And written by a name that epitomizes orthodoxy and truth—John MacArthur. Enough said. It speaks for itself."

Derek W. H. Thomas, Senior Minister, First Presbyterian Church, Columbia, South Carolina; Teaching Fellow, Ligonier Ministries; Chancellor's Professor, Reformed Theological Seminary

"This volume is the life achievement of almost fifty years of preaching in one pulpit by this world-class expositor, John MacArthur. He has stood, week after week, even decade after decade, plumbing the depths of the biblical text and connecting its truths together, leading to this well-constructed body of divinity. Here is the crown jewel from this brilliant pastor and author that will cause the truth of Scripture to shine even brighter before our eyes."

Steven J. Lawson, President, OnePassion Ministries; Professor of Preaching, The Master's Seminary; Teaching Fellow, Ligonier Ministries

"For decades John MacArthur has exemplified expository preaching, putting on full display the Word of God for the people of God. This systematic theology demonstrates how his verse-by-verse exposition naturally blossoms into a robust, colorful theological mosaic. This book is the theological dessert at the end of an expository meal. Regardless of your theological heritage, I encourage every Christian to sit under the doctrinal teaching of MacArthur. Certainly, you will walk away saturated in Scripture, left in total awe after relishing the majesty and glory of our gracious God."

Matthew Barrett, Associate Professor of Christian Theology, Midwestern Baptist Theological Seminary; Executive Editor, Credo Magazine; editor, *Reformation Theology*

"In addition to presenting orthodox theology common to historic Protestants, MacArthur defends an unusual combination of views that evangelicals debate, such as young-earth creationism, Calvinist soteriology, credobaptism, elder-rule polity, complementarianism, cessationism, and traditional dispensationalism (or what he calls futuristic premillennialism). He argues in a clear and orderly way that is worth engaging even if you disagree."

Andy Naselli, Associate Professor of Systematic Theology and New Testament, Bethlehem College and Seminary; Elder, Bethlehem Baptist Church, Minneapolis

"As a professor of theology, I am able to recommend this single volume on systematic theology to my students and tell them with confidence that this is a book I can endorse from cover to cover. I especially appreciate the dispensational aspects of this work and the way it consistently and firmly grounds the doctrines in the biblical text."

Kevin D. Zuber, Professor of Theology, The Master's Seminary; contributor, *Evidence for the Rapture* and *The Moody Bible Commentary*

ESSENTIAL CHRISTIAN DOCTRINE

ESSENTIAL CHRISTIAN DOCTRINE

A Handbook on Biblical Truth

JOHN MACARTHUR

GENERAL EDITOR

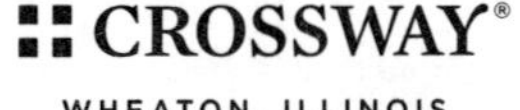

WHEATON, ILLINOIS

Essential Christian Doctrine: A Handbook on Biblical Truth

Published by Crossway
1300 Crescent Street
Wheaton, Illinois 60187

Cover design: Tim Green, Faceout Studios

Cover image: Shutterstock #575008792

First printing 2021

Printed in the United States of America

There are also citations of the Revised Standard Version (RSV) and the Holman Christian Standard Version (HCSB).

Italics in Scripture quotations have been added.

Hardcover ISBN: 978-1-4335-7185-5
ePub ISBN: 978-1-4335-7188-6
PDF ISBN: 978-1-4335-7186-2
Mobipocket ISBN: 978-1-4335-7187-9

Library of Congress Cataloging-in-Publication Data

Names: MacArthur, John, 1939- editor.
Title: Essential Christian doctrine : a handbook on biblical truth / general editor, John MacArthur.
Description: Wheaton, Illinois : Crossway, [2021] | Includes bibliographical references and index.
Identifiers: LCCN 2020038522 (print) | LCCN 2020038523 (ebook) | ISBN 9781433571855 (hardcover) | ISBN 9781433571879 (mobi) | ISBN 9781433571862 (pdf) | ISBN 9781433571886 (epub)
Subjects: LCSH: Theology, Doctrinal.
Classification: LCC BT65 .E76 2021 (print) | LCC BT65 (ebook) | DDC 230—dc23
LC record available at https://lccn.loc.gov/2020038522
LC ebook record available at https://lccn.loc.gov/2020038523

Crossway is a publishing ministry of Good News Publishers.

LB 30 29 28 27 26 25 24 23 22 21
15 14 13 12 11 10 9 8 7 6 5 4 3 2 1

CONTENTS

ILLUSTRATIONS AND TABLES

PREFACE

THE OBJECTIVE OF STUDYING Scripture is not merely to equip the believer to repeat its words; it is to equip him to understand the accurate *sense* of its words—the *truth* that the Scripture yields. Rising out of the Bible in all its forms—whether it is history, prophecy, poetry, narrative, or instruction—is propositional truth, definitive doctrine authored by the Holy Spirit that becomes the framework of both Christian theology and Christian living.

While some would consider doctrine divisive, doctrine is the one reality that unites the people of God around the truth. Any other kind of unity is superficial and sentimental.

In 2017, Crossway published *Biblical Doctrine*, which was a systematic summary of doctrine that is the foundation of The Master's Seminary. I was thrilled to oversee its publication and grateful for the investment made into that volume by Dr. Richard Mayhue and the faculty of The Master's Seminary. In particular, I have special appreciation for Nathan Busenitz and Michael Riccardi for all their work in bringing that project to fruition. We are gratified that the book has had a far-reaching response. It is now available not only in English but also in French, Spanish, and German, with eleven more languages in the process of translation. We are grateful for this global interest and are assured it will serve to bring honor and glory to our Lord in his church.

Realizing, however, the length and detail of the book, it became apparent that we needed to create a condensed version—a work that would retain the doctrinal clarity of the original but would be more accessible to those reluctant to embark upon a 1,000-page volume. The result is the book you hold in your hands. It is condensed only in length, not in substance. It retains the core biblical definitions of all the doctrines discussed in *Biblical Doctrine*, so that the dedicated and discerning reader will be able to grasp the full breadth of Christian theology. While the original is intended as a reference book, this one is designed to be read from cover to cover. Anyone who does that will find an accurate, consistent, biblical presentation of essential Christian doctrine.

It is a profound joy to be able to provide in these 300-plus pages a theological education to every reader. These are not speculations; this is God's truth systematized from Genesis to Revelation, revealing one author—the Spirit of God—and demonstrating that the Bible is so consistent as to be its own interpreter. As a result of reading, the student of this book will also learn hermeneutics—the science of biblical interpretation—by seeing how all the passages are faithfully interpreted leading to the accuracy and consistency of doctrine.

I am grateful to Professor Michael Riccardi and Dr. Kevin Zuber for their oversight and dedication in condensing the original work. I also want to thank Dr. Peter Sammons, Dr. Brad Klassen, Professor Chris Burnett, and TMS graduates Herald Gandi and Kevin VanTongeren for their work on the first drafts of the project.

It is my prayer that a generation of faithful Christians will enjoy unity in the truth. May God be pleased to use this volume to that end, to the praise of the glory of his grace.

JOHN MACARTHUR
Pastor, Grace Community Church
Chancellor, The Master's University and Seminary

ABBREVIATIONS

Standard Abbreviations

ca.	about, approximately
cf.	confer, compare
chap.	chapter
e.g.	*exempli gratia* (Lat., "for example")
esp.	especially
Gk.	Greek
Heb.	Hebrew
i.e.	*id est* (Lat., "that is")
Lat.	Latin
lit.	literally
mg.	marginal reading (in Scripture citations)

Resource Abbreviations

MNTC	MacArthur New Testament Commentary
MSJ	*The Master's Seminary Journal*

1

INTRODUCTION

Prolegomena

THE TERM *PROLEGOMENA* ORIGINATED from the combination of two Greek words, *pro*, meaning "before," and *legō*, meaning "to say," which together convey the general sense of "to say beforehand" or "to say in advance." A prolegomena chapter serves as a prologue or a preliminary discussion that introduces and defines the central content of the work that follows. These prefatory comments include assumptions, definitions, methodology, and purposes, thereby providing a context for understanding the subsequent content. Here the prolegomena discussion is organized by giving answers to a series of significant questions that will prepare the reader for the rest of this study.

What Is Theology?

Christian theology is the study of the divine revelation in the Bible. It has God as its perpetual centerpiece, God's Word as its source, and godliness as its aim. As Alva McClain puts it, summarizing Romans 11:36,

> Out of God all things come—He is the origin. Through God all things exist—He is the sustainer of all things. Unto God—back to God—He is the goal. There is the circle of eternity: *out, through, back.*[1]

David Wells has crafted a notable working definition of Christian theology:

> Theology is the sustained effort to know the character, will, and acts of the triune God as he has disclosed and interpreted these for his people in Scripture . . . in order that we might know him, learn to think our thoughts

1 Alva J. McClain, *Romans: The Gospel of God's Grace* (Chicago: Moody Press, 1973), 204.

after him, live our lives in his world on his terms, and by thought and action project his truth into our own time and culture.[2]

The apostle John died in about AD 98. With his writing of Revelation, the canon of Scripture was completed and closed. It did not take long for succeeding generations to begin writing about scriptural truth. Some of the more significant authors and their volumes include the following:

- Unknown author, *The Didache* (ca. 110)
- Irenaeus (ca. 120–202), *Proof of the Apostolic Preaching*
- Clement of Alexandria (ca. 150–ca. 215), *Stromata*
- Origen (ca. 184–ca. 254), *On First Principles*
- Gregory of Nazianzus (ca. 330–ca. 389), *Five Theological Orations*
- Augustine (354–430), *Enchiridion*
- John of Damascus (ca. 675–ca. 749), *An Exact Exposition of the Orthodox Faith*
- Peter Lombard (ca. 1095–ca. 1169), *Four Books of Sentences*
- Thomas Aquinas (1225–1274), *Summa Theologica*
- John Calvin (1509–1564), *Institutes of the Christian Religion*
- Thomas Watson (ca. 1620–1686), *A Body of Divinity*
- Francis Turretin (1623–1687), *Institutes of Elenctic Theology*
- John Gill (1697–1771), *A Body of Doctrinal Divinity*
- John Dick (1764–1833), *Lectures on Theology*

Why Study Theology?

Scottish pastor and theologian John Dick answered this penetrating query with seven profound responses. A better and more succinct answer would be difficult to come by:[3]

1. "To ascertain the character of God in its aspect towards us"
2. "To contemplate the display of his attributes in his works and dispensations"
3. "To discover his designs toward man in his original and his present state"
4. "To know this mighty Being, as far as he may be known, [which] is the noblest aim of the human understanding"
5. "To learn our duty to him, the means of enjoying his favor, the hopes which we are authorized to entertain, and the wonderful expedient by which our fallen race is restored to purity and happiness"

2 David Wells, "The Theologian's Craft," in *Doing Theology in Today's World: Essays in Honor of Kenneth S. Kantzer*, ed. John D. Woodbridge and Thomas Edward McComisky (Grand Rapids, MI: Zondervan, 1991), 172.

3 John Dick, *Lectures on Theology* (Cincinnati, OH: Applegate, 1856), 6.

6. "To love him, the most worthy exercise of our affections"
7. "To serve him, the most honourable and delightful purpose to which we can devote our time and talents"

What Are the Various Major Kinds of Theology?

1. *Biblical theology*: The organization of Scripture thematically by biblical chronology or by biblical author with respect to the progressive revelation of the Bible (properly a component of systematic theology)
2. *Dogmatic theology*: The organization of Scripture with an emphasis on favored or selected church creeds
3. *Exegetical theology*: The methodical organization of Scripture by dealing exegetically with individual texts of the Bible (properly a component of both biblical and systematic theology)
4. *Historical theology*: The historical study of doctrinal developments after the apostolic era to the present time
5. *Natural theology*: The study of what can be known about God by human reason alone through the empirical study of the natural world
6. *Pastoral/practical theology*: The organization of Scripture with an emphasis on the personal application of doctrinal truth in the lives of the church and individual Christians
7. *Systematic theology*: The organization of Scripture by a synthesis of scriptural teaching, summarized using major categories that encompass the entirety of God's written revelation (developed from exegetical and biblical theology)

What Is Systematic Theology?

The term *systematic* comes from the compound Greek word made up of *syn*, "together," and *histanai*, "to set up," meaning "to set up together" or "to systematize." As noted above, *theology* comes from the Greek word *theologia*, "a word about God." Etymologically, *systematic theology* involves the orderly bringing together of words about God or a bringing together of biblical truth in an organized fashion. Consider Charles Spurgeon's response to those who object to a systematic approach to theology:

> Systematic theology is to the Bible what science is to nature. To suppose that all the other works of God are orderly and systematic, and the greater the work the more perfect the system: and that the greatest of all His works,

> in which all His perfections are transcendently displayed, should have no plan or system, is altogether absurd.[4]

Systematic theology answers the question, what does the completed canon of Scripture teach about any one theme or topic? For example, what does the Bible teach from Genesis to Revelation about the deity of Jesus Christ? A basic definition of systematic theology, then, would be "the ordered exposition of Christian doctrines."[5]

A systematic theology must display (1) hermeneutical integrity, (2) doctrinal coherence, (3) ethical relevance, (4) worldview explicability, and (5) traditional continuity. Where these are present and operative, one will find a good systematizing that will be of value to the student of Scripture. As he carefully examines every detail of the text in preparation to expound it, systematic theology allows him to also view the whole theological picture—one that has taken into account not only the studied conclusions from church history but also the progress of revelation culminating in the complete revelation of God.

One's understanding of systematic theology could be framed by the following observations from John Murray:

> When we properly weigh the proposition that the Scriptures are the deposit of special revelation, that they are the oracles of God, that in them God encounters and addresses us, discloses to us his incomprehensible majesty, summons us to the knowledge and fulfillment of his will, unveils to us the mystery of his counsel, and unfolds the purposes of his grace, then systematic theology, of all sciences and disciplines, is seen to be the most noble, not one of cold, impass[ive] reflection but one that stirs adoring wonder and claims the most consecrated exercise of all our powers. It is the most noble of all studies because its province is the whole counsel of God and seeks, as no other discipline, to set forth the riches of God's revelation in the orderly and embracive manner which is its peculiar method and function. All other departments of theological discipline contribute their findings to systematic theology and it brings all the wealth of knowledge derived from these disciplines to bear upon the more inclusive systemization which it undertakes.[6]

Systematic theology aims to expound in a comprehensive and thematically organized fashion the biblical doctrines focused on the persons of the triune God, their purposes, and their plans in relationship to the world and humanity. It begins

4 Charles Spurgeon, as quoted in Iain H. Murray, *The Forgotten Spurgeon* (London: Banner of Truth, 1973), 9.

5 James L. Garrett, *Systematic Theology: Biblical, Historical, and Evangelical* (Grand Rapids, MI: Eerdmans, 1990), 1:8.

6 John Murray, "Systematic Theology," in *The Collected Writings of John Murray*, 4 vols. (Edinburgh: Banner of Truth, 1982), 4:4.

with informing the intellect (knowing and understanding). The intellect shapes what we believe and love in our heart. Our will desires what we love and repudiates what we hate. Our actions then accord with what we want most. The mind shapes the affections, which shape the will, which directs the actions. Theology is not fully finished until it has warmed the heart (affections) and prompted the volition (will) to act in obedience to its content.[7]

What Are the Categories of Systematic Theology?

1. *Bibliology*: The doctrine of the inspiration, inerrancy, authority, and canonicity of the Bible (Gk. *biblion*, "book")
2. *Theology proper*: The doctrine of the existence and being of God, including the triunity of God (Gk. *theos*, "God")
3. *Christology*: The doctrine of the person and work of the Lord Jesus Christ (Gk. *christos*, "Christ")
4. *Pneumatology*: The doctrine of the person and work of the Holy Spirit (Gk. *pneuma*, "Spirit")
5. *Anthropology*: The doctrine of humanity (Gk. *anthrōpos*, "man")
6. *Hamartiology*: The doctrine of sin (Gk. *hamartia*, "sin")
7. *Soteriology*: The doctrine of salvation (Gk. *sōtēria*, "salvation")
8. *Angelology*: The doctrine of holy angels, Satan, and fallen angels (Gk. *angelos*, "angel")
9. *Ecclesiology*: The doctrine of the church, universal and local (Gk. *ekklēsia*, "assembly" or "church")
10. *Eschatology*: The doctrine concerning the entire scope of biblical predictive prophecy, especially end-time events, including the destination for both saved and unsaved people, heaven and hell (Gk. *eschatos*, "last things")

What Is the Relationship between Exegetical, Biblical, and Systematic Theology?[8]

All biblical theology is systematic in nature; all systematic theology is biblical in content; and both biblical and systematic theology are exegetical in the interpretive

7 William Ames observed that theology should have as its end *eupraxia*, lit., "good practice" (*The Marrow of Theology*, trans. and ed. John Dykstra Eusden [1629; repr., Grand Rapids, MI: Baker, 1997], 78).

8 The following resources represent some of the clearest definitions, distinctions, and dependencies of the three theological emphases under discussion: Richard B. Gaffin Jr., "Systematic Theology and Biblical Theology," *Westminster Theological Journal* 38.3 (1976): 281–99; Eugene Merrill, *Everlasting Dominion: A Theology of the Old Testament* (Nashville: Broadman, 2006), 1–27; Murray, "Systematic Theology," 4:1–21; Roger Nicole, "The Relationship between Biblical Theology and Systematic Theology," in *Evangelical Roots: A Tribute to Wilbur Smith*, ed. Kenneth S. Kantzer

process. Therefore, the key question is not which one is the best approach to theology but rather, how do the three interrelate with each other?

To use a construction metaphor,

- exegetical theology supplies the building material for the foundation and structure;
- biblical theology provides the foundational support for the structure; and
- systematic theology serves as the structure built on the foundation.

Exegetical theology involves the methodical organization of Scripture by dealing exegetically with the individual texts of the Bible. This is properly an initial component of both biblical and systematic theology. As a result, every word, sentence, and paragraph of Scripture is examined in detail.

Biblical theology is characterized by the organization of Scripture thematically by biblical chronology or biblical author with respect to the progressive revelation of the Bible. This is properly a component of systematic theology. It serves as a bridge from exegetical theology to systematic theology.

Systematic theology is the organization of Scripture by a synthesis of scriptural teaching, summarized by major categories that encompass the entirety of God's written revelation. Systematic theology develops out of exegetical and biblical theology and pulls all the teaching of Scripture together as a whole. Again, Murray is helpful in making sense of these connections:

> Hence exposition of the Scripture is basic to systematic theology. Its task is not simply the exposition of particular passages. That is the task of exegesis. Systematics must coordinate the teaching of particular passages and systematize this teaching under the appropriate topics. There is thus a synthesis that belongs to systematics that does not belong to exegesis as such. But to the extent to which systematic theology synthesizes the teaching of Scripture, and this is its main purpose, it is apparent how dependent it is upon the science of exegesis. It cannot coordinate and relate the teaching of particular passages without knowing what the teaching is. So exegesis is basic to its objective. This needs to be emphasized. Systematic theology has gravely suffered, indeed has deserted its vocation, when it has been divorced from meticulous attention to biblical exegesis. This is one reason why the charge mentioned above has so much to yield support to the indictment. Systematics becomes lifeless and fails in its mandate just to the extent to which it has become detached from exegesis. And the guarantee against a stereotyped dogmatics is that systematic theology be constantly enriched,

(Nashville: Thomas Nelson, 1978), 185–93; and Charles Caldwell Ryrie, *Biblical Theology of the New Testament* (Chicago: Moody Press, 1959), 11–24.

> deepened, and expanded by the treasures increasingly drawn from the Word of God. Exegesis keeps systematics not only in direct contact with the Word but it ever imparts to systematics the power which is derived from that Word. The Word is living and powerful.[9]

One other approach to theology should be mentioned. Historical theology examines how exegetical and theological convictions developed over time. It takes into consideration the conclusions reached by prior generations of godly interpreters of Scripture.

What Are the Benefits and Limitations of Systematic Theology?

All Scripture, whether examined exegetically in particular texts or categorically within the full scope of the Bible, is spiritually profitable to accomplish at least four divine purposes (2 Tim. 3:16):

1. For establishing "teaching" or doctrine, that is, God's inspired self-disclosure about himself, his created world, and his redemptive plan to save and sanctify sinners
2. For confrontation or "reproof" of sin, whether in the form of false teaching or disobedient living
3. For "correction" of error in thinking and behaving so that the repentant one can be restored to the place of pleasing God
4. For "training," so that believers can be habitually trained to practice the righteousness of the Lord Jesus Christ—sinning less and obeying more

Scripture provides the only complete, wholly accurate, and trustworthy teaching about God, and it will sufficiently accomplish these four things for equipping "the man of God" (2 Tim. 3:17).

BENEFITS

Systematic theology can provide several benefits:

1. An unabridged collection of biblical truth
2. An orderly synthesis and summation of biblical doctrine
3. An imperative to take the gospel to the ends of the earth
4. A repository of truth for expositional preaching and teaching
5. A scriptural basis for Christian behavior in the church, the home, and the world
6. A defense of biblical doctrine against false teaching
7. A biblical response to ethical and social malpractice in the world

9 Murray, "Systematic Theology," 4:17.

As James Leo Garrett Jr. puts it,

> Systematic theology is beneficial as an extension of the teaching function of the churches, for the orderly and integrated formulation of biblical truths, for the undergirding of the preaching of preachers and lay Christians, for the defense of gospel truth against error that has invaded the church, for the legitimation of the gospel before philosophy and culture, as the foundation for Christian personal and social ethics, and for more effective universal propagation of the gospel and interaction with adherents of non-Christian religions.[10]

LIMITATIONS[11]

Systematic theology can be limited by the following factors:

1. The silence of the Bible on a particular topic (Deut. 29:29; John 20:30; 21:25)
2. A theologian's partial knowledge/understanding of the entire Bible (Luke 24:25–27, 32; 2 Pet. 3:16)
3. The inadequacy of human language (1 Cor. 2:13–14; 2 Cor. 12:4)
4. The finiteness of the human mind (Job 11:7–12; 38:1–39:30; Rom. 11:33–35)
5. The lack of spiritual discernment/growth (1 Cor. 3:1–3; Heb. 5:11–13)

What Is the Relationship of Systematic Theology to Doctrine?

Doctrine represents teaching that is considered authoritative. When Christ taught, the crowds were amazed at his authority (Matt. 7:28–29; Mark 1:22, 27; Luke 4:32). A church's "doctrinal" statement contains a body of teaching used as the standard of authoritative orthodoxy.

In the Old Testament, the Hebrew word *laqakh* means "what is received" or "accepted teaching" (Deut. 32:2; Job 11:4; Prov. 4:2; Isa. 29:24). It can be variously translated as "instruction," "learning," or "teaching."

In the New Testament, two Greek words are translated as "doctrine," "instruction," or "teaching": *didachē* (referring to the content of teaching) and *didaskalia* (referring to the activity of teaching). Paul used both words together in 2 Timothy 4:2–3 and Titus 1:9.

In Latin, *docere*, "to teach," *doctrina*, "what is being taught," and *doctor*, "the one who is teaching," all contribute to the meaning of the English word *doctrine*.

10 James Leo Garrett Jr., "Why Systematic Theology?," *Criswell Theological Review* 3.2 (1989): 281.

11 This material is adapted from Augustus Hopkins Strong, *Systematic Theology: A Compendium and Commonplace-Book Designed for the Use of Theological Students* (Old Tappan, NJ: Fleming H. Revell, 1907), 34–36.

The content may be informational (to be believed) or practical (to be lived out). It does not necessarily refer to categorized truth.

Biblically speaking, the word *doctrine* is a rather amorphous term that takes shape only in context. It refers to general teaching (systematized or not, true or false), such as the "teaching of Balaam" (Rev. 2:14) or "human teachings" (Col. 2:22), in contrast to biblical teaching such as Christ's teaching (Matt. 7:28) or Paul's teaching (2 Tim. 3:10).

Biblical doctrine, therefore, refers to the teaching of Scripture, whether it be proclamational, expositional, or categorical. That makes all Scripture "doctrinal," whether it be read, taught, preached, or systematized into theological categories. Systematic biblical doctrine (systematic theology) refers to a categorical summation of biblical teaching that follows normally employed themes or categories.

A survey of Scripture shows that all doctrine or teaching can generally be classified into one of two categories, depending on its source:

- with regard to origin—from God the Creator (John 7:16; Acts 13:12) or from God's creation (Col. 2:22; 1 Tim. 4:1)
- with regard to truth content (2 Thess. 2:11–12)—true or false
- with regard to human source (1 Thess. 2:13)—biblical or unbiblical
- with regard to quality (1 Tim. 1:10; 6:3)—sound or unsound
- with regard to acceptability (1 Tim. 1:3; Heb. 13:9)—familiar or strange
- with regard to retention (Rev. 2:24)—to hold or not to hold
- with regard to benefit (1 Tim. 4:6)—good or bad
- with regard to value (2 Tim. 3:16)—profitable or unprofitable

The modern theological use of the term *doctrine* is too narrow, distorts the primary biblical use of the term, and can be misleading. It is far better in discussing *doctrine* to use the term in its broader sense of "teaching" (which certainly includes systematized truth but is not limited to this use) rather than to use *doctrine* in its secondary sense as though this were the only sense. The teaching of Scripture serves as the yardstick, gauge, standard, paradigm, pattern, measure, and plumb line by which all other teaching on any given subject is determined to be true or false, received or rejected, sound or unsound, orthodox or heretical.

Sound biblical doctrine has many implications for the life of Christ's church:

1. Sound doctrine exposes and confronts sin and false doctrine (1 Tim. 1:8–11, esp. 1:10; 4:1–6).
2. Sound doctrine marks a good servant of Christ Jesus (1 Tim. 4:6; see also 1 Tim. 4:13, 16; Titus 2:1).
3. Sound doctrine is rewarded with double honor for elders (1 Tim. 5:17).
4. Sound doctrine conforms to godliness (1 Tim. 6:3; Titus 2:10).

5. Sound doctrine is included in the apostolic example to follow (2 Tim. 3:10).
6. Sound doctrine is essential to equipping pastors (2 Tim. 3:16–17).
7. Sound doctrine is the continual mandate for preachers (2 Tim. 4:2–4).
8. Sound doctrine is a basic qualification for eldership (Titus 1:9).

Scripture teaches that there will always be opposition to sound doctrine, both by humans (Matt. 15:2–6; Mark 11:18; 1 Tim. 1:3, 10; 2 Tim. 4:3; Titus 1:9) and by Satan and demons (1 Tim. 4:1). The Bible outlines several antidotes/corrections to false doctrine:

1. Speaking the truth of sound doctrine in love (Eph. 4:15)
2. Teaching sound doctrine (1 Tim. 4:6; 2 Tim. 4:2)
3. Holding fast to sound doctrine (Titus 1:9; Rev. 2:24–25)
4. Refuting false doctrine (Titus 1:9)
5. Rejecting and turning away from teachers of false doctrine (Rom. 16:17; 2 John 9–10)

There is a direct, inseparable relationship between sound doctrine and sanctified living, something Scripture teaches clearly and consistently (Rom. 15:4; 1 Tim. 4:16; 6:1, 3; 2 Tim. 3:10; Titus 2:1–4, 7–10). The reverse is also true—where there is false belief, there will be sinful behavior (Titus 1:16). In spite of Scripture's clear emphasis on both purity of doctrine and purity of life, a number of mistaken notions have arisen concerning the relationship between what a person believes and how a person should live. These wrong ideas include the following:

1. Right doctrine automatically leads to godliness.
2. It doesn't matter how a person lives so long as he or she has right doctrine.
3. Doctrine deadens, spiritually speaking.
4. There is no connection between what one believes and how one lives.
5. Christianity is life, not doctrine.
6. Doctrine is irrelevant.
7. Doctrine divides.
8. Doctrine drives people away.

In contrast to the negativity aimed at doctrine, the absence of sound doctrine and the presence of false doctrine will always lead to sinful behavior. Without sound doctrine, there is no scriptural basis to delineate right from wrong, no doctrinal authority to correct sin, and no biblical encouragement to motivate godly living.

On the other hand, the spiritual value of sound doctrine is incalculable:

1. Sound doctrine is spiritually profitable (2 Tim. 3:16–17).
2. Spiritual blessings are promised for obedience (Rev. 1:3; 22:7).

3. Sound doctrine guards against sin (e.g., Job, Joseph, Daniel, Christ).
4. Sound doctrine delineates between truth and error (2 Cor. 11:1–15; 2 Tim. 3:16–17).
5. Sound doctrine was central to Christ's ministry (Matt. 7:28–29; Mark 4:2; Luke 4:32).
6. Sound doctrine was central in the early church (Acts 2:42; 5:28; 13:12).
7. Sound doctrine was central to apostolic ministry (Paul: Acts 13:12; 17:19; Gal. 2:11–21; John: 2 John 9–10).
8. Martyrs gave their lives for sound doctrine (Christ: Mark 11:18; Stephen: Acts 7:54–60; James: Acts 12:2; Paul: 2 Tim. 4:1–8).
9. Christ and the apostles left a mandate to pass sound doctrine on to the next generation (Christ: Matt. 28:20; Paul: 2 Tim. 2:2).
10. Churches were commended for sound doctrine or condemned for lack of sound doctrine (Ephesus, commended: Rev. 2:2, 6; Pergamum and Thyatira, condemned: Rev. 2:14–15, 20).
11. Established sound doctrine anticipates and prepares for eras when sound doctrine is out of season (2 Tim. 4:3).
12. Sound doctrine protects the church from false teachers (Titus 1:9).
13. Sound doctrine provides true spiritual adornment for believers (Titus 2:10).
14. Sound biblical teaching and sound systematic doctrine are inseparably connected to "theology." Whether it be viewed expositionally in a text of Scripture or categorized comprehensively from all Scripture, biblical teaching cannot be disconnected from its identification with theology. Put another way, all biblical teaching is theological in nature, and all Christian theology is biblical in content.

What Is the Overarching and Unifying Theme of Scripture?[12]

The broad theme of *king/kingdom* (human and divine) appears throughout the Bible. With the exceptions of Leviticus, Ruth, and Joel, the Old Testament explicitly mentions this theme in thirty-six of its thirty-nine books. Except for Philippians, Titus, Philemon, and 1, 2, and 3 John, the New Testament directly mentions the subject in twenty-one of its twenty-seven books. All in all, fifty-seven of the sixty-six canonical books include the kingdom theme (86 percent).

The Hebrew words for "king," "kingdom," "reign," and "throne" appear over three thousand times in the Old Testament, while the Greek words for these terms appear 160 times in the New Testament. The first Old Testament mention occurs

12 Adapted from Richard L. Mayhue, "The Kingdom of God: An Introduction," *MSJ* 23.2 (2012): 167–72. Used by permission of *MSJ*.

in Genesis 10:10 and the last in Malachi 1:14. The initial appearance in the New Testament comes in Matthew 1:6 and the last in Revelation 22:5.

The exact expression "kingdom of God" does not appear in the Old Testament. In the New Testament, Matthew alone uses the phrase "kingdom of heaven," but he uses it interchangeably with "kingdom of God" (Matt. 19:23–24). And where he uses "kingdom of heaven" in passages that parallel other Gospels, those Gospel writers use "kingdom of God" (cf. Matt. 13:11 with Luke 8:10), thus establishing the correspondence between these two phrases.

Jesus never precisely defined "kingdom of heaven/God" in the Gospels, although he often illustrated it (e.g., Matt. 13:19, 24, 44, 45, 47, 52). Surprisingly, no one ever asked Christ for a definition. It can be assumed that they at least thought they understood the basic idea from the Old Testament, even if their ideas were mistaken.

Most telling, perhaps, is the plethora of *King* titles given to Christ in the New Testament:

- "King of Israel" (John 1:49; 12:13)
- "King of the Jews" (John 18:39; 19:3, 19, 21)
- "King of kings" (1 Tim. 6:15; Rev. 17:14; 19:16)
- "King of the ages, immortal, invisible" (1 Tim. 1:17)
- "King of the nations" (Rev. 15:3)

Christ's reign is said to be forever and ever (Rev. 11:15; cf. 22:5).

A biblical study of God's kingdom leads one to conclude that it is multifaceted, multidimensional, multifocal, multifactorial, and multifarious. It certainly could not be considered monolithic in character.

The idea of God's kingdom encompasses every stage of biblical revelation. For instance,

- God is King of eternity (pre-Genesis 1, Revelation 21–22, post-Revelation 22)
- God is King of creation (Genesis 1–2)
- God is King of history (Genesis 1–Revelation 20)
- God is King of redemption (Genesis 3–Revelation 20)
- God is King of the earth (Genesis 1–Revelation 20)
- God is King of heaven (pre-Genesis 1, Genesis 1–Revelation 22, post-Revelation 22)

All *kingdom of God* passages can be summarized by recognizing several broad aspects. First is the *universal kingdom*, which includes the rule of God that has been, is, and forever will be over all that exists in time and space. Second is God's *mediatorial kingdom*, in which he rules on earth through divinely chosen human representatives. Third is the *spiritual or redemptive aspect of God's kingdom*, which uniquely deals with a person's salvation and personal relationship with God through Christ. When Scripture uses the word "kingdom" to refer to God's kingdom, it could point to any one aspect of the kingdom or several of its parts together. Careful interpretation in context will determine the particulars for a given biblical text.

With these ideas in mind, it is proposed that *God as King* and *the kingdom of God* should together be seriously considered as the grand, overarching theme of Scripture. A number of other candidates for the main theme of Scripture have been considered in the past, such as the glory of God, redemption, grace, Christ, covenant, and promise. Each possibility explains a part of God's kingdom, but only *God's kingdom* explains the whole.

From before the beginning until after the end, from the beginning to the end, both in and beyond time and space, God appears as the ultimate King. God is central to and the core of all things eternal and temporal. The kingdom of God convincingly qualifies as the unifying theme of Scripture.

John Bright succinctly and eloquently captured this thinking as follows:

> Old Testament and New Testament thus stand together as the two acts of a single drama. Act I points to its conclusion in Act II, and without it the play is an incomplete, unsatisfying thing. But Act II must be read in the light of Act I, else its meaning will be missed. For the play is organically one. The Bible is one book. Had we to give that book a title, we might with justice call it "The Book of the Coming Kingdom of God." That is, indeed, its central theme everywhere.[13]

The authors of this volume would edit Dr. Bright's brilliant summary only by deleting one word, "Coming." For God's kingdom has been, is, and forevermore shall be.

The kingdom of God can be explained in this manner: The eternal triune God created a kingdom and two kingdom citizens (Adam and Eve) who were to exercise dominion over it. But an enemy deceived them, seduced them into breaking allegiance to the King, and caused them to rebel against their sovereign Creator. God intervened with consequential curses that exist to this day. Ever since, he

13 John Bright, *The Kingdom of God: The Biblical Concept and Its Meaning for the Church* (New York: Abingdon-Cokesbury, 1953), 197; see also 7, 244. See Alva J. McClain, *The Greatness of the Kingdom: An Inductive Study of the Kingdom of God* (Chicago: Moody Press, 1959), 4–53; George N. H. Peters, *The Theocratic Kingdom of Our Lord Jesus, the Christ, as Covenanted in the Old Testament and Presented in the New Testament*, 3 vols. (1884; repr., Grand Rapids, MI: Kregel, 1978), 1:29–33; Erich Sauer, *From Eternity to Eternity: An Outline of the Divine Purposes* (1954; repr., Grand Rapids, MI: Eerdmans, 1994), 89.

has been redeeming sinful, rebellious people to be restored as qualified kingdom citizens, both now in a spiritual sense and later in a kingdom-on-earth sense. Finally, the Enemy will be vanquished forever, as will sin. Thus, Revelation 21–22 describes the final and eternal expression of the kingdom of God, where the triune God will restore the kingdom to its original purity with the curse having been removed and the new heaven and the new earth becoming the everlasting abode of God and his people.

What Are the Major Motifs of Scripture?[14]

The Bible is a collection of sixty-six books inspired by God. These documents are gathered into two Testaments, the Old (thirty-nine) and the New (twenty-seven). Prophets, priests, kings, and leaders from the nation of Israel wrote the Old Testament books in Hebrew (with some passages in Aramaic). The apostles and their associates wrote the New Testament books in Greek.

The Old Testament record starts with the creation of the universe and closes about four hundred years before the first coming of Jesus Christ. The flow of history through the Old Testament moves along the following lines:

1. Creation of the universe
2. Fall of man
3. Judgment flood over the earth
4. Abraham, Isaac, Jacob (Israel)—fathers of the chosen nation
5. The history of Israel
   a. Exile in Egypt (430 years)
   b. Exodus and wilderness wanderings (40 years)
   c. Conquest of Canaan (7 years)
   d. Era of the judges (350 years)
   e. United kingdom—Saul, David, Solomon (110 years)
   f. Divided kingdom—Judah and Israel (350 years)
   g. Exile in Babylon (70 years)
   h. Return and rebuilding of the land (140 years)

The details of this history are explained in the thirty-nine books, which can be divided into five categories:

1. The Law—5 (Genesis–Deuteronomy)
2. History—12 (Joshua–Esther)
3. Wisdom—5 (Job–Song of Solomon)

14 This section is adapted from John MacArthur, ed., *The MacArthur Study Bible: English Standard Version* (Wheaton, IL: Crossway, 2010), xi–xv. Charts and notes from *The MacArthur Study Bible: English Standard Version* originate with *The MacArthur Study Bible*, copyright © 1997 by Thomas Nelson. Used by permission of Thomas Nelson/HarperCollins Christian Publishing.

4. Major Prophets—5 (Isaiah–Daniel)
5. Minor Prophets—12 (Hosea–Malachi)

The completion of the Old Testament was followed by four hundred years of silence, during which time God did not speak through prophets or inspire any Scripture. That silence was broken by the arrival of John the Baptist announcing that the promised Savior had come. The New Testament records the rest of the story, from the birth of Christ to the culmination of all history and the final eternal state. So the two Testaments go from creation to consummation, eternity past to eternity future.

While the thirty-nine Old Testament books major on the history of Israel and the promise of the coming Savior, the twenty-seven New Testament books major on the person of Christ and the establishment of the church. The four Gospels give the record of his birth, life, death, resurrection, and ascension. Each of the four writers views the greatest and most important event of history, the coming of the God-man, Jesus Christ, from a different perspective. Matthew looks at him through the perspective of his kingdom, Mark through the perspective of his servanthood, Luke through the perspective of his humanness, and John through the perspective of his deity.

The book of Acts tells the story of the impact of the life, death, and resurrection of Jesus Christ, the Lord Savior—from his ascension, the consequent coming of the Holy Spirit, and the birth of the church through the early years of gospel preaching by the apostles and their associates. Acts records the establishment of the church in Judea, in Samaria, and into the Roman Empire.

The twenty-one Epistles were written to churches and individuals to explain the significance of the person and work of Jesus Christ, with its implications for life and witness until he returns.

The New Testament closes with Revelation, which starts by picturing the current church age and culminates with Christ's return to establish his earthly kingdom, bringing judgment on the ungodly and glory and blessing for believers. Following the millennial reign of the Lord Savior will be the last judgment, leading to the eternal state. All believers of all history enter the ultimate eternal glory prepared for them, and all the ungodly are consigned to hell to be punished forever.

To understand the Bible, it is essential to grasp the sweep of that history from creation to consummation. It is also crucial to keep in focus the unifying theme of Scripture. The one constant theme unfolding throughout the whole Bible is this: God, for his own glory, has chosen to create and gather to himself a group of people to be the subjects of his eternal kingdom, who will praise, honor, and serve him forever and through whom he will display his wisdom, power, mercy, grace, and glory. To gather his chosen ones, God must redeem them from sin.

The Bible reveals God's plan for this redemption from its inception in eternity past to its completion in eternity future. Covenants, promises, and epochs are all secondary to the one continuous plan of redemption.

There is one God. The Bible has one divine Source. Scripture is one book. It has one plan of grace, recorded from initiation through execution to consummation. From predestination to glorification, the Bible is the story of God redeeming his chosen people for the praise of his glory.

As God's redemptive purposes and plan unfold in Scripture, five recurring motifs are constantly emphasized. Everything revealed on the pages of both the Old Testament and the New is associated with these five categories. Scripture is always teaching or illustrating (1) the character and attributes of God; (2) the tragedy of sin and disobedience to God's holy standard; (3) the blessedness of faith and obedience to God's standard; (4) the need for a Savior by whose righteousness and substitution sinners can be forgiven, declared just, and transformed to obey God's standard; and (5) the coming glorious end of redemptive history in the Lord Savior's earthly kingdom and the subsequent eternal reign and glory of God and Christ. While reading through the Bible, one should be able to relate each portion of Scripture to these dominant topics, recognizing that what is introduced in the Old Testament is also made clearer in the New Testament. Looking at these five categories separately gives an overview of the Bible.

THE REVELATION OF THE CHARACTER OF GOD

Above all else, Scripture is God's self-revelation. He reveals himself as the sovereign God of the universe who has chosen to make man and to make himself known to man. In that self-revelation he has established his standard of absolute holiness. From Adam and Eve through Cain and Abel and to everyone before and after the law of Moses, the standard of righteousness has been established and is sustained in Scripture to the last page of the New Testament. Violation of it produces judgment, both temporal and eternal.

In the Old Testament, God revealed himself by the following means:

1. Creation (the heavens and the earth)
2. Creation of mankind, who was made in his image
3. Angels
4. Signs, wonders, and miracles
5. Visions
6. Spoken words by prophets and others
7. Written Scripture (Old Testament)

In the New Testament, God revealed himself again by the same means but more clearly and fully:

1. Creation (the heavens and the earth)
2. Incarnation of the God-man, Jesus Christ, who is the very image of God
3. Angels
4. Signs, wonders, and miracles
5. Visions
6. Spoken words by Christ, apostles, and prophets
7. Written Scripture (New Testament)

THE REVELATION OF DIVINE JUDGMENT FOR SIN AND DISOBEDIENCE

Scripture repeatedly deals with the matter of man's sin, which leads to divine judgment. Account after account in Scripture demonstrates the deadly effects in time and eternity of violating God's standard. There are 1,189 chapters in the Bible. Only four of them do not involve a fallen world: the first two and the last two—before the fall and after the creation of the new heaven and new earth. The rest chronicle sin's tragedy and God's redemptive grace in Christ Jesus.

In the Old Testament, God showed the disaster of sin—starting with Adam and Eve and carrying on to Cain and Abel, the patriarchs, Moses and Israel, the kings, the priests, some prophets, and the Gentile nations. Throughout the Old Testament is the relentless record of continual devastation produced by sin and disobedience to God's law.

In the New Testament, the tragedy of sin becomes clearer. The teaching of Jesus and the apostles begins and ends with a call to repentance. King Herod, the Jewish leaders, and the nation of Israel—along with Pilate, Rome, and the rest of the world—all reject the Lord Savior, spurn the truth of God, and thus condemn themselves. The chronicle of sin continues unabated to the end of the age and the return of Christ in judgment. New Testament disobedience is even more flagrant than Old Testament disobedience because it involves the rejection of the Lord Savior Jesus Christ in the brighter light of New Testament revelation.

THE REVELATION OF DIVINE BLESSING FOR FAITH AND OBEDIENCE

Scripture repeatedly promises wonderful rewards in time and eternity that come to people who trust God and seek to obey him. In the Old Testament, God showed the blessedness of repentance from sin, faith in himself, and obedience to his Word—from Abel, through the patriarchs, to the remnant in Israel, and even on to the Gentiles who believed (such as the people of Nineveh).

God's will, his moral law, and his standard for man were always made known. To those who faced their inability to keep God's standard, who recognized their sin, who confessed their impotence to please God by their own works, and who asked him for forgiveness and grace—to those came merciful redemption and blessing for time and eternity.

In the New Testament, God again showed the full blessedness of redemption from sin for repentant people. There were those who responded to the preaching of repentance by John the Baptist. Others repented at the preaching of Jesus. Still others from Israel obeyed the gospel through the apostles' preaching. And finally, many Gentiles all over the Roman Empire believed the gospel. To all those and to all who will believe throughout all history, God promises blessing, both in this world and in the world to come.

THE REVELATION OF THE LORD SAVIOR AND HIS SACRIFICE FOR SIN

This is the heart of both the Old Testament, which Jesus said spoke of him in type and prophecy, and the New Testament, which gives the biblical record of his coming. The promise of blessing is dependent on grace and mercy given to the sinner. Mercy means that sin is not held against the sinner. Such forgiveness depends on a payment of sin's penalty to satisfy holy justice, which demands a substitute—one to die in the sinner's place. God's chosen substitute—the only one who qualified—was Jesus. Salvation is always by the same gracious means, whether during Old Testament or New Testament times. When any sinner comes to God in repentant faith, acknowledging that he has no power to save himself from the deserved judgment of divine wrath, believing in Christ, and pleading for mercy, God's promise of forgiveness is granted. God then declares him righteous because the sacrifice and obedience of Christ is credited to his account. In the Old Testament, God justified sinners that same way, in anticipation of Christ's atoning work. There is, therefore, a continuity of grace and salvation through all redemptive history. Various covenants, promises, and epochs do not alter that fundamental continuity, nor does the discontinuity between the Old Testament witness-nation, Israel, and the New Testament witness-people, the church. A fundamental continuity is centered on the cross, which was no interruption in the plan of God but is the very thing to which all else points.

Throughout the Old Testament, the Savior-sacrifice is promised. In Genesis, he is the seed of the woman who will destroy Satan. In Zechariah, he is the "pierced" one to whom Israel turns and by whom God opens the fountain of forgiveness to all who mourn over their sin (Zech. 12:10). He is the very one symbolized in the sacrificial system of the Mosaic law. He is the suffering substitute of whom the prophets speak. Throughout the Old Testament, he is the Messiah who would die for the transgressions of his people; from beginning to end, the Old Testament presents the theme of the Lord Savior as a sacrifice for sin. It is solely because of his perfect sacrifice for sin that God graciously forgives repentant believers.

In the New Testament, the Lord Savior came and actually accomplished the promised sacrifice for sin on the cross. Having fulfilled all righteousness by his perfect life, he satisfied justice by his death. Thus God himself atoned for sin, at a cost too great for the human mind to fathom. Now he graciously supplies all the merit necessary for his people to be the objects of his favor. That is what Scripture means when it speaks of salvation by grace.

THE REVELATION OF THE KINGDOM AND GLORY OF THE LORD SAVIOR

This crucial component of Scripture brings the whole story to its God-ordained consummation. Redemptive history is controlled by God so as to culminate in his eternal glory. Redemptive history will end with the same precision and exactness with which it began. The truths of eschatology are neither vague nor unclear—nor are they unimportant. As in any book, how the story ends is both compelling and critically important—and so it is with the Bible. Scripture notes several very specific features of the end planned by God.

In the Old Testament, there is repeated mention of an earthly kingdom ruled by the Messiah, the Lord Savior, who will come to reign. Associated with that kingdom will be the salvation of Israel, the salvation of Gentiles, the renewal of the earth from the effects of the curse, and the bodily resurrection of God's people who have died. Finally, the Old Testament predicts that God will create a new heaven and new earth—which will be the eternal state of the godly—and a final hell for the ungodly.

The New Testament clarifies and expands these features. The King is rejected and executed, but he promises to come back in glory, bringing judgment, resurrection, and his kingdom for all who believe. Innumerable Gentiles from every nation will be included among the redeemed. Israel will be saved and grafted back into the root of blessing, from which she has been temporarily excised. Israel's promised kingdom will be enjoyed with the Lord reigning on the throne in the renewed earth, exercising power over the whole world and receiving due honor and worship. Following that kingdom will come the dissolution of the renewed but still sin-stained creation and the subsequent creation of a new heaven and new earth—which will be the eternal state, separate forever from the ungodly in hell.

How Does Systematic Theology Relate to One's Worldview?[15]

A worldview comprises one's collection of presuppositions, convictions, and values from which a person tries to understand and make sense out of the world and life. As Ronald Nash puts it, "A world-view is a conceptual scheme by which we consciously or unconsciously place or fit everything we believe and

15 This section is adapted from Richard L. Mayhue, "Introduction," in *Think Biblically: Recovering a Christian Worldview*, ed. John MacArthur (Wheaton, IL: Crossway, 2003), 13–16. Used by permission of Crossway, a publishing ministry of Good News Publishers, Wheaton, IL.

by which we interpret and judge reality."[16] Similarly, Gary Phillips and William Brown explain, "A worldview is, first of all, *an explanation and interpretation of the world* and second, *an application of this view to life.*"[17]

Every worldview begins with *presuppositions*—beliefs that one presumes to be true without supporting evidence from other sources or systems. Making sense of reality, in part or in whole, requires that one adopt an interpretive stance, since there is no "neutral" thought in the universe. This becomes the foundation on which one builds.

What are the presuppositions of a Christian worldview that is solidly rooted and grounded in Scripture? Carl F. H. Henry, an important Christian thinker in the last half of the twentieth century, answers the question very simply by saying that "evangelical theology dares harbor one and only one presupposition: the living and personal God intelligibly known in his revelation."[18] This one major presupposition, which underlies a proper Christian worldview, breaks down into two parts. First, God exists eternally as the personal, transcendent, triune Creator. Second, God has revealed his character, purposes, and will in the infallible and inerrant pages of his special revelation, the Bible.

What is the Christian worldview? The following definition is offered as a working model:

> The Christian worldview sees and understands God the Creator and his creation—that is, man and the world—primarily through the lens of God's special revelation, the holy Scriptures, and secondarily through God's natural revelation in creation as interpreted by human reason and reconciled by and with Scripture, for the purpose of believing and behaving in accord with God's will and, thereby, glorifying God with one's mind and life, both now and in eternity.

What are some of the benefits of embracing the Christian worldview? A biblical worldview provides compelling answers to the most crucial of life's questions:

1. How did the world and all that is in it come into being?
2. By what standard can I determine whether a knowledge claim is true or false?
3. How does/should the world function?
4. What is the nature of a human being?

16 Ronald H. Nash, *Faith and Reason: Searching for a Rational Faith* (Grand Rapids, MI: Zondervan, 1988), 24.

17 W. Gary Phillips and William E. Brown, *Making Sense of Your World from a Biblical Viewpoint* (Chicago: Moody Press, 1991), 29, italics original.

18 Carl F. H. Henry, *God, Revelation, and Authority*, vol. 1, *God Who Speaks and Shows: Preliminary Considerations* (1976; repr., Wheaton, IL: Crossway, 1999), 212.

5. What is one's personal purpose of existence?
6. How should one live?
7. Is there any personal hope for the future?
8. What happens to a person at and after death?
9. Why is it possible to know anything at all?
10. How does one determine what is right and wrong?
11. What is the meaning of human history?
12. What does the future hold?

Christians in the twenty-first century face the same basic questions about this world and life that confronted the earliest humans in Genesis. They also had to sift through various worldviews to answer the above questions. This has been true throughout history. Consider what faced Joseph (Genesis 37–50) and Moses (Exodus 2–14) in Egypt, or Elijah when he encountered Jezebel and her pagan prophets (1 Kings 17–19), or Daniel in Babylon (Daniel 1–6), or Nehemiah in Persia (Nehemiah 1–2), or Paul in Athens (Acts 17). They discerned the difference between truth and error, right and wrong, because they placed their faith in the living God and his revealed Word.

What distinguishes the Christian worldview from other worldviews? At the heart of the matter, a Christian worldview contrasts with competing worldviews in that it (1) recognizes the triune God of the Bible as the unique source of all truth, and (2) relates all truth back to an understanding of God and his purposes for this life and the next.

There are at least two mistaken notions about the Christian worldview, especially among Christians. The first is that a Christian view of the world and life will differ on *all* points from other worldviews. While this is not always true (e.g., all worldviews accept the law of gravity), the Christian worldview will differ and be unique on the most important points, especially as they relate to the character of God, the nature and value of Scripture, and the exclusivity of Jesus Christ as Savior and Lord. The second misperception is that the Bible contains all that we need to know in every sense. Common sense should put an end to this misdirected thought; for example, Scripture does not give instructions for how to change the oil in one's car. However, it is true that the Bible alone contains all that Christians need to know about their spiritual life and godliness through a knowledge of the one true God, which is the highest and most important level of knowledge (2 Pet. 1:2–4).

How and in what life contexts does a Christian worldview prove to be necessary? First, in the world of *scholarship* the Christian worldview is offered not as one of many equals or possibilities but as the one true view of life whose single source of truth and reality is the Creator God. Thus, it serves as a bright light reflecting the glory of God amid intellectual darkness.

Second, a Christian worldview must be used as an essential tool in *evangelism*, to answer the questions and objections of the unbeliever. However, it must be clearly understood that, in the final analysis, it is the gospel that has the power to bring an individual to salvation (Rom. 1:16–17).

Finally, a Christian worldview is foundational in the realm of *discipleship*, to inform and mature a true believer in Christ with regard to the implications and ramifications of one's Christian faith. It provides a framework by which one (1) can understand the world and all of its reality from God's perspective and (2) can order one's life according to God's will.

What should be the ultimate goal of embracing the Christian worldview? Why is the Christian worldview worth recovering? Jeremiah passes along God's direct answer:

> Thus says the LORD: "Let not the wise man boast in his wisdom, let not the mighty man boast in his might, let not the rich man boast in his riches, but let him who boasts boast in this, that he understands and knows me, that I am the LORD who practices steadfast love, justice, and righteousness in the earth. For in these things I delight, declares the LORD." (Jer. 9:23–24)

Man's chief end is to know and glorify God. Yet the knowledge of God is impossible apart from a Christian worldview.

Where do systematic theology and one's worldview intersect? First, both are erected on the same shared presupposition with its two parts: (1) the personal existence of the eternal God and (2) his self-revelation in Scripture. Second, a Christian worldview is dependent on systematic theology to know and understand God's truth, for systematic theology is nothing other than organizing all that God has revealed for the purpose of rightly knowing and living unto him. Third, a Christian worldview is dependent on systematic theology to know and embrace God's worldview as revealed in Scripture, for it is only as we think Christianly that we learn to think God's own thoughts after him. Finally, systematic theology is dependent on a Christian worldview in order to consistently and properly apply the truth of Scripture for living according to the will of God, for God's glory.

How Does Systematic Theology Relate to One's Mind?[19]

Systematic theology is entirely about God's mind as found in Scripture. It is not about what humans think independently apart from the Bible. The necessary characteristics of the Christian's mind are discussed next because they qualify

19 This section is adapted from Mayhue, "Cultivating a Biblical Mind-Set," in MacArthur, *Think Biblically*, 42–53. Used by permission of Crossway.

one to learn and teach Christian theology, whose source is Scripture and whose centerpiece is the triune God.

THE REDEEMED MIND

As a result of salvation, the mind of a newly redeemed person knows and comprehends the glory of God (2 Cor. 4:6). Whereas this person was previously blinded by Satan (2 Cor. 4:4), he or she now possesses "the helmet of salvation" (Eph. 6:17) to protect the mind against the "schemes" (a mind-related term in the Greek, Eph. 6:11) of Satan. No longer is this one left vulnerable against the Devil, as he or she was before salvation. This new person (2 Cor. 5:17) now has a knowledge of God and his will that he or she previously lacked (1 John 5:18–20).

THE RENEWED MIND

When a person enters into a personal relationship with Jesus Christ, he or she becomes a new creation (2 Cor. 5:17) who sings "a new song" (Ps. 98:1). The mind acquires a new way to think and a capacity to put off old, sinful ways of thinking. Unquestionably, God is in the business of mind renewal for Christians (Rom. 12:2; Eph. 4:23; Col. 3:10).

The Bible says to "set your minds on things that are above, not on things that are on earth" (Col. 3:2). Paul put this concept in military terms: "We destroy arguments and every lofty opinion raised against the knowledge of God, and take every thought captive to obey Christ" (2 Cor. 10:5). How do we do this? Scripture reveals the mind of God (1 Cor. 2:16)—not all of his mind, to be sure, but all that God wisely determined to reveal to us. To think like God, one must think like Scripture. That's why Paul encouraged the Colossians to let the Word of Christ dwell within them richly (Col. 3:16).

Harry Blamires, an Englishman with extraordinary understanding about the Christian mind, puts this quite well:

> To think christianly is to think in terms of Revelation. For the secularist, God and theology are the playthings of the mind. For the Christian, God is real, and Christian theology describes His truth revealed to us. For the secular mind, religion is essentially a matter of theory: for the Christian mind, Christianity is a matter of acts and facts. The acts and facts which are the basis of our faith are recorded in the Bible.[20]

At salvation, Christians are given a regenerated mental ability to comprehend spiritual truth. After salvation, Christians need to readjust their thinking chiefly by

20 Harry Blamires, *The Christian Mind: How Should a Christian Think?* (1963; repr., Ann Arbor, MI: Servant, 1978), 110–11.

mind renewal, using the Bible as the means to do so. The ultimate goal is to have a full knowledge of God and his will (Rom. 12:1–2; Eph. 1:17–18; Col. 1:9–10).

THE ILLUMINATED MIND

The Bible says that believers need God's help to understand God's Word (1 Cor. 2:12–13). Consequently, the Spirit of God enlightens the minds of believers, so that they might comprehend, embrace, and obey the truths revealed in Scripture. Theologians call this *illumination*.

A great prayer to offer as one studies Scripture is, "Open my eyes, that I may behold wondrous things out of your law" (Ps. 119:18). It acknowledges an indispensable need for God's light in Scripture. So do texts like Psalm 119:33–34, "Teach me, O Lord, the way of your statutes; and I will keep it to the end. Give me understanding, that I may keep your law and observe it with my whole heart" (see also Ps. 119:102).

God wants Christians to know and understand and obey. So he gives them the help that they need through his Holy Spirit. Believers, like the men to whom Jesus spoke on the road to Emmaus, require God's assistance: "Then he opened their minds to understand the Scriptures" (Luke 24:45). God's ministry of illumination, by which he gives light on the meaning of the Bible, is affirmed in texts such as Psalm 119:130; Ephesians 1:18–19; and 1 John 2:27.

The truth about God illuminating Scripture for Christians should greatly encourage the believer. While it does not eliminate the need for gifted men to teach (Eph. 4:11–12; 2 Tim. 4:2) or the hard labor of serious Bible study (2 Tim. 2:15), it does promise that there is no need to be enslaved to church dogma or to be led astray by false teachers. Primary dependence for learning Scripture needs to be on the author of Scripture—God himself.

THE CHRISTLIKE MIND

When one thinks like God wants him to think and acts like God wants him to act, then one will receive God's blessing for obedience (Rev. 1:3). Spiritually, the Christian will be that obedient child, that pure bride, and that healthy sheep in Christ's flock who experiences the greatest intimacy with God.

It is brazen idolatry to reject the mind of God in Scripture and worship at the altar of one's own independent thinking. A believer's greatest intimacy with the Lord occurs when the Lord's thoughts prevail and one's behavior then models that of Christ.

Christians should be altogether glad to embrace the certain and true mind of God the Father (Rom. 11:34), God the Son (1 Cor. 2:16), and God the Spirit (Rom. 8:27). In contrast to Peter, who was tempted by Satan to set his mind on the things of man, believers are to set their minds on the things of God (Matt. 16:23; Col.

3:2). This has to do not so much with different categories or disciplines of thought but rather with the way things are viewed from a divine perspective. Christians should stand in awe of God's mind, as did the apostle Paul (Rom. 11:33–36).

God's view is the only true view that accurately corresponds to all reality. God's mind sets the standard for which believers are to strive but which they will never fully achieve. Put another way, man's thoughts will never exceed, equal, or even come close to God's. Over 2,500 years ago, the prophet Isaiah said this very thing (Isa. 55:8–9).

The ultimate pattern of Christian-mindedness is the Lord Jesus Christ. Paul declares, "But we have the mind of Christ" (1 Cor. 2:16). How can this be? We have it with the Bible, which is God's sufficient, special revelation (2 Tim. 3:16–17; 2 Pet. 1:3). In Philippians 2:5, Paul instructs, "Have this mind among yourselves, which is yours in Christ Jesus." The apostle is specifically pointing to Christ's mindset of sacrifice for God's glory (Phil. 2:7) and submission to God's will (Phil. 2:8). By following Christ's model, Christians can train their minds to become more like his.

THE TESTED MIND

The Christian mind should be a repository of God's revealed truth. It should not waver, compromise, or bend in the face of opposing ideas or seemingly superior arguments (2 Tim. 1:7). Truth originates not with humans but with God. Therefore, Christians should be the champions of truth in a world filled with lies that are deceivingly disguised as and falsely declared to be the truth.

It was God who invited the nation of Israel, saying, "Come now, let us reason together" (Isa. 1:18). The subject matter to be considered was repentance from sin and salvation (Isa. 1:16–20). By application, the same invitation is extended to every person alive.

However, while a commitment to think Christianly honors Christ, it is not without opposition. Satan would have believers think contrary to God's Word and then act disobediently to God's will.

Remember that before one becomes a Christian, his or her mind is blinded by the Devil: "The god of this world has blinded the minds of the unbelievers, to keep them from seeing the light of the gospel of the glory of Christ, who is the image of God" (2 Cor. 4:4). Even after salvation, Satan continues his intellectual rampage. Thus Paul had great concern for the Corinthian church: "But I am afraid that as the serpent deceived Eve by his cunning, your thoughts will be led astray from a sincere and pure devotion to Christ" (2 Cor. 11:3). Eve had allowed Satan to do some thinking for her. Then she did some of her own thinking independent of God. When her conclusions differed from God's, she chose to act on her conclusions rather than on God's commands, which is sin (Gen. 3:1–7).

Satan aims his fiery darts (Eph. 6:16) at the minds of believers (2 Cor. 11:3), making their thought life the battlefield for spiritual conquest. Scriptural accounts abound of those who succumbed, like Eve (Genesis 3) and Peter (Matt. 16:13–23). Others walked away from the fray as victors, like Job (Job 1:1–2:10) and Christ (Matt. 4:1–11). When Christians fall, it is most likely that they have forgotten to wear the helmet of salvation or to wield the sword of truth (Eph. 6:17).

In warning believers about life's ongoing, never-ending battle with Satan, Paul on two occasions tells about the schemes or designs of the Devil. He uses two different Greek words, but both relate to the mind (2 Cor. 2:11; Eph. 6:11). Since no one is immune from these attacks, the Christian must heed Peter's strong exhortation: "Therefore, preparing your minds for action, and being sober-minded, set your hope fully on the grace that will be brought to you at the revelation of Jesus Christ" (1 Pet. 1:13; see 3:15).

So far, this discussion has focused on a preventive or defensive military posture regarding the mind. The majority of Scripture deals with personal protection. However, Paul also addresses how to go on the intellectual offensive (2 Cor. 10:4–5). These offensive "weapons" (10:4) certainly feature the Word of God wielded by a Christian's mind in the context of worldview warfare. In this context of mind battle, the "strongholds" (10:4) are "arguments" (10:5) and "every lofty opinion raised against the knowledge of God" (10:5). In other words, any philosophy, worldview, apologetic, or other kind of teaching that undermines, minimizes, contradicts, or tries to eliminate the Christian worldview or any part of it is to be met head-on with an aggressive, offensive battle plan. God's intended end is the destruction ("destroy" is used twice in 10:4–5) of that which does not correspond to Scripture's clear teaching about God and his created world.

In the historical context of 2 Corinthians, Paul opposed any teaching on any subject that had come into the church and did not correspond to his apostolic instruction. Whether an unbeliever or a believer was responsible, whether the idea came from scholars or the uneducated, whether the teaching found wide acceptance or not, all thoughts or opinions that were not *for* the knowledge of God were to be considered *against* the knowledge of God. Therefore, they were to be targeted for intellectual battle and ultimate elimination. Thus, in today's context, all intellectual activities (e.g., reading, listening to the radio, viewing television and movies, studying in formal academia, engaging in casual conversations) must always be pursued using the filtering lens of a Christian theological worldview to determine whether they are allied with the truth of Scripture or are enemies of which to be wary.

THE PROFITABLE MIND

Psalm 119 provides detailed insight into a Christian's new relation to the Bible, which reveals the mind of Christ. First, a believer will develop a great love for and tremendous delight in the Scriptures (119:47–48). Second, a believer in Christ will have a strong desire to know God's Word as the best way to know God (119:16, 93, 176). Third, knowing God will then lead to a Christian obeying him (119:44–45).

Meditation

To hear something once is not enough for most people. To briefly ponder something profound does not allow sufficient time to grasp and fully understand its significance. This proves to be most true with God's mind in Scripture. Psalm 119 testifies to the importance and blessing of lingering long over God's Word.

The idea of meditating sometimes lends itself to misunderstanding. Meditation involves prolonged thought or pondering. An American figure of speech for meditating is "chewing" on a thought. Some have also likened it to the rumination process of the cow's four-stomach digestive system. A vivid picture comes from a coffee percolator. The water goes up a small tube and drains down through the coffee grounds. After enough cycles, the flavor of the coffee beans has been transferred to the water, which is then called coffee. So it is that Christians need to cycle their thoughts through the grounds of God's Word until they start to think like God and then act in a godly manner.

Scripture commands believers to meditate on three areas:

1. God (Pss. 27:4; 63:6)
2. God's Word (Josh. 1:8; Ps. 1:2)
3. God's works (Pss. 143:5; 145:5)

All 176 verses of Psalm 119 extol the virtue of living according to the mind of God. Meditation is mentioned at least seven times as the habit of one who loves God and desires a closer intimacy with him: "O how I love your law! It is my meditation all the day. . . . My eyes are awake before the watches of the night, that I may meditate on your promise" (119:97, 148; see also vv. 15, 23, 27, 48, 78, 99). In contrast, an aspect of Eve's sin can be attributed to her failure to adequately meditate on God's clear and sufficient word (Gen. 2:16–17; cf. 3:3).

Meditating on God's Word will purify the mind of old thoughts that are not of God and reinforce new thoughts from Scripture. It also puts a protective shield around the mind to block and reject incoming thoughts that contradict God. That is the scriptural process of renewing the mind.

Think on These Things

Someone has suggested that the mind is the taproot of the soul. That being so, one needs to carefully and effectively feed his or her soul by sinking one's taproot deep into God's mind in Scripture. One may ask, "What food will feed my soul?" Paul's menu for the mind includes thought entrées that are (1) "true," (2) "honorable," (3) "just," (4) "pure," (5) "lovely," (6) "commendable," (7) "excellen[t]," and (8) "worthy of praise" (Phil. 4:8). In meditating on God's Word and thinking on these things, Christians will avoid setting their minds on earthly things (Phil. 3:19) and being double-minded (James 1:6–8).

THE BALANCED MIND

Are divine revelation and human reason like oil and water—do they never mix? Christians have sometimes reached two erroneous extremes in dealing with divine revelation versus human reason. On one end of the spectrum is *anti-intellectualism*, which basically concludes that if a subject matter is not discussed in the Bible, then it is not worthy of serious study or thought. This unbiblical approach to learning and thinking leads to cultural and intellectual withdrawal. At the opposite extreme is *hyper-intellectualism*, which embraces natural revelation at a higher level of value and credibility than God's special revelation in Scripture; when the two are in conflict, natural revelation is the preferred source of truth. This unbiblical approach results in withdrawal from Scripture.

Both errors must be rejected. The believer must appropriate knowledge from both special and general revelation. However, the creation and our faculties of reason and deduction by which we study the creation (i.e., general revelation) are fallen, fallible, and corrupted by sin. Scripture, on the other hand, is infallible and inerrant and therefore must take precedence over general revelation. Where the Bible speaks to an intellectual discipline, its truth is superior. Where the Bible does not so speak, God has given us the whole world of creation to explore for knowledge—but with the caveat that man's ability to draw conclusions from nature is not infallible like God's Word. This is especially true of thinkers who continually reject their need for Christ's salvation. This does not necessarily mean that their facts are wrong or even that their basic ideas are in error. However, it does guarantee that their worldview is not in accord with God's perspective, and therefore their conclusions ought to be subjected to critical evaluation according to Scripture.

Unmistakably, from the perspective of a Christian worldview, believers are to engage their own minds and the minds of others to the best of their ability and as opportunity allows. However, several wise cautions are in order:

1. Becoming a scholar and trying to change the way one's generation thinks is secondary to becoming a Christian and changing the way one personally thinks about Christ.

2. Formal education in a range of disciplines is secondary to gospel education—namely, obeying the Great Commission (Matt. 28:18–20) and taking the gospel to the ends of the earth, to every creature.
3. General revelation *points* to a higher power, while special revelation *personally introduces* this higher power as the triune God of Scripture, who created the world and all that is in it (see Isaiah 40–48, where Yahweh reminds Israel of this critical truth) and who provided the only Redeemer in the Lord Jesus Christ.
4. To know about the truth is not nearly as important as personally and redemptively being in fellowship with the Truth, Jesus Christ (John 14:6), who is the only source of eternal life.
5. The New Testament church was not mandated to intellectualize their world, nor was this their practice. Rather, they "gospelized" it by proclaiming the saving grace of Jesus Christ to all without distinction, from key political leaders like King Agrippa (Acts 25:23–26:32) to lowly imprisoned slaves like Onesimus (Philem. 10).
6. To moralize, politicize, or intellectualize society without first seeing spiritual conversion is to guarantee only a brief and generally inconsistent change that is shallow, not deep; temporary, not lasting; and ultimately damning, not saving.

It bears repeating that both special and general revelation are necessary for cultivating a biblical mindset. However, the study of special revelation is the priority, followed in the second place by learning from natural revelation. Solomon, the wisest man who ever lived (1 Kings 3:12; 4:29–34), wrote the same advice almost three thousand years ago. His are the most authoritative statements on the subject of the mind and knowledge, since they are Scripture (Prov. 1:7; 9:10; see also 1 Cor. 1:20–21).

The beginning and end of Christian theology is a *knowledge of God* (2 Cor. 2:14; 4:6; Eph. 1:17; Col. 1:10; 2 Pet. 1:2–3, 8; 3:18) and a *knowledge of the truth* (1 Tim. 2:4; 2 Tim. 2:25; Titus 1:1). Above all, at the very center of a Christian worldview is the Lord Jesus Christ, "in whom are hidden all the treasures of wisdom and knowledge" (Col. 2:3). Nothing can be fully understood if God is not known first.

How Does Systematic Theology Relate to One's Personal Life?[21]

Godliness, Christlikeness, and Christian spirituality all describe a Christian becoming more like God. The most powerful way to effect this change is by letting

21 For more on this topic, see Benjamin B. Warfield, "The Religious Life of Theological Students," in *Selected Shorter Writings of Benjamin B. Warfield*, ed. John E. Meeter, 2 vols. (Nutley, NJ: Presbyterian & Reformed, 1970), 1:411–25.

the Word of God dwell in one richly (Col. 3:16). When one embraces Scripture without reservation, it will energetically work God's will in the believer's life (1 Thess. 2:13). The process could be basically defined as follows:

> Christian spirituality involves growing to be like God in character and conduct by personally submitting to the transforming work of God's Word and God's Spirit.

INTIMACY AND MATURITY

There is no better way to saturate one's mind with Scripture than by sitting under expository preaching and studying systematic theology. Both will enhance one's spiritual maturity. The author of Hebrews rejoiced that Jewish Christians had exhibited the intimacy of childlike faith (Heb. 5:12–13) but deplored their lack of advancement to the maturity of meat. So he exhorted, "Therefore let us leave the elementary doctrine of Christ and go on to maturity" (Heb. 6:1). Paul wrote to the Corinthians with similar disappointment (1 Cor. 3:1–3).

Intimacy deals fundamentally with one's personal relationship with the Father, Son, and Holy Spirit in godwardness. Maturity is the result of intimacy reflecting God's abiding, growing presence in Christians in regard to godliness (John 15:1–11). Just as a baby or young child, although not yet mature, can enjoy intimacy with a parent, so should a new Christian with the freshly found Savior. This intimacy fuels the maturing process, whereby a child grows into parental likeness.

Intimacy without maturity results in spiritually infantile behavior instead of spiritually adult responses. In contrast, maturity without intimacy results in a stale, joyless Christianity that can easily deteriorate into legalism and sometimes even a major fall into sin. However, Scripture teaches that when intimacy and maturity complement and feed off each other, the result is a strong, vibrant Christian life. Genuine spirituality, then, must be marked by both intimacy and maturity.

Scripture is essential for growing in spiritual maturity. Jesus, Paul, and James each directly communicated God's clear and frequent pressing demand for spiritual development in the true believer, providing key words for understanding spiritual maturity. We are to be perfect (Matt. 5:48), to be built up to mature manhood (Eph. 4:11–13), to be presented mature in Christ (Col. 1:28), complete and equipped for every good work (2 Tim. 3:16–17), and lacking in nothing (James 1:2–4).

The quickest way to grasp the essence of maturity is to read about the obedience of such people as Abel, Noah, Abraham, Sarah, Isaac, Jacob, and Joseph in Genesis. But one should not quit there. Sixty-five more books of the Bible contain additional stirring accounts of spiritual maturity. This canonical "hall of faith" serves as the ultimate example of God's affirmation of intimate faith and mature faithfulness.

Hebrews 11 chronicles spiritual maturity at its best. But notice that an exhortation immediately follows Hebrews 11, calling for the same kind of maturity in those who received the letter (Heb. 12:1–3). That exhortation is accompanied by a warning about the Father's discipline of those who persist in immaturity (12:4–11). Imperfect earthly parenthood is but a faint reflection of God's flawlessly consistent response to those who by faith in the Lord Jesus Christ have been born again into God's family (John 1:12–13).

A saint of old, Epaphras, prayed that the Christians at Colossae would stand perfect and fully assured in all the will of God (Col. 4:12). May God, in similar fashion, commend these compelling biblical truths about spiritual maturity to our stewardship of worship and obedience for his great glory.

HOLINESS

Christians have been saved to be holy and to live holy lives (1 Pet. 1:14–16). What does it mean to be holy? Both the Hebrew and Greek words for "to be holy" (which appear about two thousand times in Scripture) basically mean "to be set aside for something special." Thus, God is holy in that he sets himself apart from creation, humanity, and all pagan gods by the fact of his deity and sinlessness. That's why the angels sing of God, "Holy, holy, holy" (Isa. 6:3; Rev. 4:8), and why Scripture declares him to be holy (e.g., Ps. 99:9; Isa. 43:15).

Thus, the idea of holiness takes on a spiritual meaning among the people of God based on the holy character of God. For instance, the high priest of God had inscribed across his headpiece "Holy to the Lord" (Ex. 39:30). The high priest was especially set apart by God to intercede on behalf of a sinful nation to a holy God for the forgiveness of their transgressions.

Holiness embodies the very essence of Christianity. The holy Savior has saved sinners to be a holy people (1 Pet. 2:4–10). That's why one of the most common biblical names for a believer is *saint*, which simply and wonderfully means "saved and set apart" (Rom. 1:7; 1 Cor. 1:2).

When one considers that a holy God saves, it is no surprise to learn that he gives his Holy Spirit to every believer at salvation. A primary purpose of this gift is to equip believers with the power to live a holy life (1 Thess. 4:7–8; 1 John 3:24; 4:13).

So God wants Christians to share his holiness (Heb. 12:10) and to present themselves as slaves of righteousness, which will result in holiness (Rom. 6:19): "Since we have these promises, beloved, let us cleanse ourselves from every defilement of body and spirit, bringing holiness to completion in the fear of God" (2 Cor. 7:1). Thus the author of Hebrews writes, "Strive for peace with everyone, and for the holiness without which no one will see the Lord" (Heb. 12:14). Holiness is the core of a Christian's experience.

Spiritual maturity springs out of holiness. Scottish theologian John Brown boils holiness down to a definition that we can all understand and pursue:

> Holiness does not consist in mystic speculations, enthusiastic fervours, or uncommanded austerities; it consists in thinking as God thinks, and willing as God wills. God's mind and will are to be known from his word; and, so far as I really understand and believe God's word, God's mind becomes my mind, God's will becomes my will, and according to the measure of my faith, I become holy.[22]

SANCTIFICATION[23]

Closely connected with holiness is *sanctification*. In many New Testament uses, the word means "salvation" (Acts 20:32; 1 Cor. 1:2). Sanctification, or being set apart in salvation, should result in believers being set apart for Christian living.

Sanctification not only includes the immediate act and fact of salvation but also involves a progressive or growing experience of greater holiness and less sinfulness. It expresses God's will and fulfills the purpose of God's salvation call (1 Thess. 4:3–7). Sanctification includes one's responsibility to participate in continuing what God's Spirit began in salvation (2 Tim. 2:21; Rev. 22:11).

Christians are constantly exhorted to pursue in their Christian experience what God has declared to be true of them in salvation. Believers are also promised that what is not now complete, God will ultimately finish in glory (Phil. 2:12–13; 1 Thess. 5:23). These passages express one of the great paradoxes of Scripture: Christians are to become what they already are and one day will be. Such certainty of the Christian's future is captured in texts like these:

> For everyone who calls on the name of the Lord will be saved. (Rom. 10:13)
>
> For the word of the cross is folly to those who are perishing, but to us who are being saved it is the power of God. (1 Cor. 1:18)
>
> Besides this you know the time, that the hour has come for you to wake from sleep. For salvation is nearer to us now than when we first believed. (Rom. 13:11)

Sanctification involves the spiritual process that is pictured by a body growing into adulthood (Heb. 5:11–14) or a tree bearing fruit (Ps. 1:3). Growth is not always easy or uniform; however, it should be the direction of a true Christian's life.

22 John Brown, *Expository Discourses on the First Epistle of Peter*, 2 vols. (Edinburgh: William Oliphant, 1866), 1:117.

23 For a more detailed discussion of sanctification, see "Sanctification," in chap. 7, "Salvation" (p. 342).

Several obstacles face the believer in this lifelong pursuit. Christians need to know about these obstacles and stay on guard to avoid them or to correct them if they become a part of one's thinking:

1. One may think more highly of self than one ought and not pursue holiness as one should (Rom. 12:3).
2. One may presume upon salvation and assume that since one is saved, holy living is optional (Rom. 6:1–2).
3. One may have been erroneously taught about the nature of Christian living and so neglect the lordship of Christ (1 Pet. 3:15).
4. One may lack the zeal or energy to make holiness a priority (2 Cor. 7:1).
5. One may think that he or she is saved but not truly *be* saved and then try to live a holy life in the power of the flesh (Matt. 13:5–7, 20–22).

Nature teaches that growth is normal and to be expected; conversely, a lack of growth should sound an alarm that something is seriously wrong. Scripture teaches this same principle in a spiritual sense. Frequently, Acts reports that the early church grew and expanded (see Acts 2:41; 4:4; 5:14; 6:7; 9:31, 35, 42; 11:21; 14:1, 21; 16:5; 17:12). God also has expectations for individual growth in the Christian's life. These exhortations of Scripture need to be taken seriously (1 Pet. 2:2; 2 Pet. 3:18).

The chief agents for this growth are God's Word (John 17:17; 1 Pet. 2:2) and God's Spirit (Eph. 5:15–21). When growth occurs, one can quickly acknowledge God as the cause (1 Cor. 3:6–7; Col. 2:19). The Holy Spirit plays a prominent role in providing a true believer with the assurance of salvation. His assurance connects directly with growth (Rom. 8:16–17; 1 John 3:24).

Having formerly been spiritually dead but now made alive to God, the believer can check his vital signs to substantiate the fact that he is indeed alive, because he walks in the works that God has prepared (Eph. 2:1–10). In order to check one's spiritual health, here are some of the most important vital signs of a true Christian:

1. Christian fruit (John 15:8)
2. Love for God's people (John 13:35)
3. Concern for personal holiness (1 Pet. 1:13–21)
4. Love for God's Word (1 Pet. 2:2–3)
5. A desire to obey (John 14:15, 21, 23)
6. A sense of intimacy with God (Rom. 8:14–17)
7. Perseverance (Phil. 1:27–28)
8. Fellowship with God's people (Heb. 10:24–25)
9. A desire to glorify God (Matt. 5:13–16)
10. Witness to Christ's personal reality (1 Pet. 3:15)

As a result of testing their spiritual vital signs, Christians are not to linger or remain at the childhood level but are to grow up in all things. As this individual maturity or growth occurs, it extends to the building up and growth of the corporate body of Christ (Eph. 4:14–16).

Spirituality involves God's Spirit taking God's Word and maturing God's people through the ministry of God's servants for the spiritual growth of individual believers, which results in the growth of Christ's body. This is the ultimate goal of systematic theology—to increasingly think and then act in accord with God's will as one matures in the Christian faith.

How Does Systematic Theology Relate to One's Ministry?

The noted theologian Benjamin Warfield gave the following answer to this vital question:

> If such be the value and use of doctrine, the systematic theologian is preeminently a preacher of the gospel; and the end of his work is obviously not merely the logical arrangement of the truths which come under his hand, but the moving of men, through their power, to love God with all their hearts and their neighbors as themselves; to choose their portion with the Saviour of their souls; to find and hold Him precious; and to recognize and yield to the sweet influences of the Holy Spirit whom He has sent. With such truth as this he will not dare to deal in a cold and merely scientific spirit, but will justly and necessarily permit its preciousness and its practical destination to determine the spirit in which he handles it, and to awaken the reverential love with which alone he should investigate its reciprocal relations. For this he needs to be suffused at all times with a sense of the unspeakable worth of the revelation which lies before him as the source of his material, and with the personal bearings of its separate truths on his own heart and life; he needs to have had and to be having a full, rich, and deep religious experience of the great doctrines with which he deals; he needs to be living close to his God, to be resting always on the bosom of his Redeemer, to be filled at all times with the manifest influences of the Holy Spirit. The student of systematic theology needs a very sensitive religious nature, a most thoroughly consecrated heart, and an outpouring of the Holy Ghost upon him, such as will fill him with that spiritual discernment, without which all native intellect is in vain. He needs to be not merely a student, not merely a thinker, not merely a systematizer, not merely a teacher—he needs to be like the beloved disciple himself in the highest, truest, and holiest sense, a divine.[24]

24 Benjamin B. Warfield, "The Idea of Systematic Theology," in *The Works of Benjamin B. Warfield*, vol. 9, *Studies in Theology* (1933; repr., Grand Rapids, MI: Baker, 2003), 86–87.

Questions:

1. What are the terms used to define, and what is the definition of, theology?
2. What are the "various major kinds" of theology?
3. What is the definition of systematic theology?
4. What are the "categories" of systematic theology?
5. What are the "benefits and limitations" of systematic theology?
6. What are the implications of sound doctrine for the life of the church?
7. What is "the overarching and unifying theme of Scripture"?
8. In what ways is Scripture a revelation of God?
9. What is a "worldview," and how does systematic theology relate to one's worldview?
10. How does systematic theology relate to one's mind and life?

2

GOD'S WORD

Bibliology

THE BIBLE IS FUNDAMENTAL to evangelical theology because it provides the sole infallible and ultimate authority for a truly Christian worldview. That the Bible should play such an exclusive role is only reasonable, since from beginning to end it consistently claims to be God's Word to man. There can be no higher, more authoritative source of knowledge than this Word. Without it there is no true theology.

More than 2,500 times in the Old Testament the biblical writers assert that God spoke what was written within its pages. What the prophets spoke and wrote was synonymous with the Word of God that had come to them (Ex. 24:3). To believe the prophets was to believe God. To disobey them was nothing less than rebellion against God himself.

The phrase "the word of God" occurs more than forty times in the New Testament. Jesus and his apostles testified that the Old Testament writings were the words of God (Matt. 15:6; Rom. 3:2). They looked to the Old Testament as the basis for their teaching, and boldly equated their own words with the words of God himself. The Word of God is what Jesus preached (Luke 5:1; John 3:34). It is what the apostles taught (Acts 4:31; 1 Thess. 2:13). It is what formed the church (Acts 6:7; 12:24; 19:20).

As "the holy Scriptures" (Rom. 1:2), "the oracles of God" (Rom. 3:2), "the word of truth" (2 Tim. 2:15), and "the sacred writings" (2 Tim. 3:15), the Bible possesses unparalleled authority in establishing doctrine, identifying and correcting error, and instructing in righteousness (2 Tim. 3:16). It can never be supplanted or amended by a different authority, for it always contains that which is perfect for achieving its purpose (Ps. 19:7–11; Isa. 55:10–11; Rom. 1:16–17; 2 Tim. 3:16–17; Heb. 4:12).

God's Word declares that its content is without error and is never misleading in whatever it asserts or describes (Pss. 12:6; 119:140; Prov. 30:5). Its promises never fail, for God can never lie (Num. 23:19; Matt. 5:18; John 10:35; Titus 1:2; Heb. 6:18). Since it is absolutely true, it is totally trustworthy. Since it comes directly from God, it is universally binding.

According to Scripture, the person and word of God are so interrelated that the text of Scripture unequivocally reflects the qualities of its ultimate author. God is true, pure, unchanging, reliable, living, and active; therefore, so is his Word. God himself has given his Word the same glory as he has given his name, which is the sum of his character (Ps. 138:2). No other source of knowledge, no other literature written by humankind, possesses such qualities or functions.

The Inspiration of Scripture

God freely initiated the revelation of himself to humankind. The means he used were varied (Heb. 1:1–3), but the most thorough and understandable self-disclosures were through the written propositions of Scripture (1 Cor. 2:6–16). The written Word of God is unique in that it is the only source of knowledge that clearly explains man's plight and God's accomplishment of salvation through a Savior.

The knowledge of God was captured in the writings of Scripture by the special activity of the Holy Spirit in the writings of the biblical authors. This activity is known as *inspiration*. Zechariah describes this activity when he writes of "the law and the words that the Lord of hosts had sent by his Spirit through the former prophets" (Zech. 7:12). Paul refers to this same process by stating that "all Scripture is breathed out by God" (2 Tim. 3:16). Peter also states that "no prophecy was ever produced by the will of man, but men spoke from God as they were carried along by the Holy Spirit" (2 Pet. 1:21).

Through this process of inspiration, God ensured that the particular knowledge he determined to disclose would be revealed to its intended audience perfectly, without error, omission, or defect. Through the process of inspiration, God also ensured that this knowledge would be revealed intelligibly to humankind, in the language and thought structures of human beings.

REVELATION AND INSPIRATION

The finite creature and the infinite Creator differ fundamentally. God enjoys infinite and perfect knowledge. He always knows everything innately and exhaustively. He never learns; he always knows. On the other hand, humankind possesses a finite and dependent knowledge. Man must always learn, and he cannot know anything about his infinite Creator unless the Creator reveals it.

This revelation comes in two forms: general revelation (Ps. 19:1–6) and special revelation (vv. 7–11).

General Revelation

General revelation is God's witness of himself through creation. David states that this witness is unavoidable: "The heavens declare the glory of God, and the sky above proclaims his handiwork" (Ps. 19:1). This witness is also continuous: "Day to day pours out speech, and night to night reveals knowledge" (v. 2). This general witness is nonverbal in nature: "There is no speech, nor are there words, whose voice is not heard" (v. 3). And this witness is universally accessible to everyone at all times and in every place: "Their voice goes out through all the earth, and their words to the end of the world" (v. 4; cf. Acts 14:17; 17:23–31; Rom. 1:18–25; 10:18).

The kind of knowledge that can be discerned from general revelation includes an appreciation of God's wisdom and power. The more a person examines the vastness of space or the finest particles of molecular structure, the more he is compelled to recognize with wonder the greatness of the Creator. The way the hydrologic cycle works to water the earth, provide food, and preserve life attests to the goodness of its Creator. The fact that rain falls on the fields of those who love and worship God as well as those who do not reveals God's love for all his creatures (Matt. 5:45; Acts 14:17). God's providential care and governance of the human race can also be included as a part of general revelation (Acts 17:26).

Another form of general revelation can be observed in humanity's inherent acknowledgment of the existence of right and wrong and the need for justice (Rom. 2:14–15). Solomon also affirms that man instinctively knows there is more to life than this temporal existence, since God "has put eternity into man's heart" (Eccles. 3:11).

While general revelation conveys a great deal of knowledge about the Creator, it has a fixed content and purpose. Its clarity and unavoidable nature leaves humanity without excuse for failing to recognize and appreciate the nature of their Creator (Rom. 1:19–20). However, its purpose is not to prescribe the way by which fallen humanity might obtain reconciliation with its Creator. That end—redemption—is exclusively the purview of special revelation. Consequently, no one can be saved by the content of general revelation alone (Rom. 10:5–17; 1 Cor. 1:18–2:5).

Special Revelation

Special revelation is God's disclosure of himself in a more personal and detailed manner than that provided by general revelation. God has provided this special knowledge through (1) direct acts, (2) dreams and visions, (3) Christ's incarnation, and (4) Scripture.

God has revealed himself uniquely by direct acts at various times and in various ways throughout redemptive history. He spoke directly with Adam in the garden (Gen. 2:16–17; 3:9, 11). He spoke to Moses individually and confirmed his authority through unique signs and wonders (Deut. 34:10–12). He audibly confirmed his Son to others on three separate occasions during his earthly ministry (Matt. 3:17; 17:5; John 12:28). He performed special seasons of miracles at pivotal moments in the unfolding of his redemptive plan.

God has also revealed himself uniquely through dreams and visions. He revealed special knowledge to Joseph in the form of dreams (Gen. 37:6–7, 9). He gave Isaiah a personal vision of the Son of God in his preincarnate glory (Isaiah 6; John 12:41). The apostle John saw a vision of the resurrected and ascended Jesus Christ (Rev. 1:10–16). In each case, the dream or vision provided the human recipient with special knowledge of God's character and will.

The climax of God's special revelation occurred at the incarnation of his Son (Heb. 1:1–2). The Son of God took on human nature and dwelt among humankind as the ultimate act of the revelation of God to men (John 1:1–5, 14, 18). While he was not generally recognized for who he was because of the hardness of human hearts (Isa. 53:2; John 1:10–11), he nevertheless revealed God to humankind unlike any other medium of revelation (John 1:18; 14:9–10; Col. 1:15; Heb. 1:3).

Another form of special revelation is the written text of Scripture. Certainly, the Scriptures are not of the same category as the revelation of God's Son. The Scriptures serve to point to the Son, not to themselves (John 5:36–40). On the other hand, the revelation of God's Son can be authoritatively known today only through the Bible. Thus, while the writer of Hebrews proclaims Jesus as the climax of God's revelatory activity (Heb. 1:1–3), he then proceeds to admonish his readers to "pay much closer attention to what we have heard" (Heb. 2:1)—that is, to the apostolic witness concerning this Son of God. This witness is captured in the pages of Scripture. Without Scripture, Jesus could not be truly known.

While both general and special revelation effectively communicate knowledge about God, they are marked by differences. First, the current medium of general revelation will one day pass away (Isa. 40:8; Matt. 24:35; 1 Pet. 1:24). However, the medium of God's Word will endure forever (Ps. 119:89; Isa. 40:8; Matt. 24:35; 1 Pet. 1:25). Second, the medium of general revelation suffers under the curse of sin and corruption (Gen. 3:1–24; Rom. 8:20–23). It was once "very good" (Gen. 1:31) but now shows signs of infertility, deformity, vanity, and death (Eccles. 1:2). However, the medium of Scripture is inspired by God and entirely perfect and holy (Pss. 19:7–9; 119:140 NASB). Third, the purpose of general revelation is limited compared to that of special revelation in Scripture. While general revelation reveals the character of God through his handiwork and leaves fallen human beings without excuse for their rejection of him (Rom. 1:18–20), the special revelation of God's Word brings knowledge of Jesus and the way of salvation through faith in him (Rom. 10:13–17).

DEFINITION OF INSPIRATION

Scholars have proposed various theories for explaining the divine process of inspiration. The main views can be summarized as follows.

Dictation Theory of Inspiration. This view contends that God gave the human writers of the Bible the specific words to write without their own involvement or understanding. The process of inspiration simply involved penning the words of the Bible verbatim, much like a secretary does for an executive.

Scripture certainly includes instances of divine dictation (Ex. 34:27; Revelation 2–3). But this is by no means the only approach of inspiration, nor is it pervasive throughout the Bible. The key argument against this view is that every book of the Bible exhibits evidence of the human writer's personality and involvement (cf. Deut. 3:23–25; Ps. 42:5, 11; Luke 1:1–4; Gal. 6:11; 2 Pet. 3:15–16; Jude 3).

Still, the question remains, how could the Bible be the words of men like Jeremiah and Paul and at the same time be God's words as well? Part of the answer to this question is that God made Jeremiah, Paul, and the other writers of Scripture into men who could faithfully communicate his knowledge by forming their very personalities long before they ever wrote (Jer. 1:4–10; Gal. 1:15). By his careful providence, God taught his select spokesmen what to speak (Ex. 4:10–12; 2 Pet. 1:20–21) so that they could communicate exactly what God wanted them to communicate, within the scope of their own unique personalities and styles. As such, the Scripture can freely testify that both the Lord and Hosea spoke the words of Hosea 11:1 (Matt. 2:15), that both the Holy Spirit and David spoke Psalm 110 (Mark 12:36), that both the Holy Spirit and Isaiah spoke Isaiah 6:9–10 (Acts 28:25–27), and that every other word of Scripture is the product of both God's direct influence and the conscious, direct participation of the human writer.

Partial or Conceptual Theory of Inspiration. Advocates of this view argue that God's superintendence of the writing of Scripture never reached the level of actual words. Instead, God merely impressed upon the biblical writers the general ideas he desired to communicate, giving the writers freedom to choose how to articulate these concepts.

According to this view, only the concepts of Scripture can be considered inspired by God and therefore authoritative and true. The actual words by which those concepts are described can be tainted by error since they are the product of fallen human writers. This understanding of inspiration is found among those who contend that the Bible *contains* the Word of God but is not in its entirety the Word of God. Proponents argue that while God desires to communicate knowledge about himself and his will, he accommodated this knowledge in such a way as to allow for inaccuracy and error in how it was expressed. It then becomes the responsibility of the reader to distinguish between that which is inaccurate in the expressions of the human writer and that which is true according to the general concept intended by God.

However, it is important to recognize that Scripture never makes a distinction between its general concepts and the specific forms of their expression. Instead, Scripture consistently claims to be entirely truthful (Pss. 12:6; 19:7–9; 119:160; Prov. 30:5; 2 Tim. 2:15). According to Scripture's own witness, inspiration extends to all that is in Scripture, not just to certain parts (2 Tim. 3:16; 2 Pet. 1:20–21). God expresses great concern for every part of his Word and forbids any tampering with the wording of his commandments (Deut. 4:2; 12:32; Prov. 30:6; Rev. 22:18–19). Jesus himself affirmed that God's Word is truth (John 17:17), and that divine authority extended even to the smallest markings of its original expression (Matt. 5:18).

Natural Theory of Inspiration. Proponents of this view argue that the biblical writers found inspiration for their writing not directly from God but from themselves and their experiences. In the same way that other gifted composers and authors have been "inspired" to compose their great masterpieces, the biblical writers were moved naturally in the writing of Scripture.

The obvious objection to this view is that it denies the Bible's own testimony of divine authorship (2 Tim. 3:16; 2 Pet. 1:20–21). This view exalts the human writers of the Bible but denies that God was directly involved in its composition. It makes the Bible a human product alone—a book about God but superintended by man. While the biblical writers may have possessed exceptional skill and profound insight, they were still beset by some degree of ignorance, limitation, and error. At a human level it would have been impossible to prevent the inclusion of these features into the text of Scripture. Hence, the Bible is not really that different from any other great literary classic. Thus, proponents of this view inevitably deny Scripture's authority, necessity, and inerrancy.

The Biblical View: Verbal, Plenary Inspiration. This view contends that God inspired every word recorded by the human writers in each of the sixty-six books of the Bible in their original form. As such, any text of Scripture is at once the true, authoritative Word of God and the intended word of the biblical writer. No distinction can be made in any text between the divine and human components.

This view affirms that both the general concepts and the specific expressions are divinely authoritative and inerrant, that the process of inspiration preserved both God's ultimate agency in the writing of Scripture and the human writers' personal involvement. Such inspiration is described as *verbal* (Lat. *verbum*, "word") in that the influence of the Holy Spirit extends to the very choice of words and grammar. It is also described as *plenary* (Lat. *plenus*, "full") in that it is characteristic of every part and kind of literature found in the Bible—to historical works like Genesis just as much as to doctrinal treatises like Romans.

This view reflects what Paul asserted in 2 Timothy 3:16, "All Scripture is breathed out by God," and what Peter asserted in 2 Peter 1:21, "men spoke from God as they were carried along by the Holy Spirit." God produced the Scriptures by superintending the human writer's own thoughts as he produced the Scriptures. This resulted in a product that is both authoritative and inerrant because of its divine authorship, and intelligible to humankind because of its human authorship.

The Process of Inspiration

The processes by which the books of the Bible were composed are many and varied. At times, God gave Moses specific words to write (Ex. 34:27). At other times, God used the thoughts Moses himself was thinking (Deut. 3:23–26). Some of David's psalms were drawn from his own unique experiences (Psalms 32; 51), while others were built upon experiences David shared with others (Psalm 23). Solomon searched out and collected many proverbs (Eccles. 12:9), and then he and others compiled them into what is now the book of Proverbs (Prov. 1:1; 10:1; 25:1). Luke composed his Gospel after meticulous research (Luke 1:1–4). Jude set out to write a general letter of encouragement before changing his mind to write a letter urging the defense of the gospel (Jude 3).

Even the writing process itself was unique to the writers and the books they composed. Jeremiah dictated to his scribe, Baruch, the words God gave him. Yet even though Baruch did the writing, the words are never attributed to him; they are always considered either the words of Jeremiah or the words of God (cf. Jeremiah 36). While Paul may have occasionally written letters by his own hand (Philem. 19), he often dictated his letters to an amanuensis (a scribe or secretary), including only a few words from his own hand at the end to certify the letter's authenticity (cf. 1 Cor. 16:21; Col. 4:18; 2 Thess. 3:17). Through all these approaches to composition, God the Holy Spirit was superintending every word of what was written.

Peter provides the most succinct description of the process of composition: "knowing this first of all, that no prophecy of Scripture comes from someone's own interpretation. For no prophecy was ever produced by the will of man, but men spoke from God as they were carried along by the Holy Spirit" (2 Pet. 1:20–21). That the "prophecy of Scripture" does not come "from someone's own interpretation" indicates that the meaning of the biblical text did not ultimately originate in the intent of the human writer. What was written was not produced by the singular effort or "will of man." Rather, God's will is the ultimate cause of these writings, and he brought them into being through the Holy Spirit's direct influence on those he chose as his instruments to reveal his knowledge. Indeed, "men spoke" from and for God, but they did so as they were "carried along" by the Holy Spirit. Conscious of this reality, David testifies that "The Spirit of the LORD speaks by me; his word is on my tongue" (2 Sam. 23:2).

Paul's assertion that "All Scripture is breathed out by God" (2 Tim. 3:16) is also crucial to an understanding of the process of inspiration. First, Paul asserts that all that belongs to the category of "Scripture" is inspired by God. Certainly, the most direct reference of the term "Scripture" is to the Old Testament—"the sacred writings" Paul referred to in the previous verse (2 Tim. 3:15). But the term "Scripture" need not be restricted to the thirty-nine books of the Old Testament. What Paul emphasizes here is not a specific collection of books but a kind of literature. Consequently, the term applies by extension to those writings that were being composed during Paul's time—the writings of the New Testament—that were characterized by the same qualities as the Old Testament. Thus, in 1 Timothy 5:18 Paul joins a citation from the Old Testament ("You shall not muzzle an ox when it treads out the grain," Deut. 25:4), with a statement from Luke's Gospel ("The laborer deserves his wages," Luke 10:7), and calls them both "Scripture." Further, Peter refers to Paul's writings and compares them to "the other Scriptures" (2 Pet. 3:16), implying that Paul's writings are also considered to be Scripture.

Second, Paul asserts that all that belongs to this category of Scripture must be recognized as having been "breathed out by God." The term *theopneustos*—found nowhere else in the New Testament—is a combination of the words "God" and "to breathe out, blow." While the term has been rendered as "inspired" in many translations due to the influence of the term *inspirata* used in the Latin Vulgate, it is better understood as "expired." Expiration is the process of exhaling air out of the lungs. It is the action that happens when the voice is used. Therefore, Paul's use of the term *theopneustos* emphasizes the origin and delivery of Scripture. All that is properly defined as Scripture has been "exhaled out of the lungs of God," metaphorically speaking. It has been "spoken" by God's voice. He is responsible for the process of its communication from its origin as a thought in his own mind to its articulation in human words captured in the written text.

Objections to Inspiration

Objections to this understanding of inspiration commonly focus on the fallible nature of the human writers. Since the human component in Scripture is acknowledged, and since to be human is to err (so it is claimed), then Scripture must contain error. To deny error in Scripture, they say, is to deny its human component.

Indeed, the men God used were not perfect. Scripture does not hide this fact. Moses grievously sinned and was not permitted to enter the Promised Land (Num. 20:9–12). David deeply displeased the Lord through his sin with Bathsheba

(2 Samuel 11). Paul openly acknowledged his imperfection even after two decades of ministry as an apostle (Phil. 3:12–13).

At the same time, Scripture is unequivocal in its testimony regarding the inerrant nature of its text. As one can draw a straight line with a crooked stick, God produced an inerrant Bible using imperfect men. This process did not involve the suspension of the human writers' humanity, nor a temporary impartation of a divine nature. Rather, it involved the preservation of the writers' humanity with the Spirit's special protection against error. After all, while to err is to be human, to be human is not necessarily to err. Human beings are capable of making true statements—especially so when directly guided by the Holy Spirit.

Obvious analogies can be found in the incarnation of Jesus Christ. Scripture records the miraculous conception of the Son of God in the womb of Mary (Matt. 1:18–25; Luke 1:26–38). Mary was marked by sin just like every other descendant of Adam, and yet God used her as the vessel to bear the sinless Jesus. Analogously, God was able to use fallible human writers to produce a faultless text. Moreover, in the incarnation the Son of God took on human nature, and that human nature did not compromise the Son's sinless essence (Heb. 4:15; 1 Pet. 2:22; 1 John 3:5). In the same way, the divine and human intents could concur to produce inerrant Scripture.

PREPARATION FOR INSPIRATION

Behind the composition of the sixty-six books of the Bible was a divine superintendence that providentially orchestrated every aspect of its creation.

Preparation of the Writings

Divine providence prepared not only the biblical writers but also the historical contexts in which they wrote. Every detail of the political, social, economic, linguistic, geographic, and even meteorological spheres was specially designed by God to aid in the revelation of his knowledge.

The Pentateuch was written by Moses in the immediate context of Israel's delivery out of slavery in Egypt and on the eve of her conquest of the Promised Land. These grand historical circumstances of slavery, redemption, and promise provided the best backdrop for the composition of that literature which was to serve as the foundation for the rest of God's redemptive revelation. The Psalms were commonly written amid particular historical contexts that displayed the human writers' need for God and God's amazing works in response. Such historical circumstances vividly highlight God's worthiness of worship. The prophetic books are filled with references that identify the historical fulfillments of God's warnings and promises, serving in turn to demonstrate the trustworthiness of God's Word. Since God's promises of judgment and redemption are fulfilled exactly as described in the past, there can be certainty that those promises that remain unfulfilled to this day will one day be realized just as they are described.

A survey of the New Testament reveals the same testimony. Paul states regarding the revelation of God's Son, "But when the fullness of time had come, God sent forth his Son, born of woman, born under the law" (Gal. 4:4). In the same way, the writings of the New Testament all came into being at "the fullness of time." Whether Luke's Gospel to Theophilus, Paul's letter to Philemon, or John's revelation of Jesus Christ to the seven churches of Asia Minor, all the books of the New Testament testify to God's careful preparation of circumstances that would best occasion the revelation of the knowledge he intended to communicate.

Preparation of the Writers

God also prepared the writers themselves. Orchestrating everything from their place in their family lineage to the nature of their personal experiences to the development of their own unique writing style and vocabulary, God providentially prepared each writer of Scripture to be the ideal instrument through which he would reveal his knowledge to humanity.

Regarding God's preparation of Moses, Stephen stated, "At this time Moses was born; and he was beautiful in God's sight. And he was brought up for three months in his father's house, and when he was exposed, Pharaoh's daughter adopted him and brought him up as her own son. And Moses was instructed in all the wisdom of the Egyptians, and he was mighty in his words and deeds" (Acts 7:20–22). This exceptional upbringing produced the ideal instrument for God to use to rescue his people from slavery and compose the first five books of the Bible.

Scripture itself testifies that David's experience as a shepherd prepared him to lead the nation of Israel: "He chose David his servant and took him from the sheepfolds; from following the nursing ewes he brought him to shepherd Jacob his people, Israel his inheritance" (Ps. 78:70–71). This shepherding background also uniquely prepared David to write psalms like Psalm 23. Such personal preparation is also noted with respect to Jeremiah the prophet. To him the Lord states, "Before I formed you in the womb I knew you, and before you were born I consecrated you; I appointed you a prophet to the nations" (Jer. 1:5). With no reason to conclude that David and Jeremiah were unique, such individual preparation can be assumed for all of the prophets of the Old Testament.

The same can be recognized in the preparation of the New Testament writers. Paul, the writer of thirteen of the New Testament's twenty-seven books, testified that God had set him apart before his birth in order to reveal his Son to him and make him a preacher to the Gentiles (Gal. 1:15). Paul's unique background in Pharisaism made him the ideal instrument to record divine knowledge concerning the doctrine of justification by grace alone through faith alone in Christ alone. Similarly, Luke's education as a physician (Col. 4:14) contributed to his ability for careful investigation (Luke 1:1–4)—a skill of vital importance for the composition of his Gospel and the book of Acts. The same is true of each of the New Testament writers.

PROOFS OF INSPIRATION

God has not left his written word without proof of its divine nature. From beginning to end and in manifold ways, God testifies that the writings of Scripture are "breathed out" by him.

Old Testament Proofs of Inspiration

The Old Testament Is Identified as the Words of God. Time after time, Old Testament writers state that what was recorded was what "God said" (e.g., Ex. 17:14; 19:3, 6–7; 20:1; 24:4; 34:27). Ezra called the Old Testament "the words of the God of Israel" (Ezra 9:4). The Psalter begins by identifying the law of Moses as "the law of the LORD" (Ps. 1:2). Twenty-four times in Psalm 119 the psalmist calls Scripture the "word(s) of the LORD." The prophets introduced their messages with statements like "hear the word of the LORD" (1 Kings 22:19; 2 Kings 20:16). There was no hesitancy on the part of the Old Testament writers to equate what they wrote with the words of the Almighty.

The Old Testament Records Direct Speech by God. The first book of the Bible begins with a record of the direct speech of God: "And God said, 'Let there be light,' and there was light" (Gen. 1:3; cf. vv. 6, 9, 11, etc.). This record of direct speech continues with the instructions God gave to Adam and Eve (Gen. 1:26, 28–29; 2:16–17), as well as his judgments and promises in light of their fall into sin (Gen. 3:13–19). Genesis records direct speech between God and other individuals as well. God called Abram from the land of Ur and spoke directly to him on multiple occasions (Gen. 12:1–3; 15:1–21). Exodus 3:1–4:23 provides a detailed account of God's direct speech to Moses at the burning bush. The books of Exodus, Leviticus, Numbers, and Deuteronomy are filled with quotations of God's direct speech to human beings, particularly to Moses. Following the death of Moses, God spoke directly with Joshua, instructing him about his role in conquering the Promised Land (Josh. 1:8–9). This pattern continues throughout the Old Testament.

The Old Testament Authorizes the Prophets as God's Spokesmen. Beginning with Moses (Ex. 3:15), God's prophets were recognized as authoritative messengers from God speaking directly on his behalf. Moses was told to go directly to Pharaoh and address him on God's behalf by saying, "Thus says the LORD" (Ex. 4:22). That pattern is followed throughout the Old Testament by God's prophets, including Joshua (Josh. 7:13; 24:2, 27), Gideon (Judg. 6:7–18), Samuel (1 Sam. 10:18; 15:2), Nathan (2 Sam. 12:7, 11), and many others (e.g., 1 Kings 11:31; 12:24; 13:1–2;

13:21; 14:3–7). When a prophet speaks for God, one of the common formulas used to introduce the content is "thus says the LORD." The prophet can even speak for God in the first person (e.g., 1 Kings 20:13). David recognized that God was speaking through him when he stated, "The Spirit of the LORD speaks by me; his word is on my tongue" (2 Sam. 23:2). That prophets could speak directly for God led to counterfeit attempts to reproduce that authority, which is why God provided instruction for discerning between true and false prophets (Deut. 12:32; 13:1–5; 18:15–22).

Jesus's View of the Scriptures

There can be no better witness to a correct understanding of the inspiration and authority of Scripture than that provided by Jesus Christ himself.

Jesus Affirmed the Authority of the Old Testament. In his every reference to the Old Testament Scriptures, Jesus assumed and upheld their universal authority.

For example, Jesus appealed to the authority of the Old Testament in response to each of the temptations of Satan (Matt. 4:1–11; Luke 4:1–13). Jesus also appealed to the authority of the Old Testament to resolve matters of faith and practice. When his disciples were charged with breaking the Sabbath, Jesus referred to principles derived from the Mosaic law, quoting from 1 Samuel 21:6 as the biblical justification for their actions (Matt. 12:1–8). When asked about divorce, Jesus appealed to both Genesis 2:23–24 and Deuteronomy 24:1–4 (Matt. 19:3–9). Directly asserting the authority of the Old Testament, Jesus repeatedly asked his opponents, "Have you not read?" (Matt. 12:3, 5; 19:4; 21:16, 42; 22:31; Mark 2:25; 12:10, 24, 26; Luke 6:3).

Jesus also appealed to the authority of the Old Testament to testify to his identity. In response to the religious leaders who criticized his act of healing on the Sabbath, Jesus claimed equality with God and based this assertion on several proofs: the witness of John the Baptist (John 5:33–35); the testimony of his own works (5:36); the testimony of his heavenly Father (5:37–38); and the testimony of the Old Testament Scriptures—specifically the books of Moses (5:39–47). After his resurrection he also appealed to the Old Testament Scriptures to confirm his identity, admonishing his disciples for their doubts (Luke 24:25–27, 44–49). In fact, Jesus affirmed that the testimony of the Old Testament supersedes even that of the miracle of resurrection: "If they do not hear Moses and the Prophets, neither will they be convinced if someone should rise from the dead" (Luke 16:31).

Jesus also submitted to and promoted the authority of the Old Testament. In the Sermon on the Mount he stated that he had not come to abolish the Law or the Prophets but to fulfill them (Matt. 5:17). He stated that any violation of the Scriptures would have eternal consequences (Matt. 5:18–19). He defined the Golden

Rule as the core of the Scripture's teaching (Matt. 7:12). As Paul would say later, Jesus, the Son of God, was one "born under the law" (Gal. 4:4).

Jesus Affirmed the Inspiration of the Old Testament. Jesus did not accept the authority of the Old Testament merely because it was the popular perspective of first-century Jewish culture. He affirmed the authority of the Old Testament because he received it as the product of divine inspiration.

First, Jesus affirmed the divine and human authorship of the Bible. He repeatedly recognized the men who wrote the Old Testament, including Moses (John 5:45–47), David (Luke 20:42), Isaiah (Matt. 13:14), and Daniel (Matt. 24:15–16). At the same time, he described these writings as the product of the Holy Spirit. Jesus identified both David and the Holy Spirit as the author of Psalm 110 (Mark 12:36). He interchangeably referred to portions of the Old Testament as the words of God and the work of human writers like Moses and Isaiah (Matt. 15:1–11). For Jesus there was no difference between "God says," "the Scripture says," or "David himself says."

Second, Jesus affirmed that the inspiration of the Old Testament was both *verbal* and *plenary* in nature. Affirming its plenary inspiration, Jesus quoted from or alluded to every major division of literature in the Hebrew Bible (the Law, the Prophets, and the Writings). Affirming its verbal inspiration, Jesus based central arguments of his teaching on individual phrases, words, and even letters of the Old Testament text. In John 10:34–35, Jesus defended his claim to deity by directing his opponents' attention to one word from a phrase in Psalm 82:6, reminding his listeners that "Scripture cannot be broken" (John 10:35). When challenged by the Sadducees on the subject of the resurrection, Jesus based the whole of his rebuttal on the tense of a single Hebrew verb (Matt. 22:32). To display the Pharisees' ignorance of the meaning and significance of the Old Testament, Jesus referred to Psalm 110:1 and David's addressing his son (Jesus) as "Lord" (Matt. 22:41–45). Jesus attested to the extent of the Old Testament's verbal inspiration when he rebuked the Pharisees with these words: "it is easier for heaven and earth to pass away than for one dot of the Law to become void" (Luke 16:17).

Third, Jesus affirmed the necessity of the fulfillment of the Old Testament. Every prophecy recorded in the Old Testament must come to pass for the very reason that it is God's Word. He cited Psalm 35:19 or 69:4 as the reason for the world's hatred of him (John 15:18–25). He referred to Psalm 41:9 as the basis for Judas's betrayal (John 13:18). He cited Zechariah 13:7 as proof that the rest of his disciples would fall away at his crucifixion (Matt. 26:31). His arrest in the garden of Gethsemane was a fulfillment of Scripture (Matt. 26:56). Even as he hung on the cross he deliberately fulfilled the Scriptures to the letter (John 19:28–30). Jesus believed his entire mission was a fulfillment of that which had already been written (Mark 9:12–13; Luke 4:21; 20:17; 24:44–46; John 5:39). While the disciples did not understand this initially, they eventually "remembered that these things had been written about him and had been done to him" (John 12:16; cf. Luke 24:44–46).

Jesus Affirmed the Historicity of the Old Testament. In addition to affirming the authority and inspiration of the Old Testament, Jesus declared unwavering confidence in the veracity of its historical accounts.

Jesus affirmed the historicity of persons in the Old Testament. In every reference to Old Testament individuals, Jesus treated them as historical figures. When discussing the topic of divorce, Jesus confirmed the historical account of the creation of Adam and Eve and rested his entire teaching on marriage upon the details described in Genesis 1–2 (Matt. 19:4–5). Jesus upheld the historicity of Genesis 4, affirming Abel's existence and murder (Matt. 23:35). Jesus affirmed the historicity of Noah (Matt. 24:37–38; Luke 17:26–27); Abraham, Isaac, and Jacob (Matt. 8:11; 22:32; Luke 13:28; John 8:56); Lot and his wife (Luke 17:28, 32); Moses (John 3:14; 5:45; 7:19); David (Matt. 12:3; 22:43–45); Solomon (Matt. 6:29; Luke 11:31); the queen of Sheba (Matt. 12:42; Luke 11:31); Elijah and the widow in Sidon (Luke 4:25–26); Elisha and Naaman (Luke 4:27); Jonah (Matt. 12:39–41; Luke 11:29–32); Zechariah (Matt. 23:35; Luke 11:51); and Daniel (Matt. 24:15). In all his references to Old Testament persons, Jesus never corrects or deviates from the Old Testament records.

Jesus also affirmed the historicity of places and events in the Old Testament. Remarkably, he commonly cited those accounts most miraculous in nature. He attested to the destruction of Sodom and Gomorrah (Matt. 11:20–24; cf. Matt. 10:15). He confirmed Jonah's three days inside a great fish (Matt. 12:40) and Nineveh's great repentance (Luke 11:30–32). He affirmed a historical flood in the days of Noah that was no less global than will be the judgment of the Son in the future day of the Lord (Matt. 24:38–39). Jesus confirmed that God provided manna for Israel when they wandered in the wilderness for forty years (John 6:49). Ultimately, Jesus did not refer to these events as if they were "once upon a time." He based the certainty of his own words and work on the veracity of those accounts (e.g., Matt. 12:38–42 and Jonah 1:17).

Jesus also affirmed the historicity of the authorship of the Old Testament. On a number of occasions Jesus cited the human writer of Old Testament books by name. For example, Jesus attributed the authorship of the Pentateuch directly to Moses (Matt. 8:4; Mark 12:26; John 5:45–46). In addition, Jesus affirmed that David wrote Psalm 110 (Matt. 22:43–44), that Isaiah wrote the book of Isaiah (Matt. 13:14–15), and that Daniel wrote the book of Daniel (Matt. 24:15). Consequently, to deny the authorship of these books as stated in the Old Testament is to ascribe error to Jesus himself.

Jesus Anticipated the Writing of New Testament Scripture. Just as Jesus affirmed the authority, inspiration, and historicity of the Old Testament, he also anticipated the testimony about himself that would be written after his ascension—writings that would make up the New Testament.

First, Jesus professed that his own words were the Father's words. He repeatedly declared that when he spoke, he spoke the words given to him by the Father. They were of no less authority and permanence than the words of the Old Testament. In the upper room, Jesus asked his disciples, "Do you not believe that I am in the Father and the Father is in me? The words that I say to you I do not speak on my own authority, but the Father who dwells in me does his works" (John 14:10; cf. John 12:49–50). Even in his prayer in the garden of Gethsemane Jesus states, "Now they know that everything that you have given me is from you. For I have given them the words that you gave me, and they have received them and have come to know in truth that I came from you; and they have believed that you sent me" (John 17:7–8). Jesus was a prophet "like" Moses (Deut. 18:15) but far greater than he. To see Jesus was to see the Father (John 14:9), and so to hear from Jesus was to hear from the Father (John 17:8, 14). As the climax of God's self-revelation (John 1:18; Heb. 1:1–3), Jesus's words would need to be preserved and proclaimed with no less reverence than the words of the Old Testament. Jesus himself noted this when he stated, "Heaven and earth will pass away, but my words will not pass away" (Matt. 24:35; cf. Mark 13:31; Luke 21:33).

Second, Jesus prepared apostles to be the messengers of his Word (Luke 6:13). Jesus's act of designating a select group of disciples to be his "apostles" or "authorized messengers" indicates his intent to spread his word with accuracy and authority. These apostles first had to be with Jesus (Mark 3:14), to hear his words and see his works for an extended period of time so that after his ascension they would be ready to proclaim his Word as personal witnesses to the truth (Luke 24:44–48). They would function as his mouthpiece just as the prophets of old functioned as mouthpieces of the Lord.

Third, Jesus promised his disciples the inspiration of the Holy Spirit. This "Helper" (John 14:26; 15:26; 16:7) was the same Spirit who inspired the Old Testament Scriptures. He was also the same Spirit who would give the apostles the very words to speak (Matt. 10:16–20) just as God had done for Moses (Ex. 4:12). He was the "Spirit of truth," who would ensure the accuracy of their witness (John 15:26–27).

Fourth, Jesus pledged that his apostles would receive revelation beyond what he had personally given them. There would be more truth to come, at the proper time (John 16:12–14). The source of this revelation would be the Holy Spirit, just as it was in the Old Testament, and the focus of this revelation would continue to be the person of Jesus Christ, just as it also was in the Old Testament.

Finally, Jesus prayed that the future church would grow and be sanctified on the basis of the apostles' words. Only the Word of God could bring about faith and sanctification (John 17:17). Yet Jesus prays for those in the future who would "believe in me through their word"—i.e., through the word of the apostles (John 17:20). The Word of God would become *their* word. Their word would be the Word of God.

All of these actions on Jesus's part point to his anticipation of the composition of new writings that would serve as the enduring and faithful testimony of his life. These new writings—the apostolic/prophetic witness to the arrival of the promised Messiah—would share the same inspiration, authority, veracity, and permanence as the writings of the Old Testament that prophesied of his coming.

New Testament Proofs of Inspiration

The New Testament gives a clear and consistent witness to the inspiration and authority of the Old Testament. But it does not end there. It also testifies to the inspiration and authority of the New Testament writings themselves.

The New Testament Writers Treated the Old Testament as the Word of God. Matthew states that the words Isaiah recorded were nothing less than "what the Lord had spoken by the prophet" (Matt. 1:22–23; cf. Isa. 7:14; Matt. 2:14–15; cf. Hos. 11:1). John recognizes the authoritative nature of the Old Testament by pointing to its exact fulfillment in the death and resurrection of Jesus Christ (John 19:24, 36–37; 20:6). The writer of Hebrews introduces a citation of Psalm 95:7–11 with the words, "as the Holy Spirit says" (Heb. 3:7). He quotes the words of Moses in Genesis 2:2 but attributes them to God himself (Heb. 4:4). This same writer later cites Jeremiah 31:31–34 and again attributes these words to God (Heb. 8:8–12) and then specifically to the Holy Spirit (Heb. 10:15–17).

The apostle Paul acknowledged openly, "I worship the God of our fathers, believing everything laid down by the Law and written in the Prophets" (Acts 24:14). He contended to Agrippa that he proclaimed nothing concerning the Christ "but what the prophets and Moses said would come to pass" (Acts 26:22). He believed the Old Testament to be the authoritative basis for his preaching (1 Cor. 15:3–4). He believed that the Old Testament prophets accurately conveyed the intent of the Holy Spirit (Acts 28:25).

To buttress his arguments, Paul in his letters often introduced citations from the Old Testament with the formula, "the Scripture says" (Rom. 4:3; 9:17; 10:11; 11:2; Gal. 4:30; 1 Tim. 5:18) or the even more prevalent "it is written" (Rom. 1:17; 2:24; 3:4, 10; 8:36; etc.). For Paul, Scripture was self-authenticating and needed no external affirmation to establish its authority. The text of Scripture and the voice of God were so interchangeable that Paul says it was "the Scripture" that "preached the gospel beforehand to Abraham" (Gal. 3:8), and it was "the Scripture" that "imprisoned everything under sin" (Gal. 3:22). Paul described the Old Testament as "the oracles of God" (Rom. 3:2), a description that identifies the Scriptures as God's own sayings. He further declared that the Old Testament was "breathed out by God and profitable for teaching, for reproof, for correction, and for training in righteousness, that the man of God may be complete, equipped for every good work" (2 Tim. 3:16–17).

The reverence of the New Testament writers for the Old Testament can also be observed in their affirmation of its historical accuracy. Such significant events as the creation of Adam and Eve (1 Cor. 11:8–12; 1 Tim. 2:13; Jude 14), the details of the fall of Adam and Eve into sin (Rom. 5:12–21; 1 Cor. 15:21–22, 45; 2 Cor. 11:3; 1 Tim. 2:14), the global flood (Heb. 11:7; 1 Pet. 3:20; 2 Pet. 2:5), and the destruction of Sodom and Gomorrah (2 Pet. 2:6; Jude 7) are all treated as consistent with historical reality. God said it. Therefore, it is true.

The New Testament Writers Recognized Their Own Writings as Scripture. There are more evidences of Paul's awareness of the inspired and authoritative nature of his own writings than there are in many books of the Old Testament. Paul claimed to speak the word of God (2 Cor. 2:17; 4:2; 1 Thess. 2:13) and not his own message (2 Cor. 4:5). He viewed himself as a messenger of the very words of Christ (1 Cor. 11:23–25; 15:3; Gal. 1:12). He believed that the church was built upon his words and the words of other New Testament apostles and prophets (1 Cor. 3:10; Eph. 2:19–20). He claimed that the Holy Spirit was the agent of direct revelation through him (1 Cor. 2:1–4, 12–13; Eph. 3:1–5). He stated that what he wrote was part of the authoritative standard for Christ's church, and that to reject his words was to place oneself outside of that church (Rom. 16:25–26; 1 Cor. 7:17; 14:37–38; 2 Cor. 13:10; Gal. 1:9; 2 Thess. 3:6, 14). His teachings were to have authority over all the churches (1 Cor. 4:17; 7:17; 11:16). He commanded the public reading of his letters during the church's worship services (Col. 4:16; 1 Thess. 5:27), consciously placing his writings on the same level as the Old Testament Scriptures, which were also to be read publicly (1 Tim. 4:13).

But Paul was not alone in recognizing the inspired nature of his own writings. The apostle Peter recognized Paul's letters as having this quality as well (2 Pet. 3:16). Similarly, Paul recognized the inspired nature of Luke's Gospel, pairing a quotation of Luke 10:7 with a quotation of Deuteronomy 25:4 and calling both of them "Scripture" (1 Tim. 5:18). The apostle John began the final book of the New Testament canon with the unambiguous title, "The revelation of Jesus Christ" (Rev. 1:1). As a testimony to the inspired nature of his work, he included special blessings to his readers (Rev. 1:3; 22:7). He also noted that it was Jesus himself who commanded him to "write" the contents of the book (Rev. 1:11, 19; 2:1, 8, 12, 18; 3:1, 7, 14).

Critics of Scripture often claim that the biblical writers—particularly those of the New Testament—were ignorant of the inspired nature of their writings. Inspiration, they claim, is not a quality which they themselves recognized in their own works; it is a fabricated ideal foisted upon those works by certain readers. Such a claim, however, reflects the critics' own ignorance—and worse, their own blindness. The self-witness of the Old and New Testaments to their own inspiration is simply irrefutable.

The Authority of Scripture

The doctrine of the authority of Scripture raises an important question: How does one become convinced that the Bible really is the Word of God?

The concept of authority is and always has been the crucial issue in any discussion about truth. Truth assertions require justification, and justification of these assertions requires authority. Where is such authority to be found? Can the contents of Scripture, for example, be believed on the basis of its own testimony? Or are other authorities needed to justify belief in its claims?

The appropriate approach to this question begins with a proper definition of *authority*. Authority may be defined as the "power or right to enforce obedience; moral or legal supremacy; the right to command or give a final decision."[1] In human history, such authority has been centered in sources such as *self* (one's subjective intuition or reasoning), *tradition* (an established set of religious or cultural convictions), or *community* (a collection of people with shared experiences and values).

In a biblical worldview, original and ultimate authority resides with God alone. He did not acquire authority through some cosmic struggle. It was not bestowed on him by something or someone in his creation. He has always possessed his authority unwaveringly by virtue of his essence as the Almighty.

Accordingly, any authority that exists outside of God ultimately belongs to God and is dependent on him and thus subject to his authority. Such authority is by nature delegated or derived authority. As Paul states, "there is no authority except from God, and those that exist have been instituted by God" (Rom. 13:1; cf. John 19:11). With this in mind, we return to the fundamental question, what justifies belief in the Bible's contents?

SECONDARY SOURCES

Those who appeal to an authority outside of Scripture to justify belief in Scripture typically appeal to one of three main sources: (1) rational evidences, (2) church tradition, or (3) personal intuition.

1 The New Shorter Oxford English Dictionary, s.v., "authority."

Rational Evidences

Those who appeal to rational evidences believe the trustworthiness of the Bible must be supported by rationalistic or scientific evidences. Proponents believe that it is their responsibility to prove (or disprove) that the historical narratives of Scripture are consistent with the clear and self-evident dictates of human reason and scientific method.

Archaeological evidences provide one significant example. If the Bible's accounts of historical figures or events are to be believed, the details of the text must be confirmed by archaeological discoveries. Where such evidences affirm the Bible's narrative, those accounts can be believed. Where such evidences are absent, the Bible's narrative can be held only tentatively. Where such evidences appear to contradict the Bible's narrative, one must determine whether the archeological sources are incorrect or misleading or one's understanding of the Bible must be amended.

Scientific evidences are often cited in the effort to prove or disprove the miraculous portions of Scripture. Some endeavor to prove the reliability of miraculous accounts in Scripture by attempting to locate analogous events in history. Others attempt to disprove the reliability of these same accounts by pointing to the absence of such analogous events. For both camps, reason and empiricism are viewed as the authorities which grant approval to (or withhold it from) Scripture.

Church Tradition

A second suggested source of authority for affirming the believability of Scripture is the church's authority. This includes the declarations made by church councils, historical theologians, and other ecclesiastical bodies. The authority of all or some of these sources are claimed as necessary for justifying belief in the contents of Scripture.

The Roman Catholic Church operates according to this principle. According to Roman Catholicism, the Bible is to be believed as the Word of God because the Church granted it such a status. The Church itself decided which books would comprise Holy Scripture and delegated to those books their authority. Many other ecclesiastical traditions are based on this same principle. People adhering to such traditions believe what they believe not because they find it in the Bible but because their denomination, a favorite ecclesiastical document, or a beloved historical hero teaches it.

Personal Intuition

A third source of authority for justifying belief in Scripture is personal intuition. Whenever a text of Scripture evokes a desired experience or feeling, it is believed as true and authoritative. Whenever a text creates discomfort or offense, it is viewed with skepticism or denial. The authority of Scripture is thus derived from the reader's own personal authority.

The practical outworking of this view can be observed in those who accept or reject certain teachings of Scripture based on the favorability of those teachings to their internal sensibilities. For example, God can be sovereign only to the extent that one feels it does not violate his own sense of liberty as a human being. Man can be sinful only to the extent that such a belief does not violate one's personal sense of worth and goodness. In the end, those who place ultimate authority in personal intuition inevitably create gods in their own image.

Ultimately, neither reason, tradition, nor experience can serve as the ultimate authority in justifying belief in the contents of Scripture. At the same time, this is not to say that supporting evidences for the veracity of the biblical record will never be found in these sources. Indeed, there are a great many witnesses to the truthfulness of Scripture in archaeology, science, reason, and experience. The biblical record does correspond to reality. And as Paul argued with respect to the resurrection of Christ, historical accuracy matters (1 Cor. 15:17–19). But such sources of knowledge must be kept in their rightful place. They are secondary. They do not grant authority to the Bible. They themselves have a derived authority only to the degree that they submit to, and agree with, the Bible's teaching.

PRIMARY SOURCE

The names and titles of God and the descriptions of his character and works demonstrate his absolute authority over all his creation. There is no one above him. Therefore, there is nothing above his Word.

Scripture's Unassailable Authority

God's absolute authority is brought to bear on humankind through his Word. This is not a limitation for God, but a delight. As stated in Isaiah, "The LORD was pleased, for his righteousness' sake, to magnify his law and make it glorious" (Isa. 42:21). The psalmist bows and gives thanks to God because "you have exalted above all things your name and your word" (Ps. 138:2). In response to those who scrutinized his Word, Jesus declared that "The one who rejects me and does not receive my words has a judge; the word that I have spoken will judge him on the last day" (John 12:48). Similarly, the writer of Hebrews states, "For the word of God is living and active, sharper than any two-edged sword, piercing to the division of soul and of spirit, of joints and of marrow, and discerning the thoughts and intentions of the heart. And no creature is hidden from his sight, but all are naked and exposed to the eyes of him to whom we must give account" (Heb. 4:12–13).

Given that God's unassailable authority is mediated through his Word, it follows that this Word cannot be subjected to the scrutiny of those whom God's Word itself judges. In the same way that God's general revelation "declares" knowledge about God independent of human investigation and approval (Ps. 19:1), so God's written revelation declares his knowledge independent of human judgment.

After all, this is the very essence of revelation. Revelation is knowledge that is declared from above, not knowledge that is sought, investigated, or scrutinized from below. Its authority is derived only from the God who breathed it out; it is not ascribed by its recipients. Consequently, the acceptable response to revelation can never be skepticism. It must be belief, submission, and obedience. It must be a response of reverence (Isa. 66:2).

Scripture's Clarity and Sufficiency

Two qualities of Scripture are particularly important to the discussion of authority: clarity and sufficiency. The *clarity* of Scripture refers to its accessibility. The knowledge of God contained in the Bible has been revealed in such a way that it can be sufficiently understood in and of itself by those who seek it. Stated negatively, the Bible is not a collection of mysterious writings that requires the assistance of some other knowledge to render it understandable. Scripture is so clear that it judges and illuminates everything else.

Thus, a common metaphor used to describe God's Word is *light* (Pss. 19:8; 119:105; Prov. 6:23; 2 Pet. 1:19). Scripture is intended for everyone, not just the educated or the religious elite (Deut. 6:6–8; Neh. 8:1–3, 12; Phil. 1:1; 2 Tim. 3:15). Its purpose is to make the young and foolish wise (Pss. 19:7; 119:130). It declares clearly God's expectations for humanity (Deut. 30:11–14; 2 Tim. 3:16–17).

Certainly, the objective clarity of God's Word does not on its own cure the moral and intellectual blindness of unbelievers. To them the Bible is fundamentally obscure (1 Cor. 2:14; 2 Cor. 4:4), but such a perception evidences their own spiritual condition and God's judgment on them (Isa. 6:9–10; Matt. 13:13–15), not Scripture's inadequacy. Neither does Scripture's inherent clarity negate the believer's own need for study (2 Tim. 2:15), his need for divine enablement (Ps. 119:18), or his need for the ministry of pastors and teachers (Eph. 4:11–12). It also does not imply that every tenet of God's Word is equally understandable, or that God's truth is simplistic (2 Pet. 3:15–18). Instead, Scripture's quality of clarity indicates that its truth is accessible in and of itself to those who seek it.

That God's Word is clear indicates that it mediates his authority effectively. The same is true of the knowledge God reveals through general revelation (Rom. 1:18–20). Because general revelation is inherently clear, it renders humanity "without excuse" (Rom. 1:20). Analogously, the clarity of God's revelation of himself in his written Word means that his authority is mediated efficaciously in its purposes as well.

The Bible is also *sufficient* in and of itself to carry out the intentions God has for it (Ps. 19:7–11). It contains all the knowledge needed to bring a person to saving faith (Rom. 10:17; 2 Tim. 3:15). It is the singular source of knowledge that sanctifies (John 17:17). It is more reliable than even the most amazing spiritual experience (2 Pet. 1:19–20). It contains that which teaches, reproves, corrects, trains, and equips the believer for every good work (2 Tim. 3:17). By itself, without any help from other so-called sources of knowledge, the Bible is sufficient to accomplish all the purposes God has designed for it (Isa. 55:10–11).

That God's Word is sufficient for its intended purposes indicates, once again, that it mediates God's authority effectively. It does not lack power or information to achieve its goals. No other source of authority is required to augment or affirm it. Its knowledge does not need to be supplemented, integrated, or aligned with any other so-called truth in order to reveal God to man and bring man to God. It lacks nothing.

Consequently, it is the duty of the preacher to herald God's word with authority (2 Tim. 4:2; Titus 2:15). He does this as an ambassador entrusted with his king's decree, not as a pundit who assumes the liberty to incorporate his own wisdom or to moderate God's decrees with human experience, tradition, or philosophy. Furthermore, it is the obligation of the recipient of this Word to trust and obey. The height of love for God will be demonstrated in the believer's unqualified submission to God's authority as mediated in his Word (Isa. 66:2; John 14:15). It is this submission to the authority of this Word that best evidences the presence of saving faith (1 John 2:3). Conversely, it is the epitome of sin to question the clarity, wisdom, and veracity of this Word (Gen. 3:1–7).

The Testimony of the Holy Spirit

Even though God's Word has unmitigated authority, it does not operate alone. Essential to the recognition of Scripture's authority is the ministry of the Holy Spirit.

The authority of Scripture is recognized by the believer as a result of the Spirit's internal testimony. This ministry of the Spirit is not the communication of new revelation, as if the Spirit uses Scripture as a springboard to reveal new knowledge from God not already present in the text. Nor does this ministry of the Spirit remove the need for study by mystically granting to the believer instant absolute comprehension of the biblical text. Rather, the Spirit works alongside the text of Scripture to confirm its divine nature, authority, necessity, and truthfulness, giving the believer a certainty that it is the Word of God. So important is this ministry of the Spirit that Paul often asked for it in his prayers for believers (e.g., Eph. 1:17–19; 3:14–19; Col. 1:9–12).

This is not to suggest that Scripture has a defect that must be corrected through the activity of the Spirit. After all, this same Spirit inspired Scripture (2 Pet. 1:20–21). Rather, God's purposes of salvation and sanctification require both a *means* and an *agent*. Consequently, both the Word and the Spirit are necessary for salvation (James 1:18; 1 Pet. 1:23; John 3:3–8) and for sanctification (John 17:17; 2 Thess. 2:13; 1 Pet. 1:2). True power is observed when the Spirit and the

Word are both at work (1 Cor. 2:4; 1 Thess. 1:5). It is for this reason Paul calls the Word of God "the sword of the Spirit" (Eph. 6:17).

In light of this affirming ministry of the Holy Spirit, it is important to note that the believer himself does not grant authority to the Bible. Such authority is not his to bestow. Rather, the believer merely recognizes this authority as inherent in Scripture as the Holy Spirit testifies to it.

The Inerrancy of Scripture

The inerrancy of Scripture is a doctrine that critics have challenged particularly since the Enlightenment period (ca. 1650–1815). The assault on inerrancy is a direct attack on the doctrine of inspiration and the absolute veracity of the Word of God. No less is at stake in this issue than the trustworthiness of God himself.

ACCOMMODATION AND INERRANCY

There is an undeniable difference between God and humankind. God is infinite. Humankind is limited—and worse, corrupted by sin. Consequently, some have concluded that human language is always and necessarily imperfect and corrupt. They argue that by using human language to communicate his truth, God could only express himself inadequately, and was forced to incorporate error as he moved human writers to record it.

Several observations must be made in response. First, it is vital to understand that human language did not evolve as a human invention. Human language was a gift from God, and the capacity to use it was a component of the image of God instilled in humanity. According to Scripture, the first human words spoken were spoken by God to Adam and Eve in the garden of Eden (Gen. 1:28–31). In the innocence of that garden, human language became the perfect medium by which Adam and Eve could enjoy fellowship with God and with each other.

Adam's sin certainly brought corruption into the world. But even in his response to sin, God did not abandon human language. He communicated both his judgment and his redemptive promise using human words (Gen. 3:14–19). In fact, the enduring efficacy of human language even after the fall is seen in the potential of men who consolidated their forces to build a tower in defiance of God (Gen. 11:1–9). The Lord specifically identified the efficacy of their language as the reason for his judgment (Gen. 11:6).

As a result, God introduced confusion into language as judgment at Babel (Gen. 11:7, 9). But once again, God did not abandon human language as his effective medium of communication with men. Beginning in Genesis 12, God begins to put his redemptive plan into action by calling a man named Abram. God spoke to Abram in the words of human language (Gen. 12:1–3), and Abram obeyed in response (Gen. 12:4). The rest of the biblical account never describes any frustration with human language on God's part. To the contrary, the Scriptures testify over and over that human language was the effective medium of God's communication. Ultimately, this efficacy was demonstrated in the incarnation of his Son. The Word of God, full of grace and truth, became flesh (John 1:14), and he, too, used human language—without error.

Historically, the term "accommodation" referred to God's employment of figures and expressions that were common to man. He did not reveal himself in some deified language that required man to ascend to heaven in order to understand God, but he himself came down to meet man where he was (Deut. 30:11–14). He even used human traits to describe himself. This was nothing less than God's gracious condescension—his benevolent act of stooping down to humanity to communicate at its level, as a father stoops to use the simple sounds of his infant child.

However, some scholars have in recent times redefined accommodation as God's obligation to include error in the inscripturation of his Word in order to preserve the genuinely human contribution of the human writers. Rather than pointing to God's grace and benevolence, the notion of accommodation now is used to insist on Scripture's error and inadequacy. They argue that because God used the means of insufficient, corrupt language, and because he used fallible writers, error was inevitable. They contend that while Scripture can and does communicate general truths adequately, it nevertheless includes errors in the details.

This view of accommodation must be rejected for numerous reasons. Three are most important here. First, it commits the logical fallacy of equating finiteness with sin and error. Human language is fully capable of making statements of truth—a reality vividly demonstrated by the fact that the incarnate Word came teaching and preaching (Matt. 9:35). Moreover, human personality is not overridden if God superintended the writing of Scripture in such a way as to protect the human writers from error. The Spirit's ministry of inspiration enabled the human writers to write according to their full human potential—and at the same time without fault or error.

Second, the unanimous witness of Scripture affirms its total veracity. It claims repeatedly to be truthful (Pss. 12:6; 18:30; 119:142, 160; John 17:17; 2 Cor. 6:7; Col. 1:5; 2 Tim. 2:15; James 1:18). God's commands to leave it unaltered demonstrate that what was written is precisely what he intended it to say (Deut. 4:2; 12:32; Prov. 30:5–6; Rev. 22:18–19). God takes ownership of this Word in its written form, and he is a God who cannot lie (Num. 23:19; Titus 1:2; Heb. 6:18).

Third, this modern view of accommodation directly casts a shadow on the character of God. To insist that God used inadequate and corrupted means to communicate his knowledge questions not only God's power but also his wisdom and his love. Moreover, it casts a shadow on the very doctrine of the incarnation itself. If human language always necessarily bears the stain of corruption, then what is to be made of the teachings of the God-man Jesus Christ?

INFALLIBILITY AND INERRANCY

Inerrancy means "without error." When applied to Scripture, it means that the Bible is without error in its original manuscripts. Consequently, when interpreted as originally intended, the biblical text will never affirm anything that is untrue or contrary to reality.

Historically, the term *infallibility* has been used to refer to the same general quality as inerrancy. Infallibility means "unable to mislead or fail," and when applied to Scripture it means that the biblical text—when interpreted correctly—will never mislead its reader. However, beginning in the 1960s, certain theologians began using the term *infallibility* in a new way. Convinced that the Bible did indeed contain factual errors, yet eager to maintain their influence within evangelical circles, these scholars deliberately avoided the use of the term inerrancy and instead employed the term infallibility. Moreover, when using the term infallibility, these scholars intended something different. Rather than maintaining the traditional definition, these scholars limited its extent, instead affirming that the Bible is "unable to mislead or fail" only in terms of its teachings about faith and practice. They believed that where Scripture treated matters of history and science it *could* mislead the reader when read according to its original intent.

On the one hand, this shift created significant confusion in the church. This new movement of scholars continued to use the term infallibility to describe Scripture but at the same time asserted things about the historical details of Scripture which did not coincide with the term's traditional definition. On the other hand, this shift in terminology forced other evangelical scholars to focus significant attention on the issue of inerrancy and to respond with a careful analysis of Scripture's own self-witness concerning its absolute inerrancy. This new focus led to the creation of the International Council on Biblical Inerrancy, with the Chicago Statement on Biblical Inerrancy (1978) being one of its fruits.[2]

EXPLANATION OF INERRANCY

As with any term used to express a profound concept, certain qualifications and explanations are necessary in explaining the term inerrancy.

First, affirmation of the doctrine of inerrancy is not predicated on scientific evidence. The doctrine of inerrancy is predicated on the reality of inspiration, and is a necessary affirmation in light of Scripture's self-witness and of the character of

2 The Chicago Statement on Biblical Inerrancy can be found in John MacArthur, ed., *The Inerrant Word: Biblical Historical, Theological, and Pastoral Perspectives* (Wheaton, IL: Crossway, 2016), 378–83.

God. (Thus, we ought to argue for inerrancy deductively, not merely inductively.) Certainly, the historical veracity of Scripture does enjoy agreement from historical and empirical evidences. But it is not possible nor necessary to establish inerrancy based on scientific data. This is due to the fact that some things described in Scripture are simply not reproducible for scrutiny today. Moreover, scientific arguments commonly cited as proof against Scripture's inerrancy are themselves filled with error. Not only are the fields of science themselves undergoing constant modification, but scientific "facts" are never objective interpretations. As Paul stated, the unbeliever reads everything around him through truth-suppressing spectacles (Rom. 1:18). In the end, the only sure standard of truth is God's verbal revelation, and the clear, propositional testimony it provides to its own inerrancy is sufficient justification for the affirmation of this doctrine.

Second, the doctrine of inerrancy relates to the original writings produced by the biblical authors. It is these original works—called *autographs*—that were completely without error as the result of divine inspiration. None of these original manuscripts are in existence today. Instead, copies were made and soon thereafter copies of copies. Inspiration did not extend to the process of copying, so the quality of inerrancy extended to the product of the copying only to the degree that the copy matched the original. Naturally, errors were introduced as the process continued. Thus, when speaking of inerrancy today, the notion of absolute inerrancy must be properly limited to the original text. Subsequent copies possess derived or relative inerrancy, based on their conformity to the original standard.

Does this then render the doctrine of inerrancy invalid today, since these original manuscripts no longer exist? It does not. Our consideration, below, of the doctrines of transmission and preservation will explain this issue in greater detail, but it can be stated here that God has providentially preserved sufficient copies of the original writings that an accurate reproduction of the original autographs is possible. Through the process of textual analysis and comparison (a process called *textual criticism*), scholars know where instances of textual deviations exist and are confident of the original readings in more than 99 percent of the cases. Furthermore, today's battle over the doctrine of inerrancy is generally not related to textual matters. The battle focuses predominantly on issues like the veracity of the biblical record regarding the plagues of Egypt (Exodus 7–12), the fall of Jericho (Joshua 6), or the resurrection of certain individuals from the dead at the moment of Jesus's death (Matt. 27:51–53). Those who deny inerrancy generally do not argue that the problem today is the absence of the originals. They argue that the biblical writers themselves, and the process of inspiration that guided them, were susceptible to error. Ultimately, they make their claims of error against the original text itself.

Third, the doctrine of inerrancy allows for the customary use of language. For example, the Bible makes frequent use of estimates (1 Chron. 5:21; Isa. 37:36; Matt. 14:21). Such approximations are not factual errors; they are even expected in historical reporting. Scientifically imprecise statements also do not necessarily imply error. They are simply part of the way language is used outside of scientific journals and laboratories.

Phenomenological language is also no violation of inerrancy. Joshua prayed for the sun "to stand still," and the text reads that "the sun stood still, and the moon stopped, until the nation took vengeance on their enemies" (Josh. 10:12–13). This geocentric description in no way violates inerrancy. Language allows for truth to be conveyed from the perspective of the writer or speaker, just as meteorologists to this day continue to speak of "sunrise" and "sunset," even though they know full well that it is the earth that moves in relation to the sun, not the sun in relation to the earth.

Inerrancy allows for New Testament writers to paraphrase the Old Testament as they cite it in their writings. Inerrancy also does not require strict adherence to grammatical norms. A statement can be grammatically unconventional, unique to a particular writer, and still be understandable and truthful. A writer can even invent a brand-new word without violating truth. A quotation of direct speech can be truncated and summarized, as Luke does with Paul's sermons in the book of Acts.[3] When reporting on historical events, writers can select which details to include and arrange them according to their own particular literary structure, as the four Gospel writers do in the New Testament. Once again, such practices do not violate inerrancy.

The Preservation of Scripture

The Word of God has been the target of assaults from the moment of Satan's first onslaught in the garden of Eden (Gen. 3:1–5). Jehoiakim even attempted to destroy an original portion of it with fire (Jeremiah 36). The battle against the Bible continues to this day, but God has stated that such attacks are futile (Ps. 119:89, 160; Isa. 40:8; Matt. 5:18; 24:35; Luke 16:17; 1 Pet. 1:24–25). God will ensure that his Word is preserved.

NATURE OF PRESERVATION

The preservation of Scripture refers to God's act of preserving through time the written record of his special revelation. This preservation begins with direct commands and promptings to record his words in written form (e.g., Ex. 34:27; Rev. 1:11). It continues through the specific instructions he gave to his people to

3 See Simon J. Kistemaker, "The Speeches in Acts," *Criswell Theological Review* 5.1 (1990): 31–41.

preserve and copy those words (e.g., Deut. 17:18). It also includes the providential way in which God has kept his Word by the diligent efforts of human agents.

The Westminster Confession of 1646 describes the doctrine of preservation this way: "The Old Testament in Hebrew . . . and the New Testament in Greek . . . being immediately inspired by God, and by his singular care and providence kept pure in all ages, are therefore authentical; so as in all controversies of religion, the Church is finally to appeal unto them" (1.8). An examination of Scripture indicates that God has indeed promised to preserve his Word.

First, the Bible establishes the reality of God's *direct, eternal preservation*. Psalm 119:89 states, "Forever, O LORD, your word is firmly fixed in the heavens." The psalmist goes on to say, "Long have I known from your testimonies that you have founded them forever" (Ps. 119:152). Isaiah contrasts the transitory nature of man with the eternally enduring perfection of God's Word: "The grass withers, the flower fades, but the word of our God will stand forever" (Isa. 40:8; cf. 1 Pet. 1:24–25).

Jesus speaks of the lasting nature of God's Word in this way: "For truly, I say to you, until heaven and earth pass away, not an iota, not a dot, will pass from the Law until all is accomplished" (Matt. 5:18). The term "iota" refers to the smallest letter in the Hebrew alphabet; the "dot" refers to the small stroke of a pen that would distinguish one Hebrew letter from another (cf. also Luke 16:17). While Jesus's direct emphasis in this statement focused on the notion of fulfillment, the preservation of the Word is nonetheless assumed. Jesus spoke with the same kind of absolute certainty with respect to the preservation of his own teaching (Matt. 24:35).

But God does not take the same, direct approach to the preservation of his Word on earth as he does in heaven. Here, Scripture testifies to a *mediated, relative preservation,* whereby God preserves his Word—sometimes miraculously, sometimes providentially—through his people, to whom he has given the responsibility to protect and transmit it.

This is evidenced first of all from the repeated commands God gave to his people to take great care not to add anything to or take anything from his Word (Deut. 4:2; 12:32; Prov. 30:6; Jer. 26:2; Rev. 22:18–19). These commands did not forbid the copying of God's Word but actually provided the standard for it. Thus, upon their enthronement, Israel's kings were to write their own copy of the Law—a copy which was to be carefully approved by the Levitical priests (Deut. 17:18). The final standard was always the originally autograph.

Another example of the mediated preservation of God's Word can be seen in Moses's destruction of the tablets which contained the Ten Commandments. These stone tablets were "written with the finger of God" (Ex. 31:18), but when Moses smashed them in response to Israel's sin (Ex. 32:19), these original autographs of the Ten Commandments were destroyed, even before the people heard them taught or before any copies could have been made. For a moment of time, these words of God ceased to exist on earth. God later used Moses to restore these words verbatim through a new set of stone tablets (Ex. 34:1–2, 27–28).

A similar example is seen in Jeremiah 36. God commanded Jeremiah to record on a scroll the words he had given to him and deliver it to Judah. Jeremiah did this with the scribal assistance of Baruch (Jer. 36:1–4). Upon hearing the reading of the contents of this original manuscript, Jehoiakim, king of Judah, burned the entire scroll (Jer. 36:23). Again, for a moment of time, the original record of God's verbal revelation as given through Jeremiah ceased to exist on earth. But once again, because the original had been destroyed before any copies had been made, God miraculously restored the text through a fresh act of inspiration (Jer. 36:27–28, 32).

While God has acted directly at times to restore portions of his Word that had been completely destroyed, he has also allowed his Word for a time to be lost. For example, he did not prevent the temple priests from misplacing the book of the Law for more than fifty years (2 Kings 22:8–10; 2 Chron. 34:14–16). Because of Judah's rejection of his Word, he used the carelessness of the priests to obscure his Word from their sight—a judgment similar to his act of obscuring his Word from the understanding of those who are disobedient (Isa. 6:9–10).

Another example can be seen in contemporary copies of God's Word. At least two words are missing from every extant copy of 1 Samuel dating back at least two thousand years (see 1 Sam. 13:1). The significance of this omission is minimal. The missing words are numbers related to Saul's age at the time he became king and the number of years he reigned as king. This knowledge, however, is not lost. Based on the testimony of the rest of 1 Samuel and other books of the Old Testament, a reasonable supposition can be made concerning the numbers that should appear in this text. These missing words nonetheless demonstrate that the earthly preservation of Scripture is not always a guaranteed or miraculous act of God. He has entrusted his people with the responsibility to retain his Word through diligent effort.

If God does not directly and flawlessly preserve his Word on earth, can the copies still be considered inspired and authoritative? The answer to this question is found in the concept of *derived authority.* To the extent that the copies reflect the wording of the original, they maintain their divine, authoritative quality. An illustration of this can again be seen in God's instructions to kings concerning the copying of the Law (Deut. 17:18–20). Each successive king was to copy the Law with painstaking accuracy. However, the copy had to be checked for accuracy by the Levitical priests. Once it was certified, the king was then to read his copy of the Law for the remainder of his life, obeying it as the very words of God. The quality of the copy—its consistency with the original—determined the nature of its authority.

CANONICITY AND PRESERVATION

The Bible traces its origin to one ultimate author: God. Yet this Word contains sixty-six works of literature written by more than forty men. It begins with the book of Genesis, written by Moses around 1405 BC, and extends over fifteen centuries to the book of Revelation, written by the apostle John around AD 95. This raises significant questions: How were these works recognized as part of this collection?

Definition of Canon

The term "canon" comes from the Greek word *kanōn*, which originally meant a "reed" or a "rod." Since a rod was frequently used as a measuring stick, the word came to convey the idea of a "standard" or "rule."

It was not until the middle of the fourth century AD that the term was used to speak of the authoritative collection of books recognized as the product of divine inspiration. Athanasius (AD 295–373) first applied the term *canon* to Scripture in the *Decrees of the Council of Nicaea*, published shortly after AD 350. In these writings, he referred to *The Shepherd of Hermas* as not being part of the "canon." Shortly thereafter, the Council of Laodicea used the terms "canonical" and "non-canonical" to refer to books either accepted as part of the Bible or rejected as not inspired by God. It is in this sense—the sense of "standard"—that the term has been understood in reference to the Scriptures.

There are two primary ways in which the canon of Scripture has been defined. The view of the Roman Catholic Church is that the Bible is an authoritative collection of writings. However, that authority was conferred on the books of Scripture by the Church itself.

The biblical view understands that the canon is a collection of divinely authoritative writings. Its authority is inherent, not derived from human agents. God's people do not create God's word; God's word creates God's people (1 Pet. 1:23–25; cf. James 1:18). It is not a church or the people of God that determines which books to make authoritative. Rather, the people of God *recognize* the inspired nature that these writings already possess. Rightly understood, the canonization of Scripture is a process not of conferring but of recognizing authority.

Criteria for Recognizing Canonicity

Three general principles were used through the centuries to recognize canonical writings—the writings that constitute inspired revelation.

First, any inspired writing had to have been authored by a recognized prophet or apostle of God—or by someone closely associated with one, as in the case of the writers of Mark, Luke, Hebrews, James, and Jude. No authoritative spokesman for God is self-appointed (Ezekiel 13). His authority must come from a divine commission. Second, any inspired writing would not contradict any previous work of Scripture. God cannot contradict himself. Therefore, any word from him will be consistent with the foundation of revelation he has already provided (Deut. 13:1–5; Acts 17:11). Contradictory works must be rejected (2 Thess. 2:1–3, 15). Third, if a book was truly inspired, the people of God would be able to come to a consensus about it. This consensus would be achieved through the Holy Spirit's ministry of internal witness—testifying among his people as to which works were indeed the words of God (e.g., 1 Cor. 14:37–38; 1 John 4:6).

By the time of Christ, the entire Old Testament had been written and acknowledged by the Jewish community as the Word of God. This recognized collection of works—categorized as books of the Law, the Prophets, and the Writings (cf. Luke 24:27, 44)—conforms to the contents of the Old Testament found in Protestant Bibles today. This collection never contained the Apocrypha, the fourteen extrabiblical writings written during the intertestamental period. While respected for their historical insights, the Apocrypha was rejected by the Jewish people as uninspired and non-authoritative.

The collection of the New Testament came together in roughly the same manner. By the end of the fourth century AD, after the various individual writings of the New Testament had gone through a period of circulation and collection, representatives of the Christian church recognized the twenty-seven books of the New Testament using the same three criteria. These books were believed to possess the same qualities of inspiration and authority that marked the books of the Old Testament. The church did not confer authority on these books. It simply recognized such authority as inherent in the writings themselves.

Completion of the Canon

The issue of adding to the content of Scripture is a serious one. While many today treat the possibility of ongoing verbal revelation with a cavalier attitude, the Bible does warn of severe consequences to the one who would add to God's words without divine authorization (Deut. 4:2; 12:32; Prov. 30:6; Rev. 22:18–19). But any astute observer will point out that several of these warnings were written early in the history of the compilation of Scripture. Obviously, works were added after the warnings in Deuteronomy and Proverbs were written. Could it be that additional works could be added after the book of Revelation, despite its warning?

Several observations lead to the conclusion that the canon of Scripture is indeed closed. First, the book of Revelation is unique to Scripture in that it describes with unparalleled detail the end-time events that precede eternity future. As Genesis began Scripture by describing the beginning of time (Genesis 1–2), the book of Revelation ends Scripture by explaining the end of this age and the age to come

(Revelation 20–22). By their contents, Genesis and Revelation are the perfectly matched bookends to Scripture.

Second, just as there was prophetic silence after Malachi completed the Old Testament canon, so there was silence after John recorded the book of Revelation. With the passing of this last apostle and eyewitness of the life of Christ, the era of revelatory activity closed. It would be bizarre to think that a new book of inspired revelation would appear today, after almost two millennia of revelatory silence and two thousand years of church history.

Third, Paul asserted that the New Testament church was built on the foundation of the New Testament apostles and prophets (Eph. 2:20). The apostles and prophets were those instruments of divine revelation while the New Testament was being composed. Once the foundation of revelation had been laid in the completed canon, there was no need for additional revelation from God in this life.

Finally, the early church—those who lived closest in time to the apostles and were their disciples—believed that, with the composition of the book of Revelation and the death of John, the canon had closed.

TEXTUAL CRITICISM AND PRESERVATION

After the extent of the biblical canon has been determined, the next issue of importance relates to the original text of each of its books. As already stated, this task is necessitated by the fact that none of the original autographs of the biblical books have survived.

It is at this point that textual criticism enters the discussion. Textual criticism is the intricate science of examining and comparing the ancient copies and translations of the biblical writings in order to determine the original text that gave rise to these copies. Textual criticism, sometimes called "lower criticism," is different than "higher criticism" in that higher criticism attempts to assess the historical veracity of the original text. Textual criticism, on the other hand, focuses solely on identifying the original text without making any attempt to decide its truthfulness.

The process of textual criticism begins with a careful collection and examination of existing copies of the biblical text in question in an attempt to discern which of the copies are of greater or lesser influence in the discussion. Issues like the age of the manuscript copy and the location where it was found are part of this consideration. Variant readings are then painstakingly identified and compared among the copies in the attempt to understand why these divergent readings may have been introduced in the history of textual transmission. Finally, based on the weight of the manuscript evidence and the ability to explain the origins of the variant readings, the textual critic proposes what he believes to be the rendering of the original text.

The process of textual criticism involves varying levels of complexity when comparing the text of the New Testament with the text of the Old Testament.

For example, there is a massive amount of manuscript evidence for the text of the New Testament. Some Greek manuscripts date back to within a generation of the original writing of the text. There are far fewer existing copies of the Old Testament writings. Many of the copies of Old Testament texts date to more than a thousand years after the original writing. Even the reliability of some of the oldest witnesses—like the Dead Sea scrolls—remains hotly debated.

Nevertheless, when all the textual evidence for both Testaments is evaluated, most scholars affirm that the current versions of the Hebrew Old Testament and Greek New Testament upon which our modern translations are based are reliable. The variant readings have been identified and examined, and the vast majority of them are easily resolvable. Common discrepancies include things as obvious and insignificant as spelling errors, accidental omission of words, the transposition of words or phrases in a sentence, and the like. Other variants can be quickly identified as explanatory insertions or deliberate alterations by the copyists for various reasons. Moreover, unlike any other work of antiquity, the Bible has received the greatest scrutiny with respect to its text. At the same time, the Bible enjoys the most reliable and greatest number of copies when compared to any other literature of antiquity. Furthermore, advances in computer technology have allowed more exact analysis than ever before. When these considerations are taken into account, the text of the Bible today can easily be received as a faithful representation of the text originally composed by the biblical writers.[4]

The Necessity of Scripture

As Jesus taught the Word of God to crowds, he was often moved to compassion for them "because they were harassed and helpless, like sheep without a shepherd" (Matt. 9:36). He reminded his disciples that "The harvest is plentiful, but the laborers are few; therefore pray earnestly to the Lord of the harvest to send out laborers into his harvest" (9:37–38). What the people needed was the Word of God. Sadly, many of those with the responsibility of teaching this word had substituted for it human wisdom and tradition. In response, Jesus echoed the words of Isaiah: "This people honors me with their lips, but their heart is far from me; in vain do they worship me, teaching as doctrines the commandments of men" (Matt. 15:8–9; cf. Isa. 29:13). "Man shall not live by bread alone," Jesus stated, "but by every word that comes from the mouth of God" (Matt. 4:4; cf. Deut. 8:3).

4 For a helpful introduction to Old Testament textual criticism, see Ellis R. Brotzman, *Old Testament Textual Criticism: A Practical Introduction* (Grand Rapids, MI: Baker, 1993). For an introduction to New Testament textual criticism, see the relevant discussion in James White, *The King James Only Controversy: Can You Trust Modern Translations?*, updated and expanded ed. (Minneapolis: Bethany, 2009).

The teaching and preaching of the Word of God was not only the need of Jesus's age. It is the need of every age. The members of the early church recognized this and "devoted themselves to the apostles' teaching" (Acts 2:42). The apostles themselves refused to become sidetracked by secondary responsibilities, insisting that "it is not right that we should give up preaching the word of God to serve tables" (Acts 6:2).

The New Testament letters overflow with exhortations to make the teaching and preaching of the Word of God the very heart of Christian ministry. Candidates for church leadership were required to be "able to give instruction in sound doctrine and also to rebuke those who contradict it" (Titus 1:9; cf. 2 Tim. 2:2, 24). Paul repeatedly exhorted Timothy to "teach and preach" this Word (1 Tim. 4:11, 13, 16; 6:2). This was an expectation he exemplified wherever he went, as is demonstrated in his address to the elders at Ephesus: "I did not shrink from declaring to you the whole counsel of God" (Acts 20:27).

As Paul prepared for his impending death, he gave to Timothy what amounts to the clarion call of all Christian ministry today:

> I charge you in the presence of God and of Christ Jesus, who is to judge the living and the dead, and by his appearing and his kingdom: preach the word; be ready in season and out of season; reprove, rebuke, and exhort, with complete patience and teaching. For the time is coming when people will not endure sound teaching, but having itching ears they will accumulate for themselves teachers to suit their own passions, and will turn away from listening to the truth and wander off into myths. (2 Tim. 4:1–4)

Only this Word mediates God's saving and sanctifying knowledge to humankind. Only through this Word can human beings come to know and walk with God personally. If this Word is removed from the center, there can be no truly Christian ministry.

The Obligation to Scripture

The Scripture is no ordinary book. In fact, it is the only book breathed out by God (2 Tim. 3:16). This inspired quality brings with it unassailable authority. Through it God mediates his lordship, wisdom, and love to humankind. Its contents are about eternal life and death. Readers cannot merely move their eyes over its words. Apprehension of its contents is not enough. Scripture brings with it definite obligations (James 1:22–25).

The primary obligation is to *receive it by faith as the Word of God.* When Paul preached in Thessalonica, the people not only listened to his words but treated them as the very words of God. His subsequent commendation to them serves as the model for all who read Paul's words in Scripture, as well as the words of any of the biblical writers:

> And we also thank God constantly for this, that when you received the word of God, which you heard from us, you accepted it not as the word of men but as what it really is, the word of God, which is at work in you believers. (1 Thess. 2:13)

A second obligation is to *seek the Lord for understanding.* The psalmist understood that God was the ultimate author of the Scriptures and that it was most appropriate to solicit his aid in understanding it:

> Open my eyes, that I may behold wondrous things out of your law. (Ps. 119:18; see Acts 6:4)

Another obligation is to *feed on the Scriptures as a way of life.* The Bible figuratively describes Scripture as milk (1 Pet. 2:2), bread (Deut. 8:3; Matt. 4:4), solid food (1 Cor. 3:2), and honey (Ps. 19:10). Job testified to the effectiveness of this spiritual "menu":

> I have not departed from the commandment of his lips;
> I have treasured the words of his mouth more than my portion of food. (Job 23:12; see Jer. 15:16)

A further obligation is to *study the Scriptures meticulously.* Ezra understood that, before he could teach the Word of God to Israel, it was imperative that he first personally obey it. And before he could obey, it was imperative that he study it:

> For Ezra had set his heart to study the Law of the Lord, and to do it and to teach his statutes and rules in Israel. (Ezra 7:10; cf. 2 Tim. 2:15)

Throughout his writings, the apostle John regularly emphasized the reader's obligation *to apply the Scriptures in daily living.* He made it clear that obedience was not an option. If one loves Jesus Christ, that person will keep his commandments (John 14:15, 21, 23):

> This is love, that we walk according to his commandments. (2 John 6)

> I have no greater joy than to hear that my children are walking in the truth. (3 John 4)

When Paul wrote his last set of instructions to Timothy, he reminded him of his obligation to *preach and teach the Word of God:*

> I charge you in the presence of God and of Christ Jesus, who is to judge the living and the dead, and by his appearing and his kingdom: preach the

> word; be ready in season and out of season; reprove, rebuke, and exhort, with complete patience and teaching. (2 Tim. 4:1–2)

Isaiah's words best summarize the obligation any reader has when coming across the words of Scripture—to *tremble in response to God's Word:*

> But this is the one to whom I will look:
> he who is humble and contrite in spirit
> and trembles at my word. (Isa. 66:2)

Questions:

1. What is "general revelation" and what is its value in terms of knowing God and his ways?
2. What are the different forms of "special revelation"? What is the unique value of each in terms of knowing God and his ways?
3. What are the various theories for explaining the divine process of inspiration?
4. What is the true view and definition of inspiration? What are the key texts that teach inspiration?
5. How did God providentially prepare (historical contexts and human authors) for the production of his Word?
6. What are the various proofs of inspiration?
7. What did Jesus himself affirm about the inspiration of the Old and New Testaments?
8. What did the New Testament authors themselves believe about the inspiration of the Bible?
9. How do secondary sources of confirmation contribute to our assurance that the Bible is the Word of God? And what is the primary source of confidence in the authority of the Scriptures?
10. What is meant by the clarity and sufficiency of Scripture?
11. How does one's definition of "accommodation" (and "infallibility") relate to one's understanding of inerrancy?
12. Since we no longer have the inspired "autographs" (original manuscripts), how can we trust the copies and translations of the Bible we use today? What is "textual criticism"?
13. What are the various aspects of (the nature of) the divine preservation of the Scriptures?
14. What is the definition of "the canon" as it relates to the compilation of the books of the Bible? How is "canonicity" recognized?
15. What are the believer's obligations to Scripture?

3

GOD THE FATHER

Theology Proper

THE BIBLE'S TEACHING ABOUT God's existence, attributes (perfections), and triunity, and about his works in decreeing, creating, and ruling over all things outside himself, is vital for systematic theology and for the believer's faith and life.

The Existence of God

There is only one God, "the only true God" (John 17:3), the triune God of the Bible. The Bible does not begin with human reasoning or rationalistic arguments for the existence of God but with the foundational presupposition that God exists and that he existed "in the beginning" (Gen. 1:1), before the beginning of all things outside himself. Theology proper is rightly derived from God's own inspired, inerrant Word, which is God's testimony about himself.

SCRIPTURAL ASSERTIONS

In considering the existence of God, God's own inspired testimony (2 Tim. 3:16) must be accepted as unique and perfectly reliable. Other evidences of God's existence must be evaluated and accepted only as they align with the Bible's statements about God.

First, the Bible requires that everyone who wants to be properly related to God must first believe that he exists (Heb. 11:6). Scripture calls those who reject God's existence "fools" and "wicked" (Pss. 14:1; 53:1; Ps. 10:4). Second, the Bible states that God is eternal (Deut. 33:27)—without beginning, without ending, and without succession of moments in his experience (see Ps. 90:2; Isa. 44:6; 41:4; 57:15). Third, scriptural proof of God's existence is found in God's own proclamations of his unique "is-ness," his "being." He "is" without dependence on anything else. It is not so much that God *has* "being" as it is that he *is* "being" itself. As God himself asserted to Moses, "'I AM WHO I AM.' . . . 'Say . . . , "I AM has sent me to you"'" (Ex. 3:14). God's existence *is* existence. Thus, the existence of anything at all presupposes the existence of the God from whom all existence derives. Paul affirmed, "In him we live and move and have our being" (Acts 17:28), and, "from him and through him and to him are all things" (Rom. 11:36). God exists, has life in himself, and is the source of all existence and life, for he "gives to all mankind life and breath and everything" (Acts 17:24–25). This means that Scripture's testimony of God's existence is self-attesting and self-authenticating.

THE KNOWABILITY AND INCOMPREHENSIBILITY OF GOD

God has revealed the fact of his existence in Scripture, and he makes himself known through written human language in the Bible. Scripture teaches that man may know God truly, yet not exhaustively or comprehensively.

God's Sufficient Knowability

The Bible affirms that God can be known, even known in a personal relationship (Jer. 24:7; 31:34; John 17:3). He had a relationship with Adam and Eve (Gen. 3:8). He spoke directly with Moses (Ex. 3:3–4; 19:10, 24), even "as a man speaks to his friend" (Ex. 33:11). He was personally present in the tabernacle and in the temple on the mercy seat, where he communed with Israel (Ex. 25:22; 29:42; 1 Sam. 4:4; 1 Kings 8:10–11). God personally indwells the church collectively (1 Cor. 3:16) as well as each individual believer (Eph. 3:17; cf. John 14:23), whom he regards as friends (James 2:23).

God's Incomprehensibility

While God can be known truly, he can never be known comprehensively or exhaustively. Humans are limited to time and space and are corrupted by indwelling sin (Rom. 7:15–23), while God's being is infinite (Ps. 147:5; 1 Tim. 1:17). Apart from regeneration, men are rebellious toward God and darkened in their understanding (2 Cor. 4:3–4; Eph. 4:17–19). Man cannot see God and live (Ex. 33:20; Lev. 16:2). God "dwells in unapproachable light, whom no one has ever seen or can see" (1 Tim. 6:16; cf. John 1:18; 6:46). The spiritual form of God's essence is not revealed to man (Deut. 4:12, 15). The depths of God are known only by God (1 Cor. 2:11).

Even though man can know the many things God has revealed about himself in nature and in Scripture, nevertheless "the secret things belong to the LORD our God" (Deut. 29:29). Simply put, God's mind, knowledge, understanding, and thoughts transcend man's comprehension and intellectual capacity (see Pss. 139:6, 17–18; 147:5; Isa. 55:9). When we have exhausted all our efforts to understand God—even when we come to know him truly—we are constrained to confess with Job, "Behold, these are but the outskirts of his ways, and how small a whisper do we hear of him!" (Job 26:14).

ASSESSMENT OF "NATURAL PROOFS"

Belief in God's existence must be grounded in Scripture, for it is the sole infallible witness to God's mind. All other evidence of God's existence, while extensive, must nevertheless be subordinate to Scripture. The Bible affirms that God has also revealed himself in his creation (Rom. 1:20), in the human conscience (Rom. 2:14–15), and in history (Acts 14:17), which he controls. This is referred to as *general* or *natural* revelation. However, this revelation must never be considered independent of Scripture. On his own, fallen man will mistake and distort the revelation of God in nature (Rom. 1:18). Even the Christian needs the guidance of Scripture to properly assess God's revelation of himself in nature (1 Cor. 2:12).[1]

Inadequacy of the "Natural Proofs"

By themselves the "natural proofs" for the existence of God do not conclusively prove the existence of any god, much less the God of the Bible. This is not surprising, since at least some of these so-called "proofs" were derived from pagan philosophers such as Plato (ca. 428–348 BC) and Aristotle (ca. 384–322 BC).

The Ontological Argument. The ontological argument[2] is an argument that begins with existence (Gk. *ontos*, "being"). The classic Christian form of the ontological argument was put forth by Anselm of Canterbury (1033–1109) in his *Monologion* and *Proslogion*.[3] Anselm argued that we can think of something absolutely perfect ("something than which nothing greater can be thought"). But if that thing we are thinking of does not actually exist, then it is not absolutely perfect, since existing is better than not existing. Thus, if the thing we are imagining does not exist, we can think of something even greater than it—something that actually does exist. So, Anselm concluded, an absolutely perfect thing must necessarily exist, and that absolutely perfect thing is God.

1 See John Calvin, *Institutes of the Christian Religion*, ed. John T. McNeill, trans. Ford Lewis Battles, Library of Christian Classics (1559; repr., Philadelphia: Westminster John Knox, 1960), 1.6.1. Calvin (1509–1564) graphically portrayed this last point, comparing the Scriptures to "spectacles" that give people a clear manifestation of the true God. For more on general versus special revelation, see the sections in chap. 2 titled "General Revelation" and "Special Revelation" (pp. 53–55).

2 For more on the ontological argument, the reader should consult: John M. Frame, *Apologetics to the Glory of God: An Introduction* (Phillipsburg, NJ: P&R, 1994), 115–16; John M. Frame, *A History of Western Philosophy and Theology* (Phillipsburg, NJ: P&R, 2015), 63–70; Frederick Copleston, *A History of Philosophy* (London: Search Press, 1946), 1:163–206.

3 See Anselm, *Proslogion* 2, in Anselm of Canterbury, *The Major Works*, ed. Brian Davies and G. R. Evans, Oxford World's Classics (Oxford: Oxford University Press, 1998), 87.

An important caution to keep in mind is that many nonevangelical thinkers have also held various forms of this argument, including René Descartes (1596–1650), Baruch Spinoza (1632–1677), Gottfried Wilhelm von Leibniz (1646–1716), George Hegel (1770–1831), and Charles Hartshorne (1897–2000), but their version of this argument did not lead them to the God of the Bible.

The Cosmological Argument. Another "natural proof" is the argument from the created realm to an Ultimate Cause for it all: every effect must have a cause. Several of Thomas Aquinas's (1225–1274) famous "Five Ways" (*Summa Theologiae*, Ia.2.3; first, second, and third) use various forms of this argument of proving the existence of God. Aquinas taught that there cannot be an infinite regress of causes, so there must be an "unmoved mover" ("first way"), a "first cause" ("second way"), an original and absolutely "necessary being" sufficient to produce all created things ("third way"). Aquinas concluded that the "unmoved mover," "first cause," and "necessary being" is God.[4]

Once again we must be cautious. The Muslim philosopher Al-Ghazali (1058–1111) used a form of the cosmological argument to argue for the existence of Allah. And the cosmological argument was later held by the nonevangelical Enlightenment philosopher Gottfried Wilhelm von Leibniz. The cosmological argument did not lead them to the God of the Bible.

The Teleological Argument. Another "natural proof" is the teleological argument, the argument from design. This argument holds that the complex order, design, purpose, and intelligence in the universe is the result of the work of an intelligent, purposeful designer, who is God.

Like the others, while sound, this argument has also been made by non-Christians such as Plato, Aristotle, and Immanuel Kant (1724–1804). Therefore, this argument also does not necessarily point people to the true God.

The Moral Argument. The moral argument proposes that man's conscience and moral values imply a moral creator of man's conscience and the source of those moral values. Aquinas's "fourth way" is a form of the moral argument. He argues from the gradation of beings to an ultimately perfect being, who must be their cause. This ultimate being must be the cause of all the perfections (e.g., goodness, morality, etc.) that characterize lesser beings. And this ultimate being, he said, "we call God."

Again, however, the Enlightenment philosopher Immanuel Kant also asserted a form of the moral argument, and he denied both the Trinity and the incarnation.

4 See Thomas Aquinas, *The Summa Theologica*, trans. Fathers of the English Dominican Province, ed. Kevin Knight, 2nd ed., 1.2.3, http://www.newadvent.org/summa/1002.htm#article3.

In summary, these "natural proofs" represent a theology based on man's reason and do not necessarily lead to the triune God of the Bible. These "natural proofs" are not proofs of the existence of any god without first presupposing what a god is.

Limited Usefulness of the "Natural Proofs" of God's Existence

These cautions should serve as a warning: humanly crafted arguments do not prove the triune God of Scripture. Still, when derived from the Bible, they are forms of biblical truth and can be used by the Holy Spirit to convict people of the truthfulness of such arguments. Here are some observations:

First, using unaided human reason (which does not presuppose the self-attesting existence of God nor the self-authenticating truth of Scripture), these natural "proofs" do not logically prove the existence of the true God. For those who suppress the truth in unrighteousness (Rom. 1:18), they do not "work." In spite of the fact that God has given sufficient evidence of his own existence in creation and conscience, unregenerate man suppresses the truth of general revelation in unrighteousness (Rom. 1:18–21).

Furthermore, man's depravity reaches even to man's mind—his thinking is futile, his understanding is darkened, he walks in ignorance (Eph. 4:17–18), and he cannot understand the things God has revealed in creation (2 Cor. 2:14). Believers cannot and should not rely on the "natural proofs" as evidence for the existence of the true God.

Only by the miracle of regeneration, in which God quickens the unbelieving heart by shining into it the light of the knowledge of his glory (2 Cor. 4:6) will a fallen, sinful person come to a true knowledge of the triune God. Regeneration happens only by the proclamation of the gospel that Jesus Christ is Lord (2 Cor. 4:5). Only the gift of saving faith, imparted by the Holy Spirit through the Word of God (Rom. 10:17; James 1:18; 1 Pet. 1:23–25), supplies the basis for the knowledge of God (Heb. 11:1, 6). Christians believe that God exists because God has shone the light of his self-authenticating glory into their hearts through the Word of God.[5]

The Names of God

God's names are important because they reveal aspects of who he is in himself, in his actions within himself, and in relation to his creation. God's names represent him so personally that how one treats God's name is equivalent to how one treats God (Mal. 1:6–7, 11–14; cf. Ps. 138:2).

5 For more on the self-authenticating glory of Scripture as the proper warrant for faith, see John Piper, *A Peculiar Glory: How the Christian Scriptures Reveal Their Complete Truthfulness* (Wheaton, IL: Crossway, 2016).

YAHWEH AND COMPOUNDS

Yahweh

The most common name (6,800x) for God—Yahweh—is derived from the tetragrammaton (the four Hebrew consonants transliterated into English as "YHWH"). God identified himself at the burning bush (Ex. 3:13–15) as "I AM WHO I AM" and "I AM" (3:14), and said that this name, "LORD" (Yahweh) is "my name forever" (Ex. 3:15). Although this name of God was known before the time of the burning bush (e.g., Gen. 4:26; 5:29; 9:26; 14:22), God told Moses, "By my name the LORD I did not make myself known . . ." (Ex. 6:3) The explanation is that although in the days of the patriarchs God was addressed as Yahweh, they did not relate to God with the full understanding that Yahweh was "his name."[6]

After the Babylonian exile the people of Israel began, out of reverence, to refrain from vocalizing the name "Yahweh." When the biblical text was read orally, instead of "Yahweh" they usually spoke the Hebrew name *adonai*. The translators of the Greek Septuagint and the writers of the New Testament (under the inspiration of the Holy Spirit) respected this Jewish tradition, writing the Greek word *kyrios* ("Lord") when quoting an Old Testament passage with the name Yahweh.

When the Masoretes created the system of vowel pointing for the Hebrew Bible, they pointed "YHWH" with the vowels from the name *Adonai*. This pointing led Latin-writing Christians to transliterate the Masoretic writing of "YHWH" with its vowel markings as "Iehovah." In English this became "Jehovah." Some early English Bibles used "Jehovah" for "YHWH," but most modern English versions translate "YHWH" as "LORD," generally set in small caps to differentiate it from *adonai*.

The meaning of Yahweh is important for theology. Derived from the Hebrew verb for being (*hayah*), the basic meaning of "Yahweh" is "he is" or "he will be." So the name indicates that God is pure being and is perfectly self-sufficient. The name implies that he had no beginning, will have no ending, and is ever present. He does not derive his existence from anyone or anything but is self-existent from all eternity.

Furthermore, this name indicates the constancy of his being amid the changing conditions of his creation. For example, as Yahweh, he had been and would be present as (1) the Revealer of himself and his will, (2) the Redeemer (Gen. 1:1–2:3 compared with Gen. 2:4–25; 9:26–27; Ex. 3:15–16; 6:26; Deut. 7:9; Ps. 19:1–6 compared with Ps. 19:7–14; Isa. 26:4), (3) the Eternal One (Isa. 41:4; 48:12), (4) the Life Giver (Gen. 2:4–25; Ezek. 37:13–14, 27), and (5) the supreme Judge of all creation (Ezek. 6:13–14; 7:27; 11:10; 12:16). In sum, the name Yahweh means that God is—that he is eternal, simple, self-existent, and present at every event in time.

6 See Gustav Friedrich Oehler, *Theology of the Old Testament*, 2nd ed. (1884; repr., n.c.: HardPress, 2012), 97.

Yahweh Compounds

The relevance of God's name, especially in his relations with his people, is seen through the compound forms in which his name appears in Scripture.

Yahweh-tsabaoth. God is "the LORD of hosts" or "armies." Because he is and will be who he is, God created, governs, and leads the angels as the "armies" of heaven (Ps. 24:10; Isa. 6:1–5; 9:7; Hag. 2:6–9; Zech. 4:6) and his people as his "armies" (Ex. 7:4; 12:41; 1 Sam. 17:45) to accomplish his purposes in his creation.

Yahweh-yireh. God is "the LORD" who "will provide" or "will see" (Gen. 22:14). Because he is and will be who he is, God will see and provide what is needed to fulfill his promises. In Genesis 22:14, Abraham remembered God by this name because God had provided a ram to sacrifice in place of Isaac.

Yahweh-nissi. God is "The LORD Is My Banner" (Ex. 17:15). Because he is and will be who he is, God will be the "banner" or "standard" that will lead his people to victory over their enemies. In Exodus 17:15, Moses worshiped God as the One who gave his people victory over Amalek.

Yahweh-shalom. God is "The LORD Is Peace" (Judg. 6:24). Because he is and will be who he is, God, through the angel of the Lord, sent Gideon to "save Israel" from the Midianites (Judg. 6:14). The angel of the Lord gave Gideon a sign—that the angel's staff consumed Gideon's sacrifice with fire—to assure him that he was sending Gideon and would go with him to give him victory.

Yahweh-roiy. God is "the LORD is my shepherd" (Ps. 23:1). Because he is and will be who he is, according to Psalm 23, God will provide everything his people need in this life, in death, and forever. He will guide and protect his people.

Yahweh-tsidkenu. God is "the LORD is our righteousness" (Jer. 23:6). Because he is and will be who he is, in the future God will establish the Messiah as the Davidic King, and "he shall reign as king and deal wisely, and shall execute justice and righteousness in the land" (Jer. 23:5).

EL AND COMPOUNDS

El, *Eloah*, and *Elohim*

The Hebrew names *el*, *eloah*, and *elohim* (when used of the true God) indicate God's supreme power, strength, and might. When depicting the true God, *el* is used with the article (e.g., Gen. 31:13; 46:3; Pss. 68:20; 77:14) or with other modifiers, e.g., "the God of your father" (Gen. 49:25), "God my exceeding joy" (Ps. 43:4), "the God of heaven" (Ps. 136:26), "the faithful God" (Deut. 7:9), "the Everlasting God" (Gen. 21:33), and "the living God" (Josh. 3:10; Pss. 42:2; 84:2).

The name *elohim* is a plural (*-im*) of the root *el* (appearing more than two thousand times). Referring to the true God, it is probably a plural of intensity,[7] indicating that God has such a vast fullness to his power that a plural name is appropriate to him. This name appears at the beginning of the biblical revelation (Gen. 1:1) and is used in many passages interchangeably with the singular *el* and other singular names of God (e.g., Deut. 7:9; Josh. 24:19). This plural form does not prove that God is triune, but it certainly is compatible with later biblical revelation of the triunity of God (cf. Gen. 1:26; 3:22; 11:7).

El/Elohim Compounds

Again, when used of the true God, the Hebrew name *el* is often used with modifiers resulting in a compound name.

El Shaddai. The term *shaddai* comes from the Hebrew root *shadad*, referring to power. With respect to the true God, *shaddai* has been traditionally translated "almighty," referring to God's omnipotence. Being almighty, God provides (Gen. 17:1; 28:3–4; 35:11; 43:14; 48:3–4; 49:25), protects (Ps. 91:1) and chastens in judgment (Ruth 1:20–21; Job 5:17; 6:4; 21:20; Ps. 68:14; Isa. 13:6; Joel 1:15). The New Testament uses the Greek word *pantokratōr* ("Almighty") to refer to the Old Testament concept of God as *shaddai*, thus confirming that *shaddai* refers to God as omnipotent, (cf. 2 Cor. 6:18; Rev. 1:8; 4:8; 11:17; 15:3; 16:7, 14; 19:6, 15; 21:22).

El Elyon. Translated "God Most High," this title refers to the supreme sovereignty of God. *El elyon* is usually used in the Old Testament in relation to Gentiles and the enemies of God and his people (Gen. 14:18–22; Num. 24:16; Deut. 32:8; Pss. 91:1, 9; 92:1; 97:9; Dan. 3:26; 4:2, 17, 24–25, 34; 5:18, 21; 7:25). As such, God has supreme authority over heaven (Isa. 14:13–14; Dan. 4:35, 37) and earth (Deut. 32:8; 2 Sam. 22:14–15; Pss. 9:2–5; 21:7; 47:2–4; 57:2–3; 82:6–8; 83:16–18; 91:9–12; Dan. 5:18–21).

El/Elohey Olam. This name indicates God is eternal or "the Everlasting God" (Gen. 21:33). In Isaiah 40:28, the plural form of God's name is used (cf. Pss. 90:2; 93:2; 103:17).

ADON/ADONAI: LORD

Although the tetragrammaton, YHWH, is often pointed with the vowels in *adonai* ("my Lord"), this Hebrew name/title for God (or its absolute form, *adon* ["Lord"]) is also used as a name for God. In general use, the title is used for a general recognition of superiority (Gen. 24:18; 32:5; 44:7; Ruth 2:13), a master

7 Heinrich Friedrich Wilhelm Gesenius, *Gesenius' Hebrew Grammar*, ed. E. Kautzsch, rev. A. E. Cowley, 2nd ed. (1910; repr., Oxford, UK: Clarendon, 1976), 246.d.

(Ex. 21:4–8), an owner (1 Kings 16:24), a husband (Gen. 18:12), or a king (Gen. 40:1; Judg. 3:25; 1 Sam. 22:12; Jer. 22:18; 34:5). When used of the true God, *adonai* indicates that he possesses supreme sovereignty and ultimate authority over all things external to himself.

TSUR: ROCK

The Bible depicts God as "the Rock," comparing him to a physical rock in order to communicate his impregnable strength and thus his perfect reliability (e.g., Deut. 32:4, 15, 18, 30–31; Pss. 18:2, 31, 46; 19:14; 28:1; 31:2–3; 42:9; 62:2, 6–7; 71:3; 78:35; 89:26; 92:15; 94:22; 95:1; 144:1; Isa. 17:10; 26:4; 30:29; 44:8). The Hebrew word *tsur* depicts a cliff or quarry (Isa. 51:1). Sometimes Scripture uses a metaphor so frequently that the metaphor becomes virtually a name or a title (e.g., the "Word," in reference to the Son, cf. John 1:1–2). The expression "the Rock" is used as a name or title of God. The apostle Paul speaks of preincarnate Messiah as the Rock that cared for Israel and the "spiritual Rock that followed them" (1 Cor. 10:1–4).[8]

AB: FATHER

Since the New Testament applies the name "Father" to the first person of the Trinity, when the Old Testament depicts God as "father," this Hebrew description should be considered a name/title of God. God is the "father" of Israel in Deuteronomy 32:6 (cf. 32:18; see also Ps. 89:26; Isa. 63:16; 64:8; Jer. 3:4, 19). The theme of God as Father is expanded in the New Testament, which reveals that the first person of the Trinity is especially the Father of the second person of the Trinity, the Son of God (Matt. 7:21; John 5:17; Rom. 15:6; 1 Cor. 15:24; 2 Cor. 1:3; 11:31; Eph. 1:3; Col. 1:3; 1 Pet. 1:3; Rev. 2:27; 3:5, 21), and is the Father of believers (Matt. 6:8–9, 14–15, 18, 26, 32).

Father is an eternal name, indicating that there was never a time when the first person was not the Father of the second person, his only begotten Son. As the unbegotten Father, the first person of the Trinity is the eternal Prime Mover in all his relationships and works.

The Attributes (Perfections) of God

The attributes of God are his characteristics, the various qualities of his nature. The term *perfections*, derived from the Greek term *aretas* ("excellencies") in 1 Peter 2:9, is more fitting than *attributes* because *perfections* specifies that the characteristics of God are each perfect and inherently characterize the God who is perfect.

8 Robert Duncan Culver, *Systematic Theology: Biblical and Historical* (Fearn, Ross-shire, Scotland: Mentor, 2005), 56.

CLASSIFICATIONS

Many theologians have sought to categorize the divine perfections. The Bible does not explicitly establish categories, so the schemes of classification should not be uncritically accepted.

Negative and Positive

One scheme of classification (negative and positive) is based on (1) negative perfections, or those that are the opposite of creaturely limitations (e.g., infinite, incorporeal); and (2) positive perfections, or those that are present in man but are characteristic of God in an infinitely perfect way (e.g., goodness, holiness, righteousness, justice).

The problem with these categories is that they overlap. When one makes a negative assertion about God, he has a positive concept in mind, even though he might not be able to articulate it. For example, to say that God is immutable (negative) entails that one consciously knows that God is constant and faithful (positive). The reverse is true as well.

Natural and Moral (Greatness and Goodness; Constitution and Personality)

Natural perfections are said to belong to God's "constitution" (e.g., self-existence, simplicity, infinity), whereas moral perfections are those belonging to his will, which make him a moral being (e.g., goodness, truth, love, holiness).

The problem with this classification is that moral attributes characterize God's essence just as much as natural attributes. Perfections of goodness are also perfections of God's greatness (Psalm 145), and perfections of personality are also perfections of God's constitution.

Absolute and Relative

The absolute perfections are said to characterize God's essence considered in and of itself (e.g., self-existence, infinity, spirituality), whereas the relative perfections characterize God's essence considered in God's relation to his creation (e.g., omniscience, omnipresence).

The problem in this instance is that this classification assumes that man can know about God in his essence, but the truth is that all of God's perfections are relative, revealed in relation to his creation. Conversely, even the so-called relative perfections are absolute, because they are eternally active in the relationships between the members of the Trinity, in God's essential existence.

Immanent/Intransitive versus Emanant/Transitive/Operative

According to this classification, the former are perfections that function outside the divine essence but remain immanent in God (e.g., immensity, eternity, simplicity), whereas the latter are perfections that produce things external to God (e.g., omnipotence, goodness, justice).

Contrary to this classification, man cannot know any characteristic of God as it is in his essence but only as his character is revealed in his works. Further, the operative and causative perfections must also be immanent and intransitive in God; otherwise, God would need something outside himself to be complete.

Incommunicable and Communicable

The incommunicable perfections are those characteristics unique to God (e.g., self-existence, simplicity, immensity), whereas the communicable perfections are those characteristics transferable in part to humans (e.g., goodness, righteousness, love).

A problem with this categorization is that even the incommunicable perfections are at least somewhat like human characteristics, or no one could understand anything about God's perfections. Also, God's communicable perfections are not completely like human characteristics, or God would not be greater than man in every way.

Nevertheless, many theologians have used, and continue to use, this categorization; and it can be useful if it can help people focus on how God is unique compared to mankind. Also, this categorization stresses both the transcendence and the immanence of God, denying both pantheism and deism.

THE INCOMMUNICABLE PERFECTIONS

God's perfections are identical to his essence, and they actively integrate with (i.e., complement and qualify) each other. When considering the perfections, one must remember that one is learning about God himself, not something outside of or beside God.[9]

Independence (Aseity)

God is independent of all things. He is perfectly self-sufficient, not depending on anything outside himself for anything, and is therefore the eternal, foundational being, the source of life and sustenance for all other beings. He is self-existent, having life in and of himself (Ex. 3:14; John 5:26), and he existed before all things, and through him alone all things exist (Ps. 90:2; 1 Cor. 8:6; Rev. 4:11). He is the source of everything (Deut. 32:39; Isa. 45:5–7; 54:16; John 5:26; 1 Cor. 8:6) and he depends on nothing; all things depend on him (Rom. 11:36). He needs nothing, being all-sufficient (Job 22:2–3; Acts 17:25).

9 For fuller treatments of the attributes of God, see Herman Bavinck, *Reformed Dogmatics*, vol. 2, *God and Creation*, ed. John Bolt, trans. John Vriend (Grand Rapids, MI: Baker Academic, 2004); Stephen Charnock, *The Existence and Attributes of God* (1853; repr., Grand Rapids, MI: Baker, 1996); Arthur W. Pink, *The Attributes of God* (Grand Rapids, MI: Baker, 2006).

Immutability

God's immutability is his perfect unchangeability in his essence, character, purpose, and promises. He is eternally the same (Ps. 102:25–27) and he does not change (Mal. 3:6; James 1:17). He is incorruptible, alone having immortality, always remaining the same (Rom. 1:23; 1 Tim. 1:17; 6:15–16; Heb. 1:11–12). His faithfulness never lessens (Lam. 3:22–23).

Tensions are apparent to people when they read passages asserting God's unchangeability alongside passages stating that God repents (e.g., Gen. 6:6; Ex. 32:12; 1 Sam. 15:11, 35; Jer. 18:10; Amos 7:3, 6; Jonah 3:9–10; 4:2) or changes his purpose (e.g., Gen. 18:23–32; Ex. 32:10–14; Jonah 3:10). However, these perceived "changes" are not changes in God himself but only apparent changes as he reveals himself to people. God never changes, but creatures do change, and outward circumstances change. Thus, God's actions do not imply a change of essence or purpose.

The language of God "repenting" or "changing" in some way is anthropopathic language—figurative expressions that communicate to man on his level of understanding about God's dispositions or actions. But God's "changes" are never genuine changes at all; they may be so perceived by us, but God's perfection prohibits him from changing either for the better or for the worse. His eternal omniscience means he could never decide that a different course of action is better or wiser than that which he has already decreed. And his pure actuality means that he can undergo no change of state whatsoever.

Infinity

God's infinity describes his nature as perfectly transcending (existing and acting beyond) all limitations of time and space. God's infinitude with regard to time is called his eternity or omni-temporality, and his infinitude with regard to space is called his immensity or omnipresence.

Eternity

God perfectly transcends all limitations of time (2 Pet. 3:8). He is God eternal (Isa. 40:28), and he inhabits eternity (Isa. 57:15). He existed before creation (Gen. 1:1; John 1:1; 17:5, 24). He was, is, and is to come all at once (Ex. 3:14; Rev. 1:4, 8). He is from everlasting to everlasting (Pss. 90:2; 93:2).

God's Essence as "Timeless." The biblical statement "In the beginning, God . . ." (Gen. 1:1) indicates that God existed before "the beginning," which commenced on "the first day" (Gen. 1:5). God existed before the first moment of "the first day" of all reality outside himself. Therefore, God's existence is outside the bounds of time. While God interacts with his creation and his creatures from moment to moment, God himself transcends time; he cannot be limited by it in any way.

In his essence, God exists in an eternal "present." He always "was and is" with "the first" of time and with "the last" of time (Isa. 41:4; cf. 44:6). God is not confined or conditioned by limits or lengths of time (cf. Ps. 90:1–4; 2 Pet. 3:8). To say he is "timeless" means that both the beginning and the end (of time) are consciously experienced and are "present" realities to God. Since the expression "the beginning and the end" (Rev. 21:6; 22:13) is probably a merism (a statement of opposites to indicate totality), it means God controls every moment as consciously experienced, "present" realities.

Immensity and Omnipresence

God perfectly transcends all limitation of space, and yet is present with every point of space with all that he is. Transcendence means that God is greater than, and independent of, the creation. Immensity refers to the fact that God transcends and fills all space. His omnipresence indicates that God is present with every point of space in his entire being. He fills heaven and earth, so nothing is hidden from his presence, and he is both close and far off (Ps. 139:7–10; Jer. 23:23–24; Acts 17:27–28); thus heaven and earth cannot contain him (1 Kings 8:27; 2 Chron. 2:6; Isa. 66:1; Acts 7:48–49). He dwells in, and has his throne in, heaven (Deut. 26:15; 2 Sam. 22:7; 1 Kings 8:32; Pss. 11:4; 33:13; 115:3, 16; Isa. 63:15; Matt. 5:34; 6:9; John 14:2; Eph. 1:20; Heb. 1:3; Rev. 1:4–5), but he also dwells in the midst of his people (Ex. 20:24; 25:8; 40:34–35; Deut. 12:11; 1 Sam. 4:4; 2 Sam. 6:2; 1 Kings 8:10–11; 2 Kings 19:15). He is close (relationally) to the righteous (Pss. 11:7; 51:19; Isa. 57:15).

Specifics of Immensity and Omnipresence. God transcends space. God is not diffused through space so that only part of him is in each place. Neither is God bound to one place. God is fully present in every place. His immensity does not mean he is separate from creation in a deistic sense, even though it does mean he is distinct from and greater than creation. God upholds the created order by being entirely present with every point of space. This is true, for example, in both heaven and hell (Rev. 14:9–10) and in the righteous and the wicked.

Unity: Numerical Oneness

God's unity is his perfect uniqueness and simplicity of essence, so that neither is he more than one essence nor is the divine essence compounded or multiform. God is only one being (Deut. 6:4; Mark 12:29); he is unique; there is only one God (Deut. 4:35; 32:39; Ps. 18:31; Isa. 40:18; 43:10–11; 44:6; 45:5)—a uniqueness that is not contradicted by, but is revealed in, Jesus Christ (John 17:3; Rom. 3:30; 1 Cor. 8:4–6; 1 Tim. 2:5).

Unity: Simplicity

God's simplicity is his indivisibility, his perfect lack of composition. This means that each of, and all of, his perfections *are* his essence. This perfection can be expressed by stating that God *is*, and does not merely *have*, truth, righteousness, wisdom, spirit, light, life, love, and holiness (Jer. 10:10; 23:6; John 1:4–5, 9; 4:24; 14:6; 1 Cor. 1:30; 1 John 1:5; 4:8, 16). Such passages reveal God as the complete fullness of each respective quality.

Compatibility of God's Simplicity with the Doctrine of the Trinity. God's simplicity does not contradict the doctrine of the Trinity, but rather is the foundation of biblical monotheism.[10] God's essence is not composed of three persons. Rather, the uncompounded, undivided divine essence is possessed in full by each of the three persons. The various personal properties unique to each person are not things added to the divine essence but are only distinctions of personal subsistence and of relationship. In all the external works of the Trinity, each person acts without dividing the divine essence.

Omniscience

God's omniscience is his perfect knowledge of (a) himself, (b) all actual things outside himself, and (c) all things that do not become reality, in one eternal and simple (uncompounded) act of knowing. One should note that this definition does not say that God knows things that are "possible," because in God's eternal mind and plan there are only actual things, not possible things. He does know what would have occurred if circumstances had been different, but since in his mind and plan they never would occur, they are not "possibilities." Only what is in God's plan is "possible," because only that could ever become reality in time."[11] God knows: all things (2 Chron. 16:9; Isa. 40:13; Rom. 11:34; Heb. 4:13; 1 John 3:20); things that are contingent from a human perspective (1 Sam. 23:10–13; 2 Kings 13:19; Ps. 81:12–16; Jer. 26:2–7; 38:17–20; Ezek. 3:4–6; Matt. 11:21); future things (Isa. 41:22–26; 42:8–9; 43:9–12; 44:6–8; 46:9–11); the heart of man (1 Kings 8:39; Ps. 7:9; Prov. 15:11; Jer. 11:20; 17:9–10; 20:12; Luke 16:15; Rom. 8:27; 1 Thess. 2:4; 1 John 3:20); people before they are conceived (Ps. 139:13–16; Jer. 1:5; Rom. 8:28–30; Rev. 13:8; 17:8); the days and geographical limits ordained for each person (Pss. 31:15; 39:4–5; 139:7–16; Job 14:5; Acts 17:26).

God's knowledge is eternal and *a priori*; it is perfect, never increasing (Isa. 40:13–14; Rom. 11:34); it precedes all things outside God, never being derived from reality outside himself (Rom. 8:29; 1 Cor. 2:7; Eph. 1:4–5; 2 Tim. 1:9); and

10 See James E. Dolezal, *All That Is in God: Evangelical Theology and the Challenge of Classical Christian Theism* (Grand Rapids, MI: Reformation Heritage Books, 2017), 105–34.

11 Here we reject all forms of "middle knowledge," whether the classic Molinist conception or the so-called "compatibilistic" reformulation. See below on "The Nature of God's Knowledge."

it is definite—clearly defined, precise, certain, sure, and comprehensive (Ps. 139:1–3; Heb. 4:13)

The major effects of God's knowledge in time include the creation of the physical realm (Pss. 104:24; 136:5); the formation of the church (Eph. 3:10); all of God's actions in time, including the application of salvation (Rom. 11:33); and worship from man (Job 11:7–9; Ps. 139:17–18; Rom. 11:33).

The Nature of God's Knowledge. The knowledge God has is intuitive, inherent, and immediate, not resulting from observing and reasoning in successive moments of time. At the same time, it does have logical structure. God's knowledge refers to his activity, not merely to content, and it is simple and simultaneous in its exertion. He knows everything totally, all at once, not one thing only before he knows another thing. Yet he also knows the differences and the order existing between all things.

God's knowledge is comprehensive and completely conscious. Man's knowledge is partial and mostly unconscious. God's knowledge is "pure act," never passive (knowledge based on learning) like man's, but rather is eternally willed by him. And it is immediate, not deistic. That is, God is not removed from the things he knows. He always has direct, immediate perception of all that he knows. (On God's foreknowledge, see the discussion of *proginōskō* under "The Decree of Election," below, p. 120).

Omnipotence

God's omnipotence describes his ability to do anything consistent with his nature. Power belongs to God (Pss. 62:11; 96:7; Rev. 4:11; 5:12; 7:12; 19:1). God does whatever he pleases (Ps. 115:3; Isa. 14:24, 27; 46:10; 55:11; Dan. 4:35) and nothing is too hard for God; nothing is impossible (Gen. 18:14; Job 42:2; Jer. 32:27; Zech. 8:6; Matt. 3:9; 19:26; 26:53; Luke 1:37; 18:27; Eph. 3:20). God's works reveal his omnipotence (Psalms 8; 18; 19; 24; 29; 33; 104): creation (Genesis 1; Ps. 8:3; Isa. 42:5; 44:24; 45:12, 18; 48:13; Zech. 12:1; Rom. 1:20); providence (Heb. 1:3); and redemption (Rom. 1:16; 1 Cor. 1:24).

There are things that Scripture says God is unable to do because they would contradict his character, nature, or revealed will: repent or lie (Num. 23:19; 1 Sam. 15:29; Heb. 6:18); deny himself (2 Tim. 2:13); be tempted (James 1:13); or change (James 1:17; Mal. 3:6).

Perfection

The perfection of God speaks not only of his moral perfection—that is, that he is perfectly holy, just, and good—but also that God is the sum total of all conceivable perfections. God is morally perfect (Matt. 5:48). God's way is perfect, so his Word is perfectly true (2 Sam. 22:31). God's work is perfect in that his acts are perfectly truthful and just (Deut. 32:4).

THE COMMUNICABLE PERFECTIONS

Spirituality and Invisibility

God is spirit (John 4:24), thus invisible and noncorporeal. His essence cannot be perceived by the physical senses. God's form is not seen (Deut. 4:12, 15; John 1:18; 5:37; 6:46; 1 Tim. 6:16; 1 John 4:12, 20) because it is not physical. God is eternal (Ps. 90:1–2), omnipresent (Ps. 139:7–12), and invisible (Rom. 1:20; Col. 1:15–16; 1 Tim. 1:17; Heb. 11:27; see also Ex. 33:20).

If God is invisible, how will believers see God after the resurrection, as some texts suggest (Job 19:26; Ps. 17:15; Matt. 5:8; 1 John 3:2; Rev. 22:4)? These statements about seeing God and his face actually refer to a comparatively greater spiritual vision of God's revelation of himself, not to a physical vision of his essence. In the eternal state, the believer's spiritual perception of God will reach beyond what physical senses can see. In Scripture, God's "face" (Matt. 18:10) is an anthropomorphism for God's external mediation of his presence.[12]

Wisdom

God's wisdom is his perfect knowledge of how to act skillfully so that he will accomplish all his good pleasure—to glorify himself. This definition is based on the Hebrew word for "wisdom," *hokmah*, which can mean "skill."

The scriptural evidence for this attribute is visible in that God created by his wisdom (Job 9:4; 37–41; Pss. 19:1–7; 104:1–34; Prov. 8:22–31; Isa. 40:28; Jer. 10:12) and that God redeems by his wisdom (Deut. 4:6–8; Rom. 11:25–33 [esp. 11:33]; 16:25–27 [esp. 16:27]; 1 Cor. 2:6–13; Eph. 3:10–11; Rev. 5:12). God is the very source of wisdom itself (Prov. 2:6; 9:10; James 1:5). Moreover, he is omnisapient (Lat. *sapientia*, "wisdom") meaning that he is all-wise (Job 12:13; Ps. 147:5; Isa. 40:28; Rom. 11:33; 16:27).

Truth and Faithfulness

God's truth and faithfulness are the perfect correspondence of God's nature with what God should be, with the reliability of his words and deeds, and with the accuracy of his knowledge, thoughts, and words. All of God's words are true and faithful (2 Sam. 7:28; Pss. 19:9; 25:10; 33:4; 111:7; 119:86, 142, 151; Dan. 4:37; John 17:17; Eph. 1:13). He cannot lie or repent like humans can (Num. 23:19; 1 Sam. 15:29). He is the only real God; thus, he is true, in contrast to the false gods (Deut. 32:21; Pss. 96:5; 97:7; 115:4–8; Isa. 44:9–10; John 14:6; 17:3; 1 John 5:20). God keeps his covenants (Deut. 4:31; 7:9; Neh. 1:5; Ps. 40:11; Dan. 9:4).

12 For more on the object of the beatific vision in relation to God's invisibility, see Michael Riccardi, "Seeking His Face: A Biblical and Theological Study of the Face of God" (master's thesis, The Master's Seminary, 2015).

God is a rock of refuge, because of his dependable firmness (Deut. 32:4, 15, 18, 30, 37; Pss. 18:2–3; 31:6; 36:5; 43:2–3; 54:7; 57:3; 71:22; 143:1; 146:6; Isa. 26:4).

God is true metaphysically; he is what God should be. He is not like the false gods, which are vanities and lies (Pss. 96:5; 97:7; 115:4–8; Isa. 44:9–10). God is true ethically; his revelation of himself is perfectly reliable (Ex. 34:6; Num. 23:19; Deut. 32:4; Pss. 25:10; 31:6; Jer. 10:8, 10; John 14:6; 17:3; Rom. 3:4; Titus 1:2; Heb. 6:18; 1 John 5:20–21). This means that God is absolutely faithful (Deut. 7:9; Ps. 89:33; Isa. 49:7; Lam. 3:22–23; 1 Cor. 1:9; 2 Tim. 2:13; Heb. 6:17–18; 10:23). God is also true logically; he knows everything as it really is.

Goodness

God's goodness means that he is the perfect sum, source, and standard of that which is wholesome, virtuous, beneficial, and beautiful. God is good (Ps. 34:8) and there is no one good except God (Matt. 5:48; Mark 10:18; Luke 18:19). All creatures are called to praise his goodness (1 Chron. 16:34; 2 Chron. 5:13; Pss. 106:1; 107:1; 118:1; 136:1; Jer. 33:11).

God is the absolute good (Mark 10:18; Luke 6:35; 18:19). As such he cannot be pleased with anything short of absolute perfection. Hence, in an ultimate sense he can be pleased with only himself. Consequently, when he loves his creatures, he loves them with a chief regard to himself, whom they reflect by being created in his image. God is the source of all his creatures' blessings (James 1:17). He is the highest good (Lat. *summum bonum*) for his creatures—the proper goal of all who strive for true goodness.

Love

God's perfect love is his determination to give of himself to himself and to others, and it is his affection for himself and his people.

This definition affirms that God has affections, but that God's affections are not passions by which he is driven but active principles by which God expresses his holy dispositions. God is not unfeeling or incapable of compassion, but as pure act, God undergoes no emotional fluctuations.

God's essence is love (1 John 4:8, 16)—a love ultimately expressed among the three persons of the Trinity (John 3:35; 5:20; 10:17; 14:31; 15:9; 17:24, 26). That this love includes affection is seen by the use of the Greek verb *phileō* for the love that the Father has for the Son (John 5:20). The Old Testament testifies abundantly to God's love (Deut. 4:37; 7:8, 13; 10:15; 23:5; 2 Chron. 2:11; Isa. 43:4; 48:14; 63:9; Jer. 31:3; Hos. 11:1, 4; 14:4; Zeph. 3:17; Mal. 1:2). God's love is manifested in Christ's sacrifice for sin (John 3:16; 14:23; 15:13; 16:27; 17:23; Rom. 5:7–8; 8:37; 9:13; Gal. 2:20; 1 John 4:9–10). In John 16:27, God the Father's love for believers includes affection, as attested by the use of the verb *phileō* for the Father's love.

Grace

God's grace describes God as perfectly bestowing favor on those who cannot merit it because they have forsaken it and are under the sentence of divine condemnation. Grace is God's unmerited favor (Heb. *khen*; Gk. *charis*). God's grace is manifested in Jesus Christ (John 1:14; 1 Pet. 1:13); is abundant (Ex. 34:6; 2 Chron. 30:9; Neh. 9:17; Pss. 86:15; 103:8; 111:4; 116:5; Jonah 4:2; Joel 2:13; Zech. 12:10); does not allow for works of merit (John 1:17; Rom. 4:4, 16; 6:14, 23; 11:5–6; Gal. 5:3–4; Eph. 2:7–9). God's gifts of spiritual and earthly blessings are called "grace" (Rom. 6:1; 12:6–8; Eph. 4:7–12; Phil. 1:2; Col. 1:2; James 4:6). Israel was chosen and blessed by God due only to God's grace (Ex. 15:13, 16; 19:4; 34:6–7; Deut. 4:37; 7:7–8; 8:14, 17–18; 9:5, 27; 33:3; Isa. 35:10; 43:1, 15, 21; 54:5; 63:9; Jer. 3:4, 19; 31:9, 20; Ezek. 16:60–63; Hos. 8:14; 11:1). In the New Testament, God's grace is especially his free, unmerited favor toward sinners in giving them salvation from sin (Rom. 3:24; 5:15; 6:23; Eph. 1:6–7; 2:4–9; 2 Thess. 2:16; Titus 3:7; 1 Pet. 5:10). This is special, effectual, saving grace, in distinction to common grace, which is God's general care for his creation.

Mercy

God's mercy (Heb. *rakhamim*; Gk. *eleos, oiktirmos*) describes him as perfectly having deep compassion for creatures (people), such that he demonstrates benevolent goodness to those in a pitiable or miserable condition, even though they do not deserve it. He is a God of mercy (Ex. 34:6; Deut. 4:31; 2 Chron. 30:9; Pss. 86:15; 103:8; 111:4; 112:4; 145:8), whose mercy is manifold (Ex. 20:6; Deut. 5:10; 2 Sam. 24:14; Neh. 9:19; Pss. 51:1–2; 57:10; 86:5; Dan. 9:9, 18) and does not fail (Lam. 3:22). God gives mercy by bestowing salvation, including sustenance in the Christian life and final salvation at Christ's return (Rom. 9:23; 11:30; 1 Cor. 7:25; 2 Cor. 4:1; Eph. 2:4; Phil. 2:27; 1 Tim. 1:2, 13, 16; 2 Tim. 1:18; Heb. 4:16; 1 Pet. 1:3; 2:10; 2 John 3; Jude 2, 21). God is called the "Father of mercies" (2 Cor. 1:3), and Christ often displayed mercy (Matt. 9:36; 14:14; 20:34; cf. Heb. 2:17).

Longsuffering

God's longsuffering speaks of his being perfectly placid in himself and patient toward sinners in spite of their continual disobedience. God does not "lose his temper" but always acts calmly with proper regard. He is always tranquil. God is even patient with those deserving divine punishment (Ex. 34:6; Num. 14:18; Neh. 9:17; Pss. 86:15; 103:8–9; 145:8; Jer. 15:15; Joel 2:13; Jonah 4:2; Nah. 1:3). God's longsuffering is shown to sinners especially through Jesus Christ (Rom. 2:4; 9:22–23; 1 Tim. 1:16; 2 Pet. 3:9, 15).

Holiness

God's holiness is his inherent and absolute greatness, in which he is perfectly distinct above everything outside himself and is absolutely morally separate from sin. This definition is centered on the concept of separation, which is signified by the Hebrew and Greek words for "holy" (Heb. *qadosh*; Gk. *hosios*, *hagios*).

There are two aspects of God's holiness in the evidence found in Scripture.

Majestic Holiness. This speaks to the fact that God is inherently great and therefore is transcendently distinct from all his creatures in infinite majesty. He is majestically unique. This sense of God's holiness qualifies all his other attributes, and all these qualify his holiness. This transcendent distinction is asserted by both the Old Testament (Ex. 15:11; 1 Sam. 2:2; 2 Chron. 30:27; Pss. 5:7; 22:3; 48:1; 71:22; 89:18; 97:12; 98:1; 99:3, 5, 9; 103:1; 105:3; 145:21; Prov. 30:3; Isa. 5:16; 6:3; 10:20; 29:23; 43:14–15; 49:7; 54:5; 57:15; Jer. 51:5; Hos. 11:9; Hab. 1:12) and the New Testament (Mark 1:24; Luke 1:49; 4:34; John 17:11; Rev. 4:8; 6:10; 15:4).

Ethical, Moral Holiness. God is also morally pure and most certainly separate from sin. He is morally and ethically perfect, abhorring sin and demanding purity in his moral creatures (Lev. 11:44; 19:2; 20:26; 22:32; Josh. 24:19; Job 34:10; Pss. 5:5; 7:11; Isa. 1:12–17; Ezek. 39:7; Amos 2:7; 5:21–23; Hab. 1:13; Zech. 8:17; 1 Pet. 1:15–16).

Righteousness (Justice)

God's righteousness is his perfect, absolute justice in and toward himself; his prevention of any violation of the justice of his character; and his revelation of himself in acts of justice. Both the Old Testament Hebrew term (*tsedeqah*) and the New Testament Greek term (*dikaiosynē*) for "righteousness" carry the sense of conformity to a standard.

Categorization and Scriptural Evidence. The Bible describes two kinds of justice:

Rectoral justice. This is God's rectitude (from the Lat. *rectus*, "straight") as the moral Ruler, Lawgiver, and Judge of the world—imposing law with promises of reward and punishment (Deut. 4:8; 2 Sam. 23:3; Pss. 9:4; 99:4; 119:7, 62, 75, 106; Isa. 33:22; Luke 1:6; Rom. 1:32; 7:12; 8:4; 9:31; James 4:12).

Distributive justice. This aspect of God's righteousness is his exactness and rightness in the execution of law, in distributing reward and punishment (1 Kings 8:32; 2 Chron. 6:23; Ps. 7:11; Isa. 3:10–11; 11:4; 16:5; 31:1; Rom. 2:6; 2 Tim. 4:8; 1 Pet. 1:17). Distributive justice includes retributive justice and remunerative justice. Retributive justice is God's inflicting of punishment for disobeying his law (2 Chron. 12:5–6; Ezra 9:15; Neh. 9:26–30; Ps. 129:4; Isa. 5:15–16; Jer. 11:20; Ezek. 28:22; 36:23; 38:16–23; 39:27; 43:8; Dan. 9:14; Hos. 10:2; Zeph. 3:5; Rom. 1:32; 2:9; 12:19; 2 Thess. 1:8; Rev. 15:3; 16:5, 7; 19:2, 11). Remunerative justice is God's distributing of rewards for obeying his law (Deut. 7:9, 12–13; 2 Chron. 6:14–15; Ps. 58:11; Matt. 25:21, 34; Rom. 2:7; Heb. 11:26). God is not required to give rewards for obedience, since man is required to obey God, but he does graciously give them (Job 41:11; Luke 17:10; 1 Cor. 4:7).

God's Holiness and Righteousness in Salvation. A holy and righteous God demands holiness and righteousness of people who would be rightly related to him (Lev. 11:44; Ps. 29:2; 1 Pet. 1:15–16). God stands in absolute, essential opposition to sin, so he must judge and punish sin.

God manifested his holiness and righteousness in his past salvation of Israel and will do so in his future salvation of his people. For example, in Ezekiel 39:21–29, God judges and restores Israel in order to maintain and manifest his holiness. Many passages similarly show that God manifests his holiness and righteousness by separating from, judging, and saving Israel (*his holiness:* Lev. 20:26; Pss. 98:1; 99:9; 105:3; 106:47; 108:7; 111:9; Isa. 10:20; 12:6; 41:14, 20; 43:3, 14; 45:11; 47:4; 49:7; 52:10; 55:5; Ezek. 36:21–23; Hos. 11:9; *his righteousness:* Neh. 9:8; Pss. 72:2; 85:13; 116:5; Isa. 45:21–25; Jer. 33:15; Mal. 4:2). In the salvation of sinners, the righteousness of God is revealed (Rom. 1:17) in Christ. In Christ God judges sin and imputes righteousness on the basis of faith, and he accepts sinners as holy without compromising his righteousness (Rom. 3:25–26; cf. Rom. 3:21–30; 4:6, 25; 5:1, 9; 8:30, 33; 1 Cor. 6:11; Gal. 2:16–17; 3:24).

Jealousy

God's jealousy is his zealous protectiveness of all that belongs to him (himself, his name, his glory, his people, his sole right to receive worship and ultimate obedience, his land, and his city). God's name is "Jealous" (Ex. 34:14) and he is jealous for his holy name and glory (Ezek. 39:25). God is jealous to be the only God worshiped and served (Ex. 20:5; Deut. 4:24; 5:9; 6:15; 29:18–20; 32:16, 21; 1 Kings 14:22; Pss. 78:58–59; 79:1–7; 1 Cor. 10:22). God jealously takes vengeance on his enemies (Isa. 42:13; 59:16–20; Ezek. 5:13; 36:5; 38:19; Nah. 1:2; Zeph. 3:8). God jealously chastens his sinning people (Ps. 79:1–7; Ezek. 16:42; 23:25). God restores his people by his jealousy (2 Kings 19:31; Isa. 37:32; 63:15).

Will

God's will is his perfect determination and sovereign ordination of all things, pertaining both to himself (including his decrees and actions) and to his creation (including the events of history and the thoughts and actions of people), all unto the magnification of his utmost glory. Everything depends on the will of God:[13] creation and preservation (Ps. 135:6; Jer. 18:6; Rev. 4:11); the smallest things (Matt. 10:29); man's life and destiny (Isa. 45:9; Acts 18:21; Rom. 15:32; James 4:15); government (Prov. 21:1; Dan. 4:17, 25, 32, 35); election and reprobation (Rom. 9:15–16, 18; Eph. 1:11–12); the suffering of Christ (Luke 22:42; Acts 2:23; 4:27–28).

13 Louis Berkhof, *Systematic Theology*, 4th ed. (1932; repr., Grand Rapids, MI: Eerdmans, 1996), 76.

God's will is sovereignly independent of everything outside himself.[14] He acts according to his own pleasure (Ps. 115:3; Prov. 21:1; Dan. 4:35). He does not give account to anyone (Job 33:13; Isa. 46:10; Matt. 20:15; Rom. 9:19–20). He is pictured as the potter, his creatures as clay (Job 10:9; 33:6; Isa. 29:16; 64:8; Jer. 18:1–10; Rom. 9:19–24). No one can prevent him from doing as he pleases (Job 9:2–13; 11:10; Isa. 10:15; Dan. 4:35). Man does not have the right to demand that God express his will in particular ways (Matt. 20:13–16; Rom. 9:20–21).

A distinction must made between God's decretive will and his preceptive will.

Decretive will. This refers to God's will understood in terms of his decree. This is God's good pleasure, his eternal, unchangeable counsel or decree in which he has foreordained all things. God's decretive will characterizes all of God's essence, so it is eternal, immutable, independent, and omnipotent (Pss. 33:11; 115:3; Dan. 4:25, 35; Matt. 11:25–26; Rom. 9:18; Eph. 1:4; Rev. 4:11). (For more on this, see the discussion of "The Decree of God," below.)

Preceptive will. This is God's will as understood in terms of his "precepts." This consists of God's precepts in the law and in the gospel for man's conduct (Matt. 7:21; 12:50; John 7:17; Rom. 12:2; 1 Thess. 4:3–8; 5:18; Heb. 13:21; 1 John 2:17). It is often called God's "revealed" will. God reveals his preceptive will by means of Scripture's "precepts," i.e., laws, commands, prohibitions, teachings, warnings, and judgments.

God's decretive will and preceptive will must be held in tension. To deny his preceptive will is to commit injustice against God's holiness and to ignore the gravity of sin, but to deny God's decretive will is to deny his omniscience, wisdom, omnipotence, and sovereignty.[15] (For more on this, see the discussion of "The Decree of God," below.)

Blessedness

God's blessedness speaks of God as being perfectly delighted with himself. "Blessedness" is the Greek word *makarios*, meaning "the happiness due to a sense of great privilege." The same idea is found in the Latin *beatus*, the word behind the English words *beatify*, *beatitude*, and *blessed*. Since God is absolutely perfect, sovereign, and unhindered in all his purposes and works to glorify his name, he is supremely happy—the happiest being conceivable (cf. 1 Tim. 1:11, "the blessed God"; 6:15, "the blessed and only Sovereign"). (For more on this theme, see "Perfection," above.)

14 Bavinck, *Doctrine of God*, 228–29.

15 For more on these two aspects of the divine will, see John Piper, "Are There Two Wills in God?," in *Still Sovereign: Contemporary Perspectives on Election, Foreknowledge, and Grace*, ed. Thomas R. Schreiner and Bruce A. Ware (Grand Rapids, MI: Baker, 2000), 107–31.

Glory

God's glory is his supreme significance and splendor. The Hebrew word for "glory," *kabod*, has the sense of "weight," and, in figurative extension, "significance." The words *hod* and *hadar* have the sense of "splendor." The Greek word for "glory," *doxa*, also has the primary meaning of "splendor" or "brightness."

Most passages referring to God's glory speak of his manifested glory. Such manifestation is sourced in the glory of God's essence (Eph. 3:16; Phil. 4:19; Rev. 15:8). God manifested his glory to creation (1 Chron. 16:26–29; Pss. 29:3; 96:6; 104:1–5; 111:4; 113:4) and to Israel (Ex. 16:7, 10; 24:16; 33:18–23; Lev. 9:6, 23; Num. 14:10; 16:19; Deut. 5:24). God's glory filled the tabernacle and the temple (Ex. 29:43; 40:34; 1 Kings 8:11). God's "splendor" was given to Israel (Ezek. 16:14). In heaven, God's manifested glory was associated with God's holiness (Isa. 6:3). On earth, God's glory was seen as a cloud (1 Kings 8:10–11; Isa. 6:4) and a consuming fire (Ex. 24:17; Lev. 9:24). God later manifested his glory in Christ (John 1:14; 2 Cor. 4:4–6) and in the church (Rom. 15:7; 2 Cor. 3:18; Eph. 5:27).

The Trinity[16]

The classic Christian doctrine of the Trinity has been summarized in the Athanasian Creed, which succinctly captures the biblical truth: "We worship one God in Trinity, and Trinity in Unity; neither confounding the Persons: nor dividing the Substance."[17] (Though it bears his name, Athanasius [AD 295–373] is not the author. It was likely composed in the fifth or sixth century AD.) God is absolutely and eternally one essence subsisting in three distinct and ordered persons without division and without replication of the essence.

The triunity of God is neither illogical nor derived from human philosophy. It is a doctrine unquestionably taught in the Bible. While it may be ultimately incomprehensible, it is not contrary to reason but can be rationally explained, supported, and understood through biblical revelation.

EXPLANATION

One Simple God/Three Persons

There is only one God, and he exists as one simple (uncompounded, indivisible) essence (Deut. 6:4; Mark 12:29; John 17:3; James 2:19) (See "Unity: Numerical Oneness" and "Unity: Simplicity," above.)

16 For a supplementary discussion of the triunity of God, refer to the section in chap. 5 titled, "Deity and Triunity of the Holy Spirit" (p. 189).

17 In Philip Schaff, *The Creeds of Christendom*, vol. 2, *The Greek and Latin Creeds* (New York: Harper & Row, 1877), 66.

The one God exists eternally as three distinct persons (also known as *subsistences* or *hypostases*). Scripture clearly reveals that there are three divine persons (Matt. 3:16–17; 4:1; John 1:18; 3:16; 5:20–22; 14:26; 15:26; 16:13–15). The distinctions between the persons is further specified by the following ancient illustration, variously referred to as "The Shield of the Trinity" or "The Shield of the Faith" (the earliest attestation dates to the early thirteenth century AD):[18]

Fig. 3.1: The Shield of the Trinity

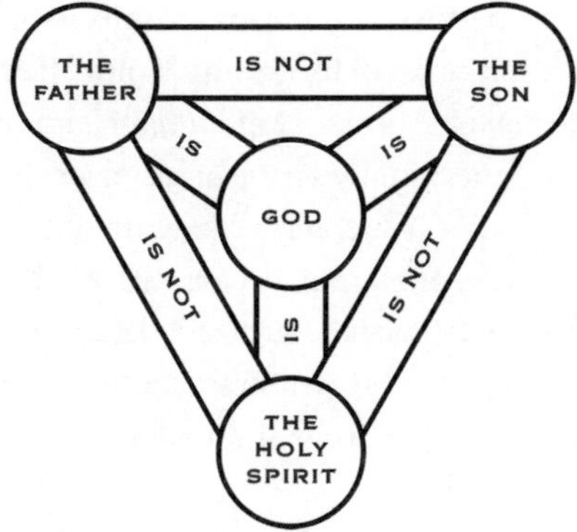

1. The Father is God.
2. The Son is God.
3. The Holy Spirit is God.
1. The Father is not the Son.
2. The Father is not the Holy Spirit.
3. The Son is not the Holy Spirit.

Essential Coequality

Each person of the Trinity (also known as the Godhead) possesses the entire simple (undivided) essence of God. The three persons, though distinct from one another, are coequal in every perfection of the divine essence. They are *essentially* (or, *ontologically*) coequal.

Personal Distinctions

While each person of the Trinity equally possesses the full, undivided divine essence, these persons are genuinely distinct from one another. The explanation

18 The "Shield of the Trinity" (or "Shield of the Faith") has appeared in various forms since the early thirteenth century. For a brief explanation of this illustration and another example of it, see Frederick Roth Webber and Ralph Adams Cram, *Church Symbolism: An Explanation of the More Important Symbols of the Old and New Testament, the Primitive, the Mediaeval and the Modern Church*, 2nd ed. (1938; repr., Whitefish, MT: Kessinger, 2010), 44–46.

for this must be found in Scripture. The persons of the Trinity are spoken of as "Father," "Son," and "Holy Spirit." These designations, also called the modes of subsistence,[19] reveal the personal properties that distinguish each member of the Trinity from the others. They describe the modes of relationship between the persons of the Trinity.

By calling the first person of the Trinity "Father" (Lat. *pater*), Scripture intends to attribute the personal property of *paternity* to him with respect to the Son. By calling the second person of the Trinity "Son" (Lat. *filius*), Scripture intends to attribute the personal property of *filiation*, or sonship, to him with respect to the Father. By calling the third person of the Trinity "Spirit" (Lat. *spiritum*), Scripture intends to attribute the personal property of *spiration*, or procession, to him with respect to the Father and the Son. By virtue of his paternity, the Father is unbegotten but eternally begets (or "generates," Gk. *gennaō*) the Son. By virtue of his filiation, the Son is begotten, or eternally generated, by the Father.[20]

These distinct modes of relationship establish a definite order (Lat. *taxis*) within the Trinity, so that it is proper to say (with respect to their relationship only, not with respect to their essence, glory, or majesty) that the Father is first, the Son is second, and the Spirit is third.

These acts of eternal generation and eternal procession are sometimes called the *opera ad intra*, or the internal works, of the Trinity. They pertain to the inner life of the Trinity. They differ from the *opera ad extra*, or the external works, which produce effects outside of God, that is, on the creation. Scripture ascribes God's various works in the economy of redemption to a particular member of the Trinity: the Father—the Creator (1 Pet. 4:19); the Son—Redeemer and Mediator (Rom. 3:24; Eph. 1:7; 1 Tim. 2:5); the Spirit—the agent of sanctification (2 Thess. 2:13; 1 Pet. 1:2).[21]

Nevertheless, in all *ad extra* works, all three persons of the Trinity work inseparably together (John 14:10). Though one person or another may be emphasized in a particular work, no one person does any work exclusive of the other two persons, for, as the classic dictum states, the external works of the Trinity are undivided (Lat. *opera Trinitatis ad extra indivisa sunt*). In the economy of redemption, the

19 The use of the phrase "modes of subsistence" should not be confused with the error of Modalistic Monarchianism (or Modalism), which is rightly rejected as a heresy.

20 These concepts are best summarized by the Athanasian Creed; see Schaff, *Creeds of Christendom*, 2:67–68. For more on eternal generation and eternal procession, see below, "Three Persons with Divine Relations: Eternal Generation and Eternal Procession".

21 Another way of stating this is that the *plan* of redemption is attributed to the Father, the *accomplishment* of redemption is attributed to the Son, and the *application* of redemption is attributed to the Spirit. Still another alternative is to say that in the economy of redemption, all things are *from* the Father, *through* the Son, and *in* the Spirit.

Son submits to the Father (John 5:30; 6:38) because he was eternally generated by the Father.[22] The Spirit is sent by the Father and the Son (John 14:26; 15:26) because he eternally proceeds from the Father and the Son. None of this implies a rank or hierarchy of *essence* within the Trinity, for each person fully possesses the undivided divine essence. (See the discussion on "Eternal Generation and Eternal Procession" below, p. 118).

A Mystery. The Trinity is a mystery in the sense that it is suprarational, ultimately beyond human comprehension. It is partly intelligible to man only because God has revealed it in Scripture and in Jesus Christ. Consequently, the doctrine must be accepted by faith, based on how the Godhead is revealed in Scripture. And it must be articulated in such a way that the essence of God is not divided and the distinctions and the coequality of being between the three persons are not compromised.

Illustrations. The Trinity has no perfect analogies in human experience. Theologians have attempted to find a perfect illustration of the Trinity, but all these attempts have either divided the essence, compromised the distinction between the three persons, or lost sight of God's *personal* essence. Nothing in the creation is exactly like the Trinity.

OLD TESTAMENT INDICATIONS

The Plural Name Elohim *and Titles for God*

The *-im* in *elohim* is a plural ending. This allows for, but does not necessitate, a plurality in God. Such plurals (*-im*) often have other connotations, such as to show honor, or to denote intensity. However, considering the New Testament's revelation of the triune God, *elohim* is at least a divine preparation for the later more complete revelation of God as triune.

Two texts (Eccles. 12:1, "your Creator"; and Isa. 54:5, "your Maker") use plural Hebrew participles in titles for God. However, as noted, plurals in Hebrew can have other connotations, so these titles do not prove that God is more than one person. Still, they are compatible with the New Testament revelation of the Trinity.

God Speaking of Himself as Plural

In other Old Testament texts, God speaks of himself in terms that suggest more than one person is in view: Genesis 1:26, "Let *us* make man in our image"; Genesis 11:7, "Come, let *us* go down and there confuse their language"; Genesis 3:22, "Behold, the man has become like one of *us*"; Isaiah 6:8, "Whom shall I send, and who will go for *us*?" These passages show God speaking of himself as both singular and plural. As with the name *elohim*, these plurals could be plurals of

22 This is in contrast to the teaching of some who say that the *ad extra* submission of the Son to the Father is rooted in a kind of eternal functional subordination (*ad intra*) of the Son to the Father.

intensity. But the progressive clarity of the New Testament concerning the Trinity argues that these plurals constitute God's assertions that he is one and yet plural.

More Than One Person as "God"

In some Old Testament passages more than one person is called "God" or "Lord." In Psalm 45:6–7, the Messiah is referred to as "God" (*elohim*) and is enthroned, having been anointed by "God" (*elohim*). Hebrews 1:8–9 indicates that "God" will say the words of Psalm 45:6–7 to "the Son," who will be enthroned as "God" by "God."

Psalm 110:1 reads, "The LORD says to my Lord: 'Sit at my right hand, until I make your enemies your footstool.'" In this messianic psalm—the Old Testament text most frequently quoted and alluded to in the New Testament—Yahweh speaks of the Messiah with the words "my Lord" (Heb. *adonai*). The New Testament quotations of this verse identify Jesus as the "Lord" of whom the "LORD" was speaking (Matt. 22:41–45; Mark 12:35–37; Luke 20:41–44; Acts 2:32–36).

Yahweh's Son

There are a few Old Testament passages that say that God has a "son," such as Psalm 2:2, 6–7. The New Testament applies this passage to Jesus as the eternal, divine Son (Heb. 1:1–3).

"One" in Deuteronomy 6:4

Deuteronomy 6:4, traditionally called the "Shema," states, "Hear, O Israel: The LORD our God, the LORD is one." (Heb. *shema* means "listen," or "hear.") This affirms that Yahweh is the one true God and is only "one." The word for "one" (Heb. *ekhad*) here affirms God's unity but allows for a unity in diversity (see Genesis 2:24, where the same word is used for marital oneness—"one flesh"). If the intention had been to assert that God is only one person, another Hebrew word, *yakhid*, would have been used, because *yakhid*, has the sense of "only, solitary" (see Ps. 68:6). Deuteronomy 6:4 is an affirmation of monotheism, but not of Unitarianism. It does not contradict the doctrine of the Trinity (see 1 Cor. 8:6) and even allows for God to be more than one person.

The Angel of Yahweh (Angel of God)[23]

A mysterious angel, sometimes called the "angel of the LORD," appears several times throughout the Old Testament. In some passages this angel is *called* Yahweh and God, but in other passages he is the one *speaking to* Yahweh—he is Yahweh, yet he is distinct from Yahweh. Yahweh sent the angel of Yahweh (Ex. 23:20–23;

23 For a more extensive discussion regarding the angel of the Lord, see the section in chap. 8 titled, "Identifying the Angel of the Lord" (p. 380).

32:34; Num. 20:16); the angel of Yahweh and Yahweh spoke to each other (Zech. 1:12–13).

Proofs that this angel was divine include the following: "of Yahweh" is the angel's very name (Ex. 23:20–21); his name was used interchangeably with God's name (Gen. 16:7, 13; 21:17, 19–20; 22:11, 14; 31:11, 13; 48:15–16; Ex. 3:2, 4; Judg. 6:11, 14, 16, 20–21, 23; 13:3, 22–23); when the angel of Yahweh made promises, God made them (Gen. 16:10; 22:15–17; cf. 12:2; 13:16); he accepted sacrifices (Gen. 22:11–13; Judg. 6:21; 13:16, 19–22); people who saw the angel of Yahweh identified him by name as divine (Gen. 16:11–13; Judg. 6:22–23; 13:21–22); the angel of Yahweh could forgive sins (Ex. 23:21; Zech. 3:3–4); he claimed to be "God" (Gen. 31:11, 13; Ex. 3:2–6).

The Holy Spirit as Divine

Old Testament passages assert that the Holy Spirit is divine and has divine perfections: the Spirit is the source of divine wisdom, power, and knowledge (Isa. 11:2); is omnipresent (Psalm 139:7); was involved in the original act of creation and in the work of preserving what God has created (Gen. 1:2; Job 26:13; 34:14–15; Pss. 33:6; 104:30); restrains sin (Gen. 6:3; Isa. 63:10). These Old Testament texts are complemented by the fuller revelation in the New Testament (see below). Furthermore, Jesus's Jewish contemporaries, especially his disciples, seemed to understand that the Holy Spirit is a distinct, divine person (Matt. 1:20; 3:11; Luke 1:15, 35; 11:13; 12:10; John 14:26; 20:22). Clearly, they either drew this concept from the Old Testament or at least saw it as fully consistent with it.

The Word of God

The Old Testament concept of God's "word" (Heb. *dabar*) also prepared the way for the New Testament's clearer revelation of the doctrine of the Trinity. In the Old Testament it was revealed that God created by means of his word (Gen. 1:3, 6, 9, 11, 14, 20, 22, 24; Pss. 33:6, 9; 104:7; 147:18; 148:8); extended providential care by means of his word (Deut. 8:3; Pss. 106:9; 147:15–18); saved by means of his word (i.e., gave life [Deut. 32:47; Ps. 119:25], guided [Ps. 119:105], chastened [Isa. 9:8] by his word). Furthermore, God's word has God's power: it breaks and cuts (Isa. 9:8–10); it consumes like fire (Jer. 5:14); it destroys like a hammer (Jer. 23:29); it accomplishes God's purpose (Isa. 55:11); and it heals (Ps. 107:20). These divine works of the "word" foreshadow the New Testament revelation of the Son of God as the divine "Word."

Three Distinct, Divine Persons. In Isaiah 61:1–2, "the LORD" (Yahweh), "the Spirit of the Lord," and the speaker, who is the Messiah, are distinct persons. The Messiah's comments start in verse 1 and continue through verse 9 (see NKJV). The Messiah speaks in verse 8: "I the LORD love justice." Thus the Messiah is sent by Yahweh and calls himself Yahweh. There are at least two divine persons in this passage, and because "the Spirit" is named, this context advances the preparation for the New Testament doctrine of the Trinity.

Likewise, in Isaiah 63:7–10 there is "the LORD" (Yahweh), "his Holy Spirit," and "the angel of his presence," i.e., the angel of Yahweh. Thus, there are at least two divine persons in this context. The Holy Spirit is here a person, because he is "grieved" (63:10), and this indicates the Holy Spirit is also divine, since it was the people's grieving of him through rebellion that resulted in divine retribution.

Similarly, in Isaiah 48:12, 16, there are at least two divine entities: "the Lord GOD" and "his Spirit" (Isa. 48:16). The personhood of the Spirit is not immediately evident in this context, but when combined with Isaiah 63:7–10, it is clear that the Spirit is a divine person. Is there a third divine entity in these verses? Both the NASB and NKJV rightly hold that this is so. Thus, the Messiah is speaking; he is the "I am" and has been "sent" by "the Lord GOD" and "his Spirit." In such a construction, the speaker and "the Lord GOD" are both divine persons, and "the Spirit" must also be divine.[24]

Other indications include an emphasis on the number three, especially in threefold formulae, such as the seraphim praising Yahweh as "holy, holy, holy" (Isa. 6:3) and in the Aaronic benediction in Numbers 6:24–27. The ancient church saw in this threefold blessing an indication of the Trinity, especially in light of the baptismal formula (cf. Matt. 28:19). In Numbers 6:27, Yahweh said that this threefold blessing would put Yahweh's "name" on the people of Israel.[25] Another threefold construction is Jacob's threefold blessing of Joseph and his sons in Genesis 48:15–16.

Other emphases on the number three can be seen in the following passages: Genesis 15:9; 30:36; 40:10, 16; Exodus 3:18; 19:11; 23:14; Leviticus 19:23; Numbers 19:12; 22:23–41; 31:19; Jeremiah 7:4 ("the temple of the LORD" three times). Perhaps the use of three in ceremonial worship was meant to testify to Israel's God being three yet one.

NEW TESTAMENT EVIDENCE

The Old Testament clearly teaches there is only one God. Some passages do allow for and even indicate that there is more than one divine person in God. However, conclusive evidence for the Trinity is revealed in the New Testament.

Only One God

Jesus repeats Deuteronomy 6:4 in Mark 12:29: "The Lord our God, the Lord is one." In John 17:3, Jesus calls God the Father "the only true God": cf. "God is one" (Rom. 3:30; James 2:19); "there is no God but one" (1 Cor. 8:4); and "there

24 The ESV, HCSB, NIV, and RSV do not make these distinctions as clearly.

25 Peter Toon, *Our Triune God: A Biblical Portrayal of the Trinity* (Wheaton, IL: Victor, 1996), 102.

is one God" (1 Tim. 2:5). The New Testament maintains that there is only one God but also refers to each of the three persons of the Trinity—the Father, the Son, and the Holy Spirit—as equally divine in names, nature, prerogatives, and works.

More Than One Person Associated with God

In some New Testament passages, the speaker or writer associates two persons with God. In John 5:17–18, Jesus claimed that he had the same authority as "my Father" and in John 10:30, Jesus said, "I and the Father are one" (see also John 16:15; 17:10). Because of these claims the Jewish leaders wanted to kill him, because he "was even calling God his own Father, making himself equal with God" (John 5:18; cf. John 10:33, "You, being a man, make yourself God"). In 1 Corinthians 8:6 Paul makes reference to "one God, the Father" and "one Lord, Jesus Christ" and attributes to both of them the work of creation and the source of existence. For Paul, both the Father and the Lord Jesus Christ are the source of grace and peace (1 Cor. 1:3; Eph. 1:2). John says believers in the millennium will be priests of both God the Father and Christ (Rev. 20:6).

Three Persons Declared to Be God

The Father Is God. In the New Testament, each of the three persons of the Trinity are called "God." The name God (Gk. *theos*) combines with the name Father in many passages (e.g., John 6:27; Rom. 15:6; 1 Cor. 8:6; 15:24; Eph. 4:6; James 3:9). When the name *theos* appears in the New Testament by itself in reference to the true God, it usually designates the first person of the Trinity, God the Father (e.g., James 1:5; 1 Pet. 3:18).[26]

Jesus Is God. Jesus's words claim that he is divine (cf. Matt. 26:63–64; Mark 14:61–62; Luke 22:67–71). In John's Gospel, Jesus repeatedly used the expression "I am" (Gk. *ego eimi*). Some of these statements are connected with metaphors: "I am . . .": "the bread of life" (John 6:35, 48); "the light of the world" (John 8:12); "the door" (John 10:9); "the good shepherd" (John 10:11, 14); "the resurrection and the life" (John 11:25). But many of these statements are absolute, without any qualifiers (e.g., John 8:24, 28, 58; 13:19; 18:5–8; cf. Mark 14:62). In all of these, Jesus is claiming to be the "I am" (Gk. *ego eimi*; cf. Ex. 3:14–15), the one who bears the Old Testament divine name of Yahweh (see esp. John 8:58).

Jesus also claims that the Father sent him, that he came from heaven, and that he had divine authority to do the works of the Father (John 3:13; 5:26–37; 6:31–58; 8:42; 16:28–30). Jesus also says that he has a special relationship with "my Father" that no one else has (e.g., Matt. 7:21; 10:32–33; 11:25–27; Luke 22:29;

26 Murray J. Harris, *Jesus as God: The New Testament Use of* Theos *in Reference to Jesus* (Grand Rapids, MI: Baker, 1992), 21–50.

24:49; John 2:16; 5:19–23; 8:36–38; 10:29–30, 36–38; 14:2–3, 11–12, 23; 15:8–10, 15; 16:10, 26–28; 17:1–26; 20:17).

John the Baptist says that Jesus is "the Lord" (John 1:15, 23, 30) and "the Son of God" (John 1:34). God the Father calls Jesus "my beloved Son" (Matt. 3:16–17; 17:5). Angels announce that Jesus is "the Son of God" (Luke 1:31–35) and "the Lord" (Luke 2:11)—in the latter passage, "Lord" is a divine name because it is a divine name in the near context (Luke 2:9, 15). In Matthew 14:33, the disciples worship Jesus as "the Son of God." Peter confesses that Jesus is "the Son of the living God" (Matt. 16:16), and Thomas confesses that the risen Jesus is "my Lord and my God" (John 20:27–29). Before Jesus's birth, he is called "Lord" by Elizabeth (Luke 1:43) and Zechariah (Luke 1:76). A centurion at the crucifixion affirms, "Truly this man was the Son of God!" (Mark 15:39).

The New Testament writers affirm Jesus's deity: he is "God with us" (Matt. 1:23); he is called "Lord" (Acts 2:34–36; cf. Ps. 110:1); he "is over all, the eternally blessed God" (Rom. 9:5 NKJV); "Jesus is Lord" (1 Cor. 2:8; 12; Rom. 10:9; 14:8–9). Jesus Christ is "the Lord of glory" (1 Cor. 2:8) and "one Lord, Jesus Christ" (1 Cor. 8:6). Paul proclaims that Jesus existed "in the form of God" (Phil. 2:6) and in Jesus "the whole fullness of deity dwells bodily" (Col. 2:9).

Several passages identify Jesus as "God" in a specific way that employs a rule of Greek grammar. This rule begins by noting a typical expression or construction in Greek: the article + a first noun or participle + the Greek conjunction (*kai*) + no article + a second noun or participle. The rule states that since there is no article before the second noun then "the latter (noun or participle) . . . denotes a farther description" of the person described by the first noun or participle.[27] Classic examples of this construction are Titus 2:13 ("our great God and Savior Jesus Christ"), 2 Peter 1:1 ("our God and Savior Jesus Christ"), and 2 Peter 2:20 ("the Lord and Savior Jesus Christ," NASB). According to the rule, the construction in these passages means that Jesus is not only "Savior" but also "God" and "Lord."

In John 12:36–40, John quotes Isaiah 53:1 and Isaiah 6:10. He asserts that these texts were fulfilled by Jesus and that they explain why the crowds did not believe in him (12:37). John explains, "Isaiah said these things because he saw his glory and spoke of him" (12:41). The pronouns "his" and "him" in this verse refer to the "he" of verse 37, which refers to "Jesus" in verse 36. Thus, John identifies Jesus as the "Lord" (Heb. *adonai*) of Isaiah 6:1, whom Isaiah saw "sitting upon a throne," and the "LORD [Yahweh] of hosts" of Isaiah 6:3,

27 This rule is called the Granville Sharp Rule. See Granville Sharp, *Remarks on the Uses of the Definitive Article in the Greek Text of the New Testament* (Philadelphia: B. B. Hopkins, 1807), 3.

whose "glory" fills "the whole earth." According to John, Jesus is the "Lord" and "LORD" of Isaiah 6:1–3.

Other New Testament passages also refer to Jesus by using Old Testament passages referring to Yahweh: cf. Acts 2:21 and Romans 10:13 with Joel 2:32; cf. Hebrews 1:10–12 with Psalm 102:25–27; cf. Ephesians 4:7–8 with Psalm 68:18.

The Holy Spirit Is God. The New Testament also identifies the Holy Spirit as divine. His titles associate him with the other persons of the Trinity: "Spirit of God" (Matt. 3:16); "Spirit of the Lord" (Luke 4:18); "Spirit of your Father" (Matt. 10:20); "my Spirit" (Acts 2:17–18); "Spirit of Christ" (Rom. 8:9); "the Lord, the Spirit" (2 Cor. 3:17–18 NASB).

In Acts 5:3–4, 9, Peter says that in lying to the Holy Spirit, Ananias and Sapphira had "not lied to man but to God." Paul declares, "The Lord is the Spirit," and refers to the Spirit as "the Lord, the Spirit" (2 Cor. 3:17–18 NASB), and says that "God's Spirit" indwells the church, because the church is "God's temple" (1 Cor. 3:16). In Ephesians 2:22, Paul states that it is "by the Spirit" that the church is "being built together into a dwelling place for God."

The New Testament attributes to the Spirit the words that the Old Testament attributed to God. In Acts 28:25–27, Paul says that the Holy Spirit spoke "through Isaiah" the words of Isaiah 6:9–10, even though in Isaiah 6, it was "the voice of the Lord" who said these words (Isa. 6:8). The same correspondence between words of New Testament passages and Old Testament passages is visible in the following couplets: Hebrews 3:7–11 with Psalm 95:7–11; Hebrews 10:15–17 with Jeremiah 31:31–34.

Three Persons with Divine Perfections

The New Testament depicts each person of the Trinity as having characteristics that are divine perfections. Table 3.1 provides a summary of select attributes shared by all three persons.

Table 3.1: The Trinity: Three Persons with Divine Perfections

	Eternal	Omnipotent	Omniscient	Omnipresent	Immutable	Loving	Holy	Truth
Father	Deut. 33:27	Matt. 19:26	Luke 16:15	1 Kings 8:27	Mal. 3:6	1 John 4:8	Lev. 11:45	John 3:33
Son	John 1:1	Rev 1:8	John 16:30	Matt. 28:20	Heb. 1:10–12; 13:8	Eph. 5:2	Heb. 7:26–27	John 14:6
Spirit	Heb. 9:14	Luke 1:35, 37	1 Cor. 2:10–11	Ps. 139:7	Heb. 9:14	Rom. 15:30	Rom. 1:4	John 15:26

Three Persons with Divine Prerogatives
According to the New Testament, each person of the Trinity exercises divine prerogatives, as table 3.2 summarizes.

Table 3.2: The Trinity: Three Persons with Divine Prerogatives

	Receive Worship	Give Commands	Forgive Sin	Judge
Father	John 4:23; James 3:9	John 14:31	Matt. 6:14	Gen. 18:25
Son	John 20:28; Heb. 1:6	John 15:12, 14	Mark 2:8–12	John 5:22
Spirit	Eph. 4:30[28]	Acts 8:29	Matt. 12:32	Judg. 3:10

Three Persons Performing Divine Actions
As shown by table 3.3, the New Testament specifies that each person of the Trinity performs divine acts.

Table 3.3: The Trinity: Three Persons Performing Divine Actions

	Creates	Sustains	Reveals	Raises Dead
Father	Gen. 1:1; 1 Cor. 8:6	Matt. 6:26	Heb. 1:1–2	John 5:21
Son	John 1:3; 1 Cor. 8:6	Col 1:17; Heb. 1:3	Matt. 5:22–48	John 5:25
Spirit	Gen. 1:2; Ps. 33:6	Job 34:14–15; Eph. 3:16	John 16:13; 2 Pet. 1:21	Rom. 8:11

Three Persons with Divine Relations: Eternal Generation and Eternal Procession
The eternal relations of the persons of the Trinity are expressed in this way: The Father eternally begets the Son and eternally spirates[29] the Holy Spirit. The Son is eternally begotten of the Father and eternally spirates the Holy Spirit. The Spirit eternally proceeds from the Father and the Son.

The eternal generation of the Son and the eternal procession of the Spirit are two of the most misunderstood doctrines of classic Trinitarianism. Although Scripture expressly speaks of the Father's begetting the Son (Ps. 2:7) and the Spirit's

28 See also 1 Thess. 5:19 and Heb. 10:23. While none of these passages explicitly affirms that the Holy Spirit has the prerogative to be worshiped as God, they nevertheless state that people should not "grieve," "quench," or "outrage" the Holy Spirit. These negative expressions, however, are, by implication, positively commanding people to do the opposite of these actions—that is, to obey, honor, and worship the Holy Spirit.

29 This is a unique word used by theologians to speak of the means by which the Holy Spirit "proceeds from the Father" (John 15:26). The term comes from the Latin *spirare*, "to breathe." It is the same word from which "spirit" derives.

proceeding from the Father (John 15:26), the Bible gives no clear and complete explanation of what those expressions mean.

This "eternal" begetting and breathing are quite unlike the corresponding creaturely activities. In the human realm, begetting occurs only once, at a definite point in time; but adding the adjective *eternal* changes the idea in a most radical way. To say Christ is "eternally begotten of the Father" does not indicate his beginning, for he "was" in the sense of "existed already," "in the beginning with God" (John 1:2–3). There never was a time when the Son did not exist.

To say Christ is eternally begotten of the Father (see Ps. 2:7; Acts 13:33; Heb. 1:5; 5:5) is to describe the unique filial relationship between the first and second persons of the Trinity as eternal. It describes the eternal, necessary, and self-differentiating act of God the Father by which he generates the personal subsistence of the Son and thereby communicates to the Son the entire divine essence (cf. John 5:26).[30] It is the sole property that distinguishes the Son from the Father and the Spirit, who each subsist in the identical divine nature.

However, the Spirit is not begotten; his mode of subsistence is *procession*. Similar to eternal generation, the procession of the Spirit from the Father and the Son[31] describes the eternal, necessary, and self-differentiating act of the Father and the Son by which they spirate the personal subsistence of the Spirit and thereby communicate to him the entire divine essence[32]; it is the very thing that distinguishes the Spirit from the Father and the Son.

Scripture does not define the difference between generation and procession, but the terminology befits the names Son and Spirit. It seems best to take the terms as indicting distinct relationships in the Godhead; in that way the terms *begetting* and *proceeding* are purposeful and important, even if we cannot fully explain how the two modes of subsistence differ from each other.[33]

The Decree, Election, Problem of Evil

THE DECREE OF GOD

God's decree is his eternal plan or purpose, whereby, according to his sovereign will, and for his glory, he has foreordained everything that comes to pass.[34]

30 Berkhof, *Systematic Theology*, 94.

31 The Western church (as opposed to the Eastern Orthodox church) holds that the Holy Spirit proceeds from the Father *and the Son*—Lat. *Filioque*.

32 Berkhof, *Systematic Theology*, 97.

33 John Owen aptly asked, perhaps echoing Acts 8:33 (cf. Isa. 53:8 in the Septuagint), "Who can declare the generation of the Son, the procession of the Spirit, or the difference of the one from the other?" (*On Temptation and the Mortification of Sin in Believers* [Philadelphia: Presbyterian Board of Publication, 1880], 268).

34 See The Westminster Confession of Faith (3.1).

The Nature of God's Decree[35]

The following characteristics reveal the nature of God's decree.

First, God's decree is eternal, before time began. Paul calls God's plan his eternal purpose (Eph. 3:11) and explicitly teaches that "God decreed before the ages" (1 Cor. 2:7) to save his own, and that this was "before the foundation of the world" (Eph. 1:4; cf. 2 Tim. 1:9; cf. Jesus's similar words in Matt. 25:34).

Second, since God's sovereign decree is eternal, it is unconditional. Since God was the only entity present in eternity past (Isa. 43:10; 44:24), it is impossible that anything external to God influenced his decree (cf. Gen. 1:1; John 1:1–3). Thus, every decision which is a part of God's decree was a free decision in accordance with his "good pleasure" (Phil. 2:13; c.f. Pss. 115:3; 135:6; Isa. 46:10; 48:14).

Third, God's sovereign decree is immutable and efficacious. Just as nothing could influence God's sovereign decree from its inception in eternity past, nothing in time can change it either (cf. Ps. 33:10–11); thus, "none can stay his hand" or call him to account for his actions (Dan. 4:35; cf. Isa. 14:27). Job affirms, "I know that you can do all things, and that no purpose of yours can be thwarted" (Job 42:2).

Finally, God's sovereign decree is also exhaustive, or comprehensive. In Isaiah 46:10 (NASB), Yahweh asserts that he will accomplish *all* his good pleasure and establish *all* things according to his purpose. "God causes *all things* to work together" according to his purpose (Rom. 8:28 NASB) and works "*all things* according to the counsel of his will" (Eph. 1:11). Simply stated, the Lord does *whatever* he pleases (see Pss. 115:3; 135:6).

God exercises specific and meticulous providential governance of all things. He causes various kinds of weather (cf. Job 37:12–13; cf. 37:6–12; Ps. 148:8), the sun to shine (Matt. 5:45), plants to grow (Ps. 104:14). He determines the life span of birds (Matt. 10:29) and humans (Job 14:5; Ps. 139:16), the boundaries of nations (Acts 17:26), seemingly random events (lots or dice, cf. Prov. 16:33). He removes and sets up kings (Dan. 2:2; cf. Prov. 21:1). "For from him and through him and to him are *all* things" (Rom. 11:36).

THE DECREE OF ELECTION

God's sovereign decree extends to the plan of redemption. Indeed, the doctrine of God's eternal and universal decree and the doctrines of predestination and election are not separate doctrines; the latter are subsets of the former.

35 This section is adapted from Mike Riccardi, "I Will Surely Tell of the Decree of the Lord," *The Cripplegate* (blog), August 28, 2015, http://thecripplegate.com/i-will-surely-tell-of-the-decree-of-the-lord/. Used by permission of the author.

The Decree of God and Predestination

The term *predestination* is often employed as a synonym for God's decree, since he predestines all things. However, it is also used more narrowly to summarize God's dealings with fallen man concerning salvation, and in that sense it has a twofold meaning: election and reprobation.

The Biblical Concept of Election

The decree of election is the free and sovereign choice of God, made in eternity past, to set his love on certain individuals, and, on the basis of nothing in themselves but solely because of the good pleasure of his will, to choose them to be saved from sin and damnation and to inherit the blessings of eternal life through the mediatorial work of Christ.

Both the terminology and the concept of election are taught explicitly throughout Scripture. In Ephesians 1:4–5, Paul writes that the Father "*chose* [Gk. *eklegomai*] us in him [Christ] before the foundation of the world, that we should be holy and blameless before him. In love he *predestined* [Gk. *proorizō*] us for adoption to himself as sons." In Romans 8:29–30, he says, "For those whom he [the Father] foreknew [Gk. *proginōskō*] he also *predestined* [Gk. *proorizō*] to be conformed to the image of his Son, in order that he might be the firstborn among many brothers. And those whom he *predestined* [Gk. *proorizō*] he also called." In the next chapter, Paul illustrates God's absolute freedom in salvation by pointing to his discriminating choice between the twins, Jacob and Esau: "Jacob I loved, but Esau I hated" (Rom. 9:11–13; see more on these verses below). Perhaps the clearest statement on God's sovereign election in salvation comes in Paul's remarks to the Thessalonians: "God has *chosen* [Gk. *haireomai*] you from the beginning *for salvation* [*eis sōtērian*] through sanctification by the Spirit and faith in the truth" (2 Thess. 2:13 NASB).

The New Testament also calls certain individuals "the elect" (Gk. *hoi eklektoi*); that is, the specific objects of God's saving choice. Often believers are called "God's chosen ones" (Col. 3:12; cf. Titus 1:1) or "those who are elect" (1 Pet. 1:1; cf. 1 Thess. 1:4). Christ was delivered over to death for "God's elect" (Rom. 8:32–34). God gives "justice to his elect, who cry to him . . ." (Luke 18:7). Other references to the elect include Matthew 24:22, 31; Mark 13:20, 27; 2 Timothy 2:9–10.

The Categories of Election

In some instances people are chosen, or elected, to an office or an area of service: for leadership over the nation of Israel (Moses, Num. 16:5–7; Zerubbabel, Hag. 2:23); for the priesthood (the tribe of Levi, Deut. 18:1–5; 21:5; 1 Chron. 15:2); for kingship (cf. Deut. 17:15; 1 Sam. 10:24; 1 Chron. 28:4–6; 29:1); for the office of prophet (cf. Jer. 1:5). The Father chose the Son for the task of accomplishing salvation (Isa. 42:1; Luke 9:35; 1 Pet. 1:20; 2:4, 6). Jesus himself chose twelve of his disciples for apostolic service (Mark 3:13–15; Luke 6:13; John 6:70; 13:18; 15:16, 19; Acts 1:2, 24).

Scripture additionally speaks of corporate election—the choice of certain nations or groups to enjoy special privileges or perform unique services to God. God chose Israel to be the recipient of his covenant love and blessings (see Deut. 7:6–7; Deut. 10:15 NASB; cf. 4:37; 1 Kings 3:8; Isa. 41:8; 44:1; 45:4; Amos 3:2). God's choice of that nation is irrevocable. Indeed, a time is coming when "all Israel will be saved" (Rom. 11:26), for "God has not rejected his people whom he foreknew [Gk. *proginōskō*]" (Rom. 11:2). "As regards *election* [Gk. *eklogē*]," Paul says, "they are beloved for the sake of their forefathers. For the gifts and the calling of God are irrevocable" (Rom. 11:28–29).

Also, Scripture clearly teaches that God chooses certain individuals for salvation. God declared of Abraham, "For I have chosen him . . . so that the Lord may bring to Abraham what he has promised him" (Gen. 18:19; cf. Neh. 9:7). He chose Isaac over Ishmael (Gen. 17:19–21; 21:12; cf. Rom. 9:7–9) and Jacob over Esau (Rom. 9:10–13).

The New Testament makes the relationship between election and salvation explicit. God's foreknowledge and predestination are linked with the effectual call, justification, sanctification, and glorification (Rom. 8:29–30). Of the Gentiles in Pisidian Antioch, Luke notes, many who "were appointed [Gk. *tassō*] to eternal life believed" (Acts 13:48)—that is, they believed because they were appointed to eternal life. Paul declared of the Thessalonians that God had "destined [them] . . . to obtain salvation [Gk. *etheto . . . eis peripoiēsin sōtērias*]" (1 Thess. 5:9). And he explicitly proclaimed, "God has chosen you from the beginning for salvation" (2 Thess. 2:13 NASB). In the case of the nation of Israel, though the majority had rejected the Messiah and were hardened, "the elect obtained" salvation by the grace of God (Rom. 11:7).

Some contend that election is corporate rather than individual. They claim God does not choose specific persons to receive salvation but rather he chooses to save a class or category of people. They point to Paul's statement that God "chose *us* in [Christ] before the foundation of the world" (Eph. 1:4). Since the "us" is plural, they claim this election is of the church, a corporate body.[36] But this understanding of Ephesians 1:4 is unlikely. Had Paul used the first-person singular *me*, he would have communicated that God had chosen only him; he could not have used the second person singular *you*, for he was writing to all the saints (Eph. 1:1) at Ephesus, not merely one individual; using the second person

36 William G. MacDonald, "The Biblical Doctrine of Election," in *The Grace of God, the Will of Man: A Case for Arminianism*, ed. Clark H. Pinnock (Grand Rapids, MI: Zondervan, 1989), 219–26.

plural *you* would have meant that only the Ephesians were elect. He used the first-person plural *us* to communicate that God had chosen each individual believer in Christ according to his sovereign pleasure.

Another argument for corporate election is built on Paul's doctrine that believers are chosen in Christ. Since Christ is God's archetypal elect one (Isa. 42:1; Luke 9:35; 1 Pet. 1:20; 2:4, 6), God has chosen only Christ as an individual; believers become part of the elect at the moment of faith by virtue of their union with Christ.[37] However, this view fails to do justice to the fact that Paul says that God "chose *us*" in Christ (Eph. 1:4); the object of God's election is "us," not "him." Also, Paul says God chose the foolish, the weak, and base—that is, fallen human individuals, to prevent such individuals from boasting before him (1 Cor. 1:27–31 NASB). Finally, the church is made up of individual members, whom God knows personally by name (Ex. 33:12, 17; Isa. 45:4; cf. John 10:14). The corporate view of election does not fit the facts of Paul's doctrine of election.

The Basis of Election

God's choice of certain individuals is made not on the basis of any virtue or worthiness that God sees in those individuals, but solely because of the sovereign and good pleasure of God's will. The choice is *unconditional.* As Moses told the people of Israel, God set his love on his people in election because he loved them. It was not because they were more numerous or worthy than other nations, but rather, "it is because the LORD loves you and is keeping the oath that he swore to your fathers" (Deut. 7:7–8). God chooses his people not according to their deeds or beliefs, but according to the sovereign freedom of his will (Eph. 1:5).

The Arminian Doctrine of Conditional Election. Arminian theologians reject unconditional election. They take Paul's comment on God's foreknowledge in Romans 8:29 to say that God chose those whom he saw would believe when, in eternity past, he "looked down the corridors of time" and discovered that, according to their own free will, they believed in Christ. In short, he chose to save on the basis of their foreseen faith. Since the rest would reject Christ, he decided not to save them on the basis of their lack of faith. This view is often called the *foreseen faith* view, the *prescient* view, or the *simple foreknowledge* view of election.

There are several significant problems with the prescient view of election. For instance, this view suggests that God looks ahead and learns things. But this is impossible, since God is omniscient. Furthermore, what God would see if he "looked ahead" is the outworking of his own sovereign decree. As has been

37 Karl Barth, *Church Dogmatics*, trans. G. T. Thompson, G. W. Bromiley, et al., ed. G. W. Bromiley and T. F. Torrance, vol. 2, part 2 (Edinburgh: T&T Clark, 1957), 94–194; Markus Barth, *Ephesians 1–3: A New Translation with Introduction and Commentary*, Anchor Bible 34, ed. William Foxwell Albright and David Noel Freedman (Garden City, NY: Doubleday, 1974), 107–9.

demonstrated above, God "works all things according to the counsel of his will" (Eph. 1:11; cf. Pss. 115:3; 135:6; Isa. 46:10; Dan. 4:35). Thus, God does not form his decree because he knows the future; rather, he knows the future because he has decreed the future.[38]

Also, conditional election seems to undermine the doctrine of salvation by grace alone (*sola gratia*). By grounding God's electing purpose in man's foreseen faith and not in God's sovereign will, this view makes man (and his choice to exercise his free will to trust Jesus) the determinative cause of salvation, rather than God. On this view, what ultimately differentiates the saved person from the unsaved is not something God has done but something man has done. But Paul affirms that God has chosen the foolish, and the weak, and the base—not the wise, the strong, or the faithful—"so that no man may boast before God. But by *His* doing you are in Christ Jesus" (1 Cor. 1:27–30 NASB).

The prescient view of election also fundamentally misunderstands the nature of God's foreknowledge, especially as taught in Romans 8:29. This verse says that God foreknew particular *persons* themselves ("For *those whom* he foreknew," Rom. 8:28–29), not the faith or actions of persons.

Furthermore, the Greek verb *proginōskō* in Romans 8:29 speaks not of simple foreknowledge but of the knowledge that characterizes an intimate personal relationship (cf. Rom. 11:2, of the intimate relationship between God and Israel; 1 Pet. 1:20, of the intimate knowledge of personal relationship between the Father and the Son).

This understanding of *proginōskō* is substantiated by its Old Testament Hebrew counterpart, *yada'*, which, though often used to speak of simple knowledge, many times carries the connotation of intimate, personal knowledge (see Gen. 4:1 [KJV], "Adam knew [*yada'*] his wife again, and she bore a son and called his name Seth" [cf. Gen. 4:25; cf. 4:17; 19:5, 8; 24:16; 38:26; Judg. 11:39; 19:25; 21:11–12; 1 Sam. 1:19]). So personal and intimate is the knowledge connoted by *yada'* that it adequately describes the sexual union between a husband and a wife. (See similar uses in Gen. 18:19; Ex. 33:12, 17.)

The term *yada'* is the Hebrew counterpart not only to *proginōskō* but also to its cognate *ginōskō*, and is used in similar ways. To those who named Christ but never did the will of his Father, Jesus declares, "I never knew [*ginōskō*] you" (Matt. 7:23). In 1 Corinthians 8:3, Paul defines the believer and lover of God as one who is "known [*ginōskō*] by God" (cf. Gal. 4:9), and in 2 Timothy 2:19, he declares, "The Lord knows [*ginōskō*] those who are his" (cf. John 10:15, 27). The knowledge indicated in these instances is the intimate knowledge of relationship.

38 For a helpful summary of the distinction between God's necessary knowledge and his free knowledge, as well as the relationship between God's knowledge and God's decree, see Berkhof, *Systematic Theology*, 102.

Therefore, the testimony of *proginōskō*, its close cognate *ginōskō*, and their Old Testament counterpart, *yada*ʿ, confirms that the sense of God's knowledge used in Romans 8:29 speaks not of a simple knowledge of facts but rather of an intimate, covenant relationship grounded in God's sovereign choice and marked by his favor and love. Simply put, to foreknow is to "forelove." Love was the motivation of God's choice, and the good pleasure of God's will was its basis (Eph. 1:4–5).

God's Unconditional, Electing Love. Scripture explicitly testifies to the timing of unconditional election. The Father loved the Son "before the foundation of the world" (John 17:24), foreknew the Son "before the foundation of the world" (1 Pet. 1:20), and the elect were loved and foreknown "before the foundation of the world" (Eph. s1:4). God's election was by a grace that was "granted us in Christ Jesus *from all eternity*" (2 Tim. 1:9 NASB). This timing of election rules out personal merit as its ground, since no temporal circumstances or personal characteristics influenced the Father's election.

Paul develops and illustrates this concept further in Romans 9:6–18, where he speaks of God's choice of Jacob over Esau (see 9:11–13). Here Paul makes the point that God's choice comes before either man had done, or could have done, anything good or bad. Rather, God chose Jacob over Esau "in order that God's purpose of election might continue" (9:11)—according to his own sovereign purpose. God's election is "not because of works but because of him who calls" (9:11). He states unequivocally that the choice was *not* because of works at all, in any sense. Rather, it was because of *him* who calls.

Paul recognizes that when his doctrine confronts fallen human reasoning, the response will be to charge God with injustice (Rom. 9:14). However, the doctrine of conditional election would never draw this objection. Who would accuse God of being unjust for choosing to save people on the basis of their foreseen acceptance or rejection of Jesus?

Paul continues, "I will have mercy on whom I have mercy, and I will have compassion on whom I have compassion" (Rom. 9:15; cf. Ex. 33:19), and he concludes, "So then it [election] does not depend on the man who wills [Gk. *ou tou thelontos*] or the man who runs [Gk. *oude tou trechontos*], but on God who has mercy" (Rom. 9:16 NASB). Paul unequivocally denies that human will and human effort have anything to do with God's election to salvation. Rather, election depends on *God* who has mercy; thus election is unconditional.

THE DECREE OF REPROBATION

The Lord Jesus teaches that few will enter the narrow gate that leads to life but that many will travel the broad way to destruction (Matt. 7:13–14). He teaches that there will be both sheep and goats—those who inherit eternal life, and others who go away into eternal punishment (Matt. 25:46).

Because God's decree is exhaustive, the doctrine of predestination extends not only to his decision to elect some unto salvation but also to his decision *not* to elect others and thus to leave them to the destruction that their sins deserve; this is the decree of reprobation.

The Statement of the Doctrine

The decree of reprobation is the free and sovereign choice of God, made in eternity past, to pass over certain individuals, choosing not to set his saving love on them but instead determining to punish them for their sins unto the magnification of his justice.[39]

The doctrine of reprobation is a difficult doctrine to contemplate. Calvin himself called it a *decretum horribile*, "a fearful decree."[40] The unregenerate who recoil from the doctrines of eternal judgment and everlasting suffering are equally offended by the doctrine of reprobation. Even many Christians who embrace the doctrine of election nevertheless balk at the doctrine of reprobation. Thus, it is necessary to state the doctrine of reprobation precisely.

In the first place, reprobation is often mistaken with the doctrine of equal ultimacy—that God is equally as active in working unbelief in the heart of the reprobate as he is in working faith in the heart of the elect. It pictures God in eternity past contemplating all humanity as yet unfallen and morally neutral and arbitrarily deciding to work sin and unbelief in the reprobate in order to be justified in consigning them to eternal punishment. Though this is what many think of when they hear the terms *reprobation* or *double predestination*, it is a gross caricature of the biblical doctrine of reprobation that is utterly foreign to Scripture, repugnant to the love and justice of God, and an aberration of historic Calvinism that has been rejected throughout Reformed orthodoxy.[41]

Instead, Scripture teaches an unequal ultimacy with regard to election and reprobation—that is, while God does indeed decree both the salvation of some and the damnation of others, there is an asymmetry in these decrees. This is observed in Romans 9:22–23, for example, where Paul uses the active voice to speak of God's involvement in election ("vessels of mercy, which he has prepared beforehand for glory") and the passive voice to speak of his involvement in reprobation ("vessels of wrath prepared for destruction"). When God chose some and not others for

39 Berkhof, *Systematic Theology*, 118.

40 Calvin, *Institutes of the Christian Religion*, 3.23.7. It is important to note, as Wayne Grudem does, that "[Calvin's] Latin word *horribilis* does not mean 'hateful' but rather 'fearful, awe-inspiring'" (*Systematic Theology: An Introduction to Biblical Doctrine* (Grand Rapids, MI: Zondervan, 1994), 685n23.

41 R. C. Sproul rightly notes that the doctrine of equal ultimacy has been identified with hyper-Calvinism, which he prefers to call "sub-Calvinism" or "anti-Calvinism" (*Chosen by God* [Wheaton, IL: Tyndale, 1986], 142).

salvation, he regarded them not as morally neutral but as already-fallen creatures. That is, from eternity God conceived of or contemplated all people in light of their fall in Adam and thus as sinful creatures.[42] In the case of the elect, he actively intervenes to sovereignly quicken them from spiritual death unto new life in Christ. In the case of the nonelect, however, he does not intervene but simply passes them by, leaving them in their state of sin and lostness. Thus, the elect receive mercy, but the nonelect receive justice, being rightly condemned as their sins deserve. God cannot be charged with unrighteousness, because all are guilty and because he is not obligated to show grace to any.

It is important to understand exactly how election and reprobation are unequal or asymmetrical. To be precise, there are two elements of the decree of reprobation: (1) the decision to pass over some, called *preterition*; and (2) the determination to condemn those passed over, called *precondemnation*. On the one hand, preterition is a negative or passive action on God's part (God simply passes over man and leaves him in his state of sinfulness) and precondemnation is a positive action in which God actively determines to visit judicial punishment on sin—the "vessels of wrath" are "prepared for destruction" (Rom. 9:22), destined to disobedience (1 Pet. 2:8), and "designated for this condemnation" (Jude 4).[43] On the other hand, precondemnation is conditional (for God assigns men to condemnation on the basis, the condition, of their sin and guilt) but preterition is unconditional (for God's decision not to choose someone for salvation is based on nothing in that individual; it is a sovereign act of God's good pleasure). Thus, preterition is passive and unconditional, while precondemnation is active and conditional.

The Vindication of the Doctrine

The doctrine of reprobation is taught in the Bible, and we are obliged to reverently submit our minds and our emotions to the infinite wisdom of God's revelation, trusting that what he says and does is right and just (Rom. 3:4).

In the first place, reprobation is a necessary implication of the biblical teaching concerning election. The very existence of a category of persons called *elect*

42 This discussion relates to the issues surrounding two terms: supralapsarianism and infralapsarianism. Supralapsarianism ("above the fall") teaches that God's decrees of election and reprobation logically preceded his decrees to create and to ordain the fall. Infralapsarianism ("after the fall") teaches the opposite, namely, that election and reprobation were logically subsequent to God's decrees to create and to ordain the fall. We hold to infralapsarianism. For a helpful introduction to the doctrine of the order of the divine decrees, see Berkhof, *Systematic Theology*, 118–25; Lorraine Boettner, *The Reformed Doctrine of Predestination* (1932; repr., Phillipsburg, NJ: Presbyterian & Reformed, 1991), 126–32.

43 Though these are passive verbs, they are what grammarians call "divine passives," indicating that God is the implied agent. See Daniel B. Wallace, *Greek Grammar beyond the Basics: An Exegetical Syntax of the New Testament* (Grand Rapids, MI: Zondervan, 1996), 437–38.

(Matt. 24:22; Luke 18:7; Rom. 8:33; 11:7; 2 Tim. 2:10; 1 Pet. 1:1) necessarily implies a category of persons who are *nonelect*.

Furthermore, reprobation is explicitly taught in the New Testament. Peter speaks of unbelievers who "stumble because they disobey the word, as they were destined to do" (1 Pet. 2:8). Jude speaks of the false teachers, "certain people . . . who long ago were designated [Gk. *prographō*, "to write beforehand"] for this condemnation" (Jude 4). God's reprobation of these false teachers is a script written in eternity past. They are among those "whose name[s] ha[ve] not been written before the foundation of the world in the book of life of the Lamb" (Rev. 13:8; cf. 17:8; 20:15; 21:27).

The clearest portion of Scripture affirming the doctrine of reprobation is Romans 9. God's dealings with Pharaoh illustrate the truth that "he has mercy on whomever he wills, and he hardens whomever he wills" (9:18), and that he does so in order to demonstrate his power and proclaim his name throughout the earth (cf. 9:17, 22). Since God inviolably determines the destiny of both the saved and the lost (cf. 9:11, 16), Paul anticipates this objection: "You will say to me then, 'Why does he still find fault? For who can resist his will?'" (9:19). In effect, "If no one can resist God's sovereign will or decree, how can he justly hold people accountable for that which they are unable to do?"[44] Paul answers those who would reproach God by reminding them that mere mortals are in no position to call God to account: "But who are you, O man, to answer back to God? Will what is molded say to its molder, 'Why have you made me like this?'" (9:20). Paul then continues with this analogy and pictures God as a potter, likening the election of some to fashioning a clay vessel for honorable use and likening the reprobation of others to fashioning another clay vessel for dishonorable use (9:21). In defending God's freedom to do what he wishes with what is his own (cf. Matt. 20:15), Paul then goes on to describe the elect as "vessels of mercy, which he has prepared beforehand for glory" and the reprobate as "vessels of wrath prepared for destruction" (Rom. 9:22–23). These vessels could have been "prepared" only by the potter himself, and Paul clearly indicates that those whom the potter hardens (9:18) are those whom he has fitted for destruction.

While these passages are enough to vindicate the doctrine of reprobation, Scripture also speaks clearly concerning the means God employs to bring about

44 Those who hold the doctrines of conditional election and libertarian free will can make no sense of this objection. They posit that God's will is in fact resistible, the very thing that Paul assumes *not* to be the case as a matter of course. Paul asks rhetorically, "For who can resist his will?," indicating that the obvious response is, "No one!" The only way it could make any sense for Paul to raise this objection at this point in his argument is if (1) God commands all people to repent and believe, (2) they lack the moral ability to do so, but (3) God still holds them accountable to repent and believe and will punish them for their failure to do so.

the destruction he has decreed for the reprobate. Because Paul himself used God's dealings with Pharaoh to illustrate reprobation, it is appropriate to consider God's hardening of Pharaoh's heart as evidence of the means of reprobation (Ex. 4:21; 8:19; 9:7; 10:1; 11:10; 14:4, 8). The Lord's purpose was to display the glory of his redeeming power in the deliverance of Israel from slavery, and in order to do so, he hardened Pharaoh's heart on numerous occasions (cf. also Deut. 2:30; Josh. 11:20; 1 Sam. 2:25). In the same way, his purpose in reprobation is to justly punish the sins of those he has not chosen to save, hardening their hearts as the means to achieving that end. Paul explicitly teaches this idea in 2 Thessalonians 2:11–12: "Therefore God sends them a strong delusion, so that they may believe what is false, in order that all may be condemned who did not believe the truth but had pleasure in unrighteousness." Because God had decreed the condemnation of these unbelievers, he also ordained the means by which that condemnation would be brought about, in this case by purposefully deceiving them. Elsewhere he is said to have blinded the eyes and hardened the hearts of the unbelieving precisely so that they would not see, understand, and repent (John 12:37–40; cf. Isa. 6:9–10). Jesus's own response to this reality is to publicly thank the Father for hiding truth from the wise and understanding and yet revealing it to little children, which he attributes to no other basis than the good pleasure of the Father's will (Matt. 11:25–26). Thus it is plain that God has ordained both the ends and the means of reprobation.

The Justification of God[45]

The chief charge leveled against the doctrine of reprobation is that it is incompatible with the justice of God. However, God is not subject to fallen human notions of fairness, nor will he be tried at the bar of human reason. Paul's rebuke is apropos: "But who are you, O man, to answer back to God?" (Rom. 9:20). All such accusations are born of the erroneous presumption that if God gives grace to any of his creatures, he must give grace to all. Boettner says, "Many people talk as if salvation were a matter of human birthright. And, forgetful of the fact that man had lost his supremely favorable chance in Adam, they inform us that God would be unjust if He did not give all guilty creatures an opportunity to be saved."[46] Yet it undermines the very nature of grace to suppose that it is *owed* to sinful human beings. Truly, the question concerning God's decree of predestination is not, why did God not choose *everybody*? but rather, how can it be that this supremely holy God would choose *anybody*?

45 This section is adapted from Mike Riccardi, "God and Evil: Why the Ultimate Cause Is Not the Chargeable Cause," *The Cripplegate* (blog), October 9, 2015, http://thecripplegate.com/god-and-evil-why-the-ultimate-cause-is-not-the-chargeable-cause/. Used by permission of the author.

46 Boettner, *Reformed Doctrine of Predestination*, 116.

And this is precisely the defense that Paul gives in Romans 9:22–23. The arrogant objector is rebuked severely and told to put his hand over his mouth. But to the submissive worshiper, Paul gives another answer. He says, "What if God, desiring to show his wrath and to make known his power, has endured with much patience vessels of wrath prepared for destruction, in order to make known the riches of his glory for vessels of mercy, which he has prepared beforehand for glory?" God has ordained sin and evil—even the eternal punishment of the wicked—to display to the elect the full glories of his name.[47]

God has ordained whatever comes to pass—even the preparation of vessels of wrath unto destruction—in order that his people might enjoy the fullest display of his glory. To those who would find fault in God for this, we must remember that God's pursuit of his own glory is, as Edwards said, "in order to the happiness of the creature . . . because the creature's happiness consists in the knowledge of God."[48] Our knowledge of God would be imperfect if we did not see the full expression of his attributes: grace, mercy, forgiveness, justice, righteousness, and the rest of the panoply of his perfections. And yet none of those attributes could be expressed fully if there were not sin to punish and to forgive or sinners to whom to be gracious or on whom to exercise justice. God is not less glorious but more glorious because he has ordained evil, and the more he magnifies his glory, the greater is his love to his people. Surely God cannot be charged with unrighteousness for doing that which amounts to the greatest benefit for those who are his.

Neither do the doctrines of election and reprobation undermine the reality that all are commanded to repent and believe the gospel. Indeed, immediately following what is the most exalted teaching on divine sovereignty, in Romans 9, Paul just as clearly teaches human responsibility in Romans 10. He declares that "everyone who calls on the name of the Lord will be saved" (10:13), mandates that preachers of the gospel be sent to call all to repentance (10:14–17), and pictures God's loving benevolence even to the obstinate by depicting him as one who stretches out his hands and calls them to salvation (10:21). The sinner's responsibility is not to discern the secret counsels of God's decree but rather to heed the clear commands of Scripture to repent and believe the gospel (Mark 1:15; Acts 17:30).

47 None has explained this better than Jonathan Edwards, in "The 'Miscellanies' no. 348," in *The "Miscellanies": Entry Nos. a–z, aa–zz, 1–500*, ed. Thomas A. Schafer, vol. 13 of *The Works of Jonathan Edwards* (New Haven, CT: Yale University Press, 1994), 419–21. For the full quote, see John MacArthur and Richard Mayhue, gen. eds., *Biblical Doctrine* (Wheaton, IL: Crossway, 2017), 509.

48 Edwards, "'Miscellanies' no. 348," 419-21.

ANSWERING OBJECTIONS

Objection 1: The Decree of God Is Contrary to the Free Moral Agency of Man

Response: Agents may properly be said to be free so long as their acts are uncoerced. People are free to act within the confines of their nature. Since all people are fallen in Adam, their nature is corrupted by sin, and they are therefore not free to choose righteousness. Nevertheless, they still freely make their moral choices according to their thinking and desires. Those choices arise from a fallen human nature, which is fundamentally opposed to obeying God. So people act freely in their sin and are not coerced by God to act against their nature. God's decree extends to the uncoerced choices of agents free to act within the bounds of their nature (cf., e.g., Gen. 50:19–20; Acts 2:23; 4:27–28).

Objection 2: The Decree of God Discourages Human Effort

Response: The decree is not addressed to men "as a rule of action" and cannot be such a rule because the content of the decree is not known until after events have occurred. But God has ordained a rule of life and belief in the Bible, so that man has the guidance available to do righteous deeds. Again, man is free in the decree to do according to his thoughts and desires, and God does not coercively prevent him from doing good. Also, God's decree includes free human choices that are determined by God to bring about his ordained ends.

For God to render an act certain by his decree is not to *compel* one to perform that act. The crucifixion of Christ took place "by the predetermined plan and foreknowledge of God" (Acts 2:23a), and yet the Jews and Romans acted without coercion, according to their own evil inclinations (Acts 2:23b). Just because God has decreed an event, thereby rendering it certain, does not mean that he coerces people to go against their thoughts and desires. As long as God does not coerce a person to act, a human action may be determined by God and thus certain to occur, and yet the person remains free to do as he or she pleases.[49]

Objection 3: The Decree of God Is Fatalism

Response: Fatalism is impersonal, is unintelligent, and has no intended ultimate end. In contrast, God's sovereign determination of his decree is the personal act of the God who is perfect wisdom, omniscience, justice, love, and grace. Further, one of the ends of the decree is people being saved from sin and living forever in eternal blessedness. Fatalism allows for no free acts, casting humanity as impersonally coerced by cosmic forces. But the decree of God includes no moral coercion. Fatalism also has no distinction between right and wrong, no moral meaning in

49 Here we affirm the compatibilistic freedom of inclination and reject the libertarian freedom of indifference. For more on compatibilism, see "Compatibilistic Theodicy," below.

the universe. But the decree of God is based on his eternal, perfect righteousness and results in believers living in unsullied moral goodness forever.

Objection 4: The Decree of God Makes God the Chargeable Cause of Sin[50]
Response: It must be admitted that sin is a part of God's eternal plan, for he "works *all* things according to the counsel of his will" (Eph. 1:11). He did not merely allow Joseph's brothers to sell him into slavery in Egypt but *meant* their sinful action for his most wise and holy ends (Gen. 45:5–8; 50:20).

However, while God is properly said to ordain—and thus to be the Ultimate Cause of—all things, he is never the proper chargeable cause of evil. Scripture distinguishes between the (1) Ultimate Cause of an action and (2) the proximate and efficient causes of an action, indicating that only the proximate and efficient causes are blameworthy for an evil action. Because God is never the efficient cause of evil and because he always ordains evil for good, he incurs no guilt.

This theodicy is substantiated by numerous passages (cf. Gen. 45:5–8; 50:20; Isa. 10:1–8; 2 Sam. 24:1; 1 Chron. 21:1; Hab. 1:6, 11), but the clearest example comes from the apostolic record of the crucifixion, the most evil event in history.

Wicked men were rightly to blame for the crucifixion of Christ (Acts 4:27), and Peter openly indicted them (Acts 2:23, 36). And yet Peter also explicitly said it was "according to the definite plan and foreknowledge of God" (Acts 2:23). Thus, God is the *Ultimate* Cause of the crucifixion, godless men were the *efficient* cause, the Jews were accountable as a *proximate* cause (again, see Acts 2:23). And yet God, by whose hand all these things ultimately came about, is not the chargeable cause of any evil, because, while the perpetrators meant it for evil, God meant it for good.

SUMMARY

Paul concludes his treatment of the doctrines of election and reprobation by bowing in worship before the magnificence of this sovereign God: "Oh, the depth of the riches and wisdom and knowledge of God! How unsearchable are his judgments and how inscrutable his ways!" (Rom. 11:33). The same must be so for us who are the beneficiaries of such glorious grace—the doctrines of sovereign election and reprobation should lead us to bow our minds in humble wonder of the God whose wisdom is inscrutable and whose grace is so bountiful as to save such wretched rebels as ourselves. "To him be glory forever. Amen" (Rom. 11:36).

50 This section is adapted from Mike Riccardi, "God and Evil: Why the Ultimate Cause Is Not the Chargeable Cause," *The Cripplegate* (blog), October 9, 2015, http://thecripplegate.com/god-and-evil-why-the-ultimate-cause-is-not-the-chargeable-cause/. Used by permission of the author.

The Problem of Evil and Theodicy

One of the most persistent arguments against the existence of God and his decree is based on the existence of physical (e.g., catastrophes, illness, pain, death) and moral (sin) evil in the world. The question is, If God is real, perfectly good, and omnipotent, how can evil exist? In more detail, stated as a proposition, If God were all-good and all-powerful, he would desire and be able to prevent evil. But there *is* evil. Therefore, there is no all-powerful, all-good God.[51]

The Christian response to the problem of evil is called theodicy, which comes from the Greek words *theos* and *dikē*, which combined mean "judicial hearing of God" (for *dikē*, see 2 Thess. 1:9; Jude 7), or the "justification of God." Theodicy is the vindication of God's justice against the charge that the presence of evil proves him to be unjust, impotent, both, or nonexistent.

BIBLICAL THEODICY

God provides his own theodicy in his Word.[52] God does not explain his actions; rather, he asserts that he is to be trusted. Genesis 3 records the beginning of moral and physical evil, yet God does not explain the origin of evil in Satan. When Adam sinned, he implied that God was at fault, but God did not defend himself and instead condemned Adam. In Genesis 22, God does not explain how his command to sacrifice Isaac harmonizes with his goodness. According to Exodus 33:19, God will not submit to man's judgment but will show grace and mercy to whomever he wills without needing to explain his actions.

In the book of Job, God never explains why Job had to suffer as a response to Satan's charges. Job himself wanted to question God but was questioned *by* God instead (Job 38–41). In Ezekiel 18:25–30, God does not defend himself against Israel's charge of injustice but rather condemns Israel for injustice.

In Romans 3:4–6, Paul does not ask questions about God's fairness but rather rebukes such questions by asserting God's rights as the sovereign Lord. In Romans 9:15–20, Paul affirms God's sovereign right to do as he pleases, and that man is disobedient in complaining against God. God is not obligated to explain his actions so as to satisfy human intellect with respect to the problem of evil. Nevertheless, in Romans 9:22–23, he does give the answer that God ordains sin and the punishment of the reprobate in order to magnify the fullness of his glory in the revelation of all of his attributes.[53]

51 Adapted from Frame, *Apologetics to the Glory of God*, 150.

52 See Frame, *Apologetics to the Glory of God*, 171–90. The treatment in the next few sections builds on Frame's principles for establishing a true biblical theodicy.

53 See above on "The Justification of God" (p. 129).

A BIBLICAL PERSPECTIVE ON EVIL

God's perspective on the matter of good and evil is the only right and reliable perspective.

First, God gives perspective on the past. God has always vindicated his ways with his people by bringing periods of suffering to an end by acts of mercy and grace. During the four hundred years of Israel's bondage in Egypt, and when enemies oppressed the nation (as in the times of the Judges), and at the time of the nation's captivity, God's goodness and power to prevent evil might have been questioned. But eventually there was God's gracious deliverance, his powerful, gracious preservation, and his faithful restoration of the nation back to the land (cf. Ezra and Nehemiah). This pattern appeared time and again in the Old Testament—God's people suffered (because of their own sin and/or because of their enemies) but God's mercy and grace delivered or restored them. Naturally, they questioned God's goodness and justice in those times of suffering, but God's mercy had the final word. God's perspective never stops with the suffering or evil; his perspective—on all events in time—always includes grace and mercy. In other words, from God's perspective there really is no "problem of evil."

Second, God gives perspective on the present. Scripture shows us that God has always used and is now presently using evil to fulfill his purposes for good. While not giving exhaustive explanations of all evil and while calling for patience amid adversities, Scripture shows some ways in which God uses evil to further his purposes: to display divine grace and justice (Rom. 3:26; 5:8, 20–21; 9:17); to judge evil in the present and future (Matt. 23:35; John 5:14); to redeem through Christ's sufferings (1 Pet. 3:18); to expand gospel witness through the suffering of Christ's people (Col. 1:24); to shock unbelievers, get their attention, and call for a change of heart (Zech. 13:7–9; Luke 13:1–5; John 9); to discipline believers (Heb. 12:3–17); and to vindicate himself (Rom. 3:26).

God assures us that he always has a good purpose in ordaining evil—for the magnification of his own glory (Rom. 9:22–23) and for the good of his people in every event (Rom. 8:28). This shows us that the solution to the problem of evil must be theocentric, not anthropocentric. It must not have as its aim to make us feel happier or freer, or even to satisfy our intellectual curiosity, but rather to glorify God. Man's true happiness comes only through God-glorifying ways: obedience, self-denial, and suffering while anticipating final glory.

Third, God gives perspective on the future. Scripture promises that God will finally be vindicated and believers fully delivered from evil. In the future, suffering will end in glory for believers, and prosperity will end in judgment for the wicked (Psalm 73; Isaiah 40; Matthew 25; Luke 1:46–55). When God's ways seem to us to be unjust in the present, we must remember his past acts (Hab. 3:1–18) and wait for God's glory and judgment (Hab. 2:2–3). In the future consummation, no one will doubt God's justice and mercy.

Finally, Scripture provides proper perspective by serving as the means by which God gives a new heart to believers. Through the Word of God, the Spirit saves and transforms doubt into faith, humbling people of their prideful autonomy and leading them to give thanks for God's mercy. Through his Word, God gives a new heart by which one sees Christ, believes, and praises (1 Cor. 2:12–13). The change of values given with the new heart lifts one's eyes past the evils of this life to the God who will finally end evil and is even now using it for his purpose. This new perspective is the Christian's theodicy.

COMPATIBILISTIC THEODICY

Compatibilism holds that, when properly defined, human responsibility and divine determinism are complementary ideas; that is, it is both logically consistent and biblically necessary to affirm that God decretally determines the free choices of human beings.

Some theologians adopt a view of freedom that is commonly called "libertarian free will." They contend that a person can be said to be free only if they have the power of contrary choice, the freedom to do otherwise than they have done. However, because God works all things according the counsel of his will (Eph. 1:11), no one has the freedom to choose contrary to God's decree. Thus, libertarian freedom is incompatible with the comprehensive decree of God.

On the other hand, compatibilism contends that one's will is genuinely free so long as that person is not coerced but acts according to his own desires and inclinations. It is the lack of compulsion that makes an action free (cf. Philem. 14), not the ability to choose contrary to God's predetermined plan. Though God turns the king's heart wherever he will (Prov. 21:1), the king is never conscious of having been overruled or coerced; he acts according to his inclinations, and thus freely. For this reason, the king is justly held responsible for his choices, even though they have been decreed by God. God may send Assyria to plunder Israel (Isa. 10:6), and yet nevertheless hold them responsible for it (Isa. 10:5), because they freely act according to their evil inclinations (Isa. 10:7). He may raise up the Chaldeans to seize dwellings not their own (Hab. 1:6), and yet nevertheless hold them guilty for it (Hab. 1:11), because they do so in the service of idols rather than Yahweh (Hab. 1:11). The anger of the Lord may incite David to number Israel (2 Sam. 24:1) and yet David be justly held responsible for it (2 Sam. 24:10, 15; cf. 1 Chron. 21:1).

Because the will of the natural man is enslaved to sin (Rom. 6:16), man's natural inclinations are always and only toward evil. Human beings are free to act within the boundaries of our nature, but our unregenerate nature is only sinful. We are free to sin as we choose, but we are not free to choose righteously (Rom. 8:7–8; 1 Cor. 2:14). For that, our nature must be supernaturally changed by the miracle of regeneration (John 3:6). Therefore, when unregenerate people sin, they sin freely according to their inclination—even though every event has been decreed by God from before the foundation of the world—and therefore they are justly held accountable.

It is often objected that it would be unjust for God to hold people responsible for that which they are unable to do. Indeed, Paul addresses this very objection in Romans 9. After clearly stating that, with respect to salvation, God has mercy on whom he wills and hardens whom he wills (v. 18), Paul raises this objection: "You will say to me then, 'Why does he still find fault? For who can resist his will?'" (v. 19). In other words, since no one can resist what God's will has decreed, how can be it just for him to hold people at fault? First, it must be observed that those are precisely the premises of compatibilism: God is exhaustively sovereign, and man is nevertheless responsible. Those who hold to libertarian free will find themselves arguing with the apostle Paul. Second, Paul's answer is simply that fallen creatures are in no place to call into question the justice of the Creator: "On the contrary, who are you, O man, who answers back to God? The thing molded will not say to the molder, 'Why did you make me like this,' will it?" (v. 20 NASB). Paul does not explain *how* God's absolute sovereignty is compatible with human responsibility; he simply asserts that it *is*. Those who desire to accept the Bible's theodicy must therefore reject libertarian freedom and embrace compatibilism.

Creation[54]

God's creation is defined as his work by his Word and for his glory in creating the universe out of nothing so that its original condition was without spiritual or physical corruption.

DIVINE CREATION

The following features summarize the main biblical assertions regarding the divine creation of the universe.

The Beginning of the Universe and Time

The universe had a beginning, and that beginning began with the first moment of time (Gen. 1:1; Matt. 19:4, 8; Mark 10:6; John 1:1–2; 17:5; Heb. 1:10). Since God, who exists outside of time, created "in the beginning," the beginning must also include time. God began to create in the first moment of time, the beginning of the first day (Gen. 1:5).

54 For a supplementary discussion of creation, consult chap. 6, "Man and Sin."

Creation Was Rapid and Out of Nothing

God created the universe in six literal twenty-four-hour days, and he created it by his Word *ex nihilo* ("out of nothing") (Gen. 1:1–31; 2:7; Ex. 20:11; 31:17; Pss. 33:6, 9; 148:1–6; Isa. 45:18; John 1:3; Acts 4:24; 14:15; 17:24–25; Rom. 4:17; 2 Cor. 4:6; Col. 1:16; Heb. 1:2–3; 11:3; 2 Pet. 3:5; Rev. 4:11; 10:6). This is sometimes called *fiat creationism*. God created the first physical energy and matter because none existed when he began his creation acts. He is thus the only cause of the beginning of the universe. He also created man as special and distinct from all other creatures, in the image of God.

The Universe Is Distinct from and Dependent on God

The universe was created by God, is distinct from him, yet is dependent on him (Job 12:10; Pss. 104:30; 139:7–10; Isa. 42:5; Jer. 23:24; Acts 17:24–28; Eph. 4:6; Col. 1:15–17; Heb. 1:3). God is greater than what he created.

The Universe Was Created by the Triune God

The triune God is the Creator. God the Father initiated the divine work of creation and governed it (1 Cor. 8:6). As the Father's means, God the Son created the universe, since he is the eternal Word of the Father who spoke all things into being (John 1:3; 1 Cor. 8:6; Col. 1:15–17; Heb. 1:10). The Holy Spirit also participated in the divine work of creating the universe (Gen. 1:2; Job 26:13; 33:4; Ps. 104:30; Isa. 40:12–13). This work was not distributed; rather, each person of the Trinity acted in concert with the other two persons. God the Father is the source; God the Son is the means; and the Holy Spirit is the agent of the acts of creation.

God's Creation Was a Free Act

God acted freely in creating (Eph. 1:11; Rev. 4:11). The creation is not necessary to the essence of God. The creation is dependent on the sovereign decree of God, so the creation is not in itself a necessity for God to be God. (see "The Decree of God," above).

Man Was Created Directly, Climactically, and Specially

God created Adam and Eve directly and specially as the climax of the divine work of creation (Gen. 2:7, 21–23). Adam was created first, "of dust from the ground," and then Eve was formed by God from one of Adam's ribs. God created man not from other beings over eons of time but from the ground on the literal sixth day of creation. When God formed Eve out of Adam, they became the first marriage partners and the pattern for all marriages (Gen. 2:24).

Man Was Created to Rule the Earth

God created Adam and Eve and commanded them to rule the earth (Gen. 1:27–31). They were God's servants to govern the earth for him.

All Creatures Were to Reproduce "According to Their Kinds"
God created each creature to reproduce "according to its kind" (Gen. 1:11, 12, 21, 24, 25). As a result, there would be inviolable boundaries in each kind's genetic nature.

All Things Were Created Mature
God created all things mature, with the appearance of age. Living things were created ready to reproduce, including plant life (Gen. 1:12), animals (vv. 20–25), and humans (vv. 26–30). Adam and Eve were created ready to be given dominion over the world. Indeed, the entire universe was created with all systems in mature operation. For example, the stars were created with their light already reaching the earth (vv. 14–19).

The Universe Was Created "Very Good"
God created completely and perfectly; the universe was "very good" by his standard of perfection for creation (Gen. 1:31). At this point, there was no corruption or death (cf. Rom. 5:12). This is incompatible with Darwinian evolution, which requires decay and death before the entrance of sin into the world.

The Purpose of Creation Was to Glorify God
God created to manifest his glory (Isa. 43:7; 60:21; 61:3; Ezek. 36:21–22; 39:7; Luke 2:14; Rom. 9:17; 11:36; 1 Cor. 15:28; Eph. 1:5–6, 9, 12, 14; 3:9–10; Col. 1:16).[55] God would not have purposed an ultimate end other than himself, since he is superior to everything outside himself. Only having his own glory as his primary purpose would preserve God's independence and sovereignty. Furthermore, no other ultimate purpose would encompass all things, and any lesser purpose would be subject to failure, since creatures are finite.

Divine Miracles[56]

The Bible defines a miracle as God's suspension of the ordinary workings of providence so as to act directly and supernaturally. Four different Hebrew words in the Old Testament reveal the various shades of meaning of "miracle": *pele'* has the basic idea of "wonder" (Ex. 15:11; Ps. 77:11); *'ot* indicates a "sign" that establishes a certainty (Ex. 4:8–9; Num. 14:22; Deut. 4:34); *geburah* means "strength" or "might" (Pss. 145:4, 11–12; 150:2); *mophet* basically means "wonder," "sign," or "portent," frequently in conjunction with *'ot* (Deut. 4:34; 6:22; Neh. 9:10).

55 Berkhof, *Systematic Theology*, 136.

56 This discussion of divine miracles is adapted from Richard Mayhue, *The Healing Promise: Is It Always God's Will to Heal?* (Fearn, Ross-shire, Scotland: Mentor, 1997), 164–73. Used by permission of Christian Focus. For more on the temporary nature and revelatory function of miracles, see the section in chap. 5 titled, "Temporary Gifts (Revelatory/Confirmatory)," p. 213.

The New Testament uses four Greek words that correspond exactly to the Old Testament Hebrew terms: *teras* ("wonder") describes the miracle that startles or imposes and is always accompanied by *semeion* ("sign"); it is comparable to *mophet* and *pele'* (see Deut. 4:34 in the Septuagint; see Acts 2:22; Heb. 2:4); *semeion* ("sign") leads a person to something beyond the miracle; it points to something else; it is comparable to *'ot* (see Num. 14:22 in the Septuagint); *dynamis* ("power" or "miracle") pictures the power behind the act and points to a new and higher power; it corresponds to *geburah* (see Ps. 144:4 in the Septuagint); *ergon* ("work") is used by Jesus in the Gospels to describe distinctive works that no one else did (see John 15:24).

Divine Providence

Divine providence is God's preserving his creation, operating in every event in the world, and directing the things in the universe to his appointed end for them. God's providence is meticulous, encompassing the grandest and minutest aspects of life: the universe as a whole (Ps. 103:19; Dan. 4:35; Eph. 1:11), the physical realm (Job 37:1–13; Pss. 104:14; 135:6; Matt. 5:45), the animals (Ps. 104:21, 28; Matt. 6:26; 10:29), the nations (Job 12:23; Pss. 22:28; 66:7; Acts 17:26), man's birth and life (1 Sam. 1:19–20; Ps. 139:16; Isa. 45:5; Gal. 1:15–16), man's successes and failures (Ps. 75:6–7; Luke 1:52), things apparently accidental or unimportant (Prov. 16:33; Matt. 10:30), protection of his people (Pss. 4:8; 5:12; 63:8; 121:3; Rom. 8:28), provision for his people (Gen. 22:8, 14; Deut. 8:3; Phil. 4:19), answering prayers (1 Sam. 1:9–19; 2 Chron. 33:13; Ps. 65:2; Matt. 7:7; Luke 18:7–8), and judging the wicked (Pss. 7:12–13; 11:6).[57]

An important distinction in studying God's providence is between his general providence and his special or specific providence. God's general providence involves his control of the whole universe (Ps. 103:19; Dan. 2:31–45; Eph. 1:11). His special/specific providence encompasses his control of the details of the universe, including the details of history (Acts 2:23) and the details in the lives of individual people, especially the elect (Eph. 1:3–12).

CAUTION: "LAWS OF NATURE"?

The "laws of nature" are not rules outside of God that God is bound to follow. These "laws" are under God's sovereign control, so he has the right and the power to order them as he will or to suspend the natural order and work miracles. These "laws" do not operate apart from God; they do not close the universe to

57 Philip Schaff, *History of the Christian Church* (Grand Rapids, MI: Associated Publishers & Authors, n.d.), 3:168. See also John M. Frame, *Systematic Theology: An Introduction to Christian Belief* (Phillipsburg, NJ: P&R, 2013), 146–70. Frame lists the following under God's universal control: the natural world, human history, individual human life, human decisions, sins, faith, and salvation.

his interference. Rather, they are the personal means that God has ordained to operate the universe. These "laws" are God's *normal* way of producing order and certain effects in the universe, but he is free to work in a *super-normal* (supernatural) way, often by using the laws in differing combinations, resulting in various effects.

DIVINE PRESERVATION[58]

There are three major aspects to God's providence, the first being his *preservation* of the universe. The ever-active work of God the Son maintains everything he created with all the characteristics and dynamics he gave them.

God sustains the breath of people and animals, and if he were to "gather to himself his spirit and his breath, all flesh would perish together, and man would return to dust" (Job 34:14–15; cf. Ps. 104:29). Even "the heavens and earth that now exist are stored up for fire, being kept until the day of judgment and destruction of the ungodly" (2 Pet. 3:7).

DIVINE CONCURRENCE[59]

The second major aspect of God's providence is his *concurrence* in all events. God's concurrence is his operation with created things, causing them to act (whether directly or by ordaining through secondary causes) in accord with their inherent properties.

Examples of concurrence permeate the Scriptures. Joseph's brothers sold him into slavery (Gen. 37:28), and yet Joseph said that it was God and *not* his brothers who sent him to Egypt (Gen. 45:5–8). Joseph's brothers and God *intended* the same evil act for opposite purposes (Gen. 50:20). The Lord said that he would be with Moses's mouth to enable him to speak for God (Ex. 4:11–12). Thus, Moses spoke his own words, and yet God spoke *his* own words by Moses. The Lord turned the heart of the king of Assyria to help the people in building the temple (Ezra 6:22). Judas, Annas, Caiaphas, and Pilate conspired to murder Jesus (Acts 2:23; 4:27), and yet all was accomplished "by the predetermined plan and foreknowledge of God" (Acts 2:23 NASB; Acts 4:28). God's concurrence in all events does not implicate him in sin. (See the discussion of "Compatibilistic Theodicy," above, as well as the response to the objection that God's decree makes him the chargeable cause of sin [pp. 132 and 135].)

In concurrence, God (the first, or ultimate, cause) uses secondary causes (i.e., indirect causes; e.g., a person's own actions, the forces of nature) to accomplish his purposes. But God sovereignly directs the actions of secondary causes to his

58 Grudem, *Systematic Theology*, 316–17. See also Frame, *Systematic Theology*, 174.

59 Berkhof, *Systematic Theology*, 171–75; Frame, *Systematic Theology*, 180–82; Grudem, *Systematic Theology*, 317–22.

intended ends. Concurrence is not a cooperative synergism, which would involve partial participation by both God and man. Rather, both are entirely, simultaneously engaged in producing an action but God's will is ultimately behind all, determining all. God does not coerce man to violate his nature in any act (just as he does not violate the properties of natural forces) but uses man's actions to accomplish his will. In this way, God—not the forces of nature, not man—is in control. Of course, God can also work by direct causation if he so chooses.

DIVINE GOVERNANCE

The third major aspect of God's providence is his divine *governance* of all things. This is his continual active rule over the whole created order.

God governs as King of the universe[60] and as King he retains and exercises sovereign rule in and over all matters in the universe (Matt. 11:25; Acts 17:24; 1 Tim. 1:17; 6:15; Rev. 1:6; 19:6).

God adapts his governance to the nature of the creatures. God mediately governs humans in their moral choices by "moral influences, such as circumstances, motives, instruction, persuasion, and example," and also through direct divine operation by the Holy Spirit in their inner nature.[61]

God's governance extends over all his works—past, present, and future (Pss. 22:28–29; 103:17–19; Dan. 4:34–35; 1 Tim. 6:15). It is detailed, even over the smallest things (Matt. 10:29–31), over things that might commonly be ascribed to chance (Prov. 16:33), and over both good and evil human actions (Phil. 2:13; Acts 14:16).

Questions:

1. How do the two truths of God's "knowability" and "incomprehensibility" fit together without contradiction?
2. What are the "natural proofs" or arguments for God's existence? What are their limitations and how are they useful?
3. What is the significance of the name "Yahweh"? And of "Elohim"?
4. What are the various attempts to classify the attributes of God, and how are they helpful or not helpful?
5. Is knowing the attributes of God a "practical exercise"? Identify and state the practical value of several of the attributes of God.

60 For an expanded discussion of God's kingship, see "What Is the Overarching and Unifying Theme of Scripture?" in chap. 1, "Introduction," above; and see chap. 10, "The Future," below.

61 Berkhof, *Systematic Theology*, 176. See also Frame, *Systematic Theology*, 172–74; Grudem, *Systematic Theology*, 331–32.

6. How can one describe and explain the Trinity using terms such as "subsistences," "hypostases," "co-equality," and the names "Father, Son, and Holy Spirit"?
7. What is the distinction between "*opera ad intra*" and "*opera ad extra*?"
8. What are the Scriptural indications of the Trinity in the Old Testament? (terms and texts)
9. What are the Scriptural indications of the Trinity in the New Testament? (terms and texts)
10. What is (and what are the characteristics of) the "decree of God"?
11. What are the key texts and arguments for (the basis of) the doctrine of election?
12. What are the key texts and arguments for (the vindication of) the doctrine of reprobation?
13. What are the objections (and answers to the objections) to the decree of God?
14. How is the "problem of evil" addressed by the doctrine of the decree of God?
15. How do the doctrines of creation, providence, concurrence, and governance help to explain the doctrine of the decree of God?

4

GOD THE SON

Christology

THE BIBLICAL WITNESS CONCERNING the second person of the Godhead, the Lord and Savior Jesus Christ, is woven like a scarlet thread throughout the entirety of the written Word of God.

Preincarnate Christ

The biblical witness affirms that the incarnate person of Jesus Christ is fully and truly God and fully and truly human; it is a tenet that the early church defended time and time again. However, the Son of God existed as the second person of the Trinity from eternity past and will do so to eternity future.

ETERNITY PAST

Triunity

The inerrant Scriptures clearly teach that the one God subsists in three coequal, consubstantial, and coeternal persons. Both Testaments make reference to distinctions between the persons in the Godhead—Father, Son, and Holy Spirit. Each subsists in the divine essence as a distinct person, each performs individual (yet inseparable) operations, and to each is ascribed divine attributes. (For a full treatment on the doctrine of the Trinity, see the discussion in chap. 3.)

The second person of the Trinity was "with God" (John 1:1), a phrase that indicates a distinctly separate identity. The persons of the Godhead can give and receive love from one another (John 17:24), they communicate with one another and about one another (Matt. 26:39), they appear distinctly in the scene of Jesus's baptism (Matt. 3:16–17), and the Trinitarian baptismal formula indicates distinct identity and coequality of the persons (Matt. 28:19). The Son is distinct from the

Father both in the inner life of the Trinity and in the economy of redemption (Phil. 2:6–7; Heb. 10:5–7; see "Old Testament Appearances," p. 146).[1]

Preexistence

The second person of the Trinity, God the Son, was eternally preexistent with his Father in glory (John 17:5) and he eternally knew the Father's love (John 17:24). In his incarnation he was sent to earth from heaven by his Father (John 6:38; 17:3; 1 John 4:9; cf. John 3:16).

The Bible identifies the Son as the Creator: "All things were made through him, and without him was not any thing made that was made" (John 1:3; see 1:10; 1 Cor. 8:6; Col. 1:16–17; Heb. 1:2, 10). Therefore, he preexisted all things, for the Creator of all things must have existed prior to the creation of all things.

He is eternal in his nature and existence, as John 1:1 affirms: "In the beginning was the Word, and the Word was with God, and the Word was God." This is an absolute "beginning." It marks the point when the eternally (pre-)existent Creator, the Son, "began" the temporary, finite existence of the creation. "You, Lord, laid the foundation of the earth in the beginning, and the heavens are the work of your hands . . ." (Heb. 1:10–12; see Ps. 102:25–27). The Son's existence is "from of old, from ancient days" (Mic. 5:2), and he is called "Everlasting Father" (Isa. 9:6). Isaiah affirms the "child is born" but the preexistent Son is "given" (Isa. 9:6; cf. Gal. 4:4). Christ has always existed as the Son of God but became a child only at the moment of his miraculous conception.

ETERNAL SON OF GOD[2]

As the second person of the Trinity ("the Word," John 1:1), Jesus Christ existed from eternity past. Was this eternal existence *as* the *Son*? Two major views have arisen: eternal sonship and incarnational sonship.

Incarnational sonship argues that his sonship began with Christ's voluntary submission at his incarnation (see John 5:18; Phil. 2:5–8). In Hebrews 1:5, the Father says, "You are my Son, *today* I have begotten you" and "I *will be* to him a

1 William G. T. Shedd identified several actions of relationship between the persons of the Trinity: "One divine person loves another, John 3:35; dwells in another, John 14:10, 11; suffers from another, Zech. 13:7; knows another, Matt. 11:27; addresses another, Heb. 1:8; is the way to another, John 14:6; speaks of another, Luke 3:22; glorifies another, John 17:5; confers with another, Gen. 1:26, 11:7; plans with another, Isa. 9:6; sends another, Gen. 16:7, John 14:26; rewards another, Phil. 2:5–11; Heb. 2:9" (*Dogmatic Theology*, 3 vols. [1889; repr., Minneapolis: Klock & Klock, 1979], 1:279).

2 This section is adapted from John MacArthur's 1999 revision of his earlier position on the sonship issue, articulated most clearly in MacArthur, "Reexamining the Eternal Sonship of Christ," *Journal for Biblical Manhood and Womanhood* 6.1 (2001): 21–23. Used by permission of the *Journal for Biblical Manhood and Womanhood.*

father, and he *shall be* to me a son" (cf. Ps. 2:7). Since begetting normally speaks of a person's origin, and sons are generally subordinate to their fathers, the text appears to teach that Jesus's sonship had a temporal beginning.

The eternal sonship view rests on the observation that the title *Son of God*, when applied to Christ in Scripture, seems to always speak of his essential deity and absolute equality with God, not his voluntary submission. So when Jesus was called "Son of God," it was understood categorically by all as a title of deity, declaring him equal with God and (more significantly) of the same essence as the Father (cf. Matt. 3:17; 17:5; 2 Pet. 3:17; John 5:18–23). Since Jesus's sonship signifies his deity and absolute equality with the Father, it cannot be a title that pertains only to his incarnation.

The begetting spoken of in Psalm 2 and Hebrews 1 is not an event that took place in time. The context of Psalm 2:7 refers to the eternal "decree" of God, so the "begetting" should be understood as figurative, not literal.

Theologians—since the First Council of Constantinople (381)—express this doctrine by the terms *eternal generation*. It is a difficult concept to grasp, but it is biblical. Scripture refers to Christ as "the only Son from the Father" (John 1:14; see 1:18; 3:16, 18). The Greek word translated "the only Son" (ESV) is *monogenēs*, sometimes translated as "only begotten" (KJV, NASB). Within the last seventy years, scholars have advanced the idea that the term speaks fundamentally of uniqueness rather than begetting.[3] However, more recent scholarship has presented a persuasive argument that uniqueness is owing to the fact that a *monogenēs* is the only begotten child.[4] Thus, *monogenēs* refers to the Son's utter uniqueness as one who is from the Father and yet of the very same essence as the Father (cf. Ps. 2:7; John 5:26). The notion of "begetting," or "begotten" does not apply to the Son in a physical sense, for he is as eternal as the Father (cf. John 8:58; Col. 1:15–17). The begetting referred to in Psalm 2:7 and John 1:14 clearly refers to something more than the conception of Christ's humanity in Mary's womb. It refers to the facts that the Son (1) is not a created being (John 1:1–3) and (2) shares the same essence as the Father (cf. John 10:30).

If Christ's sonship is all about his deity, some may wonder why this sonship applies only to the second person of the Godhead and not to the third, the Holy Spirit. This is mysterious, but Scripture clearly reveals that, while the three persons

3 They argue that term is derived from *monos* (only) and *genos* (kind) rather than *monos* and *gennaō* (beget). This is largely based on a single study by Dale L. Moody, "God's Only Son: The Translation of John 3:16 in the Revised Standard Version," *Journal of Biblical Literature* 72 (1953): 213–19.

4 See Charles Lee Irons, "A Lexical Defence of the Johannine 'Only Begotten,'" in *Retrieving Eternal Generation*, ed. Fred Sanders and Scott R. Swain (Grand Rapids, MI: Zondervan, 2017), 98–116. Irons persuasively argues that the *-genēs* stem derives from *gennao* rather than *genos*, and thus that "only begotten" is the proper translation, which refers to the Son's eternal generation.

of the Trinity are coequal, they are still distinct persons. The chief characteristics that distinguish the persons are revealed by the names Father, Son, and Holy Spirit, with the properties of paternity, filiation, and spiration: the Father is begotten of none, but eternally begets the Son; the Son is eternally begotten by the Father; and the Spirit eternally proceeds from both the Father and the Son. While these truths are ultimately incomprehensible, they are biblical and must be affirmed as part of the historic teaching of Christianity.[5]

In light of the arguments presented above against incarnational sonship, the divine declarations concerning the Son at his birth (Mark 1:1; Luke 1:32, 35), his baptism (Matt. 3:17), and his transfiguration (Matt. 17:5) express the Father's approval and endorsement, not the initial appointment of the second person of the Godhead to the position and role of Son.

OLD TESTAMENT APPEARANCES[6]

Certain appearances of God in the Old Testament are referred to as "theophanies." One such theophany occurred on Mount Sinai (Exodus 19). A number of these theophanies involves the ministry of one called "the angel of the LORD [Yahweh]" (cf. Gen. 16:7–13; Ex. 3:2–4; Judg. 6:11–23). The term "messenger" might provide a better translation than "angel," because this title denotes the function or office of the individual, not his nature.

These appearances "reveal, at least in a partial manner, something about [God] Himself, or His will, to the recipient."[7] Since it is the Son (Word) who reveals God (John 1:18; Matt. 11:27), it is proper to see such appearances as the preincarnate Son of God (i.e., a christophany).[8]

OLD TESTAMENT ACTIVITIES

The works of the second person of the Godhead in the Old Testament include creation, providence, revelation, and judgment. These are acts of deity and demonstrate that he is God.

Creation

The New Testament emphatically asserts that the Son is Creator (cf. John 1:3, 10; Col. 1:16; Heb. 1:2, 10). The Son created all things by his spoken word—he spoke

5 For further discussion on the eternal generation of the Son, see "Personal Distinctions," in chap. 3, "God the Father" (p. 109).

6 This section is adapted from William D. Barrick, "Inspiration and the Trinity," *MSJ* 24.2 (2013): 182–84. Used by permission of *MSJ*.

7 James A. Borland, *Christ in the Old Testament: Old Testament Appearances of Christ in Human Form*, rev. ed. (Fearn, Ross-shire, Scotland: Mentor, 1999), 24.

8 Cf. Borland, *Christ in the Old Testament*, 17. For a more thorough discussion regarding the "angel of the LORD," see the section in chap. 8 titled, "Identifying the Angel of the Lord" (p. 380).

all things into existence (see the repetition of "God said" in Gen. 1:3, 6, 9, 11, 14, 20, 24, and the direct declarations in Ps. 33:6 and Heb. 11:3).

Providence

The Son of God, as Messiah, acts providentially, personally, and directly to intervene in world history to establish the kingdom of God on earth (see Dan. 2:31–46; Matt. 23:37–25:46; Rev. 11:15). Christ has continually upheld the creation, sustaining and directing it in its role related to God's kingdom program (Heb. 1:3)—more than just preserving all things as in Colossians 1:17.

In the Old Testament, God's goodness in his providence emerges in the actions of one who appears to be the second person of the Godhead. Psalm 23 speaks of Yahweh as shepherd—one who cares for and provides. His goodness pursues his people all the days of their lives (Ps. 23:6). In John 10:11, Jesus identified himself as that good shepherd.

Revelation[9]

The second person of the Godhead fulfilled a vital role in the production of the Bible. The Old Testament speaks often of the appearance of God for the purpose of delivering his people, leading them, or communicating with them. Since some of these events consist of appearances by the Son of God (see "Old Testament Appearances," p. 146), they reveal the role of the second person of the Godhead in giving revelation leading to the production of Scripture. In the New Testament, Jesus himself confirms that the Father sent his Word by his messenger (cf. John 12:49; 14:10; 17:6–8, 14). The Son of God appears in both Testaments as one speaking to God's people. Thus, the Bible reveals that the divine spokesman is the Son of God himself, the very One whom the apostle John describes as "the Word" in the opening of his Gospel (John 1:1).

Judgment

The Son of God will judge both the wicked and the righteous (Matt. 25:31, 41); he is appointed as the Judge of all (John 5:22–23). Authority to bring judgment rests on the fact that he is the Son of Man (John 5:27; cf. Dan. 7:13–14), "the one appointed by God to be judge of the living and the dead" (Acts 10:42; cf. Rom. 2:16).

Jesus said that, in his first coming, he "did not come to judge the world but to save the world" (John 12:47). However, at his second coming, Jesus will judge those who reject him and do not give heed to his words.

Besides judging the unrighteous, Jesus will also sit in an evaluative judgment of believers for the purpose of rewarding them, at the "judgment seat of Christ" (2 Cor. 5:10; cf. 2 Tim. 4:8).

9 This section is adapted from Barrick, "Inspiration and the Trinity," 180–85. Used by permission of *MSJ*.

OLD TESTAMENT PROPHECIES

Jesus said to his opponents, "You search the Scriptures because you think that in them you have eternal life; and it is they that bear witness about me" (John 5:39). After his crucifixion and resurrection, Jesus expounded from the Scriptures ("Moses and all the Prophets," Luke 24:27) "everything written" concerning himself in the Law, the Prophets and the Psalms (Luke 24:44). This is the only time in Scripture that the Psalms are included with the Law and the Prophets with reference to the Messiah. Psalms that Jesus might have referred to include Psalm 2:1–12 (cf. Acts 4:25–26; 13:33; Heb. 1:5; 5:5); Psalm 22:1–31 (cf. Matt. 27:35–46; John 19:23–24; Heb. 2:12; 5:5); Psalm 69:20–21, 25 (cf. Matt. 27:34, 48; Acts 1:15–20); Psalm 110:1–7 (cf. Matt. 22:43–45; Acts. 2:33–35; Heb. 1:13; 5:6–10; 6:20; 7:24); and Psalm 118:22–23 (cf. Matt. 21:42; Mark 12:10–11; Luke 20:17; Acts 4:8–12; 1 Pet. 2:7).

The Jews themselves read the Hebrew Bible in such a way that many came to understand its prophecies as direct predictions of the coming Messiah. However, it is incorrect to read the Lord Jesus Christ into every Old Testament text. This practice ignores the true prophecies, rejects the essential hermeneutic of authorial intent, kills authentic exegesis and exposition, and makes the Old Testament meaningless to its original Jewish readers.

Following are a few key examples of Old Testament prophecies of Christ.

The Messiah Is the Seed of the Woman (Gen. 3:1)

God's verdict regarding the serpent was not completed with the curse of crawling on its belly in Genesis 3:14. He continued, "I will put enmity between you and the woman, and between your offspring (lit., seed) and her offspring" (Gen. 3:15). The serpent would enter into a kind of warfare with Eve and her offspring, and it would involve its own offspring.

Genesis 3:15 does not simply depict a conflict between good people and evil people. There is a kingdom of evil over which Satan rules. He was the one who empowered the serpent and who was ultimately responsible for what happened. The New Testament confirms such an interpretation in Romans 16:20 and in Revelation 12:9. Satan will bruise the heal of the offspring of the woman.

Furthermore, the offspring of the woman refers to some descendant of the woman who will ultimately become the ruler over a kingdom of good. That future individual will finally defeat Satan and put an end to the conflict between the two kingdoms: "He shall bruise your head" (Gen. 3:15). The crushing of the head symbolizes total defeat. The New Testament writers understood that the offspring of the woman is the Messiah (see Matt. 1:23; Gal. 4:4; 1 Tim. 2:15; Heb. 2:14; 1 John 3:8). The rest of Scripture echoes Genesis 3:15 with its two protagonists of the *head* and the *heel* (Ps. 22:16; Luke 24:39–40; Rev. 13:3). Such an interpretation makes this verse the first messianic prophecy in Scripture. Thus, Genesis 3:15 is called the *protoevangelium* ("the first gospel"), because it is the earliest prophecy promising a future deliverer.

The Messiah Is the Son of God (Psalm 2)

The New Testament treats Psalm 2 as prophetic and messianic, citing it seven times in the Gospels, five times in Revelation, three times in Hebrews, twice in Acts, and once in Philippians. Psalm 2:1–3 reveals a worldwide rebellion against God's anointed. In verses 4–6 God confirms his chosen king over the nations, and in verses 7–9 he confirms that his king is also his Son. Then he invites the world to contemplate his Son and to render full obedience to him (vv. 10–12). God demands that world leaders render to his Son spiritual service and fear by their submission to him. Spiritual blessing accrues to those who "take refuge in" God's Son—something never promised for submitting to a human king (compare Psalm 2 and Isaiah 9:6).

Trinitarian References to Messiah

A number of passages in the book of Isaiah identify three distinct divine persons (cf. Isa. 42:1; 48:16; 61:1; 63:7–10). In these texts (1) the Lord's servant will be sent by (2) the Lord, and the Lord will empower him with (3) his Spirit. Jesus confirms that Isaiah 61:1 speaks of him as the Lord's servant (Luke 4:17–21). Such specificity regarding distinct persons of the Godhead can be traced back to much earlier Old Testament references to multiple divine persons (cf. Gen. 1:1–2; 18:17, 22–33; Josh. 5:13–15).

The Messiah Is the Mediator between God and Man (Job 33:23–28)

Job spoke of his need of a "mediator." Job admitted that God was so just or righteous that a person could not be just in God's presence (Job 9:2). People are sinners and can have no fellowship with their just and holy God. They need a mediator. Job faced a hopeless future unless someone would intervene on his behalf (Job 33:24–28). In Job 19:25, Job had expressed his conviction that his Redeemer lived and would stand on the earth in the latter days.

Job's Redeemer-Mediator must be both God and man (Job 9:32–33; 16:21). According to Job 33:23, that individual is an "angel" ("messenger"), a "mediator," and "one of a thousand" (meaning "one of a kind"). This individual is able to declare what is right (Job 33:33) and to deliver Job from the pit by means of the "ransom" that this mediator possesses (Job 33:24). The apostle Paul affirms that Jesus Christ is that mediator (1 Tim. 2:5).

The Messiah Is Prophet, Priest, and King

The promise of the prophetic office of the Messiah appears first in Deuteronomy 18 in the revelation concerning a prophet greater than Moses (Deut. 18:15–22;

cf. Heb. 3:1–3). Prophets like Moses (and other prophets who followed him, from Joshua to Malachi) fulfilled a mediatorial office.

In Acts 3:22–23, the apostle Peter declared that the Messiah fulfilled the prophecy of Deuteronomy 18:15–22 (cf. Acts 7:35–38; and Ex. 3:2). First-century Jews understood Moses's prophecy as a reference to their Messiah (John 1:21, 25), and the people of Jerusalem recognized Jesus as a prophet (Matt. 21:11; see Luke 7:16; 24:19). Jesus knew himself to be a prophet (cf. Luke 13:33).

In the future, that prophet, the high priesthood, and the kingship over God's people will be combined in *one* person. The Old Testament announced that this person would also bear the title "the Branch" (Isa. 4:2; 11:1; Jer. 23:5–6; 33:14–22; Zech. 3:8; 6:12). Zechariah 6:12–13 specifically revealed that this Messiah-Priest-King would build the temple about which Haggai had prophesied (Hag. 2:1–9). One may compare these Old Testament references to "the Branch" to the individual emphases of the four New Testament Gospels: Matthew: kingly aspect, "David, a righteous Branch, . . . a king" (Jer. 23:5; 33:15); Mark: servant aspect, "My servant the Branch" (Zech. 3:8); Luke: human aspect, "The man, whose name is Branch" (Zech. 6:12); John: divine aspect, "The Branch of Yahweh" (Isa. 4:2).[10]

Of course, the future High Priest is the Lord Jesus Christ himself (cf. Heb. 5:5–6). But this high priesthood is "after the order of Melchizedek," the King-priest of Salem (cf. Gen. 14:18–20). His kingship is affirmed in in Hebrews 7:14, where the writer points out that David and his descendants are of the tribe of Judah: "For it is evident that our Lord was descended from Judah"—the tribe of kings (cf. Gen. 49:10). Jesus's high priesthood is greater than any priesthood Israel ever experienced, and his kingship is forever (see Psalm 110).[11]

Incarnate Christ

INCARNATION

Deity

Jesus was and is the God-man—truly and fully God as well as truly and fully human. In his incarnation he manifested outwardly his internal divine essence (Gk. *morphē*, "form," Phil. 2:6). Christ possessed the divine glory (John 1:14; 17:5; see Isa. 42:8). Thus, the writer of Hebrews most emphatically proclaims that Christ was the exact representation of the divine nature (Heb. 1:3; see Col. 1:15). The second person of the Trinity was not only "with God" at creation, he

10 Walter C. Kaiser Jr. and Tiberius Rata, *Walking the Ancient Paths: A Commentary on Jeremiah* (Bellingham, WA: Lexham, 2019), 277.

11 Alva J. McClain's *The Greatness of the Kingdom: An Inductive Study of the Kingdom of God* (Chicago: Moody Press, 1968) makes these arguments more cogently and exhaustively than any other volume of Christian theology. See also Paul N. Benware, *Understanding End Times Prophecy: A Comprehensive Approach* (Chicago: Moody Press, 1995), 135–45, 279–89.

was himself God (John 1:1–3). By creating the universe, the second person accomplished a work that only God could accomplish (note that the Hebrew word *bara'*, "create," takes only God as its subject).

As God, Jesus is the worthy recipient of worship (see Heb. 1:6; cf. Matt. 2:2; 14:33; Phil. 2:10–11). Doxologies in the New Testament even ascribe glory to Christ in a fashion reminiscent of the Old Testament doxology in 1 Chronicles 29:10–11 (see Heb. 13:20–21; 1 Pet. 4:11; 2 Pet. 3:18; Rev. 4:11; 5:9–10). Thus, Christ ought to be worshiped as the God of the Old Testament was worshiped.

Prayer to Jesus Christ constitutes yet another evidence for his deity. Jesus instructed his disciples to pray to him (John 14:14; 15:16; 16:23–24). Acts 1:24–25 records that the disciples prayed to Christ for guidance, and Stephen voiced two prayerful requests to Jesus (Acts 7:59–60). In Damascus, Ananias instructed Saul to be baptized and to call on the name of Jesus (Acts 22:16). Paul wrote that "everyone who calls on the name of the Lord will be saved" (Rom. 10:13; see 1 Cor. 1:2). Paul also appealed to Christ to remove the "messenger of Satan" from him (2 Cor. 12:7–8). Indeed, the New Testament closes with a prayer to Christ: "Come, Lord Jesus!" (Rev. 22:20).

Worship includes more than just prayer; it also involves praise. In Ephesians 5:18–20 Paul urges his readers to speak in hymns of praise (Eph. 5:19) addressed "to the Lord," referring to Christ (Eph. 5:20). The song of praise in Revelation 5:9–10 also focuses on the Lord Jesus. Two biblical hymns in the early church voice praise to Jesus: Philippians 2:6–11 and 1 Timothy 3:16.

All believers are admonished to "the fear of the LORD" (2 Chron. 19:9; Ps. 111:10; see Deut. 6:2; 8:6; 10:12). Jesus Christ is also the object of such fear (Col. 3:22–24; see Eph. 5:21, "out of reverence for Christ"; NASB, "in the fear of Christ"), and that godly fear forms a key section of "the song of the Lamb" (Rev. 15:3–4).

The second person of the Godhead also fully exhibits and exercises all the divine characteristics and attributes of God, such as eternality (Mic. 5:2; John 1:1; 8:58; Col. 1:17); glory (Matt. 16:27; 24:30; Luke 9:32; John 17:5); holiness (Luke 4:34; John 6:69; Heb. 7:26); immutability (Heb. 1:10–12; cf. Ps. 102:25–27; Heb. 13:8); omnipotence (1 Cor. 1:23–24; Heb. 1:2–3); omniscience (John 1:47–49; 21:17; Acts 1:24; 1 Cor. 4:5); self-existence (aseity) (John 1:1–3; Col. 1:16–17; Rev. 1:8, 17–18); sovereignty (Eph. 1:21; Col. 2:10; 1 Pet. 3:22).

According to the New Testament writers, Jesus is "the image of the invisible God" (Col. 1:15; see 2 Cor. 4:4; Heb. 1:3). Therefore, anyone who saw Christ could be said to have seen the Father (John 12:45; 14:7–10). In other words, the attributes and characteristics of the Father reside also in the person of his Son.

The Bible mentions many different titles for the Son of God. Some key titles of his deity are listed here (titles appropriately associated with his humanity will be listed under that discussion below, p. 155).

- "The Lord," or *adonai* (Ps. 110:1 with Matt. 22:41–45; Rom. 10:9–10; Phil. 2:9–11)
- "Wisdom"/"Wisdom of God" (Proverbs 8; Luke 11:49; 1 Cor. 1:24)
- "Immanuel," or "God with us" (Isa. 7:14; Matt. 1:23)
- "Mighty God" (Isa. 9:6)
- "Wonderful Counselor" (Isa. 9:6)
- "the Lord," or Yahweh (Isa. 40:3 with Mark 1:3; Joel 2:32 with Rom. 10:13)
- "Creator" (of Israel, Isa. 43:15; of souls, 1 Pet. 4:19; and of all things, with this title implied, John 1:3; Col. 1:16; Heb. 1:2)
- "The angel [messenger] of the Lord" (see Zech. 1:11–21, where 1:20 identifies the angel as Yahweh, while 1:12–13 shows him praying to Yahweh as a distinct person)
- "The Son of God" (Mark 1:1; John 3:18; 5:25; Rom. 1:4; Eph. 4:13; Rev. 2:18)
- "The Holy One" (Mark 1:24; John 6:69; Acts 3:14; Rev. 3:7)
- "Son of the Most High" (Luke 1:32)
- "The Word" (John 1:1)
- "The only begotten" (*monogenēs* = unique one; John 1:14, 18; 3:16, 18; 1 John 4:9 NASB)
- "I am" (John 6:35; 8:12; 10:7, 11; 11:25; 14:6; 15:1; cf. "I am," Ex. 3:13–14)
- "God" (John 20:28; Rom. 9:5)
- "King of kings" (1 Tim. 6:15; Rev. 17:14; 19:16; see Dan. 4:37)
- "The Almighty" (Rev. 1:8)
- "The Alpha and the Omega" (Rev. 1:8)
- "The Lord God" (Rev. 1:8)
- "The first and the last" (Rev. 1:17; 2:8)

Kenosis[12]

In his incarnation, the eternal Son made himself of no reputation by taking on a full and true human nature in addition to his divine nature. The biblical basis for this fact is found in Philippians 2:5–7. Drawing from the Greek word for "emptied himself" (v. 6), *kenoō*, theologians refer to this as the "kenosis," or "emptying." The apostle Paul affirms that, "though he was in the form of God" (Phil. 2:6, i.e., preexistent deity), Christ (the Son) voluntarily took on himself the form of a slave (Gk. *doulos*).

That Christ "was in the form [Gk. *morphē*] of God" (Phil. 2:6) is a reference to the reality of Christ's deity, just as "taking the form [*morphē*] of a slave" (Phil. 2:7,

12 Portions of this section are adapted from Mike Riccardi, "On the Incarnation: Avoiding Heresy and Pursuing Humility," *The Cripplegate* (blog), June 7, 2013, http://thecripplegate.com/on-the-incarnation-avoiding-heresy-and-pursuing-humility/ (used by permission of the author).

author's trans.) speaks about the reality of his slavery. "Form" (*morphē*) does not mean that Christ became a slave only in appearance; *morphē* specifically denotes the essential, unchanging character of something—what something is, in and of itself. The mind of Christ "is revealed in two sublime self-renunciatory acts, the one described as a *kenōsis*, the other as a *tapeinōsis*. In the former he 'emptied himself,' stooping from God to humanity; in the latter he 'humbled himself,' stooping from humanity to death."[13]

There have been serious misunderstandings about this "self-emptying." Named for the "emptying" spoken of in the *kenōsis*, kenotic theology posits that Christ emptied himself of some aspect of his deity during his incarnation, or that Christ retained his essential attributes of deity (e.g., holiness, grace) but surrendered his relative attributes (e.g., omniscience, immutability).

However, it is by definition impossible for the eternal, immutable God to cease to exist as God. Even in his incarnation, the Lord Jesus could say, "I and the Father are one" (John 10:30); this was a metaphysical statement of the Son's shared essence with the Father. The Jews clearly understood this, as their reaction indicated (John 10:33). He claimed that to see him was to see the Father (John 14:9), that he had "authority over all flesh" (John 17:2), and he received worship from his disciples (John 20:28). In Christ's transfiguration, his deity was revealed visibly, as he peeled back the veil of his humanity and allowed the expression of his own divine essence to shine forth (Matt. 17:2; see "Transfiguration," p. 162). So then, the Son did not empty himself of his deity or his divine attributes in his incarnation.

So what does "emptied himself" (Phil. 2:6) mean? While the verb *kenoō* means "to empty," it is used exclusively in a metaphorical sense in the New Testament. It never means "to pour out," as in "pouring his divine attributes out." Instead, *kenoō* means "to make void," "to nullify," or "to make of no effect." So, to ask, Of what did Christ empty himself? is to ask the wrong question. Christ himself is the object of this emptying; he nullified *himself* (cf. the KJV "made himself of no reputation," Phil. 2:7).

Christ made himself of no reputation precisely *by taking on* a human nature, "by taking the form of a servant, being born in the likeness of men" (Phil. 2:7), by adding to his divine nature a full and true humanity. His was an emptying by addition, not by subtraction. Although taking on a full human nature, the Son of God fully retained his full divine nature, attributes, and prerogatives.

In the state of humiliation, the Son of God fully possessed his divine nature, attributes, and prerogatives but did not fully express them. At times he expressed them (e.g., his miracles, cf. Luke 5:3–10). But he submitted himself to the life of

13 Alva J. McClain, "The Doctrine of the Kenosis in Philippians 2:5–8," *MSJ* 9.1 (1998): 90.

a slave (Phil. 2:7; cf. 2 Cor. 8:9). He concealed his divine glory and left the worship of saints and angels to be "despised and rejected by men" (Isa. 53:3). As the suffering servant of Yahweh, he surrendered himself to the will of the Father in everything (John 5:19, 30).

No so-called kenotic theology can be consistent with Scripture if the incarnate Christ could not have asserted "equality with God" (Phil. 2:6).[14]

Virgin Birth

The victorious "offspring" (or "seed") of the woman in Genesis 3:15 will not be the offspring of a man (see Gal. 4:4). By omitting any relationship to Adam, God suggests that the promised offspring will not partake of Adam's sin. As the first Adam was fathered by God (see Luke 3:38, "Adam, the son of God"), so the second Adam, Jesus Christ, was fathered by God, not by a human male (Matt. 1:18–20).

During the reign of King Ahaz, king of Judah, the prophet Isaiah received a revelation from God to pass on to the king: "Therefore the Lord himself will give you a sign. Behold, the virgin shall conceive and bear a son, and shall call his name Immanuel" (Isa. 7:14). According to Matthew 1:22–23, that prophecy was fulfilled at the miraculous conception of Jesus in the womb of the Virgin Mary. Some critics object to this interpretation, arguing that the term Isaiah used (Heb. *'almah*) merely refers to a "young woman of marriageable age," not a woman who has never had relations with a man. These scholars argue that another term (Heb. *betulah*) is the correct term for "virgin" as such. However, the word *'almah* does refer to a young woman who has not had intimate relations with a man in other texts (see Gen. 24:43; Ex. 2:8; Song 1:3). Furthermore, the suggestion that *betulah* is the correct Hebrew word for "virgin" seems to be contradicted by the use of the term in Genesis 24:16, which adds "whom no man had known" in order to make *betulah* ("maiden") refer to a virgin. The term *'almah* requires no such qualification. The Septuagint, the ancient Jewish translation of the Old Testament into Greek, translates the Hebrew term with *parthenos*, the same word appearing in the New Testament at Matthew 1:23.

The doctrine of the virgin conception and birth of Jesus is significant for several reasons. First, the integrity of the Gospel record concerning Jesus rests heavily on the truth of the virgin birth. If Matthew and Luke are undependable in their accounts of the virginal conception and birth of Jesus, then their entire histories of Jesus become suspect.

Second, the virgin birth allows for the preexistence of the divine person and nature. The eternal Son of God existed before the miraculous conception in Mary's womb. Natural conception would have produced a second person, but

14 For more on the doctrine of the kenosis, see Michael Riccardi, "Veiled in Flesh the Godhead See: A Study of the Kenosis of Christ," *MSJ* 30.1 (Spring 2019): 103–27.

Jesus, as the God-man, is but one person with two natures. As Isaiah said, "For to us a child is born, to us a son is given" (Isa. 9:6; see previous comment on this verse, under "Preexistence").

Third, without a virgin conception of Jesus, there can be no guarantee of his sinlessness. The descendants of Adam are sinners because Adam sinned; the descendants of Adam die (Rom. 3:23; 5:12–19; 6:23; see Ps. 51:5). Death can occur before an infant knows the difference between right and wrong and before that little one is even capable of understanding the gospel of salvation through Jesus Christ. Infant death necessitates the doctrine of original sin, for there is no death apart from sin. The sinless Jesus can experience death according to his human nature only as a result of God imputing to him all of the elect's sin and guilt (2 Cor. 5:21).

Fourth, the elimination of the virgin birth would jeopardize the entirety of Jesus's life and ministry and the attendant doctrines. If any single doctrine within the biblical teaching concerning Jesus failed, it would lead one to question everything concerning him in the New Testament record.

Lastly, the virgin conception/birth of Jesus ought to be part of the Christian's confession of faith. Jesus's birth gave him a body of flesh. The spirit of antichrist denies that Jesus came in flesh (1 John 4:1–3; 2 John 7). The believer's confession states that Jesus took on himself flesh and blood (Heb. 2:14) in order to put away sin (1 John 3:5). That confession appears in the first line of the early Christian hymn cited by Paul in 1 Timothy 3:16: "He was manifested in the flesh."

Humanity

The Bible mentions many different titles for Jesus in his humanity:

- The "offspring" or seed of the woman (Gen. 3:15; Gal. 4:4)
- "Redeemer" (Job 19:25–27; Gal. 3:13)
- "Messiah" or "Anointed" (Heb.) and "Christ" (Gk.) (Ps. 2:2; John 1:41; 4:25; Acts 18:28)
- "Servant" (Isa. 52:13; Acts 4:27)
- "Jesus" (Matt. 1:21)
- "Son of David" (Matt. 12:23; 21:9; Mark 12:35–37; Rom. 1:1–4)
- "Son of Man" (Mark 2:10; John 12:34; Acts 7:56; Rev. 1:13; see Dan. 7:13)
- "Chosen One" (Luke 9:35; cf. Matt. 12:18; 1 Pet. 1:20)
- "The Lamb of God"/"the Lamb" (John 1:29; Rev. 5:6, 8, 12, 13)
- "The firstborn," or preeminent one (Rom. 8:29; Col. 1:15; Heb. 1:6)
- "The last Adam" (1 Cor. 15:45–49; cf. Rom. 5:14; 1 Cor. 15:21–22)
- "Mediator" (1 Tim. 2:5–6)
- "High priest" (Heb. 3:1)
- "Lawgiver and judge" (James 4:12; see Matt. 28:18)

- "Advocate" (1 John 2:1)
- "The Lion of the tribe of Judah" (Rev. 5:5)
- "The Root of David" (Rev. 5:5)

The Hypostatic Union. Two ecumenical councils—Nicaea (325) and Chalcedon (451)—affirmed that Jesus was truly God and that Jesus was at the same time truly human. This "hypostatic union" of the two natures was without confusion, without change, without division, and without separation.[15]

He is but one person subsisting in two natures—the divine and the human. He therefore has a divine will and a human will, as each nature possesses its own will. In John 17:24, Christ's divine will appears in his Trinitarian relationship to the Father before the foundation of the world. In the garden of Gethsemane, Jesus subjects his human will to the Father's will (Matt. 26:39).

Jesus experienced birth (Matt. 2:1), growth (Luke 2:40), exhaustion (John 4:6), sleep (Mark 4:38), hunger (Matt. 4:2; 21:18), thirst (John 4:7; 19:28), anger (Mark 3:5), sorrow (Matt. 26:37), weeping (Luke 19:41; John 11:35), compassion (Matt. 9:36), love (Mark 10:21; John 11:3, 5, 36), joy (Luke 10:21; John 15:11), temptation (Matt. 4:1; Heb. 4:15), prayer (Matt. 14:23; Heb. 5:7), suffering (Matt. 16:21; Luke 22:44; Heb. 2:18), and death (Mark 15:37–39; Luke 23:44–46; John 12:24, 33; Rom. 5:6, 8; Phil. 2:8). Jesus was, indeed, truly and completely human—at the same time as being truly and completely God.

Hebrews 2:17–18 addresses the necessity for, and the great blessing accruing from, his humanity: "Therefore he had to be made like his brothers in every respect, so that he might become a merciful and faithful high priest in the service of God, to make propitiation for the sins of the people. For because he himself has suffered when tempted, he is able to help those who are being tempted."

John Walvoord observes that "while the attributes of one nature are never attributed to the other [nature], the attributes of both natures are properly attributed to His person."[16] That is, whatever can be said of one of Christ's natures can be rightly said of Christ as a whole person. In Acts 20:28, Paul does not mean that the divine nature has blood, for God is spirit (cf. John 4:24). But because "blood" is a property of Christ's human nature and "God" is a property of his divine nature, Paul can say of Jesus that God purchased the church with his own blood. The

15 The key portions of the Chalcedonian definition of the hypostatic union are the words: ". . . the same Son, our Lord Jesus Christ, the same perfect in Godhead and also perfect in manhood; truly God and truly man . . . one and the same Christ, Son, Lord, Only-begotten, to be acknowledged in two natures, inconfusedly, unchangeably, indivisibly, inseparably; the distinction of natures being by no means taken away by the union, but rather the property of each nature being preserved, and concurring in one Person and one Subsistence . . ." (in Philip Schaff, *The Creeds of Christendom*, vol. 2, *The Greek and Latin Creeds* [New York: Harper & Row, 1877], 62–63).

16 John F. Walvoord, *Jesus Christ Our Lord* (Chicago: Moody Press, 1969), 116.

properties of each nature may be predicated of the one person. Walvoord helpfully provides seven classifications, summarized below, by which to distinguish between biblical references to the natures and person of Christ:[17]

1. Biblical references to Christ's whole person, in which both natures are essential: Isa. 9:6–7; Matthew 1:21; Hebrews 4:14.
2. References to the whole person, but the attributes are true of his deity: John 2:24–25; John 3:13; 5:17.
3. References to the whole person, but the attributes are true of his humanity: Matthew 4:1–2; Luke 2:7; 2:40; John 4:6.
4. Apparent contradiction in references describing the whole person according to an attribute of his divine nature but predicated of his human nature: Acts 20:28; Revelation 1:17–18.
5. Apparent contradiction in references describing the whole person according to an attribute of his human nature but predicated of his deity: John 6:62; Romans 9:5.
6. References describing the whole person according to his deity but predicated of both natures: Luke 23:43; John 6:11; 6:61; Colossians 3:3–4.
7. References describing the whole person according to his humanity but predicated of both natures: Matthew 27:46 (here is the cry from Jesus, "Eli, Eli, lema sabachthani?" that is, "My God, my God, why have you forsaken me?" Because God cannot leave or abandon God, in this cry Jesus is temporarily abandoned according to his humanity. As the God-man, Jesus dies with respect to his humanity, for the divine nature cannot die); John 5:27.

Thus, a biblical theology of the person and natures of Christ must rest on a careful reading of the Scriptures coupled with a recognition of our limited understanding.

Christ's Limited Knowledge. In Mark 13:32 (cf. Matt. 24:36) Jesus says, "But concerning that day or that hour, no one knows, not even the angels in heaven, nor the Son, but only the Father." However, Jesus spoke these words during the time of his incarnation, and this limit to his knowledge pertained only to his true human nature. Even during his incarnation he remained omniscient as far as his divine nature was concerned.

Erroneous Views on the Person of Christ

Erroneous concepts of Jesus arise out of a careless and undiscerning reading of the Bible, which is compounded by man's fallen nature and the enmity of

17 Walvoord, *Jesus Christ Our Lord*, 117–18.

unbelievers. This has led to many errant ideas concerning the person of Christ. In the early church, many such errors arose and challenged the Christological orthodoxy of Bible-believers.

Ebionism. This heresy insisted on the humanity of Christ to the exclusion of his deity. It denied the preexistence of Christ—a view influenced by first-century Jewish teachings. This heresy died out by the fifth century.

Gnosticism. This heresy began as a movement with roots in Greek (Platonic) philosophy (and other mystical elements) preceding the New Testament church. However, by the second century Gnosticism gradually assimilated Christian elements. Gnosticism's main tenet echoed Plato's concept of matter being evil and spirit being good. Proponents believed that a series of emanations had come from "God" and each one became progressively more matter and less spirit—thus more evil and less good. One of these, the Demiurge, was responsible for the evil material world, and the Gnostics equated this Demiurge with Yahweh of the Old Testament. The Demiurge was depicted by the Gnostics as antagonistic to the spiritual "Christ." This "Christ" did not have a real human body (see "Docetism," below). Salvation for Gnostics consisted of a special *gnosis* (or knowledge) that only the elite possessed.

Adoptionism/Modalism. Some in the early church accepted a view holding that God adopted (thus the term *Adoptionism*) the man Jesus as his son at some point following his birth—either at his baptism or his resurrection. The Adoptionists are one of the Monarchianist groups, those who denied the Trinity and referred to one God as one ruler or monarch. Monarchianism emphasized the oneness of God—a Unitarian view. They believed God merely appeared in three different modes—Father, Son, Spirit. An early Modalist was Sabellius (hence Sabellianism), who was excommunicated in AD 217.

Docetism. The Docetists derive their name from the Greek term *dokeō*, meaning "seem" or "appear." They held to the deity of Christ while rejecting his true humanity. Because they held that material existence is inherently evil (Platonism), they believed that Jesus had no body and thus the Son of God appeared on earth as an illusion, a kind of theophany.

Arianism. The Arian heresy arose out of the teachings of Arius (AD 250–336), an elder in the church at Alexandria, Egypt. It was the most serious heresy of the early church. Arians viewed Christ as merely a created being and held that Christ was not of the *same* substance as God but of a *similar* substance.

The Councils of Nicaea (AD 325) and Constantinople (AD 381) responded to this heresy. The debate centered on the presence or absence of an *iota* ("i") in a single Greek word: *homoiousia* ("similar substance") or *homoousia* ("same substance"). The difference boiled down to whether or not Christ was genuinely God, and the councils declared its conviction from Scripture that Christ was truly and fully both God and man. Athanasius (AD 295–373), who later became bishop of Alexandria, rose in defense of the biblical testimony concerning the true deity of Jesus Christ. The councils resulted in the affirmation that Christ was "God of God, Light of Light, very God of very God, begotten, not made, being of one substance with the Father."

Apollinarianism. The Apollinarians—named for Apollinaris (ca. AD 315–ca. 392), bishop of Laodicea—denied Christ's full humanity, agreeing that he had a human body but denying that he possessed a human soul.

The Council of Constantinople condemned Apollinarian teachings as heretical in AD 381, and the Council of Chalcedon did likewise in AD 451.

Nestorianism. Nestorius of Constantinople (ca. AD 381–ca. 451) attributed a dual personality to Christ—two persons and two natures, rather than one person and two natures.

Eutychianism. Another controversy was called Monophysitism ("one nature") or Eutychianism, referring to its originator, Eutyches of Constantinople (ca. AD 378–ca. 454). Eutyches held that the deity and humanity of Christ were not distinguished—the two were fused together into a third nature that ultimately could not be confessed to be either God or man. A variation of Eutychianism that asserted that Christ had only one will became known as Monotheletism. The Council of Chalcedon condemned Eutychianism in AD 451, and the Third Council of Constantinople condemned Monotheletism in AD 680.

CHRIST'S LIFE

Baptism[18]

When John the Baptist baptized Jesus (Mark 1:1–10; John 1:19–31; Acts 19:4) the purpose was to reveal the personal presence of the Messiah in fulfillment of the Old Testament prophecies. John the Baptist identified the Messiah as "the Lamb of God, who takes away the sin of the world" (John 1:29).

Jesus explained the purpose of his baptism: "It is fitting for us to fulfill all righteousness" (Matt. 3:15). By submitting to John's baptism, Christ obeyed the will of God and identified himself with sinners. He would ultimately bear their sins so that his perfect righteousness might be credited to them (2 Cor. 5:21). This

18 Adapted from John MacArthur, ed., *The MacArthur Study Bible: English Standard Version* (Wheaton, IL: Crossway, 2010), 1364. Used by permission of Thomas Nelson/HarperCollins Christian Publishing.

act of obedience in baptism was a necessary part of the righteous life he lived that would be imputed to believers. It marked his identification with those whose sins he would bear (Isa. 53:11; 1 Pet. 3:18) and it publicly affirmed his messiahship by testimony directly from heaven (Matt. 3:17; cf. Ps. 2:7 and Isa. 42:1).[19]

Temptation

After John baptized Jesus (Matt. 3:13–17), the Holy Spirit led Jesus into the wilderness, to be tempted by Satan (Matt. 4:1–11). The Spirit's involvement in leading Jesus into the temptation demonstrates that this testing accorded with God's sovereign purpose.

Satan's temptations attacked Jesus according to his humanity, since God himself (and therefore Jesus according to his divine nature) "cannot be tempted with evil" (James 1:13). God never acts even as the agent tempting anyone to evil. However, according to his sovereign design, he does ordain that Satan, demons, or other human agents tempt us, and God uses those temptations for his own wise and holy purposes (Job 1–2; Luke 22:31–32; 2 Cor. 12:7–10). In accord with the categories listed in 1 John 2:16, Satan tempted Jesus with hunger as one of "the desires of the flesh" (Matt. 4:2–3; 1 John 2:16), with putting God to the test as an exhibition of "the pride of life" (Matt. 4:5–6; 1 John 2:16), and with the possession of the kingdoms of the world and all their glory to fulfill "the desires of the eyes" (Matt. 4:8–9; 1 John 2:16). Through this specific time of testing as throughout his earthly life, Jesus was tempted "in every respect . . . as we are, yet without sin" (Heb. 4:15).

The Bible is explicit that Jesus *did* not sin (1 John 3:5), but *could* he have sinned, whether in thought or deed? This is to raise the question of the peccability or impeccability of Christ. Those who argue for the peccability of Christ—that he could have sinned even though he did not—focus on two main points. First, they say, since even unfallen humans are capable of sinning (cf. Gen. 3:1–6), and since in his incarnation Jesus assumed a full and true human nature, he also must have been capable of sinning. To argue otherwise, they claim, is to compromise the genuine humanity of Christ. Second, peccability advocates argue that the inability to sin would undermine the genuineness of Christ's temptations; the ability to be tempted implies the ability to sin. Thus, to argue that Jesus was unable to sin is to compromise the clear biblical teaching that he was in every respect tempted as we are (Heb. 4:15).

The Scriptures, however, testify that Christ was not able to sin. In the first place, in John 14:30, Jesus states that the ruler of this world (Satan, cf. Eph 2:2; 1 John 5:19) "[had] nothing in [him]" (NASB). That is to say, there was nothing

19 For more on the significance of Jesus's baptism, see the section in chap. 7 titled, "The Obedience of Christ" (p. 268).

in Jesus but perfect purity and eager readiness to do the Father's will (John 4:34). For Jesus to have been able to sin, Satan would have had to "have" something "in" Christ—a wrong desire or willingness to sin—to exploit with external inducements, but there was no such thing. Second, in John 5:19, Jesus says, "Truly, truly, I say to you, the Son can do nothing of his own accord, but only what he sees the Father doing." Since it is beyond dispute that the Father could never sin, for Jesus to say he *can do nothing* but what he sees the Father doing is to explicitly affirm his own inability to sin.

This does not undermine Jesus's genuine humanity, as advocates of peccability claim. Though Adam and Eve were able to sin before the fall, unlike Jesus their humanity was not hypostatically united to the divine nature. But because Jesus was *both* fully and truly human *and* fully and truly divine, and because God cannot sin (James 1:13), Jesus could not have sinned. To argue otherwise is to suggest that, for the sake of being truly human, Jesus was able not to be truly God. This is to circumscribe Jesus's deity by his humanity and to deny the fundamental principle of the hypostatic union. The ability to sin is not absolutely *essential* to humanity; otherwise, we would cease to be human in our glorified state, when we will not be able to sin.

Nor does the impeccability view undermine the genuineness of Christ's temptations. The peccability view conceives of temptation as if the one tempted must always be attracted to or allured by the sin in question. But to be attracted to or allured by sin is itself sinful; a desire for an illicit end is itself an illicit desire (cf. Matt. 5:27–28; Col. 3:5). Because Jesus was tempted in every respect as we are, yet *without* sin (Heb. 4:15), Jesus's temptations never included the internal pull to disobedience that so often characterizes our temptations (cf. James 1:14), for Jesus regarded it as his *food*—his nourishment and sustenance—to do the Father's will (John 4:34). Rather than enticements from within, Jesus's temptations were inducements to sin from without (cf. Matt. 4:1–11). The perfect purity of his thinking, affections, and desires meant that Jesus could not but have emerged victorious over his temptations. Scripture often speaks of our trials as refining our faith by fire, as gold is refined (cf. 1 Pet. 1:7). If the gold is genuine, however, there is no possibility that it could be consumed by the fire of testing. The test proves the purity of the gold, and the gold's inability to fail the test does not make the fire any less genuine. In the same way, nor does Jesus's impeccability render his temptations any less genuine. In fact, since he never yielded to the temptations, he endured their full force. Thus, temptation for Jesus was more real and more powerful than for any other human being.

The account of Jesus's temptation raises the matter of Jesus's relationship to and dependence on the Holy Spirit. Several Old Testament prophecies foretold that the Messiah would depend on the Holy Spirit (see Isa. 11:2–3; 42:1; 61:1–3).

Christ's dependence on the Holy Spirit can be witnessed in his conception (Matt. 1:20), his baptism (Matt. 3:16–17), and his temptation in the wilderness (Matt. 4:1). Christ relied on the Spirit for power in his ministry (Luke 4:14) and especially in his preaching (Luke 4:17–22, fulfilling Isa. 61:1–2; Matt. 12:15–21, fulfilling Isa. 42:1–3). Christ "through the Holy Spirit" gave commandments to his chosen apostles (Acts 1:2), and he "cast out demons by the Spirit of God" (Matt. 12:28 NASB). When Jesus healed, he did so, according to his human nature, by the power of the Spirit (Acts 10:38). The Holy Spirit enabled Jesus to endure the hours of trial before and during the crucifixion—the inner agonies of Gethsemane, the humiliation before Pilate and Herod, the scourging and crown of thorns, the road to Golgotha, and the crucifixion. Jesus offered himself as a sacrifice on the cross through the Spirit (cf. Heb. 9:14). In Christ's resurrection from the dead, all three persons of the Godhead played a role (cf. Rom. 8:11; cf. John 10:17–18; see also John 2:19–22). From conception through resurrection, and, by inference, even through glorification, Jesus was sustained by the Holy Spirit according to his human nature.

Transfiguration

The event known as the transfiguration came at a turning point in Jesus's ministry and gave the disciples assurance that Christ was the Messiah. Jesus had predicted his coming death (Matt. 16:21), and this preview of glory was meant to reassure the disciples that the kingdom he promised would be established. He introduced that truth himself in Matthew 16:28: "Truly, I say to you, there are some standing here who will not taste death until they see the Son of Man coming in his kingdom." Peter later spoke of the transfiguration in similar terms (cf. 2 Pet. 1:16–18).

The brilliant light of Christ's countenance during the transfiguration ("his face shone like the sun, and his clothes became white as light," Matt. 17:2) portended the glory of "the Son of Man coming on the clouds of heaven with power and great glory" (Matt. 24:30). The apostle John described a similar vision of Christ's glory in Revelation 1:14–16 (see also Rev. 19:11–16).

The apostle Paul called Jesus "the Lord of glory" (1 Cor. 2:8; cf. Heb. 1:1–3; 2 Cor. 4:3–6). The transfiguration event most powerfully and dramatically demonstrated that Jesus was the true glory of God. Though Christ's first coming was in humility, the second will be in glory, robed in light.

CHRIST'S TEACHING

Jesus's teachings reveal the fact that he was a master teacher and storyteller who possessed knowledge and wisdom beyond any other person. In every setting and with every hearer, Jesus displayed a mastery of communication.

His Parables

There is no better example of Jesus as a master teacher than his teaching in parables. A parable consists of what could be a long analogy but is cast in the form of an ingeniously simple and often brief story taken from everyday life. Jesus excelled in the use of parables. His parables "epitomize the plain, powerful profundity of His message and His teaching style."[20] However, some interpreters misunderstand and misrepresent the method and meaning of Jesus's parables.

First, Jesus did not speak in parables solely to make his teaching accessible to the multitudes.[21] Early in his ministry, Jesus employed many graphic analogies (see Matt. 5:13–16) whose meaning was fairly clear in the context of his teaching. However, parables required *more explanation* (see Matt. 13:36), and Jesus employed them *to obscure* the truth from unbelievers as a judgment while at the same time making it clearer to his disciples (Matt. 13:11–12). At one point in his Galilean ministry, Jesus began speaking to the multitudes *only* in parables (Matt. 13:34). This veiling of the truth acted as both judgment and mercy. It was judgment because it kept them in the darkness that they loved (see John 3:19), but it was mercy because they had already rejected the light, so any exposure to more truth would only have increased their eternal condemnation.

Second, Jesus did not use parables because they were a better method of teaching than didactic discourses or sermonic exhortation. Actually, the four Gospels record more discourses (at least forty-five[22]) than parables (thirty-nine).

Jesus's parables are not allegorical stories with hidden, complex meanings. Jesus's parables have one main, uncomplicated point, and the details of the parable do not have some symbolic or spiritual meaning. When a parable's symbolism tends to be more complex, Jesus usually explains the symbolism for his hearers, so that they will not miss his main point.[23]

As a master teacher, Jesus handled tough questions from critics but showed understanding for his students. He communicated well with all classes and age groups. And his teaching was always grounded in divine revelation.

CHRIST'S MIRACLES

Jesus proved his deity and his role as Messiah by means of many miracles (Matt. 11:4–5). Prophets and apostles also wrought miracles, but by a power outside themselves (Ex. 14:13; Josh. 3:5; Acts 3:12). Jesus's miracles came

20 John MacArthur, *Parables: The Mysteries of God's Kingdom Revealed through the Stories Jesus Told* (Nashville: Thomas Nelson, 2015), xiii.

21 This paragraph is adapted from MacArthur, *MacArthur Study Bible: English Standard Version*, 1382. Used by permission of Thomas Nelson/HarperCollins Christian Publishing.

22 See the chart in W. Graham Scroggie, *A Guide to the Gospels* (Old Tappan, NJ: Revell, n.d.), 556–57.

23 MacArthur, *Parables*, chaps. 1–3.

about through his inherent divine power (Matt. 4:23–24; John 10:25, 37–38; 15:24; 20:30–31).

Jesus's miracles sometimes resulted in belief (John 2:11; 9:30–33; 11:45) or created a willingness in his hearers to listen to his teachings (Mark 12:37; Luke 5:15). However, most people rejected Jesus despite his miracles. Miracles do not necessarily convince people to believe in the Lord or in his gospel message (Matt. 13:58; Luke 16:31; John 2:23–25; 12:37; 15:24).

Jesus Christ's miracles demonstrate his deity, his supernatural origin, his power as Creator, and his authority as the sovereign Lord of all creation. His ministry confronted the anti-supernatural worldview of his day and equally confronts the present worldview committed to the uniformitarian naturalism of secular scientists. As has been said, "It is impossible to remove the supernatural elements from Jesus's life and work, as anti-supernaturalist critics have attempted to do. The historical Jesus of Nazareth and the divine Christ are inseparably linked, for they are one and the same person. Jesus was and is the God-man."[24]

HIS ARREST AND TRIALS

What significance do Jesus's arrest and trials have for the biblical doctrine of Christ? The biblical accounts of the arrest and trials of Jesus are not just historical data but are explicit proof of his messiahship.

Jesus's Arrest

The prophetic depiction of the Messiah being accused and led away to judgment implied something like an arrest (Isa. 53:8), and he himself announced his arrest beforehand (Matt. 17:22; 20:18). The arrest reveals the perfect plan of God and the willing obedience of Christ to that plan, no matter the consequences for him personally (Matt. 26:39; Acts 2:23).

Prior to his trials, the Jewish leaders had already hatched a conspiracy to "arrest Jesus by stealth and kill him" (Matt. 26:4). The leaders were so convinced that Jesus was a false prophet and a blasphemer that they willingly accepted responsibility for his death (Matt. 27:25).

But the arrest, scourging, and death of Jesus is to be explained by more than the hatred of evil men. The Jewish leaders, Herod, and Pontius Pilate had all conspired to murder Jesus (Matt. 27:2, 26; Luke 23:12; cf. Acts 4:27) but this was all by the "predetermined plan and foreknowledge of God" (Acts 2:23 NASB). The "hands of godless men . . . put him to death" (Acts 2:23 NASB) but this was "to do whatever [God's] hand and [God's] plan had predestined to take place" (Acts 4:28). As Isaiah prophesied, "Yet it was the will of the Lord to crush him" (Isa. 53:10). Indeed, all was according to the pre-creation plan of the omniscient God (cf. 1 Pet. 1:18–21).

24 John MacArthur, *John 1–11*, MNTC (Chicago: Moody Press, 2006), 76.

At the time of his arrest, Jesus provided additional external evidence of his deity. When his pursuers told him they were seeking "Jesus of Nazareth" (John 18:3–5), he identified himself, saying, "I am he." Instantly, "they drew back and fell to the ground" (John 18:5–6). The power of his spoken word and of his presence caused the soldiers and officers to fall to the ground; even Judas fell. "He" is not in the Greek in the declaration "I am he." Jesus's declaration was simply "I am," the title of deity revealed in Exodus 3:14. This is the final such self-declaration spoken by Jesus during his earthly ministry (see "The 'I Am' Statements," below, for a list of all these declarations in the Gospel of John; similar statements occur only three times in the other Gospels: Matt. 22:32; Mark 6:50; 14:62).

The "I Am" Statements[25]

Twenty-three times we find our Lord's meaningful "I am" (egō eimi) in the Greek text of this Gospel (John 4:26; 6:20, 35, 41, 48, 51; 8:12, 18, 24, 28, 58; 10:7, 9, 11, 14; 11:25; 13:19; 14:6; 15:1, 5; 18:5, 6, 8). In several of these, he joins his "I am" with seven tremendous metaphors that are expressive of his saving relationship toward the world:

"I am the bread of life" (John 6:35, 48, 51).
"I am the light of the world" (John 8:12).
"I am the door of the sheep" (John 10:7, 9).
"I am the good shepherd" (John 10:11, 14).
"I am the resurrection and the life" (John 11:25).
"I am the way, the truth, and the life" (John 14:6).
"I am the true vine" (John 15:1, 5).

There were additional proofs of Christ's deity during his arrest. When Peter drew his sword and sliced off the ear of Malchus, the servant of the high priest (John 18:10), Jesus miraculously reattached it (Luke 22:51). Jesus also said he could command "more than twelve legions of angels" to come to his aid (Matt. 26:53–54).

God himself had foreordained the very minutest details of how Jesus would die (Acts 2:23; 4:27–28). Therefore, dying was Christ's consummate act of submission to the Father's will. In all this, Jesus himself was in absolute control (see John 10:17–18). These events at his arrest display his divine sovereignty and purposeful fulfillment of the Old Testament prophecies concerning him.

25 Reproduced from MacArthur, *MacArthur Study Bible: English Standard Version*, 1550. Used by permission of Thomas Nelson/HarperCollins Christian Publishing.

Jesus's Trials

The Sanhedrin. As is clear in the Gospel accounts, Jesus's trials consisted of a religious trial by the Sanhedrin and a civil trial by the secular rulers, Pilate and Herod (cf. Luke chapters 22 and 23).[26] The Sanhedrin had been patterned after the council of elders in Numbers 11:16. However, by Jesus's time, the Sanhedrin had become a corrupt and politically motivated body, more an extension of Roman power than a court of justice. It was dominated by the Sadducees, who openly denied the supernatural elements of the Old Testament. They were eager to do the bidding of Rome in order to keep their power. Sheer political expediency, and a desire to placate the Romans, was their motive for conspiring to carry out the arrest and crucifixion of Christ (see John 11:47–53).

Principles of Justice. However, in spite of the corruption, certain principles were established to ensure that trials were both fair and merciful. In capital cases: (1) There had to be two credible witnesses against the accused, and the accused had the right to present counterevidence; false accusers were severely sanctioned (cf. Deut. 19:16–19). (2) The council had to observe a full day of fasting between the passing of sentence and the execution of the criminal. That requirement prevented hasty trials and executions. (3) To maintain fairness, the council could try cases only where an outside party—not a member of the council—had brought the charges. (4) The council had to presume the accused to be innocent until they reached an official guilty verdict. (5) Criminal trials were not to be convened at night, and if a trial was already underway when nighttime fell, court was to be recessed until the following day.

Nearly all these regulations were openly flouted in the trial of Christ. His trial was unjust and illegal by virtually every principle of jurisprudence known at the time. The trial the Sanhedrin imposed on him was one extended act of deliberate injustice, the greatest miscarriage of justice in the history of the world.

The Religious Trials. Jesus was taken first to Annas, the father-in-law of Caiaphas (and *de facto* high priest), before whom he would face his first legal trial (John 18:12–14). The trial under Annas consisted of a preliminary examination (John 18:12–14, 19–23). When Annas questioned Jesus about his teaching, Jesus directed him to those who had heard him, whereupon he was struck by one of the officers. When Jesus indicated that everyone knew he was right about the need for witnesses, no one responded, because his Jewish opponents had no intention

26 Cf. John MacArthur, *One Perfect Life: The Complete Story of the Lord Jesus* (Nashville: Thomas Nelson, 2012), 437*na*. The following description of the Great Sanhedrin and its trial system is adapted from John MacArthur, *The Murder of Jesus: A Study of How Jesus Died* (Nashville: Thomas Nelson, 2004), 102–5. Used by permission of Thomas Nelson/HarperCollins Christian Publishing.

of providing a fair trial (John 11:47–57). Annas remanded him over to Caiaphas and the Sanhedrin (John 18:24).

A session before the Sanhedrin then followed, with Caiaphas chairing the formal council (Matt. 26:57–27:2). Although they had sought out many false witnesses, those witnesses failed to agree in their accusations and Jesus maintained his silence. He saw no need for defense against such a weak showing. Finally, Caiaphas asked him to declare whether he was indeed "the Christ, the Son of God" (Matt. 26:63). Jesus affirmed the identification, appealing to Psalm 110:1 and Daniel 7:13. With that, Caiaphas tore his clothes and declared Jesus guilty of blasphemy, and the council called for his execution. Of course, Jesus spoke the truth concerning his deity. They began to abuse him, but Jesus never glibly used the powers of his deity, and he didn't use them now, to prevent his suffering and death.

The Civil Trials. The third trial took place before the Roman governor, Pontius Pilate, opening the civil phase of Jesus's trials (John 18:28–38). The accusation the Jewish authorities brought against Jesus in this civil court was not blasphemy (their verdict in the religious trial) but sedition. They deliberately lied by accusing Jesus of telling people not to pay taxes to Caesar (Luke 23:2; see 20:20–25) and of claiming himself to be king. Pilate focused on the accusation that he claimed he was "King of the Jews" (John 18:33). Jesus responded by saying that his kingdom was "not of this world" (John 18:36). His kingdom was not a part of this world, not established by human effort, and not part of the evil world system. For now, his kingdom presented no physical or political threat to either Israel or Rome.

Jesus did not deny that he was king but indicated a higher purpose for his coming: "to bear witness to the truth" (John 18:37). Further exchanges only mystified Pilate, but he had reached his conclusion: he found no guilt in Jesus worthy of death (John 18:38). The Jews renewed their accusations and their call for Jesus's death, but Jesus maintained his silence, to Pilate's amazement (Matt. 27:12–14). Jesus may have remained silent in fulfillment of prophecy (Isa. 42:1–2; 53:7) or because Pilate had declared him innocent (Luke 23:4; John 18:38)—or both. However, the ferocity of the people made Pilate afraid to exonerate Jesus. When he discovered Jesus was a Galilean, that gave him an excuse to send him to Herod (Luke 23:5–6).

Jesus's fourth trial continued in the political realm with his appearance before Herod Antipas (Luke 23:6–12).[27] Herod Antipas was a member of the Herodian dynasty. He had killed John the Baptist a year or two earlier (Matt. 14:1–12). No one was more curious or more eager than Herod to meet Jesus firsthand. But

27 The following description of Jesus's appearance before Herod Antipas is adapted from MacArthur, *Murder of Jesus*, 176–78. Used by permission of Thomas Nelson/HarperCollins Christian Publishing.

Jesus refused to satisfy Herod's cynical curiosity. In front of Herod he remained utterly and completely silent. Jesus knew of Herod's treatment of John the Baptist. Any words offered to such an evil heart would be wasted. Silence was the only appropriate response under such circumstances.

After a short time, Herod grew tired of questioning Jesus, and he and his soldiers "treated him with contempt and mocked him . . . [and] sent him back to Pilate" (Luke 23:11). Luke adds, "And Herod and Pilate became friends with each other that very day, for before this they had been at enmity with each other" (Luke 23:12). It was an unholy alliance, a friendship based on the one thing they had in common: their cowardly and contemptuous treatment of Christ—even though both Herod and Pilate had found Jesus innocent of any of the Jewish charges of sedition (Luke 23:13–16).

When Herod returned Jesus to Pilate for the fifth and final trial (Matt. 27:15–26; Mark 15:6–15; Luke 23:13–25; John 18:39–19:16), Pilate proceeded to seek a way to release Jesus by offering to make him the freed prisoner customarily released on the Passover, but the Jews would not allow it, calling instead for Barabbas to be released (Matt. 27:18–22). Washing his hands to symbolize his guiltlessness, Pilate announced that the Jews themselves were guilty of this innocent man's blood (Matt. 27:24). Pilate released Barabbas, had Jesus flogged, and delivered him over to the Roman executioners for crucifixion (Matt. 27:26).

Jesus's Execution[28]

Suffering Prior to Crucifixion. The Roman soldiers had no idea whom they were tormenting. They had their orders to scourge and crucify Jesus, but the cruel mockery they heaped on him revealed their own wickedness.

They stripped him of his garments, apart from the robe they fashioned for him. The robe was likely made from an old tunic—probably a garment that had been discarded by one of the soldiers. Matthew says that the robe was scarlet (Matt. 27:28), but Mark and John call it "purple" (Mark 15:17; John 19:2)—suggesting that it was a badly faded tunic—a mockery of royal colors.

To continue mocking Jesus's claim that he was a king, the soldiers fashioned a crown of thorns. These were no doubt the longest, sharpest thorns that could be found—some with two-inch barbed quills that would penetrate deep into his head as the crown was pressed hard on him. The reed in his hand to represent a scepter was a further attempt to lampoon his claim of royalty.

The soldiers mocked Jesus: "Hail, King of the Jews!" They spat on him. One soldier used the reed to strike him repeatedly on his head. The apostle John records that they also beat him with their hands (John 19:3). But Jesus "did not revile in

28 The following description of Jesus's suffering and crucifixion is adapted from MacArthur, *Murder of Jesus*, 190–206. Used by permission of Thomas Nelson/HarperCollins Christian Publishing.

return" (1 Pet. 2:23). Jesus knew these things were part of the Father's plan for him, so he suffered them all willingly and patiently. He endured the mocking, the flogging, the humiliation, and the shame (Isa. 50:6–7).

And then they "led him away to crucify him" (Matt. 27:31). Victims of crucifixion were forced to carry their own cross, but for someone in Jesus's severely weakened condition, this would have been virtually impossible. So "they found a man of Cyrene, Simon by name. They compelled this man to carry his cross" (Matt. 27:32).

Christ's last public message was given on the road to Calvary (see Luke 23:27–31). Part of the message was a reference to Hosea 10:8: "They shall say to the mountains, 'Cover us,' and to the hills, 'Fall on us.'" It was a dire warning of disaster to come.

In accord with the Law (Num. 15:35; cf. Heb. 13:12), Jesus's crucifixion took place outside the city, but in accord with Roman custom it was in a heavily trafficked location, carefully selected to make him a public spectacle.

Matthew writes, "they offered him wine to drink, mixed with gall, but when he tasted it, he would not drink it" (Matt. 27:34). Mark 15:23 says that the bitter substance was myrrh, which acts as a mild narcotic. It may have been offered for its numbing effect but, because he did not want his senses numbed, he spat it out. He had come to the cross to be a sin bearer, and he would feel the full effect of the sin he bore. The vinegar and gall fulfilled a messianic prophecy from Psalm 69:19–21.

Crucifixion. The intense shame of the crucifixion was accompanied by an equally intense physical pain, and yet even in that unparalleled suffering, Christ spoke forth words of truth and grace.

The prophecies concerning crucifixion. The prophecy of Genesis 3:15 mentioned that the "seed" of the woman would be wounded on the heel; this pointed to the cross. Psalm 22 describes the process of crucifixion hundreds of years before the Romans perfected the practice.

The method and effects of crucifixion. Psalm 22:16 has, "They have pierced my hands and feet" (cf. Luke 24:39–40; see the exchange with Thomas [John 20:25 and 27]). This is an exact prophecy and description of the manner of Christ's execution. Christ was nailed to the cross, rather than being lashed by leather thongs. This nailing was likely through the wrists and heels of the feet (again, Gen. 3:15)

After the victim was nailed in place, soldiers would elevate the top of the cross and slide the foot into a deep posthole. The cross would drop with a jarring blow into the bottom of the hole, causing a bone-wrenching pain throughout the body, as major joints were suddenly twisted out of their natural position, thus fulfilling Psalm 22, which reads, "I am poured out like water, and all my bones are out of joint" (Ps. 22:14).

Death normally came from slow suffocation. The victim's body would hang in such a way that the diaphragm was severely constricted. Once strength or feeling in the legs was gone, the victim would be unable to push up in order to breathe, and death would occur quickly. That is why the Romans sometimes broke the legs below the knees—to hasten the process (see John 19:31). For the members of the Sanhedrin, the fact that Jesus hung there dying so helplessly was proof that he was not who he claimed to be. They mocked him for his trust in God (Matt. 27:42–43). But in doing so their words were an almost verbatim fulfillment of the prophecy of Psalm 22:8.

As always, Jesus did not revile those who reviled him; his only words as he hung on the cross were a tender plea to God for mercy on their behalf (Luke 23:34).

Jesus's seven last sayings on the cross. As Christ hung on Calvary's cross, he spoke seven times. The last words uttered by a person before death have often held significance for their loved ones. Those from Christ's lips are unparalleled in their richness[29] and are weighted with deep theological significance that helps believers better understand his person, character, suffering, and redemptive work.

1. A plea for forgiveness: "Father, forgive them, for they know not what they do" (Luke 23:34).

Divine forgiveness consists of God forgoing his rightful retribution that sinners deserve for their sins committed against him. As the God-man, Christ's forgiveness comes from a sympathetic and compassionate human nature combined with divine power, righteousness, holiness, mercy, and grace through his deity (see Ex. 34:6–7).

2. A promise of salvation: "Truly, I say to you, today you will be with me in paradise" (Luke 23:43).

The second saying from the cross came as a response to the heartfelt request of one of the criminals crucified alongside Jesus, who said, "Jesus, remember me when you come into your kingdom" (Luke 23:39–42). Jesus knew that this man's words revealed a truly repentant heart, broken over his own sin and desiring the mercy and forgiveness of the Savior. The promise reveals Christ's deity in that only God can know the state of the heart and the ultimate destiny of any individual.

29 See MacArthur, *Murder of Jesus*, 209–24.

3. A provision for his mother: "Woman, behold, your son! . . . Behold, your mother!" (John 19:26–27).

One of the most poignant episodes occurring during Jesus's crucifixion finds Jesus addressing the mother who had given him his humanity (Isa. 49:1). Simeon's prophecy had come to its bitter fruition (see Luke 2:34–35). In Jesus's statement here, Mary's son gave all his attention to her and her need for care. To John, the disciple nearest to the heart of Jesus, the Savior committed the care of his most precious earthly relationship—his mother. In this, the perfect man demonstrated his fulfillment of the command to honor one's parents (Ex. 20:12; Eph. 6:2–3).

4. A petition to the Father: "My God, my God, why have you forsaken me?" (Matt. 27:46).

The significance of this cry from Jesus's lips is unfathomable. Herein lies the mystery of the hypostatic union (see "Humanity," p. 155). The presence of darkness (Matt. 27:45) symbolized both the loss of fellowship's light and the reality of abandonment. However, the Father and the Son were not separated in their being or in their essence through this experience. The unity of the Trinity remained intact.

The physical pains of crucifixion were nothing compared to the wrath of the Father poured out on Jesus. And now, in that period of darkness, in some incomprehensible way, the Father had abandoned him. "Though there was surely no interruption in the Father's love for Him *as a Son*, God nonetheless turned away from Him and forsook Him *as our Substitute*."[30]

The substitutionary aspect of Christ's death does not rest on his physical death alone. Christ had to bear the outpouring of God's unmitigated wrath against sin in order to satisfy justice completely. True substitutionary atonement therefore involved a painful sense of estrangement from the Father, expressed by Christ in his heartfelt petition: "My God, my God, why have you forsaken me?" Although it was temporary, the agony Christ experienced in absorbing the Father's wrath was the full equivalent of hell.[31]

This is the suffering that Jesus anticipated in the garden of Gethsemane when he prayed, "Let this cup pass from me" (Matt. 26:39). The "cup" refers to the greatest

30 MacArthur, *Murder of Jesus*, 221.

31 This is to be distinguished from the heretical doctrines of certain charismatic leaders who teach that Jesus actually became a sinner on the cross, or that he literally went to hell to undergo further punishment. Rather, as our substitute, Jesus bore the very punishment that was due to his people: the Father's wrath in all its fullness. While the wrath poured out on sinners in hell is eternal, Jesus, because of the dignity and worth of his person, could extinguish the infinite wrath of God in only three hours of suffering. In this sense, he bore the full weight of every curse and penalty our sins deserve.

of all suffering for the perfectly sinless God-man—the wrath of God poured out on him when he was made to be a sin offering. A cup is often the symbol of divine wrath against sin in the Old Testament (Isa. 51:17, 22; Jer. 25:15–17, 27–29; Lam. 4:21–22; Ezek. 23:31–34; Hab. 2:16). Christ would "bear the sins of many" (Heb. 9:28), and the fullness of divine wrath would fall on him (Isa. 53:10–11; 2 Cor. 5:21). This was the price of the sin he bore, which he paid in full. His cry of anguish in Matthew 27:46 reflected the extreme bitterness of the cup of wrath he was soon to receive.

5. A plea for relief: "I thirst" (John 19:28).

A single word in the Greek text, Jesus's fifth saying from the cross reveals the humanness of this experience—physical thirst arising out of intense exhaustion and physical agony. Yet this very concise saying reveals more than his humanity; it reveals his knowledge of the Scriptures and his determination to fulfill all that the Scriptures said about him. The psalmist had written, "For my thirst they gave me sour wine to drink" (Ps. 69:21). John made a point of saying that Jesus's statement was "to fulfill the Scripture" (John 19:28).

6. A proclamation of victory: "It is finished" (John 19:30).

The sixth saying of Jesus from the cross, like the previous saying, is but a single word in the Greek text: *Tetelestai!* His cry was triumphant and full of rich meaning since the Greek form implies that the state of completion would continue. Jesus did not refer to his earthly life as being over; he meant that he had completed the work the Father had given him to accomplish. In fact, the statement in Psalm 22:31 is, "He has done it"—also just one word in the Hebrew. Jesus celebrated the greatest triumph in the history of the universe, because his atoning work was finished. All the prophecies of the Scripture regarding the Messiah's redemptive work had been fulfilled, and God's justice was fully satisfied. Sin's ransom was paid in full; the wages of sin were settled forever for all of God's chosen throughout all history. All that remained for Christ to do was to die so that he might rise from the dead. Nothing can be added to the finished work of Christ for salvation.

7. A prayer of consummation: "Father, into your hands I commit my spirit!" (Luke 23:46).

Christ addressed his final statement from the cross to the Father, as he had in the first ("Father, forgive them, for they know not what they do," Luke 23:34) and the fourth ("My God, my God, why have you forsaken me?" Matt. 27:46). These three statements were prayers—the prayers of the Son of Man. In his humanity,

Jesus lived as a man of prayer and he died as a man of prayer (see Matt. 14:23; 19:13; 26:36–44; Heb. 5:7).

Christ died as no other man has ever died. In one sense, he was murdered by the hands of wicked men (Acts 2:23). In another sense, the Father sent him to the cross and put him to grief (Isa. 53:10). However, in still another sense, no one took Jesus's life. He himself gave it up willingly for those whom he loved selflessly and sacrificially (John 10:17–18).

HIS DEATH AND ATONEMENT[32]

How Jesus died is one thing; why he died is infinitely more important. The biblical fact is that his death was necessary, determined from before the foundation of the earth, and a necessity for the salvation of sinners.

Christ's Death

Christian theology focuses on the saving work of Jesus Christ in his substitutionary death and his resurrection from the dead. These two truths form the gospel's core message regarding salvation (see 1 Cor. 15:1–5; cf. Paul's defense Acts 26:22–23).

The apostle Peter, speaking of "the salvation of your souls," outlined the same two-part work of Christ with regard to the gospel (cf. 1 Pet. 1:9–12).

Christ's Atonement

Old Testament Revelation about Sacrifice.[33] Penal substitution means that Christ gave himself to suffer and die by bearing the full penalty for sin in the place of all the sinners whom God saves. God prepared mankind for the atoning, substitutionary sacrifice of Christ by providing early instruction about sacrifice. The Old Testament presents twelve basic principles regarding animal sacrifices:

1. Only believers should offer Old Testament sacrifices—believers who should be indoctrinated and obedient (i.e., exhibiting right teaching and right behavior). Leviticus 1:2–3 and 2:1 speak of Israelite believers, while Leviticus 17:8 and 22:18, 25 speak of foreign believers (cf. Num. 15:14–16; Isa. 56:6–8).
2. Old Testament sacrifices should be the outward demonstration of a vital faith. Without faith the sacrifices are worthless (Heb. 11:4; see 1 Sam. 15:22–23; Ps. 51:15–19; Isa. 1:11–15; Mic. 6:6–8).
3. Old Testament sacrifices do not save from sin or forgive sins. Levitical sacrifices include no provision for removing or doing away with any

32 A full treatment of the atonement of Christ is found in chap. 7.

33 This section is adapted from William D. Barrick, "Penal Substitution in the Old Testament," *MSJ* 20.2 (2009): 2, 6–8. Used by permission of *MSJ*.

individual's sinful nature. Animal sacrifices are insufficient to fully and finally atone for the sins of human beings—only a human life can fully atone for a human life (cf. Lev. 1:3 with Ps. 49:5–9; see Gal. 3:10–14; Heb. 10:1–18; 1 Pet. 1:18–19).

4. Old Testament sacrifices do not eliminate temporal punishment for sin, especially willful, defiant sin. Many sins require capital punishment—no animal sacrifice can avail for such sin (Lev. 24:10–23; Num. 15:30).
5. Old Testament sacrifices have as their chief object fellowship with God. They outwardly symbolize forgiveness for sins, which brought a measured reconciliation with the covenant-keeping God of Israel (Ex. 29:42–43; 30:36).
6. Old Testament sacrifices declare, emphasize, and magnify sin and its consequences (Rom. 3:19–20; 5:20; 7:5–11; Gal. 3:21–22).
7. Old Testament sacrifices declare, emphasize, and magnify God's holiness, righteousness, love, grace, mercy, and sovereignty (Ps. 119:62; Neh. 9:13; Matt. 23:23; Rom. 7:12). This expresses the dual function of sacrifice in the Old Testament. On the one hand, sin leads mankind *away from God*.[34] On the other hand, sacrifice, which by its bloodshed displays the terrible nature and consequences of sin, is theocentric, turning sinners' attention *to God*. Their sacrifices propitiate God's just wrath and reconcile them to God.
8. Old Testament sacrifices demonstrate that the Mosaic legislation offers the Old Testament believer no independent access to God (Heb. 9:8–10).
9. Old Testament sacrifices demonstrate that God's desire with regard to his people's offerings (giving) does not exceed their normal ability. The sacrificial objects (cattle, sheep, goats, doves; flour, oil, wine, and frankincense) are all immediately available to the individual Israelite.
10. Old Testament sacrifices emphasize the ministry of the priesthood (Lev. 1:9; 2:8; 4:20; 6:6; Hebrews 5–10; 1 Pet. 2:5).
11. Old Testament sacrifices involve the recognition of God's covenant with his people (Lev. 2:13; Ps. 50:5, 16).
12. God commands Old Testament sacrifices in part to sustain the priesthood. The covenant community provides for those who minister (Lev. 7:34–35; Neh. 13:5; Mal. 3:8–10).

In summary, by offering sacrifices, the Old Testament believer identifies himself outwardly with the covenant God and his covenant people. That outward demonstration ought to be the result of true faith. However, when that initiating faith is absent, the sacrifice is worthless—an empty gesture, devoid of any spiritual

34 Norman H. Snaith, *The Distinctive Ideas of the Old Testament* (New York: Schocken, 1964), 60.

value (i.e., a false confession). God hates false sacrifice and cannot accept it as true worship (see 1 Sam. 15:22; Ps. 50:7–15; Isa. 1:13–15).

With these principles in mind, the reader can consider how the Old Testament deals with penal substitutionary sacrifices. The ram provided by the "angel [messenger] of the LORD" as a substitute for Isaac in Genesis 22:1–14 illustrates the giving of a life as a substitute. Isaac's own death "was enacted through a substitute, an animal whose literal death provided full satisfaction to God's demands."[35]

Old Testament Revelation about Christ's Substitutionary Sacrifice.[36] To understand the relationship of the Old Testament sacrificial system to the person of the Messiah, several key texts must be examined more closely. The most significant of these texts are Exodus 12 (the Passover festival), Leviticus 16 (the Day of Atonement), and, perhaps most important of all, Isaiah 52:13–53:12.

Exodus 12: The Passover. God instituted the Passover observance, in which the lamb of the Passover served as a substitutionary sacrifice for the Israelites' firstborn sons. In Exodus 12:3, the Lord instructs Moses concerning the sacrifice of the Passover lamb: "Every man shall take a lamb according to their fathers' houses, a lamb for a household." The phrase "for a household" might imply substitution. In Exodus 12:12, the Lord says that he will execute judgment as he passes through the land of Egypt. Israelites who follow the instructions and apply the blood of the slaughtered lamb to the doorposts of their houses will escape that judgment (Ex. 12:13, 23, 27); the obedient Israelites do indeed escape death (v. 30).

In the Passover sacrifice, the Lord graciously spares guilty Israelites by means of the sacrificial blood of animals and preserves his own holiness by fulfilling his promises to deliver his people out of Egypt (Ex. 12:12–13; see Lev. 22:32–33). "The obvious symbolism is that a death has taken place, and this death substitutes for the death of the firstborn."[37] The New Testament confirms the substitutionary nature of the Passover sacrifice. In 1 Corinthians 5:7, Paul, at minimum, draws an analogy between the substitutionary nature of the Passover lamb and Christ's sacrificial death on the cross. Thus, it is no surprise to see that Jesus was crucified during Passover (Matt. 26:2).

Leviticus 16: The Day of Atonement. Of all the sacrifices and festivals, the Day of Atonement exceeds all others in its significance to Israel's relationship to Yahweh. The institution of this festival comes soon after God's judgment on the

35 Eugene Merrill, *Everlasting Dominion: A Theology of the Old Testament* (Nashville: Broadman, 2006), 236.

36 This section is adapted from Barrick, "Penal Substitution in the Old Testament," 8–21. Used by permission of *MSJ.*

37 Leon Morris, *The Apostolic Preaching of the Cross*, 3rd ed. (Grand Rapids, MI: Eerdmans, 1965), 117.

priests Nadab and Abihu (Lev. 10:1–20). Emphasis thus falls on the necessity of atonement even for the priests' sins. If the priests are defiled, they cannot mediate between the people and God. Without mediators, sinful Israelites cannot approach God's presence, and God's presence cannot continue to reside in their midst.

The "scapegoat" (Lev. 16:8–10) symbolizes the removal of sin from the presence of God's glory in the midst of his people (see Ps. 103:12; Mic. 7:19). On the Day of Atonement, both the scapegoat and the other goat sufficed as a sin offering (Lev. 16:5). Some interpreters see an allusion to the scapegoat in Isaiah 53:6 and Hebrews 13:12.[38]

The description of laying hands on the head of the goat (Lev. 16:21–22) pictures the legal transfer of sins from Israel to the living goat. It serves as their substitute—condemned to die in the wilderness, isolated from Israel. The scapegoat carries away on it "all [the] iniquities" of the Israelites (16:22). In addition, Leviticus 16:24, 29–34 indicates that the entire ritual provides atonement for the sins of the priests as well as the people. The Day of Atonement ritual displays the penal aspect of substitution. The Hebrew word for "ransom" (*koper*) represents the concept of "substitute" because it depicts the means by which evil or guilt is transferred and thereby eliminated. The use of the term *koper* as "ransom" relates explicitly to both substitution and penalty.

The Day of Atonement stands as the central observance of the sacrificial system in the book of Leviticus. The Day of Atonement provides a symbol of the real atonement by the Lord Jesus Christ (Hebrews 8–10). The chief point of Hebrews (see Heb. 8:1) is in direct contrast to the chief point of the Mosaic law (see Heb. 9:8).

Isaiah 52:13–53:12: The suffering servant's sacrifice. This is truly the first Gospel, as it reveals, seven hundred years before his coming, the life and work of the one true and perfect Sacrifice who actually took away sin. Isaiah first describes the sufferings of the servant of Yahweh, whose griefs and sorrows are not his own. That fact identifies the servant's sufferings as substitutionary: "Surely he has borne our griefs and carried our sorrows" (Isa. 53:4). The substitutionary imagery of Isaiah 53:6—"The Lord has laid on him the iniquity of us all"—is drawn straight from Leviticus 16. The vicarious elements in Christ's sufferings in his death relate quite closely to the substitutionary elements in Isaiah 52:13–53:12. Second, the language of Isaiah 53 clearly includes the penal aspect (see 53:5, "pierced . . . crushed . . . chastisement . . . wounds"). Third, key New Testament references include an apparent echo of Isaiah 53, such as in Matthew 26:28: "For this is my blood of the

38 E.g., Mark F. Rooker, *Leviticus*, New American Commentary 3A (Nashville: Broadman, 2000), 221, 226.

covenant, which is poured out for many for the forgiveness of sins" (see also Rom. 8:3; Gal. 1:4; Heb. 5:3; 10:8, 18, 26; 13:11; 1 Pet. 3:18; 1 John 2:2; 4:10).

The servant of Yahweh in Isaiah voluntarily bore the penalty for the iniquities of "many." His sacrificial death did not occur by some sort of abuse or forced action. Rather, he purposefully decided, accepted, and submitted to his suffering. Isaiah 53:10 ("when his soul makes an offering for guilt") and 53:12 ("poured out his soul to death") make that same point regarding the servant's voluntary sacrifice.

Indeed, Yahweh's servant meets all the requirements for being a substitutionary sacrifice: (1) identification with condemned sinners ("for the transgression of my people," Isa. 53:8), (2) being blameless and without any stain or spot to mar his sacrifice ("no violence . . . no deceit," 53:9; "the righteous one," 53:11), and (3) being acceptable to Yahweh ("it was the will of the LORD to crush him," 53:10).

The New Testament writers rightly understood the plain intent of Isaiah, finding every reason to take the text as directly messianic. The parallels between the servant passage in Isaiah and Mark 10:43–45 are examples: The suffering servant of Yahweh (Isa. 52:13) is the "slave of all" (Mark 10:44; cf. Isa. 53:6, "of us all"), who is "great" (Mark 10:43) because he is "high and lifted up, and shall be exalted" (Isa. 52:13). As "slave," he gave himself (lit., "his soul") as a guilt offering (Isa. 53:10)—the direct equivalent of "to give his life [lit., soul] as a ransom" (Mark 10:45). The servant's guilt offering/ransom went above and beyond the penalty of death to cover intentional as well as unintentional sin in the place of "many" (Mark 10:45; Isa. 52:14–15; 53:12).

The atoning work of Christ accomplished salvation for the elect. Jesus Christ is Savior—"there is salvation in no one else, for there is no other name under heaven given among men by which we must be saved" (Acts 4:12; see 2 Tim. 1:10; Titus 2:13). Christ's blood cleanses from sin (Heb. 13:12; 1 John 1:7). He is the Mediator of the new covenant (Heb. 12:24). As Savior, Christ gives life to believers in the present (2 Cor. 4:10; 2 Tim. 1:1) and is himself the pattern for the future resurrection of believers (2 Cor. 4:14; 1 Thess. 4:14). Christ, by his atoning work, is the Shepherd who makes it possible for believers to do good works (Heb. 13:20–21). He is the One in whom the church is placed and is blessed (Eph. 2:13).

HIS RESURRECTION AND ASCENSION

Without the resurrection of Christ, his sacrificial death fails to provide the ground for salvation from sin (1 Cor. 15:13–19). Therefore, no consideration of the biblical teaching regarding the work of Christ can end with his atoning death.

Old Testament Revelation about Christ's Resurrection

Since both Jesus and the New Testament writers declare that the significant facts concerning Christ had already been revealed through the prophets of the Old

Testament (Luke 24:25–27, 44–47; Acts 2:25–32; 1 Cor. 15:3–4), it is important to consider the textual evidence supporting their claim.

Several Old Testament references to the Messiah's resurrection appear in Job and the Psalter (see Job 19:25–27). Paul cites Psalm 16:10 and affirms that Christ's resurrection was prerequisite to his someday occupying David's throne on earth (Acts 13:34–37).

In Acts 2:30–35, Peter cites Psalm 16:10 between a citation from 2 Samuel 7 (the Davidic covenant) and Psalm 110, a key Messianic psalm. This indicates that all three texts should be considered Messianic and that the Resurrection of the Messiah should have been expected.

Thus, the very fact that the Messiah takes his seat at the right hand of the Father proves that he has risen from the dead. His exaltation (equivalent to his glory) assumes that he is no longer in the grave. Since David is not sitting at the right hand of the Father, it is obvious to Peter that David was speaking not of himself but of his future descendant, the greater Son of David. Jesus already used Psalm 110:1 to reveal to the Pharisees that he was indeed the Lord (Matt. 22:41–46), so Peter is merely passing on what Jesus taught.

New Testament History of Christ's Resurrection

Jesus himself announced beforehand that he would rise from the dead (see Matt. 17:9; Luke 18:31–33; John 2:19–22), and indeed, all four Gospel writers are unanimous in recording that Jesus rose from the dead on the first day of the week (Matt. 28:1–10; Mark 16:1–11; Luke 24:1–12; John 20:1–10).

New Testament Doctrine of Christ's Resurrection

When Jesus rose from the dead, he experienced a bodily resurrection entailing his full humanity. His resurrection body allowed him to digest food (Luke 24:41–43; see Acts 10:41); other human beings who were still in their mortal flesh could touch Jesus's body (Matt. 28:9; see Luke 24:38–40; John 20:17); and the wounds of Jesus's crucifixion remained present and visible in his resurrected body, as witnessed by Thomas (John 20:25–29). Some of the vast and glorious results Christ's resurrection achieved include:

1. The fulfillment of Old Testament prophecies (Old Testament Revelation about Christ's Resurrection," see above).
2. The fulfillment of Jesus's own predictions ("New Testament History of Christ's Resurrection," see above).
3. Confirmation of the Son's deity (Rom. 1:4).
4. The perfection of Jesus's obedience to his Father's will (John 10:17–18).
5. Proof that the Father accepted the atoning work of Christ in his sacrificial death on the cross (Rom. 4:25).
6. Securing regeneration for the elect (1 Pet. 1:3).

7. Assurance that believers will not perish due to their sins (1 Cor. 15:17–18).
8. Securing the justification of believers and assurance that they will never be condemned by God (Rom. 8:1–11, 31–34).
9. Opening the way for Christ to send the Holy Spirit to indwell believers and form them into the church, the body of Christ (John 16:7).
10. Declaration of Christ as Head of the church and ruler of creation (Eph. 1:19–23; Col. 1:15–19).
11. Encouragement to establish the first day of the week for worshiping Christ and serving him in local assemblies (Matt. 28:1; John 20:19; Acts 20:7; 1 Cor. 16:2).
12. The guarantee of a future resurrection life for all believers (John 5:26–29; 14:19; Rom. 4:25; 6:5–10; 1 Cor. 15:20, 23).
13. Confirmation of the future fulfillment of the Davidic covenant (Acts 2:29–36; 13:34–37).
14. The guarantee that Christ will judge the world (John 5:24–30; Acts 17:31).
15. The glorification and exaltation of the Son with the glory he once shared with the Father (John 17:5; Phil. 2:8–9; 1 Pet. 1:10–11, 20–21).

There exists no greater event in redemption history than the resurrection of Christ, because it completes and validates his sacrificial death and advances the program of the kingdom with an eternally living King. The resurrection must be believed in order for someone to experience salvation (Rom. 10:9–10).

The Resurrected Christ's Ascension

Scripture teaches that Christ ascended back into heaven to be seated at the right hand of his Father (Acts 2:33; cf. Heb. 1:8) and to the glory he had known with the Father (John 17:5; cf. John 16:5). The disciples had heard from Jesus that he was going to ascend to his Father (John 16:16–17; see 7:33–34; 8:21; 14:19, 28–29), and Jesus fulfilled his declarations, physically departing from the earth and ascending to heaven from the Mount of Olives (Acts 1:9–11). The Father received him into his glory (1 Tim. 3:16), and Christ is now seated on the throne of the Father (Rev. 3:21), at his right hand (Acts 5:31; Eph. 1:19–20), the throne of the universal and eternal kingdom of God (Mark 16:19; Acts 5:31; 7:55–56; Eph. 1:19–20). His session on the Father's throne testifies to the reality of his completed work of redemption (Heb. 10:12–13; 12:2).

Christ's ascension was confirmed by the visions of Stephen (Acts 7:55–56), Paul (Acts 9:3–5; 22:6–8; 26:13–15), and John (Rev. 4:1; 5:6). For Paul, Jesus's ascension left a lasting impression and was a key element in his salvation experience—the living, risen, ascended, heavenly Messiah spoke to him from heaven.

The Glorified Christ[39]

HEAVENLY INTERCESSOR

Christ's present ministry in glory on behalf of his people occurs in his heavenly intercession. He has ascended to the right hand of the Father, where he mediates as the believers' advocate and High Priest (Rom. 8:34; Heb. 7:25; 9:24; 1 John 2:1). There the Savior "is interceding for us" (Rom. 8:34), serving as the exalted High Priest for all believers (cf. Heb. 8:1–2; cf. John 17). Thus, the hope of godly Job has been realized: "Even now, behold, my witness is in heaven, and he who testifies for me is on high" (Job 16:19).

RAPTURE

All the remaining aspects of the post-resurrection ministry of Christ relate to his future work. His church awaits his call to the true church, which is his body, to come up to be with him. This is the "rapture" of the church (cf. 1 Thess. 4:13–18). As Jesus died and rose again, so too will those who have died in Christ (1 Cor. 15:51–58; 1 Thess. 4:14). There is no judgment connected to this event; it is for believers. This imminent, divine collection of believers into heaven, as Jesus promised (John 14:1–3) is a sign-less event and is the next one on the redemptive schedule.

Paul lived and spoke as if this event could happen in his lifetime; that is, he believed that it was imminent (Rom. 13:11; 1 Cor. 6:14; 10:11; 16:22; Phil. 3:20–21; 1 Tim. 6:14; Titus 2:13).

The phrase "the Lord himself will descend" (1 Thess. 4:16) fulfills the pledge by Jesus in John 14:1–3. Until then, he remains in heaven (1 Thess. 1:10; Heb. 1:1–3). Believers who have died will rise first (1 Thess. 4:16; 1 Cor. 15:52). Those alive at the rapture will accompany those dead, who rise first, and all will "meet the Lord in the air" (1 Thess. 4:17).

JUDGMENT SEAT[40]

The Lord Jesus Christ—the Judge of all people (John 5:22–23)—will judge believers at what is called the judgment seat of Christ (2 Cor. 5:10; cf. 1 Cor. 3:10–15). The term "judgment seat" metaphorically refers to the place where the Lord will sit to evaluate believers' lives for the purpose of giving them eternal rewards. The seat (*bēma*) refers to an elevated platform where victorious Greek athletes went to receive their crowns, or to the place of judging, as when Jesus stood before Pontius Pilate (Matt. 27:19; John 19:13). Corinth had such a platform where both

39 For a more thorough discussion of these themes, see chap. 10, "The Future."

40 This section is adapted from MacArthur, *MacArthur Study Bible: English Standard Version*, 1723. Used by permission of Thomas Nelson/HarperCollins Christian Publishing.

athletic rewards and legal verdicts were dispensed (Acts 18:12–16). At the *bēma*, Christ will judge the actions that occur during the believer's earthly life. This does not include sins, since their penalty was paid in full at the cross (Eph. 1:7).

SECOND COMING

The Greek term *parousia* (Matt. 24:3, 27, 37, 39; 2 Thess. 2:8; James 5:7–8) literally means "presence." In the New Testament, this term points to a unique and distinct "coming." The New Testament writers use this term at times to designate the second coming of Christ (it is also used to refer to the rapture, in 1 Thess. 2:19; 3:13; 4:15; 5:23). Another Greek noun, *apokalypsis* (1 Cor. 1:7; 2 Thess. 1:7; 1 Pet. 1:7, 13; 4:13), meaning "to uncover or unveil," also describes the revelation of Christ at his second coming as King over all.

Jesus will return to earth with divine power and glory to judge the living inhabitants of the earth (Matt. 24:30; 25:31–46; Luke 9:26; see Dan. 7:13; Titus 2:13; 2 Pet. 3:12; Jude 14; Rev. 1:7). The prophets of the Old Testament speak often of God's future judgment. Zephaniah explicitly portrays the judgment of God by presenting the Messiah as "a mighty one" who will bring salvation to the earth (Zeph. 3:17; cf. Zeph. 1:3 in Matt. 13:41; Zeph. 1:15 in Matt. 24:29).

The Father has already given all authority to the Son for the execution of judgment (John 5:27; see Matt. 25:31–32).

MILLENNIAL REIGN[41]

Returning with his raptured and glorified church, Christ will establish his millennial kingdom on earth (Acts 1:9–11; 1 Thess. 4:13–18; Rev. 20:1–6). Six times Revelation 20 mentions Christ's kingdom that will last a thousand years. These references refer to a literal thousand-year period during which Jesus Christ will reign on the earth in fulfillment of both numerous Old Testament prophecies (2 Sam. 7:12–16; Psalm 2; Isa. 11:6–12; 24:23; Amos 9:8–15; Mic. 4:1–8; Zech. 14:1–11) and Jesus's own teaching (Matt. 24:29–31, 36–44).

In the realm of society, Christ will abolish warfare and establish peace (Isa. 9:7; Mic. 4:3–4). Justice will prevail in every class and race of mankind (Ps. 72:4; Isa. 65:21–22), and God will reclaim social devastation (Ps. 72:16; Isa. 61:4).

In the political realm, Christ will establish himself as the international absolute ruler (Ps. 2:8–10; Isa. 2:2–4) and will establish his world capital at Jerusalem (Jer. 3:17). In his kingdom, Christ will put an end to the nations' animosity toward Jews (Zech. 8:13, 23).

41 This section is adapted from William D. Barrick, "The Kingdom of God in the Old Testament," *MSJ* 23.2 (2012): 179–80, 184. Used by permission of *MSJ*.

Ecclesiastically, Christ will rule as Priest-King over Israel and the world community (Ps. 110:4; Zech. 6:12–13). In the messianic kingdom, Israel will become the religious leader of the world (Ex. 19:6; Isa. 61:6, 9), and the world's religious capital will be Jerusalem (Zech. 14:16–17). As a result, the temple in Israel will be the focal point of worship (Ezekiel 40–48; Hag. 2:6–9).

In the millennial kingdom the vice-regency of mankind over creation that Adam was to exercise—but lost in the fall—will be restored by Christ in his reign. The purpose of God for his creation and the rule over it that man was to implement, as depicted in Psalm 8:3–9, will come to fruition. Jesus Christ, as the ultimate "son of man" (Ps. 8:4), will fulfill mankind's role as the human race's only perfect representative. Hebrews 2:5–14 reveals that "we do not yet see everything in subjection" to Christ (2:8), because his mediatorial kingdom has not begun. In the end, even the currently reigning prince of this world, Satan (John 12:31; Eph. 2:2), will come under Christ's reign and kingdom power. As long as Satan reigns as prince of this world, the Davidic reign of Christ has yet to be established. For that reason, Jesus taught his disciples to pray, "Your kingdom come" (Matt. 6:10). "Amen. Come, Lord Jesus!" (Rev. 22:20).

GREAT WHITE THRONE JUDGMENT

After the millennial kingdom, Christ will judge the unbelieving dead at the great white throne (Rev. 20:11–15). As the Mediator between God and mankind (1 Tim. 2:5); the Head of his body, the church (Eph. 1:22; 5:23; Col. 1:18); and the coming universal King who will reign on the throne of David (Isa. 9:6–7; Ezek. 37:24–28; Luke 1:31–33), Christ is the final Judge of all who fail to place their trust in him as Lord and Savior (Matt. 25:14–46; Acts 17:30–31).

ETERNITY FUTURE

At the end of this world's history, God will gather everything to himself in the new heaven and new earth that he will create (Rev. 21:1–5). The new eternal state will be totally unified under Christ (cf. 1 Cor. 15:27–28).

The paradise of eternity is thus revealed as a magnificent kingdom. But the real glory of eternity future rests in the fact that all believers will reside in the presence of the Lord Jesus Christ, in a glorious communion with God in Christ. The man Christ Jesus will be the center of the divine glory in heaven, from whence it will be diffused unto all the saints (cf. John 17:24).

Indeed, such communion with Christ seems to be the import of Scripture speaking jointly of God and the Lamb (the slain Savior) when revealing the happiness of the saints in heaven: "For the Lamb in the midst of the throne will be their shepherd, and he will guide them to springs of living water, and God will wipe away every tear from their eyes" (Rev. 7:17; cf. Rev. 21:3–4). Finally, the apostle

John declares, "And I saw no temple in the city, for its temple is the Lord God the Almighty and the Lamb. And the city has no need of sun or moon to shine on it, for the glory of God gives it light, and its lamp is the Lamb" (Rev. 21:22–23).

Questions:

1. What is the Scriptural teaching for the "preexistence" of Jesus Christ?
2. What are the works of the Son (second member of the Trinity) in the Old Testament?
3. What are the key messianic prophecies in the Old Testament?
4. What are the key proofs of the deity of Jesus Christ? (texts and titles)
5. What is meant by the *kenosis*?
6. Why is it important to affirm the virgin birth of Jesus Christ?
7. What are the key proofs of the humanity of Jesus Christ?
8. What is meant by the *hypostatic union*?
9. What are the erroneous views that attempt to explain the relationship of the two natures (deity and humanity) of Christ?
10. What are the key events of the life of Christ and why are they significant (what do they teach us about him and his ministry)?
11. How do the Old Testament sacrifices (esp. Leviticus 16) and prophecies (esp. Isaiah 53) reveal and explain the meaning and significance of the death of Jesus Christ on the cross?
12. Why is the bodily resurrection of Jesus significant for the believer's faith and hope?
13. What are the aspects of the glorified Christ, and why are they meaningful for believers living today?

5

GOD THE HOLY SPIRIT

Pneumatology

THIS CHAPTER INTRODUCES THE Holy Spirit, the third person of the triune Godhead. The truth about the Holy Spirit appears throughout Scripture, from Genesis to Revelation.

Introduction to the Holy Spirit

BIBLICAL SURVEY

The Hebrew word *ruakh* appears 378 times in the Old Testament, and 79 of those refer specifically to the Holy Spirit. The identical Aramaic word occurs 11 times (in Daniel only). *Ruakh* primarily means "spirit" (1 Sam. 16:14), "wind" (Ex. 10:13), or "breath" (Gen. 6:17). Context almost always determines the intended reference: e.g., the Spirit of God (Gen. 6:3); the spirit of man (Job 10:12); an attitude (Prov. 16:18); the immaterial part of man (Ps. 31:5).

The Holy Spirit is referred to from the time of creation (Gen. 1:2) all the way to the last Old Testament book (Mal. 2:15). God's Spirit appears most frequently in Isaiah (15 times), Ezekiel (15 times), Numbers (7 times), Judges (7 times), 1 Samuel (7 times), and Psalms (5 times).

New Testament revelation about the Holy Spirit is more extensive. The word *pneuma* occurs 379 times in the New Testament and it refers to the Holy Spirit on more than 245 of these occasions. *Pneuma* refers to the Holy Spirit in twenty-three books (Philemon, James, 2 John, and 3 John excepted). The Holy Spirit appears throughout the New Testament, from Matthew 1:18 to Revelation 21:10. The Holy Spirit is mentioned most frequently in Acts

(56 times), Romans (28 times), and 1 Corinthians (22 times). One of the most dominant themes is that the Holy Spirit is a gift from God to every believer (Rom. 5:5; 2 Cor. 1:22; 5:5; Gal. 3:5; Eph. 1:13–14; 1 Thess. 4:8; 1 John 3:24; 4:13).

PERSONHOOD AND DEITY OF THE HOLY SPIRIT

The Holy Spirit is a person, as are God the Father and God the Son. He is mentioned more than 320 times as such in the Bible. Personhood is not measured by physical, bodily elements but is rather determined by the possession of three basic characteristics: (1) cognition/intellect, (2) volition/will, and (3) emotion/affection.[1] Since the Bible provides more than sufficient evidence that the Holy Spirit possesses all three essentials of personhood, the Spirit is recognized as the third person of the triune Godhead.

Examples of his cognition/intellect: he knows, and he counsels and imparts wisdom (Isa. 11:2); he possesses a mind (Rom. 8:27; 1 Cor. 2:10–13); he inspired Scripture and provides truth (Acts 1:16; Heb. 3:7; 10:15; 1 Pet. 1:11; 2 Pet. 1:21; cf. John 14:17, 26; 15:26; 16:13; 1 John 4:6); he testifies (John 15:26; 1 John 5:7–8).

Examples of his affection/emotion: he experiences joy (1 Thess. 1:6); he grieves over sin (Isa. 63:10; Eph. 4:30); he loves (Rom. 5:5; 15:30; Gal. 5:22).

Examples of his volition/will: he contends with sinners (Gen. 6:3; Acts 7:51); he directs believers and distributes spiritual gifts (Acts 16:6–7; cf. 1 Cor. 12:11; Heb. 2:4).

NAMES AND ATTRIBUTES OF THE HOLY SPIRIT

One of the chief evidences for the triunity of the Godhead involves the designations (names) of the Holy Spirit in relation to the Father and to the Son.

For instance, in relation to the Father he is called: "his Spirit" (Num. 11:29; Rom. 8:11); "your [Holy] Spirit" (Ps. 139:7; 51:11); "the Spirit of God" (Gen. 1:2; Matt. 3:16; 1 Cor. 2:11) and ". . . of our God" (1 Cor. 6:11) and ". . . of the living God" (2 Cor. 3:3) and ". . . of the Lord God" (Isa. 61:1).

In relation to the Son he is called: "the Spirit of Jesus" (Acts 16:7) and "of Christ" (Rom. 8:9; 1 Pet. 1:11; cf. Phil. 1:19); "the Spirit of his Son" (Gal. 4:6).

Other designations are unique to the Holy Spirit: He is "the eternal Spirit" (Heb. 9:14); "your good Spirit" (Ps. 143:10); "the Holy Spirit" (Matt. 1:18); or simply "the Spirit" (Num. 11:17; Matt. 4:1).

Key attributes of the Spirit include: he is "the Spirit of counsel and might" (Isa. 11:2); "of faith" (2 Cor. 4:13); "of glory" (1 Pet. 4:14); "of grace" (Heb. 10:29; cf. Zech. 12:10); "of holiness" (Rom. 1:4); "of life" (Rom. 8:2); "of truth" (John 14:17;

1 The language of "affection" and "emotion" does not mean God's affections are involuntary passions as is often true of human emotions. As the Westminster Confession states, God is "without body, parts, or passions, immutable" (2.1). See "Immutability," in chap. 3, "God the Father" (p. 98).

15:26; 16:13; 1 John 4:6; cf. 1 John 5:6); "of wisdom and understanding" (Isa. 11:2; Eph. 1:17). He is quintessentially "the Helper" (John 14:26; 15:26; 16:7).

WORD PICTURES OF THE HOLY SPIRIT

The Bible uses several metaphors that describe key ministries of the Holy Spirit. These ministries are mostly unique to the New Testament and the Spirit's ministry to Christ, to the apostles, and to believers.

Clothing (Luke 24:49)

God the Son told the disciples that he would send "the promise of my Father" so that they could be "clothed" (Gk. *endyō*) with "power from on high" (Luke 24:49). A comparison of this passage with John 14:16–17 shows that the "promise" is the Holy Spirit. God sovereignly clothes his people with the Spirit (cf. Col. 3:12–14).

Dove (Matt. 3:16; Mark 1:10; Luke 3:22; John 1:32)

The dove was a symbol of innocence and blamelessness (Gk. *akeraios*, Matt. 10:16; see *akeraio*, used in Rom. 16:19 and Phil. 2:15 of believers) and even righteousness. Thus, at Christ's baptism the Son identified his ministry as one of fulfilling all righteousness (Matt. 3:15) and the Spirit (pictured by the dove, which represented righteousness) inaugurated Christ's ministry of righteousness (Matt. 3:16).

Fire (Acts 2:3)

The presence of God is often pictured by fire (Ex. 3:2–6; 13:21; Lev. 9:24; Acts 7:30–33). The use of fire in Acts 2:3 occurs on the day of Pentecost and most appropriately portrays the visible presence of the Holy Spirit.

Oil (2 Cor. 1:21; 1 John 2:20, 27)

Anointing with oil in Scripture symbolized appointment to an important position: the priesthood (Ex. 40:12–15); David to be king of Israel (1 Sam. 16:13); Jesus's disciples to be apostles (2 Cor. 1:21; cf. Acts 2:1–4.). Christ—*the* "anointed one" (Heb. *meshiakh* and Gk. *christos*)—was anointed with the Holy Spirit (Acts 4:27; 10:38) for ministry. Believers, called a royal priesthood (1 Pet. 2:9), are anointed with the Holy Spirit so they can know the truth about Christ (1 John 2:20, 27). Paul was anointed with the Holy Spirit for his apostleship (2 Cor. 1:21–22).

Pledge (2 Cor. 1:22; 5:5; Eph. 1:14)

Three times (2 Cor. 1:22; 5:5; Eph. 1:14), the Holy Spirit is said to be given to every believer as a guarantee (Gk. *arrabōn*, "down payment, earnest, or pledge") of his or her full salvation. The Spirit is God's pledge that what he began when a person first believed in Christ will be completed (Phil. 1:6).

Seal (2 Cor. 1:22; Eph. 1:13; 4:30)
A seal is a sign of security. The Father set his seal on the Son (John 6:27). God set his seal on the apostles (2 Cor. 1:22). The Lord set his seal on believers (Eph. 1:13; 4:30). The seal that God placed on all believers (Gk. *sphragizō*) is the Holy Spirit.

Water (John 7:38–39; Acts 1:5; 2:33; 1 Cor. 12:13 [2x]; Titus 3:5–6)
The Holy Spirit is pictured as (1) life-giving water (John 7:38–39; 1 Cor. 12:13b; Titus 3:5–6); (2) life-enabling water (Acts 1:5; 2:33); and (3) life-sustaining water (1 Cor. 12:13a).

Paul spoke of the Holy Spirit as being water in a salvific sense when it is consumed (1 Cor. 12:13b; cf. John 4:14). Christ spoke about the Holy Spirit being rivers of living water (John 7:38–39; cf. Ezek. 36:25–27). Paul pictured the Holy Spirit as water being poured out for the washing of regeneration (Titus 3:5–6). At the time of Christ's millennial kingdom, God will pour out his Spirit redemptively on the house of Israel (Isa. 32:15; 44:3; Ezek. 39:29; Joel 2:28–29).

Wind (John 3:8; Acts 2:2; 2 Pet. 1:21)
The Greek word *pneuma* can be translated "spirit" (Matt. 5:3), "Spirit" (Matt. 1:18), "wind" (John 3:8), or "breath" (Rev. 13:15), as context determines. In John 3:8, Jesus likened the phenomenon of wind to the work of God's Spirit in salvation in that it is invisible, unexpected, unpredictable, yet always powerfully accomplishing its end (cf. Ezek. 37:9–14).

Luke pictured the sound of the coming of the Holy Spirit on Pentecost as that of a mighty rushing wind (Acts 2:2).

Peter described the writing of Scripture using wind (as wind carries along a ship at sea) as an illustration of the Holy Spirit's work of inspiration (2 Pet. 1:21). Thus, the Holy Spirit "carried along" the apostles in writing the New Testament.

MINISTRIES OF THE HOLY SPIRIT

The Holy Spirit ministered to the Lord Jesus Christ in several significant ways: he prophesied of him (Isa. 11:1–2; 42:1–4; 61:1–3; Zech. 12:10); accomplished his virgin conception and birth (Matt. 1:18, 20; Luke 1:34–35); anointed and empowered him (Matt. 3:13–17; Mark 1:9–11; Luke 3:21–22; John 1:29–34; cf. Matt. 12:15–21; Luke 4:17–21; cf. also Matt. 12:28; Luke 4:14–15; 11:20; Acts 10:38); filled and led him (Luke 4:1–2; John 3:34; cf. Matt. 4:1; Mark 1:12; Luke 4:1, 14; Acts 1:2); and raised him from the dead (Rom. 1:4; 8:11).

Similarly, the Spirit also ministers to Christ's people. Christ promised the disciples that upon his departure he would send them "the Helper," the Holy Spirit (John 16:7). For believers, the Spirit convicts (John 16:8–11); regenerates (John 3:5–6, 8; Titus 3:5); illuminates (1 Cor. 2:10–13); adopts (Rom. 8:15); baptizes (1 Cor. 12:13); seals (2 Cor. 1:22; Eph. 1:13–14; 4:30); indwells (Rom. 8:9–11;

1 Cor. 3:16; 6:19); teaches (John 14:26; Acts 15:28; 1 John 2:20, 27); bears witness (Acts 5:32; Rom. 8:16; 9:1; 1 John 5:6–8); empowers (Ex. 31:1–3; Judg. 13:25; Acts 1:8); fills (Luke 4:1; Acts 2:4; Eph. 5:18); strengthens (Eph. 3:16); calls to ministry (Acts 13:2–4); sanctifies (Rom. 15:16; 1 Cor. 6:11; 2 Thess. 2:13; 1 Pet. 1:2); and intercedes (Rom. 8:26–27; Eph. 6:18; Jude 20; see 1 John 5:14–15). In addition, the Spirit provides fellowship (2 Cor. 13:14; Phil. 2:1); liberty (2 Cor. 3:17–18); life and peace (Rom. 8:6); power (Rom. 15:13; 1 Cor. 2:4; Eph. 3:16); wisdom (Isa. 11:2); and unity (Eph. 2:18; 4:3–4).

SINS AGAINST THE HOLY SPIRIT

Believers may sin against the Holy Spirit by grieving, lying to, testing, and neglecting him (Eph. 4:30; Acts 5:3; 5:9; Gal. 3:3–6; 5:17) and by quenching him (1 Thess. 5:19).

Unbelievers sin against the Holy Spirit by blaspheming him (Matt. 12:31; Mark 3:29; Luke 12:10); rebelling against/resisting him (Gen. 6:3 [NASB]; Neh. 9:30; Isa. 30:1; 63:10; Acts 7:51; Gal. 5:17); or insulting/provoking him (Heb. 3:10; 10:29).

Deity and Triunity of the Holy Spirit

The deity and triunity of the Holy Spirit have occasionally been called into question (see also chap. 3, "God the Father"; and chap. 4, "God the Son"). When this has occurred, it is because the content of Scripture has been disregarded, due either to simple unbelief or faulty human reasoning supplanting God's inspired Word. The Bible teaches the deity of the Holy Spirit.

DEITY

Attributions

In Acts 5, Peter confronted Ananias, asking, "Why has Satan filled your heart to lie to the Holy Spirit?" (5:3), and then he indicted him: "You have not lied to man but to God" (5:4). Peter equated a lie to the Holy Spirit with a lie to God, thereby identifying the Holy Spirit as God.

Since the words of Yahweh are at times attributed to the Holy Spirit (cf. Ps. 95:8–11 with Heb. 3:7–11; Isa. 6:8–10 with Acts 28:25–27; and Jer. 31:33–34 with Heb. 10:15–17) the Holy Spirit is equated with Yahweh.

Christians are called "God's temple" (1 Cor. 3:16; 6:19) because the Holy Spirit, who is God, dwells in them (Rom. 8:9, 11; 2 Tim. 1:14).

God's work of forming the church (1 Cor. 12:18, 24, 28) is also attributed to the Holy Spirit (1 Cor. 12:11), indicating he is God.

Jesus said, "Whoever blasphemes against the Holy Spirit never has forgiveness but is guilty of an eternal sin" (Mark 3:29; see Matt. 12:31–32; Luke 12:10).

This passage again demonstrates the deity of the Holy Spirit, since only God can be blasphemed.[2]

Attributes, Actions, and Associations

The Holy Spirit possesses the perfections of God: eternality (Heb. 9:14); glory (1 Pet. 4:14; cf. Isa. 42:8; 48:11); holiness (Ps. 51:11; Isa. 63:10–11; Matt. 1:18; Rom. 1:4); omnipotence (Gen. 1:1–2; Luke 1:35; Rom. 1:4); omnipresence (Ps. 139:7–10; cf. Jer. 23:24); omniscience (Isa. 40:13; 1 Cor. 2:10–11). These divine characteristics certify that the Holy Spirit is indeed God.

The Holy Spirit's actions include creation (Gen. 1:2; Job 26:13; 33:4), inspiration (2 Pet. 1:20–21), regeneration (John 3:5–8; Titus 3:5), and sanctification (2 Thess. 2:13; 1 Pet. 1:2), and these are the actions of God.

Several passages in Scripture clearly associate the Holy Spirit with the other members of the Godhead: Matthew 28:19, the baptism instructions; 1 Corinthians 2:10–13, the Father (God) and the Spirit complement each other equally in the revelation, illumination, and interpretation of God's Word; 2 Corinthians 13:14, all three members of the Godhead are mentioned and set on equal footing in this Pauline Trinitarian benediction; Revelation 1:4–6, this Johannine Trinitarian invocation links the Father, the Spirit, and the Son together as coequals. In John 14:16, 26; 15:26; 16:7 the Spirit is called "another Helper" (Gk. *allos*, "another of the same kind"), where the other Helper in view is Jesus, a member of the triune Godhead.

Erroneous Views

The most serious historical heresies regarding the Holy Spirit fall into two categories: (1) the denial that the Holy Spirit was a person, and (2) the denial that the Holy Spirit was eternal God, which was consequently a denial of God's triunity.

Sabellianism. This late-second- or early-third-century heresy proposed that there was one God in three manifestations or modes, and thus it was also known as Modalism. It has also at times been called Monarchianism because it radically affirmed "the one God" (monarch; monotheism). Those who held this view believed they were protecting the doctrine of one God from the false teaching that there were three gods. In doing so, however, they rejected God's triunity.

Arianism. This early- to mid-fourth-century heresy taught that the one God created the Son in eternity past, who in turn created the Holy Spirit. While this false teaching affirmed the personhood of both Christ and the Holy Spirit (un-

2 For a discussion of the nature of the blasphemy against the Holy Spirit, see "The Blasphemy against the Holy Spirit and Apostasy," below (p. 195); and "The Unpardonable Sin," in chap. 6, "Man and Sin" (p. 259).

like Sabellianism), it denied their deity and consequently God's triunity. Like Sabellianism, Arianism taught that the Godhead consisted of one person with the essence of deity. This false doctrine was confronted at the Council of Nicaea (AD 325) and the Council of Constantinople (AD 381).

Socinianism. This sixteenth-century aberration affirmed the personhood of Christ while denying his deity. It also denied the Holy Spirit's personhood and deity, thus denying God's triunity. Various modern Unitarian movements affirm much of Socinianism.

TRIUNITY[3]

As the doctrinal statement of The Master's Seminary puts it, "We teach that there is but one living and true God (Deut. 6:4; Isa. 45:5–7; 1 Cor. 8:4), an infinite, all-knowing Spirit (John 4:24), perfect in all His attributes, one in essence, eternally existing in three persons—Father, Son, and Holy Spirit (Matt. 28:19; 2 Cor. 13:14)—each equally deserving worship and obedience." There is one God who eternally subsists in three distinct consubstantial, coequal, and coeternal persons.

While no one text declares or explains the fullness associated with the incomprehensible triune God (Isa. 40:28), God's triunity appears implicitly and explicitly throughout the Bible.

In several Old Testament texts God uses the plural pronoun "us" in reference to himself (cf. Gen. 1:26; 3:22–23; Isa. 6:8). This allows for a plurality in the Godhead. The Hebrew word translated "one" (*ʾehad*) in Deuteronomy 6:4 hints at a plurality, "the LORD is one." This term (*ʾehad*) frequently communicates the idea of unity in diversity: e.g., Genesis 1:5, one day in two parts, evening and morning; Genesis 2:24, one couple in two partners; Exodus 24:3, one voice in many people; Exodus 26:6, one tabernacle in multiple parts; Numbers 13:23, one cluster in many grapes. Therefore in Deuteronomy 6:4 *ʾehad* can be understood to refer to the one God in three persons.

Later, in the progress of revelation, Isaiah writes of three persons when referring to the one God of Israel: "the Lord GOD," "me" (i.e., Christ), and "his Spirit" (Isa. 48:16). Isaiah 61:1 similarly says, "The Spirit of the Lord GOD is upon me," that is, upon Christ; and in fact Christ interpreted this text in just such a manner in Luke 4:18–19.

In the further progress of God's written revelation, the New Testament evidence becomes more direct and frequent in showing that Father, Son, and Holy Spirit are of the same divine essence and are coequal, one God in three

3 This section is adapted from Richard Mayhue, "Editorial: One God—Three Persons," *MSJ* 24.2 (2013): 161–65. Used by permission of *MSJ*. For a more thorough discussion of the triunity of God, refer to chap. 3, "God the Father."

persons, expressing unity in diversity. All three appear together in numerous New Testament texts (see Matt. 3:16–17; 28:19; Luke 1:35; John 15:26; cf. 14:16, 26; 16:7–10, 14–15; Rom. 8:11; 15:30; 2 Cor. 13:14; Heb. 9:13–14; 1 John 4:2; Jude 20–21).

A key text among the Trinitarian passages comes in Ephesians 1:3–14, which speaks of each person's involvement in the salvation of believers: the Father elects (1:3–6), the Son redeems (1:7–12), and the Spirit seals (1:13–14).

With the completed canon of Scripture, the early church fathers wrote about the Trinity with greater clarity. For instance, Irenaeus (ca. AD 120–202) clearly referred to "God, the Father, uncreated, beyond grasp, invisible, one God the maker of all"; and to "the Word of God, the Son of God, Christ Jesus our Lord"; and to "the Holy Spirit, through whom the prophets prophesied and the patriarchs were taught about God." Also, Gregory of Nazianzus (ca. AD 330–ca. 389) wrote, "The Son is not Father; . . . yet he is whatever the Father is. The Spirit is not Son. . . . Yet whatever the Son is, he is. The three are a single whole in their Godhead and the single whole is three in personalities."[4]

Finally, Augustine (AD 354–430) wrote, "Whatever . . . is spoken of God in respect to himself, is both spoken singly of each person, that is, of the Father, and the Son, and the Holy Spirit; and together of the Trinity itself, not plurally but in the singular."[5] Also, when early councils of bishops began to compose creedal statements, they affirmed the truth of the Trinity. For instance, The Niceno-Constantinopolitan Creed (ca. AD 381)[6] and the (Pseudo) Athanasian Creed (ca. AD 375–525):

> And the Catholic faith is this: That we worship one God in Trinity, and Trinity in Unity;
>
> Neither confounding the persons: nor dividing the Substance [Essence].
>
> For there is one person of the Father: another of the Son: and another of the Holy Ghost.
>
> But the Godhead of the Father, of the Son, and of the Holy Ghost, is all one: the Glory equal, the Majesty coeternal.[7]

4 See Irenaeus, *Proof of the Apostolic Preaching*, trans. Joseph P. Smith, Ancient Christian Writers 16 (London: Longmans, Green, 1952), 50; Gregory of Nazianzus, *On God and Christ: The Five Theological Orations and Two Letters to Cledonius*, trans. Fredrick Williams and Lionel Wickham (Crestwood, NY: St. Vladimir's Seminary Press, 2002), 122–23.

5 Augustine, *On the Holy Trinity*, in *A Select Library of the Nicene and Post-Nicene Fathers of the Christian Church*, ed. Philip Schaff (New York: Charles Scribner's Sons, 1905), 3:92 (5.8.9).

6 See Philip Schaff, *The Creeds of Christendom*, vol. 2, *The Greek and Latin Creeds* (New York: Harper & Brothers, 1889), 58–59.

7 In Schaff, *Creeds of Christendom*, 2:66.

In this creed are at least seven lines of thought that affirm the Trinity:

1. The Father is God.
2. The Son is God.
3. The Holy Spirit is God.
4. The Father is not the Son.
5. The Father is not the Holy Spirit.
6. The Son is not the Holy Spirit.
7. There is exactly one God.[8]

The Work of the Holy Spirit in Salvation

Scripture teaches that the saving benefits purchased by Christ's cross are applied to believers through the work of the Holy Spirit.[9]

REGENERATION

The first step in the Spirit's application of salvation is regeneration. Fundamental to understanding regeneration is the reality that every human being who has ever lived has suffered from spiritual deadness (Rom. 3:23; Eph. 2:1, 5). Only God the Father, God the Son, and God the Holy Spirit can give new spiritual life to those who were previously dead in their sins (Rom. 8:2, 6, 10–11). Regeneration directly addresses this gracious act of God.

Word Pictures

Scripture pictures regeneration using four different images: (1) spiritual birth, (2) spiritual cleansing, (3) spiritual creation, and (4) spiritual resurrection.

Spiritual Birth (Titus 3:5). The Greek word normally translated "regeneration" is *palingenesia*—a combination of *palin* ("again") and *genesia* ("to be born"), so literally "born again" (see Gal. 4:29). The word appears twice in the New Testament: Matthew 19:28 uses it to refer to the millennium as a regenerated world; in Titus 3:5 it refers to salvation. First Peter 1:3, 23 uses the Greek term *anagennaō*, which also literally means "born again." In John 3, Jesus told Nicodemus, "You must be born again," using two Greek words that literally mean "born from above" and that refer to spiritual rebirth by God, who dwells above (John 3:3, 7; see James 1:17). John's first epistle repeatedly refers to being born of God (1 John 2:29; 3:9; 4:7; 5:1, 4, 18).

Spiritual Cleansing (Titus 3:5). Paul twice uses the Greek word *loutron* to refer to those who are filthy with sin (Isa. 64:6) being washed clean by regeneration

8 See the illustration titled "The Shield of the Trinity," in chap. 3 (p. 109).

9 For more on the doctrine of salvation, particularly with respect to the Holy Spirit's work of regeneration, see chap. 7, "Salvation," esp. "The Internal Call: Regeneration" (p. 300).

(Eph. 5:26; Titus 3:5). After Paul recounts the many heinous sins of the Corinthians (1 Cor. 6:9–10), he uses the Greek word *apolouō* to describe their being washed, which he associates with the sanctification of salvation and justification (1 Cor. 6:11).

Spiritual Creation (Titus 3:5). In Titus 3:5, Paul uses the Greek word *anakainōsis*, which literally means "new again" and is translated "renewal." This is a compound word using *kainos*, which means "new in quality," in contrast to *neos*, which means "new in time." Paul employed both words for "new"; when emphasizing newness in quality of life, he chose *kainos* to describe God's redemptive creation (2 Cor. 5:17; Gal. 6:15; Eph. 4:24); when intending the newness in time of spiritual life renewal, he turned to *neos* (Col. 3:10). Because of regeneration in the sense of spiritual renewal, Christians have a new nature (2 Cor. 5:17) with new spiritual capacities (Rom. 6:18, 20; 1 Cor. 12:3). The regenerated believer is in a condition even better than that of Adam (before the fall); Adam was merely innocent, but the regenerated believer is now the Holy Spirit's spiritual re-creation in the image of righteousness.

Spiritual Resurrection (John 6:63). Both Paul (2 Cor. 3:6) and John (John 6:63) declare that the Spirit gives life. Elsewhere, Scripture states that God gives life (John 5:21; Rom. 4:17; 6:13; Eph. 2:5; Col. 2:13). John reveals that Christ gives life (John 5:21). A coordinated Trinitarian effort is involved in bringing spiritual life.

The Old Testament

It is clear that Old Testament believers, like New Testament believers, experienced regeneration. Since only those who are "born again"—that is, regenerated—can be in the kingdom of God (John 3:3, 5, 7), and since Old Testament believers were salvifically in the kingdom of God, Old Testament saints were necessarily regenerated. Approaching it from a different angle, since it is impossible for a believer to be justified by God without being regenerated, and since Old Testament believers were justified (Gen. 15:6; Rom. 4:1–12; see Ps. 32:1–2), then Old Testament saints were regenerated.

Trinitarian Involvement

All three members of the Godhead were involved in some aspect of regeneration, since Scripture says that all three give life: the Father (John 1:13; 2 Cor. 5:17–19; Eph. 2:4–6; Col. 2:13; James 1:18; 1 Pet. 1:3; 1 John 5:11); the Son (John 1:12; 5:21); the Holy Spirit (John 3:3, 5–7; 6:63; Titus 3:5).

The Holy Spirit and God's Word

Salvation comes only by God's will, not by human will (John 1:13; Eph. 2:8–10; James 1:18). Scripture emphasizes that it is by the complementary interaction of God's Spirit (John 3:3, 5–7; Gal. 3:2–3, 14; 1 Thess. 1:5; Titus 3:5) with God's Word (Rom. 1:16; 1 Thess. 1:5; 2:13; 1 Pet. 1:23) that regeneration takes place.

Therefore, regeneration involves the triune God's instantaneous impartation of eternal spiritual life to people who were formerly spiritually dead but have embraced Christ by faith because of God's grace. This act of efficacious grace is entirely by the Holy Spirit through the Word of God.

The Blasphemy against the Holy Spirit and Apostasy

Scripture identifies two instances in which people decisively exclude themselves from the Spirit's regenerating work. First, there are those who commit the unpardonable or unforgiveable sin, the blasphemy against the Holy Spirit (Matt. 12:31–32; Mark 3:28–30; Luke 12:10). In Matthew 12 Jesus identified the Pharisees' failure to believe in him and their accusations against him (12:24) as blasphemy against the Holy Spirit (12:31), for it was by the Spirit that he performed his works of compassion and power. Such blasphemy is unforgiveable (Matt. 12:32). The Pharisees' refusal to accept what they knew to be true, and their slanderous charge against him, proved they were past the point of repentance and forgiveness.

Second, those people who counterfeit their profession of faith in Christ are described by the term *apostasy*, a term that means "to fall away." These people outwardly and temporarily give the appearance of being truly regenerated by the Spirit, but because they eventually fall away and abandon the faith (e.g., Heb. 2:1–3; 3:7–13; 6:4–6; 2 Pet. 2:20) they prove themselves to have never truly been converted (cf. 1 John 2:19). It is impossible for someone who has truly abandoned the faith in the light of full revelation to be renewed again unto repentance (Heb. 6:4–6). Apostasy consists of a hard-hearted, resolute rejection of Christ, and of regarding as false the truth of God.

Often the sensitive consciences of genuine believers who love Christ trouble them. Their sin causes them to wonder if they have committed the unpardonable sin or apostatized. But these egregious acts of hardness of heart and apostasy are not the marks of those who love Christ. Those who are troubled by their sin must continue to turn from sin and trust in the sufficiency of Christ's life, death, and resurrection to save them from God's wrath. Christ has promised to never leave his own (Matt. 28:20; Heb. 13:5) or let them be snatched away from him (John 10:28–29). God promises to finish his work of salvation (Phil. 1:6), so that nothing can separate true believers from God's love in Christ (Rom. 8:38–39). Fearful believers ought to examine themselves, repent of sin, look to Christ alone for righteousness, rejoice in the sufficiency of his saving love, and follow after him with renewed strength.

BAPTISM OF THE HOLY SPIRIT

After God's Spirit regenerates a person, at least six significant spiritual enhancements involving the Spirit take place. All six occur concurrently with salvation, but each is treated individually in Scripture.

1. Christ *baptizes* the believer with the Spirit into the body of Christ (1 Cor. 12:13).
2. The Father *seals* the believer with the Holy Spirit as a show of ownership and a guarantee of one's salvation (Eph. 1:13).
3. The Spirit *indwells* the believer (1 Cor. 3:16).
4. The Spirit *fills/controls* the believer (Eph. 5:18).
5. The Spirit *produces* spiritual fruit in the believer's life (Gal. 5:22–23).
6. The Spirit *gifts* the believer for service in the church (1 Cor. 12:4).

Christ promised the coming of the Spirit (John 14:16–17; Acts 1:4–5), and this took place on Pentecost (fifty days after Passover), which celebrated the Jewish Feast of Weeks (Ex. 34:22; also called the Feast of the Harvest, Ex. 23:16). As the Jews celebrated the firstfruits of the physical harvest (Lev. 23:15–17), the new covenant era for the church inaugurated the firstfruits of the Holy Spirit's salvation harvest (Acts 2:1–4; see Rom. 8:23; John 4:35).

Scriptural Considerations

The *expectation* of Spirit baptism appears in all four Gospels and in Acts 1. The *experience* of Spirit baptism began in Acts 2, as recalled in Acts 11. The *explanation* of Spirit baptism came later, in 1 Corinthians 12.

Expectation. Matthew 3:11–12; Mark 1:8; Luke 3:16–17; and John 1:32–34 all report John the Baptist's reference to Christ baptizing with the Holy Spirit. The Greek preposition *en* should be translated "in" or "with," since these renderings have been used earlier in the obvious sense of "by means of" with reference to water.[10] As one is immersed (*baptizō*) "in," "with," or "by means of" water, so is one baptized "in," "with," or "by means of" the Holy Spirit.

Three different baptisms appear in these texts: (1) water baptism, signifying previous repentance; (2) Spirit baptism, signifying salvation and entrance into the universal church, the body of Christ (1 Cor. 12:13); and (3) fire baptism, pointing to the judgment of unbelievers (Matt. 3:12; 25:41; Luke 3:16; John 15:6; Rev. 20:14–15).

As he prepared to ascend to heaven from the Mount of Olives, the Lord reminded his disciples of what John the Baptist had previously said concerning

10 Daniel B. Wallace, *Greek Grammar beyond the Basics: An Exegetical Syntax of the New Testament* (Grand Rapids, MI: Zondervan, 1996), 374.

Spirit baptism and indicated that the initial fulfillment would be just days away as they waited in Jerusalem (Acts 1:4–5).

Experience. On the day of Pentecost, John's and Christ's previous pronouncements came to pass (Acts 2:1–21). Luke did not explicitly record it as such; however, Peter confirmed later that it was on Pentecost that the Spirit "fell on" the apostles, for he observed that "the Holy Spirit fell upon them [the Gentiles] just as [he did] on us *at the beginning*" (Acts 11:15, emphasis added). Thus, he concluded that what was then happening to Cornelius's family (cf. Acts 10:44–46) had occurred on Pentecost.

Explanation. While the historical narratives do not provide any *explanation* as to the meaning or significance of Spirit baptism, Paul did explain its meaning in 1 Corinthians 12:13, "For in [with] one Spirit we were all baptized into one body—Jews or Greeks, slave or free—and all were made to drink of one Spirit." Simply put, Spirit baptism occurs when Jesus Christ, Lord of his church, from Pentecost on, by the Spirit, places Christians into his body, the church, at the moment a person puts faith in Christ as Savior and Lord. By Christ's doing so, Christians are immersed into and participate in the universal body of Christ by the Savior's sovereign will.

Some later events recorded in Acts appear to raise a few questions. Jesus had told his disciples to preach the gospel in Jerusalem, in Judea, in Samaria, and to the end of the earth (Acts 1:8). The apostles obeyed, and the milestones of this expansion are recounted in Acts 2; 8; 10–11; and 19. As they proceeded from Jerusalem to Ephesus, from Jew to Gentile, each progression was marked by special circumstances. As each new group was added to the church—Samaritans (Acts 8:14–19), Gentiles (10:44–48), and believers from the old covenant (19:1–7)—each group received a special welcome from the Holy Spirit. The unusual events and manifestations that appeared at these historical transition points were meant to mark the historical progress of the gospel. But they were not meant to establish the normative experience of the church for all time. By comparing these historical narratives to the pertinent didactic sections of the Epistles, it is clear that the experiences outlined in Acts 2; 8; 10–11; and 19 were exceptions to the norm, given in order to historically validate and illustrate the spread of the gospel during the unique period of transition from God-fearing Judaism to new covenant Christianity as chronicled in the book of Acts. They have not been the normative expectation and experiences of gospel ministry through the subsequent centuries up to the present time.[11]

11 See Walter C. Kaiser Jr., "The Baptism in the Holy Spirit as the Promise of the Father: A Reformed Perspective," in *Perspectives on Spirit Baptism: Five Views*, ed. Chad Owen Brand (Nashville: Broadman, 2004), 15–37.

In summary, Holy Spirit baptism is a positional act, taking place in the life of every Christian concurrently with regeneration. The texts in Acts that refer to a post-conversion baptism of the Spirit are associated with the transitional nature of the period described in Acts. First Corinthians 12:13 records the *normative* doctrine of Spirit baptism, stating that it results in a new position in the body of Christ for all Christians at the moment of faith in Christ. It can be inferred from the fleshly nature of the Corinthian Christians, to whom Paul wrote this passage, that it does not necessarily have any influence on subsequent holiness. The church, the spiritual body of Christ, is formed as believers are immersed by Christ in the Spirit and united with all other Christians, beginning with Pentecost.

SEALING WITH THE HOLY SPIRIT

The Spirit of promise (Eph. 1:13) is given by God as his guarantee of a believer's future inheritance in glory. Paul developed the theme of *sealing* using two Greek words: *sphragizō*, "to seal," and *arrabōn*, "a pledge" (2 Cor. 1:21–22; 5:5; Eph. 1:13–14; 4:30). Both of these terms originated with a secular sense, but Paul later appropriated them as spiritual word pictures to describe a significant salvation ministry involving the Holy Spirit. *Sphragizō*, or "sealing," pictured an ancient practice of placing soft wax on one's correspondence or property, which was then stamped with a unique mark that unmistakably identified the owner or originator. It symbolized security, protection, ownership, authority, and authenticity. *Arrabōn*, or "guarantee," was a financial down payment or deposit given in good faith that the remaining payment(s) would be forthcoming to complete a business transaction. It communicated the idea of a pledge to promote certainty and assurance.

In the context of salvation, the seal points to God's ownership of the believer, who has been bought with a price—the blood of God's Son Jesus Christ (1 Cor. 6:19–20). God seals the believer (2 Cor. 1:22; 5:5) with the Holy Spirit much as he earlier sealed Christ (John 6:27). Thus, the Holy Spirit is the actual seal (2 Cor. 1:22) that authenticates a Christian as a child of God.

All true believers receive the seal of the Holy Spirit because of their salvation (Rom. 8:9). Just as one is saved by grace through faith in Christ, one is also sealed by God with the Holy Spirit because of his grace.

The immediate purpose of the seal is to identify those who will one day receive the full and final benefit of salvation, namely, resurrection (Rom. 8:20–23). That is why Romans 8:23 speaks of a believer's present life as having "the firstfruits of the Spirit," since there is much more to come on the future day's resurrection and redemption of the believer's body (2 Cor. 5:4–5; Eph. 1:14; 4:30).

The Spirit is not only God's seal on believers but also God's guarantee (2 Cor. 1:22; 5:5; Eph. 1:14), God's pledge, down payment, and deposit that certifies with impeccable assurance the certainty that what God began he will also complete (Phil. 1:6). The Spirit is "the promised Holy Spirit, who is the guarantee of our inheritance until we acquire possession of it, to the praise of his glory" (Eph. 1:13–14; see John 10:28–29; Rom. 8:31–39).

The Work of the Holy Spirit in Sanctification[12]

INTRODUCTION[13]

The Titles for Believers

The New Testament employs a variety of terms to refer to believers. The term "Christian" (Gk. *Christianos*) is found on only three occasions in Scripture (Acts 11:26; 26:28; 1 Pet. 4:16). A favorite term for believers in the Gospels and Acts was "disciple" (Gk. *mathētēs*; 250x). Throughout the New Testament, there is the frequent use of "brother" (Gk. *adelphos*) and the rare appearance of "sister" (Gk. *adelphē*, Philem. 2; 2 John 13). Another striking expression is "slave" (Gk. *doulos*) in contrast to Christ as "Lord" (Gk. *kyrios*).

Each of the above five terms seems rather appropriate, even obvious. However, one additional reference to a believer is not so obvious—"saint" (Gk. *hagios*). It is the most surprising, the most intriguing, and the least deserved. Used sparsely in the Gospels and Acts, "saint" is the preferred terminology in the Epistles and Revelation.

Why "saint"? It focuses on God's attribute of holiness (cf. Isa. 6:1–8) and his design that all true believers in Christ increasingly demonstrate and emulate this quality as their mark of Christian authenticity (cf. Heb. 12:10). The Spirit of holiness (Rom. 1:4), elsewhere referred to as the Holy Spirit (Ps. 51:11; Isa. 63:11; Matt. 1:18; Jude 20), personifies this preeminent attribute. By focusing on this title for believers, the discussion that follows will explore the salvific implications of sanctification and holiness as they appear in such familiar biblical texts as Matthew 5:48, Romans 8:28–30, Philippians 1:6, 1 John 3:2–3, and Jude 24–25.

The Tenses of Salvation

Three distinct word groups in the New Testament synonymously describe salvation in terms of that which is past, present, and future: these are (1) completion/perfection (Gk. *teleioō*, *teleios*), (2) salvation (Gk. *sōzō*, *sōtēria*, *sōtērion*), (3) sanctification (Gk. *hagiazō*, *hagiasmos*, *hagios*). Each word group is used to describe salvation in each of the three tenses (identified in the following lines by

12 For a more thorough discussion of sanctification, refer to chap. 7, "Salvation."

13 This section is adapted from Richard L. Mayhue, "Sanctification: The Biblical Basics," *MSJ* 21.2 (2010): 143–57. Used by permission of *MSJ*.

the numbers 1, 2, 3). Some passages describe salvation as a past event: believers have been (1) "perfected" (Heb. 10:14); are (2) "saved" (Titus 3:5); are (3) "sanctified" (1 Cor. 6:11). Some passages describe salvation as a present event: believers (1) are experiencing "completion" (2 Cor. 7:1); (2) are "working out" their salvation (Phil. 2:12); (3) are seeing their progressive "sanctification" (1 Thess. 4:3–4, 7). Some passages describe salvation as a future event: believers (1) will "be made perfect" (Heb. 12:22–23); (2) will see "salvation" (Rom. 13:11); (3) will be "sanctif[ied] completely" (1 Thess. 5:23).

The teaching from these passages can best be summarized with these observations:

1. "Salvation," "sanctification," and "completion"/"perfection" can be used synonymously in Scripture as word groups with significant salvific importance.
2. Salvation is part of sanctification in its broadest sense, and sanctification is part of salvation in its fullest sense.
3. Therefore, salvation and sanctification are inseparable. You cannot have one without the other.
4. Each of these three word groups can describe the past, the present, or the future.
5. Each of these three word groups can describe inauguration, continuation, or culmination in the context of redemption.
6. Each of these three word groups can describe either the part or the whole of salvation.
7. A person is said by Scripture to already be what a person is actually becoming.
8. A person is commanded in the Bible to now be what one cannot completely be until eternity.

The Time Perspectives of Salvation

A study of the following verses will allow the Scriptures to speak for themselves concerning the three time perspectives of sanctification—positional, progressive, and perfective:

Positional Sanctification: Acts 20:32; 26:18, 1 Corinthians 1:2, 30; 6:11; Ephesians 5:26; 2 Thessalonians 2:13; Hebrews 10:10; 1 Peter 1:2.

Progressive Sanctification: John 17:17; Romans 6:19, 22; 2 Cor. 3:18; 7:1; 1 Thessalonians 4:3, 4, 7–8; 2 Timothy 2:21.

Perfective Sanctification: 1 Thessalonians 3:13; 5:23.

In summary, sanctification as taught in Scripture is a salvific work of God:

1. inaugurated by, and in which all three members of the Godhead participate
2. continued by God in this life unto completion in heaven

3. cannot be separated from justification or glorification
4. empowered by God's Word and God's Spirit
5. once begun, cannot be lost, stopped, or undone
6. prompts a holy response of biblical obedience to the work of the Holy Spirit from those who are genuine saints
7. does not eradicate sin from the believer until glorification
8. provides confident hope in this life because of a certain eternal hope for the next life

THE INDWELLING OF THE SPIRIT

Two views have been posited regarding the indwelling ministry of the Holy Spirit. One side understands indwelling in the Old Testament as being the same as in the New Testament.[14] The other side supports the view that the Spirit's indwelling ministry that began at Pentecost in Acts 2 differed significantly from the indwelling spoken of in the Old Testament.[15]

First, a look at what the Old and New Testaments say about the Spirit's indwelling is in order. After the evidence has been gathered, then a sound conclusion may be reached.

Old Testament

Several Old Testament believers are said to have been indwelt by the Holy Spirit. Joshua is described as "a man in whom is the Spirit" (Num. 27:18). The Spirit entered into Ezekiel to enable him for his prophetic ministry (Ezek. 2:2; 3:24). This appears to have happened on two separate occasions—the Holy Spirit departed from Ezekiel and returned for a second indwelling. Peter refers to a time when the Spirit of Christ was actively indwelling the Old Testament prophets (1 Pet. 1:10–11; the phrase "Spirit of Christ" refers to the Holy Spirit, cf. Acts 16:7; Rom. 8:9; Gal. 4:6; Phil. 1:19).

It has been claimed that Joseph and Daniel were also indwelt by God's Spirit (Gen. 41:38; Dan. 4:8–9, 18; 5:11–14; 6:3). However, this testimony may be questioned since it came from several pagan rulers (Pharaoh, Nebuchadnezzar, Belshazzar's queen, Belshazzar, and Darius) who knew nothing about God's Holy Spirit and thus are not qualified to be expert witnesses. There are several additional Old Testament texts that speak about God putting his Spirit within the heart of the nation of Israel (Ezek. 11:19; 36:26–27; 37:14). This divine promise will be fulfilled in the millennial reign of Christ after his second advent.

14 Leon J. Wood, *The Holy Spirit in the Old Testament* (Grand Rapids, MI: Zondervan, 1976), 69–70.

15 James M. Hamilton Jr., *God's Indwelling Presence: The Holy Spirit in the Old and New Testaments* (Nashville: B&H Academic, 2006).

On far more numerous occasions than indwelling, the Old Testament speaks of the Holy Spirit coming "upon" particular leaders of Israel as an act of empowerment. This was also the language used of Simeon, who held Christ as an infant in the temple (Luke 2:25–35). This language, which precludes indwelling, appears in the Old Testament from Exodus to Joel (see Ex. 31:3; 35:30–31; Num. 11:17, 25; 24:2; Deut. 34:9; Judg. 3:10; 6:34; 11:29; 14:6, 19; 15:14; 1 Sam. 10:10; 11:6; 19:23; 16:13; 19:20; 1 Chron. 12:18; 2 Chron. 15:1; 20:14; 24:20; Isa. 61:1; Ezek. 3:24; 11:5).

The Spirit also on rare occasions physically relocated people (1 Kings 18:12; 2 Kings 2:16; Ezek. 3:12, 14; 8:3; 11:1, 24; 37:1; 43:5). This also occurred in the post-Pentecost era, with Philip and John (Acts 8:39–40; Rev. 21:10).

In summary, indwelling in the Old Testament was infrequent, involved selected leaders in Israel, was temporary, and involved empowerment for a specific service.

New Testament

The Greek terms *oikeō*, *enoikeō*, and *katoikētērion* describe the Holy Spirit "dwelling within" believers, without which indwelling a person is not a true believer (Rom. 8:9; Jude 19). The six key passages discussing the Spirit's indwelling believers include Romans 8:9, 11; 1 Corinthians 3:16; 6:19; Ephesians 2:22; and 2 Timothy 1:14. In each passage *individuals* are indwelt, except in Ephesians 2:22, which seems to speak of indwelling in both an individual and a collective sense—the body of Christ, the church.

The major characteristics of indwelling in the New Testament can be summarized as follows:

1. always begins at salvation
2. inclusive of all believers individually
3. permanent
4. cohesive in the collective sense of the universal church
5. an empowerment for holy living and fruitful service

Clearly there are some very distinct contrasts with Old Testament indwelling and New Testament indwelling. So, were Old Testament saints and are New Testament believers indwelt by the Holy Spirit in the same manner?

Old and New Testament Believers Indwelt Identically?

For the following reasons, it seems that Old Testament believers were not indwelt by the Holy Spirit in the same manner as believers at Pentecost and beyond:

1. The differing characteristics mentioned show a contrast between Old Testament and New Testament indwelling.
2. While all Old Testament believers, like New Testament believers, were regenerated by the power of God's Spirit, nowhere does Scripture teach that indwelling was a necessary component of salvation in the Old Testament.

3. In John 7:39, Jesus explicitly said that the Holy Spirit had not yet been given in the sense of Spirit baptism, Spirit indwelling, and Spirit filling for all believers.
4. In John 14:17, Christ said of the Holy Spirit, "He dwells with you and will be in you." The Greek verb *menō*, here translated "dwells," would be more appropriately rendered "abides," since neither *oikeō*, *enoikeō*, nor *katoikētērion* is used. Thus, while in the future the Spirit "will be *in*" believers, in the present he only "dwells *with*" them.
5. In John 13–17, Jesus told the apostles to expect something significant to occur, because when he departed, the Holy Spirit would be sent in his place. The old covenant was being replaced by the new covenant (Hebrews 8). Indwelling of the Holy Spirit would be a part of the new.
6. There would be no need for Scripture to speak explicitly of the few indwellings in the Old Testament if all Old Testament saints had been indwelt.
7. First Samuel 16:14 records that the Holy Spirit departed from Saul, and in Psalm 51:11, David prays that God would not take the Holy Spirit from him. These passages make the best sense if they are understood to speak of Holy Spirit empowerment and not salvation.
8. New Testament indwelling refers not only to individuals but also corporately to the church. Since the church did not begin until Pentecost, the Old Testament would have had no indwelling like that in the New Testament.

FILLING WITH THE SPIRIT

The Holy Spirit's filling ministry occurred in both the Old and New Testaments. References to the Spirit's filling are seen first in Exodus 31:3 and last in Colossians 1:9. Three periods reveal variations of emphasis and manifestation: (1) pre-Pentecost (Genesis to John, ca. 1440 BC–AD 30), (2) Pentecost (Acts 1–2, AD 30), and (3) post-Pentecost (Acts 3 until the rapture, AD 30 until the rapture).

The Hebrew word *male'* (Gk. *empimplēmi* [Septuagint]) is used in the Old Testament. The New Testament employs three Greek terms that are different but very similar in meaning: (1) *pimplēmi*, (2) *plērēs*, and (3) *plēroō*. All these words carry the basic idea of domination or total control. When describing the work of the Holy Spirit, they convey the general idea of divine sovereignty as the cause and human submission as the effect.

Pre-Pentecost

Old Testament. With regards to the filling ministry of the Holy Spirit, the pre-Pentecost era can be split into two broad periods. First, the whole Old Testament period.

Occasions. Mentions of "filling" occurred during (1) the building of the tabernacle (Ex. 31:2–3; 35:31–35, ca. 1444 BC); (2) the leadership of Joshua (Deut. 34:9, ca. 1405 BC; (3) the building of Solomon's temple (1 Kings 7:14, 40, 45, ca. 966 BC); and (4) the ministry of Micah (Mic. 3:8 [see Zech. 4:6], ca. 700 BC).

Observations. The specific occasions of filling in the Old Testament were noticeably infrequent and involved the Holy Spirit equipping or enabling selected leaders to carry out God's plans at special times in Israel's history. This indwelling did not involve Spirit-produced character. Holy Spirit filling seems very much like these other Old Testament descriptions: "the Spirit rested on them" (Num. 11:26); God "put his Spirit on them" (Num. 11:29); and "the Spirit of God came upon him" (Num. 24:2).

Gospels. The second period prior to Pentecost is the time of Jesus's ministry.

Occasions. "Filling" is mentioned explicitly only four times in the Gospels—all by Luke: John the Baptist (Luke 1:15); Elizabeth (Luke 1:41); Zechariah (Luke 1:67); Christ (Luke 4:1; see Luke 3:22). In two instances there is an implicit filling: Jesus (implicitly) "filled" as a child (Luke 2:40); Christ (implicitly) caused a filling when he breathed on the disciples, saying, "Receive the Holy Spirit" (John 20:22). This act may be understood as Christ's pledge that the Holy Spirit would be coming at Pentecost, just as he promised (John 14:26–27; Acts 1:4; 2:4).

Observations. As with the Old Testament, filling in the Gospels involved Spirit enablement for selected individuals for very unique, unrepeated ministries. From the first Old Testament mention of "filling" until the final Gospel mention—the entire pre-Pentecost period, lasting about 1,475 years—only nine individuals (not including the eleven disciples) are cited as having been filled by the Holy Spirit. Clearly, Spirit fillings prior to Pentecost were rare, limited, and very exceptional.

Pentecost

Occasion. After Christ's resurrection and ascension to heaven (Acts 1:1–11), the eleven (plus Matthias, Acts 1:13, 15–26), family members (Acts 1:14), and other believers (Acts 1:15) gathered in Jerusalem to wait and pray for what Christ promised in the upper room (John 13–17) and in Acts 1:4–5 regarding the imminent ministry of the Holy Spirit.

The Holy Spirit arrived on the day of Pentecost (Acts 2:1–4) and all 120 believers were baptized by Christ with the Holy Spirit into the church (see "Baptism," p. 409; 1 Cor. 12:13). A new phase in God's program (from Israel to the church) began. These 120 were filled with the Holy Spirit (Acts 2:3–4) and were Spirit-enabled to speak in languages that they did not previously know (Acts 2:4–12). Additionally, they all were filled by the Holy Spirit in the sense of Spirit-produced character (cf. Eph. 5:18–21).

Observations. Special Spirit enablement continued, as had been the historical pattern, but on Pentecost, filling became the experience of all Christians, not just a few selected individuals for special occasions. A new dimension involving Spirit-produced character for all Christians also commenced on Pentecost (Eph. 5:18–21).

Post-Pentecost

The Holy Spirit continued to enable select individuals and several select groups of people for ministry, up to and including Paul's first missionary journey (Acts 11:24; 13:9, 52). It can be assumed that the Holy Spirit continued to produce godly character in all Christians (cf. Eph. 5:18–21).

Until ca. AD 48. The period from Pentecost through Paul's first missionary journey gives further illustrations of Spirit filling in the church age. Scripture records eight occasions of Holy Spirit enablement from AD 30 to 48: Peter (Acts 4:8); Christians (Acts 4:31); the seven (Acts 6:3, 5); Stephen (Acts 7:55; see 6:10); Paul (Acts 9:17); Barnabas (Acts 11:24); Paul (Acts 13:9–11); Paul, Barnabas, and others (Acts 13:52).

AD 48 and Beyond. From Acts 14 through Revelation 22 there are no mentions of "filling" that relate to enablement or equipping as had been the case in the Old Testament, the Gospels, Pentecost, and the period after Pentecost through the first missionary journey. It is thus assumed that the "filling" described in Ephesians 5:18–21 prevailed as the exclusive form of filling beginning with the second missionary journey, which commenced in Acts 14.

Ephesians 5:18–21.[16] Paul wrote, "And do not get drunk with wine, for that is debauchery, but be filled with the Spirit" (5:18). The apostle begins with what being filled is *not*.

Being filled with the Holy Spirit is not a dramatic experience of being energized and spiritualized into a state of advanced godliness; it is not some temporary effect that results in ecstatic experiences; it is not a notion at the other extreme, stoically trying to do what God wants us to do, with the Holy Spirit's blessing, in our own power; it is not the same as possessing or being indwelt by the Holy Spirit (he indwells every believer at the moment of salvation; cf. Rom. 8:9); it does not describe a process of receiving the Spirit progressively by degrees, since a Christian not only possesses the Holy Spirit but also possesses him in his fullness; it is not the same as the baptism of the Spirit (see above on 1 Cor. 12:13 and baptism of the Spirit); it is not the same as being sealed or secured by the Spirit. Sealing is

16 This section is adapted from John MacArthur, *Ephesians*, MNTC (Chicago: Moody Press, 1986), 247–48. Used by permission of Moody Publishers.

an accomplished fact (Eph. 1:13). Also, nowhere are believers commanded to be indwelt, baptized, or sealed by the Holy Spirit. The only command is to be filled.

Paul uses the term "fill" in regard to salvation in Philippians 1:11 ("fruit of righteousness"; see also James 3:18). He also employs "fill" to explain sanctification here in Ephesians 5:18–21 (see Col. 1:9–10). Ephesians 1:23 and 3:19 are echoes of 5:18, while Romans 15:13–14 and Colossians 3:12–4:6 parallel the larger context in Ephesians 5:15–6:9. Paul's focus assumes the Ephesians' salvation, and in 5:18–21 he explains their responsibility in the sanctification process as being filled with the Spirit.

Command. Unlike all previous mentions of Spirit "filling," in Ephesians 5:18 Paul commands believers to *continue* being filled with or controlled by the Holy Spirit. He employs an imperative to insist that they continuously submit to the Holy Spirit's control because it is God's will (Eph. 5:17).

Conditions. Christians obey this command by not grieving the Holy Spirit (Eph. 4:30) or quenching the Holy Spirit (1 Thess. 5:19) with sinful habits (cf. Eph. 5:18) or by lying to the Holy Spirit (cf. Acts 5:3, 9).

Christians need to walk wisely (Eph. 5:15) and to walk by and live in the Spirit (Gal. 5:16, 25)—which is by God's Word applied by God's Spirit. Knowing Scripture produces the effect of being filled with the Spirit (cf. Col. 3:12–4:6 with Eph. 5:15–6:9).

Confirmations. The chief characteristic of one's salvation and subsequent sanctification is an ongoing, habitual, growing obedience to God's Word that is empowered by the indwelling Holy Spirit. Ephesians 5:19–6:9 illustrates some primary particulars. The evidence of the Spirit's filling includes offering a continuous and grateful response to the Lord regardless of one's life circumstances (Eph. 5:20; see 1 Thess. 5:18). It also includes living in a humble relationship with others, including other Christians (Eph. 5:21), wives with husbands (Eph. 5:22–24), husbands with wives (Eph. 5:25–33), children with parents (Eph. 6:1–3), parents with children (Eph. 6:4), employees with employers (Eph. 6:5–8), and employers with employees (Eph. 6:9).

All the representative indicators in Ephesians 5–6 are expanded on in other New Testament texts such as 1 Corinthians 13:4–7; Galatians 5:22–23; and 2 Peter 1:5–11.

THE FRUIT OF THE SPIRIT

Living by the Spirit produces fruit (Gal. 5:22–23; cf. John 15; Phil. 1:11). Paul wrote extensively about the work of the Spirit in Galatians. He first discussed the Holy Spirit's work of salvation (Gal. 3:2–3, 5, 14; 4:6, 29; 5:5) and then followed with the Holy Spirit's work of sanctification (Gal. 5:16–18, 22–25). There he contrasted the spoils of the flesh (Gal. 5:19–21) with the fruit of the Spirit (Gal. 5:22–23).

Later, in Ephesians, he similarly spoke of the unfruitful deeds of darkness (Eph. 5:3–7, 11) compared to the fruit of the light (Eph. 5:8–9).

All in all, Spirit-produced fruit can be defined as Christian thinking and living in obedience to Scripture that honors God. It can be classified using six categories:

1. fruit of attitudes (Gal. 5:22–23; Eph. 5:9)
2. fruit of actions (Col. 1:10; Titus 3:8, 14)
3. fruit of worship (Heb. 13:15)
4. fruit of gospel telling (Rom. 1:13; Col. 1:5–6)
5. fruit of truth telling (Eph. 5:9; 1 John 4:2)
6. fruit of abundant giving (Rom. 15:26–28; 2 Cor. 9:6–8, 13; Phil. 4:17)

The Galatians were urged to "walk by the Spirit" (Gal. 5:16, 25), to be "led by the Spirit" (Gal. 5:18), to bear "the fruit of the Spirit" (Gal. 5:22–23), and in so doing to "live by the Spirit" (Gal. 5:25). Fruit (Gk. *karpos*) in Galatians 5:22 is singular, not plural, so true believers will manifest all these elements simultaneously. The nine representative qualities (Gal. 5:23, "such things") refer to the whole work of the Spirit's sanctifying labor in the life of one who has been declared righteous by faith in the Lord Jesus Christ. This picture is similar in kind to the fifteen facets of the diamond called "love" in 1 Corinthians 13:4–7, the qualities of an elder (1 Tim. 3:1–7; Titus 1:6–9), and the qualities commended to and commanded of believers in Christ (Col. 3:12–17; 2 Pet. 1:5–11).

Not surprisingly, Paul begins his discussion of spiritual fruit with the characteristic of love (cf. John 13:35; see 15:8).

Love. Christ's substitutionary death provided the ultimate example of love (Gk. *agapē*). He said, "Greater love has no one than this, that someone lay down his life for his friends" (John 15:13). Paul called for this supreme love to be characteristic of a husband's love for his wife: "Husbands, love your wives, as Christ loved the church and gave himself up for her" (Eph. 5:25). First Corinthians 13:8 promises that "love never fails" (NASB).

Thus, love is a communicable divine attribute that is central to the Father's character (1 John 4:8), put on display by Christ at the cross, and enabled in believers by the Holy Spirit. Love can be defined broadly as the conscious, sacrificial, and volitional commitment to the welfare of another person, in obedience to God's Word (2 John 6), regardless of that person's response or what one does or does not receive from him or her, or what love costs one to give.

Joy.[17] Joy (Gk. *chara*) is a happiness based on unchanging divine promises and eternal spiritual realities. It is the sense of well-being experienced by one who

17 This section is adapted from John MacArthur, ed., *The MacArthur Study Bible: English Standard Version* (Wheaton, IL: Crossway, 2010), 1751. Charts and notes from *The MacArthur Study Bible:*

knows that all is well between oneself and the Lord (1 Pet. 1:8). Joy is not the result of favorable circumstances but is a deep, abiding inner thankfulness to God for his goodness that is not diminished or interrupted even when one's circumstances are the most painful and severe (John 16:20–22; 1 Thess. 1:6). Joy is a gift from God, and as such, believers are not to "manufacture" it but to delight in the blessings they already possess (Phil. 4:4).

Peace.[18] Peace (Gk. *eirēnē*) results in an ordered, settled, and undisturbed response to whatever life brings one's way (Phil. 4:6). This peace is beyond human understanding (Phil. 4:7), an inner calm that results from confidence in one's saving relationship with Christ. The verb form of the Greek term denotes binding together and is reflected in the expression "having it all together." Like joy, peace is not determined by one's circumstances (John 14:27; Rom. 8:28; Phil. 4:7, 9).

Patience. Patience (Gk. *makrothymia*) involves self-restraint that does not retaliate reactively. It endures injuries inflicted by others without the need for revenge and willingly accepts irritating or painful situations. *Longsuffering* captures the essential sense in one word. Paul displayed patience (2 Cor. 6:1–10, esp. 6:6), and both James (James 5:7–11) and Peter (1 Pet. 3:20; 2 Pet. 3:15) commended the fruit of patience.

Kindness. Kindness (Gk. *chrēstotēs*) is expressed as a tender, gentle concern for others that actively seeks ways to serve them. The Father (Rom. 2:4; Titus 3:4) and the Son (Matt. 11:30) displayed kindness in the act of salvation. Believers are to be kind toward one another (Eph. 4:32; Col. 3:12) and are to commend themselves to others through kindness (2 Cor. 6:6).

Goodness. Goodness (Gk. *agathōsynē*) exhibits an actively determined capacity to deal with people in the best interest of God's glory, even when confrontation and correction are required. Goodness is associated with the "fruit of the light" (Eph. 5:9). The Greek word for "goodness" appears nowhere in Greek literature except in the Bible, where in the Septuagint translation of the Old Testament, "goodness" is said to be an attribute of God (Neh. 9:25).

Faithfulness. Faithfulness (Gk. *pistis*) is an inner commitment that consistently expresses itself as an outward loyalty that remains true to one's spiritual convictions. The eleventh chapter of Hebrews recounts the faith and faithfulness of notable Old Testament saints. God exemplifies faithfulness in his own divine

---

English Standard Version originate with *The MacArthur Study Bible*, copyright © 1997 by Thomas Nelson. Used by permission of Thomas Nelson/HarperCollins Christian Publishing.

18 This section is adapted from MacArthur, *MacArthur Study Bible: English Standard Version*, 1751. Used by permission of Thomas Nelson/HarperCollins Christian Publishing.

character (Rom. 3:3). The saints in Daniel's seventieth week are urged to be faithful in the face of possible martyrdom (Rev. 13:10; 14:12).

Gentleness. Gentleness (Gk. *prautēs*), sometimes translated "meekness," basically pictures controlled strength expressed by a humble heart. In its ancient secular sense, the Greek term meant a gentle breeze or a tamed beast, that is, strength used for good, not evil. Paul characterized Christ in this manner (2 Cor. 10:1; see Matt. 11:29). Gentleness describes three attitudes: (1) submission to the will of God (Col. 3:12); (2) teachability (James 1:21); and (3) consideration of others (Eph. 4:2).

Self-Control. Self-control (Gk. *enkrateia*), which literally means "in strength," refers to an inward restraint of appetites and passions resulting in a spiritual mastery that submits consistently to the greater cause of God's will, not man's. This is a commended quality of godliness (2 Pet. 1:6), one with which Paul described the discipline of a winning athlete (1 Cor. 9:25). To the church in Crete pastored by Titus, Paul listed this consistently practiced quality as an identifiable trait of an elder (Titus 1:8).

In summary, the New Testament uses the imagery of fruit to contrast Christians with non-Christians, who lack the Holy Spirit's work of sanctification. First, the lack of fruit identifies an unbeliever, while abundant fruit authenticates a true believer (Matt. 13:18–23; esp. 13:23; John 15:2–6). Second, believers bear good fruit, while unbelievers produce rotten fruit (Matt. 7:16–20; 12:33; Luke 6:43–44; Gal. 5:19–23).

Spiritual Gifts for Serving the Church

In the New Testament, every believer is gifted to serve in the body of Christ, the church.

Several New Testament Greek words help to explain how this works. First, *charis* (Rom. 12:6; 1 Pet. 4:10), normally translated "grace," indicates undeserved or unearned favor. It is the basis for the term *charisma* (Rom. 11:29; 12:6; 1 Cor. 1:7; 12:4, 9, 28, 30–31; Eph. 4:7; 1 Pet. 4:10), which means "grace gift." Both words are used together in Romans 12:6 and 1 Peter 4:10 to provide the fullest sense of spiritual giftedness in the church. Second, *pneumatikos*, used in 1 Corinthians 12:1 and 14:1 in the context of gifts, adds the dimension of being *spiritual* as opposed to being *natural* (see *psychikos* in 1 Cor. 2:14–15; 15:46). In other words, these are gifts associated with the Holy Spirit that have a spiritual nature and that are given for a spiritual purpose. Finally, *merismos* (Heb. 2:4) conveys the idea that the originator and distributor of these gifts is God, not humans.

New Testament spiritual gifts are in a sense Trinitarian. God the Father has planned for and appointed the gifts (1 Cor. 12:18, 28). God the Son has purchased these gifts (Eph. 4:7–8, 11). God the Holy Spirit indwells and empowers people with spiritual gifts (1 Cor. 12:11). All three persons of the Godhead are involved (1 Cor. 12:4–6).

OVERVIEW OF GIFTS

At least seven gift lists can be found in the New Testament. No two lists are identical; thus, they are representative, not exhaustive: see 1 Corinthians 12–13, Romans 12, Ephesians 4, and 1 Peter 4.

While the lists primarily discuss gifts given by the Holy Spirit, several speak to both gifts and gifted offices. Apostles, prophets, and teachers are included with gifts in 1 Corinthians 12:28–30. In contrast, Ephesians 4:11 exclusively lists apostles, prophets, evangelists, and shepherds/teachers.

The following observations constitute some of the most important descriptions and conclusions from God's revelation concerning spiritual gifts:

1. Salvation is a *charisma* gift, that is, an undeserved gift by God's grace (Rom. 6:23; Eph. 2:8; Titus 2:11).
2. The Holy Spirit is also a *charisma* gift, that is, an undeserved gift by God's grace (Rom. 5:5; 1 Thess. 4:8; 1 John 3:24; 4:13; also see Acts 2:38; 10:45; Heb. 6:4).
3. Like Spirit baptism, spiritual gifts accompany salvation.
4. God's will, not human will, determines individual giftedness (1 Cor. 12:11, 18, 24; Heb. 2:4).
5. Spiritual gifts are permanent and irrevocable (Rom. 11:29).
6. Spiritual gifts received with salvation should be distinguished from natural talents possessed from physical birth (1 Cor. 12:11). However, the Holy Spirit can certainly use both kinds of giftedness for his own divine purposes.
7. Spiritual giftedness alone does not necessarily make a Christian spiritual, as demonstrated by the Corinthian church (1 Cor. 14:20). Spiritual character is the highest priority (Col. 1:28).
8. All Christians, without exception, are gifted (1 Cor. 12:7, 11; Eph. 4:7; 1 Pet. 4:10) and can have more than one gift. Each one has a unique combination of gifts.
9. The Holy Spirit produces a variety of gifts (1 Cor. 12:4), which Christians employ in a variety of ministries (1 Cor. 12:5–6) with a variety of outcomes (1 Cor. 12:6).
10. Individual giftedness enhances the corporate good (1 Cor. 12:7) through Christians serving one another (1 Pet. 4:10).
11. Gifts are to be exercised in love (1 Cor. 13:8, 13), because without love, the practice of giftedness is useless (1 Cor. 13:1–3).

12. Gifts differ according to God's grace given (Rom. 12:6; Eph. 4:7) and are to be ministered by Christians as good stewards of God's grace (1 Pet. 4:10).
13. Scripture commands Christians to exercise their gifts (Rom. 12:6; Eph. 4:11–14) as a human responsibility and obligation.
14. The primary purpose of permanent gifts is for the edification of the church (1 Cor. 14:4–5, 12, 17, 26; see Eph. 4:12–13).
15. The fruitful exercise of one's giftedness brings God glory (1 Pet. 4:11).

TEMPORARY GIFTS (REVELATORY/CONFIRMATORY)[19]

The following discussion addresses both temporary gifts that ceased with the apostolic age[20] and permanent gifts that continue to the end of the church age. The seven gift lists record temporary and permanent gifts in three ways. First, two lists emphasize temporary gifts (1 Cor. 12:8–10; 13:8–9). Second, two lists focus on permanent gifts (Rom. 12:6–8; 1 Pet. 4:10–11). Finally, three lists recount a mix of temporary and permanent gifts (1 Cor. 12:28–30; 13:1–3; Eph. 4:11). The temporary gifts served both revelatory and confirmatory purposes in authenticating God's special messengers and the inauguration of the new covenant era.

First, consider Peter's inspired comment in Acts 2:22: "Men of Israel, hear these words: Jesus of Nazareth, a man attested to you by God with mighty works and wonders and signs that God did through him in your midst, as you yourselves know . . ." Here Peter essentially echoed Christ, who asserted that his works certified his claims to deity and messiahship (John 11:47–48).

Second, Paul made a direct statement about miracles in relationship to the apostles in 2 Corinthians 12:12. He noted that the marks (*sēmeia*) of an apostle were signs, wonders, and miracles—supernatural phenomena to authenticate the apostolic messenger and thus validate his message (Acts 2:43; 5:12; Rom. 15:19; Heb. 2:1–4). This is similar to the Old Testament prophets—God fulfilled the prophets' messages and performed miracles through them (see Deut. 13:1–5; 18:21–22) to distinguish between true and false prophets.

Third, the author of Hebrews (Heb. 2:3–4) argued that God used miracles to authenticate the salvation message.

These passages teach that God's primary purpose for the miracles was *to authenticate his messengers (prophets and apostles) as bearing a true revelation*

19 Much of the following discussion of miracles and temporary gifts is adapted from Richard Mayhue, *The Healing Promise: Is It Always God's Will to Heal?* (Fearn, Ross-shire, Scotland: Mentor, 1997), 167–72. Used by permission of Christian Focus.

20 For a more thorough discussion concerning specific temporary gifts and their cessation, refer to chap. 9, "The Church." Also consult the articles in two *Master's Seminary Journal* issues devoted to cessationism and the revelatory gifts: *MSJ* 14.2 (2003): 143–327, and *MSJ* 25.2 (2014): 17–93.

from God. This was true of both temporary revelatory gifts and temporary confirmatory gifts.

The Biblical Pattern of Authenticating Miracles

A review of biblical history reveals three major periods during which God performed miracles through human agency. Such miracles through human agents did occur in other eras, but only rarely by comparison. These three major periods include the following:

1. The ministries of Moses and Joshua, ca. 1450–1390 BC
2. The ministries of Elijah and Elisha, ca. 860–800 BC
3. The ministries of Christ and his apostles, ca. AD 30–60

Still, even in those periods, miracles were not the norm for all of God's servants. Speaking of John the Baptist, the Lord said, "I tell you, among those born of women none is greater than John. Yet the one who is least in the kingdom of God is greater than he" (Luke 7:28). Yet John the apostle writes of the Baptizer, "John did no sign, but everything that John said about this man was true" (John 10:41). Later, John's message was vindicated by Christ's miracles. So the stature of a man of God was primarily evidenced not by sign miracles but by the truthfulness of his message.

Caution from Extrabiblical History

Reports of miracles are not limited to biblical history or even Christianity. In fact, if the mere number of alleged miracles were used to measure the authenticity of a religion, true Christianity would be eclipsed by false religion. The fact that alleged miracles happen outside the Christian faith should cause Christians to be wary of those who claim to do the miraculous.

The history of alleged miracles within the sphere of Christianity since AD 100 is abundant in the area of healing. Noted theologian Benjamin Warfield observed,

> There is little or no evidence at all for miracle-working during the first fifty years of the postapostolic church; it is slight and unimportant for the next fifty years; it grows more abundant during the next century (the third); and it becomes abundant and precise only in the fourth century, to increase still further in the fifth and beyond. Thus, if the evidence is worth anything at all, instead of a regularly progressing decrease, there was a steadily growing increase of miracle-working from the beginning on.[21]

Christians need to heed history's warnings regardless of their own position on miracles done through human agents. Satan will do all that he can to mislead and

21 Benjamin B. Warfield, *Counterfeit Miracles* (1918; repr. Edinburgh: Banner of Truth, 1972), 10.

deceive Christians along the dead-end path of alleged miracles (2 Cor. 11:13–15). Those who have participated in this deception will one day approach Jesus with claims of having done miracles in his name, only to hear him say, "I never knew you; depart from me, you workers of lawlessness" (Matt. 7:23).

The Cessation of Revelatory and Confirmatory Gifts

Have miracles and temporary gifts through human agents really continued beyond the apostolic age? There is no single, explicitly clear biblical statement that specifies whether miracles through men and temporary gifts ceased with the apostles or continued, but if one consults the whole counsel of God, one will find the answer. The case for the cessation of the revelatory sign gifts can be made in response to three questions.[22]

The "What" Question. First, what *are* the biblical gifts of prophecy, tongues, and healing? Prophecy was the infallible proclamation of direct, infallible revelation from God (Deut. 13:1–5; 18:20–22). The biblical gift of tongues was the supernatural ability, granted by the Spirit, of select Christians to speak in previously unlearned human languages (Acts 2:1–11; 1 Cor. 12:30), alongside someone gifted to interpret tongues (1 Cor. 14:28), practiced in the assembly of the church (1 Cor. 14:26) for the edification of believers (1 Cor. 14:5, 26) and as a sign of judgment to unbelievers (1 Cor. 14:21–22). The gift of healing was the supernatural ability to, at will (e.g., Acts 16:18), instantaneously (e.g., Mark 1:42) and irreversibly (e.g., Matt. 14:36; Luke 5:12–13) heal even organic illness and defects (John 9:1–37; Acts 3:1–10) in such a way that is obvious even to the most hostile detractors (e.g., Matt. 12:24; Acts 4:16–17).

It is appropriate, then, to ask whether the most faithful servants of Christ's church have seen these gifts, biblically defined, being practiced since the foundation of the church. Neither in history nor in the present have *these* gifts continued. Though some might use the biblical terminology, the supposed "gifts" presently practiced bear little resemblance to the biblical originals. Prophecy has been redefined to be inclusive of fallible personal impressions; tongues has been redefined as a private prayer language; and healing has been redefined as progressive, incomplete, and reversible. If Scripture teaches that the New Testament gifts of prophecy, tongues, and healing continue today, it is difficult to explain why the Spirit is manifestly not giving *those* gifts to believers, but rather is giving these admittedly different contemporary counterparts.

22 We are indebted to Dr. Nathan Busenitz for this conceptual outline. For a fuller defense of cessationism, see John MacArthur, *Strange Fire: The Danger of Offending the Holy Spirit with Counterfeit Worship* (Nashville: Thomas Nelson, 2013).

The "Why" Question. Second, why were these gifts given? What purpose were they intended to serve? Hebrews 2:3–4 teaches that the purpose of the revelatory gifts was fundamentally to authenticate the messengers of the gospel: "[The gospel] was declared at first by the Lord, and it was *attested* to us by those who heard, while God also *bore witness* by signs and wonders and by various miracles and by gifts of the Holy Spirit distributed according to his will." The revelatory gifts were given to confirm the proclamation of the gospel, being a testimony of God to the authenticity of the apostles' message (cf. Acts 2:22; Rom. 15:18–19; 2 Cor. 12:12).

Such authentication was necessary because the apostles were bringing a new message and new revelation—first to a Jewish community that had been severely warned not to add to Yahweh's words, and then to a Gentile world that regarded it as foolishness. They could not simply claim to have received new revelation and expect to be accepted in the synagogues. Therefore, God confirmed their message by testifying to their genuine commission from him through the miraculous gifts.

But do we stand in need of such authenticating revelation today? No, because we possess today what first-century believers did not: the completed canon of Scripture, the full revelation of God's mind to his people. Now, the fully sufficient sixty-six books of the Old and New Testaments are their own self-authentication. God grounds our faith in the apostolic message not in continuing signs and wonders but in the sufficient Scriptures. These testify to the glory of Christ better than Peter's eyewitness account of the transfiguration (2 Pet. 1:16–21)—better than even the resurrection of the dead (Luke 16:31). The purpose of the revelatory gifts has been superseded by the Scriptures themselves.

The "When" Question. Third, can we say for sure *when* the gifts ceased? As Paul unfolds the mystery of the new man, the church, he speaks of it as a spiritual household: "So then you are . . . members of the household of God, built on the foundation of the apostles and prophets, Christ Jesus himself being the cornerstone, in whom the whole structure, being joined together, grows into a holy temple in the Lord" (Eph. 2:19–21). The key thought is that the spiritual household of the church is built on the *foundation* of the apostles and prophets of the New Testament (cf. 3:5), with Christ as the cornerstone in that foundation. In the church's infancy, this new spiritual organism had not yet received the fullness of new covenant revelation. The apostles and prophets were the revelation-bearing officers of the church. They were thus considered its foundation because the Word of God is the foundation of the church, and that Word of God was still being progressively revealed through them.

But writing the Scriptures was not the only function of the apostles and prophets. The apostles practiced the gifts of healings and miracles, since these are called "signs of a true apostle" (2 Cor. 12:12). The prophets obviously practiced the gift of prophecy. But under the rubric of "prophets" in Ephesians 2:20 we ought also to admit the gift of tongues, because interpreted tongues were virtually equivalent to prophecy (1 Cor. 14:27–29). Thus, prophecy, tongues, and healings and miracles all come under the rubric of "apostles and prophets," who are the foundation of the church.

When one builds a building, one does not continue laying the foundation until the building is done. The foundation is laid, and then the building is built on top of it. Christ continues to build his church (cf. Eph. 4:16), but the foundation was laid when the revelatory ministry of the apostles and prophets had been completed and the fullness of God's revelation was set forth in Scripture. The church then was built on that revelatory foundation—not by adding revelation but by standing on that which was already revealed, proclaiming it, and going forth in its saving and sanctifying power.

In summary, when did the gifts of prophecy, tongues, and miracles and healings cease? They ceased when "the apostles and prophets" ceased, that is, when the foundation of the church had been decisively laid by the completion of the canon of Scripture. Any attempt to exercise such gifts today is to level the building that has been built, to tear up its foundation, and to seek to lay it again.

The following nine temporary, miraculous gifts/offices served revelatory or confirmatory purposes and ceased at the completion of the apostolic era because their purposes had been accomplished:

1. Apostle (1 Cor. 12:28; Eph. 4:11): Men directly commissioned by the risen Christ and sent out to found and establish the church.
2. Distinguishing between spirits (1 Cor. 12:10): The divine enablement to discern true from false statements made by people who deceptively claimed that their words were prophetic revelations from God.
3. Healing (1 Cor. 12:9, 28, 30): The divine enablement to restore the sick to immediate health (which did not necessarily require a faith response by those being healed; e.g., Acts 3:7; 9:40; 16:18; 20:10).
4. Miracles (1 Cor. 12:28): The divine enablement to perform works of power that contravene or exacerbate the normal processes of nature.
5. Prophecy (1 Cor. 12:10; Eph. 4:11): The divine enablement of receiving and communicating direct verbal revelation from God to man.
6. Tongues (1 Cor. 12:10, 28; 13:1): The divine enablement to speak in a real, human language that had not been previously learned.
7. Interpretation of tongues (1 Cor. 12:10, 30; see 14:26–28): The divine enablement to interpret the words of one speaking in tongues.
8. Utterance of knowledge (1 Cor. 12:8; 13:2, 8): The divine enablement to communicate a direct word of insight from the Lord to guide the local

church in understanding a prophecy (deemed a revelatory gift because it is linked with prophecy in 13:8).

9. Utterance of wisdom (1 Cor. 12:8): The divine enablement to give a direct word from the Lord to skillfully guide the local church in a specific decision (deemed a revelatory gift because it is connected with the word of knowledge, which is linked to prophecy in 13:8).

PERMANENT GIFTS (SPEAKING/SERVING)

The following eleven permanent, ministering gifts/offices involve speaking and serving purposes that have continued beyond the apostolic era to this present time:

1. Evangelist (Eph. 4:11): The divine enablement to effectively explain, exhort, and apply the gospel to the unsaved.
2. Exhorting (Rom. 12:8): The divine enablement to effectively incite practical holiness in heart and action through encouragement, comfort, admonishment, and entreaty.
3. Faith (1 Cor. 12:9; 13:2): The divine enablement to trust God in all details of his work even when the outcome seems uncertain. This gift produces stellar assurance that God will accomplish his purposes.
4. Giving (Rom. 12:8; 1 Cor. 13:3): The divine enablement to generously, joyfully, and sacrificially give earthly possessions to the Lord for the work of the ministry.
5. Helping/serving (Rom. 12:7; 1 Cor. 12:28): The divine enablement to sacrificially and submissively help meet the needs of other Christians.
6. Leading/administrating (Rom. 12:8; 1 Cor. 12:28): The divine enablement to zealously govern Christians toward the goal of accomplishing the will of God.
7. Mercy (Rom. 12:8): The divine enablement to cheerfully detect, empathize with, and assist in meeting the physical, emotional, and spiritual needs of other people.
8. Prophecy/preaching (Rom. 12:6): The nonrevelatory, divine enablement to "forthtell," that is, to proclaim the Scriptures.
9. Shepherd/teacher (Eph. 4:11): The divine enablement to shepherd Christians by leading, providing, feeding, protecting, and otherwise caring for them.
10. Spiritual discernment (1 Cor. 12:10): The divine enablement to identify forms of doctrinal error and religious deception. This represents the permanent, ministry aspect of discernment. As "the father of lies" (John 8:44), Satan continually seeks to counterfeit the true work of God by disguising himself as an angel of light (cf. 2 Cor. 11:14), working primarily through false teachers, who dispense "doctrines of demons" (1 Tim. 4:1

NASB). There are those in the church today who have been given a significant ability to identify falsehood by comparing it to biblical truth.

11. Teaching (Rom. 12:7; 1 Cor. 12:28): The divine enablement to clearly interpret, explain, and apply the Scriptures to Christians.

IMPORTANT ISSUES

Believers naturally have a number of questions and concerns about spiritual gifts. Note, therefore, these observations: It is probably better to think each believer receives "a giftedness" rather than "a gift." That is, each Christian has a unique blend of several gifts—a capacity that is spiritual in source and nature (1 Cor. 1:7; 7:7; 1 Pet. 4:10)—not just one exclusive gift. Furthermore, salvation itself is a *charisma*, that is, a free gift (Rom. 6:23), and the Holy Spirt himself is a gift as a part of salvation (Rom. 5:5; 1 Thess. 4:8; 1 John 3:24; 4:13). Yet, every believer has a unique "giftedness," a "manifestation of the Spirit for the common good" (1 Cor. 12:7). Spiritual gifts are diverse (1 Cor. 12:12–27); of the several gift lists in the New Testament, no two are the same (Rom. 12:6–8; 1 Cor. 12:8–10, 28–30; 13:1–3, 8; cf. 1 Cor. 7:7). The kind of spiritual gifts people are given does not necessarily indicate their level of spirituality. In the lists of qualities desired for church leaders and mature believers, spiritual gifts are not emphasized (Gal. 5:22–23; 1 Tim. 3:1–7; Titus 1:5–9; cf. 1 Cor. 13:4–7).

How should Christians identify their gift or "giftedness"? Since spiritual gifts are mostly meant to be used in the context of the local church, it is likely that as Christians serve one another, others will recognize and comment on an individual's spiritual giftedness. An individual may have a personal inclination for some area of service or ministry, so that by serving in that area one is able to maximize a particular ministry with minimum effort. Above all, it should be remembered that spiritual gifts are meant to build up the church (1 Cor. 14:12) and serve one another (1 Cor. 12:7; 1 Pet. 4:10)—they are not for self-exaltation but for the edification of others (1 Pet. 4:10) and for God's glory (1 Pet. 4:11).

The Work of the Holy Spirit in Creation

Very little is written in Scripture about the Holy Spirit and creation (see "Creation," in chap. 3, "God the Father" [p. 136]). Yet the Holy Spirit's participation appears in the very first chapter of the Bible, exactly where one would expect to find it. When God said, "Let us make man in our image, after our likeness," he used the plural pronoun three times (Gen. 1:26). Here the Scriptures undeniably imply that God the Father, God the Son, and God the Holy Spirit were all three involved in creation. Genesis 1:2 actually describes one aspect of the Holy Spirit's contribution. (See also Job 26:13 and Psalm 33:6.)

The Holy Spirit and Scripture[23]

The Spirit of truth (John 14:17, 26; 15:26; 16:7, 13; 1 John 4:6; 5:7) has been actively engaged in every aspect of mediating God's Word, from revelation and inspiration to application.

Christ taught that, in his absence, the Paraclete would come alongside the apostles to equip and exhort them to continue teaching what Christ had taught (John 14:16, 26), to help the disciples bear witness to Christ (John 15:26–27), and to help the disciples convict the world with their message of truth (John 16:7–11). In all four of these passages in John's Gospel, the Greek term *paraklētos* is best translated "Helper." John's emphasis is on the Paraclete helping the disciples specifically to *know* and *remember* and *preach* the truth about Christ. The first five chapters of Acts further confirm that the Paraclete came and helped the disciples to know the truth and to declare it with power (Acts 1:8; 2:4, 33; 4:8, 31; 5:32).

This work of the Spirit with the apostles lays the foundation of the Holy Spirit's ministry with relation to Scripture. Paul spoke of this aspect of the Spirit's ministry in 1 Corinthians 2:10–16, addressing the Spirit's work of revelation and inspiration (2:10–11), instruction (2:12–13), and illumination, affirmation, and utilization (2:14–16).

REVELATION AND INSPIRATION

The term *revelation* generally refers to the divine disclosure, whether by general or special means, of what was previously unknowable to humans (1 Cor. 2:10–11). Inspiration applies only to the written Word of God, whereby the Holy Spirit protects God's revelation through human writers from error in order to provide a completely true and trustworthy writing, down to the very words used (2 Tim. 3:16–17). Peter further explained inspiration by stating that the prophecies of Scripture were made not by an act of human will but rather by men who were directed by the Holy Spirit (2 Pet. 1:20–21). John was in the Spirit (Rev. 1:10) when he received inspired revelation from the "seven spirits" (Rev. 1:4), an idiom that refers to the Holy Spirit using the number of perfection (seven), which speaks of the Spirit's fullness (see Rev. 4:5; 5:6).

The Holy Spirit's role in revelation finds confirmation from many who spoke on behalf of God: in the Old Testament (see 2 Sam. 23:2; Neh. 9:20, 30; Isa. 63:11, 14; Hag. 2:5; Ezek. 3:24, 27; Mic. 3:8; Zech. 7:12); and in the New Testament (see Acts 2:25–26; Matt. 10:20; Mark 13:11; Luke 12:12; Acts 11:28; 1 Cor. 2:10; 1 Pet. 1:10–12). The Holy Spirit gave aid not only in revelation but also in inspiration (see Isa. 59:21; John 16:13; Eph. 3:5; Rev. 1:4, 10).

23 For a more thorough discussion of Scripture, refer to chap. 2, "God's Word."

At times, the New Testament authors speak specifically of scriptural texts that were both revealed and inspired by the Holy Spirit: Matthew (Matt. 22:43); Mark (Mark 12:36, citing Ps. 110:1); Luke (Acts 1:16, 20, citing Pss. 41:9; 69:25; 109:8; Acts 4:25–26, citing Ps. 2:1–2); (Acts 28:25–27, citing Isa. 6:9–10); the author of Hebrews (Heb. 3:7–11, citing Ps. 95:7–11; Heb. 9:1–8, citing Exodus 25–26).

INSTRUCTION, ILLUMINATION, AND AFFIRMATION

The Spirit is given to instruct and teach believers (cf. Neh. 9:20; 1 Cor. 2:13; 1 John 2:27; see also 1 Cor. 2:14–16). Paul prayed for the Ephesians that "the God of our Lord Jesus Christ, the Father of glory, may give you the Spirit of wisdom and of revelation in the knowledge of him, having the eyes of your hearts enlightened, that you may know . . ." (Eph. 1:17–18).

Psalm 119 most frequently mentions the human need for divine instruction. On nine occasions, the psalmist urgently petitions, "Teach me your statutes" (Ps. 119:12, 26, 33, 64, 66, 68, 108, 124, 135). It can be assumed that he looked to the Holy Spirit for instruction. What Christ did for the disciples in opening their minds to understand the Scripture (Luke 24:45), the Holy Spirit does for Christians.

Illumination can refer either to one's salvation (2 Cor. 4:4, 6; see Acts 26:18; Heb. 6:4) or to a believer's need for greater understanding of or enlightenment regarding the Bible. The psalmist who prayed for the Holy Spirit to teach also asked for illumination: "Open my eyes that I may behold wondrous things out of your law" (Ps. 119:18; see also 119:27, 34, 73, 125, 144, 169; Eph. 1:18). Then he testified to the benefit of illumination: "The unfolding of your words gives light; it imparts understanding to the simple" (Ps. 119:130).

While Holy Spirit illumination is indispensably helpful, there are certain things that it is not and certain things that it cannot do. Illumination does not function apart from God's Word (Ps. 119:18; Luke 24:45). It does not guarantee that every Christian will agree doctrinally, because the human element can cause false doctrine (Gal. 2:11–21). Nor does it mean that everything about God is knowable (Deut. 29:29), or that human teachers are unnecessary (Eph. 4:11; 1 Tim. 3:2; 2 Tim. 4:2). Illumination is not a one-time experience nor a substitute for dedicated personal Bible study (2 Tim. 2:15).

In addition to instructing and illuminating the Christian, the Holy Spirit also bears witness to the believer that Scripture is truthful and trustworthy. At least three New Testament texts speak to this aspect of the Spirit's ministry in regard to God's Word (Acts 5:32; Heb. 10:15; 1 John 5:6). By far the most stellar and unimpeachable witness to the Bible is the Spirit of Truth (John 14:17).

UTILIZATION

Not only is the Holy Spirit involved in the delivery and teaching aspects of Scripture (1 Cor. 2:4–5; 1 Thess. 1:5); he also empowers believers in their obedience. The very similar outcomes from letting the word of Christ dwell in a believer (Col. 3:16–17) and from letting the Holy Spirit control the believer's life (Eph. 5:18–20) illustrate that, in addition to the intellectual side of knowing Scripture, the Holy Spirit is equally involved in energizing the volition of believers in obeying Scripture.

The Spirit also provides Christians with and helps them employ spiritual weaponry in battling the spiritual darkness of Satan and demons. A vital part of the Christian's armament is "the sword of the Spirit, which is the word of God" (Eph. 6:17). So, whether it involves walking in the way of Christ or fighting for the glory of Christ, the inseparable connection of the Holy Spirit with Scripture propels the believer onward to victory.

Questions:

1. What are the aspects of personhood and what are the scriptural proofs that the Spirit is a person?
2. What are the several word pictures or metaphors in Scripture that illustrate the qualities or ministries of the Spirit?
3. What are the ministries of the Spirit to Christ? To believers?
4. How do believers/unbelievers sin against the Spirit?
5. What are the attributions, attributes, actions, and associations of the Spirit?
6. What are the erroneous views noted in this chapter about the Spirit?
7. What are the arguments or proofs for the Spirit in relationship to the triunity of God?
8. How are the Spirit's ministries of regeneration, baptism, and sealing defined and defended?
9. What are the differences between the Spirit's work of indwelling in the Old Testament and the New Testament?
10. How is the Spirit's work of filling distinguished from other ministries of the Spirit?
11. What are the different historical eras that inform the Spirit's ministry of filling?
12. What is the "fruit of the Spirit," why is it important, and how is it to be produced?
13. What are the different types of spiritual gifts?
14. Why is distinguishing the types of spiritual gifts important?
15. What are the ministries of the Spirit with respect to Scripture?

6

MAN AND SIN

Anthropology and Hamartiology

Introduction to Man

IMPORTANCE OF ANTHROPOLOGY

Anthropology is the study of humankind (from the Gk. *anthrōpos*, "man" or "mankind"). Secular schools offer courses on anthropology, but they do so from a man-centered perspective. To properly understand man, one must do so from a Bible-based and God-centered perspective.

Biblical anthropology is important. First, it is a topic that deals with ultimate questions: Who am I? Why am I here? What is my purpose in life? Where am I headed?

Second, created last, on the sixth day of creation week, man is unique and is the high point creation. "He is crowned as king of the lower creation and is given dominion over all the inferior creatures."[1]

Third, anthropology helps us understand our relationship to God. Since man is a creature in God's image, we learn how he is supposed to act and relate to God.

Fourth, a biblical anthropology addresses and instructs us on specific issues like abortion, euthanasia, homosexuality, transgenderism, and environmentalism. Much of the world's confusion and sin in regard to these issues stems from

1 Louis Berkhof, *Systematic Theology*, 4th ed. (1939; repr., Grand Rapids, MI: Eerdmans, 1991), 183.

a faulty view of God and man. A biblical anthropology guides us in applying a Christian worldview to critical matters facing our world.

Fifth, a biblical view of man refutes false philosophies and ideologies, such as secular humanism, scientific naturalism, Darwinian evolution, Marxist communism, Freudian psychology, and postmodernism. It also exposes erroneous notions about man in the false religions of Hinduism and Buddhism, among others.

Although humanity consists of both male and female, it is appropriate to use the term *man* to refer to humanity. The Hebrew term translated "man" in the Bible, *'adam*, is used for both mankind in general and man as a male, distinct from a woman. The universal sense of *'adam* is found in Genesis 1:27 and 5:1–2. In both passages, *'adam* (or "man") includes male and female. So, there is scriptural support for using *man* for mankind. Yet *'adam* (or "man") is also used of the male as distinct from the female (as in Gen. 2:22 and 25). This does not reflect a negative bias against women. This chapter will use terms like *humanity*, *humankind*, and *persons* to refer to mankind in general, but *man* in its broader meaning is also appropriate and will be used.[2]

DIVINE SUDDEN CREATIONISM[3]

The origin of the physical universe has emerged as one of the most significant biblical battlegrounds in the twenty-first century. A full discussion of the various creation views is beyond the purpose of this chapter, but the position presented here is "divine sudden creationism."[4] This is the view presented in Scripture and is the context for understanding the creation of man on day six. Key truths, including the greatness and power of God, are lost when one abandons the plain sense of Genesis 1 and 2 that the earth was created directly by God in six literal days.

The creation of the universe was not a long process, nor was the creation of man. The power and glory of God were manifested in a sudden creation, which included both earth and man. Specific statements about God's power in creation occur throughout Scripture (cf. Neh. 9:6; Isa. 44:24; Jer. 32:17; Acts 14:15; Heb. 1:10; Rev. 4:11). This creation was *ex nihilo*—the material and spiritual creation came into being from nothing (cf. Heb. 11:3; Ps. 33:6, 9; Rom. 4:17).

In addition to these strong affirmations that God created the universe, the Bible also makes definitive assertions concerning the nature of the creation. In Exodus 20:8–11, Moses illustrates how the fourth commandment of Sabbath rest should be celebrated by referring to creation as the model. Man is to labor for

2 See Wayne Grudem, *Systematic Theology: An Introduction to Biblical Doctrine* (Grand Rapids, MI: Zondervan, 1994), 439–40.

3 This section is adapted from Richard Mayhue, "Editorial: Scripture on Creation," *MSJ* 23.1 (2012): 1–6. Used by permission of *MSJ*.

4 For more on this view, see the section in chap. 3 titled, "Creation" (p. 146).

six days because God made the heaven and the earth in six days. Since the days of work were measured in twenty-four-hour segments, the periods for creation that served as the prototype also had to be of equal duration. Unless days of equal length were intended, the illustration would be meaningless.

Scripture attributes the work of creation to God's power (Rom. 1:20), for his glory (Ps. 19:1), and revealing his dominion (Ps. 97:9). Such statements are in harmony with the view of divine sudden creation. Only sudden creationism testifies to God's power from the start. The truth that man was created in the image of God (Gen. 1:26) seems to indicate a divine sudden creation, since that image was not the result of a long evolutionary process. New Testament statements about Christ's role in creation fit best with the view of sudden creation (cf. John 1:3; Col. 1:16), and in Mark 10:6 Jesus claimed that man was a part of the creation "from the beginning" and not a subsequent development.

Evidence for sudden creationism can also be gleaned by looking at the coming glorification of believers. In a moment, God will resurrect and glorify the bodies of his people (Dan. 12:2; John 5:29; Rom. 8:23; 1 Cor. 15:51; 1 Thess. 4:16–17). They will be instantly re-created from the dust of the earth. This is like a repeat of the creation of Adam, only this time, not just one body but millions will be re-created.

In addition, what God will do to this earth at the end of its existence is evidence for sudden creationism. In a rapid exertion of divine power, God will destroy the present, cursed earth and universe in a fiery atomic implosion. In its place he will create a "new heavens and a new earth" (2 Pet. 3:10–13). God will suddenly create the new universe out of nothing, just as he suddenly created this present universe.

Genesis 1–2 also contains support for God creating the earth in a short period of time. First, the term translated "day" (Heb. *yom*) in Genesis 1 refers to either the period of light within a twenty-four-hour cycle or the entire period of both darkness and light (twenty-four hours). The one exception is Genesis 2:4, where "day" refers to the entire period of creation.

Second, the Hebrew word for "day" (*yom*), when accompanied by a numerical adjective such as "third" or "fourth" (i.e., an ordinal), is never used figuratively. It is always a twenty-four-hour period. In addition, the Hebrew plural for "day" is never used figuratively in the Old Testament outside a creation context (e.g., Ex. 20:9).

Third, the terms "evening" and "morning" in Genesis 1 are never used figuratively in the Old Testament. They always describe a twenty-four-hour day. God defines "day" in Genesis 1:5 as a period of light and then darkness. After creating light (Gen. 1:3) and causing a spatial separation between the darkness and the light with respect to earth (v. 5), God established the cycle of light and darkness as a principle measurement of time—one day (v. 5). This cycle is one full rotation of the earth on its axis or a twenty-four-hour day.

Together, these points show that God created the earth and everything in it in six consecutive twenty-four-hour days. The human species did not evolve from lower life forms but was created by divine fiat, through the exertion of God's divine will, from lifeless dust (Gen. 2:7; 3:19; Eccles. 3:20; 12:7).[5]

ADAM AS A HISTORICAL PERSON

Genesis presents Adam as a real historical man. The simplest and most natural interpretation of Genesis 1 declares that God created the specific person Adam on the sixth day of creation. Genesis 2 then offers more detail on the creation of Adam and Eve. Adam's connection with other historical persons supports the claim that he was indeed a specific person. Adam is the father of Cain, Abel, and Seth (Gen. 4:1–2, 25; 5:1–3). Adam is also said to have had conjugal relations with his wife, Eve, to bear Cain and Seth, and Genesis 5:3 further states that Adam fathered Seth at age 130. These details cannot be legitimately identified as poetic or figurative language describing something other than reality.

The New Testament also affirms Adam as a historical figure. Jesus's genealogy in Luke includes Adam (3:38; cf. 1 Chron. 1:1). The apostle Paul clearly believed in a literal Adam. His comments about Adam and Jesus in Romans 5:12–21 make sense only if both are historical persons. Adam brings death, guilt, and condemnation to all who are in him (i.e., all who possess human life, with the exception of the Lord Jesus), while Christ Jesus brings life, righteousness, and justification to all who are granted spiritual life through their faith-union with him. If Adam is not a person, then the comparison collapses, including Jesus's role as the One who represents mankind as Savior.

In similar fashion, Paul contrasts Adam and Jesus several times in 1 Corinthians 15 (15:22, 45, 47, 49). Paul's point is that just as we humans bear the image of Adam, so with the coming glorification we will bear the image of Jesus. The comparison assumes that both Adam and Jesus are historical persons who represent humanity (cf. 1 Tim. 2:13).

The historicity of Adam is not a trivial matter. A literal Adam is foundational for understanding the origin and history of the human race, the nature of humanity, the origin of sin, the beginning of human and animal death, the need for salvation, the basis for historical events in Genesis, the reason for functional order within the church, and even the future existence of mankind.[6]

5 For a more thorough biblical defense of a young earth and of literal six-day creationism, see Terry Mortenson and Thane H. Ury, eds., *Coming to Grips with Genesis: Biblical Authority and the Age of the Earth* (Green Forest, AZ: Master Books, 2008).

6 For a further defense of the historicity of Adam, see William D. Barrick, "A Historical Adam: Young-Earth Creation View," in *Four Views on the Historical Adam*, ed. Matthew Barrett and

Created in God's Image

MAN CREATED DIRECTLY BY GOD

Genesis 1 reveals the creation of "the heavens and the earth" (1:1) and all things material and immaterial (see Col. 1:16) in six literal days (Gen. 1:3–31). For the first five days and the beginning of day six, the phrases "Let there be . . ." or "Let there . . ." are used to describe God's creative acts (Gen. 1:3, 6, 9, 11, 14, 20, 24). Yet with the creation of man, a different phrase is used: "Let us make man . . ." (Gen. 1:26). This shift stresses that man has a unique significance within God's creation.

Genesis 2 is wholly devoted to the creation of mankind, including how the first man and woman were made. Also, various terms such as "make"/"made," (Heb. *'asah*) (1:26; 31; 2:18; 5:1; 6:7), "create," (Heb. *bara'*) (1:27; 5:1–2) and "form" (Heb. *yatsar*) (2:7, 8) emphasize God's active involvement in the creation of man.

God's direct creation of man is affirmed throughout Scripture (cf. Ps. 100:3; Matt. 19:4; James 3:9).

Man's creation by God means human existence is not autonomous but is dependent on God. Paul made this clear in Acts 17:28 when he declared, "In him we live and move and have our being." The only reason we are alive is because God exists, created us, and sustains our lives.

Second, direct creation means that man is not God. Man is neither divine nor the highest being in existence. A metaphysical or ontological gap exists between God and man. Man can never be God, nor should he seek to be God.

Third, as a creature, man is obligated to submit to God. Man is not free to do whatever he desires, as if his actions have no consequences with God (cf. Eccles. 11:9). Everything man does must be viewed in light of God's will for him.

Fourth, man has a unique role in God's creation. Genesis 1:26–28 reveals that man is called to multiply, to fill the earth, and to subdue it. The psalmist declared, "the earth he has given to the children of man" (Ps. 115:16), and in eternity, man will reign on the new earth (see Rev. 21:1; 22:5).

Fifth, man was created to give God glory. Isaiah 43:6–7 reveals that God says that his people are created for his glory: ". . . everyone who is called by my name, whom I created for my glory." Everything man does should be for the glory of God (1 Cor. 10:31).

MAN AS THE IMAGE OF GOD (*IMAGO DEI*)

Scripture reveals that man is made in God's "image" and "likeness" (Gen. 1:26–27; 5:1–2; 9:6; 1 Cor. 11:7; James 3:9). The Hebrew term for "image" (*tselem*) signifies a "copy" but also carries the idea of "representation." The Hebrew term for

---

Ardel B. Caneday, Counterpoints: Bible and Theology (Grand Rapids, MI: Zondervan, 2013), 197–227.

"likeness" (*demuth*) can refer to "pattern," "shape," or "form." It signifies something patterned after an original. Its use in Genesis 1:26 indicates that man is patterned after God; he is a son of God. This understanding is supported by Genesis 5:3, which reveals that Seth was a son in the "likeness" of his father, Adam. To join these two meanings together, we can conclude that because he is a son of God, man may function as God's representative.

Implications of Humans Being Made in God's Image

Though human beings are not divine, the fact that they are created in the "image" and "likeness" of God carries significant truths. First, the image of God is affirmed for all persons—male and female alike (Gen. 1:27), and, by extension, for every ethnicity (cf. Acts 17:26). While distinct genders, both male and female are equal as persons and equal in value.

Second, even after the fall (see Genesis 3), all people still possess the image and likeness of God. This is affirmed in Genesis 5:1–3 for all the offspring of Adam and Eve. Genesis 9:6 says that capital punishment is the appropriate penalty for murder since man is the image of God, and James 3:9 condemns cursing people since they are "made in the likeness of God." This affirms that people after the fall still bear something of God's likeness. The image was marred with the curse, but the image and likeness of God, though distorted, was not obliterated.

Third, the image of God explains mankind's capacity to live in relationship with others. The three persons of the triune God—Father, Son, and Holy Spirit—have enjoyed perfect, personal, eternally loving communion with one another from eternity. God is love, and that love was perfectly expressed in eternity past within the Trinity (John 5:20; 17:24, 26). Thus, man is designed in the image of God as a relational being, who is not only able to relate to other people and to God in a loving way but is also required to do so in order to experience fulfillment (Gen. 2:18, 22–24).

Fourth, because man is made in the image of God, he is charged and enabled to "rule" and "subdue" the earth on God's behalf (Gen. 1:26 and 28). The Hebrew term for "rule," used twice in Genesis 1:26–28, is *radah* and means "have dominion," "rule," or "dominate."[7] Later, in Psalm 110:2, the term refers to the Messiah's future rule: "The LORD sends forth from Zion your mighty scepter. Rule [*radah*] in the midst of your enemies." Also, the Hebrew word translated "subdue" in Genesis 1:28 is *kabash*, which means "bring into bondage," even by forceful means (cf. 2 Sam. 8:11). Man's right to rule the creation is affirmed in Psalm 8:4–8, a text quoted in Hebrews 2:5–9, which states that in "the world to come," mankind will rule over the earth. Humanity will do so through the ultimate man—Jesus the

7 See Francis Brown, S. R. Driver, and Charles A. Briggs, *A Hebrew and English Lexicon of the Old Testament* (Oxford: Clarendon, 1962), 921.

Messiah, who will also share his reign with those united to him (see 1 Cor. 15:27; Rev. 5:10). Man is God's image bearer who functions as a mediator-king on earth. God tasks mankind to manage the world as his representatives.

How Is Man the Image of God?

How exactly is man in God's image? The *substantive* view says that the image of God is a characteristic within the makeup of man—the physical body of man or physical characteristic, or a psychological or spiritual quality, such as reason, memory, will, or moral capacity. The *functional* view asserts that the image of God is something humans do, such as ruling and subduing the earth or having dominion over creation (Gen. 1:26–28). The *relational* view claims that relationship is the image of God. This perspective was popular with neoorthodox and existential theologians.

It is probably best to understand that the image of God is substantive or structural to man and that function and relationship are the *consequences* of man being the image of God structurally. Since man is the image of God, he is able to exercise dominion and experience relationships. According to Genesis 1:26–28, man is made in God's image (Gen. 1:26a), and *then* he is tasked with ruling and subduing the earth and being in relationship (Gen. 1:26b–28).

The image's structure permeates man's being and consists of the complex qualities and attributes of man that make him human. This includes his physical and spiritual components. All that makes one a human person is related to the image of God. The following characteristics help to further define man as an image bearer:

Ontologically, man is a living, personal, self-conscious, active being with personality. He is a complex unity of soul/spirit and body.

Volitionally, man has a will and the ability to select between various choices. He can discern right from wrong. This volitional aspect separates man from the animals and other creatures mentioned in Genesis 1–2.

Intellectually, man has a rational mind. He is aware of himself, his environment, other people, and God. He can think critically and logically. He possesses memory, imagination, creativity, and language skills for communicating and understanding the thoughts of others.

Emotionally, a human experiences a wide range of emotions and feelings, such as fear, anger, guilt, anxiety, regret, shame, happiness, and joy.

Relationally, man is equipped to participate in relationships with God and with other people. Jesus said that the greatest commandments are to love God and to love others (Matt. 22:36–40). Only *persons* can give and receive love.

Functionally, man has what he needs to fill, rule, and subdue the earth on God's behalf for God's glory. Males and females have bodies able to reproduce and to interact with a physical environment. Humanity possesses the ingenuity to implement a successful strategy for the earth.

JESUS AS THE IMAGE OF GOD

Jesus Christ is the quintessence of the image of God. He is the "last Adam" (1 Cor. 15:45) and "the image of the invisible God" (Col. 1:15). The Greek term for "image" is *eikōn* and compares to the Hebrew term for image, *tselem*. It conveys both "representation" and "manifestation." God is spirit and is thus invisible, but Jesus as the God-man is the image of the invisible God.

Hebrews 1:3 declares, "He [Jesus] is the radiance of the glory of God and the exact imprint of his nature." "Imprint" (Gk. *charaktēr*) refers to a "stamp" or "impress"; therefore Jesus as the last Adam is the perfect imprint or stamp of God. When we look at Jesus, we see everything God intended for man.

The Human Constitution

Scripture uses various terms to refer to human persons. Five of the more common terms are *body*, *soul*, *spirit*, *heart*, and *conscience*. It is helpful to examine each of these.

BODY

Man's constitution includes a physical component. According to Genesis 2:7, "The Lord God formed the man of dust from the ground." A link exists between earth and man. Man comes from the ground. Just as the creation is material, God's image bearers possess a material element, often called a "body."

In the Old Testament, two primary Hebrew terms refer to "body." *Gewiyyah* occurs twelve times for either a living body (Gen. 47:18; Neh. 9:37) or a dead carcass (1 Sam. 31:10, 12). *Basar*, often translated "flesh," occurs 266 times. It refers to (1) a blood relative (Gen. 29:14; 2 Sam. 5:1); (2) humanity collectively (Gen. 6:12–13; Job 34:15); (3) every living thing (Gen. 9:15–17); (4) the material substance of the body (Gen. 2:23; 17:14; Job 19:26); (5) the whole person (Lev. 17:11; Pss. 16:9; 63:1; Eccles. 4:5); and (6) the person as weak, dependent, and temporary (Gen. 6:3; 2 Chron. 32:8; Ps. 78:39; Isa. 40:6).

In the New Testament, the Greek word for "body" is *sōma*. It can refer to (1) the physical body (Mark 5:29; Rom. 8:11; Gal. 6:17; James 2:16); (2) the whole person (Rom. 12:1; Eph. 5:28; Phil. 1:20); and (3) the fallen, carnal nature (Rom. 6:6; 8:13; Phil. 3:21).

Genesis 1:31 states that everything God made was "very good." This includes the human body. Although the human body is a "lowly body" (Phil. 3:21) and is subject to death (Rom. 7:24), believers can look forward to the resurrection of the body at the rapture (1 Thess. 4:13–18). Because Jesus died and was raised bodily, he is the firstfruits of the resurrection to life eternal and the guarantee that others will be raised bodily as well (1 Cor. 15:20–24). Believers can look forward to a glorified body whose source is heaven (2 Cor. 5:1–5).This is a great hope for

Christians who "await a Savior, the Lord Jesus Christ, who will transform our lowly body to be like his glorious body" (Phil. 3:20–21). Old Testament saints and martyred saints during the tribulation period will be resurrected at the time of Jesus's kingdom (Dan. 12:2; Rev. 20:4).

Bodily resurrection, though, is not just for believers. The wicked will be resurrected for eternal punishment (cf. John 5:28–29; Rev. 20:11–15).

SOUL

Another important aspect of man's nature is the *soul* (Heb. *nephesh*; Gk. *psychē*). The Hebrew word *nephesh* often refers to a person in his entirety as a living being (Gen. 2:7). In most of its uses, *nephesh* is synonymous with being a person.

There are also places where *nephesh* carries the narrower sense of referring to only the immaterial part of a person (cf. Gen. 35:18), and at times *nephesh* refers to the life principle that animates the body (cf. Lev. 17:11). It can also be linked with interior functions of the person, such as intellect, will, and emotions (Lam. 3:20)

The Greek New Testament word for "soul," *psychē*, occurs around 110 times. It is translated as "soul," "life," and "I." This term denotes (1) the whole person (Acts 2:41; Rom. 13:1; 2 Cor. 12:15); (2) the essential being or seat of personal identity, often in relation to God and salvation (Matt. 10:28, 39; Luke 1:46; John 12:25); (3) the inner life of the body (Acts 20:10; Eph. 6:6); (4) the intellect (Acts 14:2; Phil. 1:27); (5) the will (Matt. 22:37; Eph. 6:6); (6) the emotions (Matt. 26:38; Mark 14:34); and (7) the moral and spiritual life (Heb. 6:19; 1 Pet. 1:22; 3 John 2).

At physical death, the soul survives (cf. Luke 12:20; Rev. 20:4). Ultimately, all souls will be united with resurrected bodies (Rev. 6:9–11; 20:4).

SPIRIT

The immaterial part of man is also referred to as "spirit." The Hebrew word for "spirit" is *ruakh* and is used for wind (Gen. 8:1; Amos 4:13), physical breath (Job 9:18; Ps. 135:17), the Spirit of God (Pss. 51:11; 106:33 [ESV mg.]; Isa. 42:1), and the life force of lower creatures (Gen. 6:17; Eccles. 3:19, 21).

In regard to human beings, *ruakh* refers to (1) the whole person (Ps. 31:5; Ezek. 21:7); (2) the power that brings life to the body (Gen. 2:7; Judg. 15:19; Job 27:3); (3) mental capacities: intellect (Gen. 41:8; Ezek. 20:32), spiritual understanding (Job 20:3; 32:8), wisdom (Ex. 28:3), will (Dan. 5:20), and emotions (1 Sam. 1:15; Prov. 15:13); and (4) the openness of the soul to God (Ps. 51:10; Isa. 26:9).

The Greek term for "spirit" is *pneuma*. It connotes the life force that animates the body and departs at death (Matt. 27:50; Acts 7:59; James 2:26; Rev. 11:11). It often refers to interaction with God and the spiritual realm (Rom. 1:9; 8:16; 1 Cor. 14:14; Rev. 21:10). It is also commonly used of the Holy Spirit (Gal. 5:18).

In sum, *ruakh* and *pneuma* are used in Scripture to refer to (1) wind or breath (Gen. 8:1; John 3:8), (2) an attitude or disposition (Matt. 5:3), (3) the Holy Spirit (Gen. 1:2; Matt. 1:18, 20), (4) angelic spirits (1 Sam. 16:14; Matt. 8:16; Luke 7:21), and (5) the human spirit (Gen. 41:8; Acts 17:16).

HEART

In the Bible, the heart is not so much the physical organ but the seat of a person's thoughts, attitudes, motivations, and actions. The Hebrew words for "heart" are *leb* and *lebab* and can refer to the whole person (Ps. 22:26) or to the core of the inner life (Ex. 7:3, 13; Ps. 9:1; Jer. 17:9). "The springs of life" (Prov. 4:23), both good and evil thoughts (Gen. 6:5; 1 Kings 3:12; Job 8:10), intentions (Ex. 35:5; Dan. 5:20), emotions and passions (Deut. 19:6; 1 Sam. 1:8), and actions all flow from the heart. Conscience is linked with the heart (1 Sam. 24:5; Job 27:6).

The Greek word for "heart" is *kardia*. It refers to the governing faculty of the person (Matt. 18:35; Rom. 6:17; 2 Cor. 5:12). Jesus reaffirmed the Old Testament teaching that all thoughts and deeds flow from the heart (Matt. 15:19; cf. Luke 6:45). The heart is also the source of the intellect (Matt. 9:4; cf. Acts 8:22).

All people are born with a dark and evil heart that is "deceitful . . . desperately sick" (Jer. 17:9). Unbelieving hearts are foolish and darkened (cf. Rom. 1:21). But believers receive new hearts (Ezek. 36:26) that are by grace pure (cf. Matt. 5:8), good (cf. Luke 8:15), and sincere (cf. Heb. 10:22). The Christian experiences a new heart that loves God, desires to obey him, is purified, and produces good fruit.

CONSCIENCE

The conscience is a God-given faculty of moral evaluation concerning right and wrong, good and evil. A conscience provides a person with self-awareness and rational capacity, and alerts a person concerning the morality of his or her actions. The conscience functions like a divine moral referee.

Although the concept is clearly there, the Old Testament has no specific term for "conscience." For example, Solomon asked God for "an understanding mind" so he could "discern between good and evil" (1 Kings 3:9). Abigail told David that he should "have no cause of grief or pangs of conscience for having shed blood without cause" (1 Sam. 25:31).

The Greek term for "conscience" is *syneidēsis*, which occurs mostly in Paul's writings. In Romans 2:14–15 Paul writes of the conscience of the Gentiles who lack access to the written Mosaic law yet still know what God requires of them. All people are born with an innate knowledge of right and wrong based on God's law—that is the conscience.

THREE VIEWS OF THE HUMAN CONSTITUTION

Monism

Monism is the view that the human person is one material element; there is no soul or immaterial part. Secular materialism asserts that matter is the only substance in the universe, no spiritual entities exist, and mental and spiritual activities are chemical products of the brain. At physical death, there is no immaterial part to survive.

Dichotomism

Dichotomism holds that man is a two-part being consisting of a body and an immaterial element called either "soul" or "spirit." No real distinction exists between the two terms, which are interchangeable. Dichotomism, then, affirms the human person as a combination of body and soul/spirit. While a person has a physical body, the soul/spirit animates the body and survives physical death. Christian dichotomists point to Genesis 2:7—God formed man from the ground (material) and breathed life into him (immaterial). They also point to Matthew 10:28, where Jesus seemed to affirm a distinction between body and soul.

Trichotomism

Trichotomism also affirms that man consists of multiple parts, but it holds that man is a three-part being comprising body, soul, and spirit. The first element of man is the body, which is the material part of a person. The second part is the soul, which is the psychological element of man; soul is the basis of reason, emotion, personality, and social interaction. The third part is the spirit, which is usually identified as the religious element that perceives and responds to spiritual matters and to God. Whereas the soul is said to interact with horizontal areas related to man's experience with people and nature, the spirit interacts with vertical matters such as man's experience with God. The presence of spirit allegedly distinguishes humans from animals.

Two passages that seem to distinguish "spirit" and "soul" are 1 Thessalonians 5:23 (which also mentions "body") and Hebrews 4:12.

Trichotomism was popular among the Alexandrian fathers of the early church, especially Clement of Alexandria (ca. 150–ca. 215) and Origen (ca. 184–ca. 254).

Evaluation of the Three Views

Materialistic monism must be rejected since it denies the existence of God and all spiritual realities.

Christian forms of monism rightly assert that the human person is a unified self, but they fail to recognize diversity within the unity. The Bible affirms a distinction between body and soul (Matt. 10:28) and an immaterial part that survives physical death (Rev. 6:9–11).

Both dichotomism and trichotomism correctly affirm that man consists of more than matter. The dividing issue centers on whether there exists a substantive distinction between soul and spirit. The biblical evidence indicates that there does not. "Soul" and "spirit" are used interchangeably in Scripture, and both terms indicate similar functions in relating with God, other people, and nature. So, it is difficult to argue that they are distinct parts of a person. Some verses even place "soul" and "spirit" together in parallel form, showing that the same concept is in view (cf. Job 7:11; Isa. 26:9; Luke 1:46–47).

The uses of the terms "spirit" and "soul" in 1 Thessalonians 5:23 and Hebrews 4:12 do not actually support trichotomism. They are different terms for the same immaterial aspect of the person, used together for emphasis, as in Luke 10:27, where Jesus mentions loving God with all one's "heart," "soul," "strength," and "mind." Terms like "heart," "soul," "spirit" are overlapping concepts, not distinguishable parts.

However, since Scripture presents a person as a unified yet complex self, the designation "complex unity" is preferable to dichotomism.[8] The material (body) and immaterial (soul/spirit) function together in one person, embracing both unity and diversity.

God's salvation eventually brings restoration to the whole person. The Holy Spirit regenerates dead sinners, making them spiritually alive to God (Titus 3:5), yet Jesus will also redeem and glorify their bodies (Rom. 8:23; Phil. 3:20–21).

The Origin of the Soul

There are three main views concerning the origin of the soul: preexistence, creationism, and traducianism.

Preexistence is the belief (Plato, et al.) that souls preexisted before conception. Origen (ca. 184–ca. 254) taught that God originally created a fixed number of spirits, some of which were joined to material bodies and became humans. Islam also holds to a form of preexistence before birth. This view has no biblical support.

"Creationism" (narrowly applying the term to this one issue) teaches that each individual soul is created by God and is added to a natural human body. Scriptural support for this view is drawn from several passages: Genesis 2:7 (God breathed a soul into man); Ecclesiastes 12:7 ("the spirit returns to God who gave it"); Isaiah 42:5 (God "gives breath to the people on it [the earth] and spirit to those who walk in it"); Zechariah 12:1 (God "formed the spirit of man within him"); Hebrews 12:9 (God is "the Father of spirits"). The creationist view can be found in church history; Jerome (ca. 340–420), Thomas Aquinas (1225–1274),

8 See James R. Beck and Bruce Demarest, *The Human Person in Theology and Psychology: A Biblical Anthropology for the Twenty-First Century* (Grand Rapids, MI: Kregel, 2005), 137.

and John Calvin (1509–1564) affirmed this view. An important weakness of applying a "creationist" view to this issue is that God's direct-creation acts are said to have ceased on the sixth day of creation.

Traducianism says the soul is transmitted from parents to children by the natural procreation process, just as the body is. While God certainly is man's Creator, and while Adam's body and soul were directly and uniquely created by God, God uses the secondary means of human procreation to provide each person both a body and a soul. Adherents of the traducianist view in church history include Tertullian (ca. 160–ca. 220), Gregory of Nyssa (ca. 330–ca. 395), and Martin Luther (1483–1546). While definitive Scriptural evidence is lacking, the traducianist position seems best. God is man's Creator, but God also ordained human procreation for the filling of the earth (Gen. 1:28). God uses natural means for procreation, yet he is the Ultimate Cause of the process. As a complex unity of body and soul/spirit, our entire being, including the soul, is a result of the God-ordained procreation process.

Gender

GENDER CREATED BY GOD

Despite the modern confusion about gender and gender roles, the Bible is clear that God created gender and human sexuality (Gen. 1:27; cf. Matt. 19:4). Gender is not fluid or flexible; it is not determined by one's preferences or feelings and it did not occur by accident or through an evolutionary process. The first man was directly created male by God (Gen. 2:7). Later, God took a rib from the man and fashioned it into the first woman (Gen. 2:21–22). Thus, the man and the woman were not created in the same way. This difference points to the functional distinctions between men and women. The roles that men and women have in society, the family, and the church are grounded in the differences between men and women that God instituted at creation.

The objective reality of gender is not only grounded in the biblical account of creation but is assumed in the practical application of God's law (cf. Deut. 22:5). Deviating from God's plans for gender and sexuality is rebellion against God (see Rom. 1:24–27).

GENDER, MARRIAGE, AND PROCREATION

Male and female were created for relationship, not isolation. Man was created to need a "helper" (cf. Gen. 2:18a) and woman was created to be that helper (Heb. *'ezer*) (cf. Gen. 2:18b).

When God made the woman from Adam's rib, he brought her before the man (Gen. 2:23), and Adam immediately realized that the woman was the suitable companion for him.

God's intent for man and woman (Gen. 2:24) was a lifelong commitment of unity—"one flesh" in marriage. The term "joined" (v. 24 NASB) (Heb. *dabaq*) means "strong personal attachment and devotion" and involves the sexual union at the heart of the oneness, as well as the children, who are one from two. Yet the unity of marriage goes beyond that, involving mutual dependence in all areas of life. Oneness and intimacy should permeate the marriage relationship.

Marriage has only one definition, and it is sanctioned by God: the union of one man and one woman (Gen. 2:23–24). Marriage is to be a public, formal, and officially recognized covenant between a man and a woman. Prolonged conjugal cohabitation does not establish and is not equivalent to marriage (John 4:18). Where a valid marriage has been established prior to faith in Christ, the couple should keep the covenant and remain married (1 Cor. 7:24)

The man-woman relationship in marriage is designed for procreation. The biological structures of male and female have been designed by God to produce children. According to Genesis 1:28, God blessed the male and female and said, "Be fruitful and multiply and fill the earth." The procreation command given to Adam was repeated to Noah (Gen. 9:1, 7). Not all marriages lead to having children, but arrangements that preclude natural procreation in principle (i.e., homosexual arrangements) do not reflect God's original design for marriage. Homosexual unions cannot rightly be called "marriages," since they involve only one gender, possess no ability to procreate, and cannot provide the kind of sexual companionship God intended.

HOMOSEXUALITY[9]

Deviations and perversions of God's marriage design began immediately after the fall. The sexual innocence of the first couple (Gen. 2:25) was soon replaced with guilt and shame (Gen. 3:7; 8–10).

Sexual perversion also spread quickly. Polygamy appears in Genesis 4:19. Demonic sexual perversion occurs in Genesis 6:2. Other deviations include lewdness (Gen. 9:22), adultery (or near adultery) (12:15–19), fornication (16:4), incest (19:36), rape (34:2), prostitution (38:15), and sexual harassment (39:7). Homosexuality appears on a large scale in Genesis 19.

Marriage is good and holy, but homosexuality is a perverse rebellion that threatens God's intent for marriage and family. The Bible presents homosexuality as sin and explicitly states that practicing homosexuals will not inherit God's kingdom (1 Cor. 6:9–10). Homosexuality perverts God's design that marriage reflects Christ's relationship to his church (cf. Eph. 5:31–32). By tampering with

9 This section is adapted from John MacArthur, "God's Word on Homosexuality: The Truth about Sin and the Reality of Forgiveness," *MSJ* 19.2 (2008): 153–74. Used by permission of *MSJ*.

the participants of marriage, homosexual activity or homosexual marriage distorts the gospel picture that God intended marriage to portray.

In Genesis 1:27, the Hebrew words for "male" and "female" are emphatic, giving the sense of "the one male and the one female." This is God's paradigm for marriage. Based on this paradigm of one man and one woman established at creation, the rest of Scripture strictly forbids any sexual activity outside of marriage—including all fornication (Acts 15:29; 1 Cor. 6:9; Heb. 13:4), adultery (Ex. 20:14; Lev. 20:10; Matt. 19:18), bestiality (Ex. 22:19; Lev. 18:23; 20:15–16; Deut. 27:21), and homosexuality (Lev. 18:22; 20:13; Rom. 1:26–27).

Homosexuality in Genesis

God's opposition to homosexual behavior is illustrated in his response to the perversions of the men at Sodom in Genesis 19. The very term *sodomy*, coming from this incident, refers to the homosexual behavior practiced by the Sodomites. Lot recognized their homosexual passions as inherently wicked (Gen. 19:7), and because the Sodomites were so perverse, the Lord destroyed the entire city with fire and brimstone (Gen. 18:20–33; 19:23–29; cf. 2 Pet. 2:6 and Jude 7).

Sodom establishes that depraved men cannot pursue sensuality and ungodliness and escape God's judgment (Matt. 25:41; Rom. 1:18; 2:5, 8; Eph. 5:6; 1 Thess. 2:16; 2 Thess. 1:8; Heb. 10:26–27; Rev. 6:17). Scripture refers back to Sodom and Gomorrah more than twenty times as an illustration and warning concerning what will happen to those who live such ungodly lives (cf. Matt. 10:14–15; 11:23–24; Luke 17:28–32).

Homosexuality and the Mosaic Code

The Mosaic legal code declares that homosexuality is detestable in the sight of God (Lev. 18:22 and 29; 20:13). Homosexuality is listed in Leviticus 18 and 20 in the context of other sexual sins and is treated as morally equal to adultery, incest, and bestiality. The fact that Christians are no longer under the Mosaic code does not mean that God's attitudes toward these sexual sins, including homosexuality, have changed. The New Testament reaffirms that homosexual activity is sin.

God's view of homosexual behavior is revealed in the word "abomination." The word occurs repeatedly in this context (Lev. 18:22, 26, 27, 29, 30; 20:13) and is also a term found frequently in the book of Deuteronomy (see Deut. 7:25; 12:31; 17:1, 4; 18:9–14; 27:15). Just as idolatry is a perpetual offense to God's moral character, so also is any perversion of God's design for marriage.

Homosexuality and Romans 1

The apostle Paul reiterates the prohibition against homosexuality in Romans 1:26–27. Both male homosexuality and lesbianism are in view in this passage. God's judgment falls on both because they involve unnatural acts. The word translated "relations" (Gk. *chrēsis*) was a common way to speak of sexual intercourse and in this context refers to homosexual acts. Such behavior stems from "dishonorable passions" driven by selfish lust, not love. Marriage is a sacred institution, and any sexual activity with someone other than one's spouse is strictly forbidden by God (Gal. 5:19; Heb. 13:4). This includes not only fornication and adultery but any form of homosexuality, since these are contrary to the divine design established at creation.

Personhood

BEGINNING OF PERSONHOOD

While various views concerning the beginning of personhood have been offered, only one is biblical. This is the view that personhood begins at conception.

Scientific fact demonstrates that human life begins at conception, when all twenty-three pairs of chromosomes are complete. The fertilized egg then contains a complete and fixed genetic structure (DNA).[10] The manifestation of personhood appears rapidly after conception. The Bible makes reference to babies in the womb in personal terms: for instance, Rebekah's children (Gen. 25:21–22; cf. Rom. 9:10–13), Job (Job 3:3), Jeremiah (Jer. 1:5), and John the Baptist (Luke 1:41). Other passages refer to God's intimate knowledge of and involvement with people in the womb (e.g., Job 10:8–11; Ps. 139:13–16; Isa. 44:24). Exodus 21:22–25 strongly shows that the unborn are to be considered persons. This passage indicates that if a pregnant woman is hit by a man and the child within her is born alive without sustaining harm, the man who struck her must pay a fine. But if the child is harmed, then the law of retaliation must be enforced, including death if the child dies ("pay life for life"). The baby in the womb must be a person, since the death penalty is required if the baby in the womb is killed. By this standard, the practice of abortion is murder since it involves the killing of a person—a human being.[11]

END OF HUMAN LIFE

Since the fall (Genesis 3, see below), human death has been the harsh and inevitable final reality. Death is "the king of terrors" (Job 18:14) and Paul referred to death as an "enemy" that must be defeated (1 Cor. 15:26).

While death is often viewed as natural, death is an intrusion into God's creation. God created humans for life, not death. In his original state, man was not created to die, though death was nonetheless a possibility if he rebelled against his Creator (Gen. 2:16–17). Jesus conquered death by his resurrection, and the

10 Beck and Demarest, *Human Person*, 43.

11 For more on this issue see Beck and Demarest, *Human Person*, 45.

fact that death will be finally removed in the coming eternal state (Rev. 21:4) demonstrates that death is not inherent to being human.

God holds sovereign control over life and death (1 Sam. 2:6; Job 12:10). In the future, death will be thrown into the lake of fire after the great white throne judgment, prior to the eternal state (Rev. 20:14).

The Bible links death with a person's final breath (Job 14:10). Genesis 25:8 says, "Abraham breathed his last and died." The same is said of Ishmael (Gen. 25:17). On the cross, "Jesus uttered a loud cry and breathed his last" (Mark 15:37).

The reality of personhood begins in the womb and extends to this final breath, the end of life. The Bible treats all humans through death as persons with dignity. Since being in God's image is structural to being human, there never comes a point when a person becomes anything less than a full person. This includes the elderly and the severely handicapped. Some argue that personhood exists only if someone can function in a certain capacity. But that makes personhood dependent on what a human does rather than on who he or she is. Understanding this point rules out the killing of people whom society might deem unworthy of living. A biblical understanding of human life places a barrier before the termination of a life simply because that person cannot "contribute to society," however that may be defined. From conception to last breath, all human beings are God's creations and should be treated as such.

DESTINY AT DEATH

Cessation of Existence

Those holding to a naturalistic worldview believe that death means the cessation of existence (e.g., the ancient philosopher Epicurus, 341–270 BC). Since naturalists believe that all of reality, including humans, consists only of matter, death of the body means (to them) a permanent end to one's existence. Since consciousness and thoughts are tied only to brain tissue, once the human body dies, all consciousness and thought totally cease. The Bible flatly denies this view (cf. Heb. 9:27).

Continuation of the Soul Only

Some (e.g., the philosophers Socrates [ca. 470–399 BC] and Plato [ca. 428–348 BC]) believe that people possess an immaterial soul that survives physical death to exist in another realm—whether in heaven or in some soulish existence—but that the physical body (which Socrates considered a prison) is temporary and will not be resurrected. Only the soul is immortal. Liberal minister Harry Emerson Fosdick (1878–1969) said, "I believe in the persistence of personality through death, but I do not believe in the resurrection of the flesh."[12]

12 Harry Emerson Fosdick, *The Modern Use of the Bible* (New York: Macmillan, 1924), 99.

Annihilationism

Annihilationism teaches that only some people—believers—will live forever, experiencing the resurrection of the body, while others—the wicked—will cease to exist. Advocates suggest that this annihilation could occur at physical death, at a coming judgment, or after a finite period of punishment in hell. Annihilationists suggest that passages that speak of "eternal" or "forever" punishment for the lost do not mean never-ending, conscious torment. It is only the consequences of being extinguished that last forever. Philip Edgcumbe Hughes (1915–1990) claimed, "Everlasting death is destruction without end . . . , the destruction of obliteration."[13] For Edward Fudge, the biblical language of a lake of fire is a symbol of "irreversible annihilation."[14]

Two assumptions undergird the annihilation view. The first is that God's character is inconsistent with conscious, eternal punishment. Allegedly, God's love cannot be harmonized with such a destiny. The second is that immortality is not inherent to man's existence. Immortality is granted to those who trust in God, while it is refused to those who are lost. It is a reward for those who receive salvation but is withheld from those who do not.

Soul Sleep

The notion of soul sleep, or *psychopannychia*, asserts that physical death brings a temporary end to one's conscious existence until a subsequent day of resurrection. This view denies an intermediate state of conscious existence after death and affirms that the souls of believers sleep rather than going immediately to heaven. Proponents claim scriptural support for soul sleep in Ecclesiastes 9:5 and Daniel 12:2. Defenders of soul sleep include Jehovah's Witnesses, Seventh-Day Adventists, and Christadelphians.

Reincarnation

Reincarnation, or the transmigration of the soul, asserts that at physical death the soul of a person inhabits another entity, such as a human or animal. Reincarnationists believe that all living things experience a cycle of births, deaths, and rebirths until they achieve an impersonal union with the highest reality (in Hinduism, "Brahman"), then the cycle of reincarnation ceases. Most individuals experience reincarnation thousands of times as determined by the law of karma. Karma functions like a law of cause and effect that determines one's existence in the next life.

13 Philip Edgcumbe Hughes, *The True Image: The Origin and Destiny of Man in Christ* (Grand Rapids, MI: Eerdmans, 1989), 405.

14 Edward W. Fudge, *The Fire That Consumes: A Biblical and Historical Study of Final Punishment* (Fallbrook, CA: Verdict, 1982), 117.

Reincarnation is held by millions of Hindus, Buddhists, and Jains. Increasing religious pluralism has brought reincarnation to Western societies. Forms of reincarnation are found in neo-paganism, witchcraft, the occult, and New Age philosophies.

Entry into an Intermediate State Awaiting Resurrection

The traditional Christian view is that the soul/spirit lives in an intermediate state between death and bodily resurrection. While the human person is a complex unity of body and soul/spirit, death causes a temporary separation of body and soul. The body returns to the ground, while the soul resides in another realm. The soul of the believer resides with God in heaven, but the soul of the unbeliever is separated from God in hell. At the coming resurrection, the souls and bodies of all people will be united forever in the final heaven or hell.

Evaluation of Views

The biblical evidence strongly sides with the view that souls enter into an intermediate state awaiting resurrection. This view is largely based on three truths: (1) the human person possesses an immaterial soul; (2) an intermediate state exists; and (3) there is a coming resurrection.

That the human person possesses an immaterial soul was discussed in previous sections on the soul and the human constitution. In regard to the intermediate state, Paul said that being separated from the body meant being with the Lord (2 Cor. 5:8; Phil. 1:23). Jesus told the thief on the cross that he would be with him in paradise that very day (Luke 23:43). Stephen, while being stoned, prayed that Jesus would receive his spirit (Acts 7:59–60). These examples refute the perspectives of the cessation of existence, reincarnation, and soul sleep. Conscious life exists after physical death.

Multiple passages also teach a coming resurrection of the body (cf. Job 19:25–26; Isa. 26:19; Dan. 12:2; John 5:28–29; Rom. 8:23; Phil. 3:21; 1 Cor. 15:23; 1 Thess. 4:13–18). The Bible's clear teaching on the coming bodily resurrection refutes the view that only the soul continues after death. The annihilation perspective denies the testimony of Scripture that the wicked will experience eternal, conscious torment. The Bible uses the language of "eternal fire" (Matt. 25:41) and says that the "smoke of their torment goes up forever and ever" (Rev. 14:11) and that "they have no rest, day or night" (Rev. 14:11). Having no rest indicates self-consciousness. Finally, Jesus set eternal life and eternal punishment side by side in Matthew 25:46: "And these [the wicked] will go away into eternal punishment, but the righteous into eternal life." As eternal life is unending for believers, so too will eternal punishment for the unbeliever be unending. The relationship between the two is symmetrical, not asymmetrical.

Man and Society

ETHNICITY AND NATIONS

An important but often neglected part of biblical anthropology concerns ethnicity and nations. How do the various people groups fit into God's purposes?

Just as God is both unity (one God) and plurality (three persons), God's image bearers evidence both unity and diversity. Humanity is unified, since all humans are descendants of Adam, yet many ethnic groups and nations exist (cf. Acts 17:26). Adam, who transcends ethnic diversity and nations, and was the head of the human race, was created, along with Eve, with the genetic ability to produce a multiplicity of races and various skin colors. When God commanded man to multiply and fill the earth (Gen. 1:26–28), this multiplying and filling would involve differing people groups.

After the global flood, Noah represented mankind as the one from whom diversity would again emerge. Noah's sons—Ham, Shem, and Japheth—became the heads of various peoples in the world (see Gen. 9:19). In Genesis 10–11, the table of nations and the account of the Tower of Babel reveal God's program involves nations and ethnicities. This is the backdrop for God's plan to use Abraham to bless all peoples (Gen. 11:27–12:3). The narratives of the Old Testament depict a wide diversity of nations and peoples and indicate that this diversity was part of God's plan from the beginning (cf. Gen. 12:3; 22:18).

The New Testament also reveals an awareness of and purpose for the nations and the peoples. As the New Testament opens, Jesus is the One who will bless both Israel and Gentiles. Thus Simeon prophesied that Jesus would be "a light for revelation to the Gentiles, and for glory to your people Israel" (Luke 2:31–32). After Jesus's death and resurrection, the gospel was proclaimed to the entire world, with Jesus himself commanding his followers, "Go therefore and make disciples of all nations" (Matt. 28:19). On the day of his ascension, Jesus affirmed the expectation of a restored kingdom for national Israel yet proclaimed the necessity of taking the gospel to all people groups of the world (Acts 1:6–8). As the book of Acts records, the gospel spread from Jerusalem to Samaria to the broader Gentile world. The Jerusalem Council also testified that the resurrected Son of David brought messianic salvation to Gentiles *as Gentiles* (Acts 15:13–18); they did not need to be incorporated into Israel or keep the Mosaic law.

The apostle Paul gave clear teaching in his epistles about ethnicity for the church. Thus, Galatians 3:28 explains that believers equally share salvation and spiritual blessings in Christ regardless of race, gender, or social status. Ephesians 2:11–3:6 says that believing Gentiles are coequal with believing Jews in the people of God and participate together in the covenants and promises mediated through Israel. Believing Gentiles do not become spiritual Jews; instead, Jews and Gentiles share common life together in the church. The unity among Jews and Gentiles is grounded in the death of Jesus and the removal of the Mosaic law (Eph. 2:13–16). Colossians 3:9–11 speaks of a renewal in Christ "in which there is no distinction between Greek and Jew, circumcised and uncircumcised, barbarian, Scythian, slave and freeman" (NASB). Salvation is equally accessible to all people groups. Any animus or hatred for others on the basis of ethnicity is thus a sinful violation of these biblical truths.

The last book of the Bible also describes universal blessings. Representatives of every tribe, tongue, people, and nation will be saved by Christ and will reign when the kingdom comes to the earth (Rev. 5:9–10). Revelation 7:4–9 reveals the salvation of both the tribes of Israel and people from all nations. Revelation 21:3 uses the Greek term *laoi* to refer to the "peoples" of God (ESV mg.), showing ethnic diversity on the new earth. Revelation 21:24, 26 testifies that nations with their kings will bring contributions to the new Jerusalem. And Revelation 22:2 says that the leaves of the tree of life maintain healing and harmony among the nations. Never again will ethnic or national hostility exist, only harmony.

HUMAN GOVERNMENT

Human government is an institution created by God to provide social order in the world.

Biblical Principles of Human Government

The apostle Paul's most extensive discussion on the purpose of government is found in Romans 13:1–7. The apostle Peter expressed the same view of human government in 1 Peter 2:13–14. Several truths come from these two passages.

1. God has appointed human government (Rom. 13:1–2) as his "servant" (Rom. 13:4). Government is part of God's common goodness to mankind.
2. Since God appointed government, resisting government is resisting God. Those who resist its authority will be judged (Rom. 13:2).
3. One purpose of government is "to punish those who do evil" (1 Pet. 2:14). Thus, the one in authority is "an avenger who carries out God's wrath on the wrongdoer" (Rom. 13:4). Government functions as God's mediator to curb evil.
4. Government has the right to carry out capital punishment: "He does not bear the sword in vain" (Rom. 13:4). When Pilate told Jesus that he had the authority to crucify him (John 19:10), Jesus did not dispute this, but he did inform Pilate that his authority came from God: "You would have no authority over me at all unless it had been given you from above" (John 19:11).
5. Another function of government is to approve and praise those who do good (Rom. 13:3; 1 Pet. 2:14). Peaceful, law-abiding citizens need not

fear the authorities. Few governments will harm those who obey their laws; rather, they seek to honor them.

6. Government is a cause for "terror" to those who do bad things (Rom. 13:3). Those who break the law must be afraid of the consequent punishment. Even the most godless governments can deter criminal behavior.
7. All people, and especially Christians, are to be "subject" to human government (Rom. 13:1, 5; 1 Pet. 2:13). The word "subject" was used of a soldier's absolute obedience to his superior. The one exception arises if obeying a civil command means disobeying a command of God (Ex. 1:7; Dan. 3:16–18; 6:7, 10). In this case, "We must obey God rather than men" (Acts 5:29).
8. Obeying government eases one's conscience (Rom. 13:5).
9. People are to pay taxes and show respect to governing authorities (Rom. 13:7). Jesus affirmed taxation when he said, "Render to Caesar the things that are Caesar's" (Matt. 22:21).

Righteous Human Government Awaiting the Messiah

While societies existed after creation, God established the power of government as a mediatorial institution after the flood. Human government was originally instituted to protect human life and punish those who unjustly took human life (Gen. 9:5–6). Here God granted government the right to inflict capital punishment on those who murder a person made in God's image. This is not to be done in acts of personal vengeance but by an established government given the responsibility and right to punish wrongdoers.

Human governments in a fallen world are always susceptible to corruption and wickedness. Even the God-given institution of the Law revealed to Moses (Exodus; Deuteronomy) could not guarantee "good government." Central to a righteous government is a righteous leader, and the only righteous leader the world will ever know is the Messiah—the Lord Jesus Christ (cf. Isa. 9:6–7; 11:4–5). When Christ returns, he will come with his angels to judge the nations of the earth (Matt. 25:31–46) and establish his reign. The twelve apostles will then rule under him with the church over a restored nation of Israel (Matt. 19:28; Rev. 2:26–27; 5:10).

Nations in the Millennial Kingdom and the Eternal State

Nations and governments will exist during Jesus's millennial kingdom. Revelation 20:3 says that Satan will be removed from the earth at that time so that "he might not deceive the nations any longer." This means that nations will exist in that era. Isaiah 2:2–4 reveals that the Lord will then make executive decisions on behalf of the nations and will establish international harmony. When the thousand-year reign of Jesus is nearing its end, Satan will be released from his prison and "will come out to deceive the nations" (Rev. 20:7–8). Those who join him from the nations will be destroyed by fire from heaven (Rev. 20:9–10).

Nations will also exist in the eternal state. Revelation 21:24, 26 refers to "nations" and "kings of the earth" that "bring their glory" into the new Jerusalem. The leaves of the tree of life will maintain harmony among these nations (Rev. 22:2), and these nations will reign over the new earth in the presence of God the Father and Jesus the Son (22:1–5).

HUMAN CULTURE

Human culture has roots in Genesis 1–2. The command for man to rule and subdue the earth and its creatures (Gen. 1:26, 28) is often referred to as the "cultural mandate," since man was to use his abilities and status as God's image bearer to control the creation on God's behalf. This included the land, vegetation, animals, birds, and aquatic creatures. In Genesis 2:15, God put Adam "in the garden of Eden to work it and keep it." Man was given an earthly vocation, and this created culture.

Culture includes works, art, music, education, and all areas where man interacts with his environment. God is the Creator of culture, and man is called to carry it out on God's behalf. The human ability to develop God-honoring culture was damaged by the fall in Genesis 3. Man came under a death sentence, and the environment and all its components were cursed. Mankind would labor hard, but the ground would work against him with thorns and thistles and would eventually consume him in death (Gen. 3:17–19). And yet culture was still in evidence and valued throughout the early stages of human history.

Jubal became the first to compose and play music. He "was the father of all those who play the lyre and pipe" (Gen. 4:21); Tubal-cain was the first to specialize in metals (Gen. 4:22). After the flood, Noah focused on agriculture: "Noah began to be a man of the soil, and he planted a vineyard" (Gen. 9:20; with unfortunate results, cf. 9:21). Culture was also adapted for collective yet nefarious uses, as depicted in Genesis 11 in the account of the Tower of Babel. The people were able to "make bricks" and build with them (Gen. 11:3, 4). The details of "brick for stone" and "bitumen for mortar" show cultural prowess in architecture, although here men used it to make a great name for themselves and to stay located in one area against God's command to multiply and fill the earth (Gen. 9:1).

During the time of Israel's patriarchs, culture focused on pasturing flocks (Gen. 37:13–17). The people constructed temporary dwelling places in winter, and in spring they sought pastures for their flocks. Later, the Hebrew people intersected with Egypt, which had a culture that was sophisticated for its day. While imprisoned in Egypt, Joseph interacted with Pharaoh's "chief cupbearer" and "chief baker" (Gen. 40:1–2). When placed in leadership in Egypt, Joseph helped the Egyptians gather grain for an upcoming drought (Gen. 41:53–57). As the Hebrew people became enslaved in Egypt, they were tasked with building "store cities" for Pharaoh (Ex. 1:11).

Moses was trained in the culture of Egypt (Acts 7:22), although his loyalty was with God's people, the Hebrews. When the Hebrews were freed from Egypt in the exodus, they plundered the wealth of the Egyptians (Ex. 12:36). The Mosaic covenant given at Sinai contained cultural instructions such as the building of the tabernacle, which would be at the center of Israel's worship life. Two gifted artisans, Bezalel and Oholiab, would head up this work (Ex. 31:2–6). Yet Israel's wicked use of culture manifested itself when the people constructed a golden calf to worship (Exodus 32). The contrast between Exodus 31 and 32 highlights culture in a fallen world. As God's image bearers, men are capable of great cultural works, yet apart from God's will, culture can be used for idolatry and wickedness.

Culture was prominent in the life of David. He was a gifted musician and psalmist. His example shows that musical instruments should be used to praise the Lord, including trumpets, tambourines, strings, pipes, and cymbals (Ps. 150:3–5). Solomon also invested much artistic effort and materials in building the glorious and beautiful first temple (1 Kings 7–8). When the queen of Sheba saw Solomon's wisdom, the temple, the food on Solomon's table, the order of his servants, and their clothes, it took her breath away (1 Kings 10:4–5). She was overwhelmed by the beauty and order of Israel's culture during this high point of Israel's kingdom.

While in captivity, Daniel and three associates became an example of being educated in the ways of Babylonian culture without compromising their devotion to the God of the Bible. They refused to partake of the king's food or worship a golden statue (Daniel 1 and 3).

While railing against Israel's covenant disobedience, the prophets of Israel also foretold of a future restoration of Israel with cultural glory (see Isa. 60:5–7 and 65:17–25).

When Jesus arrived, he proclaimed the nearness of the kingdom of God in all its dimensions (Matt. 4:17), yet both the leaders and people of Israel rejected him (Matthew 11–12). Nonetheless, Jesus's death atoned for sins and laid the basis for the reconciliation and restoration of Israel, all nations, and all things (Acts 3:21; Col. 1:20; Rev. 5:9–10). When Jesus comes again in glory, there will be a "new world." Those who left all to follow him will receive houses, family members, and lands in his kingdom (Matt. 19:28–29).

In sum, God created culture. He made a diverse world and tasked man to rule and subdue it for his glory. There is no dichotomy between God and culture or man and culture. God expects man to successfully rule over his creation (Ps. 8:4–8), although the complete fulfillment of this expectation awaits Jesus's kingdom in the "world to come" (Heb. 2:5–8). Culture in this fallen world is infested with sin, so there must also be a purging with fire of all negative remnants of a fallen world, including fallen human culture (2 Pet. 3:8–13). On the new earth, culture will always point to the glory of God. Heaven's culture will do so with absolute holy perfection.

Sin

The universal sinfulness of man is obvious and verifiable. It impacts us individually and societally. It is deeply rooted within us and is manifested continually. Throughout history, societies have consistently acknowledged man's natural sinfulness. However, in the modern Western society of the last two centuries many have attempted to deny the reality of sin. Many people today view human beings as naturally and basically good. They attribute the evils of wars, poverty, and human suffering to evil ideologies and philosophies (fascism, racism), or to inequitable economic conditions, or in some instances to evil individuals who are not typical of the rest of (basically good) humankind. The sinful behavior of individuals is explained (or even excused) as people are viewed primarily as products of their environment, social upbringing, or psychological drives or deprivations. Society has gone so far in accommodating its own depravity that it is reluctant to hold anyone morally culpable for almost any behavior. At the same time, society has shifted toward moral relativism. Today, right and wrong, good and evil, are not defined in absolute terms but are viewed subjectively. Individuals and societies, not God, are seen as having the authority to determine what is wrong. A strong majority of people now believe that truth and morals are flexible and subjective, not fixed. And they have no interest in what Scripture says. In our age of self-esteem and subjectivity, people do not like to think of themselves as evil.

SIN DEFINED

The study of sin is called *hamartiology*. This designation comes from the Greek word for "sin," *hamartia*. Sin is a multifaceted and complex reality. In the Old Testament Hebrew, *khata'* is often translated "sinning" or "sinned" (Gen. 20:6; Ex. 10:16). The word is also linked with "missing the mark" (Judg. 20:16; cf. Prov. 19:2). This term is closely related to the Greek noun *hamartia* ("sin") and its verb form *hamartanō* (cf. Rom. 3:23).

Pasha' is another strong Hebrew term for sin in the Old Testament and means "to rebel," "to trespass," or "to betray" (cf. Isa. 1:2) The Hebrew word *'abar* means "to transgress" or "to pass over." In a moral context it refers to transgressing a commandment or violating a covenant (cf. Num. 14:41; Judg. 2:20).

New Testament (Greek) words for sin include *adikia*, "unrighteousness" or "injustice" (Rom. 1:18; 2 Thess. 2:12); *planaō*, "wandering" or "straying" (2 Tim. 3:13; 2 Pet. 3:17); *anomia*, "lawlessness," i.e., rejecting God's law (1 John 3:4);

apeitheō, being disobedient and willfully obstinate toward God's will (Rom. 11:31; John 3:36); *asebeia*, "ungodliness," "wickedness," or "impiety" (Jude 18); *agnoia*, ignorance or the absence of understanding (Eph 4:18); and *parabasis*, breaking of or deviation from God's law (Rom. 2:23). These representative biblical terms demonstrate the multidimensional nature of sin.

Sin must be understood from a God-centered standpoint. At its core, sin is a violation of the Creator-creature relationship. Man exists only because God made him, and man is in every sense obligated to serve his Creator. Sin causes man to assume the role of God and to assert autonomy for himself apart from the Creator. The most all-encompassing view of sin's mainspring, therefore, is the demand for autonomy.

Because God is the Creator of everything, all creatures are obligated to obey him and to live according to his will. Satan's sin was due to pride: "I will make myself like the Most High" (Isa. 14:14). Adam's sin was disobedience and unbelief (cf. Gen. 3:6; Rom. 5:18–19). Sin, therefore, is acting autonomously and usurping the authority of God.

In his detailed treatise on the sinfulness of mankind in Romans 1–3, Paul explained how sinful creatures violated their relationship with the Creator: "They exchanged the truth about God for a lie and worshiped and served the creature rather than the Creator, who is blessed forever! Amen" (Rom. 1:25). Thus, idolatry occurs when persons exchange the worship of God for the worship of creatures. The peace and wholeness that comes only from worshiping the true God is forfeited when worship is instead directed toward creatures. By rejecting the Creator, the unbelieving heart seeks to satisfy itself with that which cannot bring lasting joy or true fulfillment—whether material possessions, success, admiration, immoral relationships, drugs, alcohol, gambling, or many other substitutes. Those who devote themselves to such things become enslaved to them (2 Pet. 2:19).

In the context of Romans 1, Paul said that foolish people with darkened hearts "exchanged the glory of the immortal God for images resembling mortal man and birds and animals and creeping things" (Rom. 1:23). He singled out homosexuality by both women and men: "For their women exchanged natural relations for those that are contrary to nature; and the men likewise gave up natural relations with women and were consumed with passion for one another, men committing shameless acts with men and receiving in themselves the due penalty for their error" (Rom. 1:26–27).

In light of these factors, we offer this short definition of sin: *Sin is any lack of conformity to God's will in attitude, thought, or action, whether committed actively or passively. The center of all sin is autonomy, which is the replacing of God with self. Always closely associated with sin are its products—pride, selfishness, idolatry, and lack of peace (shalom).*

RELATIONSHIP OF THE DOCTRINE OF SIN TO OTHER DOCTRINES

The doctrine of sin is inseparable from all other biblical doctrines. The doctrine of sin is linked to the doctrine of God, since sin is primarily against God (Ps. 51:4). The doctrine of sin directly defines mankind as fallen and affects everyone, since sin defines every life at birth; corrupts everyone's relationship with God, with other persons, and with creation; and brings all to death. The doctrine of sin obviously affects the doctrine of salvation, since sinners need to be rescued but are unable to save themselves. Because they are profoundly and pervasively sinful, sinners are in need of salvation by grace. The doctrine of sin relates to the doctrine of Jesus Christ, since Jesus is the last Adam, the suffering servant, the Messiah, and the seed of the woman (cf. Gen. 3:15)—the One who conquers sin and all its forms and effects, redeems believers, restores creation, and defeats Satan. Jesus does all this by atoning for the sins of his people. Without his perfect substitutionary death, there would be no salvation from sin. And without his resurrection and exaltation as Lord of all, man would not be able to rule over creation as God promised and expects. Both Satan and the fallen angels sinned against God and were removed from his presence. No salvation is provided for Satan and the demons who followed him. While holy angels are ministering spirits who serve people inheriting salvation (Heb. 1:14), Satan and his evil spirits are deceivers who tempt mankind to disobey God. The church is the community of people saved from sin in this age. It is also God's global ambassador for proclaiming reconciliation to sinners. The church proclaims the gospel of the forgiveness of sins found in Jesus Christ. The fallen world is dominated by sin and its effects. But one day Christ will rule in righteousness during the millennial period (Rev. 20:1–6), Satan and his demons will ultimately be thrown into the lake of fire (20:10), and sin and its effects will be finally removed with the coming eternal state (cf. Rev. 21:4).

ORIGIN OF SIN

Satan

The Bible lays the blame for the sin and death in the world on the first man, Adam (Rom. 5:12). But the sin of the first couple was prompted by the temptation of Satan through a serpent (Gen. 3:1; cf. Rev. 20:2).

Genesis does not describe Satan's fall, but the fall of Satan is probably being referred to in Ezekiel 28 and Isaiah 14. Both passages speak of human kings (of Tyre and Babylon), yet what is depicted goes far beyond any human monarch. Rather, both passages describe the first sin in the cosmos. Ezekiel 28:13 says, "You were in Eden, the garden of God." We are told that Satan was an "anointed guardian cherub . . . on the holy mountain of God" (Ezek. 28:14). The reference to "cherub" means that Satan was an angel in God's presence. Ezekiel 28:15 then states, "You were blameless in your ways from the day you were created, till unrighteousness was found in you." Isaiah 14:14 says that the desire to be like God ("the Most High") was the reason for this angelic worship leader's rebellion (Isa. 14:11–12).

Adam and Eve

Eve was deceived or beguiled (Gen. 3:1–5; cf. 2 Cor. 11:3) by the serpent and ate first from the tree and then gave the fruit to Adam (Gen. 3:6). Still, Scripture places the primary responsibility for this act on Adam, since Adam, not Eve, was the representative head of humanity. Romans 5:12 explicitly places the blame for the sin and death in the world on Adam, the representative head.

Since God cannot sin and does not tempt anyone to sin (James 1:13), and since Lucifer, the angels who followed him, and Adam and Eve were all created sinless, the question arises as to where sin originated. Many believe that since God is all-powerful, the blame for sin must belong to him. This is false. Certainly, the origin of sin is a deep and dark mystery, but God is not the chargeable cause of sin. Because created persons sinned, the capacity for sin had to exist as a possibility within them. Sin occurred because Satan, Adam, and Eve chose to act autonomously to disobey God rather than to love God. Consequently, as creatures, they cannot escape accountability to their Creator.

Sin does not surprise God. He is able to overcome sin and has even ordained it to most fully display his glory, but the blame for sin lies at the feet of the persons who choose to disobey. God's absolute sovereignty in no way undermines man's accountability.[15] This is true both for Satan and fallen angels and for Adam and Eve, who passed on their sinfulness to all their descendants.

Consequences of the Fall

PERSONAL CONSEQUENCES

Sin always disappoints and never satisfies. Adam and Eve were instantly faced with this reality. The aftermath of their sinful act reveals sin's consequences. Embracing the serpent's lie, Adam and Eve expected to become like God, enlightened and fulfilled. Yet the opposite occurred. When Eve and then Adam ate of the forbidden tree, their eyes "were opened," but not in the way they had expected (Gen. 3:7). They did not discover contentment and bliss. Instead, they experienced guilt and shame. They were immediately aware of their nakedness and sewed fig leaves together to cover themselves (Gen. 3:7).

In addition to shame came another consequence: fear. When the couple heard God walking in the garden, they "hid themselves from the presence of the LORD God" (Gen. 3:8), and Adam said, "I was afraid" (Gen. 3:10). Sin causes fear and hiding from God.

15 For more on how God's sovereignty over sin and evil does not make him the chargeable cause of either, see the section in chap. 3 titled, "The Decree, Election, Problem of Evil" (p. 119).

Another result of sin was blame. When God confronted Adam, Adam appeared to blame Eve: "The woman whom you gave to be with me, she gave me fruit of the tree, and I ate" (Gen. 3:12). In reality, Adam blamed God when he said, "The woman whom *you* gave to be with me . . ." Then, when God asked Eve what she had done, she blamed the animal, saying, "The serpent deceived me, and I ate" (Gen. 3:13). The universal default position among fallen persons is to blame someone else for their sin.

These personal consequences of sin are severe. Sin promises enlightenment and peace, but instead it brings shame, fear, and blame, as well as death (Gen. 2:17–19). And as the next section shows, the consequences reach far beyond even this.

THE FALL'S IMPACT ON RELATIONSHIPS

The negative consequences of sin go beyond personal turmoil and despair. Man was created for relationships with God, with other people, and with the creation. All three connections were damaged by the fall of man.

Relationship with God

First and most important, man's relationship with God was severed. Man became spiritually dead. (See "Spiritual Death," below).

In addition, sin brings the wrath of God, which is God's righteous displeasure toward sin (cf. Rom. 1:18; Eph. 5:6). Sin also invites God's punishment. Because he is holy and righteous, God must punish sin. Jesus said that the wicked "will go away into eternal punishment" (Matt. 25:46).

Sin creates enmity, a situation of hostility between parties. Romans 5:10 says that before salvation in Christ, people are "enemies" of God. Unbelievers are "alienated from the life of God" (Eph. 4:18). Also, "the mind that is set on the flesh is hostile to God" (Rom. 8:7). The responsibility for the enmity lies solely with man.

Relationship with People

Next, sin disrupted all human relationships. First, God said that the woman would have increased pain in childbirth, so that even the procreation of another person would be difficult (Gen. 3:16a).

Second, there would be tension between man and woman in the basic and necessary union of marriage. God told Eve, "Your desire shall be contrary to your husband, but he shall rule over you" (Gen. 3:16b). While "desire" could refer to a physical desire for her husband, a desire to control is probably in view. Genesis 4:7, which has a parallel construction, uses "desire" in a controlling sense: "And if you [Cain] do not do well, sin is crouching at the door. Its desire is contrary to you, but you must rule over it." So Genesis 3:16 predicts struggle and conflict within marriage, the most intimate love relationship.

Third, strife between persons in general society is promised and realized. Cain slew his brother Abel out of jealousy (Gen. 4:8). Lamech killed a young man who had struck him (Gen. 4:23). The history of mankind manifests continual hatred, strife, murders, and war.

Relationship with Creation

Man's sin negatively affected his relationship to the creation. Man's mandate to rule and subdue the earth and its creatures is not revoked (Ps. 8:4–8), but creation now works against man and frustrates his efforts. God told Adam, "Cursed is the ground because of you; in pain you shall eat of it all the days of your life" (Gen. 3:17). The cursed ground will lead to "pain" for man. Adam is also told, "Thorns and thistles it shall bring forth for you; and you shall eat the plants of the field. By the sweat of your face you shall eat bread" (Gen. 3:18–19a). So man's interaction with the earth will be difficult, and the earth will even consume him at death (Gen. 3:19b). God's plan for mankind's successful rule of creation remains unfulfilled. It will take the last Adam, Jesus (1 Cor. 15:45), and those who believe in him, to righteously rule the earth (Rev. 5:10). This will occur when Jesus returns and establishes his millennial reign (Rev. 20:1–6).

In sum, not only will Adam and his descendants suffer and die as individuals, but also all his relationships will suffer. Only the Lord Jesus will be able to restore mankind's relationship to God, to one another, and to the creation. As the "last Adam" (1 Cor. 15:45), he will love God and people perfectly and will manifest absolute control over creation.

THREE FORMS OF DEATH

The widespread and devastating results of sin can be summarized in one word: death. God told Adam, "But of the tree of the knowledge of good and evil you shall not eat, for in the day that you eat of it you shall surely die" (Gen. 2:17). Death is the penalty for disobedience. It is a complex concept involving (1) spiritual death, (2) physical death, and (3) eternal death.

Spiritual Death

When Adam and Eve sinned, physical death did not occur immediately. Adam lived 930 years (Gen. 5:5). Spiritual death, however, happened instantly. Spiritual death is the state of spiritual alienation from God. As a result of Adam's sin, all living people (with the exception of the Lord Jesus Christ) are born spiritually dead (Eph. 2:1, 5). For Adam and Eve, sin brought separation from God, banishment from his presence, and forfeiture of spiritual life (Gen. 3:23–24). All their descendants have likewise been born in a state of spiritual death. This deadness also renders a person unresponsive to spiritual truth (Rom. 8:7–8; 1 Cor. 2:14;

2 Cor. 4:4; Eph. 4:17–18). Only by the divine miracle of regeneration does God end spiritual death and re-create sinners, making them alive to himself (2 Cor. 4:6).

Physical Death

The process of physical death started when Adam and Eve sinned. God told Adam, "you are dust, and to dust you shall return" (Gen. 3:19). Even before any human died, animal death occurred when God killed an animal to use its skin to clothe Adam and Eve (Gen. 3:21). Human death first occurred when the initial offspring of Adam and Eve, Cain, killed his brother Abel (Gen. 4:8). The list of Adam's descendants in Genesis 5 starkly reveals that death became the end of every human life, by repeating after every person listed, ". . . and he died" (Gen. 5:5, 8, 11, 14, 17, 20, 27, 31). Besides the past exceptions of Enoch and Elijah and the future exceptions of those who will be alive at the rapture (1 Thess. 4:13–18), physical death will consume all descendants of Adam. The writer of Hebrews declares, "It is appointed for man to die once, and after that comes judgment" (Heb. 9:27). Physical life became brief after the flood. Moses said, "The years of our life are seventy, or even by reason of strength eighty; yet their span is but toil and trouble; they are soon gone, and we fly away" (Ps. 90:10).

Eternal Death

Eternal death awaits those who physically die while being spiritually dead. Those who die in unbelief will face the lake of fire forever (Rev. 20:11–15). John refers to this as "the second death" (Rev. 20:6). While it does not cause people to cease to exist, eternal death is still a kind of death since it involves everlasting ruin, punishment for sins, and separation from God's presence to bless. Only those who are delivered by the gracious work of the Lord Jesus escape eternal death. Revelation 20:6 states, "Blessed and holy is the one who shares in the first resurrection! Over such the second death has no power."

ORIGINAL SIN

The doctrine of *original sin* concerns the question of how Adam's sin affected the entire human race. While "original sin" refers to the first sin committed by Adam, it also encompasses the sinful state and condition of all people because of their relationship to Adam. It explains why people are depraved and tainted with sin from conception.

Psalm 51:5, "Behold, I was brought forth in iniquity, and in sin did my mother conceive me," and Ephesians 2:3, "We . . . were by nature children of wrath, like the rest of mankind" support the concept of original sin. Romans 5:12–21 is the most detailed Scripture passage on this topic. It is also one of the most debated sections in Romans, since several views have been proffered regarding how Adam's sin impacts mankind.

Four truths are asserted in Romans 5:12. First, sin entered the world through "one man"—Adam. Second, sin brought death. Third, death spread to all people. Fourth, the reason death spread to all people is "because all sinned." It is this last point that is most disputed. Augustine used Latin translations of Romans 5:12 that interpreted the Greek phrase *eph hō* in the sense of *in quo* ("in whom"), translating the last part of the verse as "in whom [i.e., in Adam] all sinned." He took that to mean that all people were really *in* Adam and actually participated with him in his sin (see "Realism" below). Most translations today rightly opt instead for a causal sense: "because all sinned."

The Latin mistranslation of Romans 5:12 notwithstanding, the subsequent verses do tie all human sin to Adam. In verses 18–19, Paul explains that "one trespass led to condemnation for all men," and that "by the one man's disobedience the many were made sinners." In verse 15 he also states, "many died through one man's trespass." Furthermore, the aorist tense for "sinned" (Gk. *hēmarton*) at the end of verse 12 ("because all sinned") points to a specific historical event. So, a direct connection does exist between Adam's sin and the sinfulness of Adam's descendants. But what is this connection? Several answers have been offered.

Unexplained Solidarity

One view is that Romans 5:12–21 reveals a vague, unexplained solidarity between Adam and all people. Some connection admittedly exists, but proponents of this opaque idea suggest that it cannot be known with certainty. We must be content with not knowing. This unexplained solidarity position appears to be the default for those unsatisfied with the other views mentioned below.

Bad Example

Some hold that Adam's sin is a bad example left for all people. When people sin, they choose to follow Adam's bad precedent. Humans are not actually guilty for Adam's sin, nor do they inherit a sinful nature from him. No direct transmission of sin exists between people and Adam. This Adam-as-bad-example view is historically linked with Pelagius (ca. 354–ca. 420), the British monk who rejected the doctrine that all humans possess a sin nature. He taught that people are able to obey God without divine grace. Thus, all people are like Adam when he was created, and all are free to either obey or disobey God.

This view will not do. It does not adequately grasp the sinfulness of people after Adam's fall (Eph. 2:1, 5). It also does not do justice to the comparison between Adam and Christ in Romans 5:12–21. Further, if Adam is only a bad example, does this mean that Christ is only a good example and that we are left to save ourselves? Judging by Pelagius's reliance on the freedom of the human will for salvation, one has to answer affirmatively. His condemnation for heresy at the Council of Ephesus in 431 is therefore justified.

Inherited Sinful Nature

Another view is that all people do inherit a corrupt and sinful nature from Adam. Thus, there is a real connection between Adam and his descendants, i.e., all humans. But the *guilt* for Adam's sin is *not* inherited. While the inherited sinful nature may be enough to render a person condemned by God as a sinner, this view maintains that such condemnation is not on account of Adam's guilt being imputed or reckoned to his descendants.

Variations of this perspective exist among Arminians, who have asserted that both Adam's guilt and his corruption pass to all descendants of Adam but that prevenient grace, purchased by Christ's supposed universal atonement, removes the guilt and depravity coming from Adam. No one besides Adam is held responsible for what Adam did. A person becomes responsible as a sinner only when he chooses to sin.

While rightly affirming that all persons have a corrupt nature from Adam, this view does not recognize that Adam's sin directly brings guilt to all people. Paul said, "One trespass led to *condemnation* for all men" (Rom. 5:18), an inherently legal term that establishes guilt. This verse teaches, therefore, that people receive more than just a corrupt nature, since Adam's trespass leads to condemnation. All humans are constituted sinners by Adam's action (Rom. 5:19).[16] Also, the Arminian concepts of prevenient grace and universal atonement, which removes or neutralizes guilt from Adam, have no scriptural support.[17]

Realism

Also known as the Augustinian or seminal view, *realism* asserts that all humanity was physically present in Adam when he sinned. As the first man, Adam collectively represented human nature, of which Adam's descendants are all a part. All were in Adam in seed form when he sinned. This means that Adam's descendants were in Adam's loins participating in his sin. And since everyone participated in Adam's sin, all people are morally guilty and condemned for doing so. Thus, both the corrupt nature and the guilt are passed down naturally from Adam.

Support for the realism view is drawn from Hebrews 7:9–10, which teaches that Levi—the great-grandson of Abraham—paid tithes through Abraham to Melchizedek, because Levi was "still in the loins of his ancestor [Abraham] when Melchizedek met him." In effect, the action of Abraham was the action of Levi. This could also be true of Adam and his descendants; the action (sin) of Adam was the action (sin) of his descendants.

16 See the section in chap. 7 titled, "The Ground of Justification" (p. 328).

17 See the section in chap. 7 titled, "The Author of Regeneration" (p. 301), and "The Extent of the Atonement" (p. 277).

The realism view affirms that the connection between Adam's sin and the sin of humanity is more than just a bad example from Adam or an inherited sin nature. Instead, all people actually participated in Adam's sin; the guilt and condemnation are deserved because all actually sinned. Realism offers an explanation as to how all people can appropriately be guilty for Adam's sin. When Adam sinned, all actually sinned in him. If that is so, advocates say, no one can make the charge that "innocent" people are wrongly imputed with Adam's sin, since everyone actually participated in his transgression.

However, it does not fall to us to sit in judgment on the appropriateness of God's legal declarations. The supposition that it would be unjust to impute Adam's sin to man unless we had actually participated in Adam's transgression does violence to the parallel between Adam and Christ in Romans 5:12–21. No one questions the appropriateness of the forensic imputation of Christ's righteousness to sinners. We would not say that sinners are wrongly imputed with Christ's righteousness unless they actually participated, seminally, in his obedience.

And, of course, we did not. The union between Christ and his people is not a seminal union, for Christ fathered no physical children. Rather, it is a legal union. As our representative, Christ's obedience is counted—legally imputed or judicially reckoned—by God to be *our* obedience. For the parallel between the first and last Adam to hold together (Rom. 5:12–21; cf. 1 Cor. 15:45), Adam's sin must be transmitted in the same manner as Christ's righteousness is. Therefore, because Adam was the representative of all humanity, his disobedience is counted—legally imputed or judicially reckoned—by God to be the disobedience of all who were in him. Those who would charge that such imputation is wrong or inappropriate because not everyone actually participated in Adam's sin show their inconsistency when they do not make the same charge against the imputation of Christ's righteousness. The former draws objections because it is punishment, while the latter is excused because it is a gift. As John Murray explains,

> The analogy instituted in Romans 5:12–19 (cf. 1 Cor. 15:22) presents a formidable objection to the realist construction. It is admitted by the realist that there is no "realistic" union between Christ and the justified. . . . On realist premises, therefore, a radical disparity must be posited between the character of the union that exists between Adam and his posterity, on the one hand, and the union that exists between Christ and those who are his, on the other. . . . But there is no hint of that kind of discrepancy that would obtain if the distinction between the nature of the union in the two cases were as radical as realism must suppose. . . . [And] the case is not merely that there is no hint of this kind of difference; the sustained parallelism militates against any such supposition. . . . This sustained emphasis not only upon the one man Adam and the one man Christ but also upon the

one trespass, and the one righteous act points to a basic identity in respect of *modus operandi.*[18]

Representative Headship

The most acceptable position is that Adam's sin is imputed to all who were united to him as the representative of humanity. Adam's guilt is our guilt. While affirming that a corrupt nature is passed down from Adam, representative headship teaches that all people are condemned because of their direct relationship to Adam as their head.

The representative-headship view (often called *federal headship*) asserts that the action of a representative is determinative for all members united to him. When Adam sinned, he represented all people; therefore, his sin is reckoned to his descendants.

An example of headship affecting others is found in Joshua 7 with Achan and his family. Israel's defeat at Ai was attributed to Achan, who disobeyed God. Achan alone committed this sinful action, yet his sons and daughters were stoned along with him, bearing the punishment along with Achan for his deed (Josh. 7:24–25). In a similar manner, the guilt of Adam's sin is imputed or placed on the rest of the family of mankind.

Those who affirm the representative-headship view first appeal to the parallels made with Jesus in Romans 5:12–21 (discussed above under the realism view). Romans 5:18 says that Jesus's "one act of righteousness leads to justification and life for all men," and Romans 5:19 affirms that Jesus's obedience is imputed to others as their own righteousness. The logic here suggests that if the justification and righteousness of the Lord Jesus is imputed to those who are in him, so too the guilt of Adam's sin has been imputed to those he represented. Again, the Adam-Christ parallel in Romans 5:12–21 is best explained by the idea of representation. Just as Christians are considered righteous because Christ's alien righteousness (i.e., righteousness that is external to the believer) is imputed to all who are Christ's, so too Adam's guilt is imputed to all his descendants, even though they did not personally sin when he did.

Adherents of this view also appeal to 1 Corinthians 15:22: "For as in Adam all die, so also in Christ shall all be made alive." Here death and life respectively are linked with Adam and Christ as two representatives of mankind. In addition, Romans 5:14 explicitly teaches that Adam's offspring did not commit Adam's sin ("... whose sinning was not like the transgression of Adam"). So Adam relates to his offspring as their representative head, and thus the act of Adam is imputed to others, even though the others did not actually commit the sin that Adam did.

18 John Murray, "The Imputation of Adam's Sin: Second Article," *Westminster Theological Journal* 19.1 (1956): 36.

In sum, both men—Adam and Christ—are seen as representatives of humanity, and in the case of both, the effects of their actions are placed on others. Adam is the representative of sinful humanity, and Jesus is the representative of righteous humanity. Significantly, while this view emphasizes imputation via headship with Adam, it also encompasses inherited corruption passed on from Adam to the whole of humanity.[19]

Though historically referred to as *federal headship*, the label *representative headship* is preferable since it better conveys the fact that both Adam and Christ act as the legal representatives for those who are reckoned to be in them. As explained above, this position makes the best sense of the parallels between Adam and Christ articulated in Romans 5 and 1 Corinthians 15.

Some suggest that the representative-headship view is contrary to the strong scriptural testimony that children will not be held accountable for the sins of their fathers (see Deut. 24:16 and Ezek. 18:20). However, there is no real connection between the doctrine of original sin and these passages, which address the guilt and punishment for *personal* sin.

OLD SELF AND NEW SELF

The relationship of Adam and Jesus Christ to humanity is also connected to the concepts of "old self" and "new self," found twice in Paul's letters—Ephesians 4:22–24 and Colossians 3:9–10. The Greek word for "self" in both passages is *anthropos* and refers to "man." Some justifiably translate these as "old man" and "new man."

In Colossians 3:9–10, Paul reminds his Christian readers that the old self has been "put off" while the new self has been "put on." This is a statement of fact, not a command. Christians are no longer the old self but are now the new self. This change occurred when they believed in Christ.

In regard to Ephesians 4:22–24, debate exists as to whether Paul is commanding his readers to put off the old self and put on the new self or whether he is stating a fact that Christians are already a new self, as in Colossians 3:9–10. Either way, Paul is emphasizing that in Christ a transformation has occurred. Christians have gone from being the old self to being the new self. And they are to live in light of this reality.

But what does Paul mean by "old self [man]" and "new self [man]," and how does this relate to the doctrines of man and sin? The old self is the unregenerate self, connected with Adam. It encompasses everything a person is in Adam before

19 Though the representative view has often been associated with a "covenant of works," one does not need to affirm such a covenant in order to maintain representative headship. In fact, not even all covenantalists who affirm federal headship tie it to a covenant of works (e.g., Anthony A. Hoekema, *Created in God's Image* [Grand Rapids, MI: Eerdmans, 1994], 161n65).

union with Christ. The new self is the regenerate self, united with Christ, who replaces the old man. When a person becomes a Christian, he puts on the new self and becomes a "new creation" in Christ (2 Cor. 5:17). He is no longer the old man—the unregenerate self. The new self in Christ is reality. Still, Christians struggle with the flesh, and they must continually put aside fleshly desires. They must walk by the power of the Holy Spirit so that they do "not gratify the desires of the flesh" (Gal. 5:16).

These paradigms of "old man" and "new man" are important distinctions contrasting humanity in Adam and humanity in Christ. One is either in Adam or in Christ; no other option exists. According to Romans 5:18–19, being in Adam means death, guilt, and condemnation. Being in Christ, however, means life, justification, and righteousness.

TOTAL DEPRAVITY

The Bible teaches what has been called total (or pervasive) depravity to describe the corruption and pollution of sin passed down from Adam. Total depravity emphasizes the devastating impact of sin on the person and covers three related concepts: (1) the pollution and corruption of all aspects of a person; (2) the complete inability of a person to please God; and (3) universality, in that all humankind are conceived and born as sinners. Together these show the abysmal state of unredeemed humanity, all of whom are both unable and unwilling to glorify God.

Total depravity does not mean that unsaved people always act as badly as possible. Nor does it mean that unsaved people cannot do relative acts of goodness. Unbelievers can do good things for society, their friends, and their family. These acts have a relative goodness, which corresponds with something Jesus said: "If you then, who are evil, know how to give good gifts to your children . . ." (Matt. 7:11).

Concerning the first feature of total depravity, sin is total or pervasive in that all components of a person are polluted by sin. No part of man escapes. This includes both the material and immaterial aspects of a person—both body and soul. The body decays and is headed for physical death, and along the way, the body functions as an instrument for evil activity. The spiritual part of man is also fully corrupt. This includes all of man's thinking, reasoning, desires, and affections. Thus, Paul concludes, "To the defiled and unbelieving, nothing is pure; but both their minds and their consciences are defiled" (Titus 1:15). Speaking of the godless, Paul refers to "the futility of their minds" (Eph. 4:17). The heart is also debased. Jeremiah 17:9 says, "The heart is deceitful above all things, and desperately sick; who can understand it?" Jesus also teaches that it is from the heart that wicked deeds occur (Mark 7:21–23). On multiple occasions the Bible addresses both corrupt thinking and an evil heart. Paul said, "They are darkened in their understanding, alienated from the life of God because of the ignorance that is in them, due to their hardness of heart" (Eph. 4:18). Also, sinful mankind "became futile in their thinking, and their foolish hearts were darkened" (Rom. 1:21).

Second, sin is total in that man is incapable of pleasing God on his own. Paul states, "For the mind that is set on the flesh is hostile to God, for it does not submit to God's law; indeed, it *cannot*. Those who are in the flesh cannot please God" (Rom. 8:7–8; cf. John 6:44; 1 Cor. 2:14). And Jesus says, "Apart from me you can do nothing" (John 15:5).

Third, sin is universal in that all humans are sinners. First Kings 8:46 declares, "For there is no one who does not sin." And Psalm 14:3 states, "They have all turned aside; together they have become corrupt; there is none who does good, not even one." The entire section of Romans 1:18–3:20 is dedicated to showing that all people are sinners and unable to save themselves, concluding that "all have sinned and fall short of the glory of God" (Rom. 3:23).

Therefore, man's spiritual state is not one of relative neutrality, in which he is able to accept or reject God and his gospel. He is an active hater of God (Rom. 8:7) who cannot accept spiritual truth (1 Cor. 2:14). The total depravity of man demonstrates the absolute sovereignty of God in salvation. Man can do nothing. God must accomplish all as a gift of sovereign grace.

Sin Issues

ARE SOME SINS WORSE THAN OTHERS?

Are all sins the same in God's eyes, or are some sins worse than others? All sins are the same in the sense that each renders a person guilty and worthy of God's wrath. The root of all sin is autonomy and replacement of God with self. However small a sin may appear, it is an assertion that the person is acting independently of God. Breaking any command is an assault against the divine Lawgiver (cf. James 2:10–11). Even one sin against an infinitely holy God demands an infinite punishment.

At the same time, Scripture does speak of the reality that some sins are considered greater than others. When being shown abominations in the temple, Ezekiel was told, "You will see still greater abominations that they commit" (Ezek. 8:13). Jesus explained that those who delivered him to Pilate committed "the greater sin" (John 19:11). In Matthew 11:20–24, Jesus said that the Jewish cities that heard the kingdom message would fare worse on judgment day than the Gentile cities that did not. Greater knowledge brings greater responsibility. In Luke 12:47–48, Jesus taught that a servant who knew the Master's will but did not do it would be treated more harshly than one who did not know the Master's will. Also, James said that a stricter judgment awaits teachers: "Not many of you should become teachers, my brothers, for you know that we who teach will be judged with greater strictness" (James 3:1).

These two biblical realities are harmonized by considering that there is both a quantitative and a qualitative aspect to sin and punishment. All mankind is guilty of sinning against an infinitely holy God. Therefore, all who die without repenting and trusting in Christ face the same quantitatively eternal punishment for their sins. And yet, because God is strictly just, he will punish those who have committed qualitatively greater offenses with a qualitatively greater punishment. The character of their suffering will be exactly proportional to the crimes they have committed (e.g., 2 Pet. 2:17; Jude 13).

THE UNPARDONABLE SIN

In Matthew 12:31–32 Jesus spoke of the unforgivable sin. The context for Jesus's statement is his confrontations with the contentious Pharisees. In 12:22–24, the Pharisees accused Jesus of casting out demons by the power of Satan. The truth was that Jesus cast out demons by the power of the Holy Spirit to demonstrate that the kingdom had come upon the people (12:28). This was the correct significance of his miracles. Casting out demons by the Holy Spirit showed that God's kingdom was at work through the Messiah. In effect and in fact, the Pharisees were denying the work of the Holy Spirit. This was derogatory, blasphemous, and a willful and final rejection of the Holy Spirit who is working through Jesus, by attributing God's work in Christ to Satan.

The reality is that all who finally reject the Lord Jesus in this life, never embracing him in saving faith, will not be pardoned, since forgiveness is offered only to those who believe in him. Though the unpardonable sin described in Matthew 12 involved final hardness of heart against Jesus when he was on earth, the unrepentant rejection of the Lord Jesus Christ is always a sin that remains unforgiven, since forgiveness is found only through repentant faith in Christ. Conversely, anyone who comes to Christ in true repentance and genuine faith will be forgiven (cf. John 6:37; Rom. 10:9).[20]

SIN LEADING TO DEATH

In 1 John 5:16, the apostle John mentions two types of sin concerning a fellow Christian ("brother"). First, he says that there is a sin that does not lead to death. And second, he speaks of a sin that does lead to death. What is the "sin that leads to death"? It is possible that John is referring to a professing believer who demonstrates through habitual sin that he is not an authentic Christian (1 John 3:6). So the sin in question concerns an unbeliever's sin that leads to eternal death.

20 For more on the unpardonable sin, see the section in chap. 5 titled "The Blasphemy against the Holy Spirit and Apostasy" (p. 195).

Apostasy is unforgivable. Praying for restoration in this case is futile because God has already set the rejecter's future (Heb. 6:6).

Another view is that the sin leading to death could refer to a true believer whose life, like that of some at Corinth (1 Cor. 11:29–30), brought shame to Christ, and thus God's discipline resulted in premature death. The Christian's sin is so serious that God takes the person's life. For example, Ananias and Sapphira died on the spot when they lied to the Holy Spirit in front of the church (Acts 5:1–11).

Both of these views reflect biblical truth, and it is difficult to know with certainty which one John intended. In both cases, John concludes that prayer for those committing a sin leading to death will not produce the results that one might anticipate because the prayer is not in accord with God's will (1 John 5:14–15).

ARE THERE MORTAL AND VENIAL SINS?

The Roman Catholic Church promotes the concepts of mortal sins and venial sins. Allegedly, mortal sins are intentional and serious (murder, adultery, fornication) and result in the loss of justification and in spiritual death. If a person dies with a mortal sin on his soul, he is lost forever. The remedy for a mortal sin is the sacrament of penance, which restores one to justification. A venial sin is a lesser or forgivable sin that does not break fellowship with God or result in the soul being eternally separated from God. For example, intentional slander is a mortal sin, while an unintentionally unkind comment may be only a venial sin.

The Bible does not affirm the differentiation of mortal and venial sins—nor the supposed sacramental, penitential remedies for them. All sins establish legal guilt, and without faith in Christ sinners are worthy of eternal separation from God. The categories of mortal and venial sins operate within a faulty view of salvation, in which justification is viewed as a process during which a person can commit certain sins that remove him from a relationship with God, while other sins do not sever that fellowship. The biblical view is that at the moment of saving faith, the Christian is declared righteous (justification by faith alone) because of the imputed righteousness of Christ (Rom. 4:3–5). All sins are forgiven so that nothing can separate the Christian from fellowship with God (Rom. 8:1, 38–39). Furthermore, the Roman Catholic idea of meritorious penance as necessary for the removal of a mortal sin is an error that strikes at the sufficiency of Jesus's atoning sacrifice for sin. Rather than looking to his own acts of penance, the Christian looks to Christ's sacrifice as the full payment for all his sin (Heb. 10:10–18).

SIN AND THE CHRISTIAN

The Bible does not teach the possibility of moral perfection[21] in this life or before the resurrection, so Christians will sin (cf. 1 John 1:8). But when a person trusts in Christ, he receives both forgiveness of sins and Christ's righteousness and is eternally freed from condemnation (Rom. 8:1). Christ died for our sins (1 Cor. 15:3), so all sins—past, present, and future—are forgiven. God, who began a good work in us, will be faithful to complete what he started (Phil. 1:6). Sin will not remove a Christian from God's love; indeed, Paul says that nothing "will be able to separate us from the love of God in Christ Jesus our Lord" (Rom. 8:39).

However, while instances of personal sin cannot break the believer's *union* with Christ, they do have a negative impact on the believer's *communion* with Christ. When Christians sin, they grieve the Holy Spirit (Eph. 4:30). Sin also brings God's discipline (cf. Heb. 12:6; Rev. 3:19).

Sin in the life of a Christian is a serious matter. It harms one's spiritual growth and testimony for Christ. While Christians will never face judicial punishment for sins, they will stand before the judgment seat of Christ to give an account for their deeds done in the body, whether good or bad (2 Cor. 5:10). The dross will be burned away, and the eternal reward will reflect what remains (1 Cor. 3:12–15).

THE COMING "MAN OF SIN"

Before Christ's second coming, the Bible predicts a specific "man of sin," an ultimate Antichrist figure, who will be the consummate embodiment of sin and evil. During the coming day of the Lord, this person will be Satan's counterfeit to the Lord Jesus (2 Thess. 2:3–4). Jesus is the God-man who is the embodiment of righteousness and love. But Satan's man will be the opposite. Paul called him "the man of lawlessness" and "the son of destruction" (2 Thess. 2:3).

The conditions surrounding this "man of lawlessness" are detailed in 2 Thessalonians 2. There Paul refuted the erroneous belief that the "day of the Lord" had already begun. He revealed that two events would coincide with the coming of the day of the Lord, and since neither of those events had occurred, the day of the Lord could not yet have arrived. The first event would be a massive rebellion in which a great apostasy against God would occur. The second would be the arrival of the man of sin—"the man of lawlessness . . . the son of destruction"—who would oppose God and demand worship of himself (2 Thess. 2:3–4). The word for "lawlessness" comes from the Greek term *anomia*, which means "against law" or "lawless." In this context it means "to be opposed to God's law and purposes."

21 For more on the biblical refutation of the doctrine of perfectionism, see the section in chap. 7 titled, "Perfected Sanctification" (p. 345).

This passage goes on to describe the activity of this man of sin (see 2 Thess. 2:4–10). He will oppose God and exalt himself (2 Thess. 2:4) and he will also sit in God's temple in Jerusalem and declare himself to be God (see Dan. 9:27; Matt. 24:15). The eschatological man of lawlessness will do his work "by the activity of Satan" (2 Thess. 2:9–10). Just as Jesus did his miracles in the power of the Holy Spirit, this man will be empowered by Satan. He will come with "false signs and wonders" that further the "wicked deception" of lost people who are perishing.

The man of sin will have a short career (2 Thess. 2:8) and will be thrown into the lake of fire. His reign of wickedness will be replaced by the kingdom of righteousness, ruled by the Lord Jesus Christ (Isaiah 11; Zechariah 14).

GOD AND THE PROBLEM OF EVIL

The reality of evil and suffering is used by some as a reason for rejecting God. Allegedly, if God were all-good and all-powerful, then evil and suffering would not exist. But contrary to disproving God, the existence of evil and suffering can be adequately explained only from a Christian worldview rooted in the biblical perspective of creation and the fall. (See "The Problem of Evil and Theodicy," in chap. 3, "God the Father," [p. 133].[22]) The comments are appropriate here in light of sin's role in producing evil and suffering.

One must remember that God is the sovereign King of the universe, who does as he wills without needing to answer to man (Rom. 9:20). God is not on trial, and any apparent contradictions between God's existence and the reality of evil are simply that—apparent, not real. With this reality understood, several points can help one understand evil and suffering.

First, God created the world and called everything in it "very good" (Gen. 1:31). No sin or death existed during creation week. These were introduced later by Adam (Genesis 3; cf. Rom. 5:12). God told Adam that eating from the tree of the knowledge of good and evil would bring death (Gen. 2:15–17), but Adam nevertheless willfully disobeyed his Creator, to whom he was accountable. The responsibility for sin lies at the feet of sinful man. God is not the chargeable cause of evil (cf. Rom. 3:5–6; 9:14).

Second, when Adam disobeyed God, Adam introduced both moral and natural evil into the world. By sinning against God, man brought hostility into human relationships and moral evil into creation. Sin also affected the natural order. Since man was the pinnacle of creation and was tasked with ruling and subduing the rest of creation, his sin impacted all nature. God cursed the ground because of man's sin, and thus, nature now works against man (Gen. 3:17). Paul says that

22 See also the section in chap. 3 titled, "Objection 4: The Decree of God Makes God the Chargeable Cause of Sin" (p. 132).

creation was subjected to futility against its will (Rom. 8:20). The responsibility for the fallen world lies with man, not God.

But why doesn't God simply fix the world or intervene to stop tragedies and acts of evil? Part of the answer is that mankind is experiencing the consequences of sin. God made man his vice-regent, and man possessed everything he needed to rule the earth successfully. Yet when he sinned, God was not bound to shield man from the consequences of his rebellion.

Third, God has not left man alone to wallow and suffer without hope. He introduced a promise to restore creation and defeat the evil power behind the serpent (Gen. 3:15), a plan that ultimately culminates in Jesus Christ and will be fulfilled by his first and second comings. Also, God brings undeserved common goodness to mankind (Matt. 5:45). He restrains evil (2 Thess. 2:7), and he instituted the conscience to restrict the sinner's freedom (Rom. 2:14–15) and human government to punish evildoers (Rom. 13:1–7). God himself also experienced the effects of a fallen world when Jesus became a "man of sorrows" (Isa. 53:3) who lived, suffered, and died on a cross as a sin bearer under divine wrath. Jesus's death and resurrection laid the foundation for the coming restoration of all things (Col. 1:20; Rev. 5:9–10). No one can rightly say that God is a detached observer of evil and suffering. Jesus left heaven and suffered as no person has ever suffered in order to deliver sinners from eternal suffering.

Finally, a judgment day is coming when God will make all things right. He will reward what is right and punish what is wrong. Paul noted that when Jesus comes, he "will bring to light the things now hidden in darkness and will disclose the purposes of the heart. Then each one will receive his commendation from God" (1 Cor. 4:5). The righteous, who have received salvation in Christ, will experience glory far beyond the sufferings of this life (Rom. 8:18). This truth gives eternal perspective to our temporal sufferings in this fallen world. A day is coming when all tears of sorrow will be removed and when death will be no more (Rev. 21:4). Believers will experience the joys of a new earth forever, and sin will forever cease. As Paul explained, "The sting of death is sin. . . . But thanks be to God, who gives us the victory through our Lord Jesus Christ" (1 Cor. 15:56–57). And all the children of God will be forever loved by God as he has always loved his eternal Son (John 17:24–26).

Questions:

1. Why is biblical anthropology important?
2. What are the arguments for divine sudden creationism?
3. What does the Bible teach about the image of God in man, and what are the implications of that teaching?

4. What are the various terms used to refer to the human person in Scripture? (texts and definitions)
5. What are the three views of the human constitution?
6. What are the three views of the origin of the human soul?
7. What does the Bible teach about gender and the related issues of marriage and homosexuality?
8. What are the views of human destiny after death?
9. What does the Bible teach about ethnicity, human government, and human culture?
10. What is the biblical definition of sin, and how does the doctrine of sin relate to other biblical doctrines?
11. Where did sin come from?
12. What were and what are the consequences of the fall (Genesis 3)?
13. What are the various views of original sin? (texts and explanation)
14. What is "total depravity"?

7

SALVATION

Soteriology

Introduction to Soteriology

In coming to the doctrine of soteriology, the student of Scripture arrives at the pinnacle of Christian theology, for the themes and topics addressed in the study of salvation run to the very heart of the gospel and to the center of redemptive history. As has been demonstrated in chapter 6, man has utterly failed in his charge to rule over creation as God's representative on earth. He has sinned against God in Adam's disobedience and fallen from the original state of blessed fellowship he experienced in the garden. As a result, all of Adam's descendants are conceived in sin, born enemies of God, and doomed to perish eternally in hell.

And yet God is a Savior who has acted in saving grace to redeem from sin and death those who would believe. His plan of redemption began in eternity past, as God the Father set his electing love on undeserving sinners, determining to rescue them from the fall and the deserved consequences of their disobedience. The Father carried out this plan by sending the Son to accomplish redemption for those he had chosen, and then by sending the Spirit to apply redemption to those he had chosen. Thus, while the Father's plan of redemption was discussed in chapter 3, this chapter follows a Trinitarian form by examining the Son's accomplishment and the Spirit's application of redemption, shedding light on the following doctrines: atonement, calling and regeneration, repentance and faith, union with Christ, justification, adoption, sanctification, the perseverance of the saints, and glorification.

The Accomplishment of Redemption

In 1 Corinthians 15, the apostle Paul tells us that the very heart of the gospel is "that Christ died for our sins in accordance with the Scriptures, that he was buried, that he was raised on the third day in accordance with the Scriptures" (1 Cor. 15:3–4). As has been demonstrated in chapter 6, man's depravity has established the *need* for salvation. And as has been observed in chapter 3, the Father's unconditional election has formed the *plan* of salvation. But it is the atonement of God the Son that *has accomplished* that redemption in space and time. The distinctive teaching of biblical Christianity is that God himself has made full atonement for sinners—and he accomplished this by the substitutionary sacrifice of his own Son on the cross, apart from any contribution from sinners. If we are going to be fundamentally committed to the gospel, we must devote ourselves to an accurate, robust, biblical understanding of the atonement.

THE PLAN OF SALVATION AND THE MISSION OF THE SON

In chapter 3, we examined the biblical teaching concerning the Father's plan of redemption—his intention to rescue his creatures from sin and death and to restore them to a right relationship with himself. The triune God devised an eternal plan in which man's salvation would be accomplished by the Son, and in which the benefits secured by the Son's redemptive work would be applied by the Holy Spirit. The second member of the Trinity would be born by the Holy Spirit as the God-man (Matt. 1:18; Luke 1:35), live a life of perfect obedience to the Father in the power of the Spirit (Matt. 3:15; Rom. 5:18–19), lay down his life as a sacrifice for the sins of his people (John 10:14–15; Hebrews 9–10; Rev. 5:9), and rise again as the firstfruits and guarantee of their resurrection (Rom. 4:25; 1 Cor. 15:22–23, 42–57). It is essential to understand that the Son's redemptive mission is birthed out of this Trinitarian plan of salvation. The atonement he accomplished is inextricably rooted in the Father's purpose to save his chosen. Christ was not haphazardly embarking on a mission of his own devising (John 6:38) but was acting in strict accordance with the specific plan devised in the eternal councils of the Trinity.

Several passages of Scripture testify to this pretemporal, determinate plan of salvation. In the first place, many passages identify the Son's atoning work as divinely predetermined (Luke 22:22; Acts 2:23; 4:27–28; Eph. 3:11; cf. 1:9, 11; 2 Tim. 1:9; 1 Pet. 1:20). In addition, the mission of the Son is often spoken of as a matter of obedience to the Father's will, indicating both that the Father had made his will known to the Son in a prior agreement and that Jesus was acting consistently with this prior directive from his Father (John 10:18; 17:4–5; Phil. 2:8; Heb. 10:7). Third, we see the reality of this agreement in the Father's promise to reward the Son once he completed his work (Ps. 2:7–8; Isa. 53:10–12; cf. Phil. 2:9–11). Finally, perhaps the most significant aspect of the eternal plan of salvation is that the Father gives specific individuals to the Son on whose behalf he is to accomplish redemption. That is to say, the Father commissions the Son to be the representative and substitutionary sacrifice for a particular people—namely, all and only those whom the Father has chosen for salvation. Several comments from Jesus in the Gospel of John bear this out, as he speaks of accomplishing salvation for the people whom the Father has given him (John 6:37–40; 10:14–15, 29; 17:1–3, 6, 9, 24). This eternal, intra-Trinitarian plan of salvation shapes and conditions every aspect of the Son's mission as he undertakes to accomplish redemption. The atonement accomplishes the eternal purpose of the triune God.

THE CAUSE OF THE ATONEMENT

The triune God's motivation for devising this plan of redemption is twofold. In the first place, the love of God is the cause of the atonement. Some misunderstand the atonement as a loving Son overcoming an angry and wrathful Father, conceiving of the Father's love as the consequence rather than the cause of the atonement. But the Father does not love his people strictly on the grounds that Jesus died for them; rather, Jesus died for God's people because the Father loved them (John 3:16; Rom. 5:8; 1 John 4:9–10). In other words, the plan of redemption is born out of the good pleasure of the Father's free and sovereign electing love (Eph. 1:4–5, 9). It is because the Lord "set his love on . . . and chose" his people (Deut. 7:7) that he has decreed to accomplish their redemption by the atoning work of Christ.

In addition to his love, God's justice also is a cause of Christ's atonement. Once the triune God had decreed in his love to reconcile to himself those he had chosen, it was necessary that he decree to accomplish this in a way that was consistent with his justice. For God to reconcile guilty sinners to himself, sin must be punished, the broken law must be satisfied, and God's wrath must be justly assuaged. All these objectives are met in the person and work of the Lord Jesus Christ, who fulfilled the law (Matt. 3:15; Rom. 5:18–19; Gal. 4:4–5), paid sin's penalty (1 Pet. 2:24), and extinguished God's wrath (Heb. 2:17) on behalf of the elect. As Paul says, the Father put the Son forward "as a propitiation by His blood, through faith, to demonstrate His righteousness" (Rom. 3:25 NKJV). Sin is not overlooked but is punished in Christ, and therefore God "show[s] his righteousness at the present time, so that he might be just and the justifier of the one who has faith in Jesus" (Rom. 3:26).

THE NATURE OF THE ATONEMENT

Scripture employs several themes to describe what Christ accomplished on the cross. The work of Christ was a work of substitutionary sacrifice, in which the Savior bore the penalty of sin in the place of sinners (1 Pet. 2:24); it is a work of propitiation, in which God's wrath against sin is fully satisfied and exhausted in the person of our substitute (Rom. 3:25); it is a work of reconciliation, in which the alienation between man and God is overcome and peace is made (Col. 1:20, 22); it is a work of redemption, in which those enslaved to sin are ransomed by the price of the Lamb's precious blood (1 Pet. 1:18–19); and it is a work of conquest, in which sin, death, and Satan are defeated by the power of a victorious Savior (Heb. 2:14–15). Each of these themes is worthy of study and will be the subject of this section's discussion.

The Obedience of Christ

However, there is a unifying principle in Scripture that encompasses the many facets of Christ's atonement: obedience. There are three senses in which obedience encapsulates the whole of the substitutionary work of Christ. First, Scripture characterizes Christ's work as obedience to the divine plan of salvation, as discussed above (John 6:38; cf. 12:49; John 10:17–18; 14:31; Phil. 2:8; Heb. 10:7, 9).

Second, such obedience was necessary for Christ to be a suitable substitutionary sacrifice for sinners. In the Old Testament, if the penalty for sinners was to be executed on a substitute, that substitute was required to be without any spot or defect (Ex. 12:5; Lev. 22:20–21; cf. 1:3, 10; 3:1, 6; 22:18–25). The same principle extends to Christ's atoning sacrifice, he who is our Passover Lamb (1 Cor. 5:7; cf. Isa. 53:7; John 1:29; 1 Pet. 1:18–19; Rev. 5:12) and the fulfillment of the Levitical sacrifices (Heb. 9:23). For Christ to have been a fitting substitute to bear the punishment for sin in the place of sinners, he himself had to be sinless—holy, innocent, undefiled, and separate from sinners (Heb. 7:26). For this reason, Scripture links the life of Christ, in which "he learned obedience through what he suffered" (Heb. 5:8), with his fitness to become "the source of eternal salvation to all who obey him" (Heb. 5:9; cf. 2:18; 4:15).

Finally, it was necessary for Christ to be obedient to the law of God in order to provide the righteousness that is the ground of justification. God's law consisted of two key aspects: prescriptive commands that required full obedience, and penal sanctions for the breaking of those commands. Sinful man has fallen short of both, and so Christ had to remedy both. On the cross, he "redeemed us from the curse of the law by becoming a curse for us" (Gal. 3:13; cf. Deut. 21:23)—that is, by bearing God's wrath in our place. But he also lived a life of perfect obedience to provide the righteousness that is credited to us through faith (Rom. 4:3–5; Phil. 3:9). For this reason, Paul contrasts the first Adam with Christ, the last Adam (1 Cor. 15:22, 45), saying, "For as by the one man's disobedience the many were made sinners, so by the one man's obedience the many will be made righteous" (Rom. 5:19; cf. Gal. 4:4–5). Adam's sin provides an actual, lived-out record of human disobedience, which, counted to be ours through our union with him, becomes the basis on which God justly constitutes all people guilty (Rom. 5:12).

In the same way, Christ's vicarious obedience provides the actual, lived-out record of human righteousness, which, counted to be ours through our union with him, becomes the basis on which God justly constitutes guilty sinners righteous (1 Cor. 1:30; cf. Rom. 10:4; 2 Cor. 5:21). This means the Lord Jesus Christ did more than just die for our sins; he also lived to fulfill our righteousness (Matt. 3:15).[1]

Penal Substitution

Beyond the general heading of obedience to the Father, the most fundamental description one can ascribe to the atonement is that it is a work of penal substitution. That is to say, on the cross, Jesus suffered the penalty for the sins of his people (*penal*) as a substitute for them (*substitution*). Man's depravity leaves him unable to pay the penalty for his sin. However, God in his love has appointed the Lord Jesus Christ to stand in the place of sinners to bear their sin, guilt, and punishment and thereby satisfy God's wrath on their behalf.

For this reason, Isaiah characterizes the suffering servant as the one who "has borne our griefs and carried our sorrows" (Isa. 53:4), who "bore the sin of many" (Isa. 53:12). "The LORD has laid on him the iniquity of us all" (Isa. 53:6), and so "he shall bear their iniquities" (Isa. 53:11). Thus, when Jesus comes into the world, John the Baptist announces him as "the Lamb of God who takes away the sin of the world" (John 1:29)—that is, by taking sin on himself. The apostle Paul declares that "for our sake [the Father] made [Jesus] to *be* sin" (2 Cor. 5:21a) in the same sense that he makes us to become the righteousness of God (2 Cor. 5:21b): by imputation—that is, by counting our guilt to be his. The curse of the law that we were under was borne by Christ, who became a curse for us (Gal. 3:13). The apostle Peter says, "He himself bore our sins in his body on the tree, that we might die to sin and live to righteousness." Then, quoting Isaiah's account of the suffering servant, he adds, "By his wounds you have been healed" (1 Pet. 2:24; cf. Heb. 9:28). The Lord Jesus Christ bore the punishment of the sins of his people and thereby brought them blessing: "He was pierced for our transgressions; he was crushed for our iniquities; upon him was the chastisement that brought us peace" (Isa. 53:5).

In addition to these clear statements, the New Testament attaches the concept of penal substitution to the cross of Christ by using four Greek prepositions that all have a substitutionary force: *peri* ("for," 1 Pet. 3:18; 1 John 2:2; 4:10); *dia* ("because of," "for the sake of," 2 Cor. 8:9; cf. 1 Cor. 8:11); *anti* ("in place of," "instead of," Matt. 20:28; Mark 10:45); and *hyper* ("on behalf of," Luke 22:19–20; John 10:11, 15; Rom. 5:6; 2 Cor. 5:21; Gal. 2:20; Eph. 5:25; Titus 2:14; Heb. 2:9).

1 For more on what is traditionally called the active obedience of Christ, see "The Ground of Justification: Imputed Righteousness" (p. 328, below). For a fuller treatment, see John MacArthur and Richard Mayhue, gen. eds., *Biblical Doctrine* (Wheaton, IL: Crossway, 2017), 520–22, 614–18.

Penal-substitutionary atonement is woven into the fabric of new covenant revelation from beginning to end, because it is the very heart of the gospel message. In free and willing obedience to his Father, the Lord Jesus Christ has stood in the stead of sinners, has died as a sacrifice for their sin and guilt, has propitiated the Father's wrath toward them, has reconciled them to the God for whom they were created, has redeemed them out of the bondage of sin and death, and has conquered the rule of sin and Satan in their lives. Each of those themes—sacrifice, propitiation, reconciliation, redemption, and conquest—is a different facet of Christ's substitutionary work and deserves further examination.

Sacrifice. Drawing from the Old Testament's prescriptions for sacrificial worship to God, the New Testament explicitly identifies the death of Christ as a sacrifice for sins, the fulfillment of the Passover (1 Cor. 5:7; cf. Exodus 12) and the Levitical sacrifices (Heb. 9:23, 26; cf. Leviticus 16). The Passover meal was the setting of Jesus's Last Supper with his disciples, wherein he instituted the new covenant, declaring that his body would be broken and his blood poured out for them (Matt. 26:17–29; Mark 14:12–25; Luke 22:7–20). In this way he declared that his death would be the fulfillment of the feast of the Passover, the lamb slain as a substitutionary sacrifice for the redemption of his people (John 1:29; cf. 1:36; 1 Pet. 1:18–19). Just as the blood of the slain lamb protected Israel from the execution of God's judgment, so also the blood of the slain Lamb, Jesus, protects his people from the Father's wrath against their sin.

Similarly, just as the high priest entered beyond the veil into the Most Holy Place, so also Christ is the Great High Priest (cf. Heb. 3:1; 4:15; 7:26; 8:1) who has entered beyond the veil of the heavenly tabernacle (his own flesh, Heb. 10:20), into the very presence of God. And while the high priest sprinkled the blood of the sacrificial goat on the mercy seat to make atonement, the Lord Jesus sprinkled his own blood (Heb. 9:21–22; 12:24; 1 Pet. 1:2), and inasmuch as his blood is infinitely more valuable than that of goats and calves, he thus secured an eternal redemption. He is therefore the fulfillment of both the high priest and the sacrifice; he is both offerer and offering, for he "offered himself without blemish to God" (Heb. 9:14; cf. Eph. 5:2; Heb. 7:27; 9:23, 26, 28; 10:10, 12, 14). Further, he is also the fulfillment of the mercy seat, where the blood was sprinkled and wrath was averted (Rom. 3:25). Finally, Jesus is the perfect fulfilment of the scapegoat as well, the one on whom all our iniquity is laid (Isa. 53:6; 2 Cor. 5:21; 1 Pet. 2:24). As the midday sun was shrouded in darkness, the Father was, as it were, laying his hands on the head of the Son and confessing over him the sins of his people, and banishing him from his presence (Heb. 13:12; cf. Matt. 27:46). "Outside the camp," away from the presence of the Lord and of his people, was where the sacrifices were to be disposed of (Lev. 4:12, 21; 6:11; 8:17; 9:11; 16:27; cf. Heb. 13:11). It was that lonely place where the leper was isolated to bear his shame (Lev. 13:46) and where the blasphemer was to be stoned (Lev. 24:14, 23). It was to that place of shame and isolation that the Son of God was banished so that we might be welcomed into the holy presence of God.

Propitiation. By receiving the full exercise of the Father's wrath against the sins of his people, Christ satisfied God's righteous anger against sin and thus turned away his wrath from us who, had it not been for our substitute, were bound to suffer it for ourselves. This is what the New Testament identifies as propitiation (Rom. 3:24–25; Heb. 2:17; 1 John 2:2; 4:10). Some, however, have argued that "propitiation" is the wrong translation for this particular Greek term (*hilasmos, hilaskomai*). Rather than a sacrifice that turns away God's wrath, they have argued that it speaks of expiation, the cancellation or removal of sin. But there is clear biblical justification for reading *hilaskomai* as a wrath-averting sacrifice.

The Greek *hilaskomai* word group also translates the Hebrew term *kaphar*, which often means to satisfy the wrath of God. Three passages illustrate this clearly. First, when Israel committed its first act of brazen idolatry with the golden calf, God responded in wrath (Ex. 32:10). The next day, however, Moses sought to turn away God's wrath from the people: "perhaps I can make atonement for [Heb. *kaphar*; Gk. *exilaskomai* (Septuagint)] your sin" (Ex. 32:30). Second, when the people had committed sexual immorality with Moabite women and had begun worshiping the gods of Moab, the Lord again responded in wrath (Num. 25:3), manifested in a plague (Num. 25:8–9). Phinehas, one of the priests, was so incensed by such brazen rebellion that he killed the idolaters with a spear, with the result that the plague was checked (Num. 25:7–8). The Lord praised Phinehas for his righteous indignation, saying, "Phinehas . . . has turned back my wrath from the people of Israel. . . . he was jealous for his God and *made atonement for* [Heb. *kaphar*; Gk. *exilaskomai* (Septuagint)] the people of Israel" (Num. 25:11–13). Once again, propitiation is synonymous with making atonement. Third, in response to the people's mutiny against Moses and Aaron, the Lord's wrath was kindled against Israel, again in the form of a plague (Num. 16:45, 48–49). Moses told Aaron, "Take your censer, and put fire on it from off the altar and lay incense on it and carry it quickly to the congregation and make atonement for [Heb. *kaphar*; Gk. *exilaskomai* (Septuagint)] them, for *wrath* has gone out from the LORD; the plague has begun" (Num. 16:46). Aaron did as Moses said: "And he put on the incense and made atonement for [Heb. *kaphar*; Gk. *exilaskomai* (Septuagint)] the people. And he stood between the dead and the living, and the plague was stopped" (Num. 16:47–48). Once again, a clear parallelism emerges between making atonement and turning away God's wrath against sin as exercised in the form of a plague.

Therefore, when the New Testament writers use the Greek *hilaskomai* word group—that is, the same word group used to translate the Hebrew *kaphar* in the

Septuagint—it is reasonable to expect that it denotes propitiation just as it did in the Old Testament, especially given the contexts in which the term is used. For example, the first use of "propitiation" in the New Testament comes in Romans 3:25, after Paul has spent two chapters detailing how the wrath of God is kindled against the sin of all mankind (Rom. 1:18; 2:5, 8; 3:5). The thread of divine wrath has been so woven through this opening section of the letter that the reader almost expects to be confronted with how God will provide for its abatement. We see precisely that in Romans 3:21–26: God has put forward his Son, the Lord Jesus Christ, "as a propitiation by his blood, to be received by faith" (Rom. 3:25). God has satisfied his wrath against sin by the sprinkling of the blood of the spotless Lamb on the mercy seat of the heavenly altar (Heb. 9:11–15, 23–24). He has punished the sins of his people in a substitute, and thus his wrath has been turned away from them.

The significance of propitiation, then, is that it identifies Christ's work as a wrath-bearing sacrifice. Sin may not merely be overlooked but must be punished, whether in the sinner in hell or in Christ the substitute on the cross. All the wrath that God would have exercised on elect sinners in the eternal torments of hell was poured out fully on our substitute in those three terrible hours on Calvary. Because of this, there is no longer any wrath left for Christ's people. God is propitious toward them, for their sin has been paid for.

Reconciliation. Man's sin has not only incurred guilt and aroused the wrath of God but has also alienated man from God (e.g., Gen. 3:8, 22–24; Isa. 59:2). God has become man's enemy (Rom. 5:10), and the mind of man is "hostile" toward God (Rom. 8:7). For this reason, Scripture also speaks of the atonement as a work of reconciliation, whereby the ground of the enmity between God and men—namely, the guilt of sin and the punishment of God's wrath—is removed and dealt with, thus accomplishing peace (Rom. 5:10–11; 2 Cor. 5:18–19; Eph. 2:16; Col. 1:20–22).

Several characteristics of the doctrine of reconciliation emerge from these texts. First, reconciliation is a work of God, accomplished in the person of Christ through the efficacy of his blood (2 Cor. 5:18; Col. 1:20). Man does not effect this reconciliation by doing something to remove God's hostility toward his sin. Rather, sinners passively receive reconciliation as a gift through the work of Christ (Rom. 5:11). Second, Scripture presents reconciliation as a finished work accomplished by Christ's sacrifice. Each of the above passages indicates that reconciliation occurred in the past through the once-for-all death of Christ. Third, reconciliation is fundamentally forensic. This is demonstrated by the parallelism in Romans 5, where the phrase "we were reconciled to God by the death of his Son" is parallel to "we have now been justified by his blood" in the immediately preceding verse (Rom. 5:9–10). Since justification is forensic and is parallel with reconciliation, it is likely that reconciliation also ought to be understood in forensic terms. Paul removes all doubt in 2 Corinthians 5:19 when he explicitly identifies the work of reconciliation as God's "not counting [the world's] trespasses against them." "Counting" comes from the Greek word *logizomai*, the New Testament's most common term for "imputation" (e.g., Rom. 4:1–25). By imputing our sins to Christ our scapegoat, by exercising his wrath on him as our substitute, and by imputing Christ's righteousness to us (2 Cor. 5:21), God has removed the ground of his enmity against us, namely, the guilt of sin. As propitiation is the removal of God's wrath against sinners, so reconciliation is the removal of God's enmity against sinners.

Because of Christ's atonement, sinners once separated from God may be restored to loving fellowship with him whom they were created to know and worship: "For Christ also suffered once for sins, the righteous for the unrighteous, that he might bring us to God" (1 Pet. 3:18).

Redemption. Christ's atonement is also characterized as redemption, that by which man is redeemed from the bondage of sin and the law through the payment of Christ's shed blood as a ransom.

When an Israelite had become so poor that he had to sell himself into slavery, God's law made provision for his family to redeem him out of slavery by paying a price (Lev. 25:47–55). In a similar way, sinners are in bondage to sin (Rom. 6:6), and Christ has redeemed them by the ransom price of his life (Matt. 20:28; Mark 10:45; cf. 1 Tim. 2:6). For this reason, Paul can exhort believers to glorify God in their body, for "you were bought with a price" (1 Cor. 6:20; cf. 7:23). Believers have been "ransomed [NASB: "redeemed"] . . . not with perishable things such as silver or gold, but with the precious blood of Christ, like that of a lamb without blemish or spot" (1 Pet. 1:18–19). Here contrasted with silver and gold, the blood of Christ is explicitly identified as the price by which redemption is purchased. Thus, when the apostle John describes creatures in heaven worshiping the ascended Christ, he notes that they praise him for his atoning work (Rev. 5:9; cf. Acts 20:28). Christ's people—that is, those "who follow the Lamb wherever he goes"—are therefore called the "redeemed" (Rev. 14:3–4), the purchased ones, for they "have redemption through his blood" (Eph. 1:7; cf. Col. 1:14). Christ redeems sinners from the curse of the law (Gal. 3:13; cf. 4:4–5), from the penalty and power of sin (Rom. 6:18, 22; Titus 2:14; Heb. 9:15), and eventually from the presence of sin (Rom. 8:23; cf. Luke 21:28; Eph. 4:30).

Conquest. In paying the penalty of sin and freeing his people from sin and death, Jesus also accomplished a victory of conquest over Satan and the rulers, authorities, cosmic powers, and "spiritual forces of evil in the heavenly places" (Eph. 6:12). Since "the whole world lies in the power of the evil one" (1 John 5:19; cf. 2 Cor. 4:4;

Eph. 2:2), overcoming the penalty and power of sin in the lives of his people is to triumph over Satan (Matt. 12:29; cf. Luke 11:21–22). By his redemptive work on the cross, Christ dealt the decisive death blow to Satan and his kingdom of darkness, realizing—that is, inaugurating even if not yet consummating—the purpose for which he came into the world: "to destroy the works of the devil" (1 John 3:8; cf. John 12:31; 16:11). When he forgave us "all our trespasses, by canceling the record of debt that stood against us with its legal demands," setting it aside by "nailing it to the cross," he removed the ground of Satan's accusations against us (Col. 2:13–14). Therefore, Paul writes, "He disarmed the rulers and authorities and put them to open shame, by triumphing over them in him" (Col. 2:15). Through the paradoxical triumph of his death, Jesus "destroy[ed] the one who has the power of death, that is, the devil, and deliver[ed] all those who through fear of death were subject to lifelong slavery" (Heb. 2:14–15). And on the third day, Jesus displayed his conquest over the power of sin and death by rising from the grave. It was impossible for him to be held in death's clutches (Acts 2:24), for, having defeated death, "the keys of Death and Hades" belong to him (Rev. 1:17–18).

Summary. Such, then, is the character of the penal-substitutionary atonement of Christ. The guilt of our sin demanded the penalty of death, and so the Lamb of God was slain as an expiatory sacrifice on our behalf. The wrath of God was kindled against our sin, and so Christ was set forth as a propitiation to bear that wrath in our place. The pollution of our sin alienated us from God and aroused his holy enmity against us, and so by atoning for sin Christ has reconciled God to man. Obedient to sin, man was in bondage to sin through the law that exposed sin in our lives, and so Christ has paid the ransom price of his precious blood to God the Father in order to redeem us from such slavery. In doing so, he has plundered Satan's house, conquering death and its captain by the exercise of his own power.

THE SUFFICIENCY OF THE ATONEMENT[2]

If there is one description to be applied to the nature of Christ's penal-substitutionary atonement, it is that it is a perfectly sufficient sacrifice. Several features establish its perfect sufficiency.

In the first place, it is an objective atonement—a work accomplished independent of and apart from those who will eventually partake of its benefits. No cooperating work or response to grace adds to or energizes this ground of our salvation. To be sure, those who subjectively experience the benefits of the atonement must respond in repentance and faith, but such responses belong to the *application* of redemption—not its *accomplishment*—and are themselves

2 This section follows John Murray's helpful presentation in *Redemption Accomplished and Applied* (Grand Rapids, MI: Eerdmans, 1955), 51–58.

purchased by the perfect work that Christ has wrought. "It is finished!" was the triumphant cry from the cross, not "It has begun." As with the Father's work of election, which depends "not of him who wills or runs" (Rom. 9:16 ESV mg.), and with the Spirit's work of application, in which he blows where he wishes (John 3:8), so it is with the Son's work of redemption. Salvation is of the Lord (Jonah 2:9), and therefore, it has been perfectly accomplished *by* him, two thousand years ago, external to those who will reap its divine blessings.

Second, the sufficiency of the atonement is established by its finality. It is a single, finished, unrepeatable work. The Roman Catholic Church teaches precisely the opposite, demeaning the sufficiency of Christ's work by proposing to repeat his sacrifice in the ceremony of the Mass.[3] This is in explicit contrast with the consistent testimony of the book of Hebrews (Heb. 7:26–28; 9:11–12, 25–28; 10:10–14). These passages explicitly deny that Christ was to offer himself repeatedly (Heb. 9:25). To suggest such a thing is to impugn the character of Christ himself, for it was the weakness of the high priests that demanded their repeated offerings (Heb. 7:28). Yet there is no such weakness in our High Priest; he is the eternally perfect Son—holy, innocent, undefiled, and separate from sinners (Heb. 7:26). And inasmuch as the Son of God himself is intrinsically worthy, his was a better sacrifice (Heb. 9:23; cf. 8:6), of such a character as to perfect—for all time—those for whom it was offered (Heb. 10:14). Can there be any greater violence done to these texts than to suggest that Christ's sacrifice has to be repeated? Such perverse doctrine drains the cross of its very saving power, for "where there is forgiveness of these [sins], there is no longer any offering for sin" (Heb. 10:18; cf. Rom. 6:10). If there remains an offering to be given, there has been no forgiveness of sins.

3 "In the Sacrifice of the Mass and in the Sacrifice of the Cross the Sacrificial Gift and the Primary Sacrificing Priest are identical; only the nature and the mode of the offering are different. . . . According to the Thomistic view, *in every Mass Christ also performs an actual immediate sacrificial activity*, which, however, must not be conceived as a totality of many successive acts but as one single uninterrupted sacrificial act of the Transfigured Christ. The purpose of this Sacrifice is the same in the Sacrifice of the Mass as in the Sacrifice of the Cross; primarily the glorification of God, secondarily *atonement*, thanksgiving, and appeal" (Ludwig Ott, *Fundamentals of Catholic Dogma*, ed. James Canon Bastible, trans. Patrick Lynch, 4th ed. [Rockford, IL: TAN Books, 1974], 408, emphasis added). Just as striking is the following statement from Roman Catholic priest John O'Brien: "When the priest pronounces the tremendous words of consecration, he reaches up into the heavens, brings Christ down from His throne, and places Him upon our altar to be offered up again as the Victim for the sins of man. . . . While the Blessed Virgin was the human agency by which Christ became incarnate a single time, the priest brings Christ down from heaven, and renders Him present on our altar as the eternal Victim for the sins of man—not once but a thousand times! The priest speaks and lo! Christ, the eternal and omnipotent God, bows His head in humble obedience to the priest's command" (*The Faith of Millions: The Credentials of the Catholic Religion*, rev. ed. [Huntington, IN: Our Sunday Visitor, 1974], 256).

Finally, the sufficiency of the atonement is established by its efficacy. That is to say, by dying on the cross, Christ has *actually* saved his people. He came not to make salvation hypothetical, possible, or merely available but to actually "save his people from their sins" (Matt. 1:21). He came not to make men redeemable but to redeem them. He died not potentially but actually, and so he made not a provisional atonement but an actual one. As the Lord of glory prepared to yield up his spirit to the care of the Father, conscious that he had accomplished the work he came to do, he declared: "It is finished" (John 19:30). Redemption had been accomplished. Our High Priest had actually made purification for sins, and, his work completed, he sat down (Heb. 1:3). The Good Shepherd had actually taken away the sins of his sheep (1 John 3:5) by bearing them in his own body (1 Pet. 2:24). He had actually extinguished the full exercise of the Father's wrath (Rom. 3:25), having actually become a curse for us (Gal. 3:13) and thus exhaustively paying the full penalty for our sins. In so doing, he actually purchased the redemption of his people by the ransom price of his own blood (Acts 20:28; Rev. 5:9). Each of these passages is a statement of efficacious accomplishment. To artificially insert the concept of provisionality or potentiality into any of those texts is to force one's theology on the plain meaning of Scripture.

In fact, this element of efficacy has been inherent in the biblical conception of atonement from its beginning in the Levitical law (Lev. 4:20, 26, 31, 35; 5:10, 13, 16, 18; 6:7; 12:8; 14:20, 53; 19:22). When the priest made atonement, he actually atoned, and that atonement brought about its intended effect of the forgiveness of sins.[4] Thus, when the same Greek word group (*hilaskomai*, *hilasmos*, *hilastērion*) that was used to translate *kaphar* in the Septuagint appears in the New Testament to describe the atoning work of Messiah, the reader naturally understands that same efficacy to inhere in the concept of Christ's atonement. Jesus's death did not make sins forgivable; it accomplished forgiveness. His atonement was not hypothetical, potential, or provisional; it was an efficacious atonement.[5]

4 Of course, this is not to say that sins were forgiven other than through the atonement of Christ, for all the old covenant sacrifices looked forward to and derived their efficacy from Christ's final sacrifice (Rom. 3:24–26; Heb. 9:11–10:18). Nevertheless, on the basis of the work of Christ, God graciously allowed himself to be temporarily propitiated by the sacrifices he prescribed to Israel.

5 None of this is to suggest that the elect were justified or granted saving faith and repentance at the time of Christ's death in the first century. Nor is it to suggest that anyone is saved apart from faith. To assume so is to confuse the accomplishment of redemption with its application. Rather, to speak of definite atonement and accomplished salvation is to say that Christ has endured all the punishment of, paid the full penalty for, and satisfied the whole of God's wrath against the sins of his people. It is to say that he has done everything necessary to completely secure the salvation of those for whom he died—to render certain and definite the application of salvation's benefits to all those for whom Christ purchased them. It is, finally, to say that nothing can be added to Christ's work in order to invest it with power or efficacy but that because our substitute has actu-

THE EXTENT OF THE ATONEMENT

Having understood the glorious nature of Christ's atoning work, it is now necessary to answer the question of its extent. For whom did Christ die? On whose behalf did Christ offer himself as a penal-substitutionary sacrifice? For whom did he propitiate the wrath of his Father? Whom did Christ reconcile to God and redeem out of slavery to sin and Satan?

The answers given to this vital question typically fall into two general categories. The universalist school of thought answers that Christ has paid for the sins of every person who has ever lived without exception. This is often called *general, unlimited*, or *universal atonement*.[6] By contrast, *particularists* teach that Christ died as a substitute for the elect alone—for only those particular individuals whom the Father chose in eternity past and gave to the Son. While this position has long been known as *limited atonement*—that Christ's atonement is limited to the elect—many proponents have found such a label to be easily misunderstood and have preferred *definite atonement* or *particular redemption*. Throughout the discussion of soteriology in the present volume, particular redemption has been affirmed. In this section it will be defended from Scripture.

In undertaking this discussion, we must understand the precise question under consideration. Asking the question, For whom did Christ die?, is not asking, To whom should the gospel be preached? Both particularists and universalists readily acknowledge that the gospel ought to be proclaimed to all people without exception; Christ genuinely offers himself as Savior to anyone who would turn from his or her sins and trust in him for righteousness. Neither is it to ask, For the forgiveness of whose sins is Christ's work sufficient? Both sides agree that, had God chosen to save more sinners than he actually has, Christ would not have had to suffer any more than he did in order to save them. Nor is the question, Who will finally be saved? Both particularists and universalists stipulate that the benefits of Christ's salvation will be applied only to those who repent and believe in him. Thus, both particularists and universalists can subscribe to the popular dictum that the atonement is "sufficient for all, yet efficient for only the elect." This is also not a dispute over whether any nonsaving benefits resulting from the atonement accrue to the nonelect. If God had not intended to save sinners through Christ's atonement, it is likely that he would have immediately visited

---

ally borne the full penalty of sin's condemnation, "there is therefore now no condemnation for those who are in Christ Jesus" (Rom. 8:1).

6 Though *universalist* is a common designation for those who believe that all people without exception will finally be saved, that is not how it is intended here. In the discussion of the extent of the atonement, the term refers to those who believe that the atonement has a universal extent—i.e., that Christ died for all without exception—even though not all without exception will be saved. This includes Arminians, Amyraldians, and hypothetical universalists.

justice on sinful man as he did on the fallen angels (2 Pet. 2:4). Yet because God intended to save his people through Christ in the fullness of time, even those whom he will not ultimately save will have enjoyed the benefits of common grace, divine forbearance, and a temporary reprieve from divine judgment. Therefore, to avoid unnecessary confusion and contention, it ought to be acknowledged that one's position on the extent of the atonement does not necessarily affect one's answer to these other questions. Instead, the question is, In whose place did Christ stand as a substitutionary sacrifice when he bore the full fury of his Father's righteous wrath against sin? The answer is, only those who will never bear that wrath themselves, namely, the elect alone.

Another reason this discussion often leads to frustration relates to methodology. Too often, universalists cite a number of proof texts containing the words "all" or "world" and consider the matter closed, declaring the particularist interpretation a violation of the "plain reading" of the text. Yet such an approach fails to take into account the context of these isolated texts along with the rest of the teaching of Scripture and thus demonstrates that what is often claimed to be the "plain reading" is nothing more than a superficial reading.

Numerous passages of Scripture contain universalistic language while they do not speak of every individual without exception. For example, Romans 5:18 says, "Therefore, as one trespass led to condemnation for all men, so one act of righteousness leads to justification and life for all men." The so-called "plain reading" of this text would seem to require that the two phrases "all men" be interpreted identically in both halves of the verse. Such a position, however, leads either to affirming the doctrine of universal salvation or to denying the doctrine of original sin. All without exception are condemned in Adam (Rom. 5:12), yet not all indiscriminately receive justification and life (Matt. 7:13, 22–23; Rev. 21:8). In Romans 5:12–21, Paul is contrasting Adam and Christ as the two representative heads of humanity, which sheds light on his intent in 5:18. Just as Adam's actions affect all those who are in him, so also Christ's actions affect all those who are in him. Thus, considering the context can correct a superficial reading of an isolated passage of Scripture.

In other instances, universal language is simply a convention of common speech. When the Pharisees said of Jesus, "Look, the world has gone after him" (John 12:19), they did not mean that everyone alive on the earth at that time had begun to follow Christ. When Paul said, "All things are lawful for me" (1 Cor. 6:12; cf. 10:23), he did not mean that he was at liberty to do anything and everything without exception, for he acknowledged that he was not without law but was "under the law of Christ" (1 Cor. 9:21). Therefore, the presence of universal language should not automatically be read to mean "all without exception." Like anything else, universal language needs to be properly interpreted according to its context and in accordance with the entirety of biblical teaching.

Rather than volleying proof texts back and forth, it is essential to consider the clear teaching of Scripture concerning the *nature* of Christ's mission to accomplish redemption. The Bible's teaching on the nature of the atonement has significant bearing on the proper understanding of its extent. Several lines of scriptural evidence must be considered to support the particularist view of the atonement.

Trinitarian Particularism

The beginning of this chapter set forth the biblical teaching concerning the divine plan of salvation and its relationship to the Son's mission. It was demonstrated that the decision for the Son to take on human flesh and rescue sinners from death and judgment was made not unilaterally but in accordance with an agreed-upon Trinitarian plan. In perfect unity, the Father commissioned the Son to go in the power of the Holy Spirit in order to save sinners. The Father sent the Son for a specific purpose, to accomplish a particular mission (see John 4:34; cf. 6:38; 10:17–18; 17:4; Phil. 2:8; Heb. 10:7). Whatever the Son intended to accomplish on his saving mission, it was precisely that purpose for which the Father had sent him. There is a perfect unity of purpose and intention in the saving will of the Father and the saving will of the Son.

However, the Father has not chosen everyone for salvation (Rom. 8:29–30, 33; 9:22–23; Eph. 1:4–5). If the Father's election is particular and not universal, and if the Father and the Son are perfectly united in their saving will and purpose, it is impossible that the Son's atonement should be universal and not particular.[7] Yet this is the unavoidable conclusion of those who deny particular redemption. Said another way, if the atonement is universal, then either election is also universal, or the Father and Son are at cross-purposes with one another. However, Scripture refutes both notions. The saving will of the Father is expressed in his particular election (that he has chosen some, not all, to be saved), and the Son has come to do the will of his Father who sent him.

What is that will? Jesus explicitly explained, "And this is the will of him who sent me, that I should lose nothing *of all that he has given me*, but raise it up on the last day" (John 6:39). There exists a group of chosen individuals whom the Father has given the Son, and it is on *their* behalf that he accomplishes his redemptive work. They are all those who will eventually come to him (6:37) and

7 As Robert L. Reymond writes, "It is unthinkable to believe that Christ would say: 'I recognize, Father, that your election and your salvific intentions terminate upon only a portion of mankind, but because my love is more inclusive and expansive than yours, I am not satisfied to die only for those you have elected. I am going to die for everyone'" (*A New Systematic Theology of the Christian Faith*, 2nd ed. [Nashville: Thomas Nelson, 2010], 678).

believe (John 6:40) because they have been effectually drawn by the Father (6:44, 55–65); they are the sheep for whom the Son lays down his life (10:14–15, 27) and to whom he gives eternal life (6:40; 10:28; 17:2). Christ says plainly, "Yours they were, [Father,] and you gave them to me" (17:6; cf. 17:9, 24), and he clearly distinguishes them from the rest of the world (17:9). These individuals who belonged to the Father before the foundation of the world can be none other than the elect whom he has chosen for salvation. It is therefore these, and these alone, whom the Father gives to the Son, and thus it is these, and these alone, for whom the Son accomplishes redemption.

Therefore, it is not surprising to read of the many ways in which Scripture identifies a *particular* people as the beneficiaries of Christ's work on the cross. He has given his life as a ransom for *many* (Matt. 20:28; Mark 10:45; cf. Isa. 53:12; Matt. 26:28), not for all. He is the Good Shepherd, who lays down his life for his *sheep* (John 10:11–15), not for the goats who are not his (cf. John 10:26). He is the lover of the brethren who lays down his life for his *friends* (John 15:13). He is the great Redeemer, who with his own blood purchased the *church* of God (Acts 20:28). He is the bridegroom of the *church* (Rev. 19:7; cf. John 3:29), whom he loved and for whom he gave himself up (Eph. 5:25). He was delivered over for the *elect* (Rom. 8:32–33), for whom he continues to intercede (Rom. 8:34; cf. John 17:9). And he is the sanctifier of "*a people for his own possession* who are zealous for good works" (Titus 2:14).[8]

By virtue of their own unity of essence, the Father, Son, and Holy Spirit are perfectly united with respect to their saving will and purpose. Christ was sent by the authority of the Father and in the power of the Holy Spirit to save no more and no fewer people than the Father chose and the Spirit regenerates (cf. Eph. 1:3–14). The Father has elected some, not all; the Spirit regenerates some, not all. To suggest that Christ has atoned for all, not some, is to put the persons of the Trinity entirely at odds with one another; it is to be forced to say that the will of the Son is not the will of the Father and the Spirit. This not only threatens the consubstantiality of the persons of the Trinity, but it flatly contradicts Christ's own explicit statements that he had undertaken his saving mission precisely to

8 Some contend that even though Christ has died for his sheep, it does not follow that he did not also die for the goats. But there is evidence that these particularizing designations are necessarily exclusive. First, Paul identifies those for whom the Father gave up his Son as "God's elect" (Rom. 8:32–33)—a category that necessarily excludes those not chosen. Second, since Jesus says, "I lay down my life for the sheep" (John 10:14–15), just moments before he declares to the Pharisees, "You are not among my sheep" (John 10:26), it is legitimate to infer that he did not lay down his life for those Pharisees. Third, Paul makes Christ's sacrificial love for the church the pattern for the husband's love for his wife (Eph. 5:25–27), and husbands ought to love their wives in a way that is special and different from the way they love all others. In these cases, emphasis on the elect does imply exclusion of the nonelect.

do the will of his Father. As the Father has given to the Son a particular people out of the world, it is for these—his sheep, his own, the church—that Christ lays down his life. Unity in the Trinity demands a particular atonement.

Efficacious Atonement

Perhaps the most common argument from those who hold to some form of an unlimited atonement is that Christ died for all without exception in a *provisional* sense. Christ died to *provide* salvation for all yet not to infallibly secure it for anyone in particular. He has died *potentially* for all, it is said, such that the potential exists for anyone to have the benefits of his sacrifice applied to him or her through repentance and faith. The key to the universalist's argument is to cast Christ's atonement as intrinsically ineffectual.

However, as argued above, the attribute of efficacy is inherent in and essential to the biblical concept of atonement. To review, Scripture teaches that Christ has actually—not potentially, provisionally, or hypothetically, but actually—accomplished the salvation of his people by virtue of his work on the cross. It is nearly tautologous to say that when Scripture states that our substitute "bore our sins in his body on the tree" (1 Pet. 2:24), it means he *actually*, not potentially, bore our sins in his body on the tree. When Scripture says, "But he was pierced for our transgressions; he was crushed for our iniquities; upon him was the chastisement that brought us peace, and with his wounds we are healed" (Isa. 53:5), it would be exegetically monstrous to conclude that he was only potentially pierced or potentially crushed—that his chastisement brought only a potential peace or that his wounds brought only potential healing. That would be to artificially inject the concept of *potentiality* into texts that speak of efficacious, objective accomplishment. Rather, Christ was *actually* pierced, crushed, chastised, and wounded, and therefore he accomplished actual peace and actual healing. Scripture does not say, "By his wounds, you were made healable." It does not say, "By his wounds, you were put into a state in which you *might* be healed if you fulfill certain conditions that activate the hypothetically universal scope of Christ's wounds."[9] The text simply says, "By his wounds you have been healed." That is, Christ's objective, substitutionary suffering and death actually accomplished the spiritual healing of those for whom he died—those who, because of the intrinsic worth and efficacy of Christ's sacrifice, "not only may be saved, but are saved, must be saved, and cannot by any possibility run the hazard of being anything but saved."[10]

9 Borrowing language from Carl R. Trueman, "Definite Atonement View," in *Perspectives on the Extent of the Atonement: 3 Views*, ed. Andrew David Naselli and Mark A. Snoeberger (Nashville: B&H Academic, 2015), 42.

10 Charles Spurgeon, "Particular Redemption," in *The New Park Street Pulpit* (London: Alabaster & Passmore, 1856), 4:135.

The New Testament consistently portrays the efficacy of the atonement: Jesus actually expiated our sins (1 John 3:5), actually propitiated the Father's wrath against us (Rom. 3:25; Heb. 2:17–18), actually reconciled God to us (Col. 1:22), and actually purchased our redemption (Acts 20:28; Rev. 5:9). He came not to make salvation possible or to make men savable; he came to decisively save his people (Matt. 1:21). In his atoning work, Christ did not provide a hypothetical salvation but rather infallibly secured the salvation of those for whom he died by actually bearing their punishment.[11]

Since, then, Christ's atonement is inherently efficacious, and since it is agreed that not all will finally be saved, the extent of the atonement must be limited. The only other option is to suggest that God demands the payment of sin's penalty first from Christ on the cross and then again from the unbelieving sinner in hell. But such double jeopardy is wholly inconsistent with the justice of God. If there is wrath left to pour out on the unbelieving sinner, then that wrath was not satisfied by the substitutionary work of Christ. If there is a penalty left for the sinner to pay in hell, then that penalty was not paid by Christ on the cross. That leaves only two options: either (1) Christ's sacrifice was impotent and ineffective, or (2) Christ's powerful and efficacious sacrifice was accomplished for a specific number of persons. Since the former is blasphemous and explicitly contrary to Scripture, we are constrained to embrace the latter. Because Christ actually satisfied all of the Father's wrath against the sins of those for whom he substituted, one cannot affirm a universal atonement while also denying universal salvation.[12]

Ultimately, then, we find that both sides limit the atonement: the particularist limits its extent, while the universalist limits its efficacy. But an inefficacious atonement—aside from contradicting Scripture—fundamentally undermines the

11 J. I. Packer writes poignantly, "Christ did not win a hypothetical salvation for hypothetical believers, a mere possibility of salvation for any who might possibly believe, but a real salvation for his own chosen people. His precious blood really does 'save us all'; the intended effects of his self-offering do in fact follow, just because the cross was what it was. Its saving power does not depend on faith being added *to* it; its saving power is such that faith flows *from* it. The cross *secured* the full salvation of all for whom Christ died" ("Saved by His Precious Blood: An Introduction to John Owen's *The Death of Death in the Death of Christ*," in J. I. Packer and Mark Dever et al., *In My Place Condemned He Stood: Celebrating the Glory of the Atonement* [Wheaton, IL: Crossway, 2007], 123, emphasis added).

12 Again, Packer argues, "If we are going to affirm penal substitution for all without exception we must either infer universal salvation or else, to evade this inference, deny the saving efficacy of the substitution for anyone; and if we are going to affirm penal substitution as an effective saving act of God, we must either infer universal salvation or else, to evade this inference, restrict the scope of the substitution, making it a substitution for some, not all" ("What Did the Cross Achieve? The Logic of Penal Substitution," in *In My Place Condemned He Stood*, 90–91).

gospel itself, for an inefficacious atonement is no atonement at all. An atonement that is inefficacious is an atonement that does not atone.[13]

The Unity of the High Priestly Work of Christ

Borrowing the conceptual framework of the Old Testament sacrificial system, Scripture frequently speaks of Christ as the Great High Priest of his people (Heb. 2:17; 3:1; 4:14–15; 5:1, 5, 10; 6:19–20; 8:1–6; 9:11–12, 25). Therefore, except for where the New Testament explicitly contrasts Christ's priestly ministry with that of the Old Testament priests (e.g., Heb. 7:27), there is a basic continuity between them. The work of the Levitical priests thus sheds light on the extent of the atonement in the inseparable unity between the priest's work of sacrifice and his work of intercession.

On the Day of Atonement, the high priest was to slay one goat as a sacrifice for the sins of the people of Israel (Lev. 16:9). Yet the sacrificial death was not the end of the priest's work. After slaying the goat, he was required to "bring its blood inside the veil" into the Most Holy Place, and "sprinkl[e] it over the mercy seat and in front of the mercy seat" (Lev. 16:15; cf. 16:18–19). It is this twofold work—both the slaughter of the goat and the intercessory sprinkling of its blood—that accomplished atonement for Israel's sins. This was the case not only for the Day of Atonement but also for all the sacrifices that required the death of animals. The priest was first to slay the animal and then to "offer up the blood and sprinkle the blood around on the altar" (Lev. 1:5 NASB; cf. 1:11; 3:2, 8, 13; 4:6–7, 17–18, 25, 30, 34; 5:9; 7:2; 17:6).

The observation we must make from these rituals is that the scope of the priest's sacrifice is identical to the scope of his intercession. The high priest never sacrifices the goat on behalf of everyone throughout the Gentile world and then

13 Therefore, we must conclude with Spurgeon that the universalist may keep his ineffectual atonement: "The Arminians say, Christ died for all men. Ask them what they mean by it. Did Christ die so as to secure the salvation of all men? They say, 'No, certainly not.' We ask them the next question—Did Christ die so as to secure the salvation of any man in particular? They answer, 'No.' They are obliged to admit this, if they are consistent. They say, 'No; Christ has died so that any man may be saved if'—and then follow certain conditions of salvation. We say, then, we will just go back to the old statement—Christ did not die so as beyond a doubt to secure the salvation of anybody, did He? You must say 'No'; you are obliged to say so. . . . Now, who is it that limits the death of Christ? Why, you. You say that Christ did not die so as infallibly to secure the salvation of anybody. We beg your pardon, when you say we limit Christ's death; we say, 'No, my dear sir, it is you that do it.' We say Christ so died that He infallibly secured the salvation of a multitude that no man can number, who through Christ's death not only may be saved, but are saved, must be saved, and cannot by any possibility run the hazard of being anything but saved. You are welcome to your atonement; you may keep it. We will never renounce ours for the sake of it" ("Particular Redemption," 4:135).

sprinkles its blood only on behalf of Israel. No, the sacrifice and the intercession were two sides of the same atoning coin, both done on behalf of Israel alone.

The same principle applies to the unity of the twofold High Priestly ministry of Christ. The author of Hebrews depicts Christ as our Great High Priest who both offered himself as the perfect sacrifice and entered into the Most Holy Place to intercede for his people (Heb. 9:24). In other words, Christ's sacrificial offering of himself is inextricably linked to his intercessory work on behalf of his people in the presence of God (Heb. 4:14–15; 7:25; 1 John 2:1). That is, Christ intercedes for everyone for whom he died, and he died for everyone for whom he intercedes (cf. Rom. 8:29–39, esp. vv. 32–34).

Therefore, the key question is, does Christ intercede before the Father on behalf of all people without exception or on behalf of the elect alone? Surely it is the latter. Is Christ praying to the Father for the salvation and blessing of the nonelect—a request that the Father, because he does not intend to save the non-elect, will refuse his Son? Are the persons of the Trinity so divided? Here again the doctrine of unlimited atonement would drive a wedge between the will of the Father and the will of the Son, which has disastrous implications for biblical Trinitarianism. Further, Christ himself answers this question in the High Priestly Prayer of John 17. Here the Great High Priest is interceding before the Father on behalf of those for whom he will soon offer himself as a sacrifice, and he explicitly says, "I am praying for *them*. I am *not* praying for the world but for those whom you have given me, for they are yours" (John 17:9). Jesus offers his High Priestly intercession only to those whom the Father has given him (cf. John 6:37, 39, 44, 65; 10:29; 17:2, 6, 20, 24)—namely, the "elect" of Romans 8:33.

Since the priestly work of sacrifice and intercession are inextricably linked, and since it is unthinkable that Christ would refuse to intercede for those for whom he shed his precious blood, we must conclude that the extent of the atonement—like the extent of Christ's intercession—is limited to the elect.

The Argument of Romans 8:29–39

In Romans 8:29–39, Paul speaks explicitly of the extent of the atonement in verse 32 when he says that the Father did not spare his Son but gave him up "for us all." Who is the "us all" for whom Christ was given up to death? Paul answers this question in a number of ways. First, if we look for an antecedent to "for us all" (8:32), we find another "us" in verse 31, referring to those whom God is *for*. Continuing our search for an antecedent, we find that those whom God is for are those whom he foreknew, predestined, called, justified, and glorified (8:29–30). Moving forward, we learn that those for whom Christ was delivered over are those to whom God will graciously give all the saving benefits purchased by Christ's death, for "how will he not also with him graciously give us all things" (8:32)? Romans 8:33 then explicitly identifies these people as "God's elect" and those whom he justifies, and verse 34 identifies them as those for whom Christ intercedes. Finally, those for whom Christ died are those who can never be separated from the love of Christ (vv. 35–39).

Several conclusions should be drawn from these observations. First, since the nonelect do not receive all the saving benefits of God's grace as promised in Romans 8:32 (particularly being rescued from eternal punishment), they are not part of the "us all" for whom Christ was delivered over. Second, since Paul identifies the "us all" for whom Christ was delivered over to be "God's elect" in 8:33, Christ was not delivered over for those who are nonelect. Third, since all for whom Christ was delivered over will also be the beneficiaries of his intercessory ministry at the Father's right hand, and since Christ does not intercede on behalf of the nonelect, they are not included in the "us all" for whom Christ was delivered over. Fourth, since all for whom Christ was delivered over can never be separated from the love of Christ, and since the nonelect will in fact be separated from the love of Christ in eternal punishment, they are not included in the "us all" for whom Christ was delivered over. The extent of Christ's atonement is once again shown to be necessarily limited to the elect.

Making Sense of Universalistic Texts

The preceding positive arguments are sufficient to establish particular redemption as a biblical doctrine. However, the most common objection against limiting the extent of the atonement comes from several passages of Scripture that seem to explicitly contradict it by using universalistic language in relation to Christ's death: "For God so loved the *world*, that he gave his only Son" (John 3:16); Christ Jesus "gave himself as a ransom for *all*" (1 Tim. 2:6); and so on. Therefore, in order for the case for particular redemption to stand, these universalistic texts must be explained in a way that (1) harmonizes with the precepts of particular redemption and (2) is consistent with contextual, grammatical-historical interpretation.

Three categories of texts are usually presented in response to the above argumentation for particular redemption. First are texts which speak of Christ dying for "all." Second are texts which speak of Christ dying for "the world." Third are texts which seem to indicate that Christ has died for those who will finally perish. The following section will address each of the three categories, giving a key example of each.[14]

Christ Died for All. First are texts which speak of Christ dying for "all." Universalists often appeal to such texts and simply assert that "all" must always mean "all people without exception." To be sure, there are instances where that is the

14 For a more extensive discussion that addresses more texts, see MacArthur and Mayhue, *Biblical Doctrine*, pp. 554–65.

case: all people without exception "have sinned and fall short of the glory of God" (Rom. 3:23; yet even here there is one exception—the Lord Jesus Christ). But there are several passages of Scripture where "all" simply cannot mean "all without exception" (e.g., Matt. 10:22; John 18:20; Rom. 5:18; 11:32). Paul himself limits universalistic language when he comments on Psalm 8:6 in 1 Corinthians 15:27: "But when it says, 'all things are put in subjection,' it is plain that he is excepted who put all things in subjection under him." That is, in this case, "all things" does not mean "all things without exception." Therefore, "all" is not a self-defining expression. While in some contexts it may legitimately be understood to speak of every person who has ever lived (i.e., all without exception), in other contexts it may legitimately be understood to speak of all kinds of people throughout the world (i.e., all without distinction). The determining factor of the proper sense of "all" is not one's *a priori* assumptions but rather the context of the particular passage in which the word occurs. When those passages are subjected to the scrutiny of contextual exegesis, it becomes clear that none of them supports an unlimited atonement.

One of the most popular texts marshaled in support of an unlimited atonement is 1 Timothy 2:3–6, which speaks of "God our Savior, who desires all people to be saved and to come to the knowledge of the truth. For there is one God, and there is one mediator between God and men, the man Christ Jesus, who gave himself as a ransom for all, which is the testimony given at the proper time." This appears to many to teach a universal (all) atonement. However, this passage must be read in its context. When Paul wrote 1 Timothy, certain persons were teaching a "different doctrine" (1:3), "swerving" from sound teaching and wandering into "vain discussion" (1:6). These false teachers had ambitions to be "teachers of the law" (1:7), and their speculation regarding genealogies (1:4) and forbidding of marriage and certain foods (4:1–3) indicates that their false doctrine consisted of an exclusive Jewish elitism. Paul's universalistic statements throughout the letter (cf. 1 Tim. 2:2, 4, 6; 4:10) make perfect sense in light of the context of this elitist false teaching. He is not teaching that Christ died for all without exception but rather that, contrary to this false teaching, Christ died for all without distinction.[15] This conclusion is strengthened by the fact that he urges prayers to be made "for all people" (1 Tim. 2:1), by which he means not every individual throughout the entire world by name (for such would be impossible) but rather all kinds of

15 Even I. Howard Marshall, who held to an unlimited atonement, wrote, "This universalistic thrust is most probably a corrective response to an exclusive elitist understanding of salvation connected with the false teaching. . . . The context shows that the inclusion of Gentiles alongside Jews in salvation is the primary issue here" (*A Critical and Exegetical Commentary on the Pastoral Epistles*, in collaboration with Philip H. Towner, International Critical Commentary [Edinburgh: T&T Clark, 2006], 420, 427).

people: "for kings and all who are in high positions" (2:2). Also, immediately after the passage in question, Paul speaks of his apostolic appointment as a teacher of the Gentiles (2:7), indicating further that his intent is to speak of all without distinction (i.e., not just Jews but Gentiles also). Finally, it must be remembered that the ransom Jesus paid was not a potential ransom but an actual and efficacious one. If we accept the universalist interpretation of 1 Timothy 2:6, we must either (1) embrace universal final salvation or (2) denigrate the efficacy of the atonement. Instead, the particularist interpretation makes the best sense of the totality of the biblical data. Paul uses the word "all" to refer to all kinds of people in order to undermine a heretical Jewish elitism that had taken hold at Ephesus.

Christ Died for the World. In addition to passages which speak of Christ dying for "all," texts that say Christ died for "the world" or "the whole world" are also often appealed to in support of an unlimited atonement. But in the same way, they must also be interpreted according to their context. In the cases in which such passages are describing the extent of the atonement, they are properly interpreted to mean "all without distinction" rather than "all without exception." Two examples will suffice.

Perhaps the most common text brought in support of universal atonement is John 3:16. Universalists claim that, by giving his only Son over to a substitutionary and sacrificial death, God has expressed his love for the entire world, which they believe refers to every individual who will have ever lived. However, nothing in the passage demands that "world" be interpreted to mean "all without exception." In fact, there is good reason to understand it as "all without distinction." In particular, Jesus is discussing salvation with Nicodemus, "a man of the Pharisees . . . [and] a ruler of the Jews" (John 3:1). The Pharisees, like virtually all Israel in Jesus's day, regarded Gentiles as unclean and alienated from the covenant promises of God. As Jesus discusses salvation with this ruler of the Jews, he explains that God's love extends not only to Israel but also to men and women throughout the whole world—Gentiles as well as Jews. Further, one must note Jesus's own particularism in this very verse. Christ has been given up so that whoever *believes* (Gk. *pas ho pisteuōn*, lit., "all the believing ones") should not perish but have eternal life. Jesus clearly limits the scope of his atoning death to those who will eventually believe in him for salvation.

The universalist alternative would create numerous problems. For instance, if Christ had been sent to atone for every individual without exception, would that not have included those sinners who had already died and were paying for their sins in hell? But for what reason? To give them an opportunity to repent? Yet such an opportunity had passed, for they had already been undergoing divine judgment (cf. Heb. 9:27). An even greater problem would be that, by saying that Christ atoned for people who will finally perish in hell, the universalist necessarily limits the efficacy of Christ's sacrifice. If Christ can atone for someone's sins and that person can still go to hell, then something other than Christ's atonement is ultimately responsible for salvation.

Similar issues are at play in 1 John 2:2. John writes, "He is the propitiation for our sins, and not for ours only but also for the sins of the whole world." Here we have a statement of the nature of the atonement (propitiation), followed by a statement of the scope or extent of that work (the whole world). A superficial reading of the text at first seems to leave the reader in tension, because propitiation—that is, the actual satisfaction of God's wrath against sin—for all without exception would demand universal final salvation. Yet again, because Scripture teaches that not all will finally be saved (Matt. 7:13, 23; 25:31–46; 2 Thess. 1:9; Rev. 21:8), such an interpretation is untenable.

At this point there are two options. First, the universalist accepts the superficial interpretation of "whole world" to mean "all without exception" and therefore modifies the propitiatory *nature* of the atonement to mean "a potential propitiation." Such an interpretive move, however, militates against everything Scripture teaches concerning the efficacious nature of propitiation. There is no exegetical basis for such an interpretation. Alternatively, the particularist interprets the nature of propitiation in accordance with the rest of biblical teaching and seeks a way to understand "whole world" that both avoids doing violence to the grammar, context, and authorial intent of 1 John 1–2 and averts the problematic implications of universalism. Such a way is available. It is to understand "the whole world" to refer to "all without distinction" rather than "all without exception." This option fits better lexically because it respects the Bible's uniform definition of *hilasmos* as the efficacious satisfaction of wrath. It also fits better contextually, for John is writing to churches being harassed by the false teaching of sinless perfectionism (1 John 1:6–10), likely linked to an incipient Gnosticism promising that the key to spiritual victory was found in a secret knowledge that only the Gnostics possessed. Thus, when John writes of the scope of the Savior's accomplishment, he repudiates all vestiges of exclusivism: Christ is not the propitiation for our sins only, whether Jews rather than Gentiles, Gnostics rather than other Christians, or believers in Asia Minor rather than believers throughout the rest of the world. No, he is the propitiation for the sins of God's people scattered throughout the entire world.

Such an interpretation is only confirmed by the syntactical parallel in John 11:49–52. There John reports Caiaphas's prophecy concerning the death of Christ—that one man would die for the people (11:50). John then comments, "He did not say this of his own accord, but being high priest that year he prophesied that Jesus would die for the nation, and not for the nation only, but also to gather into one the children of God who are scattered abroad" (11:51–52). Note the parallelism:

> John 11:51–52: . . . that Jesus would die for the nation, and not for the nation only, but also to gather into one the children of God who are scattered abroad.
>
> 1 John 2:2: He is the propitiation for our sins, and not for ours only but also for the sins of the whole world.

Thus, this other comment from John's pen would support interpreting "the whole world" in 1 John 2:2 to mean "all without distinction," namely, the children of God who are scattered abroad throughout the whole world (cf. John 10:16). Indeed, in Revelation 5:9 John also writes explicitly of Christ's particular atonement, which he describes as being for all without distinction, for the saints sing, "Worthy are you to take the scroll and to open its seals, for you were slain, and by your blood you ransomed people for God from every tribe and language and people and nation." John does not say that the Lamb ransomed every tribe and language and people and nation, which would fit the universalist interpretation, but that he ransomed people *from* every tribe and language and people and nation—that is, not all without exception but all without distinction.

With regard to 1 John 2:2, then, the particularist interpretation of "the whole world" fits the language, context, and authorial intent of the passage; does not contradict any other passage of Scripture; parallels other passages John wrote; and avoids the undesirable interpretive conclusions of either universal final salvation or an inefficacious propitiation, one or the other of which is unavoidable in the universalist interpretation. Thus, the particularist interpretation is both biblically and theologically preferable.

Christ Died for Some Who Will Finally Perish. A final set of texts are those which suggest that some of those who are the objects of Christ's death may finally perish for their sins in hell. If Scripture teaches that some of those for whom Jesus died will eventually pay for their own sins, it becomes plain that Jesus's death was not in fact efficacious. In that case, it would not be inconsistent to say that Jesus died for all without exception even though not all without exception are saved.

However, the authors of Scripture often refer to those who eventually show themselves to be false brethren as if they were genuine believers. This is often called "the judgment of charity." That is, such people represented themselves as truly belonging to the covenant community and thus were regarded and spoken of as true believers while they remained in the church (e.g., John 12:4; Heb. 3:12–4:7). Their eventual departure from the covenant community, however, demonstrated that they never truly belonged to Christ, for nothing can separate the true believer from the love of Christ (Rom. 8:35–39; cf. John 10:27–30; Phil. 1:6). Thus, while the abuse of Christian liberty has the potential to "grieve" (Rom. 14:15) and "wound [the] conscience" of (1 Cor. 8:12) the weaker brother, a true brother for whom Christ died will never finally be lost. If such a person does fall away from the faith, they reveal themselves to have never truly been a brother in the first place (1 John 2:19).

Related to this is Peter's comment concerning the false teachers in 2 Peter 2:1. Here Peter indicates that the false teachers were "bought" or "redeemed" (Gk. *agorazō*) by the "Master" (Gk. *despotēs*) and yet will nevertheless face eternal destruction. Thus, universalists argue that Christ the Master died for all without exception, even purchasing the false teachers, but that because they are never truly saved, they will not finally partake of the saving benefits of Christ's death.

However, at least five considerations prompt us to reject this interpretation. First, in all but one instance in the New Testament (Jude 4), the word "Master" (Gk. *despotēs*) is used to indicate not the Son but the Father. Thus, Christ's redeeming work on the cross is likely not in view here. Second, *agorazō* is likely being used in a non-salvific sense, since it is never used in a salvific sense without being accompanied by a word for "price" (1 Cor. 6:20; 7:23; Rev. 5:9; 14:3, 4).[16] Third, Peter is clearly alluding to Deuteronomy 32:6, which says, "Do you thus repay the Lord, O foolish and unwise people? Is not He your Father who has bought you? He has made you and established you" (NASB). The language of "denying the Master who bought them" serves to identify the false teachers of Peter's day with the false prophets of Israel. Fourth, it is likely that Peter is granting, for the sake of argument, the premise that the false teachers are true believers. In other words, as Thomas Schreiner says, "It *appeared as if* the Lord had purchased the false teachers with his blood [2 Pet. 2:1], though they actually did not truly belong to the Lord."[17] Peter is thus sarcastically saying, "These who claim to be redeemed deny by their deeds and their doctrine the Master whom they claim has bought them. They are no better than the false prophets of Israel." Fifth, if taken to its logical conclusion, the universalist interpretation denies not only an efficacious redemption—which Scripture explicitly affirms (Eph. 1:7; Col. 1:14)—but also the doctrine of the perseverance of the saints, that is, that one who is truly redeemed cannot be lost (John 10:27–30; Rom. 8:31–39; 1 John 2:19).

16 Gary D. Long, *Definite Atonement* (Nutley, NJ: Presbyterian & Reformed, 1976), 72.

17 Thomas R. Schreiner, "'Problematic Texts' for Definite Atonement in the Pastoral and General Epistles," in David Gibson and Jonathan Gibson, *From Heaven He Came and Sought Her: Definite Atonement in Historical, Biblical, Theological, and Pastoral Perspective* (Wheaton, IL: Crossway, 2013), 390.

Summary

In summary, though several texts of Scripture employ universalistic language with respect to the scope of Christ's death, none of those texts stands under exegetical scrutiny as support for an unlimited atonement. Rather, when interpreted in context, passages that refer to Christ's death for "all" and for "the world" are used to speak of all without distinction, not all without exception, and passages that might seem to indicate that those for whom Christ died can finally perish in their sins are shown to teach no such thing.

Because Scripture reveals (1) that the three persons of the Trinity are entirely united in their saving will and purpose, (2) that atonement is never potential or provisional but always actual and efficacious, (3) that Christ's High Priestly ministry of sacrifice is coextensive with his High Priestly ministry of intercession, (4) that several passages of Scripture speak of Christ's atoning work in particularistic terms, and (5) that no passage of Scripture teaches that Christ atoned for all without exception, therefore Scripture teaches that the extent of Christ's atonement is not universal but is limited to the elect alone.

RESURRECTION, ASCENSION, AND INTERCESSION

Christ's intercessory work was not exhausted at the cross. He was not only "delivered up for our trespasses"; he was also "raised for our justification" (Rom. 4:25). Further, he also ascended to the right hand of the Father to rule over all things (Eph. 1:20–23), in which place believers are said to be seated with him (Eph. 2:6). Because he ascended, he sent the Holy Spirit to permanently indwell every member of his church (John 14:16–17; 16:7) and to empower us for holiness and service. Further still, he presently intercedes for us at the right hand of the Father (Rom. 8:34; Heb. 7:25), praying for our greatest spiritual benefit, defending us against our Accuser, sanctifying our prayers, and ministering to us in our times of need (cf. Heb. 4:16).[18]

The culmination of our study of the accomplishment of redemption must be to worship the triune God for the work of the Son. Accurate theology must always issue in transcendent doxology (see the song of the saints and angels in Rev. 5:9–13).

The Application of Redemption

Because of the sufficiency of Christ's atoning work, if a believer is asked *when* God saved him, there is a sense in which he ought to reply, "Two thousand years ago." And yet no one comes into this world saved. We are all brought forth in iniquity (Ps. 51:5), dead in our trespasses and sins (Eph. 2:1), by nature children

18 For more on Christ's resurrection, ascension, and present intercession, see chap. 4, "God the Son."

of wrath (Eph. 2:3), and enemies of God (Rom. 5:10; 8:7–8). Though all the blessings of salvation were purchased once for all at the cross, the people of God do not enjoy the benefits of Christ's work until the Holy Spirit *applies* those blessings to individual believers—until they are born of the Spirit unto repentance and faith, are united to Christ, and are thereby justified, adopted, and set apart for a life of holiness and service to God. It is for this reason that we must distinguish between the accomplishment of redemption and the application of redemption.

In the wisdom of God, the Holy Spirit does not immediately apply to the believer all the fullness of the benefits secured by Christ's work. Instead, these blessings are imparted to us progressively, in stages. Further, even those aspects of salvation that are applied simultaneously are nevertheless to be properly distinguished from one another. For instance, although we are justified and adopted in the same moment, both justification and adoption are unique blessings. Collapsing one of them into the other robs each of its distinctive glory. Like a precious diamond, the glory of the application of redemption is multifaceted and is fully comprehended only as each individual facet contributes to the brilliance of the whole. Thus, the study of soteriology is concerned to explore the distinctiveness of each aspect of the application of redemption.

THE ORDER OF SALVATION

Not only are these aspects of salvation distinct from one another, but they are also logically, and sometimes chronologically, related to one another. The *ordo salutis*, or "order of salvation," aims to define these logical and chronological relationships between the various stages of the application of redemption.[19] Some have questioned whether it is proper even to attempt such a thing, since the Bible does not provide an explicit *ordo salutis*. Yet there is a significant scriptural basis for recognizing an order to salvation (e.g., John 1:12–13; Rom. 8:29–30). To suggest that glorification is anything but the last step in the application of redemption, or to suggest that faith is given subsequent to justification, would be to violate the plain sense of several passages (glorification: Rom. 8:23; Phil. 3:20–21; justification: Rom. 3:28; 5:1). Therefore, to speak of logical order or priority is not to unnaturally foist "human logic" on the text of Scripture. Instead, it is to read out of the text the divine logic and order that the Spirit of God himself has plainly revealed. This is the goal of a biblical *ordo salutis*.

19 It is important to recognize this distinction between logical and chronological order. Certain blessings may be granted simultaneously (e.g., regeneration and faith), while nevertheless maintaining a definite order of cause and effect between the two (e.g., regeneration is the cause, not the consequence, of faith).

The Ordo Salutis *and Romans 8:29–30*

The clearest single text that speaks to the order of salvation is Romans 8:29–30. There Paul writes, "For those whom he foreknew he also predestined to be conformed to the image of his Son, in order that he might be the firstborn among many brothers. And those whom he predestined he also called, and those whom he called he also justified, and those whom he justified he also glorified." As we examine this text, we will discover the beginnings of an *ordo salutis*.

First, though foreknowledge and predestination do not belong to the application of redemption, they nevertheless fit naturally into a definite order. Even the prefixes of both words—"fore-" and "pre-"—show that foreknowledge and predestination are antecedent to the later aspects of redemption (see also Eph. 1:4–5; 1 Pet. 1:20). Thus, the eternal counsel of the Trinity, in which the Father set his electing love on those whom he meant to save, anchors all the saving activity that takes place in the accomplishment and application of redemption.

Second, Paul lists glorification last in this sequence. It is the final feature in the application of redemption, as it describes the eradication of sin and infirmity from our present bodies, truly and consummately saving us from sin and all its effects (Rom. 8:19–25; 1 Cor. 15:50–57; Phil. 3:20–21). Therefore, no matter how any other elements of salvation relate to one another, it is certain that glorification must be last in the *ordo salutis*. Calling and justification must precede glorification.

What, then, is the relationship between calling and justification? In the first place, it is to be observed that the calling Paul has in view here is the effectual call of God that results in salvation (e.g., 1 Cor. 1:9, 24, 26; 2 Tim. 1:9; 2 Pet. 1:3, 10; cf. John 11:43–44) rather than a general calling that may be rejected (e.g., Matt. 22:14; Acts 7:51). This is so because he says that all those who are thus called are also justified and glorified (Rom. 8:30). No one who hears this calling fails to receive the saving blessings of justification and glorification. Second, given that Paul lists foreknowledge and predestination first and glorification last, it is sound to conclude that he has a definite order in mind as he enumerates these various aspects of salvation. Thus, because he lists calling before justification, it is proper to understand that calling precedes justification. Therefore, the order of the application of redemption as presented in Romans 8:30 is effectual call, justification, and then glorification.

The Ordo Salutis *and Other New Testament Texts*

Romans 8:29–30 does not exhaustively treat every aspect of the application of redemption. There is no mention of regeneration, faith, or sanctification, among other saving benefits. To understand where these other doctrines fit in the order of salvation, we must examine the rest of the New Testament.

It may be easiest to place the gift of faith in the order of salvation, since Scripture is clear that faith is the condition of justification. Sinners are said to be justified "by faith" (Rom. 3:28; 5:1; Gal. 3:24), "through faith" (Gal. 2:16), and "on faith" (Phil. 3:9). A sinner will not be declared righteous in God's sight unless he believes, and it is only through the instrumentality of faith that he will lay hold of the righteousness of God in Christ. Thus, it is proper to place faith before justification, and because faith is itself the instrumental cause of justification, nothing ought to come between them. Therefore, we may add faith to our *ordo salutis* as follows: effectual call, faith, justification, and then glorification.

Further, we must also consider that saving faith is always a repentant faith, for the faith that turns to Christ for salvation necessarily turns away from sin and self-righteousness (Acts 26:17–18; 1 Thess. 1:9). This is why the gospel is preached as a call to both repent and believe (Mark 1:14–15; Acts 20:21), for one cannot exist without the other. Repentance is so vital to saving faith that the apostle James says that to sever them is to kill faith, for faith without works (i.e., "fruits in keeping with repentance," Luke 3:8) is dead (James 2:17, 26). Such is no true and saving faith but is utterly useless (James 2:20). The repentance that saves is a believing repentance, and the faith that saves is a repentant faith (cf. Matt. 4:17; Luke 24:47; John 3:16; 20:31). They are two sides of the same coin, and together they constitute conversion (cf. Acts 15:3). And because one must logically turn *from* something before he can turn *to* something else, repentance is placed before faith. Therefore, our order stands as follows: effectual call, conversion (repentance and faith), justification, and then glorification.

Significant disagreement surrounds the relationship between regeneration and faith, yet Scripture seems to clearly present faith as the consequence of the new birth. In the first place, because the natural man is dead in sin (Eph. 2:1–3) and thus unable to understand and accept the things of the Spirit of God (1 Cor. 2:14), he is absolutely incapable of faith until the Spirit quickens spiritual life in him (John 6:65). Second, Jesus declares that the new birth is the prerequisite for seeing (John 3:3) and entering (John 3:5) the kingdom of God. Seeing the kingdom is undoubtedly a figure of speech for exercising saving faith (cf. Heb. 11:1), and it cannot be disputed that one enters the kingdom at conversion (i.e., when the sinner repents and believes the gospel). It follows, then, that the new birth is logically prior to faith. Third, the apostle John says, "Everyone who believes that Jesus is the Christ has been born of God" (1 John 5:1). The verb tenses in this verse are significant. John declares that everyone who presently believes in Jesus *has been* born of God. The very same relationship (as evidenced by identical grammatical constructions) exists between the new birth and the practice of righteousness (1 John 2:29), love (1 John 4:7), and overcoming the world (1 John 5:4). Yet none of these precedes—and still less, causes—regeneration. Finally, there is good reason to believe that calling and regeneration speak of two aspects of the same reality, namely, the summons to spiritual life on the one hand and the impartation of spiritual life on the other.[20] If calling and regeneration can be thus identified with one another, it is understandable that when Paul speaks of calling in Romans 8:30, he does not need to include regeneration, for he conceives of them as one and the same act. Since it has already been demonstrated that faith is subsequent to calling, it is sound to conclude that while they are temporally simultaneous, regeneration logically precedes and gives birth to faith. Therefore, we may continue building our *ordo salutis*: effectual call/regeneration, conversion (repentance and faith), justification, and then glorification.

At this point the remaining aspects of the application of redemption are relatively easy to place. As with justification, believers are said to lay hold of the grace of adoption by faith (John 1:12; Gal. 3:26). This is good cause for considering justification and adoption to be contemporaneous blessings. However, it is proper that adoption should logically follow justification, for believers could not be justly given the legal rights of life in the family of God while they remained destitute of a right standing before him. God must first declare us righteous before welcoming us into the family of the One "whose name is Holy" (Isa. 57:15). Further, the faith by which we lay hold of justification and adoption is a faith that continuously works through love (Gal. 5:6). While regeneration, conversion, justification, and adoption all occur instantaneously, sanctification is a progressive process that takes place throughout the Christian life (2 Cor. 3:18). Thus, sanctification is subsequent to adoption but prior to glorification. The sanctification process is marked by the believer's persevering in faith (Matt. 24:13) and growing in the assurance of salvation (2 Pet. 1:10; 1 John 5:13).

Therefore, based on the foregoing biblical analysis, we find Scripture to provide the following *ordo salutis*:

1. foreknowledge/predestination/election (God's choice of some unto salvation)
2. effectual call/regeneration (the new birth)
3. conversion (repentance and faith)
4. justification (declaration of right legal standing)
5. adoption (being placed into the family of God)
6. sanctification (progressive growth in holiness)

20 In 2 Cor. 4:6, Paul compares the creation of the world by God's word (cf. Gen. 1:3; Ps. 33:6) to the regeneration of the sinner by God's word (cf. James 1:18; 1 Pet. 1:23, 25). When speaking of the creation of the world, we do not distinguish God's command to create from his act of creation. He literally spoke the universe into existence. We ought to take the same approach to the creation of spiritual life in the sinner. The call itself creates the life that it commands. Thus the effectual call ought to be identified with regeneration. For an excellent defense of this view, see appendix 3 of Matthew Barrett, *Reclaiming Monergism: The Case for Sovereign Grace in Effectual Calling and Regeneration* (Phillipsburg, NJ: P&R, 2013).

7. perseverance (remaining in Christ)
8. glorification (receiving a resurrection body)

We turn now to a more thorough discussion of these doctrines concerning the application of redemption.

THE EXTERNAL CALL: GOSPEL PROCLAMATION

When Paul speaks of the doctrine of divine calling in Romans 8:30, he has in mind God's effectual call, or regeneration, whereby God sovereignly summons the sinner out of spiritual death and into spiritual life. In fact, when the New Testament Epistles speak of divine calling, in every case they are referring to this internal, effectual call. The Gospels speak of another call, however, often termed the external call, the general call, or the gospel call. This refers to the verbal proclamation of the gospel by which all sinners are called to turn from their sin and trust in Christ for salvation (Matt. 22:14).

In other words, there is a distinction between the call of God (the internal call) and the call of the preacher (the external call). The internal call is given only to the elect and always brings the sinner to salvation. By contrast, the external call is given to all people without distinction and is often rejected. Because of this, the external call does not properly belong to the *ordo salutis*, for the saving benefits of Christ's redemption are always and only effectually applied to the elect. Nevertheless, because the external call of the gospel is the means by which God issues the effectual call of regeneration, it is a requisite component in the study of the application of redemption.

The Necessity of the External Call

Romans 10:13 declares that the external call is essential for the sinner to be able to "call" on the Lord for salvation:

> For "everyone who calls on the name of the Lord will be saved."
>
> How then will they call on him in whom they have not believed? And how are they to believe in him of whom they have never heard? And how are they to hear without someone preaching? And how are they to preach unless they are sent? As it is written, "How beautiful are the feet of those who preach the good news!" But they have not all obeyed the gospel. For Isaiah says, "Lord, who has believed what he has heard from us?" So faith comes from hearing, and hearing through the word of Christ. (Rom. 10:13–17)

This text clearly indicates that proclaiming the message of the gospel is absolutely imperative to people being saved. Sin has penetrated to the core of man's being, so that he is a sinner not only by choice but also by nature (cf. Rom. 8:7; 1 Cor. 2:14;

Eph. 2:3; 4:17–18). God's revelation of himself in the natural world (Rom. 1:19–20) is sufficient to render all inexcusably guilty before God and to convict men of their sinfulness and the coming judgment both temporally (1:21–31) and eternally (1:32). The solution to the damning spiritual condition of mankind is not found, however, in natural revelation, nor by the sinner looking within himself or to his own resources. For salvation to come to anyone, the gospel message of the life, death, burial, and resurrection of the Son of God, sent from heaven to save sinners by grace through faith apart from works, must be proclaimed to them. The word of truth is the means by which God brings about the new birth (James 1:18; 1 Pet. 1:23, 25). For this reason, the gospel is hailed as "the power of God for salvation" (Rom. 1:16–17). It is by the foolishness of the message preached that God is pleased to save those who believe (1 Cor. 1:18–21). Therefore, we must send preachers of the gospel.

The Elements of the External Call

Since the external call of the gospel is essential for salvation, we must understand what constitutes that call. At least three elements must be communicated in the proclamation of the gospel. First, the gospel preacher must explain the facts of God's holiness, man's sinfulness, and the work of Christ in accomplishing redemption. God is the Creator of all things (Ps. 24:1), and as his creature, man is accountable to God, his Judge. God is perfectly holy (Matt. 5:48); he is the essence of all that is good—so much so that he can have absolutely no fellowship with anyone who falls short of moral perfection (1 John 1:5; cf. James 2:10). And yet Scripture declares that all people have sinned against God by breaking his law and therefore fall short of the perfect standard of righteousness that is required for fellowship with him (Rom. 3:23). The verdict pronounced over the whole of mankind is, "None is righteous, no, not one" (Rom. 3:10), and the resulting sentence is death: "For the wages of sin is death" (Rom. 6:23). Because sin against an infinitely holy God demands an infinite punishment, this death is not merely physical or temporal but also spiritual and eternal. The just punishment for all sin is hell: conscious torment forever, away from the saving presence of the Lord (Matt. 13:50; 25:46; 2 Thess. 1:9; Rev. 14:11).

It is into this miserable state of affairs that God steps forth in sovereign grace. While man was helpless under the weight of sin, with no way to pay its penalty and escape its results (Rom. 5:6), God the Son became a man to live the perfectly righteous life that the sons of Adam had failed to live and to die a substitutionary death in the place of his people (Rom. 5:6, 8), absorbing in his own person the full penalty of the Father's wrath against their sin (Isa. 53:6; 2 Cor. 5:21; 1 Pet. 2:24). After dying in the stead of sinners, he was buried, and on the third day, he rose from the dead in triumph over sin and death (Rom. 4:25; 1 Cor. 15:4; Heb. 2:14–18) and ascended to the right hand of the Father in heaven (Eph. 1:20–23).

Unless a preacher accurately explains man's predicament in sin and Christ's incarnation, substitutionary atonement, and resurrection, the gospel has not been preached.

While believing these facts of the gospel is essential to salvation, it is not sufficient; indeed, even the demons believe true facts about God and his gospel (James 2:19). For a sinner to have a saving interest in Christ, he must respond to these facts by turning from sin and trusting in Christ for righteousness. Therefore, a second essential element of the external call is the preacher's earnest call for the sinner to repent and believe (Mark 1:14–15; Acts 20:21; cf. 1 Thess. 1:9). That is to say, a biblical gospel presentation calls sinners to (1) acknowledge their sin and guilt before God (Luke 15:18), (2) abandon all hope of attaining forgiveness by good works (Heb. 6:1), (3) forsake their life ruled by sin and self (Isa. 55:7; Luke 9:23), and (4) put all their trust in the righteousness of Christ alone for being accepted by and reconciled to God (Rom. 10:4, 9; Phil. 3:4–9). Only by repentant faith may a sinner subjectively lay hold of the benefits objectively purchased by Christ. Further, this call to repent and believe is to be delivered with the utmost urgency. Preachers must not present Christ to the sinner in a cold and disinterested manner; rather, driven by the fear of the Lord (2 Cor. 5:11), they are to earnestly persuade and implore men to "be reconciled to God" (2 Cor. 5:20).

A third necessary element of the external call is the promise of forgiveness of sins and eternal life. As we call sinners to repentance and faith, we must present to them the incomparable blessings promised to those who are obedient to the gospel call (John 3:16; Acts 2:38; 3:19; 13:38–39). Ultimately, the greatest promise of the gospel is that sinners once alienated from God can be reconciled to a right relationship with him (Eph. 2:18; 1 Pet. 3:18)—even to become his child (John 1:12). Therefore, a God-centered gospel presentation will not only proclaim the magnificent promises of forgiveness and eternal life but will also declare that eternal life consists in the knowledge of and communion with the triune God (John 17:3) and will present him, the Giver, as the gospel's greatest gift.

The Characteristics of the External Call

The external call to salvation as presented in the gospel is marked by several key characteristics. First, it is a general, or universal, call. That is, the good news of repentance and faith for the forgiveness of sins is to be proclaimed to all people without exception. Whereas the internal call of regeneration is given only to the elect, the external call of the gospel is to be preached indiscriminately to elect and reprobate alike. God represents himself as earnestly desiring that the wicked should repent (Ezek. 18:23, 32; 33:11; cf. 2 Cor. 5:20), and in accordance with that desire, he exuberantly calls all people to himself (Isa. 55:1, 3). He entreats sinners to seek him and is eager to have compassion on them and to forgive them (Isa. 55:6–7). Without discrimination he commands "all the ends of the earth" to turn to him and be saved (Isa. 45:22). The Lord Jesus preached the gospel even to those who rejected him (Matt. 22:2–14; Luke 14:16–24), inviting everyone who was weary to find rest in him (Matt. 11:28–30). This universality is represented in the church's Great Commission, to "make disciples of all nations" (Matt. 28:19; cf. Luke 24:47) and to "preach the gospel to every creature" (Mark 16:15 NKJV). Thus, it is no surprise to see this universality modeled in apostolic preaching, as Paul declared to the philosophers on Mars Hill that God "commands all people everywhere to repent" (Acts 17:30). Indeed, the universality of the gospel call cannot be denied.

A second characteristic of the external call is that it is a sincere, bona fide offer. Some object that because God intends only to save those whom he has chosen, the indiscriminate call of the gospel cannot be genuine on God's part. This is nothing less than a blasphemous accusation from those who have exalted their own reasoning above God's revelation. God does call all to repentance, and he represents himself as sincerely desiring the repentance of the wicked (Ezek. 18:23; cf. 18:32; 33:11). Can anyone doubt the sincerity of the God who says, "Oh, that my people would listen to me, that Israel would walk in my ways!" (Ps. 81:13; cf. Rom. 10:21)? While it may be difficult to understand how statements of compassion toward the nonelect can be reconciled with the doctrines of sovereign election and particular redemption, it is not an option to conclude that God does not mean what he says![21] The God who "has mercy on whomever he wills" and "hardens whomever he wills" (Rom. 9:18) is the God who takes no pleasure in the death of the wicked. To reason that the former is incompatible with the latter is not an option for the Bible-believing Christian.

The offer of salvation communicated in the external call of the gospel is conditioned on repentance and faith. For it to be a genuine, well-meant offer on God's part, he simply has to be sincerely disposed to provide the promised blessings upon the satisfaction of the offer's conditions. And this is precisely the case; if anyone repents and trusts in Christ, God *will* forgive and save him. However, such repentance and faith are impossible for the natural man (Rom. 8:7–8; 1 Cor. 2:14). Apart from regenerating grace, no man will ever repent and believe. Thus, in the case of the nonelect, the conditions of the offer will never be met. To suggest

21 As Berkhof comments, "The external calling is a calling in good faith, a calling that is seriously meant. It is not an invitation coupled with the hope that it will not be accepted. When God calls the sinner to accept Christ by faith, He earnestly desires this; and when He promises those who repent and believe eternal life, His promise is dependable. This follows from the very nature, from the veracity, of God. It is blasphemous to think that God would be guilty of equivocation and deception, that He would say one thing and mean another, that He would earnestly plead with the sinner to repent and believe unto salvation, and at the same time not desire it in any sense of the word" (*Systematic Theology*, 4th ed. [1932; repr., Grand Rapids, MI: Eerdmans, 1996], 462).

that God's offer is insincere—indeed, that he feigns sincerity—because he does not provide the necessary grace to overcome man's depravity is to suppose that God is obligated to give grace to all. To such a notion the Lord himself responds, "Am I not allowed to do what I choose with what belongs to me?" (Matt. 20:15). The potter has the right over the clay "to make out of the same lump one vessel for honorable use and another for dishonorable use" (Rom. 9:21). God is not obligated to give grace to anyone, let alone everyone. The deficiency in the gospel call lies in man's depravity, not in any supposed parsimony in God's grace. To suggest such a thing approaches the highest strains of blasphemy.

Finally, a third characteristic of the external call is that, in and of itself, it is not efficacious. Unlike the effectual call, the external call can be resisted. Jesus makes this distinction in his conclusion to the parable of the wedding banquet: "For many are called, but few are chosen" (Matt. 22:14). That is, many are invited to partake in the feast of the blessings of eternal life, yet because the Father has chosen only some and not all, few are effectually called. Therefore, many who are invited reject the external call. Any instance in which the gospel is preached and rejected is evidence for the inherent inefficacy of the external call (e.g., John 3:18; 6:64; 12:37; Acts 7:51; 17:32). It is for this very reason that the external call is insufficient for salvation.

THE INTERNAL CALL: REGENERATION

Because of the deficiencies of the external call, sinners stand in need of a sovereignly efficacious call, inherently powerful to overcome the effects of depravity and to bring them to repentance and saving faith. In his natural state, man is a spiritual corpse (Eph. 2:1), entirely unresponsive to the spiritual truth proclaimed in the gospel. For this reason, the natural man will always reject the gospel, for the things of the Spirit of God "are folly to him, and he is not able to understand them because they are spiritually discerned" (1 Cor. 2:14). Scripture says the natural man is spiritually blind, and so he does not see the glory of Christ in the gospel (2 Cor. 4:4; cf. Rom. 1:21–22; Eph. 4:17–18). He is also spiritually deaf; he cannot perceive the truth announced in the gospel of grace (Isa. 6:9–10; Matt. 13:15; John 8:43). Still further, man's will and affections are entirely disordered by sin (Jer. 17:9), for his heart is a heart of stone (Ezek. 11:19; 36:26), cold and unresponsive to the meaning and glory of divinely revealed truth.

"But God, being rich in mercy, because of the great love with which he loved us, even when we were dead in our trespasses, *made us alive* together with Christ" (Eph. 2:4–5). In the exercise of his sovereign pleasure, God issues an effectual call in the heart of the elect. He powerfully summons the sinner out of his spiritual death and blindness and, by virtue of the creative power of his word, imparts new spiritual life to him—giving him a new heart, along with eyes to see and ears to hear, and thus enabling him to repent and believe in Christ for salvation (Rom. 8:30; 1 Cor. 1:24; 2 Tim. 1:9; 1 Pet. 5:10; 2 Pet. 1:3). He effectually calls his people "out of darkness" and "into his marvelous light" (1 Pet. 2:9), "to himself" (Acts 2:39), into fellowship with his Son (1 Cor. 1:9) so that they belong to Christ (Rom. 1:6), and "into his own kingdom and glory" (1 Thess. 2:12). This is the divine miracle of regeneration, or the new birth.

The Author of Regeneration

The author of this radical change of man's nature cannot be man himself but rather must be the Creator of all life, including eternal life—God alone. Unlike other aspects of the application of redemption, in regeneration man is entirely passive; God is the sole active agent in bringing about the creative miracle of the new birth.

It is significant that Scripture uses the imagery of being born again to describe this work of regeneration (John 3:3–8; 1 Pet. 1:3, 23; 1 John 3:9). In the physical realm, a child makes no contribution to his conception or birth. He is entirely dependent on the will of his parents to be brought into being. In the same way, Jesus chooses this analogy to teach that dead and depraved sinners cannot contribute to their rebirth unto spiritual life but are entirely dependent on the sovereign will of God for regeneration. He declares, "Truly, truly, I say to you, unless one is born again he cannot see the kingdom of God" (John 3:3). Sin has so infected and corrupted mankind that nothing less than the wholesale renovation of the soul is required for salvation. When Nicodemus asks how this can happen, Jesus does not give him a list of religious duties by which he can cooperate with God's grace. Instead, he points to the sovereign will of God and declares, "The wind blows where it wishes" (John 3:8). As John Murray observes, "The wind is not at our beck and call; neither is the regenerative operation of the Spirit."[22] Sinful mankind cannot induce this new birth.

Aside from this vivid imagery, Scripture explicitly affirms that regeneration is an act of God alone. Those who are born again are born "not of blood nor of the will of the flesh nor of the will of man, but of God" (John 1:13). This truth precludes human effort from having any bearing on regeneration. No heritage or ancestral lineage, no man-made religion or sacramental system, and not even the decision of man's will can produce regeneration. The children of God are born *of God*. So far from depending on man's will, sinners are brought forth unto spiritual life by the exercise of *God's* will (James 1:18). While man was utterly helpless to bring himself to life, "God . . . made us alive together with Christ" (Eph. 2:4–5; cf. Col. 2:13). According to the Father's great mercy, "he has caused us to be born again" (1 Pet. 1:3).

22 Murray, *Redemption Accomplished and Applied*, 99.

The monergistic[23] work of God in regeneration is displayed perhaps most clearly in Ezekiel 36:25–27, in which God promises a day when he would bring regeneration to his people, removing their heart of stone and giving them a heart of flesh. In just these three verses, God uses the phrase "I will" six times, insisting that this spiritual heart transplant is entirely his work. In the next chapter, God illustrates his own sovereignty and man's helplessness by picturing the future regeneration of Israel as his breathing life into a valley full of dry bones (Ezek. 37:1–11). The natural man is no more able to bring himself to life than a pile of dead and dry bones could bring themselves to life. God then declares, "Behold, *I will* open your graves and raise you from your graves. . . . And *I will* put my Spirit within you, and you shall live" (Ezek. 37:12, 14).

These passages in Ezekiel point to the Holy Spirit's role in regeneration. While many texts explicitly name the person of the Father as the agent of regeneration (James 1:17–18; 1 Pet. 1:3; cf. Rom. 8:30; 1 Cor. 1:9), Scripture also indicates that the Holy Spirit participates in this work. Jesus says that to be born again is to be "born of the Spirit" (John 3:5, 6, 8; cf. 6:63). The apostle Paul says that Christ saves us by "the washing of regeneration and renewal of the Holy Spirit" (Titus 3:5). We may conclude, therefore, that while the Father is the ultimate agent of regeneration, summoning us out of death and into life, the Holy Spirit is the efficient cause of regeneration, carrying out the will of the Father by giving us spiritual life.

The Nature of Regeneration

The Greek term for "regeneration" (*palingenesia*) appears only twice in the New Testament. In Matthew 19:28, Jesus uses the word to refer to the renovation of the creation that will begin in the millennial kingdom and will come to consummation in the new heavens and the new earth. In Titus 3:5, Paul says, "He saved us, not because of works done by us in righteousness, but according to his own mercy, by the washing of regeneration and renewal of the Holy Spirit." Here we learn that regeneration is characterized by both washing and renewal. These concepts

23 *Monergism* is a word derived from the Greek *monos*, meaning "one," and *ergos*, meaning "work." It speaks of there being one agent at work. Theologians have employed this term to describe the view of regeneration argued for here, namely, that God is the sole agent at work in regeneration, while man is entirely passive. *Synergism*, on the other hand, speaks of "working together" and describes a view of regeneration in which man cooperates with God in regeneration. Wesleyan theologian and synergist John Miley wrote, "Regeneration is not an absolute work of the Spirit. . . . There are prerequisites which cannot be met without our own free agency. There must be an earnest turning of the soul to God, deep repentance for sin, and a true faith in Christ. Such are the requirements of our own agency. There is no regeneration for us without them" (*Systematic Theology*, 2 vols. [New York: Hunt & Eaton, 1892], 2:336). Such teaching is entirely contradictory to Scripture's emphasis on God's activity and man's helplessness with respect to regeneration. For a masterful defense of monergistic regeneration, see Matthew Barrett, *Salvation by Grace: The Case for Effectual Calling and Regeneration* (Phillipsburg, NJ: P&R, 2013).

are also present in John 3:5, where Jesus describes the new birth as being "born of water and the Spirit," a reference to Ezekiel 36:25–26, which metaphorically describes regeneration as being sprinkled with clean water and being given a new heart. Thus, regeneration speaks of a cleansing from sin and a creation of spiritual life. It is a purifying renovation.

This divine impartation of spiritual life is a fundamental re-creation of the whole person. Paul plainly states, "Therefore, if anyone is in Christ, he is a new creation. The old has passed away; behold, the new has come" (2 Cor. 5:17). It is not merely the sinner's spirit or soul that is a new creation, but he himself, as a whole person, is a new creation. Just as man's depravity is total—that is, just as sin has so pervaded man's nature as to leave no part of him untouched by sin's corruption—so also does regeneration reach to the totality of man. The Holy Spirit opens the blind eyes of the mind (Acts 26:18; 2 Cor. 4:4, 6; Eph. 1:18), replacing, as it were, the mind of the flesh with the mind of the Spirit (Rom. 8:5–9)—indeed, with the mind of Christ himself (1 Cor. 2:16)—so that the regenerate man understands all the things that he once could not understand (1 Cor. 2:15; cf. 1 John 2:20, 27). The Spirit removes the sinner's heart of stone and implants in him a heart of flesh capable of perceiving and loving spiritual truth (Ezek. 11:19; 36:26; cf. Deut. 30:6). The affections are thus renewed after the likeness of Christ, so that the new man hates sin (Matt. 5:4), loves righteousness (Matt. 5:6; John 3:21), thirsts for the God whom he once abhorred (Pss. 27:4; 42:1–2), and loves and rejoices in the Christ whom he once regarded as foolish (1 Pet. 1:8; cf. 2 Cor. 5:16). With renewed affections, the sinner's will is finally freed from the bondage of sin unto the liberty of righteousness. He now wants what God wants (Ps. 40:8), for the Spirit of God is at work within him "both to will and to work for his good pleasure" (Phil. 2:13; cf. Ezek. 36:27). Once bound in sin and spiritual death, man's mind, heart, and will are now renewed unto life. The regenerated sinner is truly a "new self, created after the likeness of God in true righteousness and holiness" (Eph. 4:24).

Perhaps the most vivid picture of regeneration comes in 2 Corinthians 4. Paul describes the state of the natural man when he says, "The god of this world has blinded the minds of the unbelievers, to keep them from seeing the light of the gospel of the glory of Christ, who is the image of God" (2 Cor. 4:4). To be spiritually dead (cf. Eph. 2:1) is to be devoid of the spiritual life that allows one to see the true value of the glory of Christ revealed in the gospel. The essence of spiritual death is spiritual blindness. Man's spiritual perception is so disordered by sin that he has no taste for what is objectively delightful (i.e., the gospel of the glory of Christ) but is infatuated with what is objectively repulsive and disgusting (i.e., sin and the glory of self). The unregenerate man pursues what is worthless because he is blind to its detriment, and he refuses what is most precious because he is blind to its value. Thus, when the objective beauty of Christ is held forth in the gospel message, the unregenerate man sees no glory in him, and therefore, left to himself, he will ever and always choose to reject the gospel.

What, then, is the remedy for such a miserable condition? There is no hope in man's enslaved will but only in the sovereign grace and life-giving power of God. Paul answers that the remedy for man's spiritual blindness is monergistic regeneration: "For God, who said, 'Let light shine out of darkness,' has shone in our hearts to give the light of the knowledge of the glory of God in the face of Jesus Christ" (2 Cor. 4:6). Paul compares regeneration to God's original creation of the world. In the beginning, God spoke the universe into existence from nothing (Pss. 33:6; 148:5): "And God *said*, 'Let there be light,' and there was light" (Gen. 1:3), instantly "call[ing] into existence the things that do not exist" (Rom. 4:17). In regeneration, God speaks the command into darkened and dead hearts—"Let there be light"—and instantaneously births in us the light of eternal spiritual life where it had not existed.[24] He shines the light of life into the blind heart. He gives us new spiritual eyes so that we finally see sin for what it is—in all its objective ugliness—and so finally see Christ for who he is—in all his objective beauty and glory. And when sinners finally have functioning spiritual eyes and the light necessary to see things as they actually are, they turn away in disgust from the filth of sin (repentance) and eagerly embrace the Christ whose glory they can at last see (faith).

It is for this reason that theologians speak of the regenerating grace of God as irresistible.[25] It is not that God's grace can never be resisted (Acts 7:51); rather, in the irresistible grace of regeneration, God overcomes man's natural resistance to the gospel by shining light into his heart and opening his eyes to the glory of Jesus. Irresistible grace, then, does not mean that man is coerced or forced into repentance and faith; his will is not violated. Rather, this grace *frees* man's will; it opens our eyes so we can accurately compare the glory of sin to the glory of Christ. It is impossible that anyone with restored spiritual sight through regeneration should see sin and Christ side by side and do anything but turn from sin and embrace Christ in saving faith. Thus, in regeneration man's will is not violated but transformed. As the Westminster Confession states, we come to him

24 Thus, the effectual call of regeneration creates the very life that it commands. John Murray explains, "The summons is invested with the efficacy by which we are delivered to the destination intended—we are effectively ushered into the fellowship of Christ. There is something determinate about God's call; by his sovereign power and grace it cannot fail of accomplishment" (*Redemption Accomplished and Applied*, 91).

25 *Irresistible grace* is the *I* in the acronym TULIP, which summarizes the doctrines of grace. The other letters stand for *total depravity, unconditional election, limited atonement*, and *perseverance of the saints*.

"most freely, being made willing by His grace."[26] In the final analysis, regenerating grace is irresistible because *Christ* is irresistible, for regenerating grace opens our spiritual eyes to his irresistibility.

The Means of Regeneration[27]

As the Father is the ultimate agent of regeneration and the Spirit is the efficient cause of regeneration, Scripture identifies the Word of God itself—specifically the gospel message—as the instrumental cause, or means, of regeneration (James 1:18; 1 Pet. 1:23–25; cf. 2 Thess. 2:14). It is by means of the preached gospel that the Spirit of God powerfully works to open the eyes of our hearts to the glory of Christ. While the external call is insufficient for regeneration, it is absolutely necessary, for the external call of gospel preaching is the vehicle for the internal call of regeneration. There is no faith without the preached word (Rom. 10:17).

This rules out as unbiblical any sacramental view of regeneration. Though proponents of baptismal regeneration appeal to John 3:5 to teach that the new birth is mediated through baptism, there are several reasons why we ought not to understand "born of water" to refer to Christian baptism. First, Jesus does not mention baptism anywhere in this interaction with Nicodemus but does repeatedly emphasize the necessity of faith for salvation (John 3:15, 16, 18, 36). If baptism were the instrument of the new birth, it is difficult to explain why Jesus would limit its mention to one oblique reference. Second, baptismal regeneration contradicts Jesus's statement in John 3:8 that, with respect to the new birth, the Spirit is like the wind that blows where it wishes. Such language pictures the sovereign freedom of the Spirit, an image that is incongruous with tying regeneration to a ritual, physical act of human will. John Piper aptly observes that in that case "the wind would be confined by the sacrament."[28] Third, Jesus expects Nicodemus, the teacher of Israel, to understand his teaching on the new birth (John 3:10). However, Christian baptism did not yet exist at that time. It makes little sense to admonish Nicodemus for failing to understand a practice that had not yet been instituted.

One would, however, expect Jesus to admonish Nicodemus for failing to understand Old Testament teaching on the subject, and in fact, that is the most likely explanation for his words. The Old Testament often employs the imagery of water and Spirit to symbolize spiritual cleansing and renewal, never baptism (cf. Num. 19:17–19; Isa. 4:4; 32:15; 44:3; 55:1; Joel 2:28–29; Zech. 13:1). In Ezekiel's

26 Westminster Confession (1646), in Philip Schaff, ed. *The Creeds of Christendom*, vol. 3, *The Evangelical Protestant Creeds* (1877; repr. Grand Rapids, MI: Baker, 1998), 624–25..

27 Portions of this section are adapted from John MacArthur, *John 1–11*, MNTC (Chicago: Moody Press, 2006), 104–5. Used by permission of Moody Publishers.

28 John Piper, *Finally Alive: What Happens When We Are Born Again* (Fearn, Ross-shire, Scotland: Christian Focus, 2009), 39.

prophecy of the new covenant, he famously speaks of both water and the Spirit in the context of regeneration:

> I will *sprinkle clean water* on you, and you shall be clean from all your uncleannesses, and from all your idols I will *cleanse* you. And I will give you a new heart, and a new spirit I will put within you. And I will remove the heart of stone from your flesh and give you a heart of flesh. *And I will put my Spirit within you*, and cause you to walk in my statutes and be careful to obey my rules. (Ezek. 36:25–27)

When Jesus spoke of being born of water and the Spirit, he was declaring that regeneration was a truth revealed throughout the Old Testament (e.g., Deut. 30:6; Jer. 31:31–34; Ezek. 11:18–20) and thus a truth with which Nicodemus should have been familiar. Against this Old Testament backdrop, Christ's point was unmistakable: without the spiritual washing of the soul—a cleansing accomplished by the Holy Spirit (Titus 3:5) and solely by means of the word of the gospel (Eph. 5:26; 1 Pet. 1:23–25)—no one can enter God's kingdom.[29] Given this proper understanding of John 3:5, the doctrine of baptismal regeneration is shown to be without biblical basis. The gospel itself is the sole instrument of the new birth.

The Relationship of Regeneration to Faith

One of the most common questions related to evangelical soteriology concerns the relationship between regeneration and faith. Which produces which? Does man's act of faith bring about the Spirit's work of regeneration, or does the Spirit's work of regeneration bring about man's act of faith? In numerous ways, Scripture answers in favor of the latter: regeneration is the cause, not the consequence, of saving faith.

At the outset, we must observe that regeneration and faith are distinguished not in terms of time but in terms of logical causality. Some reject the notion that regeneration causes faith because they want to avoid saying that someone might be regenerated *without* saving faith. But this is to confuse logical order with chronological order. From a temporal perspective, regeneration and faith occur simultaneously. Nevertheless, though two events may occur at the same time, one may still cause the other. To illustrate this, consider once again the imagery of 2 Corinthians 4. Paul pictures regeneration as the opening of blind eyes and faith as the spiritual perception of Christ's glory (cf. John 3:3; Heb. 11:1). Now, no time passes between a man's opening his eyes and his perception of light; they are simultaneous. However, his perception of light is causally dependent on opening

29 For a thorough examination of various interpretations for "born of water," see D. A. Carson, *The Gospel according to John*, Pillar New Testament Commentary (Grand Rapids, MI: Eerdmans, 1991), 191–96.

his eyes. Seeing does not cause him to open his eyes; his sight is the *consequence* of his eyes being opened. In the same way, though they occur in the exact same instant, the sinner's faith does not cause his regeneration; rather, the opening of the spiritual eyes in regeneration is the cause of the spiritual sight of faith.

Further, the Bible's teaching concerning the natural man's spiritual inability precludes any concept of synergism in regeneration. In his state of spiritual death (Eph. 2:1–3), man is incapable even of understanding the things of the Spirit, let alone receiving them (1 Cor. 2:14). The sinner's mind is so hostile to God that he is literally unable to submit to God's law (Rom. 8:7), and thus he cannot please God in any sense (Rom. 8:8), including the exercise of faith (Heb. 11:6). Man is blind to the value of God's glory revealed in Christ and is hopelessly enamored with sin, despite its worthlessness. To suggest that a sinner in such a state could, apart from the regenerating grace of the Holy Spirit, summon from within his own deadness the saving faith that God declares to be his sovereign gift (Eph. 2:8) is to wholly underestimate the miserable nature of man's depravity. Instead, Jesus says, "No one can come to me unless the Father who sent me draws him" (John 6:44), and, "This is why I told you that no one can come to me unless it is granted him by the Father" (John 6:65). Coming to Jesus is a synonym for believing in Jesus—for it is this kind of coming that results in salvation (John 5:40)—and the "drawing" of John 6:44 is the gift spoken of in John 6:65, both referring to the effectual, irresistible call of God in regeneration. Therefore, Jesus is teaching that, because of the sinner's depravity, no one can come to him in saving faith unless the Father grants the gift of being effectually drawn in regeneration.[30]

The apostle John also comments explicitly on the relationship between regeneration and faith. In 1 John 5:1, he writes, "Everyone who believes [presently] that Jesus is the Christ has been [antecedently] born of God, and everyone who loves the Father loves whoever has been born of him." The present participle "believes" indicates present continuous action, while the perfect passive indicative "has been born" speaks of a past action whose results continue into the present time.[31] In other words, everyone who presently believes that Jesus is the Christ

30 Some synergists object that it is inconsistent to describe the Father's drawing as effectual, since drawing connotes persuasion rather than determination. They often argue that "drawing" does not mean "dragging." Interestingly, the Greek word *helkō*, translated "draws" in John 6:44, often refers to a decisive, effectual movement like dragging. Other New Testament occurrences of *helkō* refer to fishermen hauling in a fishing net (John 21:6, 11), a soldier drawing his sword from its sheath in the midst of battle (John 18:10), angry men dragging a foreigner before their court (Acts 16:19), and a mob dragging a suspected traitor out of their city with the intent to kill him (Acts 21:30). Far from an ineffectual wooing, the Father's drawing in John 6:44 is the decisive, effectual calling of regeneration.

31 Daniel B. Wallace, *Greek Grammar beyond the Basics: An Exegetical Syntax of the New Testament* (Grand Rapids, MI: Zondervan, 1996), 573.

has been born of God. John thus represents faith as the consequence, not the cause, of the new birth.

This reading of the grammar of 1 John 5:1 is confirmed by examining a selection of grammatical parallels in the same letter. There are two other instances in which John employs a present active participle in concert with a perfect passive indicative to illustrate the relationship between the new birth and its concomitants:

> If you know that he is righteous, you may be sure that everyone who practices [presently] righteousness has been born of him [antecedently]. (1 John 2:29)

> Beloved, let us love one another, for love is from God, and whoever loves [presently] has been born of God [antecedently] and knows God. (1 John 4:7)

Both of these passages consist of precisely the same grammatical construction that appears in 1 John 5:1. In 1 John 2:29, John teaches that a habitual pattern of practiced righteousness is an indication of the new birth. Now, the causal relationship between the practice of righteousness and the new birth is not that man is born again as a result of doing good works! Paul patently contradicts such a thought in Titus 3:5, explicitly denying that the new birth comes on the basis of righteous deeds. No, the impartation of new spiritual life in regeneration is the cause of an ongoing practice of good deeds (cf. Eph. 2:10). In 1 John 4:7, John singles out a particular good work: everyone who loves has been born of God. Here again, the relationship between love and regeneration is evident: love does not cause the new birth but is the consequence of it. To suggest otherwise would undermine the gospel of salvation by grace alone. Therefore, if we must conclude that practicing righteousness (1 John 2:29) and loving the brethren (1 John 4:7) are consequences, not causes, of regeneration, we cannot conclude otherwise than that faith is also a consequence of regeneration, since 1 John 2:29, 4:7, and 5:1 are grammatically identical.[32]

Given the clarity of the biblical pictures of regeneration, the implications of man's total depravity, and the explicit comments of Jesus and the apostle John, the student of Scripture must conclude that, while regeneration and faith are experienced simultaneously, regeneration logically precedes faith and is its cause. Sinners do not believe in Christ in order to be born again but rather are born again unto believing.

32 First John 5:4 is also noteworthy. Though the grammatical construction is not identical, it is nevertheless similar. Here John speaks of the new birth in the perfect tense ("everyone who has been born of God") and of a concomitant of the new birth in the present tense ("overcomes the world"). Again, the causal relationship between the two is clear: one does not overcome the world in order to be born again, but rather one overcomes the world as a consequence of being born again. In the next sentence, John identifies the victory that overcomes the world: our faith. Once again, faith is identified as the consequence, not the cause, of the new birth.

The Results of Regeneration

The divine life birthed in the soul at regeneration does not lie stagnant after the moment of conversion. In God's bountiful grace, the Spirit continues to progressively strengthen that holy disposition born in regeneration throughout the believer's life. That is to say, regeneration results in sanctification. While a full discussion of sanctification comes later, it is worthwhile to mention several aspects of sanctification that Scripture identifies as results of the new birth.

First, the regenerated believer necessarily makes a practice of righteousness. As the apostle John says, "Everyone who practices righteousness has been born of him" (1 John 2:29). The dominating tenor of the believer's life is one of increasing holiness (Rom. 6:4; Eph. 2:10; 4:24). To put it negatively, "No one born of God makes a practice of sinning, for God's seed abides in him, and he cannot keep on sinning because he has been born of God" (1 John 3:9). Man's nature has been fundamentally changed from death in sin to life in Christ (Rom. 6:11), and he thus does not make a practice of sinning. This does not mean that the child of God has ceased entirely from sin at the moment of regeneration (Rom. 7:14–25; 8:12–13), but the believer's life is characterized by putting away patterns of sin and putting on patterns of righteousness (Eph. 4:22–24). Those who profess to be saved but do not progress in cultivating patterns of life in obedience to Christ's commands can have no assurance that they are children of God. Since the new birth is the work of the Spirit (Titus 3:5, see above), those who are born again necessarily bear the fruit of the Spirit and are increasingly characterized by love, joy, peace, patience, kindness, goodness, faithfulness, gentleness, and self-control (Gal. 5:22–23).

Second, the regenerate life is marked by overcoming the evil influences of this world system (1 John 5:4). The world is full of the lust of the flesh, the lust of the eyes, and the pride of life (1 John 2:15–17), all of which are tools of Satan, in whose power the whole world lies (1 John 5:19). He wields these tools as instruments of temptation in the lives of professing believers, earnestly desiring to cause shipwreck of their faith and thus besmirch the name of Christ (1 Tim. 1:19; cf. James 2:17). Yet John declares that the regenerate child of God overcomes these pressures and temptations through a persevering faith that walks in obedience to the Lord. The believer never finally and decisively yields to Satan's temptations, because Christ protects him (1 John 5:18). Believers need not ever live in fear of losing their salvation, for persevering faith is the heritage of those truly born from above.

Third, the child of God obeys willingly and delightfully; for him, "his commandments are not burdensome" (1 John 5:3). Self-righteous moralists may, by strong willpower, be able to bring their behavior into conformity with the external standards of God's Word (cf. Matt. 15:8), but they find such a task burdensome.

They cannot exclaim, "O how I love your law!" (Ps. 119:97), and "I delight to do your will, O my God; your law is within my heart" (Ps. 40:8). It requires a new nature, re-created in the likeness of God (Eph. 4:24), to delight in obedience. By God's grace, this is the birthright of every true child of God. The regenerated believer is not enslaved to do the duty he hates; rather, by virtue of the Spirit's work, his heart is liberated to love the law he is commanded to follow (Rom. 6:11–22).

Finally, the child of God loves his fellow believers and lives to sacrificially serve them. John writes, "Beloved, let us love one another, for love is from God, and whoever loves has been born of God and knows God" (1 John 4:7). God himself is love (1 John 4:8, 16); it is his very nature. Those who are begotten of God share in his nature (2 Pet. 1:4) and therefore will reflect his nature by serving and benefitting others (1 John 3:16–18). Those who are truly born again manifest an evident love for the church, for the child of God loves the children of God (1 John 5:1) and is devoted to meeting the needs of his brothers and sisters in Christ.

CONVERSION

When God shines the light of regeneration into the sinner's heart, he opens the person's spiritual eyes so that he can see the bankruptcy of sin and the worthiness of Christ (Acts 26:18; 2 Cor. 4:6), who is perfectly suited to forgive our sins and provide the righteousness we need for eternal life. Finally furnished with the ability to perceive reality as it is, the newly reborn soul necessarily and immediately turns away in revulsion from sin and eagerly runs to embrace Christ. That turning from sin and unbelief is *repentance*, and the eager embrace of Christ as Savior from sin and as Lord over one's life is *faith*. Together, repentance and faith make up the single act of *conversion*.

It should be apparent that repentance and faith are intimately related and even inseparable from each other—truly two sides of the same coin. In the first place, it is only reasonable; one cannot turn away from something without turning toward something else. But the inseparability of repentance and faith is also a theological necessity. To the regenerate heart, the beauty of Christ's glory is irresistibly compelling, and it outshines the false glories of sin just as the brilliance of the noonday sun renders the stars invisible. To suggest that one might embrace Christ without also decisively purposing to repudiate sin is to suggest that sin is more objectively desirable to the regenerated heart than Christ is. On the contrary, to the newly awakened sinner, Christ is an inestimably valuable treasure, and to gain him, one delightfully forsakes everything (Matt. 13:44–46; Phil. 3:8). Thus, the faith that saves is a repentant faith, just as the repentance that saves is a believing repentance. For this reason, the gospel call to salvation is a summons to both repent and believe (Mark 1:15; Acts 20:21; 26:18; 1 Thess. 1:9). In true conversion, there is always a turning *from* sin (repentance) and a simultaneous turning *to* God in Christ (faith). It is impossible that one should occur without the other.

Nevertheless, though they are simultaneous actions, in each instance in which they are named together, the New Testament lists repentance first (Mark 1:15; Acts 19:4; 20:21; Heb. 6:1), indicating a logical priority. For this reason, we will treat repentance first and then faith.

Repentance

Biblical repentance is not a mere change of thinking, though it does involve an intellectual acknowledgment of sin and a change of attitude toward it. Neither is it merely shame or sorrow for sin, although genuine repentance always involves an element of remorse. True biblical repentance is also a redirection of the human will, a purposeful decision to forsake all unrighteousness and pursue righteousness instead. Thus, genuine repentance involves the mind, the heart, and the will.[33]

Intellectually, repentance begins with a recognition of sin. We must apprehend the truly wicked nature of sin and as a result humbly acknowledge that we are sinners who have broken God's law, have fallen short of his glory, and therefore stand guilty before him. To experience the intellectual aspect of repentance is to declare with Job, "I have uttered what I did not understand" (Job 42:3; cf. 42:6), and to confess as did David, "I have sinned against the LORD" (2 Sam. 12:13; cf. Ps. 51:3–4). It is to humbly confess one's need for grace and mercy and to ask for forgiveness (Ps. 51:1–2).

Emotionally, genuine repentance is marked by a sincere sorrow, remorse, and even mourning over one's sin (cf. Matt. 5:4). Old Testament saints would often act out their sorrowful repentance by smiting their thigh (Jer. 31:19), sitting on an ash heap (Job 42:6), and donning sackcloth and ashes (Jonah 3:5–6; cf. Matt. 11:21). This true, repentant sorrow is distinct from what Paul calls "worldly grief," which produces death (2 Cor. 7:10; cf. Matt. 19:22; 27:3–5). Nevertheless, while sorrow should not be equated strictly with repentance, it is a necessary component of it and is often a powerful impulse to genuinely turning away from sin. As Paul says, "Godly grief produces a repentance that leads to salvation without regret" (2 Cor. 7:10). Thus, true repentance will always include at least some element of contrition—not sorrow for getting caught, nor sadness because of the

33 Geerhardus Vos writes, "Of the three words that are used in the Greek Gospels to describe the process, one emphasizes the emotional element of regret, sorrow over the past evil course of life, *metamélomai*; Matt. 21:29–32; a second expresses reversal of the entire mental attitude, *metanoéō*, Matt. 12:41; Luke 11:32; 15:7, 10; the third denotes a change in the direction of life, one goal being substituted for another, *epistréphomai*; Matt. 13:15 (and parallels); Luke 17:4; 22:32. Repentance is not limited to any single faculty of the mind: it engages the entire man, intellect, will and affections" (*The Teaching of Jesus concerning the Kingdom of God and the Church* [1903; repr., Nutley, NJ: Presbyterian & Reformed, 1972], 92–93).

consequences, but a spirit broken by the sense of having sinned against God and a longing to be restored to fellowship with him (Ps. 51:12, 17).

Finally, repentance involves a change of direction, a transformation of the will. Far from being only a change of mind, repentance constitutes a determination to abandon stubborn disobedience and surrender the will to Christ. The wicked forsakes his evil thoughts (Isa. 55:7); turns from his wickedness and practices justice and righteousness (Ezek. 33:19); and turns from his wicked way (Jonah 3:10; cf. 2 Chron. 7:14). Repentance is a resolute disowning of oneself and one's sinful way of life and an embrace of Christ for justifying and sanctifying righteousness. As such, while repentance is not to be strictly defined as a change in behavior, a changed life *is* the fruit that genuine repentance will inevitably bear (Isa. 1:16–17; Luke 3:8–14; Acts 26:20). Though sinners are not saved *by* good works, they are saved *for* good works (Eph. 2:10; Titus 2:14; 3:8). A person who has genuinely repented will stop doing evil and will begin to live righteously. Where there is no observable difference in conduct, there can be no confidence that repentance has taken place (Matt. 3:8; 1 John 2:3–6; 3:17).[34]

In summary, then, the Scriptures teach that repentance begins with the sinner's humble acknowledgment of his sin and need for forgiveness. Understanding the offensiveness of his sin before God produces great mourning, sorrow, and even shame and humiliation. His disgust with himself and his unrighteousness leads him to repudiate his wickedness and to decisively turn away from his life of sin. As he turns from his former way of life, he turns to trust and serve the God who is worthy of all worship. In Christ he finds forgiveness and is restored to fellowship with his Creator. Finally, he does not regard that forgiveness as the final step but lovingly, from the heart, purposes to live in obedience to the revealed will of God, empowered by the work of the Holy Spirit. The evidence of his inward repentance is thus manifested in his external deeds.

Repentance is an essential element of conversion and is therefore an indispensable element of the gospel message. Not only is repentance mentioned alongside faith in the proclamation of the gospel (Mark 1:15; Acts 20:21; Heb. 6:1), but also many biblical texts call for repentance alone to lay hold of salvation (Matt. 4:17; Mark 1:15; Luke 5:32; 13:3, 5; 24:47; Acts 2:38; 3:19; 17:30). This does not contradict the truth that faith is the sole instrument of justification. Rather, it illustrates that the relationship between repentance and faith is so intimate that the mention of the one implies the other—that one cannot turn from sin without turning to Christ in faith, and vice versa. Scripture is unmistakably clear: repentance is not an optional element but is an essential component of the true gospel.

34 John MacArthur, *The Gospel according to Jesus: What Is Authentic Faith?*, rev. ed. (Grand Rapids, MI: Zondervan, 2008), 180, 182.

Those who insist that it is possible to savingly trust in Christ without repenting of sin—to believe in Jesus as Savior but not submit to him as Lord—find themselves in direct contradiction to the gospel according to Jesus and the apostles.[35]

Faith

Whereas repentance is the act of turning *away* from sin, faith is the soul's turn *to* God and trusting in Christ for forgiveness, righteousness, and eternal life. As the miracle of the new birth banishes the blindness of spiritual death, the eyes of the sinner's re-created heart look on the glory of Jesus and delight to find in him an utterly sufficient Savior, perfectly suited to cleanse from sin, provide perfect righteousness, and satisfy the soul. Beholding the glory of God in the face of Christ (2 Cor. 4:6), the sinner embraces Jesus with all his heart, entrusting and committing himself to all that Christ is. Therefore, saving faith is a fundamental commitment of the whole person to the whole Christ; with his mind, heart, and will, the believer embraces Jesus as Savior, Advocate, Provider, Sustainer, Counselor, and Lord God.

Like repentance, then, saving faith consists of intellectual, emotional, and volitional elements: knowledge (Lat. *notitia*), assent (Lat. *assensus*), and trust (Lat. *fiducia*), respectively. The mind embraces knowledge, a recognition and understanding of the truth concerning the person and work of Christ. The heart gives assent, or the settled confidence and affirmation that Christ's salvation is suitable to one's spiritual need. The will responds with trust, the personal commitment to and appropriation of Christ as the only hope for eternal salvation.[36] Each of these components requires further elaboration.

Knowledge. The most basic element of faith is knowledge. Contemporary thought conceives of faith as the opposite of knowledge—that faith is what takes over when one does not have sufficient knowledge. However, the biblical conception of faith is not an existential leap in the dark or a sentimental, wish-upon-a-star kind of hope. So far from being an alternative to knowledge, true faith is based on knowledge; it has its sure and solid foundation in the knowledge of divinely revealed truth.

Scripture testifies to this in a number of ways. First, the Bible often represents the knowledge of particular truths as the causal ground of faith. For example, faith in Christ for salvation is grounded on "knowing that a man is not justified by the works of the Law but through faith in Christ Jesus" (Gal. 2:16 NASB). It is *because*

35 For a thorough discussion of the controversy over "Lordship salvation," as well as a thorough refutation of so-called "free grace" theology, see John MacArthur, *Gospel according to Jesus*; and MacArthur, *The Gospel according to the Apostles: The Role of Works in the Life of Faith* (1993; repr., Nashville: Thomas Nelson, 2000).

36 MacArthur, *Gospel according to the Apostles*, 27.

we know that works do not justify that we believe in Christ for salvation. Similarly, Paul grounds the believer's faith in his future resurrection on the knowledge of Christ's resurrection: "Now if we have died with Christ, we believe that we shall also live with Him, knowing [i.e., "because we know"[37]] that Christ, having been raised from the dead, is never to die again" (Rom. 6:8–9 NASB; cf. 2 Cor. 4:13–14; 1 Pet. 5:9). These passages make plain that biblical faith and knowledge of the truth are not enemies but that the latter is the ground of the former.

Second, Scripture often employs the phrase "believe that . . ." followed by propositional truth claims that identify the content of saving faith.[38] One must believe that Jesus is God (John 8:24; 13:19; cf. Ex. 3:14) and is one with the Father (John 14:10–11); that he is the Messiah and Son of God (John 11:27; 20:31; 1 John 5:1, 5) who was sent from the Father (John 11:42; 16:27, 30; 17:8, 21); that he died for sins and rose from the grave (1 Thess. 4:14; cf. Rom. 10:9); that God exists and "rewards those who seek him" (Heb. 11:6); and that sinners are saved by grace through faith alone (Acts 15:11; cf. 15:9). Since saving faith comes from hearing the gospel message concerning Christ (Rom. 10:17), knowledge of the divinely revealed facts of God's holiness, sin's penalty, Christ's identity, and what he has accomplished for sinners is the very ground of saving faith.

Clearly, then, true faith has objective substance. Believing is not a mindless leap in the dark or an ethereal kind of trust apart from knowledge. The truth of the gospel message as revealed in Christ and in Scripture provides a factual, historical, intellectual basis for our faith. We do not believe according to our subjective whims; we believe the truth (2 Thess. 2:11–12; cf. John 8:46; 1 Tim. 4:3). Faith that is not grounded in this objective, propositional truth is no faith at all.[39]

Assent. While knowing the facts is *necessary* to faith, it is not *sufficient*. It is entirely possible to know the truth without believing or embracing it. Many students of Scripture intellectually grasp its great truths yet reject them as false. Many understand the truths of the gospel while failing to repent and trust in Christ. For this reason, faith is said to have an emotional element as well as an intellectual element. Faith not only knows the truth but also assents to and wholeheartedly embraces the truth as it is revealed in Scripture. The truth is known and believed.

The writer of Hebrews speaks of this heartfelt assent as a component of faith when he defines faith as "the assurance of things hoped for, the conviction of things not seen" (Heb. 11:1). Assurance refers to a foundation, the ground on which something is built. Faith is here described as a supernatural certainty—

37 The participle *eidotes* (lit., "knowing") here bears a causal force: "because we know." See Wallace, *Greek Grammar beyond the Basics*, 631.

38 Reymond, *New Systematic Theology*, 727.

39 MacArthur, *Gospel according to the Apostles*, 29–30.

a God-wrought conviction about the truth of the Bible's promises and the trustworthiness of Christ. What cannot be seen with the physical eyes is unveiled for the spiritual eyes by faith. Later in the chapter, we learn that Moses's faith consisted of the resolute conviction that the riches of Christ's glory were more valuable than the treasures of Egypt (Heb. 11:24–27). He did not just intellectually apprehend that Christ was more precious; he was persuaded in the depths of his heart that it was true. It was Paul's resolute, faith-filled conviction of the sovereignty of Christ that fueled his endurance through the most intense suffering, for he said, "I know whom I have believed, and I am convinced that he is able to guard until that day what has been entrusted to me" (2 Tim. 1:12).

With respect to conversion, then, the one who possesses saving faith wholeheartedly embraces the truth concerning his own sinfulness and Christ's suitableness to save him. The newly awakened believer becomes absolutely convinced that he is helpless to address the inevitable misery of his spiritual condition, and he looks on Christ with the certain conviction that Christ's sufficiency is the perfect answer to his spiritual bankruptcy. By this faith the sinner is made well (cf. Mark 10:46–52).

Trust. Further still, there is more to faith than merely knowing and embracing the truth. James tells us that the demons know and believe the truth of monotheism (James 2:19). Nicodemus believed that Jesus was a teacher sent from God (John 3:2). Agrippa believed that the Old Testament spoke truth (Acts 26:27). Judas was convinced that Jesus was the Christ (Matt. 27:3–5). Yet none of these possessed saving faith. Faith begins with knowledge and assent, but it does not stop until it reaches the will's utter reliance on Christ for one's personal salvation.[40] It moves beyond "believing *that*" and arrives at "believing *in*"; it moves beyond mentally assenting to truth *about* Christ and arrives at personally trusting *in* Christ and depending *on* him for forgiveness of sins and reconciliation to God.

The apostle Paul narrates his own conversion story in Philippians 3. He characterizes the true Christian as one who puts no confidence in the flesh (Phil. 3:3), one who does not look within himself—to his inherited privileges or religious accomplishments—to acquire the righteousness that God requires. In his life as a Pharisee, Paul had indeed put full confidence in his flesh—in his heritage, social standing, religious ritualism, traditionalism, devotion, and sincerity, and even in the external observance of God's commands (Phil. 3:4–6). He trusted in these fleshly credentials to lift him up to reach the standard of God's righteousness.

40 As John Murray insightfully notes, "Faith is knowledge passing into conviction, and it is conviction passing into confidence. Faith cannot stop short of self-commitment to Christ, a transference of reliance upon ourselves and all human resources to reliance upon Christ alone for salvation. It is a receiving and resting upon him" (*Redemption Accomplished and Applied*, 111).

But that error disappeared after he met the risen Christ on the road to Damascus. When God opened the eyes of Paul's heart in regeneration, all the self-righteousness that Paul had counted on to be gain he came to regard as loss (Phil. 3:7). He counted it all rubbish in order to "gain Christ, and be found in Him, not having my own righteousness, which is from the law, but that which is through faith in Christ, the righteousness which is from God by faith" (Phil. 3:8–9 NKJV). He had turned from depending on himself for righteousness to trusting in Christ alone for righteousness (cf. Rom. 10:4; 2 Cor. 5:21).

Not only does the one with saving faith trust in Christ for righteousness, he also receives Christ as treasure. Paul regarded knowing Jesus personally to be of such surpassing value that he was willing to lose everything in his life to gain him (Phil. 3:8). Jesus himself spoke of conversion as finding a treasure (Matt. 13:44–46). The man whose heart has been awakened in regeneration is like a man who stumbles onto a priceless buried treasure. And because of the surpassing value of the treasure that is Christ Jesus, the sinner willingly forsakes everything he has so he can lay hold of the Savior whom he regards as supremely precious (Luke 9:23; 14:26–33; cf. Matt. 10:37–39). These texts caution the student of Scripture against conceiving of saving faith as that which merely uses Christ to escape punishment. Saving faith is preeminently an eager embrace of a *person*—a wholehearted, delightful reception of Christ for the fullness of who he is, namely, the source of all righteousness, life, and satisfaction for the newborn soul (Matt. 5:6; John 4:13–14; 6:35).

Finally, in this volitional aspect of faith, one not only trusts in Christ but also entrusts oneself *to* Christ, for believing in a person necessarily involves a personal commitment. The one who trusts Christ places himself in the custody of Christ for both life and death. The believer relies on the Lord's counsel, trusts in his goodness, and entrusts himself for time and eternity to his guardianship. Saving faith, then, is the sinner, in the whole of his being, embracing all of Christ. That is why Scripture often uses such metaphors for faith as looking to Jesus (John 3:14–15; cf. Num. 21:9), eating his flesh and drinking his blood (John 6:50–58; cf. 4:14), receiving him (John 1:12), and coming to him (Matt. 11:28; John 5:40; 6:35, 37, 44, 65; 7:37–38). One demonstrates his faith that bread satisfies hunger not merely by confessing, "Bread satisfies!" but by eating the bread. In the same way, one demonstrates his faith in Christ not merely by saying, "I believe!" but by coming to Christ, receiving all that he is, and entrusting to him all that the believer is. In summary, faith is leaning wholly on Christ—for redemption, for righteousness, for counsel, for fellowship, for sustenance, for direction, for help, for his lordship, and for all in life that can truly satisfy.

This means that true, saving faith necessarily works itself out in loving obedience (cf. Gal. 5:6). The eleventh chapter of Hebrews is dedicated to illustrating this sole principle. After defining the nature of true faith in the opening verses, the author scans the whole of redemptive history to demonstrate that faith *works*. Faith offers (Heb. 11:4), walks (11:5), builds (11:7), blesses (11:20–21), hides (11:23), leaves (11:24–27), conquers (11:30), and more. In short, faith obeys. It compels one to act in accordance with the truth that he professes to believe. At conversion, saving faith does nothing but passively receive the provision of Christ. Yet true faith never remains passive; it immediately goes to work—not as a means of earning divine favor but as a consequence of having received the grace of God that works mightily within us (Col. 1:29). As we work out our salvation with fear and trembling, it is God who works in us, both to will and to work for his good pleasure (Phil. 2:12–13).[41]

Gifts That Keep On Giving

Two other features of repentance and faith must not go without mention. First, both repentance and faith are sovereign gifts of God himself. While it is true that repentant faith is held out to sinners as their responsibility and the condition for their justification, the corruption of their mind, affections, and will makes it impossible for them to truly repent and believe. It is only by the sovereign work of the Spirit in regeneration, renewing our heart and opening our spiritual eyes, that we are enabled to turn from sin and self and trust in Christ alone for righteousness. For this reason, Scripture speaks of repentant faith not as a sovereign decision of the human will but as that which is supernaturally granted as a gift of God's grace. Both repentance (Acts 5:31; Acts 11:18; 2 Tim. 2:25) and faith (Acts 18:27; Eph. 2:8–9; Phil. 1:29) are sovereign gifts from God.

Second, as a divine gift, the repentant faith that saves could never be transient or temporary. It has an abiding quality that guarantees it will endure to the end, so that repentance and faith characterize the lifestyle of the true Christian. Thus, when Peter asked Jesus how often he should forgive a brother who sins against him (Matt. 18:21), Jesus responded, "If your brother sins, rebuke him, and if he repents, forgive him, and if he sins against you seven times in the day, and turns to you seven times, saying, 'I repent,' you must forgive him" (Luke 17:3–4). The principle

41 MacArthur explains, "Does this mix faith and works, as some are fond of saying? Not at all. Let there be no confusion on this point. Faith is an *internal* reality with *external* consequences. When we say that faith encompasses obedience, we are speaking of the God-given *attitude* of obedience, not trying to make *works* a part of the definition of faith. God makes the believing heart an obedient heart; that is, a heart eager to obey. Faith itself is complete before one work of obedience ever issues forth.

"But make no mistake—real faith will always produce righteous works. Faith is the root; works are the fruit. Because God Himself is the vinedresser, fruit is guaranteed. That's why whenever Scripture gives examples of faith—as here in Hebrews 11—faith inevitably is seen as obedient, working, and active" (*Gospel according to the Apostles*, 34).

is that one ought to repent as often as one sins. In his letters to the churches of Asia, Christ instructed believers (i.e., "those whom I love") at the church of Laodicea to "be zealous and repent" (Rev. 3:19), which shows that repentance is not just a one-time event at conversion but is expected even of true Christians. The Lord also taught his disciples to be in the habit of praying for forgiveness (Matt. 6:12), which necessarily requires ongoing repentance. The apostle John similarly states, "If we confess our sins, he is faithful and just to forgive us our sins and to cleanse us from all unrighteousness" (1 John 1:9). The present tense of "confess" indicates ongoing activity. Thus, believers show that they are the ones God has forgiven and cleansed because they are continually confessing their sins. In sum, though justification frees the believer from the penalty of sin, the presence of sin remains in his unredeemed flesh. Therefore, because he continues to sin against God and others, he must continue to repent. In a believer's life, a spirit of repentance must be as indwelling as is his remaining sin.

The same is true of faith.[42] The familiar words of Habakkuk 2:4, "The righteous shall live by his faith" (cf. Rom. 1:17; Gal. 3:11; Heb. 10:38), speak not of a momentary act of believing but of a living, enduring trust in God. Hebrews 3:14 emphasizes the permanence of genuine faith. Its very durability is proof of its reality: "We have come to share in Christ, if indeed we hold our original confidence firm to the end." The faith that God gives can never evaporate, and the work of salvation cannot ultimately be thwarted (1 Cor. 1:8; Phil. 1:6; Col. 1:22–23).[43] The apostle Paul summarizes the totality of the Christian life when he declares, "The life I now live in the flesh I live by faith in the Son of God, who loved me and gave himself for me" (Gal. 2:20; cf. Heb. 10:39). The Christian's life is to be distinguished by daily confession of, mourning over, and turning from sin, as well as by a persevering faith in the person of Christ and the promises of God.

UNION WITH CHRIST

One of the most precious truths in all Scripture is the doctrine of the believer's union with the Lord Jesus Christ. The concept of being united to Christ speaks of the most vital spiritual intimacy that one can imagine between the Lord and his people. While Christ relates to believers as Lord, Master, Savior, and Teacher, they are not merely associated with Christ as the object of his saving grace and love. It is not that Christians merely worship Jesus, obey him, or pray to him, though surely those privileges would be enough. Rather, they are so intimately identified with him and he with them that Scripture says they are united—he is in them and they are in him. The Lord and his people share a common spiritual

42 This paragraph is adapted from John MacArthur, "The Lordship Controversy," Grace to You, accessed April 14, 2016, http://www.gtycanada.org/Resources/Articles/A293.

43 MacArthur, *Gospel according to Jesus*, 189.

life, such that the apostle Paul could say that our life is "hidden with Christ in God" (Col. 3:3), that Christ is himself our life (Col. 3:4), and that Christ lives in us (Gal. 2:20). United to his people in this way, Christ acts as their representative and substitute; that is, that which Christ has accomplished on behalf of his people God reckons to their account, just as if they had done it themselves. Because of union with Christ, believers have been crucified with him (Gal. 2:20), have died with him (Rom. 6:8; Col. 2:20), have been buried with him (Rom. 6:3–4), have been raised with him (Eph. 2:5–6; Col. 3:1), and have even been enthroned in heaven with him (Eph. 2:6). He is thus the Mediator of all the benefits of salvation, for God our Father "has blessed us with every spiritual blessing in the heavenly places *in Christ*" (Eph. 1:3 NASB).

Such intimate spiritual union is unique to Christianity. In no other religion is the object of worship said to become the life of the worshiper. Muslims do not speak of being in Allah or in Muhammad; Buddhists never say that they are in Buddha. They may follow the teachings of their respective leaders, but Christians alone are said to be *in* Christ, united to him as their representative, substitute, and Mediator.

This concept of union with Christ is as pervasive as it is precious. Most commonly represented by the tiny preposition "in," the believer's union with Christ permeates the New Testament. Believers are often said to be "in Christ" (1 Cor. 1:30; 2 Cor. 5:17), "in the Lord" (Rom. 16:11), and "in him" (1 John 5:20). Similarly, Christ is also said to be in his people (Rom. 8:10; 2 Cor. 13:5; Eph. 3:17), a notion that Paul defines as the very "hope of glory" itself (Col. 1:27). Sometimes both of these aspects of union with Christ are presented in the same text, only further emphasizing the intimacy of the mutual indwelling of Christ and the believer (e.g., John 6:56; 15:4; 1 John 4:13). Clearly, the importance of the believer's union with Christ cannot be overstated.

Union with Christ and Soteriology

How the doctrine of union with Christ relates to the rest of soteriology has long been a matter of discussion. That is because it is not merely another phase in the application of redemption, like regeneration, faith, or justification. Instead, union with Christ is the matrix out of which all other soteriological doctrines flow. Indeed, as Paul says in Ephesians 1:3, our union with Christ is the source of every spiritual blessing we receive—from the Father's election in eternity past, to the Son's redemptive life, death, burial, and resurrection, all the way to the glorification of the saints with Christ in heaven. For this reason, the great theologian John Murray called the believer's union with Christ "the central truth of the whole doctrine of salvation."[44] It is the unifying principle of all soteriology, spanning from eternity past to eternity future.

In the first place, the Father's election is rooted in Christ. Paul says, "[The Father] chose us in him [Christ] before the foundation of the world" (Eph. 1:4). He also tells us in 2 Timothy 1:9 that God gave us grace "in Christ Jesus before the ages began." Though the Father's work of election occurred before we even existed, his choice to save his people is nevertheless in Christ. This means there was never a time when God contemplated his elect apart from their vital union to Christ.

Second, Scripture teaches that God reckoned the elect to be united with Christ throughout every act of the Son's accomplishment of redemption. It is in him we have redemption and forgiveness (Eph. 1:7; Col. 1:14). We are united to him in his perfect life of obedience. As he "fulfill[ed] all righteousness" (Matt. 3:15), so also those united to him are clothed in his righteousness (Gal. 3:27), that is, they are credited with his obedience (Rom. 5:19; cf. 1 Cor. 1:30; 15:22). This union was also the ground on which our sin could be justly imputed to Christ. The Father counts the elect to have lived Jesus's life because he counts Jesus to have lived our lives and thus he punished him accordingly (2 Cor. 5:21; 1 Pet. 2:24). That is why we are said to have "died with Christ" (Rom. 6:8; Col. 2:20; cf. Col. 3:3; 2 Tim. 2:11), "our old self [having been] crucified with him" (Rom. 6:6). Not only this, but we were "buried with him" (Rom. 6:4; Col. 2:12), raised from the dead with him (Eph. 2:6; Col. 2:12; 3:1), and even "seated . . . with him in the heavenly places in Christ Jesus" (Eph. 2:6). His life is our life, his punishment our punishment, his death our death, his resurrection our resurrection, his righteousness our righteousness, his ascension and glorification our ascension and glorification. In summary, though we had not yet been born, God nevertheless counted his people to be in union with their Savior throughout the accomplishment of his redemptive work. Christ did not live, die, and rise again for a faceless, nameless group; redemption was remarkably personal, as the body was always reckoned to be united to the head (Eph. 5:23, 25).

Third, just as the plan and accomplishment of redemption occur in Christ, so too does the application of redemption. Believers are born again unto saving faith in union with Christ. Paul describes the believer's regeneration when he says that they have been "made . . . alive together with Christ" (Eph. 2:5) and are "created in Christ Jesus" (Eph. 2:10). If anyone is united to Christ, he is a new creation (2 Cor. 5:17), which is another way of saying that one is born again in union with Christ. This impartation of new spiritual life issues immediately in repentant faith, the instrument by which one subjectively appropriates all the

44 Murray, *Redemption Accomplished and Applied*, 161.

spiritual blessings planned by the Father and purchased by the Son (Gal. 2:20). United to Christ by faith, believers lay hold of Christ's righteousness (Phil. 3:9) and so are justified in him (Gal. 2:17), for there is no condemnation for those who are in Christ Jesus (Rom. 8:1). Thus declared righteous in Christ, believers are adopted into the family of God through Christ (Eph. 1:5; cf. Gal. 3:26) and are sanctified in him for holiness and service to God (1 Cor. 1:2).

Union with Christ is also the source of the believer's progressive sanctification and perseverance. Christ is called our sanctification because our sanctification flows from him (1 Cor. 1:30). We bring forth the fruit of righteousness only as we stay connected to our vine (John 15:4–5). The members of the body grow into maturity as they receive the communication of life from their head (Eph. 4:15–16). Thus, believers "[died] to the Law through the body of Christ," because it is only as they are "joined to another, to Him who was raised from the dead," that they might walk in his resurrection life and thereby "bear fruit for God" (Rom. 7:4 NASB; cf. 6:4–11). Increasing in holiness is impossible apart from union with Christ. Further, it is on the basis of this union that true believers always persevere until the end (John 10:27–28), for while they are in Christ nothing can separate them from the Father's love (Rom. 8:38–39). Indeed, not even death severs this union, for Christians who die are called the "dead in Christ" (1 Thess. 4:14, 16).

Finally, it is on the basis of union with Christ that believers will be raised from the dead. He is the firstfruits of our resurrection, as Paul comforts the Corinthians: "But in fact Christ has been raised from the dead, the firstfruits of those who have fallen asleep. For as by a man came death, by a man has come also the resurrection of the dead. For as in Adam all die, so also in Christ shall all be made alive" (1 Cor. 15:20–22). Paul reasons elsewhere, "For if we have been united with him in a death like his, we shall certainly be united with him in a resurrection like his" (Rom. 6:5; cf. 8:17).

It is plain, therefore, that the believer's union with Christ encompasses every step of salvation, from election in eternity past to glorification in eternity future. Those whom God has chosen, whom Christ has purchased, and to whom the Spirit gives life are never contemplated apart from their union with Christ. And yet this union is not actualized in the sinner's experience before his conversion, for the apostle Paul speaks of a time when believers were "separated from Christ, alienated from the commonwealth of Israel and strangers to the covenants of promise, having no hope and without God in the world" (Eph. 2:12). He continues, "But now in Christ Jesus you who once were far off have been brought near by the blood of Christ" (Eph. 2:13). That is to say, the sinner passes from separation to union with Christ when he becomes a partaker in the gospel purchased by Jesus's blood, the benefits of which he lays hold of by faith alone (Rom. 3:25;

4:24; Gal. 3:24). It is for this reason that we treat union with Christ at this point in discussing the application of redemption.

The Nature of the Believer's Union with Christ

What exactly does it mean that believers are united to Christ? Scripture answers by illustrating the intimacy of this union with a number of metaphors. By understanding these metaphors, we can reach sound biblical conclusions concerning the nature of our union with Christ.

First, Scripture uses the picture of a building and its foundation. Paul speaks of the church as God's household, a spiritual building laid on the foundation of the divine revelation communicated by the apostles and prophets (Eph. 2:19–22). Just as every stone in a literal building is cut precisely to fit snugly, strongly, and beautifully with every other part and to rest perfectly on the foundation, so also does the unity and stability of the church depend on Christ, her foundation. It is only by being built on and permanently united to Christ, the cornerstone, that believers find their spiritual existence, support, and security to be well-founded.

Second, the believer's union with Christ is pictured as the union between the vine and its branches (John 15:4–5). Just as the branches depend on the vine for life, strength, and sustenance, so also does the believer depend on union with Christ for all spiritual nourishment and growth. Apart from Christ the vine, we the branches can bear no fruit; we are entirely useless, destitute of any spiritual vitality unless we remain connected to our vine.

Third, Scripture also uses the metaphor of marriage to portray the union between Christ and his church. The church is often pictured as Christ's bride (2 Cor. 11:2; Rev. 19:7; 21:9), and Christ as the husband and head of the church (Eph. 5:22–33). In Ephesians 5, Paul based all his instructions for the husband-wife relationship on the relationship between Christ and *his* bride. At the end of this discussion, Paul declares of marriage, "This mystery is profound; and I am saying that it refers to Christ and the church" (Eph. 5:32). The parable of marriage illustrates that the believer's union with Christ is intimate, organic (one-flesh), legal, and unbreakable.

Fourth, perhaps the greatest metaphor given to illustrate union with Christ is the union of head and body (Rom. 12:5; 1 Cor. 12:12–13, 27; Eph. 1:22–23). Also pictured in the marriage text of Ephesians 5, Paul says, "Christ is the head of the church, his body" (Eph. 5:23). The one who nourishes and cherishes his own body loves *himself* (Eph. 5:28–30), because there is such an intimate union between the head and the body. Believers' bodies are members of Christ's own body, so much so that to unite oneself to a prostitute is to unite Christ to a prostitute (1 Cor. 6:15–16). Thus, what happens to the head happens to the body, and what happens to the body happens to the head. This metaphor lays the groundwork for understanding the *legal and representational nature* of the believer's union with

Christ, where Christ obeys (Rom. 5:18–19; cf. 1 Cor. 1:30), dies (Col. 2:20), rises (Col. 3:1), and ascends (Eph. 2:6) in their place, such that they are reckoned to have done all those things. Because this union is a legal union—that is, because Christ is the representative head of his people—there is no element of Christ's earthly life, death, burial, resurrection, and ascension in which the believer does not partake, on account of being in him.

In summary, then, we can speak of at least five characteristics of the believer's union with Christ. First, it is an organic union. That is to say, Christ and believers form one body, of which he is the head and they are the members. Thus, what is true of the head is true of the body. Second, it is a legal union, fitting Christ to be the representative head of his people and fitting them to be the beneficiary of his substitutionary work of salvation. Third, it is a vital union, in which all spiritual life and vitality flows from the vine to the branches, such that the life of Christ becomes the dominating and animating principle of believers' lives (Gal. 2:20). Fourth, it may be called a spiritual union, not only because spiritual life is communicated to and strengthened within the believer but also because this union has its source in and is mediated by the Holy Spirit (Rom. 8:9–10; 1 Cor. 12:13; John 14:16–18). Finally, it is a permanent union that can never be severed, as nothing can separate us from the love of God which is in—that is, which is ours in union with—Jesus Christ our Lord (Rom. 8:38–39).

Implications of the Believer's Union with Christ

The foregoing study provides a number of implications with respect to the believer's union with Christ. First, since the Son is united to the Father and to the Spirit, believers, by their participation in Christ, are also made one with God the Father and God the Holy Spirit. Jesus thus prays that the unity of the church would reflect the unity he shares with his Father (John 17:21). Therefore, we are said to be in the Father (1 Thess. 1:1) and the Father in us (1 John 4:15). Similarly, believers are said to be in the Spirit (Rom. 8:9) and the Spirit in us (2 Tim. 1:14). In an unspeakable mystery, we who were once separated, alienated, and without God in the world are swept up into the divine life of the triune God himself (2 Pet. 1:4). This is great cause for worship.

Second, those who are one with Christ are also one with everyone else who is one with Christ. This speaks of the fundamental unity of all believers in Christ. Christians do not have a merely *personal* relationship with Jesus, but rather a *corporate* relationship with him as well, for we are united to all who are united to him. We are the unified members of his body (Rom. 12:5; 1 Cor. 12:26; Eph. 5:23), the living stones in the spiritual house built on Christ the foundation (Eph. 2:19–22; 1 Pet. 2:4–5). To suggest that one can be united to Jesus apart from his church is to tear the head from the body. There is no union with Christ that does not issue in fellowship with his church (1 Cor. 1:9; cf. 1 John 1:3). Indeed, the unity of the Trinity is the ground of Jesus's prayer for the unity of the church (John 17:21). What a motivation for diligently pursuing the unity of the Spirit in the bond of peace among all believers (Eph. 4:3)!

Finally, we must grasp the significance that every spiritual benefit received in salvation comes only through Christ. As John Owen wrote, this union "is the cause of all other graces that we are made partakers of; they are all communicated unto us by virtue of our *union* with Christ. Hence is our adoption, our justification, our sanctification, our perseverance, our fruitfulness, our resurrection, our glory."[45] It is only as we share in Christ that we have a share in what is his. No spiritual blessing in all the world is found anywhere but in Jesus. Therefore, if we are to have an interest in Christ's blessings, we must have an interest in his person. The gifts are wrapped up only in the Giver.

JUSTIFICATION

In the previous section, we examined how the believer's union with Christ is the fountain out of which every spiritual blessing flows. The immediate result of that union is God's free gift of justification, by which he declares believers to be righteous because of their union with the Righteous One, the Lord Jesus. The application of redemption continues to unfold. In regeneration, God performs that divine operation in the sinner's soul whereby he births new spiritual life in him. In conversion, God grants the necessary gifts of repentance and faith by which we are united to Christ and lay hold of the blessings of salvation. Then, in justification, God legally declares that we are no longer deemed guilty under the divine law but are forgiven and counted righteous in God's sight.

In justification, God provides the answer to mankind's most basic theological and religious question: How can sinners come to be in a right relationship with the holy God of the universe? In every age of human history, religion has answered that we can get to heaven by being good people. The various religious systems of the world concoct lists of rituals and ceremonies that must be performed to achieve a measure of righteousness that might avail in the courtroom of God. However, the answer that Jesus gave was that if man is to enter heaven, he needs a righteousness that surpasses the righteousness of even the most religiously devout people in the world (Matt. 5:20). In fact, he needs to be perfect, just as God is perfect (Matt. 5:48). If man is to be reconciled to God, he does not just need to be a good person; he needs to be a perfect person. He needs a perfect righteousness, for God himself is perfect and requires perfection.

45 John Owen, *An Exposition of the Epistle to the Hebrews*, vol. 21 in *Works of John Owen* (1648; repr., Edinburgh: Banner of Truth, 1967), 150, italics original.

At the very outset, then, it is necessary to understand that salvation is a matter of righteousness. People are condemned to eternal spiritual death because they lack the righteousness that a perfectly holy God possesses and requires for fellowship with him. And the only way sinners can ever be reconciled to God is by being given the righteousness that belongs to God himself. The gospel saves because God gives his very own righteousness to man (Rom. 1:16–17; 3:20–26; 10:3–4; 2 Cor. 5:21; Gal. 2:21; 3:21–24; Phil. 3:9). Because of this, the doctrine of justification flows from the very heart of the gospel and the soul of Christianity itself. It is, as Martin Luther said, the article by which the church stands or falls,[46] for it concerns the only way sinful man can be declared righteous in God's sight.[47]

Man's answer to this fundamental question is to try to order his life by some moral or ritualistic standard; if he does that successfully, he can contribute something to his salvation and thus achieve a righteousness acceptable to his god. Yet the Bible consistently denies that anyone can be justified by his own works. Rather, salvation is God's righteousness imputed to the believer by grace alone through faith alone in Christ alone. Take a moment to read the following passages: Romans 3:21–28; Galatians 2:16; and Galatians 3:21–26, where the distinction between faith and works is clearest.

These texts demonstrate that there are only two religions: the religion of human achievement, by which man works to contribute to his own righteousness; and the religion of divine accomplishment, whereby God accomplishes righteousness by the holy life and substitutionary death of the Son of God and then freely gives that righteousness as a gift through faith alone. The religion of human achievement encompasses every other religious system in the history of mankind—from the pursuit of nirvana in Buddhism, to the five pillars of Islam, to the sacraments and acts of penance of Roman Catholicism. Biblical Christianity is the lone religion of divine accomplishment. Because Christians are justified by faith alone, their standing before God is not in any way related to personal merit. Good works and practical holiness are not the grounds for acceptance with God. God receives as righteous those who believe, not because of any good thing he sees in them—not even because of his own sanctifying work in their lives—but solely on the basis

46 "Because if this article [i.e., justification] stands, the church stands; if this article collapses, the church collapses" (Martin Luther, *D. Martin Luthers Werke: Kritische Gesamtausgabe* [Weimar, Germany: H. Böhlau, 1883–1993], 40:3.352.3).

47 To the English reader, the intimate relationship between "righteousness" and "justification" may not be as obvious as it would have been to a Greek reader. In the original language of the New Testament, the words "righteous," "righteousness," "justify," and "justification" all come from the same root word and appear in the following respective forms: *dikaios*, *dikaiosynē*, *dikaioō*, and *dikaiōsis* (and in Hebrew: *tsaddiq*, *tsedeq/tsedaqah*, *tsadoq/tsadeq*). To be justified, then, simply means to be declared righteous in the sight of God, as will be developed more fully below.

of Christ's righteousness, which is graciously reckoned to their account through faith alone. As Paul says, "To the one who does not work but believes in him who justifies the ungodly, his faith is counted as righteousness" (Rom. 4:5).[48]

Therefore, we may define justification as that instantaneous act of God whereby, as a gift of his grace, he imputes to a believing sinner the full and perfect righteousness of Christ through faith alone and legally declares him perfectly righteous in his sight, forgiving the sinner of all unrighteousness and thus delivering him from all condemnation.[49] We will unpack the elements of that definition throughout the rest of this section.

The Nature of Justification: A Legal Declaration

Before examining any particular aspect of justification, we must be clear about what the Bible teaches concerning the nature of justification itself. Justification is a legal, or forensic, declaration of righteousness, not an actual impartation or infusion of righteousness. It describes what God *declares* about the believer, not what he *does to change* the believer. In fact, justification itself effects no actual change whatsoever in the sinner's nature or character.[50] It is an instantaneous change of one's status before God, not a gradual transformation that takes place within the one who is justified.[51]

Legal declarations like this are fairly common in everyday life. When a jury foreman announces to the court that a defendant is not guilty, the legal status of the defendant changes instantly. Seconds before, the law regarded him as "the accused," innocent until proven guilty. But as a result of the foreman's verdict, he is not guilty in the eyes of the law. Yet the jury's verdict does not *make* the man not guilty; his own actions are the basis of his guilt or innocence. Neither does it declare his life free from any and all evil. The foreman's announcement simply declares the defendant's status before the law. In a similar way, the justification spoken of in Scripture is God's divine verdict of "not guilty—fully righteous" pronounced on the sinner. In the case of justification, it is not that the accused is innocent but that another has paid in full the penalty for his crimes.

Disagreement over the nature of justification is a key issue that divides biblical Christianity from Roman Catholicism. Roman Catholic theology teaches that justification is not merely forensic but transformative. In other words, according to Roman Catholic teaching, "to justify" does not mean "to *declare* righteous" but "to *make* righteous." Now, it is true that the saving grace of God is transformative; those who are declared righteous in conversion will be progressively made

48 MacArthur, *Gospel according to the Apostles*, 69–70.

49 MacArthur, *Gospel according to Jesus*, 196.

50 MacArthur, *Gospel according to the Apostles*, 70.

51 MacArthur, *Gospel according to Jesus*, 196.

righteous throughout the course of their Christian lives. However, this progressive transformation defines the reality not of biblical justification but of sanctification. By failing to distinguish these two intimately related yet nevertheless distinct applications of redemption, Roman Catholicism collapses sanctification into justification. The inevitable consequence is that the believer's own imperfect righteousness replaces the perfect righteousness of Christ as the sole ground of justification. The result is "a righteousness of my own that comes from the law," which, as Paul says in Philippians 3:9, is not the saving righteousness of God. Failing to understand the nature of justification as a legal declaration and instead mischaracterizing it as a transformative process destroys the very foundation of the gospel.

Scripture itself testifies to this truth, for the biblical writers often use the terms for justification and righteousness in a way that must be declarative rather than transformative.[52] In the Old Testament, the word is often used in judicial contexts (Ex. 23:7; Deut. 25:1; 1 Kings 8:31–32; Job 9:15; Isa. 43:9, 26; Jer. 12:1). Once again, judges do not *make* people righteous or wicked. They do not infuse righteousness or wickedness into the character of a person. Instead, they merely declare a defendant to be either righteous or guilty. Indeed, God declares, "he who justifies the wicked and he who condemns the righteous are both alike an abomination to the Lord" (Prov. 17:15; cf. Isa. 5:23). If justification were transformative, how could it be said that making a wicked person righteous is an abomination? Transforming the character of a wicked person and infusing him with righteousness would be a righteous act! Thus, a transformative understanding of justification violates the sense of these texts. To justify the wicked is not to make him righteous but to declare him righteous when he is not.

Further, justification is shown to be declarative and not transformative in those instances in which God is the one said to be justified. In Luke 7:29 the people are said to have "declared God just" (KJV, "justified God"). If the sense of justification were transformative, this would mean the people effected a positive moral transformation in God, which is nothing short of blasphemy. The ESV properly brings out the sense in the translation: "declared . . . just." That is, God's righteousness was vindicated and demonstrated (cf. Rom. 3:26).

52 This is not to say that Scripture never uses these terms in an ethical sense (see, e.g., Ps. 11:7; 1 Tim. 6:11). However, as Thomas Schreiner notes, "The ethical use of the term in some contexts doesn't necessitate the conclusion that the term isn't forensic in other . . . texts" (*Faith Alone: The Doctrine of Justification: What the Reformers Taught . . . and Why It Still Matters*, The Five Solas [Grand Rapids, MI: Zondervan, 2015], 158n1). The question is, in those key texts that describe the saving righteousness of God granted to sinners, does context support a forensic understanding of justification? We answer in the affirmative.

In addition, justification is often clearly contrasted with condemnation (Rom. 5:18; 8:33–34; 2 Cor. 3:9; cf. Job 9:20; Ps. 94:21; Prov. 17:15). But to condemn someone does not mean to make someone wicked; it means to render a verdict and declare that he is wicked. For the parallel between justification and condemnation to hold, we must also understand that justification does not mean to make righteous but to declare righteous.

Therefore, when we turn to texts that speak of God justifying the believer in a salvific sense (e.g., Rom. 3:20–28; 4:4–5; 5:1; Gal. 2:16; 3:11, 21–26; 5:4), we ought to understand them to be referring to God's instantaneous declaration that the sinner is in a right standing before him. These passages teach that God declares the believer to be righteous as a gift of his grace, which the believer receives by faith alone apart from works.

The Ground of Justification: Imputed Righteousness

But how is such a declaration by God just? Proverbs 17:15 says, "He who justifies the wicked . . . [is] an abomination to the Lord." And yet we are told in Romans 4:5 that God justifies the *ungodly*. How can God declare to be righteous those who are actually guilty, and not participate in something abominable? The answer to that question is the doctrine of imputation, wherein sinners who are unrighteous are counted to be righteous on the basis of Christ's work. This is a twofold act; God imputes—that is, counts, credits, or reckons—our sin to Christ and punishes him in our place, and he imputes Christ's righteousness to us and grants us eternal life in him.

Forgiveness of Sins: The Imputation of Our Sin to Christ. First, God imputes our sin to Christ: "For our sake he [the Father] made him [Christ] to be sin who knew no sin" (2 Cor. 5:21). Now, in what sense did the Father "make" the Son "sin" on our behalf? In only one sense: the Father counted Jesus to have committed all the sins of all those who would ever repent and believe in him. He did not actually make Jesus a sinner; it would be blasphemous to suggest that the God-man was actually made a sinner, for God cannot sin. Instead, the Father judicially reckoned Christ to have committed the sins of those for whom he died. Just as the scapegoat bore the guilt of Israel when Aaron confessed the people's sins over its head (Lev. 16:21), so "the Lord has laid on him the iniquity of us all" (Isa. 53:6), such that Christ actually "bore our sins in his body on the tree" (1 Pet. 2:24; cf. Isa. 53:4–6). And just as the blood of the goat of the sin offering was sprinkled on the mercy seat to propitiate God's wrath (Lev. 16:15), so also was Christ "put forward as a propitiation by his blood" (Rom. 3:25).[53] Though innumerable sinners will escape

53 The word for mercy seat in Leviticus 16:15 is the same as the word for propitiation in Romans 3:25: *hilastērion*.

divine punishment, no sin will ever go unpunished, for every sin of the elect has been reckoned to Christ and has been punished in him on the cross. In this way, divine justice is fully satisfied. Sin has not been merely swept under the rug; it has been justly punished in a substitute. This is the gospel through which God demonstrates his righteousness, "so that he might be just and the justifier of the one who has faith in Jesus" (Rom. 3:26).

Therefore, because the believer's sins have been imputed to and punished in Christ, they are not counted against him but are forgiven and covered (Rom. 4:7–8). Therefore, the justified believer faces no condemnation (Rom. 8:1, 33–34) but enjoys peace with God (Rom. 5:1) and the sure hope of eternal life (Rom. 8:30; Titus 3:7).

Provision of Righteousness: The Imputation of Christ's Righteousness to Us. But the forgiveness of sins does not exhaust God's work in justification. In fact, if the only benefit believers received in justification were the forgiveness of our sins, we could not be saved. The old Sunday school definition of justification—"just as if I'd never sinned"—is inadequate, because salvation is not merely a matter of sinlessness but of righteousness (Matt. 5:20, 48). The law of God consists in both positive demands and penal sanctions. That is, it requires both (1) that God's creatures perform certain duties suitable to his righteousness and (2) that they undergo a certain punishment if they fail to perform those duties. Man has failed to do both. We do not live lives of perfect righteousness, walking in obedience to God in all things, loving him with all our heart, soul, mind, and strength, and loving our neighbors as ourselves. Nor could we pay the penalty that our disobedience demands without perishing eternally in hell. Therefore, if we are to be saved, our substitute must not only pay our penalty by absorbing the wrath of God against our sin but must also obey all the positive demands of the law that were required of us.

This twofold nature of Christ's substitutionary work is sometimes referred to as his *passive obedience* and *active obedience*.[54] Without the positive provision of righteousness, mere forgiveness would leave us in a state of innocence or moral neutrality, as Adam was before the fall—reckoned as never having sinned but as

54 John Murray explains, "The law of God has both penal sanctions and positive demands. It demands not only the full discharge of its precepts but also the infliction of penalty for all infractions and shortcomings. It is this twofold demand of the law of God which is taken into account when we speak of the active and passive obedience of Christ. Christ as the vicar of his people came under the curse and condemnation due to sin and he also fulfilled the law of God in all its positive requirements. In other words, he took care of the guilt of sin and perfectly fulfilled the demands of righteousness. He perfectly met both the penal and the preceptive requirements of God's law. The passive obedience refers to the former and the active obedience to the latter" (*Redemption Accomplished and Applied*, 21–22).

never having obeyed either. For this reason, Scripture speaks of the justified sinner being counted righteous in addition to being forgiven. The apostle Paul states, "Now to the one who works, his wages are not counted as a gift but as his due. And to the one who does not work but believes in him who justifies the ungodly, his faith is counted as righteousness" (Rom. 4:4–5; cf. Gen. 15:6; Isa. 61:10).

In the next chapter, Paul identifies the righteousness that is imputed to believers to be Christ's own righteousness. In Romans 5:12–19, Paul compares and contrasts the two representative heads of humanity: (1) Adam and (2) Christ, the "last Adam" (see 1 Cor. 15:45). His argument climaxes in Romans 5:18–19:

> Therefore, as through the one man's [Adam's] trespass there resulted condemnation to all men, so also through the one man's [Christ's] righteousness there resulted justification of life to all men. For as through the one man's disobedience the many were constituted sinners, so by the one man's obedience the many will be constituted righteous. (author's trans.)[55]

Paul's main argument is as follows: Adam disobeyed God, and his disobedience was counted for condemnation to all who were in him. In the same way, Christ obeyed God, and his obedience was counted for righteousness to all who are in him. So, far from being a "legal fiction," both the imputation of sin and the imputation of righteousness have a basis in the actual, lived-out actions of Adam and Christ.

In justification, then, God not only satisfies the penal demands of the law by imputing our sin to Christ and punishing him in our place; he also satisfies the positive demands of the law by imputing Christ's righteousness to us. We thus "become" the righteousness of God in Christ in the same way Christ was "made" sin for us: by judicial reckoning, that is, by imputation (2 Cor. 5:21). In justification, the perfect righteousness that God requires (Matt. 5:20, 48) is not worked in us in a transformative sense but is credited to us through our union with Christ, the Righteous One, who has fulfilled all righteousness on our behalf (Matt. 3:15; Rom. 10:4; 1 Cor. 1:30; Gal. 3:27). When we are "found in him," we do not have a righteousness of our own derived through commandment keeping; rather, we lay hold of the external righteousness of God that comes through faith in Christ (Phil. 3:9).[56]

55 For an explanation of this translation, see MacArthur and Richard Mayhue, *Biblical Doctrine*, p. 617nn140–41.

56 Some theologians object that because Paul uses the phrase "the righteousness of God," he therefore does not refer to the obedience of Christ. But compare 2 Pet. 1:1: "the righteousness of our God and Savior Jesus Christ." Further, the righteousness imputed to believers is the righteousness of God *precisely because* it is the righteousness of Christ (cf. Rom. 1:17; 3:21–22; 10:3–4). As Murray argues, "It is the righteousness of the God-man, a righteousness which measures up to the require-

In summary, in Christ we have a substitute who has both paid our penalty *and* achieved our righteousness. Christ accomplished forgiveness by atoning for our sins on the cross. Just as our sins were reckoned to *his* account, in the same manner his righteousness is counted as *ours*. His perfect righteousness is thus the ground on which we stand before God. Sinners are not justified because of some good thing in them; God can declare us righteous—he can justify the ungodly and yet remain just—because he graciously imputes to us the perfect righteousness of his own dear Son. Thus, the sole ground of justification is the righteousness of Christ counted to be ours as a gift by grace alone (cf. Rom. 3:24; Eph. 2:8–9; Titus 3:7).

The Means of Justification: Faith Alone

Christ's accomplishment of redemption occurred two thousand years ago, apart from any human influence. But how can the objective work of Christ be applied to me personally? By what means can my sins be imputed to Christ and his righteousness be imputed to me? The answer Scripture consistently gives is that we are justified through faith alone, apart from works. Faith unites us to Christ in his death and resurrection, so that his punishment counts for our punishment and his righteousness counts for our righteousness.

The clearest exposition of the doctrine of justification by faith alone comes in Paul's letters, especially the book of Romans (3:22–28; 5:1; 9:30; 10:4, 6, 10) and Galatians (2:16; 3:22, 24, 26). Take time to read each of those referenced verses. You will discover that one must despair of being declared righteous through his own works and trust in Christ alone for righteousness.

Although Jesus never formally explained the doctrine of justification (as Paul does in Romans and Galatians), the doctrine of *sola fide* underlies and permeates all his gospel preaching. For example, in John 5:24 Jesus declared, "Whoever hears my word . . . has passed from death to life." Without undergoing any sacrament or ritual, and without any waiting period or purgatory, the believer passes from death to life. The thief on the cross is another example. On the most meager evidence of his faith, Jesus told him he would be in heaven that very day (Luke 23:43). No sacrament or work was required for him to procure salvation.

But the one occasion where Jesus actually declared someone "justified" provides the best insight into the way he taught the doctrine. In Luke 18:9–14, Jesus tells a parable of a revered Pharisee who trusts in his own good deeds for his righteousness, in contrast to a despised tax collector who looked entirely outside of himself to God for forgiveness. In a shocking twist, Jesus declares that the believing tax

---

ments of our sinful and sin-cursed situation, a righteousness which meets all the demands of a complete and irrevocable justification, and a righteousness fulfilling all these demands because it is a righteousness of divine property and character, a righteousness undefiled and inviolable" (*Redemption Accomplished and Applied*, 128).

collector went to his house justified, while the working Pharisee remained dead in his sins. The tax collector sought God's favor not on the basis of anything that he had done—not even anything that God had accomplished in him—but only because of what God had accomplished on his behalf. He knew he owed an impossible debt that he knew he could not pay—that his best works were sin—and so he did not offer to do anything for God but looked for God to do for him what he could not do for himself. He went away without performing any works of penance, sacraments, or rituals, and yet was declared righteous. Apart from any works whatsoever, he was justified by means of faith alone.

Perhaps the clearest affirmation of justification by faith alone comes in Romans 4, as Paul turns to God's dealings with Abraham to illustrate that his gospel has ancient roots. In verse 3, he cites Genesis 15:6, noting that God imputed righteousness to Abraham by means of Abraham's faith. His works had absolutely nothing to do with it, for Paul goes on to say, "Now to the one who works, his wages are not counted as a gift but as his due. And to the one who *does not work* but believes in him who justifies the ungodly, his faith is counted as righteousness" (Rom. 4:4–5). Here Paul explicitly negates the teaching that works constitute any part of the ground of justification. If we were to perform any good work for our salvation, the righteousness that would result could never properly be called a gift. The worker earns wages. But the recipient of salvation is "justified by [God's] grace as a gift" (Rom. 3:24), and a gift can only be given apart from any work. The glorious consequence of this precious doctrine is that salvation is totally free. With an empty hand, the sinner lays hold of the righteousness of Christ through faith alone.

It is important to state that faith in Christ is not the *ground* of the believer's righteousness but merely the *means*, or instrument, through which we receive righteousness. This is an important distinction, because many people rest their hope for heaven on the fact that they had the good sense to believe the gospel. But such an understanding undermines the truth that we are saved by grace alone. Righteousness cannot be based on my faith without that righteousness becoming "a righteousness of my own" (Phil. 3:9). If saving righteousness is grounded on the sinner doing anything—even believing—it is no longer an alien righteousness given as a gift and therefore cannot be the righteousness of God that is required for salvation. In that case, faith would be made into a work, and "grace would no longer be grace" (Rom. 11:6). God's holiness is so magnificently perfect that all our righteousness must be a free gift of his sovereign grace, because we could never earn it. Thus, God declares sinners righteous not because their faith has earned them righteousness but because Christ has earned righteousness, which

God grants as a gift by the means of faith.[57] So far from being the currency by which we purchase salvation from God, faith is uniquely suited to grace (Rom. 4:16) because it is nothing more than the outstretched arm and the empty hand that confesses, "I have nothing! I am bankrupt of any spiritual resources or ability! Lord, I receive your gift of salvation in Christ."

The Result of Justification: Good Works

Perhaps the most common objection to the doctrine of *sola fide* is the accusation that the apostle James explicitly contradicts it. How can James's comment, "You see that a person is justified by works and not by faith alone" (James 2:24), be reconciled with the doctrine of justification by faith alone? The answer is that James uses the word "justified" in a different sense than Paul uses it in the above texts. In particular, James speaks of justification in the sense of "vindication" or "the demonstration of righteousness."

Scripture often uses the word "justification" in this sense. For example, we read in a confession of the early church that Christ "was manifested in the flesh" and "vindicated [KJV: "justified"] by the Spirit" (1 Tim. 3:16; cf. Luke 10:29). Certainly, the Lord Jesus stood in no need of forensic justification, of being legally declared righteous. Rather, this passage speaks of the Spirit's vindication of Christ by the many miracles he performed (Acts 2:22), as well as the ultimate vindication of the resurrection (Rom. 1:4). In the same way, James uses the term "justified" in the sense of "vindicated" or "demonstrated."

The context of James 2 also makes this clear. James is commenting on Abraham's sacrifice of Isaac according to God's commandment (2:21; cf. Gen. 22:1–14), an event that took place many years after it was declared that Abraham "believed [in] the LORD, and he counted it to him as righteousness" (Gen. 15:6). In contrast, when Paul desires to illustrate the truth of the imputation of righteousness through faith alone apart from works (Rom. 4:6), he chooses this earlier instance in Abraham's life before there was even any law for him to follow (Rom. 4:9–13). James, however, is not speaking of forensic justification and the imputation of

57 Benjamin B. Warfield's famous remarks are worthy of wholehearted affirmation: "The *saving power* of faith resides . . . not in itself, but in the Almighty Saviour on whom it rests. It is never on account of its formal nature as a psychic act that faith is conceived in Scripture to be saving,—as if this frame of mind or attitude of heart were itself a virtue with claims on God for reward. . . . It is not faith that saves, but faith in Jesus Christ. . . . It is not, strictly speaking, even faith in Christ that saves, but Christ that saves through faith. The saving power resides exclusively, not in the act of faith or the attitude of faith or the nature of faith, but in the object of faith; . . . we could not more radically misconceive [the biblical concept of faith] than by transferring to faith even the smallest fraction of that saving energy which is attributed in the Scriptures solely to Christ himself" (*The Works of Benjamin B. Warfield*, vol. 2, *Biblical Doctrines* [1932; repr., Grand Rapids, MI: Baker, 2000], 504, italics original).

righteousness. He is not teaching that good works are the ground of our salvation. Rather, he is speaking about good works that are the necessary evidence of our salvation. Abraham's faith, which was credited to him as righteousness apart from anything he had done, was vindicated by his works. In other words, Abraham's works demonstrated that his faith was true faith and not dead faith (cf. James 2:17, 26). True faith is shown by its works (James 2:18), but those works are the evidence and result of our justification and initial sanctification, not the ground of our justification.

Far from refuting the doctrine of *sola fide* in favor of the legalists, James's argument actually provides a defense of the doctrine from the attack of the opposite error: antinomianism—the teaching which denies that sanctification is the necessary fruit of justification. Whereas legalism undermines the gospel by insisting that we must add our obedience to Christ's work in order to be justified, antinomianism perverts the gospel by subtracting from the efficacy of Christ's work, denying that those who receive Christ as Savior must also submit to him as Lord. James absolutely demolishes that proposition. He explains that the "faith" of professing Christians who fail to make progress in practical holiness, but continue to walk in patterns of unrighteousness, is no true and saving faith at all. Their faith is dead (James 2:17, 26), demonic (2:19), and useless (2:20), and identifies them as the self-deceived whom Jesus has never known (Matt. 7:21–23).

In fact, John Calvin, the great Reformer and believer in *sola fide*, stood on the teaching of James 2 when he wrote, "It is therefore faith alone which justifies, and yet the faith which justifies is not alone."[58] In other words, salvation is not a *result of* good works (Eph. 2:9), but salvation does necessarily *result in* good works. This is the very purpose of our salvation: "For we are his workmanship, created in Christ Jesus *for good works*, which God prepared beforehand, that we should walk in them" (Eph. 2:10). Christ gave himself for us not only to forensically redeem us from all lawlessness but also to "purify for himself a people for his own possession who are zealous for good works" (Titus 2:14). Those who deny that good works are the necessary fruit of the justification received through faith alone make out the Lord Jesus Christ to be half a Savior—one who saves from sin's penalty but not from its power. Yet Scripture teaches that we are united with Christ not only in his death but also in his resurrection, the necessary result of which is a holy life (Rom. 6:3–6; 2 Cor. 5:14–15). All true Christians have been "set free" from sin's bondage and have become "slaves to God," resulting in sanctification (Rom. 6:1–14, 22). Therefore, while it is faith alone that saves, the faith that saves is never

58 From Calvin's "Acts of the Council of Trent with the Antidote" (1547), quoted in Schreiner, *Faith Alone*, 62.

alone but will always be accompanied by the fruit of righteousness (Phil. 1:11) wrought by the Holy Spirit in the life of the believer (Gal. 5:22–25; cf. John 15:8).[59]

Concluding Remarks Regarding Justification

In summary, justification is that aspect of the application of redemption in which God legally declares the sinner to be righteous in his sight. The ground of this declaration is the righteousness of Christ that he accomplished in the sinner's stead by (1) dying to provide forgiveness of sin and by (2) walking in perfect obedience to his Father in order to provide the righteousness required for fellowship with God. By grace alone, God imputes our sin to Christ so that he might truly bear our punishment, and he imputes Christ's righteousness to us so that we might stand before him in perfect holiness. This imputation is mediated through faith alone apart from any work on the sinner's part. Good works must follow justification, but they are the evidence—not the ground—of true and saving faith.

The doctrine of justification runs to the very heart of the gospel. It offers the only hope of salvation to guilty sinners, who, apart from Christ, have no hope of a restored relationship with the holy God of the universe, yet who, in him, are clothed with the perfect righteousness that God requires. The good news of the gospel is that this blessing is offered freely to all who would receive it, apart from any works, through faith alone. The doctrine of justification is the very foundation of the gospel promise of John 3:16, that "God so loved the world, that he gave his only Son, that whoever believes in him should not perish but have eternal life"; and of Romans 8:1, that "there is therefore now no condemnation for those who are in Christ Jesus."

ADOPTION

While it may seem impossible to improve upon such gifts as regeneration, conversion, union, and justification, the Word of God speaks of yet another spiritual blessing in the application of redemption: the Father's adoption of believers as his children.[60]

59 For a more detailed biblical case against antinomianism, especially as represented in the "No Lordship" doctrine of Zane Hodges and Charles Ryrie, see John MacArthur, *Gospel according to Jesus*; and MacArthur, *Gospel according to the Apostles*.

60 The background for the New Testament concept of adoption comes from the practice of adoption in ancient Rome, conveniently outlined in John MacArthur, *Slave: The Hidden Truth about Your Identity in Christ* (Nashville: Thomas Nelson, 2010), 155–57: "The adoption process consisted of several specific legal procedures. The first step completely terminated the adopted child's social relationship and legal connection to his natural family. The second step made him a permanent member of his new family. Additionally, any previous financial obligations were eradicated, as if they had never existed. In order for the transaction to be legally formalized, the presence of

The concept of adoption is familiar to us because it remains common in today's world, and it is a rare case when the story of any particular adoption fails to warm the heart. Through the intervention of a compassionate benefactor, adopted children are welcomed into the loving home of a new family eager to provide protection, instruction, and the hope of a future. The New Testament builds on this blessing of human adoption by using it as an analogy to describe God's fatherly love for us. We were spiritual orphans under the cruel oppression of sin and Satan. By nature, we were "children of wrath" (Eph. 2:3), "sons of disobedience" (Eph. 2:2; 5:6), and even children of the Devil himself (John 8:44). Our only home was this sin-cursed world that is fast passing away (1 John 2:17). Our only guardian was the avowed enemy of our souls (1 Pet. 5:8). Our only future was the terrifying expectation of hell's judgment (Heb. 10:27).

But God, eager to display the glory of his grace, intervened on our behalf:

> In love he predestined us for adoption . . . as sons through Jesus Christ, according to the purpose of his will, to the praise of his glorious grace, with which he has blessed us in the Beloved. (Eph. 1:4–6)

> But when the fullness of time had come, God sent forth his Son, born of woman, born under the law, to redeem those who were under the law, so that we might receive adoption as sons. (Gal. 4:4–5)

The eternal Son of God was forsaken by his Father so that we might be welcomed as sons. At great cost to himself, God took every legal measure to rescue us from sin and make us part of his family. As planned in eternity past, the Son purchased believers at Calvary, and they finally lay hold of the blessing of adoption at the time of conversion, "for," says the apostle Paul, "in Christ Jesus you are all sons of God, through faith" (Gal. 3:26; cf. John 1:12). In adoption, God legally places regenerated and justified sinners into his family, so that they become sons and daughters of God and thus enjoy all the rights and privileges of one who is a member of God's eternal family.

The Unique Blessing of Adoption

Though it has often been confused with regeneration or viewed as just another aspect of justification, the spiritual blessing of adoption is a unique privilege in

---

seven reputable witnesses was required. If necessary, their testimony would refute any potential challenge to the adoption after the father had died.

"Once the adoption was complete, the new son or daughter was then completely under both the care and control of the new father. The previous father no longer had any authority over his former child. In Roman households, the authority of the *paterfamilias* ('father of the family') was final and absolute. And that authority extended to those adopted into the household, starting at the moment of their adoption."

God's economy of redemption. We think of becoming God's children as a result of regeneration—being born again. But adoption speaks of being born into a family. Though regeneration and adoption are intimately related, Scripture nevertheless distinguishes these two blessings with respect to the author, nature, and means of each, as seen in table 7.1.

Table 7.1 Regeneration versus Adoption in Scripture

	Regeneration	**Adoption**
Author	Holy Spirit (John 3:5–6, 8; 6:63)	The Father (Eph. 1:5)
Nature	Transformative (Ezek. 36:26–27; cf. 2 Cor. 5:17)	Legal (John 1:12)
Means	Word of God (James 1:18; 1 Pet. 1:23–25)	Faith (John 1:12; Gal. 3:26)

Further, adoption should not be viewed as just a subset of the work of justification. Though both justification and adoption are declarative acts mediated through faith, they are distinct blessings. Justification is the legal declaration that one is righteous with respect to the demands of God's law. Adoption, however, is the legal declaration by the divine Judge that the justified one has been made a member of the divine Judge's family.

It is an unspeakable blessing to be granted new spiritual life in regeneration. So also is it a remarkable privilege to be freed from the penalty of sin and declared righteous in Christ. If the bestowal of God's gifts stopped at regeneration and justification, no one would question his goodness or regard his grace as deficient. But in an extravagant expression of love, God adopts believers into his family, so that we relate to him not only as the Giver of spiritual life and the provider of legal righteousness but also as our loving and compassionate Father. For this reason, adoption has rightly been designated "the highest privilege that the gospel offers"[61] and "the apex of grace and privilege" that "staggers imagination because of its amazing condescension and love."[62] Indeed, as the apostle John considered the reality of the believer's adoption, he was compelled to let out yet another apostolic burst of praise: "See what great love the Father has lavished on us, that we should be called children of God!" (1 John 3:1 NIV). How great indeed!

61 J. I. Packer, *Knowing God*, rev. ed. (Downers Grove, IL: InterVarsity Press, 1993), 206.

62 Murray, *Redemption Accomplished and Applied*, 134.

"Universal Fatherhood of God"?

The notion that believers *become* the children of God at the time of conversion deals the deathblow to the doctrine of the universal fatherhood of God—the liberal Protestant teaching that all human beings are God's children by default. It is true that Scripture sometimes speaks of God's fatherhood in universal terms. One example of this is Acts 17:28–29. However, the context of this statement clearly indicates that Paul was speaking of the reality that God is the Creator of all mankind and thus is the universal Father only in that sense. He is "the Father of spirits" (Heb. 12:9), who "gives to all mankind life and breath and everything" (Acts 17:25), and he "made from one man every nation of mankind" (Acts 17:26). Thus, "in him we live and move and have our being" (Acts 17:28).[63]

Nevertheless, the fact that God is the common Creator of all human beings does not mean that all are his children in the relational sense indicated by the doctrine of adoption. Jesus himself speaks most severely on this issue, noting that all unbelievers are children of Satan himself. He clearly distinguishes between his Father and the Pharisees' father (John 8:38), denies that God is their Father (John 8:42), and explicitly declares, "You are of your father the devil" (John 8:44). The apostle John comments on this distinction between the children of God and the children of the Devil, noting that the latter are those who do not practice righteousness (1 John 3:10). Scripture differentiates between the children of the flesh and the children of God (Rom. 9:8), the children of the slave woman and the children of the free woman (Gal. 4:22–31), and the children of light and the children of darkness (Eph. 5:8). These passages militate against any understanding of the universal fatherhood of God. Indeed, rather than being sons of God, natural humanity is described as "the sons of disobedience" (Eph. 2:2; 5:6). So far from relating naturally to God as children, all fallen human beings are "by nature children of wrath" (Eph. 2:3). Unless something drastic happens—indeed, nothing less radical than being made alive from the dead (Eph. 2:4–5)—man in his natural condition will not know the blessings of a loving Father but rather will experience the wrath of a righteous Judge. It is only to those who receive Jesus and believe in his name that authority is given to become children of God (John 1:12), for all of God's adoptive children are "sons of God through faith in Christ Jesus" (Gal. 3:26 NASB) as a result of his work of redemption (Gal. 4:5).

Therefore, rather than an *essential* fatherhood of God or a universal *creative* fatherhood of God, these passages on adoption speak of the *redemptive* fatherhood

63 This may also be Malachi's intent when he rebukes the sinful priests of his day, asking, "Have we not all one Father? Has not one God created us?" (Mal. 2:10). However, given his reference to "the covenant of our fathers" at the end of the verse, it is more likely that Malachi is referring to God's fatherhood of Israel as a covenant nation (cf. Jer. 31:9; Hos. 11:1).

of God, in which justified sinners become sons and daughters of the Father with all the rights and privileges that a member of his family enjoys.

The Privileges of Adoption

What, then, are those rights and privileges to be enjoyed by members of the family of God? The chief blessing of our adoption is that the Holy Spirit himself takes up permanent residence in our hearts, freeing us from sin and fostering our fellowship with God (Rom. 8:15–16; Gal. 4:6–7). Though we were enslaved to sin and idolatry (Gal. 4:8), the Spirit of adoption has liberated us from our slavery into "the freedom of the glory of the children of God" (Rom. 8:21; cf. 2 Cor. 3:17). We are no longer slaves of a master but permanent sons of our Father (John 8:35), and the Spirit himself bears witness in our hearts to assure us that this new relationship is genuine. So intimate is our bond with the God of the universe that the Spirit compels us to cry out to him with childlike affection, "Abba! Father!" (Rom. 8:15; Gal. 4:6). An informal Aramaic term for "father," *Abba* signifies the most endearing tenderness and intimacy between a father and a son. Aside from these two passages, "Abba" occurs only one other time in the New Testament: on the lips of Jesus himself during the darkest hour of his earthly sojourn. In Gethsemane, as the Son poured out his heart to the Father, pleading that the cup of divine wrath be removed from him, he called to him as "Abba" (Mark 14:36). It is nothing short of staggering to think that we who were once alienated from God because of our sin (Eph. 4:18) have been given the privilege of crying out to the Father in the very same way that his beloved Son did. The glory of that thought is exceeded only by the reality that his cry of "Abba" was ignored so that ours would be heard.

Because we can relate to God as our Father, we share in the richness of his loving compassion, protection, provision, and beneficence. His disposition to us is as a father to his children, eager to display kindness and to act in our greatest interests (Ps. 103:13). That disposition to compassion is illustrated by the Lord himself, who asks,

> What father among you, if his son asks for a fish, will instead of a fish give him a serpent; or if he asks for an egg, will give him a scorpion? If you then, who are evil, know how to give good gifts to your children, how much more will the heavenly Father give the Holy Spirit to those who ask him! (Luke 11:11–13)

Not only will God give us his Spirit, but as the parallel passage puts it, God will also give us the "good things" for which we ask him (Matt. 7:11). Because of this, we have no need to become anxious about our daily necessities, for the Father is happy to provide these for us (Luke 12:29–30). Immediately after these consolations from our Lord, he comforts us with the Father's beneficence in what may be the most tender words he ever spoke: "Fear not, little flock, for it is your Father's good pleasure to give you the kingdom" (Luke 12:32). God is not merely a distant, disinterested-though-generous benefactor. As a father delights to bless his children with an inheritance, it is his good pleasure—he eagerly delights—to make us sharers in the fullness of the kingdom itself.

Implied in this eagerness of God to bless his adopted children is the reality that we may approach the Lord of glory in prayer. As Jesus said, our Father is ready to give good gifts "to those who ask him" (Matt. 7:11; Luke 11:13), and he provides for the necessities of life as we seek first his kingdom (Luke 12:30–31), which is done preeminently through prayer. For this reason, when the Lord taught his disciples to pray to God, he instructed them to address him saying, "Our Father in heaven" (Matt. 6:9). What a privilege it is to approach the throne of grace with the confidence that the sovereign Lord is our heavenly Father, eager to hear our requests and bless us from his bounty!

Another privilege of our adoption as sons is the loving, fatherly discipline we receive from God. The author of Hebrews counsels us, "My son, do not regard lightly the discipline of the Lord, nor be weary when reproved by him. For the Lord disciplines the one he loves, and chastises every son whom he receives" (Heb. 12:5–6; cf. Prov. 3:11–12). When we depart from God's will and engage in sinful thoughts and actions, he will providentially order various hardships and afflictions in our lives to warn us of sin's consequences, to lead us to repentance, and to cultivate greater spiritual maturity in us (e.g., 2 Sam. 12:10–12; 1 Cor. 11:30). The author of Hebrews goes on to explain that when we experience this discipline, "God is treating [us] as sons. For what son is there whom his father does not discipline? If you are left without discipline, . . . then you are illegitimate children and not sons" (Heb. 12:7–8). Indeed, when God withdraws his discipline, it is the severest indication of his judgment, as he is giving people over to their sin and its consequences (Rom. 1:25–28). In the human realm, Scripture says that parents who withhold discipline from their children hate them (Prov. 13:24) and desire their death (Prov. 19:18). Thus, for God to discipline us as his children is sure testimony of his earnest love and sincere desire for our greatest benefit. As the author of Hebrews continues, "he disciplines us for our good, that we may share his holiness" (Heb. 12:10). Though in the moment "all discipline seems painful rather than pleasant, . . . later it yields the peaceful fruit of righteousness to those who have been trained by it" (Heb. 12:11). When we consider that there is a "holiness without which no one will see the Lord" (Heb. 12:14), we are compelled to treasure the loving discipline of our Father, for it fits us for fellowship with him. What a privilege that the God of the heavens has taken a personal interest in our spiritual welfare—not only to declare us righteous but also to work practical righteousness in us by his great grace!

Still another privilege of our adoption into God's family is the unity we enjoy with our brothers and sisters in Christ. The church is not merely a social club or a political organization knit together by common interests or shared hobbies. Rather, we are objectively united to one another as members of the same family. No wonder the early believers addressed one another as brothers and sisters (e.g., Acts 1:15–16; Rom. 12:1; 16:14; Phil. 4:1; 1 Tim. 5:1–2; cf. Matt. 12:46–50). A family is not merely a group of people with some shared interests and a subjective appreciation for one another. Instead, brothers and sisters are bound together by something much deeper—by the objective union that results from the love shared by their parents. And while brothers and sisters may not always relate to one another on the best terms, no amount of discord or conflict can break the objective bond that they share. The same is true within the family of God. Tensions and disagreements may arise between us and our brothers and sisters in Christ. But just as nothing can separate us from the loving union that we share with Christ individually (Rom. 8:38–39), nor can anything separate us from the union we share with one another corporately. It is on the basis of this objective union that we pursue "the unity of the Spirit in the bond of peace" (Eph. 4:3). As long as Christians do that, we will never be alone. We will always belong to one another. Because of the adopting grace of our Father, we face life's darkest trials alongside our brothers and sisters as the family of God.

In addition to all these privileges that we enjoy in the present time, our adoption as children of God also guarantees us a share in the future inheritance of eternal life. Paul writes that if we are adopted children, we must also necessarily be heirs. We are no longer slaves but sons, "and if a son, then an heir through God" (Gal. 4:7)—indeed, "heirs of God and fellow heirs with Christ" (Rom. 8:17). In human relations, sons and daughters inherit the estate of their parents at the time of their passing. All that belonged to the parents is bequeathed to the children as they carry on the family legacy. In a similar way, though by nature we had no rightful claim to all the riches of the kingdom of God, by grace we have become God's adopted children and have thus become legal heirs of "an inheritance that is imperishable, undefiled, and unfading, kept in heaven" for us (1 Pet. 1:4). So genuine is our inheritance that we are described as fellow heirs with Christ (Rom. 8:17). Everything that Christ will receive by divine right as the natural Son of God, we will receive by divine grace as adoptive children of God.[64] Because Christ is God's Son, all that the Father has belongs to him. And because we are in Christ, everything that is Christ's is ours, "whether . . . the world or life or death or the present or the future" (1 Cor. 3:22–23)—all things belong to the children of God. The redeemed are sure to enjoy all the blessings of heaven in God's presence, for

64 John MacArthur, *Romans 1–8*, MNTC (Chicago: Moody Press, 1991), 445.

he promises that "he who overcomes will inherit these things, and I will be his God and he will be My son" (Rev. 21:7 NASB). Chief among these heavenly blessings is the promise of a glorified body after the likeness of Christ's resurrection body, free from all sin and infirmity (1 Cor. 15:23, 42–44; Phil. 3:20–21). While in the "house" of our present body we groan under the effects of sin's curse (2 Cor. 5:2 NASB), we look forward to the consummation of our adoption as sons and daughters of God, the redemption of our bodies (Rom. 8:23).

This glorification has, in a sense, begun in this present life in the form of progressive sanctification, yet another privilege of our adoption. Just as children imitate their father, so also are we exhorted to "be imitators of God, as beloved children" (Eph. 5:1). One of the richest blessings of God's grace in salvation is that he attaches his name to his people. He graciously pursues the welfare of his people with the same zeal with which he upholds the honor of his reputation, because they bear his name (cf. Josh. 7:9; 1 Sam. 12:22; Jer. 14:7, 9; Dan. 9:17–18). As children of God, we bear the "family name" of God, and as Isaiah says, his name is Holy (Isa. 57:15; cf. 1 Chron. 29:16; Ps. 33:21; Isa. 47:4; Luke 1:49). Thus the apostle Peter exhorts us, "As obedient children, do not be conformed to the passions of your former ignorance, but as he who called you is holy, you also be holy in all your conduct, since it is written, 'You shall be holy, for I am holy'" (1 Pet. 1:14–16). If we call on this holy One as Father, we ought to live lives that resemble his holiness (1 Pet. 1:17), conducting ourselves as "blameless and innocent, *children of God* without blemish in the midst of a crooked and twisted generation" (Phil. 2:15).

The conclusion to the study of the doctrine of adoption must be a call to holiness. God's promise to us is, "I will be a father to you, and you shall be sons and daughters to me" (2 Cor. 6:18). If we enjoy such an exalted position as children adopted into the family of God, enjoying all the rights and privileges as sons and daughters of the Almighty himself, we must respond as Paul instructs in the next verse: "Since we have these promises, beloved, let us cleanse ourselves from every defilement of body and spirit, bringing holiness to completion in the fear of God" (2 Cor. 7:1). Therefore, we now turn our attention to the doctrine of sanctification.

SANCTIFICATION

Thus far in this study of the application of redemption, we have considered those benefits purchased by the work of Christ that the Spirit applies immediately to believers at the inception of the Christian life. At regeneration, the sinner is made alive, granted repentance and faith, united to Christ, declared righteous on the basis of the imputed righteousness of Christ, and adopted into the family of God. However, the blessing of sanctification is a benefit of the application of redemption that, though it begins at regeneration, is applied throughout the entirety of the Christian's life. In sanctification, God, working especially by the Holy Spirit, separates the believer unto himself (cf. 1 Cor. 1:2) and makes him increasingly holy, progressively transforming him into the image of Christ (Rom. 8:29; 2 Cor. 3:18) by subduing the power of sin in his life and enabling him to bear the fruit of obedience in his life.

The Relationship between Justification and Sanctification

Sanctification is intimately connected to justification but is not to be confused with or collapsed into justification, as in Roman Catholic theology. Justification is the once-for-all judicial declaration of righteousness that defines man's legal standing before God. Sanctification is a gradual, ongoing transformation of his nature. In justification, Christ has secured forensic righteousness *for* the believer; in sanctification, the Spirit progressively works practical righteousness *in* the believer. Justification concerns the *imputation* of righteousness, whereas sanctification concerns the *impartation* of righteousness. To confuse the two is to fundamentally undermine the gospel.[65]

Positional (Definitive) Sanctification

Though sanctification is primarily understood to be a process in which the believer is conformed into the image of Christ (e.g., Scripture speaks of believers as "those who *are being* sanctified," Heb. 10:14), that process has a definite beginning at regeneration. The present-tense aspect of sanctification is often called progressive sanctification, whereas the past-tense aspect may be called either initial, positional, or definitive sanctification.

As discussed earlier, regeneration is not only the impartation of spiritual life but is also a definitive cleansing from sin.[66] That is why Paul designates regeneration as not only a renewal but a washing as well (Titus 3:5). Thus, when the Spirit imparts spiritual life, opening the sinner's eyes to the filth of sin and the glory of Jesus (2 Cor. 4:4, 6), man's nature is sanctified—definitively transformed into a new creation (2 Cor. 5:17). The holy disposition that is strengthened throughout the believer's progressive sanctification is that same holy disposition that is born in the believer at regeneration. In this sense, regeneration is the beginning of sanctification.

For this reason, the New Testament often employs the terminology of sanctification in the past tense, characterizing the Christian as one who has been initially sanctified by God (Acts 20:32; 26:18; 1 Cor. 1:2; 6:11). Both the Old and New Testaments identify all of God's people as saints—literally, "the holy ones"

65 For more on the relationship between justification and sanctification, see "The Nature of Justification: A Legal Declaration" (p. 326), and "The Result of Justification: Good Works" (p. 333).

66 See "The Nature of Regeneration" (p. 304) and the discussion of Ezek. 36:25–27 and John 3:5 in "The Means of Regeneration" (p. 307).

(e.g., Pss. 16:3; 34:9; Dan. 7:18–27; Matt. 27:52; Acts 9:13, 32, 41; Rom. 1:7; 8:27; 1 Cor. 1:2; 2 Cor. 1:1; Eph. 1:1; 6:18; Phil. 1:1; Col. 1:2; Jude 3; Rev. 19:8). So far from identifying a spiritually elite people on the basis of their personal merits, as the Roman Catholic Church teaches, what makes a believer a saint is not his practical righteousness but his positional righteousness. All believers are saints because they have been set apart by a holy God and have been united to the holy Lord Jesus. They have been initially, or positionally, sanctified.

The most significant reality in definitive sanctification is that, through union with Christ, the believer is set free from the dominion of sin. While justification and imputed righteousness grant the Christian freedom from sin's penalty, initial sanctification grants him freedom from sin's power. This is precisely Paul's point in Romans 6:1–7:6, where he states that believers have died to sin through union with Christ, so that they would no longer be enslaved to sin. As a result, sin's legal right to rule over believers has been broken. Though once enslaved to sin, believers possess Christ's resurrection power to resist temptation, mortify sin, and pursue increasing holiness. Therefore, though the believer may struggle mightily with sin, he must never grow comfortable with sin in his life. To do so is to make peace with a dethroned enemy—to submit to a ruler who has been conquered.

This freedom from the dominion of sin is the necessary foundation for all progress in progressive sanctification. Believers can obey the imperatives of Romans 6:12–13 only because of the indicative reality of freedom from sin announced in Romans 6:11 and 14. This indicative-imperative paradigm is the difference between biblical ethics and the moralism of legalistic religion or naturalistic philosophy. It is only because of union with Christ in his death and resurrection that the believer can make any progress in practical holiness (Gal. 2:20; Col. 3:12). Therefore, any attempt at self-improvement apart from God's grace is a man-made counterfeit of sanctification. It finds no favor with God and must ultimately prove ineffective (Rom. 8:8; 14:23; Heb. 11:6). The Christian pursues practical holiness not to enter a relationship with God or to earn his love, but because he is already God's child and a recipient of his love in Christ. Thus, it is necessary to fight sin in the strength and in the freedom of that gracious reality. Believers in Christ can be victorious over sin only because—and must be victorious over sin precisely because—Christ has conquered sin in them by his death and resurrection.

Progressive Sanctification

However, this decisive victory over the dominion of sin does not leave the believer totally purified. Though the penalty of sin is paid for and the power of sin is broken, the presence of sin still remains in the believer's flesh and therefore must continually be put to death. Thus, the sanctification that begins definitively at regeneration necessarily continues throughout the entirety of the Christian life. This continuous aspect of sanctification is called progressive sanctification.

The progressive nature of sanctification is substantiated by Scripture's numerous calls to holiness in the present tense, indicating ongoing, continuous action (Rom. 8:13; 12:2; Heb. 12:14). Further, several passages explicitly assert the progressive nature of sanctification (Phil. 1:9; 3:12–14; Col. 3:9–10; 1 Thess. 3:12; 1 Pet. 2:2; 2 Pet. 3:18). Most clearly, Paul states that as believers behold the glory of Christ with the eyes of the heart, they are thereby "being transformed into the same image from one degree of glory to another" (2 Cor. 3:18). Believers are not conformed to the image of Christ in an instant; they experience a progressive transformation into his image by degrees. Thus, the Holy Spirit's work in believers will cause them to increase in sanctification throughout their Christian lives.

Perfected Sanctification

Just as sanctification has a definitive beginning at regeneration and increases throughout one's life, it will also be brought to completion at the end of the believer's life. To the degree that we behold Christ's glory in this life, to that degree are we sanctified (2 Cor. 3:18). However, because we see him imperfectly (1 Cor. 13:12), perfected sanctification awaits the day when we will see him face-to-face. As the apostle John says, "But we know that when he appears we shall be like him, *because* we shall see him as he is" (1 John 3:2).

Contrary to the doctrine of *perfectionism*, sanctification can never be completed in this life. Though Scripture often exhorts believers to holiness in language that sounds very absolute (e.g., Matt. 5:48; 1 Pet. 1:15–16), we ought not assume that a commandment to perfection implies our ability to be perfect. Scripture explicitly contradicts the assumption that the existence of a command necessarily implies man's ability to obey. For example, Jesus teaches that the moral inability to produce good fruit absolves the unbeliever neither of his responsibility to do so nor of the certain consequences of failing to do so (Matt. 7:18–19). Further, all people everywhere are held responsible to repent and believe the gospel (Acts 17:30; cf. Mark 1:15)—the very thing Scripture elsewhere declares they are unable to do (Rom. 8:7–8; 1 Cor. 2:14).

Perfectionists also appeal to other passages which speak of complete sanctification (1 Thess. 5:23), perfection and completion (Col. 1:28; James 1:4), and the inability to sin (1 John 3:6, 9). But these are misinterpretations. In 1 Thessalonians 5:23, complete sanctification refers to sanctification in the entirety of man's nature, which Paul mentions explicitly in the next phrase ("your whole spirit and soul and body"). He is praying that God would sustain their faith throughout their life and finally bring his sanctifying work to completion, perfecting both the spirit/soul and the body at the return of Christ (cf. Phil. 3:21). Passages speaking of "perfection" refer not to total sanctification but to spiritual maturity, as the word is often translated elsewhere (e.g., 1 Cor. 2:6; Heb. 5:14). John's statements are rightly understood only when one properly translates the present tense of the verb. Rather than teaching that Christians never commit any acts of sin, he is teaching that no true believer continues in an unbroken lifestyle or pattern of sinning as he did in his unregenerate state. Indeed, John's other comments from the same letter emphatically exclude any notion of sinless perfection in this life (e.g., 1 John 1:8). James comments that "we all stumble in many ways" (James 3:2), and as we daily commit sin, the Lord Jesus instructs us to daily pray for forgiveness (Matt. 6:11–12; cf. 1 John 1:9). Far from seeking to attain spiritual perfection in this life, all believers ought to cry with Paul,

> *Not* that I have already obtained this or am already perfect, but I press on to make it my own, because Christ Jesus has made me his own. Brothers, I do not consider that I have made it my own. But one thing I do: forgetting what lies behind and straining forward to what lies ahead, I press on toward the goal for the prize of the upward call of God in Christ Jesus. (Phil. 3:12–14)

Then, in a display of apostolic irony, he adds the exhortation, "Let those of us who are mature"—the same word translated elsewhere as *perfect*—"think this way, and if in anything you think otherwise, God will reveal that also to you" (Phil. 3:15). Those who are "perfect" (i.e., truly spiritually mature) are those who realize they are not perfect and who acknowledge the constant need for actively pursuing personal holiness.

The Character of Progressive Sanctification[67]

So much of the confusion over how to properly and successfully pursue sanctification comes from fundamentally misunderstanding the nature of sanctification. Followers of Christ, therefore, must understand the character of this holiness that they are commanded to pursue. While several passages of Scripture must be consulted to clarify this truth, two foundational texts stand out as especially pertinent:

> Therefore, my beloved, as you have always obeyed, so now, not only as in my presence but much more in my absence, work out your own salvation with fear and trembling, for it is God who works in you, both to will and to work for his good pleasure. (Phil. 2:12–13)

> And we all, with unveiled face, beholding the glory of the Lord, are being transformed into the same image from one degree of glory to another. For this comes from the Lord who is the Spirit. (2 Cor. 3:18)

67 Much of this section is adapted from Michael Riccardi, *Sanctification: The Christian's Pursuit of God-Given Holiness* (Sun Valley, CA: Grace Books, 2015). Used by permission of Grace Books.

These and other texts establish several conclusions concerning the nature, author, means, and dynamics of progressive sanctification.

The Nature of Sanctification. Sanctification is fundamentally a supernatural work of God performed in the inner nature of man. Paul declares that God is at work *in* believers that they may not only work for his good pleasure but even will for his good pleasure (Phil. 2:13). That is to say, God works for the believer to sanctify not merely his external actions but also his internal desires. Further, Paul speaks of sanctification as the believer's "being transformed" into the image of Christ (2 Cor. 3:18), a term that describes an inward change in fundamental character (Rom. 12:2; Eph. 3:16). Commenting on Paul's exhortations for believers to be renewed in the spirit of their minds (Eph. 4:23), Charles Hodge rightly observes that

> sanctification . . . does not consist exclusively in a series of a new kind of acts. It is the making the tree good, in order that the fruit may be good. It involves an essential change of character. As regeneration is not an act of the subject of the work, but in the language of the Bible a new birth, a new creation, a quickening or communicating a new life, . . . so sanctification in its essential nature is not holy acts, but such a change in the state of the soul, that sinful acts become more infrequent, and holy acts more and more habitual and controlling.[68]

Therefore, believers should not conceive of holiness as the reformation of external behaviors, in which people bend their will to perform duties for which they have no Godward motive; rather, believers must recognize that sanctification consists fundamentally in the miraculous inward transformation of the affections. To use Hodge's metaphor, it is not taking fruit and stapling it to the tree branch but is rather rooting the branch in the vine so that the fruit is borne via the believer's vital union with Christ. While the holy person certainly does what God commands, he does so because he loves God and loves what God loves. Sanctification is the spiritual transformation of the mind and the affections that in turn redirects the will and the actions.

The Author of Sanctification. Since sanctification is not fundamentally external but internal and supernatural, its author must be God. Consistent with this, Paul states that "it is *God* who works in you, both to will and to work for his good pleasure" (Phil. 2:13). The God of peace equips his people to "do his will" and works in them "that which is pleasing in his sight" (Heb. 13:20–21). For this reason, Scripture often employs the passive voice in key texts on sanctification,

68 Charles Hodge, *Systematic Theology* (1871–1873; repr., Grand Rapids, MI: Eerdmans, 1968), 3:226.

commanding believers not to transform themselves but to *be transformed* (e.g., Rom. 12:2; 2 Cor. 3:18). As Berkhof concludes, sanctification "consists fundamentally and primarily in a *divine* operation in the soul."[69] More specifically, Scripture identifies the Holy Spirit as the member of the Godhead who is the divine agent of sanctification (Rom. 1:4; 2 Cor. 3:18; Gal. 5:17, 22–23; 1 Pet. 1:2).

The Means of Sanctification. While sanctification is properly said to be an internal work of the Spirit, the believer is not to be idle. Scripture is replete with exhortations and imperatives to pursue holiness. Paul commands the church to "work out your own salvation with fear and trembling" precisely because God is at work within them (Phil. 2:12–13). Peter declares that, on the basis of the work of Christ, believers have been granted "all things that pertain to life and godliness," and have "escaped from the corruption that is in the world because of sinful desire" (2 Pet. 1:3–4). And he follows these precious indicatives with a rousing call to action: "For this very reason, make every effort to supplement your faith with virtue" (2 Pet. 1:5). So far from being an excuse not to work, God's sanctifying work in believers is the very ground of our efforts. We are to "strive for . . . the holiness without which no one will see the Lord" (Heb. 12:14), to "put to death the deeds of the body" (Rom. 8:13), to "flee from sexual immorality" (1 Cor. 6:18), to "pursue righteousness" (2 Tim. 2:22), and even to "cleanse ourselves from every defilement of body and spirit, bringing holiness to completion in the fear of God" (2 Cor. 7:1).

Thus, while believers cannot directly effect the inner transformation of sanctification for their souls, and while sanctification is properly said to be the Spirit's work, believers are not passive in sanctification. Instead, the Holy Spirit effects his sanctifying transformation in the hearts of believers through the use of means that must be appropriated. The Scottish Puritan Henry Scougal provides an effective illustration:

> All the art and industry of man cannot form the smallest herb, or make a stalk of corn to grow in the field; it is the energy of nature, and the influences of heaven, which produce this effect; it is God "who causeth the grass to grow, and the herb for the service of man" (Ps. 104:14); and yet nobody will say that the labours of the [farmer] are useless or unnecessary.[70]

In other words, though God causes grass to grow and makes the land produce crops, only a foolish farmer passively waits for the land to yield its produce by divine fiat. Instead, he acknowledges that God brings forth fruits and vegetables

69 Berkhof, *Systematic Theology*, 532, italics added.

70 Henry Scougal, *The Life of God in the Soul of Man: Real Religion* (1677; repr., Fearn, Ross-shire, Scotland: Christian Focus, 2012), 78–79.

from the earth by means of a farmer's labors. Similarly, in and of himself, the believer is just as powerless to effect holiness in his heart, for it is the work of God. Yet only a foolish person waits passively for his heart to spring forth in righteousness by divine fiat. Instead, the faithful Christian acknowledges that God brings forth the fruit of holiness by means of the believer's labors. Scripture's repeated calls to effort, action, and obedience are commands for believers to put ourselves in the way of those channels of sanctifying grace that the Spirit employs to conform Christ's people into his image.

The means of sanctification include the following:

1. reading and meditating on the Word of God (Pss. 1:2–3; 19:7–11; 119:105; John 17:17; Acts 20:32; 2 Tim. 3:16–17; Heb. 4:12; James 1:23–25)
2. praying (Ps. 119:37; Luke 11:9; Phil. 4:6–7; Heb. 4:16; James 4:2; 1 John 1:9)
3. fellowshipping with the saints in the context of the local church (Prov. 27:17; 1 Cor. 12:7; Eph. 4:11–16, 25; Heb. 3:12–13; 10:24–25)
4. interpreting the experiences of God's providence according to Scripture (Rom. 8:28–29), especially the experience of trials (Ps. 119:71; Rom. 5:3–5; 8:17; Phil. 3:10–11; Heb. 12:10; James 1:2–4; 1 Pet. 1:3–7)
5. keeping the commandments of God (John 15:10)

Sanctifying grace flows through all these channels, and so it is the responsibility of Christians to put themselves in the way of these blessings. Though believers cannot perform the divine operation of sanctification on their own souls, they must nevertheless pursue holiness by availing themselves of the means by which the Spirit of God accomplishes this divine operation.

The Dynamics of Sanctification. The dynamics of sanctification speak to how sanctification actually works. Why does reading and studying the Word of God sanctify? How is prayer a means of grace? Why does fellowship with other believers push the people of God to greater holiness? Paul writes, "We all, . . . beholding the glory of the Lord, are being transformed" (2 Cor. 3:18). As believers in Christ behold his glory as revealed in the Word with the eyes of their heart (Eph. 1:18), they are thereby progressively conformed into his image (see also 2 Cor. 4:17–18; Heb. 11:1, 26–27; 12:2; 1 John 3:2). The foundational means of sanctification is the spiritual sight that beholds the glory of Christ. John Owen summarizes this biblical teaching:

> Let us live in the constant contemplation of the glory of Christ, and virtue will proceed from Him to repair all our decays, to renew a right spirit within us, and to cause us to abound in all duties of obedience. . . .
>
> It will fix the soul unto that object which is suited to give it delight, complacency, and satisfaction. . . .

> when the mind is filled with thoughts of Christ and his glory, when the soul thereon cleaves unto Him with intense affections, they will cast out, or not give admittance unto, those causes of spiritual weakness and indisposition. . . .
>
> And nothing will so much excite and encourage our souls hereunto as a constant view of Christ and His glory.[71]

In other words, when the believer apprehends the glory of Christ with the eyes of faith, the sight of his beauty satisfies the soul in such a way that he does not go on seeking satisfaction in the false and fleeting pleasures of sin. The spiritual apprehension of Christ's glory conforms believers' affections to the divine will, causing them to hate sin and love righteousness. Then, sanctified affections direct the will in such a way that it desires the righteousness it has come to love and repudiates the sin it has come to hate. Finally, the internal transformation is brought to fruition externally, as the sanctified will issues in holy living.

Therefore, as the believer avails himself of the various means by which he lays hold of the Spirit's sanctifying grace, he is to look with the eyes of faith to the transforming glory of Christ revealed through those means. The Word of God is a vehicle for the glory of God (Ex. 33:18; 34:5–7; 1 Sam. 3:1, 21). Prayer is the occasion for personal communion with God, in which the worshiper seeks God's face (2 Chron. 7:14; Pss. 24:6; 27:8; 105:4; Hos. 5:15) in order that he might behold his transforming beauty (Ps. 27:4). Fellowship in the local church is an opportunity to hear the Word preached skillfully, to sing songs of worship with sanctifying lyrics drawn from biblical truth, to pray corporately as the body of Christ, and to see the gospel pictured in the ordinances of baptism and communion. Besides this, to whatever degree Christians have been imperfectly conformed to the image of Christ (Rom. 8:29; 2 Cor. 3:18), to that degree they reflect the image of his glory to one another. Finally, obedience itself is the avenue for greater disclosure of the glory of Christ to the eyes of the heart (John 14:21). When confronted with temptations to sin, believers must reason with themselves, considering that sin never delivers the satisfaction it promises. They must consider that obedience brings fuller disclosures of the Savior, who is the source of all true pleasure and satisfaction. And out of a desire for the superior pleasure that is found in Christ, they must engage in (1) the work of mortification: putting to death the deeds of the body (Rom. 8:13), that is, laying aside the old self (Eph. 4:22) and the sin that so easily entangles (Heb. 12:1) and that clouds the sight of Christ's glory; and

71 John Owen, *Meditations and Discourses on the Glory of Christ*, in *The Works of John Owen*, vol. 1, *The Glory of Christ*, ed. William H. Goold (1854–1855; repr., Edinburgh: Banner of Truth, 1967), 460–61.

(2) the work of vivification: putting on the new self (Rom. 13:14; Eph. 4:24), that is, delightfully disciplining themselves to behold Christ in Scripture, prayer, fellowship, providence, and the obedience that brings deeper communion with him.

By fighting to behold the glory of Jesus by all the means of grace, the follower of Christ will be gradually transformed into his image from the inside out. He will therefore conduct himself in a manner worthy of the gospel (Phil. 1:27) and worthy of the Lord himself (Col. 1:10), working out his salvation with fear and trembling, just as Scripture commands (Phil. 2:12). As 2 Timothy 2:21 declares, "He will be a vessel for honorable use, set apart as holy, useful to the master of the house, ready for every good work."

PERSEVERANCE

Is salvation in Christ eternally secure? Do those who truly know Jesus Christ as Savior and Lord by faith persevere in that faith to the very end of their lives? Or is there a possibility that a genuine Christian could lose his or her salvation? Can those who genuinely trust Christ for salvation later abandon their faith and thus ultimately lose their eternal life? The unified teaching of the whole Scripture answers with an emphatic *no* to each of these questions. All those who are truly born of the Spirit and united to Christ by faith are kept secure in him by God's power and thus will persevere in faith until they go to be with Christ in death or when he returns. This doctrine is often labeled the perseverance of the saints.[72]

The Preserving Power of the Triune God

The eternal security of the true believer in Christ is ultimately founded on the preserving nature of the triune God.

The Sovereign Will of the Father. First, the believer's security is grounded in the unchanging love, infinite power, and saving will of the Father. Salvation began in eternity past, when God set his saving love on his elect and granted them grace in Christ Jesus (2 Tim. 1:9), appointing Christ to be their Mediator. Scripture describes this decree as the Father giving the elect to the Son (cf. John 6:37, 39; 10:29; 17:2, 6, 9, 24) and predestining them to become conformed to the Son's image (Rom. 8:29). It is impossible for those whom the Father has predestined to Christlikeness to fail to attain that end, for "those whom he predestined he also called, and those whom he called he also justified, and those whom he justified he also glorified" (Rom. 8:30). The final consummation of the believer's salvation is so certain and sure that Paul can speak of the justified one as if he has already been glorified. All those whom God chose he also justified on the ground of the

72 For a fuller treatment of the believer's security and assurance, see John MacArthur, *Saved without a Doubt: Being Sure of Your Salvation*, 3rd ed. (Colorado Springs: David C. Cook, 2011).

righteous work of the Son, and all those whom he justified he also glorified. It is impossible that one who has been united to Christ and granted his righteousness in justification will not be glorified as well, for the Father will not fail to carry out the fullness of his electing purpose to its designed end. None for whom Christ died is subject to condemnation (Rom. 8:31–34; cf. 8:1), and nothing in all creation can separate true believers from the love of God in Christ (Rom. 8:35–39).

The Lord Jesus makes this very point in John 6:37–40. The Father wills that Christ lose *none* of those whom he has given him, and that every elect believer will possess eternal life and will be raised to everlasting glory on the last day. And the Father's will cannot be overturned by anyone or anything (Job 42:2; Pss. 33:10–11; 115:3; Isa. 46:9–10; Dan. 4:35), for he is not only graciously disposed to his people but is also sovereignly powerful to accomplish his desired ends. As Jesus says, "I give [my sheep] eternal life, and they will never perish, and no one will snatch them out of my hand. My Father, who has given them to me, is greater than all, and no one is able to snatch them out of the Father's hand" (John 10:28–29). Using the strongest negative language available in the Greek language, Jesus emphatically declares that those who belong to Christ by faith "will never perish" (John 10:28) but will have eternal life (John 3:16). He grounds the eternal security of Christ's sheep in the sovereign power of the Father who holds them in his hand. The Father is so great and mighty that no one could snatch from his hand those whom he holds forever.

For this reason, Paul expresses his confidence that "he who began a good work in you will bring it to completion at the day of Jesus Christ" (Phil. 1:6). Quite simply, God finishes what he starts. Since it was the sovereign grace of the Father—not the free will of man—that *began* the work of salvation in the lives of sinners (cf. Acts 11:18; 16:14; Eph. 2:4–9; Phil. 1:29; James 1:18), so also will God exercise that same sovereign power to bring this great work to its completion. Believers can be confident that they will persevere by the preserving power of the Father.

The Merit of the Son. Second, the believer's security is grounded in the merits of Christ's saving work and the efficacy of his present intercession. No one may bring a charge against God's elect, because Christ has died, has been raised, and intercedes for his own (Rom. 8:33–34). This is the ground upon which no one will separate believers from Christ's love (Rom. 8:35–39). Further, the Son's redeeming work accomplishes its design with perfect efficacy. As their substitute, the Son of God stood in the place of elect sinners on the cross and bore the divine punishment for their sins (1 Pet. 2:24). In doing so, he has fully propitiated the Father's wrath against his people (Rom. 3:25; Heb. 2:17; 1 John 2:2; 4:10), purchasing them out of the slave market of sin with the price of his own blood (Acts 20:28; Rev. 5:9). Not only this, but the Father has also certified, by raising Christ from the dead, that his death sufficiently atoned for sin. The resurrection was the great vindication and validation of Christ (1 Tim. 3:16), verifying that the Father had approved of his completed work and that there was no more penalty left to pay, no more wrath left to bear for those who are in him. To suggest that sinners for whom Christ offered himself as a propitiation may yet suffer the eternal penalty of God's wrath is to demean the worth of his redemptive sacrifice and to contradict the Father's testimony in the resurrection. Further still, through the Spirit's application of Christ's redemptive work, the sinner is credited with Christ's righteousness in justification. It is unthinkable that the Spirit would apply only a portion of those saving benefits purchased by Christ's redemption; a soul declared righteous on the basis of Christ's work will never be stripped of that righteousness to undergo condemnation (Rom. 8:1; cf. Acts. 13:38–39).

Moreover, Christ not only has offered an infinitely worthy sacrifice on behalf of his people but he also presently intercedes for them before the Father (Rom. 8:34). He prays particularly to ensure the eternal salvation of the elect with an intercession that is always efficacious. Jesus does not save his people in a manner in which that salvation can be forfeited or lost; he saves "to the uttermost" (Heb. 7:25)—perfectly, completely, and eternally, ensuring that salvation will not be lost. When Satan had demanded to sift Peter like wheat, Jesus responded by assuring Peter, "But I have prayed for you that your faith may not fail" (Luke 22:31–32). Jesus's intercessory prayer is enough to ensure the preservation of Peter's salvation, for he continues, "And *when*"—not "if," but "when"—"you have turned again, strengthen your brothers" (Luke 22:32). All believers are the beneficiaries of their Great High Priest's perfectly efficacious intercession and thus are kept by the power of God (1 Pet. 1:5).

The Sealing of the Spirit. Third, the believer's security is grounded in the sealing ministry of the Holy Spirit. Paul writes, "In him you also, when you heard the word of truth, the gospel of your salvation, and believed in him, were sealed with the promised Holy Spirit, who is the guarantee of our inheritance until we acquire possession of it, to the praise of his glory" (Eph. 1:13–14; cf. 4:30). In Paul's day, affixing one's seal to something expressed the concepts of security, authentication, and ownership. God seals his people with the Holy Spirit himself, giving his own Spirit to personally indwell each believer as a pledge of the future inheritance of salvation (2 Cor. 1:22; 5:5). The word translated "pledge" is a commercial term that refers to an earnest or down payment which guarantees that the rest of the promised payment will follow. God would not affix his seal of ownership to his people, causing the Holy Spirit himself to indwell them as a pledge of his earnest faithfulness to bring them to their promised inheritance, and yet fail to secure them so as to deliver fully on his promise of eternal life.

The Persevering Faith of the Child of God

While all true believers are sovereignly preserved in their salvation by the almighty power of God, his sovereignty in no way eliminates their responsibility to persevere in faith throughout their lives. Just as God's sovereignty in conversion does not mitigate the responsibility to repent and believe (Rom. 9:14–18; cf. Rom. 10:11–21), and just as God's sovereignty in sanctification does not rule out the need for sustained effort in pursuing holiness (e.g., Phil. 2:12–13; 2 Pet. 1:3–5), so also God's sovereign preservation is not at odds with the necessity of the believer's perseverance. All true believers are "by God's power . . . being guarded through faith for a salvation ready to be revealed in the last time" (1 Pet. 1:5). God's power is the decisive preserving force, but his power keeps his people *through faith*—that is, through the continuing, persevering faith that works through love in every believer (Gal. 5:6).

Therefore, Scripture issues numerous calls to persevere in faith, indicating that failure to persevere will result in a failure to lay hold of final salvation (Matt. 10:22; Matt. 24:12–13; John 8:31). Those who do not abide in his Word are shown to be false disciples—or "false brothers" (2 Cor. 11:26; Gal. 2:4)—who claim to belong to Jesus but fail to bring forth the necessary fruit that gives evidence of genuine conversion. Christ will "present you holy and blameless and above reproach before [the Father], *if indeed you continue in the faith*, stable and steadfast, not shifting from the hope of the gospel that you heard, which has been proclaimed in all creation under heaven" (Col. 1:22–23; cf. Heb. 3:14). These passages clearly indicate that the professing believer must persevere in faith and obedience if he is to finally come to salvation. Scripture gives no warrant to assure professing Christians of eternal life whose lives do not exhibit the fruit of genuine faith (James 2:14–26).

An implication of this truth is that many people may give outward signs of devotion to Christ and his church who are inwardly not true Christians. Illustrated by the seed that fell on the rocky ground, some professing Christians seem to receive the Word of God joyfully. Yet they have no root, so when tribulation and persecution come, they fall away from Christ and abandon their profession of faith (Matt. 13:3–9, 18–23). Jesus warns that some who enthusiastically profess faith in Christ and even seem to exercise miraculous gifts of the Holy Spirit will come to the day of judgment expecting to inherit salvation but will instead be sent away to destruction (Matt. 7:21–23). Interestingly, Jesus does not say, "I knew you once, but you failed to persevere and fell away from the faith," but rather, "I *never* knew you." Those who make even the sincerest professions of faith but who fail to supplement their faith with the fruit of the Spirit (2 Pet. 1:5–10; Gal. 5:22–24) were never true Christians to begin with.

This is significant, because many object to the doctrine of the perseverance of the saints on the basis of experiencing a friend or relative who professed faith in Christ but later fell away. Experience, in concert with several passages of Scripture that threaten final perdition for failing to persevere, suggests to them that true Christians may actually lose their salvation. However, Scripture teaches that those who fail to persevere to the end reveal that they were never true Christians to begin with. The apostle John writes, "They went out from us"—which is to say, certain people associated themselves with the church yet later departed—"but they were not of us; for if they had been of us, they would have continued with us. But they went out, that it might become plain that they all are not of us" (1 John 2:19).

Assurance of Salvation[73]

How, then, can one be assured that he is a true believer in Christ and will not one day fall away, revealing that he was never a true believer at all? Scripture calls upon those who profess faith in Christ to examine themselves. Paul urges the Corinthians, "Examine yourselves, to see whether you are in the faith. Test yourselves" (2 Cor. 13:5). Peter similarly exhorts the churches in his care, "Therefore, brothers, be all the more diligent to confirm your calling and election" (2 Pet. 1:10). The apostle John dedicated his entire first epistle to the subject, stating his theme at the end: "I write these things to you who believe in the name of the Son of God, that you may know that you have eternal life" (1 John 5:13).

The authors of Scripture clearly desired that believers be assured of their salvation by examining their lives for evidence of genuine spiritual life. Consider the following eleven lines of evidence—largely drawn from the tests outlined in 1 John—by which Christians can gain assurance that their faith and salvation are genuine:

1. Fellowship with the Father and the Son through the Holy Spirit (1 John 1:3; 5:1; cf. Ps. 34:8; 1 Cor. 1:9; Gal. 2:20; Heb. 4:16)
2. The ministry of the Holy Spirit in the heart (1 John 2:27; 4:13; cf. 1 Cor. 2:10, 12; Gal. 5:22–23)
3. Answered prayer (1 John 3:22; 5:14)
4. Longing for Christ's return (1 Cor. 16:22; Phil. 3:20–21; 1 John 3:1–3)
5. Spiritual discernment (1 John 4:1–6; cf. 2:12–19)
6. Acute awareness of the holiness of God and the guilt of sin (1 John 1:5–10; cf. Rom. 7:14–15; 2 Cor. 7:10)
7. Decreasing patterns of sin (1 John 3:8–9; cf. Rom. 6:14–18)
8. Increasing patterns of obedience (1 John 2:3; cf. John 8:31)
9. Rejection of worldliness (1 John 2:15; cf. James 4:4)
10. Being rejected by the world (1 John 3:13; cf. Matt. 5:10–12; John 3:19–20; 15:18–21; Phil. 1:29; 2 Tim. 3:12; 1 Pet. 4:12–14)
11. Love for fellow Christians (1 John 2:9–11; 3:10, 16–19; cf. John 13:35; 1 Thess. 4:9)

73 This section is adapted from MacArthur, *Saved without a Doubt*, 67–91. Used by permission of David C. Cook. All rights reserved.

GLORIFICATION

The final divine act in the application of redemption is glorification.[74] Glorification is the radical transformation of both the body and the soul of believers, perfecting them in holiness, and thereby fitting them for eternal life on the new earth in perfect communion with the triune God. Murray helpfully describes glorification as "the complete and final redemption of the whole person, when in the integrity of body and spirit, the people of God will be conformed to the image of the risen, exalted, and glorified Redeemer, when the very body of their humiliation will be conformed to the body of Christ's glory" (cf. Phil. 3:21).[75]

The Consummation of Salvation

The resurrection of the body is the consummation of our salvation, the climax of redemption, as the Spirit brings to completion the redemption that the Father planned and that Christ purchased (Rom. 8:19–23, 30). Those on whom the Father set his electing love he predestined for salvation, and these—whose redemption Christ purchased by dying in their place as a propitiation for their sins—enjoy the benefits of that redemption. In justification, they are freed from the penalty of sin, and in sanctification, they are freed from the power of sin. In glorification, they are finally freed from the very presence of sin in both body and soul (John 17:24; Eph. 5:27; cf. John 6:39–40, 44, 54). In this way, glorification especially magnifies Christ as the preeminent source of the beauty of holiness that is reflected in his perfected brethren (Rom. 8:29).

The doctrine of glorification is essential to the Christian faith, so much so that if it were not true we would be the most pitiable of all people (1 Cor. 15:12–19). It was the hope of a glorified body that galvanized Paul to totally surrender his natural body to the mistreatment and persecution that attended a life of gospel ministry (2 Cor. 5:1; cf. 4:14–18). The "sufferings of this present time are not worth comparing with the glory that is to be revealed to us," and so believers welcome the sufferings of Christ if it means that "we may also be glorified with him" (Rom. 8:17–18; cf. Phil. 3:10–11). Therefore, while life in a world and in a body that are both cursed by sin causes us to groan, that groaning is assuaged by the eager anticipation of "the redemption of our bodies" (Rom. 8:23).

An ageless anchor of the soul, the resurrection was the hope of even old covenant believers in Yahweh (Job 19:13–27; Dan. 12:2; John 11:24; Acts 24:14–15; Heb. 11:16). Standing on that Old Testament foundation, the reader can view

74 This brief treatment of glorification concerns the doctrine of the resurrection from a soteriological perspective. For further discussion of the resurrection in the context of eschatology, including the timing of the events, the effect on the physical creation, and the destiny of unbelievers, see chap. 10, "The Future."

75 Murray, *Redemption Accomplished and Applied*, 175.

the New Testament Epistles' explicit teaching on the resurrection of the body as a welcome elaboration and development of the ancient and living hope of the people of God. Paul reveals that as the condemnation of Adam brought the whole human race guilt and corruption unto death, in the same way, union with the second Adam will cause all believers to overcome sin and death and to be made alive in him (1 Cor. 15:22, 45). This takes place "each in his own order: Christ the firstfruits, then at his coming those who belong to Christ. Then comes the end" (1 Cor. 15:23–24; cf. 1 Thess. 4:13–17). Indeed, the dead in Christ and those alive at his coming will be glorified in the twinkling of an eye at his return (1 Cor. 15:51–53). At that time, death itself—the very last enemy—will be destroyed (1 Cor. 15:26; cf. Acts 2:24; Heb. 2:14–15; Rev. 1:17–18), which will be cause for victorious celebration:

> When the perishable puts on the imperishable, and the mortal puts on immortality, then shall come to pass the saying that is written:
>
> "Death is swallowed up in victory."
> "O death, where is your victory?
> O death, where is your sting?"
>
> The sting of death is sin, and the power of sin is the law. But thanks be to God, who gives us the victory through our Lord Jesus Christ. (1 Cor. 15:54–57)

We rejoice in the hope of the glory of God (Rom. 5:2) and bless the God and Father of our Lord Jesus Christ, because he, according to his great mercy, has caused us to be born again to this living hope of "an inheritance that is imperishable, undefiled, and unfading, kept in heaven for [us], who by God's power are being guarded through faith for a salvation ready to be revealed in the last time" (1 Pet. 1:3–5).

In the face of so great a salvation, spanning from eternity past to eternity future, the only fitting conclusion is to add our voices to the heavenly chorus—that "great multitude that no one could number, from every nation, from all tribes and peoples and languages, standing before the throne and before the Lamb, clothed in white robes, with palm branches in their hands" (Rev. 7:9). We must cry out in worship along with them, "Salvation belongs to our God who sits on the throne, and to the Lamb!" (Rev. 7:10). Thanks be to God for his inexpressible gift!

Questions:

1. What is the "Trinitarian plan of salvation"?
2. What is the twofold cause of the atonement?
3. What is meant by "penal substitutionary" atonement?

4. Why is "obedience" the unifying principle that encompasses the facets of Christ's atoning work?
5. What is the meaning and significance of these terms for the atonement: sacrifice; propitiation; reconciliation; redemption; conquest?
6. In what ways is the atonement "sufficient" and "efficacious"?
7. What are the various terms used to describe views regarding the extent of the atonement?
8. What does the unity of the High Priestly work of Christ indicate about the extent of the atonement?
9. What does the argument of Romans 8:29–39 indicate about the extent of the atonement?
10. How does each side of the debate over the extent of the atonement understand these texts: 1 Timothy 2:3–6; John 3:16; 1 John 2:2?
11. What is the *ordo salutis*?
12. What is the "external call"?
13. What is the "internal call"?
14. What is the definition and significance of "regeneration"?
15. What are the key parts of "conversion"?
16. What are the components of saving faith? (Latin terms)
17. What is meant by "union with Christ"?
18. Why is "justification by faith alone" so significant?
19. What is the nature of, and the ground of, justification?
20. What is the definition and what are the key features of these terms/concepts: adoption; sanctification; perseverance; glorification?

8

ANGELS

Angelology

Introduction to Angels

Theologies typically ignore or only minimally treat angelology. However, the Bible contains a great amount of information about spirit beings, including Satan and the angel of the Lord. Therefore, this section attempts to summarize what Scripture reveals regarding the holy and evil angels.

The Biblical Reality of Angels

The Old Testament Hebrew word *mal'akh* and the New Testament Greek word *angelos* can generally be translated "messenger," "envoy," or "ambassador" when referring to humans, but are usually translated as "angel" when referring to nonhuman, supernatural, created beings. The context in which these words appear determines whether they refer to (1) humans, (2) holy angels, (3) Satan, (4) demons, or (5) the angel of the Lord.

Scripture accounts for the history of the holy and evil angels, including Satan. God created all the angels (Neh. 9:6; Ps. 148:2–5; Col. 1:16) at the outset of his creation of the earth (cf. Job 38:4–7). Satan's fall (Ezek. 28:15) and the demons' rebellion (Rev. 12:4) would have occurred after Genesis 2 (the seventh day of creation) but before Genesis 3 (Eve's deception and Adam's disobedience).

The undeniable existence of angels can be substantiated by the hundreds of references to them in Scripture, from Genesis 3:24 to Revelation 22:16.

In the Old Testament, the largest category of references speaks of human messengers, with references to the "angel of the Lord" a close second, and only

24 occasions refer to holy angels. Neither Satan nor demons are referred to as "angels" in the Old Testament.

In the New Testament, the term "angel" appears in the Gospels, with heavy emphasis in Matthew and Luke, while Acts, the Epistles, and Hebrews record several occurrences. By far, the book of Revelation uses "angel" or "angels" more than any other New Testament section. Unlike the Old Testament, the New Testament use of the term for "angel" or "messenger" is in relation to holy angels, though some references to humans, demons, Satan, and the angel of the Lord are also in view.

The Bible includes only 26 specific historical encounters with angels (10 in the Old Testament and 16 in the New Testament). The events began with Abraham in Genesis 18 and continued until the time of John's prophetic visions in Revelation, covering a total of about 2,100 years, from ca. 2015 BC to ca. AD 95.

The Nature of Angels and Demons

SPIRITUAL QUALITIES OF ANGELS AND DEMONS

Both the holy and evil angels are immaterial spirit beings (Heb. 1:14; cf. Luke 24:39), and as such they are not bound by physical space. Scripture attests that these spirit beings are able to travel between heaven to earth (Gen. 28:12; John 1:51; cf. Dan. 9:20–23; 10:1–13, 20; Rev. 12:4, 9), and demons can take up residence in an unregenerate person (Matt. 12:43–45; Mark 1:34; cf. 1 Pet. 5:8). Holy angels have even appeared visibly (Gen. 18:2; Num. 22:31; 2 Kings 6:15–17; John 20:11–12; cf. Heb. 13:2).

From their creation (Job 38:4–7) through the end of Daniel's seventieth week, holy angels reside in the heavenly realm of God's presence, the "third heaven," or paradise (2 Cor. 12:2–3; cf. Ps. 123:1). When Christ returns to earth for his millennial reign, the angels that accompany him will serve his purposes on the earth (Matt. 25:31). Those who remain in worshipful service to God in the third heaven will reside with God and all the redeemed in the new heaven and new earth (Rev. 20:1–22:21, esp. 21:12). Demons, meanwhile, carry out their evil plans on the earth in submission to Satan, who roams the earth (1 Pet. 5:8).

In the heavenly sphere, holy angels constantly do battle with demons (Dan. 10:13, 20–21; Rev. 12:7–9). Also, as spirit beings, holy angels are "greater in might and power" than humans (2 Pet. 2:11). They seem exceptionally strong and have power to strike or slay humans, and to rescue or destroy (Gen. 19:1–26; 2 Sam. 24:10–17; 2 Kings 19:35; Isa. 37:36; Acts 12:20–23).

Nevertheless, no spirit being is omnipotent like God (Ps. 103:20; 2 Pet. 2:11), omniscient like God (Matt. 24:36), or omnipresent like God (Dan. 9:21–23; 10:10, 14).

POPULATION OF ANGELS AND DEMONS

Because angels neither procreate (Matt. 22:30) nor die, they have a fixed population from the time of their creation (Neh. 9:6). Revelation 12:4 indicates that evil angels constitute one-third of the angelic population, while elect angels make up two-thirds. The Bible nowhere places an exact number on the quantity of angels, so it is beyond our understanding.

The number of holy angels is exceeding incalculable (Deut. 33:2; Ps. 68:17; Dan. 7:10; Jude 14). Their population appears innumerable (Heb. 12:22): the host of heaven (2 Chron. 18:18; Pss. 103:21; 148:2) are like the stars (1 Kings 22:19), a multitude (Luke 2:13) of thousands of thousands (Rev. 5:11; cf. Matt. 26:53). Needless to say, there is no shortage of holy angels at God's disposal to carry out his will and to render appropriate worship and praise to their Creator.

Within their populations, angels and demons function according to powerful organizational hierarchies described by terms such as "authorities," "rulers," "powers," "dominions," and "thrones" (Rom. 8:38; 1 Cor. 15:24; Eph. 1:21; 2:2; 3:10; 6:12; Col. 1:16; 2:15; 1 Pet. 3:22). Scripture does not fully explain the order or function of these holy or evil hierarchies.

MORAL QUALITIES OF ANGELS AND DEMONS

All angels were created morally pure. Holy angels remain so in perpetuity, being called holy (Mark 8:38; Luke 9:26), elect angels (1 Tim. 5:21), sons of God (Job 1:6; 2:1), who do not need redemption from a fallen state (Heb. 2:14–16) and cannot die in the future (Luke 20:36).

Demons, on the other hand, are called unclean, lying, and evil spirits (1 Kings 22:22–23; Matt. 8:16; 10:1; Luke 7:21; Gal. 1:8). The fall of the demons appears to be described in Ezekiel 28:15, in an extended prophetic look at Satan—"You were blameless in your ways from the day you were created, till unrighteousness was found in you." The rebellion of these angels must have occurred between Genesis 2 and 3, sometime on Day 7 or after (cf. Gen. 1:31—the creation of all angels was among that which was "very good").

Holy angels will not face any judgment because they will never sin. Satan and his demons, however, will be judged at the final judgment for their immoral deeds (Matt. 25:41; 2 Pet. 2:4; Jude 6; Rev. 20:10). Indeed, they have already lost the battle over the souls of believers because "greater is he who is in [believers] than he who is in the world" (1 John 4:4 NASB). The original judgment on demons for their initial rebellion (Rev. 12:4) seems to have had several variations: one group was cast directly into the Abyss (2 Pet. 2:4; Jude 6; cf. Luke 8:31), and part of this group will be released in the middle of Daniel's seventieth week (Rev. 9:1–11); a special group of four demons were bound at the Euphrates River and will be released at the end of Daniel's seventieth week (Rev. 9:13–15); the other demons who were cast down with Satan will continue to do his treacherous bidding, but will be imprisoned with him during Christ's millennial reign, then released and eternally judged (Isa. 24:21–22; Matt. 25:41; 2 Pet. 2:4; Jude 6; Rev. 12:7–10).

PERSONHOOD OF ANGELS AND DEMONS

Holy angels possess the three identifiable traits of personhood. First, they possess intellect, as exhibited by their wisdom, singing, discourse, worship (2 Sam. 14:20; Matt. 28:5; Job 38:7; Heb. 1:6), and the ability to speak any human language. Second, they possess emotions, as seen in their joy over the repentance of sinners and their worshipful fear of God (Ps. 148:2; Luke 2:13–14; 15:10; Heb. 1:6). Third, they possess will, as demonstrated by their strong desire to understand things related to salvation (1 Pet. 1:10–12).

Demons also possess intellect (Matt. 8:29; Mark 1:24; Luke 8:26–39), including the ability to speak any human language and to author false doctrine (1 Tim. 4:1). Additionally, they express affections (Matt. 8:29; Mark 1:24; 5:7; James 2:19) and an evil will (Matt. 8:31).

As spirit beings, angels and demons are without gender and cannot reproduce after their own kind (Matt. 22:30; Mark 12:25; Luke 20:35–36). When holy angels do appear in Scripture, however, they look like men, not women (Gen. 18:2; Dan. 10:16, 18; Mark 16:5).

The Roles and Activities of Angels and Demons

HOLY ANGELS

Holy Angels are messengers of God's truth (Rev. 1:1). They are referred to in Scripture by seventeen names and titles that define their nature and function as "messengers." Five of these references are provided below.[1]

1. *Archangel* (Dan. 10:13; 1 Thess. 4:16; Jude 9): Since Daniel refers to Michael as "one of the chief princes" (the Old Testament equivalent of "archangel"), there are at least two.

2. *Cherubim* (Gen. 3:24; Ex. 25:18–22; 37:8; Ezek. 1:4–28; 10:1–20; 28:14, 16): This title expresses diligent guardianship, as depicted in a handful of accounts. For example, Ezekiel wrote that Satan was originally a "guardian cherub" (Ezek. 28:14,

1 For a full list of the names, titles, and functions of angels, see John MacArthur and Richard Mayhue, gen. eds., *Biblical Doctrine* (Wheaton, IL: Crossway, 2017), 668–70.

16); a cherub guarded the garden of Eden (Gen. 3:24); two cherubs were fashioned on the mercy seat as guarding the ark of the covenant (Ex. 25:18–22; 37:8; cf. Heb. 9:5); and the twelve angels at the twelve gates of the new Jerusalem are likely cherubim (Rev. 21:12). The four living creatures of Ezekiel 1:5–14 are later identified as cherubim (Ezek. 10:20–22).

3. *Seraphim* (Isa. 6:2, 6): This kind of angel appears only in Isaiah 6. With a name meaning "burning ones," at least two seraphim (v. 3) were concerned with God's holiness. Some have thought that cherubim, living creatures, and seraphim might be different versions of the same kind of angel.

4. *Living creatures* (Rev. 4:6; 19:4): The living creatures in Revelation 4:8, in distinction from those in Ezekiel 1:5–14, look and act like seraphim (Isa. 6:1–4) in that they have six wings and are involved in noteworthy worship (Rev. 4:6–11; 5:6–14; 7:11; 14:3; 19:4) as well as judgment (Rev. 6:1–7; 15:7).

5. *Morning stars* (Job 38:7): Satan is called "Day Star" (Isa. 14:12), and angels in general are called "stars of heaven" (Rev. 12:4).

Holy angels perform several notable activities to the glory of the triune God.

1. Worshiping, praising, and serving God in heaven (Isa. 6:1–7; Job 1:6; 2:1; 38:7; Rev. 4:6–11; 5:8–13; 7:11–12)
2. Serving Jesus in his earthly life and ministry (Matt. 2:13; 4:11; Luke 22:43; John 1:51)
3. Proclaiming God's messages of the truth (Dan. 8:16; 9:21; 10:13–14; Luke 1:19, 26–38; Acts 7:38, 53; Gal. 3:19; Heb. 2:2; Rev. 1:1; 14:6–7)
4. Acting as instruments of judgment on individuals (Matt. 13:41–42; 16:27; 2 Thess. 1:7–8), cities (Gen. 19:1, 12–13), and nations (Rev. 8:6–11:19; 12:7–9; 16:1–21), and in the imprisonment of Satan (Rev. 20:1–3)
5. Comforting and protecting believers (Dan. 10:19; Pss. 34:7; 35:5–6; 91:11–12; Matt. 18:10; Heb. 1:14), and being involved in the church (1 Cor. 4:9; 11:10; 1 Tim. 5:21)
6. Serving at Christ's second coming (Matt. 16:27; 25:31; 1 Thess. 4:16; 2 Thess. 1:7)
7. Acting as a witness in and to the church (1 Cor. 4:9; 1 Tim. 5:21) and to the mystery that is the salvation of fallen man (1 Pet. 1:12)

DEMONS

Old and New Testament names and descriptive titles for demons reveal much about their evil allegiance and nature. Some of these are listed below:

1. *Demon.* The Hebrew language did not have one word that uniformly referred to demons, but the Greek Old Testament (the Septuagint) uses the New Testament word for demon (*daimonion*) eight times to translate

several different Hebrew terms referring to demonic activity or idolatrous and immoral worship (Deut. 32:17; Ps. 91:6, cf. "Abaddon" and "Apollyon," Rev. 9:11; Pss. 96:5; 106:37; Isa. 13:21; 34:14; 65:3 NASB; 65:11, cf. "cup" and "table" of "demons," 1 Cor. 10:21). In Greek, the term occurs sixty-three times with few variations, making the term common and consistent for evil spiritual beings in the New Testament.

2. *Angel.* Demons are understood as "messengers" associated with Satan and evil (Matt. 25:41; 2 Cor. 12:7; 2 Pet. 2:4; Jude 6: Rev. 12:7, 9).
3. *Spirit* (Matt. 8:16; 12:45; Mark 9:17, 20; Luke 9:39; 10:20; 11:26; Acts 16:16, 18; Rev. 16:14). This is the essential characteristic of all angels—both elect and evil. Twenty-three times demons are described as morally impure by the title "unclean spirits" (Matt. 10:1–Rev. 18:2).
4. *Lying or deceitful spirit.* The "lying spirit" (2 Chron. 18:21) is Satan, "the father of lies" (John 8:44). Satan dispatches lying spirits (demons) to give false messages and disseminate false doctrines (1 Kings 22:22–23; 2 Chron. 18:22; 1 Tim. 4:1).
5. *Prince of Greece*, *Prince of Persia* (Dan. 10:13, 20). It appears that the ruling world power of Persia, and its conqueror Greece (Dan. 8:1–8, 20–22), each had a demon that influenced the human leadership of those nations. This demon did battle with Michael, the chief holy angel and defender of Israel (Dan. 10:21; 11:2; 12:1; cf. Jude 9; Rev. 12:7). However, these few verses do not support the erroneous teaching of territorial demons worldwide.
6. *Host of heaven.* This term can speak of evil angels (Deut. 4:19; 17:2–3; 2 Kings 17:16; 21:3, 5; 23:4–5; Isa. 24:21–22; 34:4) but can also be used for the physical bodies in the sky (Ps. 33:6; Isa. 40:26) and holy angels (1 Kings 22:19; Neh. 9:6; Luke 2:13).
7. *Star.* This generic term for all angels, both holy and evil, is used in the context of Revelation 12:4 to describe one-third of all angels rejecting God and aligning themselves with Satan.

Demons carry out several evil actions, including the following:

1. indwell humans and animals (Mark 5:1–16)
2. physically afflict people (Mark 9:17, 22)
3. terrorize humans (1 Sam. 16:14–15; 18:10; 19:9; Acts 19:13–16; 2 Cor. 12:7)
4. initiate false worship (1 Cor. 10:20–21)
5. promote false doctrines (1 Tim. 4:1)
6. perform false signs and wonders (2 Thess. 2:9; Rev. 16:13–14)
7. deceive prophets (1 Kings 22:19–23)

8. encourage idolatry (Deut. 32:17; Ps. 106:37)
9. engineer death (Judg. 9:23, 56–57)

However strong demons might be, they also have serious weaknesses and vulnerabilities:

1. They unwittingly serve God's purposes (Judg. 9:23).
2. They were terrified of Christ and the gospel (Matt. 8:29; Mark 1:24; James 2:19).
3. They obeyed Christ (Matt. 8:32), the Twelve (Matt. 10:1–8), and the Seventy-Two (Luke 10:17–20).
4. They cannot separate believers in Christ from the love of God (Rom. 8:38).
5. They can be restrained by the Holy Spirit (2 Thess. 2:6; 1 John 4:4).
6. They have been judged already by God (2 Pet. 2:4; Jude 6) and will be judged again in the future (Rev. 20:10).

DEMONIC INDWELLING AND AFFLICTION

Perhaps the most controversial question regarding demons is whether a true believer can be demonized. Since Satan cannot control the total life of one who is indwelt by the Holy Spirit, the question is whether Satan, through his demons, can exercise direct, partial control over an area of the life of a Christian. Formulating a conclusive biblical statement requires lexical, biblical, historical, theological, and practical approaches.

Along lexical lines, the New Testament describes demonic influence on humans with four phrases. The first two total 29 of the 32 occurrences: one "having" a demon and one who is "demonized." The other two phrases—"with an unclean spirit," and one "afflicted" with an unclean spirit—imply demonization. The fact that demons can "enter in," "go out," or be "cast out" (Matt. 8:16, 32; 9:33; 12:22–24; Mark 1:34; 5:8, 13) speaks to the degree of powerful control a demon can exert within the body of a demonized person. All 32 New Testament occurrences therefore refer to demonic possession rather than any lesser form of demonic influence, such as demon oppression or harassment.

There are 15 biblical accounts of demonic indwelling (4 specific incidents in the Old Testament and 11 in the New Testament). Scripture does not seem to support the idea that true believers can experience internal demon possession. Two instances of potential demonic indwelling have been debated. One concerns Saul in the Old Testament (cf. 1 Samuel 16; 18; and 19), who was "the Lord's anointed one" (1 Sam. 24:6, 10), who appeared at times to be a man of faith. Scripture records that Saul was tormented by demons, who were "upon" him (1 Sam. 16:23; 18:10; 19:9), but this does not suggest that the evil or harmful spirit existed *within* Saul.

The other instance concerns the woman bent double in Luke 13:10–17, who was suffering from "sickness caused by a spirit" (Luke 13:11). Although Jesus referred to her as "a daughter of Abraham" (Luke 13:16), it seems this is a simple designation of her Jewish ethnicity without regard to her personal faith in God. Thus, there is not one instance in Scripture where Satan or demons resided within a true believer and needed to be expelled.

Theologically, the New Testament epistles never warn believers about the possibility of demon inhabitation or about how to cast them out, even though Satan and demons are discussed rather frequently. Other theological factors confirm the conclusion that a true believer cannot be indwelt by demons:

- Cohabitation of the Holy Spirit with unclean spirits in a true believer is inconceivable (cf. 2 Cor. 6:14–18), especially in view of the Spirit's protective sealing (2 Cor. 1:21–22; Eph. 4:30).
- The believer is "delivered" from Satan and transferred to Christ's kingdom (Col. 1:13).
- Victorious conquest in Christ leaves no room for the Evil One to hold dominion in a believer's life (Rom. 8:37–39; 1 Cor. 15:57; 2 Cor. 2:14; 1 John 2:13–14; 4:4).
- The idea of demon invasion in the life of a true believer is unbiblical according to the promise of 1 John 5:18.

Practically speaking, casting out demons is necessary because demons do at times reside within people, and the result is the unyielding control of its victim. Scripture describes some of the results as epilepsy (Matt. 17:14–18), blindness (Matt. 12:22), deafness (Mark 9:25), and mutism (Matt. 9:32–33). Eviction results in healing from such afflictions. If one encounters a truly demonized person, then he must recognize the strength of the Enemy, appeal to God in prayer (see Jude 9), and use the power of Scripture (Rom. 1:16)—especially the gospel—to deal with the situation. Nevertheless, true believers have no need of demonic deliverance because the Bible convincingly reveals that true believers cannot be inhabited by Satan or demons. They can, however, be tormented, oppressed, and harassed externally, even to a severe degree (cf. 2 Cor. 12:7).

Satan

The reality of evil indicates the existence of an actual perpetrator of evil. The biblical witness affirms and describes that perpetrator as Satan in 8 Old Testament (27 occurrences) and 19 New Testament books (74 occurrences).

Satan was created as the "anointed guardian cherub," a chief angel who served in God's presence (Ezek. 28:13–16). Satan now rebelliously leads a band of evil angels (Matt. 25:41; Rev. 12:9), disguising himself as an angel of light (2 Cor. 11:14).

Satan exhibits the three basic characteristics associated with personhood: intellect (Matt. 4:1–11; 2 Cor. 2:11; Eph. 6:11; 1 Tim. 3:7; 2 Tim. 2:26), affection (1 Tim. 3:6; Rev. 12:12, 17), and will (Luke 22:31; 2 Tim. 2:26).

As a spirit being (1 Kings 22:21–23; 2 Chron. 18:20–22; Eph. 2:2), Satan can appear at times like a physical person (Matt. 4:3–11) and possesses an extraordinary mobility to travel between heaven and earth (Job 1:7; 2:2; 1 Pet. 5:8) to do his evil work in both realms (1 Kings 22:21–22; Job 1–2; Matt. 4:3–11; Rev. 12:10).

Satan possesses the highest power of created beings. His power is at least equal to that of Michael the archangel (Dan. 10:13, 21; 12:1; Jude 9; Rev. 12:7). No human being possesses the supernatural power that belongs to Satan. He is powerful in heaven (1 Kings 22:19–23; 2 Chron. 18:18–22; Job 1–2; Zech. 3:1–5; Rev. 12:7) and on earth (Job 1:7; 1 Pet. 5:8). Nevertheless, Satan possesses none of the divine attributes of his Creator, such as omnipotence, omniscience, omnipresence, immutability, or sovereignty. In fact, Satan's power is limited by God (Job 1:6–12; 2:1–6), rejected by Christ (Matt. 4:1–11; Acts 10:38), overcome by believers (James 4:7; 1 John 2:13–14; cf. Acts 26:18), and will be permanently revoked (1 Cor. 15:24; Rev. 12:9–10; 20:1–3, 7–10).

SATAN'S CHARACTER

Various names and titles for the Evil One warn of his diabolical character and intentions. Such attributions include the following:

1. *Satan.* This name appears across the Old and New Testaments, meaning "adversary," "enemy," or "opposition." He has been the chief initiator, instigator, and perpetrator of evil aggression both against and within the purposes and plans of God.
2. *Devil.* This is the second-most-used term for Satan in the Bible, referring to his slanderous accusations against true believers (Job 1–2 [Septuagint]; Zech. 3:1) and ultimately against God.
3. *Evil One.* This is the third-most-frequent name used for the Enemy (Matt. 5:37; 6:13; 13:19, 38; John 17:15; Eph. 6:16; 2 Thess. 3:3; 1 John 2:13–14; 3:12; 5:18–19). Satan's evil character stands in contrast to Christ's righteousness. The transliterated Hebrew word "Belial" (Deut. 13:13; Judg. 19:22; 1 Sam. 2:12; 1 Kings 21:13; Prov. 6:12; Nahum 1:15) refers to vile, wicked, and worthless scoundrels and troublemakers, and is applied to the Evil One, whose wickedness is unrivaled (2 Cor. 6:15). It is nothing short of ironic that Satan stands as the "accuser of our brethren" before

God to charge believers as being unworthy of God's grace in redemption and service (Zech. 3:1; Rev. 12:10).

4. *Lucifer.* Tradition has popularized this title, appearing in the KJV/NKJV in reference to the "light bearer," "day star," or "son of the dawn" in Isaiah 14:12. The title, in context, seems to describe the king of Babylon but also to describe Satan by extension. Revelation 9:1 portrays Satan as a "star fallen from heaven," and Revelation 9:11 identifies him as "king" over demons, who themselves are pictured as having been created as "stars of heaven" (Job 38:7; Rev. 12:4).
5. *Serpent.* The imagery of the crafty serpent of old (Gen. 3:1, 4, 13–14) is unmistakably identified with the Devil or Satan on four later occasions (Isa. 27:1; 2 Cor. 11:3; Rev. 12:9; 20:2). This figure is apocalyptically envisioned as a dragon (Isa. 27:1; Rev. 12:3, 7, 9; 20:2), Leviathan, the fleeing and twisting serpent (Isa. 27:1).
6. *God of this world.* The title "god" (2 Cor. 4:4; cf. Ps. 82:6) reflects Satan's position, not his nature, as he is not deity. By God's sovereign ordinance, Satan is granted superior power and position on the earth (1 John 5:19), empowering all false religions (Rev. 2:9; 3:9) and reigning over demons (Matt. 9:34; 12:24; Mark 3:22; Luke 11:15; Eph. 2:2; Rev. 9:11). The name "Beelzebul," from the patron deity of the coastal Philistine city of Ekron (2 Kings 1:2–3), means "lord, prince" and refers to Satan's authority over his evil angels (Matt. 12:24; Mark 3:22; Luke 11:15).
7. *Abaddon* (Rev. 9:11). This transliterated Hebrew word is associated with death and destruction in the Old Testament (Job 26:6; 28:22; 31:12; Ps. 88:11; Prov. 15:11; 27:20). Its Greek counterpart, "Apollyon," refers to Satan as the angelic king with dominion over demons in the bottomless pit in Revelation 9:11.

SATAN'S ACTIVITY IN HISTORY

Scripture recounts very few specific historical events involving Satan, but the instances well represent his ever-active diabolical pattern as "ruler of this world" (John 12:31; 14:30; 16:11), who is constantly at work on earth during the present age. Satan's continual activities as recorded in Scripture include the following:

- He "prowls around like a roaring lion, seeking someone to devour" (1 Pet. 5:8).
- He tells lies (John 8:44) and influences people to lie (Acts 5:3).
- He disguises himself as an angel of light (2 Cor. 11:13–15).
- He snatches the gospel from unbelieving hearts (Matt. 13:19; Mark 4:15; Luke 8:12).

- He holds unbelievers under his power (Eph. 2:2; 1 John 3:8–10; 5:19).
- He traps and deceives unbelievers, holding them captive to do his will (2 Tim. 2:26).
- He tempts believers to sin (1 Cor. 7:5; Eph. 4:27).
- He seeks to deceive the children of God (2 Cor. 11:3).
- He takes advantage of believers (2 Cor. 2:11).
- He seeks to destroy the faith of believers (Luke 22:31).
- He torments the servants of God (2 Cor. 12:7).
- He thwarts the progress of ministry (1 Thess. 2:18).
- He wages war against the church (Eph. 6:11–17).

Old Testament references to Satan include the following:

1. Creation of Satan: beginning of creation (Neh. 9:6; Job 38:7; Ps. 148:2, 5; Ezek. 28:13, 15; Col. 1:16)
2. Moral fall of Satan: post-creation (Isa. 14:12–13; Rev. 12:4)
3. Deception of Eve: post–moral fall (Gen. 3:1–6; 2 Cor. 11:1–3; 1 Tim. 2:14; Rev. 12:9; 20:2)
4. Edenic curse: post-deception (Gen. 3:15; John 16:11; Rom. 16:20)
5. Accusing Job (Job 1–2)
6. Dispute with Michael (Jude 9)
7. Provocation of David (1 Chron. 21:1)
8. Lying to Ahab (1 Kings 22:1–40; 2 Chron. 18:1–34)
9. Influencing the king of Babylon (Isa. 14:12–14)
10. Influencing the king of Tyre (Ezek. 28:12–17)
11. Accusing the high priest (Zech. 3:1–2)

New Testament references involving Satan include the following:

1. Birth of Christ (Rev. 12:4)
2. Temptation of Christ (Matt. 4:1–11; Mark 1:12–13; Luke 4:1–13)
3. Debilitating a woman (Luke 13:16)
4. Sifting of Peter (Luke 22:31)
5. Defection of Judas (Luke 22:3; John 13:2, 27)
6. Influencing the lie of Ananias (Acts 5:3)
7. Hindering Paul (1 Thess. 2:18)
8. Inflicting Paul (2 Cor. 12:7)
9. Final banishment from heaven: middle of Daniel's seventieth week (Rev. 12:7–13)
10. Empowering the Antichrist and the False Prophet: middle of Daniel's seventieth week (Rev. 13:2, 4)
11. Performing false signs: last half of Daniel's seventieth week (Rev. 16:13–14)

12. Millennial incarceration: Christ's millennial kingdom (Rev. 20:1–3)
13. Final battle: end of Christ's millennial kingdom (Rev. 20:7–9)
14. Final judgment: end of Christ's millennial kingdom (Isa. 27:1; Rev. 20:10)

SATAN'S STRATEGIES

Paul writes to the Corinthians that believers should "not be outwitted by Satan; for we are not ignorant of his designs" (2 Cor. 2:11). Understanding the schemes of the Devil helps prepare believers to resist him. Satan strategizes as a master tactician (2 Cor. 2:11; 11:3; Eph. 6:11) to ensnare people (1 Tim. 3:7; 2 Tim. 2:26) in an attempt to bring the world around to his perverted thinking and away from the pure truth of God. He began his evil activity with Adam and Eve (Gen. 3:1–24) and will continue it till the end of time (Rev. 12:9; 20:3, 8).

Spiritual Counterfeits

Satan's evil and his perversion of the truth is masked by his masterful ability to imitate God with spiritual counterfeits. Without being given new spiritual eyes through regeneration by the Holy Spirit, a person will consider Satan's lies as truth. The major counterfeits of Satan listed in Scripture include the following:

1. The Trinity, as dragon/Satan (Rev. 13:4), Beast/Antichrist (Rev. 13:4), and False Prophet (Rev. 13:11; see 16:13)
2. The kingdom, but actually the "domain of darkness" (Col. 1:13)
3. Angels (Matt. 25:41; 2 Cor. 11:14; 12:7; Rev. 12:7)
4. The throne (Rev. 2:13)
5. Churches (Rev. 2:9; 3:9)
6. Worship (Rom. 1:25; Rev. 13:4)
7. Workers (2 Cor. 11:13, 15)
8. Christs (Matt. 24:5, 24; Mark 13:22; 1 John 2:18, 22)
9. Prophets (Matt. 7:15; 24:11, 24; Mark 13:22; 2 Pet. 2:1)
10. Apostles (2 Cor. 11:13; Rev. 2:2)
11. Teachers (2 Pet. 2:1)
12. Believers (Matt. 13:38, 40; 2 Cor. 11:26; Gal. 2:4)
13. The gospel (Gal. 1:6–7)
14. Theology (1 Tim. 4:1)
15. Mysteries (2 Thess. 2:7; Rev. 2:24)
16. Miracles (Matt. 7:21–23; 2 Thess. 2:9; Rev. 16:13–14)
17. Communion (1 Cor. 10:20–21)

Satan's Objectives

Satan aims his fiery darts (Eph. 6:16) at human minds (2 Cor. 11:3). The Christian's thought life becomes the battlefield for spiritual conquest, so the believer must be spiritually strong in the mind (Matt. 22:37; Rom. 12:2; 2 Cor. 4:4; 10:5; Phil. 4:8; Col. 3:2; 1 Pet. 1:13). If Christians think in ways contrary to God's Word, they will act disobediently to God's will (cf. Prov. 23:7; 27:19). On the other hand, if believers think as God thinks and live according to his Word (Col. 3:16), then victory over Satan's schemes is assured.

The historical narratives and teaching portions of Scripture identify four of Satan's major objectives against the Christian, which are marked by specific tactics. They are briefly noted below:

1. Satan will attempt to distort or deny the truth of God's Word (Matt. 4:1–11; 13:3–4, 18–19; 16:23). He does this in at least eight ways:
   a. *Sensualism.* Replacing God's Word as the standard for determining God's best for one's life (cf. Gen. 3:1–6, in opposition to 2 Tim. 3:16–17).
   b. *Sensationalism.* Believing that immediate success is more desirable than success in God's time (cf. Matt. 4:1–11, in opposition to 1 Cor. 1:18–25).
   c. *Universalism*: Believing that humanity will share the same eternal reality just as they share the same earthly reality (Matt. 13:24–30, in opposition to John 1:12–13; 3:36; 5:24).
   d. *Rationalism.* Substituting simple childlike faith anchored in the Word of God with human reason (Matt. 16:21–23, in opposition to Isa. 55:9).
   e. *Existentialism.* Elevating oneself as master of one's soul and destiny (2 Cor. 4:4, in opposition to John 3:16–21).
   f. *Illusionism.* Affirming without support that anything that appears or claims to be of God *is* of God (2 Cor. 11:13–15, in opposition to Deut. 13:1–5; 1 John 4:1–4).
   g. *Ecumenism.* Believing that all sincere religions involve valid expressions of worshiping the true God (Rev. 2:9; 3:9, in opposition to Acts 4:12).
   h. *Humanism.* Supposing that Satan can be defeated without God's help (Jude 9, in opposition to John 15:5).

2. Satan will attempt to discredit the testimony of God's people (Acts 5:1–11; 1 Tim. 3:7). He does so in at least four ways:
   a. *Situationalism.* Viewing God's Word as flexible enough to bend depending on the context (Acts 5:1–11, in opposition to Ps. 119:89).
   b. *Individualism.* Putting one's satisfaction above one's spouse within the marriage (1 Cor. 7:1–5, in opposition to Eph. 5:22–25).
   c. *Isolationism.* Assuming one's personal reputation has no effect on anyone else (2 Sam. 12:14, in opposition to 1 Tim. 3:7; 6:1; Titus 2:5).

d. *Hedonism.* Denying home responsibilities and satisfying one's own fleshly desires while expecting the church to provide support (in opposition to 1 Tim. 5:14–15 and 2 Thess. 3:10).

3. Satan will attempt to depress or destroy the believer's enthusiasm for God's work (2 Cor. 12:7–10). He influences at least four mindsets:
   a. *Materialism.* Prizing material and physical blessings more highly than one's spiritual relationship with Jesus Christ (in opposition to Matt. 6:33).
   b. *Defeatism.* Seeing oneself as a failure, no longer useful in the King's service (cf. Luke 22:31–34, in opposition to Ps. 32:1–7).
   c. *Negativism.* Finding a person's weakness to prevent his or her effective service for God (in opposition to 2 Cor. 12:7–10; Phil. 4:13).
   d. *Pessimism.* Doubting the ability to accomplish anything significant for God due to difficult life circumstances (cf. 1 Thess. 2:17–3:2, in opposition to Ps. 37:23–24).

4. Satan will attempt to dilute the effectiveness of God's people (1 Tim. 3:6; cf. 1 Chron. 21:1–8). He does so in at least five ways:
   a. *Egotism.* Attributing personal achievements to personal abilities rather than to God's activities in one's life (cf. 1 Chron. 21:1; 1 Tim. 3:6, in opposition to Jer. 9:24–25; 1 Pet. 5:6).
   b. *Nominalism.* Believing that being saved and forgiven makes one's present lifestyle unimportant (cf. Zech. 3:1–5; 1 John 2:1–6).
   c. *Cultism.* Understanding salvation as based on works rather than on faith in Jesus Christ (cf. Luke 22:3–6, in opposition to Eph 2:8–9).
   d. *Uniformitarianism.* Withholding forgiveness and comfort to a disciplined believer despite his or her repentance and change of heart toward God (in opposition to 2 Cor. 2:5–11; Eph 4:32).
   e. *Assertivism.* Assuming it is healthy to vent one's anger frequently for lengthy periods of time (in opposition to Eph. 4:26–27; James 1:19–20).

Satan's Prototypical Assault

Satan's first assault on humans elucidates why he is known as "the father of lies" and as a "murderer from the beginning" (John 8:44): ever since he facilitated the sin of Adam and Eve, everyone in the entire human race has been born dead in sin (Eph. 2:1–3). In Genesis 3, Satan beguiled Eve (2 Cor. 11:3) into rejecting God's truthfulness and then acting independently of him. The six aspects of that assault have constituted Satan's prototypical method for attacking humanity ever since.

1. *Disguise.* In Genesis 3:1, Satan arrived, craftily disguised as a serpent. The word "crafty" is used in a negative sense to refer to trickery (cf. Josh. 9:4)

2. *Dialogue.* Satan spoke to the woman with the goal of deceiving her. Satan used three tactics on Eve that later proved fatal:
   a. He singled out Eve from her husband and entered into an apparently innocent dialogue with her. A godly marriage, however, is designed as a union where the husband and wife strengthen, encourage, edify, and build up each other.
   b. He surprised Eve with his encounter. Had Eve been practicing the presence of God, she would have understood the danger.
   c. He made a seemingly innocent inquiry. According to the Hebrew construction, it was really a question of ridicule. A modern-day paraphrase would be, "You've got to be kidding, Eve. God didn't *really* say you can't eat from any tree in the garden, did he?"

3. *Doubt.* Satan planted a seed of doubt about God's command concerning eating from the trees of the garden (Gen. 2:16–17). Eve's paraphrase of God's original words indicates that she had begun to question the certainty of death and judgment, cultivating that seed of doubt into a blatant denial of the truthfulness, applicability, and trustworthiness of God.

4. *Denial.* In Genesis 3:4–5, Satan fed Eve five lies disguised by partial truth:
   a. Eve would not die. In truth, though they did not die immediately in a physical sense, they did immediately die spiritually in their relationship with God, being spiritually separated from him because of their sin. That spiritual death led to their later physical death.
   b. God's Word is unreliable, since he said they would die but they did not. On the basis of this lie, Eve moved decisively to abandon the authority of God's Word.
   c. Man can become like God: "For God knows that when you eat of it your eyes will be opened, and you will be like God, knowing good and evil." Satan omitted the truth that Adam and Eve were susceptible to sin rather than being unchangeably holy in nature like God. As a result of their sin, all humanity has been cursed with sin and have known "good" and "evil" by experience.
   d. God wished to jealously maintain his uniqueness and not share it with anyone. Satan implied that this was bad, not good, but God was protecting his deity.
   e. The fundamental lie is, "I, Satan, have your best interest at heart. Believe me, not God."

5. *Deliberation.* Autonomous empirical research originated with Eve in Eden. Eve concluded that the only way that she could decide whether

God was right or wrong was to test him with her mind and senses. When she believed God's Word was no longer authoritative, that it no longer dictated what was right and wrong in her life, she chose to run three tests on the tree to see whether God or Satan was right (Gen. 3:6): (1) it was good for food, according to "the desires of the flesh" (1 John 2:16); (2) it had emotional or aesthetic value and was a delight to the eyes (cf. 1 John 2:16); (3) it had intellectual value, allowing her to possess wisdom like God (cf. 1 John 2:16).

6. *Death.* Adam and Eve's minds were affected, and they suddenly perceived evil (Gen. 3:7). Before, when they were naked in the garden, all was pure (Gen. 2:25), but due to sin, they suddenly knew they were naked, and so they desired to cover up their nakedness. Guilt had entered the human race—man became spiritually separated from God and hid from him (Gen. 3:9–11), and conflict arose between the man and woman as they began to shift blame for their sin (Gen. 3:12–13).

SATAN'S SERVANT ROLE

Despite Satan's powerful activities and strategies, God's sovereignty has overruled and conquered the worst that Satan could execute as "the god of this world." Even Satan's worst evil assaults will serve God's best righteous purposes. A few of the several historic occasions of such assaults mentioned in Scripture are reported below:

1. *Job 1–2.* God gave Satan authority to touch Job's possessions, family, and body, but not Job himself (Job 1:12–19; 2:3–7). Although Job lost his possessions and his children, and suffered horribly, he did not curse God but rather worshiped him (Job 1:21; 2:10). Job honored God and proved wrong Satan's accusations that Job had a merely self-serving loyalty to God. In the end, God doubly blessed Job for his sincere and Satan-tested fidelity to God (Job 42:10).
2. *1 Samuel 16.* After God's Spirit had departed from Saul (1 Sam. 16:14), a demon tormented him (1 Sam. 16:14–16, 23; 18:10; 19:9). Only the harp playing of David brought Saul relief, thus causing him to love David greatly and raise him to a position of trust. God's positioning of David providentially led to his slaying of Goliath (1 Sam. 17:26–49) and eventually to his kingship (2 Sam. 2:11; 5:4–5).
3. *1 Kings 22:19–23 and 2 Chronicles 18:18–22.* In these texts Satan appropriately fits the description of the "lying spirit" behind the false prophecy. Satan's role as ruler over demons accounts for the fact that the lying spirit influenced four hundred prophets. In the face of the uniformly positive message of the demons through the false prophets, Micaiah was proven

to be the authentic prophet, and his prediction of the defeat and death of Ahab fulfilled God's prophetic word from Elijah (1 Kings 22:37–38; cf. 21:17–19).

4. *1 Chronicles 21 and 2 Samuel 24.* In his later years, David seems to have felt he could take greater confidence in the size of his army than in the power of his God, especially in light of pressure from the people. First Chronicles 21:1 states, "Then Satan stood against Israel and incited David to number Israel." Joab strongly opposed the census, but the will of the king prevailed. Thus, David neither sought the wisdom of counselors (Prov. 11:14; 24:6) nor heeded God's counsel (cf. Ps. 33:16–17), but sinfully put his trust in himself and his army. God thus employed Satan (2 Sam. 24:1; cf. 1 Chron. 21:1) to test David's humility, and the king failed miserably.
5. *Zechariah 3.* As on several occasions, Satan stood before God to accuse Joshua the high priest, representative of the nation of Israel, of being unworthy to receive God's blessing. The Accuser's goal was that God would reject both Joshua and Israel for their "filthy garments" (Zech. 3:3–4). The Lord used the occasion of Satan's accusations to declare that Israel had not forfeited the promises that God made to Abraham and David, even though the promise awaited a future time when Israel would become faithful to the Lord (Zech. 12:10–13:1).
6. *Matthew 4.* Christ was tempted by Satan in all points of human weakness (4:1–11; cf. Heb. 4:15; 1 John 2:16). Satan's design was to get Jesus to violate the plan of God and employ the divine power that he had set aside in his humiliation (cf. Phil. 2:7). Satan's failure to tempt Christ into sin proved at least three essential truths concerning Christ's deity: his impeccability, his unswerving allegiance to the truth of God's Word, and his superiority to and authority over Satan.
7. *Luke 22.* Satan demanded to "sift" Peter like wheat, and Christ granted his request (Luke 22:31). But Christ also prayed that Peter would recover, be spiritually strengthened by the experience, and be enabled to lead the disciples (Luke 22:32). Peter experienced God's love, mercy, and grace, returned to fellowship with the disciples, and was restored by Christ to ministry (John 21:15–17). The Master reaffirmed his trust in Peter and his ability to minister.
8. *John 13.* In regard to Christ's death, Satan served God by entering Judas (Luke 22:3–6; cf. John 13:2), who began to scheme with the chief priests about how to betray Christ, and whom Christ later dispatched to quickly carry out his treachery (John 13:27). This is the supreme example of God using Satan to be the catalyst for something that God had actually planned

in eternity past—the release of believers from diabolical dominion in the kingdom of darkness (cf. Acts 2:22–24).

9. *Acts 5.* The "father of lies" (John 8:44) filled the heart of Ananias to lie to the Holy Spirit (Acts 5:3), with Sapphira as his accomplice. As a result, they were killed by God in front of the Jerusalem assembly (Acts 5:5, 10). God used Satan to impress a new heightened level of fearing God on everyone there (Acts 5:5, 11) and on all who have read about the incident since. "It is a fearful thing to fall into the hands of the living God" (Heb. 10:31).
10. *2 Corinthians 12.* God used a satanic messenger, a harassing "thorn . . . in the flesh," to keep Paul from pride after he had received a vision of the third heaven. The Old Testament usage of the figure of speech suggests Paul's thorn could have been people who were "a thorn in the side" or "a pain in the neck," very possibly because they were demon-possessed false teachers and unbelievers (see some examples in Paul's life in Acts 13:10; 2 Tim. 2:17–18; 4:14). Yet again, what Satan meant for evil, God ordained for good, driving Paul to a humble reliance on God through prayer (1 Pet. 5:6–7; 2 Cor. 12:8).
11. *Revelation 13.* At the midpoint of Daniel's seventieth week (verse 5), the satanic trinity will be introduced, including Satan (the dragon of 13:2–4; cf. 12:9; 20:2), the Antichrist (the beast of 13:1–10), and the False Prophet (the "another beast" of 13:11–17). Global deception will continue for forty-two months (13:5) until Christ's second coming (19:11–20:3) ends this diabolical dominion and King Jesus reigns for one thousand years (20:4–6). In all this, Satan functions as God's servant by setting up the occasion for the triumphant advent of Christ and the inauguration of his millennial kingdom on earth.

A CHRISTIAN'S DEFENSE AGAINST SATAN

God's Protection

Ephesians 6:10–20 records how God has designed spiritual weapons for the Christian's war against spiritual attack (cf. Rom. 13:12; 2 Cor. 6:7; 10:4). He has provided a "panoply" of weapons for both defensive and offensive use so that we would "be strong in the Lord and in the strength of his might," and "able to stand against the schemes of the devil" (Eph. 6:10–11).

1. *The belt of truth* (v. 14). Like the belt cinching up the soldier's tunic for battle, the believer "girds the loins" by having an attitude that is marked by integrity and readiness to use the Word of God to do battle (v. 17).

2. *The breastplate of righteousness* (v. 14). As a breastplate in battle protects the heart and bowels, so the Christian, figuratively, needs to protect the heart, which is the seat of the mind, and the bowels, which are the seat of emotions. Practical, personal righteousness is more protected the more the believer is sanctified by the Spirit into the image of Christ (2 Cor. 3:18; 2 Pet. 3:18).
3. *Footwear of readiness* (v. 15). The sandals of Roman soldiers were thickly soled, stable like sports cleats, and tightly bound for both quick action and durable use. The believer needs sure footing in order to withstand the Enemy's schemes. This sure footing comes from having embraced the gospel.
4. *The shield of faith* (v. 16). Just as a Roman soldier would have a shield large enough to protect from fiery darts with their smoldering pitch, so the Christian's faith is effective enough to extinguish the fiery darts of the Evil One. The greater one's subjective belief in the objective faith, the greater the victory in spiritual battle.
5. *The helmet of salvation* (v. 17; 1 Thess. 5:8). The assurance of salvation and the hope of future deliverance from the Enemy is the best defense against the crushing blows of the Enemy.
6. *The sword of the Spirit* (v. 17). This weapon is both defensive and offensive, short enough to be wielded with precise movements for effective attack (cf. Heb. 4:12). Jesus responded incisively with the Word of God to Satan's temptations and gained the victory (Matt. 4:4, 7, 10).
7. *The arsenal of prayer* (v. 18). "Praying at all times in the Spirit, with all prayer and supplication" is the most effective offensive resource the Christian has. Jesus set the model for prayer for protection: "Deliver us from the evil one" (Matt. 6:13).

God's Provisions

God has provided multiple means by which a Christian can be victorious over Satan in this life. The following provisions focus on the most important and encouraging truths found in the Bible to this end.

1. The Savior gained victory at Calvary.

   Christ's earthly ministry and atoning work at the cross means the overthrow of Satan's hold on humanity (John 12:31; Rev. 12:11), because his death destroyed the Devil's power over death (Heb. 2:14). The victory of the Savior promises final victory—believers will overcome all evil (1 John 2:13; 5:4–5) when Satan is cast into the lake of fire at the end of Christ's millennial reign to be tormented for all eternity future (Rev. 20:10).

2. Christ prays and protects.
   Jesus interceded as High Priest by praying that Christians would be protected from Satan (John 17:15, 20). All true believers are indeed protected from eternal harm (1 John 5:18), and God will never release any of his elect from his sure grip (John 10:28–29).
3. Christ sent the Holy Spirit.
   Because Christ has sent the Holy Spirit (John 14:16, 26; 15:26; 16:7), believers now have his indwelling power, which is greater than any evil influence (1 John 4:4).
4. God informs believers.
   God has forewarned believers of Satan's evil plans in Scripture so that Christians can be prepared when the spiritual battle erupts (2 Cor. 2:11; 1 Pet. 5:8). Furthermore, Christ modeled prayer for believers in spiritual battle (cf. Matt. 6:13), and Scripture instructs as to how to gain victory over Satan: submit to God, draw near to him, and resist the Devil (James 4:7–8; 1 Pet. 5:9).
5. Shepherds strengthen and encourage the church.
   Pastors are to establish and exhort the flock of God in the faith (1 Thess. 3:2), so that the Tempter will fail with his temptations (1 Thess. 3:5).

JUDGMENTS AGAINST SATAN

God has handed down and will hand down multiple judgments on rebellious Satan. Scripture outlines his judicial history.

Satan's Original Judgment

Before Satan deceived the first humans, he committed an act of highest treachery, for which he was judged. Three passages seem to describe his first act of treason.

- *Revelation 12:3–17.* Apocalyptic imagery narrates Satan's rebellion and fall from heaven with one-third of all angels, and his relentless scheming against Christ and his people.
- *Ezekiel 28:11–19.* Satan seems to be at the root of the prophecy against the evil king of Tyre, since particular references seem to surpass the human king. For example, he was in Eden, which might refer to the literal Eden (v. 13), and at his creation he was surrounded by every precious stone (v. 13), at which time he was blameless, only later to be revealed as unrighteous (v. 15).

- *Isaiah 14:4–21.* Satan seems to embody the king of Babylon in this prophecy, who, like the king of Tyre, exhibited great pride and self-deception. Isaiah narrates Satan's desire to be like God and his resultant fall and ultimate derision when he is cast into the pit.

Satan's Judgment in Eden

In Genesis 3:14–15, both Satan and the possessed serpent appear to be cursed. The serpent receives the physical curse of moving on his belly and eating dust as he goes. Satan will one day be destroyed with a crushing blow by the Messiah (Rom. 16:20; cf. John 16:11).

Satan's Judgment at Calvary

Christ came to "destroy the works of the devil" (1 John 3:8; cf. Heb. 2:14). Christ's victory on the cross signified Satan's defeat. Jesus's victory cry, "It is finished" (John 19:30), sealed his judgment over Satan (John 12:31; 16:11). The church reaffirms Satan's defeat because it is made up of those who have been delivered from his power (Acts 26:18; Col. 1:13; 2:15).

Satan's Coming Judgment

a. During the Great Tribulation

Revelation 12:7–13 reveals that, at the halfway mark of the great tribulation, all evil forces will be banished from accessing heaven. While this means that Satan and his demons will pursue believers in a particularly fierce way on the earth, they will no longer be able to accuse believers of sin in the presence of God, which has been their standard practice (Job 1:6–7; 2:1–2).

b. During the Millennium

When Jesus Christ returns to the earth to rule from Jerusalem, he will bind Satan in unbreakable chains and seal him in a bottomless pit for one thousand years (Rev. 20:1–3) so that he cannot deceive the nations (cf. Rev. 20:7–8). Presumably, all demons will be imprisoned with him (Isa. 24:21–22).

c. For Eternity

Revelation 20:10 portrays the final judgment of Satan after his futile rebellion against King Jesus is quelled in a burst of fire from heaven—Satan is sent to burn forever in the lake of fire. All of his evil forces will join him there (cf. Matt. 8:29; Luke 8:31), as well as all sinners after the great white throne judgment (Matt. 25:41; Mark 9:48; Rev. 20:14–15).

Identifying the Angel of the Lord

The Hebrew noun for "angel" or "messenger" refers to "the angel of the Lord" in about ninety uses in sixteen Old Testament books. This specific designation appears only in the Old Testament and refers to a unique, one-of-a-kind messenger. He is also called "the angel of God" (Gen. 21:17), "his angel" (Gen. 24:7, 40), "my angel" (Ex. 23:23), "the angel of his presence" (Isa. 63:9), and "the messenger of the covenant" (Mal. 3:1). Several lines of biblical evidence conclusively identify this special person as the preincarnate Christ, God the Son, who holds the same divine rights and prerogatives as God the Father.

A strong case for the angel of the Lord being the preincarnate Christ is that no created angel ever possessed the traits of deity possessed by the angel of the Lord. The Old Testament reveals the angel of the Lord as a divine person who can be referred to as Yahweh (Gen. 16:11–13; 22:9–18; 32:24–30; Ex. 3:2–6, 14; Judg. 13:21–23), as one sent from Yahweh (Ex. 23:20–23; 32:34; Num. 20:16), or as speaking with Yahweh (Zech. 1:12–13). These references indicate that the angel of the Lord is a distinct divine person. Other qualities exhibit his divine nature:

1. He claims to have a divine nature (Gen. 31:11, 13; Ex. 3:2–5; 23:20–21; Judg. 13:17–18; Mal. 3:1).
2. Witnesses identified him by name as divine (Gen. 16:11–13; Judg. 6:22–23; 13:21–22).
3. He displays divine attributes and exerts divine prerogatives (Gen. 48:16; Ex. 23:21; 33:14; Isa. 63:9; Zech. 3:3–4).
4. When the angel of Yahweh made promises, God made them (Gen. 16:10; 22:15–17; cf. 12:2; 13:16).
5. The "angel of the Lord" receives worship (Gen. 22:11–13; Ex. 3:5; Josh. 5:15; Judg. 6:21; 13:20).

Furthermore, Old Testament assertions of the deity of the angel of the Lord match New Testament assertions concerning God's eternal Son, the Lord Jesus Christ. A few of their attributes and activities can be compared:

1. By taking the name of "the Lord" (Gen. 16:11–13; 22:9–18), the "Angel" claimed to be an eternal being, just as the Lord Jesus Christ claimed (John 1:1; 8:58; 17:5).
2. The "Angel" is asserted to be God (Ex. 3:2–6; Judg. 13:17–18), and Jesus Christ is God (John 1:1; 5:18; 10:33; 2 Pet. 1:1; 1 John 5:20).
3. The distinct divinity of the Angel asserts plurality in the Godhead (Ex. 23:20–23; Isa. 6:1, 8 [with John 12:41–42]; Zech. 1:12–13), which is asserted by and about Jesus Christ (Matt. 28:19; Mark 1:9–11; John 15:26; 2 Cor. 13:14).

4. Both Christ and the "Angel" were responsible to reveal and explain God to man (John 1:18; 10:30; 12:45; 14:7, 9; 2 Cor. 4:4; Col. 1:15, 19; 2:9; Heb. 1:3).

Therefore the only identification of the "angel of the Lord" that satisfies the divine characteristics in the Old Testament and matches the distinct divine attributes and priorities in the New Testament is the preincarnate appearance (a christophany) of the second person of the triune Godhead, the eternal Son of God, the Lord Jesus Christ.

Questions in Angelology

Some frequently asked questions remain when treating angels, demons, and Satan.

WHAT ABOUT GUARDIAN ANGELS (MATT. 18:10)?

Scripture clearly says that angels are ministering spirits (Heb. 1:14), but the idea of individual guardian angels is not biblically based. While Matthew 18:10 appears to affirm guardian angels, the text rather suggests that believers are collectively served by angels in general, with multiple angels even aiding one person at the same time (cf. 2 Kings 6:17; Ps. 91:11; Luke 16:22).

SHOULD ANGELS BE WORSHIPED (COL. 2:18)?

Angels are not to be worshiped (Col. 2:18; Rev. 19:9–10; 22:8–9); angels are to worship God (Heb. 1:6; cf. Isa. 6:1–4; Rev. 5:8–14). People are prohibited from worshiping any object (Ex. 20:1–5; 34:14; Deut. 11:16; 30:17; Pss. 31:6; 97:7) at great penalty for disobedience (Ex. 32:1–10).

WHAT IS MEANT BY "SOME HAVE ENTERTAINED ANGELS UNAWARES" (HEB. 13:2)?

The teaching in Hebrews 13:2 that "some have entertained angels unawares" is given not as the ultimate motivation for hospitality but rather to reveal that one never knows how far-reaching an act of kindness might be (cf. Matt. 25:40, 45).

The writer of Hebrews is not suggesting that believers should expect angelic visitations. Rather, he is vividly implying that, when one practices biblical hospitality (1 Tim. 3:2; Titus 1:8), one may at times experience unexpected blessing, as illustrated in the early portions of the Old Testament (cf. Gen. 18:1–3; 19:1–2; Judg. 6:11–24; 13:6–20).

INTO WHAT DO ANGELS "LONG TO LOOK" (1 PET. 1:12)?

God involved holy angels in executing his plan of salvation during Jesus Christ's incarnation, temptation, humiliation, and ascension (cf. Matt. 4:11; 28:5–7;

Mark 16:4–7; Luke 1:26–35; 2:10–14; 22:41–43; 24:4–7; Acts 1:10–11). Angels are nearby to witness the fruit of salvation in the lives of believers (cf. Luke 15:7, 10; 1 Cor. 4:9; 1 Tim. 5:21; Heb. 1:14; Rev. 5:11–14). Holy angels do not themselves need to be saved. Nevertheless, they have a holy curiosity to understand the kind of mercy and grace they cannot experience. That they strain to understand the dynamics of our salvation is yet another way for them to glorify God (cf. Job 38:7; Ps. 148:2; Isa. 6:3; Luke 2:13–14; Heb. 1:6; Rev. 5:11–12; 7:11–12).

DO CHURCHES HAVE ANGELS (REV. 1:16, 20)?

The seven "stars" (Rev. 1:16) are the "messengers" (Gk. *angelos*) of the seven churches (Rev. 1:20). In context, the "stars" seem to represent human messengers, for at least three reasons: (1) the terms "star" and "messenger" are used across the canon to refer to humans (Gen. 37:9; Judg. 5:20; 1 Sam. 23:27; Job 1:14; Ezek. 23:40; Dan. 12:3; Mark 1:2; Phil. 2:25; Jude 13); (2) humans, not angels, are placed in a leadership position over the church; (3) Christ's message is to humans rather than to angels (Rev. 2:1, 8, 12, 18; 3:1, 7, 14). The seven "messengers" are therefore the human leadership of the church, namely the elders and overseers.

HOW WILL CHRISTIANS "JUDGE" ANGELS (1 COR. 6:3)?

The Greek verb meaning to "judge," "decide," or "determine" appears in 1 Corinthians 5:12, 13; 6:1, 2, and 3. The context of 1 Corinthians 5:9–6:11 conveys a judicial sense for the verb. Holy angels by nature, however, do not need adjudication, and Scripture does not even hint that they ever received or will receive judgment. Evil angels, however, have been judged and will receive ultimate judgment at the end of time (Matt. 25:41; cf. Rev. 20:10). Therefore in 1 Corinthians 6:3 Paul alludes to the final judgment of demons by Christ and all believers who will sit with Christ on his throne (Rev. 3:21) and will have authority to judge them (Rev. 20:4).

DO ISAIAH 14 AND EZEKIEL 28 REFER TO SATAN?

The primary intent of the writers in these passages was to pronounce God's judgment on the actual kings of Babylon (Isa. 14:4–21) and Tyre (Ezek. 28:1–19) while using Satan's background to illustrate the evil of their rule. The failed self-exaltation of both pagan kings to the level of God seems to have replicated the earlier attitudes, actions, and fall of the Evil One (Isa. 14:13–14; Ezek. 28:2, 6, 12–17). These kings are thus indirectly related to Satan, serving as his human surrogates in ways similar to other objects or people elsewhere in Scripture (cf. Deut. 32:17; Ps. 106:37–38; Matt. 16:23).

DOES SATAN READ MINDS?

The Devil does not have the power to know what individual people are thinking. There are at least three reasons to deny his ability to read minds: (1) As a created being (John 1:3; Col. 1:16), he does not share God's omniscience; (2) there is no biblical warrant or evidence to suggest he is all-knowing; (3) while he can know the extent of a person's moral and mental corruption due to the fall (Gen. 3:1–7), and therefore the generally degenerate quality of a person's thinking, he cannot know their specific thoughts.

HOW ARE CHRIST AND SATAN RELATED?

Christ created Satan along with all things (John 1:3, 10; 1 Cor. 8:6; Col. 1:16; Heb. 1:2). Satan is always inferior to the divine lordship and will of the triune Godhead (1 John 3:8; cf. Job 1:12; 2:6; Matt. 4:10; John 16:11; Rev. 20:9–10).

CAN SATAN OR DEMONS PERFORM MIRACLES?

Created beings are not all-powerful like their Creator. While God has worked miracles through Christ (John 11:47–48) and the apostles (Acts 4:16), he has never done so in like manner on behalf of Satan or demons. Satan has greater powers than humans (Job 1:12; 2:6) but cannot match God's omnipotence (cf. Ex. 7:11–12, 22; 8:7, 18–19), although through deception many people believe his acts are miraculous and divine (2 Thess. 2:9–10; Rev. 12:9; 13:3, 12–14; 16:13–14; 19:20; 20:3, 8, 10; cf. 1 Tim. 4:1).

ARE THERE DEMONS IN THE WORLD TODAY?

Two common extremes mark the church's understanding of the dynamics of evil spirits in the world today. On the one hand, society's ever-increasing immorality and Satan-honoring practices only accelerate the spiritually dark conditions in which evil forces thrive. The Christian community can therefore overemphasize the spiritual activities of demons in the face of the dark environment outside the church. On the other hand, the invisible nature of most demonic assaults, coupled with a materialistic indifference, leads many believers to underemphasize the spiritual war in the world. Several preliminary, general observations promote a balanced view of demonic activity:

1. We affirm the historical reality of Satan and demons, both in the past and in the present, as verified by the Bible.
2. We affirm that the Bible admonishes Christians to expect Satan and demons to operate now much as they did in both Old Testament and New Testament times (1 Pet. 5:6–11).
3. We affirm that the Bible teaches that, in living out the Christian life, one will experience real spiritual battle with Satan and his army of demons.

4. We affirm that Scripture alone, independent of personal experience or clinical data, will truthfully determine the reality of demonic experiences and provide an understanding of encounters with Satan and demons.
5. We affirm that instructions in the New Testament Epistles on how to conduct spiritual warfare were not limited to the first century (Eph. 6:10–20).

CAN CHRISTIANS "BIND" SATAN?

There is no biblical teaching that would lead one to conclude that believers can "bind" Satan. Passages that lead some people to ask this question include Matthew 12:22–29; Mark 3:27; and Luke 11:14–23. These texts, however, have nothing to do with believers binding Satan. Rather, Christ is the "stronger" man who exerts a greater power than Satan in order to bind him. Additionally, the language of "binding" and "loosing" in Matthew 16:16–19 (especially v. 19) refers to the apostles forgiving or not forgiving sin and has nothing to do with Satan (cf. Matt. 18:15–18; John 20:23).

WHO ARE THE "SONS OF GOD" IN GENESIS 6:1–4?

This is one of the most mysterious, elusive texts in the Bible and therefore one of the most difficult to interpret. Important questions include: Who are the "sons of God" (verse 2)? Who are the "Nephilim" (verse 4)? Are demons involved here?

Some introductory assumptions will help set up the discussion. First, Genesis 6:1–4 is a true and accurate historical record, and as such it must be interpreted in the context of the first five chapters of Genesis. Second, the Nephilim in 6:4 should not necessarily be considered offspring from the sons of God and daughters of men, since reproduction is after one's own kind (Gen. 1:20–25) and spirit beings cannot reproduce (Matt. 22:30; Mark 12:25). Also, the existence of post-flood Nephilim in Numbers 13:33 challenges this hybrid offspring view. What's more, supposed New Testament links to Genesis 6:1–4 (such as 1 Peter 3:19–20; 2 Peter 2:4; and Jude 6) are debatable and do not prove the hybrid offspring view. Nevertheless, an indirect angelic-human relationship might have taken place between demon-possessed men and women resulting in the Nephilim.

The three most common views of the passage follow:

1. "Sinful Sethites" View

The godly line of Seth sinfully married the ungodly female offspring of Cain. The line of Seth was thus polluted, but Noah and his Sethite family were spared in the flood. The following features support the view:

- "Sons of God" can refer to godly men (Deut. 14:1; Ps. 73:15; Isa. 43:6; Hos. 1:10). The juxtaposition of the phrase "daughters of men" could refer to a sinful line.
- The flood was a judgment on human sin, not demonic sin (Gen. 6:5–7; cf. v. 3), which is supported by the context of sin in Genesis 1–5 and corroborated by the New Testament accounts of Noah's day (Matt. 24:37–39; Luke 17:26–27). Human sin would have been perpetuated by marrying outside the faith and further contaminating the human race.

Some problems, however, remain: "Men" does not correspond exactly with "sons of God"; the phrase "daughters of men" does not seem limited to the line of Cain; the phrase "sons of God" does not seem limited to the line of Seth.

2. "Demon-Possessed Men" View

Evil angels took up bodily residence in men, who acted licentiously with the women of the world, leading to universal moral pollution. In support of this ancient view is that the phrase "sons of God" can refer to angels (Job 1:6; 2:1; 38:7) and would here explain the alleged contrast with the phrase "daughters of men."

This view, however, is not without its problems. First, neither the context of chapters 1–5 nor the passage itself clearly introduces demons as the "sons of God," and the ensuing judgment is specifically focused on humans, not demons, as further highlighted in later descriptions of Noah's day (Matt. 24:37–39; Luke 17:26–27). Second, the phrase "sons of God" never exclusively refers to demons in the Old Testament; rather, the term "angel" (Gen. 19:1, 15; 28:12; 32:1) would likely have been used if evil angels were in view.

3. "Rogue Rulers" View

"Sons of God" was an ancient phrase used to describe rulers who were represented as having a direct connection with deity and who ravaged and abused women, distorting God's holy design for marriage. There is biblical support for the title "sons of God" to refer to human rulers (Ps. 82:6; John 10:33–36). Furthermore, their sin matches later descriptions of the sinful conditions of Noah's day, and God's judgment would therefore focus on human sinners. Nevertheless, the view assumes more detail than the passage offers, and Scripture does not describe kings as being associated with deity at this period of world history.

Questions:

1. What does the Bible teach about the reality and the nature of good angels and of demons?
2. What are the moral and spiritual qualities of good angels? And of demons?

3. What are the biblical names, roles, and activities of good angels?
4. What are the biblical names and activities of demons?
5. Can a true believer be "demonized" (or "possessed by demons")?
6. What does the Bible teach about the reality of Satan?
7. What does the Bible teach about the names and character of Satan?
8. Where in history (Old Testament, New Testament, and future) does Satan make his appearance?
9. Considering Satan's strategies, what good things of God does Satan attempt to counterfeit?
10. Considering Satan's activities, what are Satan's objectives?
11. How is Satan's temptation of Eve (Genesis 3) a "prototypical Satanic assault"?
12. What does Ephesians 6 teach the believer about resisting Satan and his demons?
13. What are the judgments of Satan?
14. Who is the "angel of the Lord"? (texts and arguments)

9

THE CHURCH

Ecclesiology

CHARLES SPURGEON DESCRIBED THE church as "the dearest place on earth." Indeed, for all who know and love the Lord Jesus Christ, no place in the world should be sweeter or more cherished than the church. The church is precious for many reasons, first and foremost because the Lord Jesus died on her behalf (Eph. 5:25). As Spurgeon added, "Nothing in the world is dearer to God's heart than his church."[1]

Defining the Church

The basic term for the church in the New Testament is the Greek word *ekklēsia*, which means "those who are called out."[2] In the ancient world, an *ekklēsia* referred to a group of citizens who had been "called out" to administrate civic affairs or to defend the community in battle. In Acts 7:38 Israel is referred to as "the congregation" (*ekklēsia*) (cf. Ex. 19:17), but this is a nontechnical usage and refers to a large group, as it does in Acts 19:32 and 41, where the term refers to an angry mob in Ephesus.

Used in the specific, more technical New Testament sense of *the church* (Acts 20:28; 1 Cor. 1:2; 10:32; 11:16, 22; 15:9; 2 Cor. 1:1; Gal. 1:13; 1 Thess. 2:14; 2 Thess. 1:4; cf. Rom. 16:16), *ekklēsia* refers to the community of those who have been called out by God to faith in Jesus Christ (Rom. 1:7; 1 Cor. 1:2; Eph. 4:1; 1 Thess.

1 Charles H. Spurgeon, "The Best Donation," sermon no. 2234, preached April 5, 1891, in *The Metropolitan Tabernacle Pulpit: Containing Sermons Preached and Revised* (Pasadena, TX: Pilgrim, 1975), 37:633, 635.

2 The English word *church* derives specifically from the Greek term *kuriakos*, referring to "those who belong to the Lord."

2:12; 2 Tim. 1:9; 1 Pet. 5:10; cf. Rom. 8:28). They are those whom he predestined in eternity past, called and justified in this present life, and promised to glorify in the future (Rom. 8:30; cf. Eph. 1:11). As such, the church is not a physical building. It is not a religious institution, an ethical organization, or a sociopolitical association. The church is the assembly of the redeemed—those who have been called by God the Father to salvation as a gift to his Son (John 6:37; 10:29; 17:6, 9, 24).

The church was born on the day of Pentecost (Acts 2:1–21, 38–47). After Pentecost, the church steadily increased in numbers as the gospel was faithfully proclaimed throughout the world (Acts 2:39, 41, 47; 4:4; 5:14; 6:7; 9:31, 42; 11:21, 24; 13:48–49; 14:1; 16:5). It was "the Lord [who] added to their number day by day those who were being saved" (Acts 2:47). The advance of the gospel has continued throughout the centuries of church history and has been heralded by generations of faithful believers across the globe.

One day, the church age will reach its glorious fullness when Christ comes to rapture his own (1 Cor. 15:51–53; 1 Thess. 4:13–18). From that point forward, the church will be in the presence of her Savior for all eternity (cf. Rev. 22:3–5).

In spite of persecution from outside forces (John 15:18–25; 1 Pet. 1:6–7; 1 John 3:13), and internal threats from false teachers (2 Pet. 2:1; Jude 3–4), the Lord Jesus assured his disciples that he would build his church and that the gates of hell would not overcome it (Matt. 16:18).

CHRIST'S DESIGN FOR HIS CHURCH[3]

In Matthew 16:18, Jesus delivers seven hallmark principles for building his church.

A Permanent Foundation

Christ provided the church with a permanent foundation: "You are Peter, and *on this rock* I will build my church" (Matt. 16:18). A *rock* evokes the concept of permanence. Here Christ promised the church would not be a temporary or passing movement but would have a *lasting* relevance.

The foundation was not Peter. Christ here distinguishes between a movable, detached boulder (the basic meaning of "Cephas" and "Peter" [Gk. *petros*]) and the unshakeable, immovable foundation suitable for the church. The word Christ used for "rock" (Gk. *petra*) means "bedrock," the rock built upon by the wise builder (Matt. 7:24–25).

What or who, then, is the rock? The Old Testament pictures God as the rock in whom believers find strength and refuge (cf. 1 Sam. 2:2; Ps. 18:1–2). In 1 Corinthians, Paul identified Christ as the rock in the wilderness (1 Cor. 10:4). Paul expressed the same idea when he referred to Jesus Christ as "the foundation"

3 This section is adapted from Richard Mayhue, *What Would Jesus Say about Your Church?* (Fearn, Ross-shire, Scotland: Christian Focus, 1995), 16–20. Used by permission of Christian Focus.

(1 Cor. 3:11) that Paul himself had laid (1 Cor. 3:10). Paul laid Christ as the foundation by his *preaching* of Christ (1 Cor. 2:1–2). Just as Paul understood that his testimony of Christ was the *bedrock foundation* of the church, it seems best to take Peter's testimony of Christ— "You are the Christ, the Son of the living God" (Matt. 16:16)—as the *rock* upon which Christ would build his church. This *testimony of* Christ is the *reality of* Christ; the "rock" is Christ himself. Christ alone is the rock of redemption on which the church is being built (Acts 4:11–12).

Personal Involvement

Second, Christ promised his personal involvement: "*I* will build my church" (Matt. 16:18). Christ works through his people; he is with them (Matt. 28:20), in them (Col. 1:27), and among them constantly (Rev. 1:12–13, 20). We "are God's fellow workers" (1 Cor. 3:9) and partners with Christ in building his church. Christ's participation proves indispensable in raising up his church.

A Positive Expectation

"I *will* build my church" (Matt. 16:18). Christ's confident assertion guarantees that the church has a positive expectation. The church will be triumphant because Christ began building the church with the intention of completing her (Eph. 5:26–27). This declaration also indicates that, at the time Jesus uttered these words, the church was yet future—"I *will*."

A Powerful Advance

Jesus claimed that his church would have a powerful advance: "I will *build* my church" (Matt. 16:18). The church experienced an explosive beginning, with three thousand members being added the first day (Acts 2:41). "And the Lord added to their number day by day those who were being saved" (Acts 2:47). Before New Testament times had ended, churches had spread across the face of the Roman Empire—reaching from Jerusalem to Rome. Christ's building efforts continue to this very hour, everywhere in the world, just as he intended (cf. Mark 16:15; Luke 24:47).

A Paid-In-Full Ownership

Christ bought the church with his own blood and therefore possesses the exclusive paid-in-full ownership of the church: "I will build *my* church" (Matt. 16:18; cf. Acts 20:28). The church belongs uniquely to its Redeemer (1 Cor. 3:23; 6:19–20) and its Head (Eph. 1:22; 5:23). The Chief Shepherd owns his flock (John 10:14–15).

A People-Centered Priority

For Christ, the church has a people-centered priority: "I will build my *church*" (Matt. 16:18). The church comprises an assembly of people who have believed in Jesus Christ for eternal life (Acts 4:32). Jesus uses living stones—individual people—to build his church (1 Pet. 2:5). The goal of edification is to present every believer complete in Christ (Col. 1:28).

A Promise of Success

Jesus has promised success to the church: "I will build my church, and *the gates of hell shall not prevail against it*" (Matt. 16:18). In the Old Testament, "gates of" is used with Sheol (Isa. 38:10) and death (Job 38:17; Pss. 9:13; 107:18), both referring to physical death. But as Jesus's promise makes clear, even the threat of death cannot overpower his church. The "gates of hell" are a metaphor for death and the power of Satan (see Heb. 2:14). Christ's promise guarantees that the universal body of believers under his headship will have an enduring testimony that cannot be destroyed by this world, by Satan, or even by death (cf. 1 Cor. 15:54–57).

THE CHURCH AND THE KINGDOM

The Old Testament prophets foretold details about both the Messiah's suffering (Isa. 53:1–12) and his earthly kingdom (cf. Isa. 2:1–4; 9:6–7; Zech. 14:8–21). But the notion of a time between Christ's first and second comings, during which Gentiles would be incorporated into the people of God alongside Jewish believers (Rom. 11:11–20), was a mystery not revealed until the New Testament (cf. Eph. 3:4–7).

Although the Lord Jesus repeatedly demonstrated himself to be Israel's promised Messiah and King, the nation refused to receive him (John 1:11; 5:43; cf. Acts 2:22–23). Consequently, Jesus said to the Jewish religious leaders of his day, "the kingdom of God will be taken away from you and given to a people producing its fruits" (Matt. 21:43).

Nonetheless, Israel's rejection did not undermine the gracious promises God made in the Old Testament. Those kingdom promises will one day be literally fulfilled when the Jewish people embrace their King in saving faith (Rom. 11:25–26; Zech. 12:10; 14:8–9; cf. Rev. 20:1–6; cf. 2 Tim. 4:1). That reality is yet future. In the meantime, God is accomplishing his kingdom purposes through the church (cf. Matt. 21:43; cf. Rom. 9:25–26; 1 Pet. 2:9).

Though the physical kingdom of Christ on earth awaits its future fulfillment, the Lord Jesus brought an internal, spiritual kingdom—the realm of salvation—at his first coming (cf. Matt. 13:3–52; Luke 17:20–21). Its citizens (cf. Phil. 3:20–21) have been regenerated by the Holy Spirit (John 3:3; cf. Matt. 13:11–16). It cannot be attained through self-righteousness or legalism (Matt. 5:20; 23:13) but is characterized by "righteousness and peace and joy in the Holy Spirit" (Rom. 14:17). Present-day believers are those who have been delivered "from the domain of darkness and transferred . . . to the kingdom of his beloved Son, in whom [they] have redemption, the forgiveness of sins" (Col. 1:13–14; cf. Eph. 5:5, 8).

The spiritual kingdom of Christ grows and advances through the preaching of the gospel (Mark 1:14–15; cf. Matt. 22:1–14; 2 Cor. 7:9–11) and the "good news about the kingdom of God and the name of Jesus Christ" (Acts 8:12; cf. Matt. 4:23; 9:35; 13:19; 24:14; Acts 14:22).

As his spiritual kingdom, the church submits to Jesus Christ as her Head, Master, Lord, and King (Eph. 1:22; Col. 1:18). His law is her standard (cf. Gal. 6:2). His Word is her creed (cf. Col. 3:16). His will is her mandate (cf. Heb. 13:20–21). And his glory is her greatest ambition (cf. 2 Cor. 5:9).

THE VISIBLE AND INVISIBLE CHURCH

Not all who are part of the visible church, and who outwardly profess faith in Christ, are actually members of the invisible church (the community of those who truly possess saving faith in him) (Matt. 13:24–30; Jude 4). Jesus himself warned that many will claim to know him who in reality do not (cf. Matt. 7:21–23). This sobering warning ought to prompt all professing believers to examine themselves to ensure that they are truly in the faith (2 Cor. 13:5; cf. 1 John 2:3–11).

The New Testament also warns about false teachers who deliberately seek to threaten the church from within (Matt. 7:15; Mark 13:22; Acts 20:29–30; 2 Pet. 2:1; 1 John 4:1; Jude 3–4). When local churches or even entire denominations embrace false teaching—abandon the purity of the gospel (Gal. 1:6–9) and deny the authority of Jesus Christ (Titus 1:16; 2 Pet. 2:1; Jude 4)—they are rightly labeled "apostate," "heretical," and "false."

THE UNIVERSAL CHURCH AND LOCAL CHURCHES

All true believers throughout the church age—both those alive today and those already in heaven (cf. Heb. 12:23)—make up the universal church. Those who are part of the universal church in every generation, scattered throughout the world, are instructed to meet together regularly in local assemblies (Heb. 10:24–25). Such was clearly the pattern of the early church (cf. Acts 14:23, 27; 20:17, 28; 1 Cor. 11:18–20; Gal. 1:2; 1 Thess. 1:1).

The local church is designed to equip believers through the teaching of God's Word (Acts 2:42; 1 Tim. 4:13), to lead them in corporate worship (Eph. 5:18–20; Heb. 13:15), to protect them by the oversight of godly leaders (Acts 20:28; Heb. 13:7, 17; 1 Pet. 5:1–4), and to provide them with opportunities to serve one another (1 Pet. 4:10–11).

THE DISTINCTION BETWEEN THE CHURCH AND ISRAEL[4]

What is the relationship between the New Testament church and the nation of Israel? Proponents of "replacement theology" (also called supersessionism) insist

4 For more on this topic, see Michael J. Vlach, *Has the Church Replaced Israel? A Theological Evaluation* (Nashville: B&H Academic, 2010). Also refer to chap. 10, "The Future."

that the church is the new Israel, and that the blessings promised to the Jewish nation in the Old Testament have been transferred to the church. However, the writers of the New Testament consistently maintain a distinction between the church and Israel (cf. 1 Cor. 10:32). The New Testament presents the church as a new entity (Eph. 2:15), a mystery not fully revealed until this age (Eph. 3:1–6; 5:32; Col. 1:26–27). As noted, in Matthew 16:18 Jesus indicated that he saw the church as something yet future.

Most biblical commentators agree that, of the more than seventy uses of the term Israel in the New Testament, most of these occurrences refer to ethnic Israel (the nation or the Jewish people). However, two New Testament passages, Romans 9:6 and Galatians 6:16, are debated. In Romans 9:6, the apostle Paul writes, "not all who are descended from Israel belong to Israel." In the immediate context of Romans 9:6, Paul is speaking about Jewish believers. These are a distinct remnant of ethnic Israelites—Paul's "kinsmen according to the flesh" (Rom. 9:3) but also believers in Jesus—a group within the larger unbelieving nation (cf. Rom. 11:5). In the broader context of Romans chapters 9–11, Paul is asserting that God has not abandoned the nation of Israel in spite of her unbelief. In light of both the larger and narrower context, the "not all Israel" in Rom. 9:6a (NASB) can only refer to ethnic Israelites who have embraced their Messiah. They are "from Israel" (9:6b NASB), that is, from the nation or the Jewish people.

Galatians 6:16 is part of Paul's closing salutation to his readers: "peace and mercy be upon them, and upon the Israel of God." Some have suggested that "the Israel of God" in this passage refers to the church as a whole—equating Israel with the church. However, Paul is clearly referring to two distinct groups of people in this verse:[5] the grammar and context of the verse suggest that "the Israel of God" refers specifically to Jewish Christians and not to the entire church; the pronoun "them" ("peace and mercy be upon them") speaks of Gentile believers in the Galatian churches (cf. Acts 13:46–48).

Conflating the church and Israel can lead to significant hermeneutical and interpretive problems, in which promises and directives given specifically to the nation of Israel are spiritualized or allegorized and incorrectly applied to Gentile believers in the church. Though the church shares in the blessings of the new covenant (Luke 22:20; 2 Cor. 3:3–8; Heb. 8:7–13; 9:15), in the future God will

5 Advocates of replacement theology argue for an explicative use of *kai* in this verse (which would be translated "even"). However, such a use is uncommon and very unlikely. See Robert L. Saucy, "Israel and the Church: A Case for Discontinuity," in *Continuity and Discontinuity: Perspectives on the Relationship between the Old and New Testaments: Essays in Honor of S. Lewis Johnson, Jr.*, ed. John S. Feinberg (Wheaton, IL: Crossway, 1988), 246; and see S. Lewis Johnson Jr., "Paul and 'the Israel of God': An Exegetical and Eschatological Case-Study," in *Essays in Honor of J. Dwight Pentecost*, ed. Stanley D. Toussaint and Charles H. Dyer (Chicago: Moody Press, 1986).

again turn his attention to the nation of Israel in fulfillment of his promises to them (Rom. 11:25–26; cf. Dan. 9:24–27).

BIBLICAL METAPHORS FOR THE CHURCH[6]

The New Testament uses many analogies to depict God's relationship to his people. He is their King; they are his subjects (Matt. 25:34; 1 Cor. 4:20; Phil. 3:20; Col. 1:13–14). He is the Creator; they are his creatures (2 Cor. 5:17; Eph. 2:10). He is the Shepherd; they are his sheep (John 10:3, 11, 14, 26; Heb. 13:20; 1 Pet. 2:25; 5:2–4). He is the Master; they are his slaves (Matt. 10:24–25; Rom. 14:4; Eph. 6:9; Col. 4:1; 2 Tim. 2:21; Jude 4). He is their Father (Matt. 6:9; Rom. 1:7); they are his adopted children (John 1:12; Rom. 8:16–17, 21; Phil. 2:15; 1 John 3:1–2; cf. Rom. 8:14, 19; 2 Cor. 6:18; Gal. 3:26; 4:6; Heb. 12:7) and the members of his household (Gal. 6:10; Eph. 2:19; 1 Tim. 3:15; 1 Pet. 4:17), to the point that the Lord Jesus "is not ashamed to call them brothers" (Heb. 2:11) and "God is not ashamed to be called their God" (Heb. 11:16).

The church is further described as the bride of Christ (2 Cor. 11:2; Eph. 5:23–32; Rev. 19:7–8; 21:9) and the body of Christ (Rom. 12:4–5; 1 Cor. 12:12, 27; Eph. 4:12, 25; 5:23, 30; Col. 1:24), of which he is the Head (Eph. 1:22–23; 4:15; Col. 1:18; 2:19). Both of these metaphors emphasize the spiritual union that exists between Christ and his own (cf. Gal. 2:20).

The imagery of the body is unique in illustrating the relationship between Christ and the church.[7] Just as the human body is a marvelously complex organism, with many parts, and yet remains a unified whole, so the body of Christ is made up of many individuals and yet is a unified whole. The church is the body of Christ, of which every true believer in Christ is a member. Being the Head of the body (Eph. 1:22–23; Col. 1:18), Christ cannot be separated from his body, his church. Conversely, those who are part of his church cannot be separated from him (John 10:28–29; Rom. 8:38–39) or from each other (1 Cor. 12:12–27).

Another New Testament metaphor that illustrates the vital union that believers share with Christ is that of the vine and the branches (John 15:1–11; cf. Rom. 11:17). Just as a branch is wholly dependent on the vine for its life, nourishment, and fruit-bearing growth (John 15:4–10), so believers depend fully on the Savior as the source of their spiritual life and vitality.

6 This section is adapted from John MacArthur, *John 12–21*, MNTC (Chicago: Moody Press, 2008), 142. Used by permission of Moody Publishers.

7 Some of these metaphors are also applied to Israel in the Old Testament, such as the image of the vineyard, the flock, and the bride (see Isa. 5:1–7; 40:11; Ezek. 16:32; Hos. 3:1–5). Other images, such as the kingdom, the family, and the temple are alluded to in the Old Testament. However, the metaphor of the body is unique to the church and has no Old Testament equivalent.

The metaphor of the church as the temple of God illustrates the intimate fellowship that the church enjoys with God through Christ (John 17:21; 1 Cor. 1:9; 1 John 1:3; 2:24). Believers themselves are the temple of God, and every Christian has access to God through Christ (Heb. 4:14–16; 10:19–23). Having been built on the foundation of the Lord Jesus (1 Cor. 3:10–11; 1 Pet. 2:7), Christians are described as living stones who make up the temple of God (1 Pet. 2:4–8). The apostle Paul uses temple imagery to depict believers both individually (1 Cor. 6:19–20) and corporately (1 Cor. 3:16–17; Eph. 2:21–22).

Purposes of the Church

The church exists to display the wisdom and mercy of God in this present age (Eph. 3:10; cf. Rom. 9:23–24; 11:33; 1 Cor. 1:20–31) by proclaiming the gospel of Jesus Christ throughout the world (Matt. 28:19–20; Acts 1:8; 1 Pet. 2:9), so that sinners might be rescued from the domain of darkness (Col. 1:12–13), and so that unbelieving Israel might be provoked to jealousy and repentance (Rom. 10:19; 11:11).

Furthermore, the church exists to glorify God (Eph. 1:5–6, 12–14; 3:20–21; 2 Thess. 1:12) by actively building up its members in the faith (Eph. 4:12–16), faithfully teaching the Word (2 Tim. 2:15; 3:16–17), regularly observing the ordinances (Luke 22:19; Acts 2:38–42), proactively fostering fellowship among believers (Acts 2:42–47; 1 John 1:3), and boldly communicating the truth of the gospel to the lost (Matt. 28:19–20).

TO EXALT GOD

Because God is zealous for his glory (Isa. 48:9–11; cf. Isa. 43:6–7; 49:3), his people should likewise be consumed with a desire to glorify and exalt him (1 Cor. 10:31; cf. 6:20).

One of the primary ways in which the church exalts God is through worship and praise. Whenever the church gathers, worship ought to be the ultimate priority (cf. John 4:23–24). Worship consists of ascribing to God the honor that he is due, declaring his glory both in words of praise (e.g., Pss. 29:2; 95:6; 99:5, 9; Heb. 12:28) and through acts of obedience (Rom. 12:1). True worship necessarily includes the exaltation of Jesus Christ (cf. Phil. 2:9; cf. Acts 5:31).

TO EDIFY BELIEVERS

A key ministry of the church is the "building up" of itself (1 Cor. 14:26; 1 Thess. 5:11). This is known as "edification." Edification takes place through the ministry of the Word (Acts 20:32; 2 Tim. 3:15–17; 1 Pet. 2:2), the mentoring of godly leadership (Eph. 4:11–12), the selfless exercise of spiritual giftedness (1 Cor. 12:7; 1 Pet. 4:10), and the practice of the "one another" commands in the New Testament.

A list of those commands includes: love one another (Rom. 12:10; 13:8; 1 Thess. 3:12; 4:9; 2 Thess. 1:3; 1 Pet. 1:22; 4:8; 1 John 3:11, 23; 4:7, 11–12; 2 John 5); live in harmony with one another (Rom. 12:16; 15:5; cf. Gal. 5:26; 1 Thess. 5:13); bear one another's burdens (Gal. 6:2); confess sins to, and pray for, one another (James 5:16). The biblical context of these commands indicates that they are primarily intended to govern the believer's relationship to fellow Christians within the church. By putting these directives into practice, God's people thereby edify the body of Christ (cf. Rom. 14:19; 15:2) and exemplify the love of Christ to a watching world (John 13:35).

TO EVANGELIZE THE LOST

A church must likewise have a strong emphasis on evangelism, both locally and around the world. The church's evangelistic commission is articulated by Jesus himself in Matthew 28:18–20. This "Great Commission" indicates that true evangelism involves making disciples (not convincing unbelievers to make decisions). The pattern of disciple making was established by Jesus himself, who sought to make disciples during his earthly ministry (Mark 1:16–22; 2:14; John 8:31). His example is to be continued by his people.

Believers in the early church were characterized by a passion to preach the gospel and make disciples (cf. Acts. 2:47; 14:21). Their zeal made their enemies take notice (cf. Acts 1:8; 5:28; 19:10). The New Testament presents evangelism as the responsibility of church leaders (2 Tim. 4:5; cf. Eph. 4:11), Christian individuals (1 Pet. 3:15), and the church as a whole (1 Pet. 2:9).

Spiritual Authority in the Church

Jesus Christ is the Head of the church (Eph. 1:22; 4:15; 5:23; Col. 1:18; 2:19; cf. 1 Cor. 11:3). His sovereign lordship was bestowed on him by his heavenly Father (Matt. 11:27; John 3:35; 5:22; Acts 2:36; Phil. 2:9–11). He is the church's supreme authority. Submission to the sovereign lordship of Christ is not optional for believers, and their highest calling and supreme obligation is to submit joyfully to his commands (e.g., John 14:15, 21, 23; 15:10; 1 John 5:3; 2 John 6). That submission is expressed both individually (cf. Rom. 12:1–2; 1 Pet. 1:14–15) and corporately (cf. Col. 3:16).

GIFTED LEADERS

Christ's headship of the church is administered through godly leaders whom he has given to lead his people (1 Thess. 5:12–13; Heb. 13:7, 17). In Ephesians 4:11, Paul says of the ascended Christ, "He gave the apostles, the prophets, the evangelists, the shepherds [pastors] and teachers" (cf. 1 Cor. 12:28). Two of the groups delineated in that verse—namely, the apostles and the prophets, played a unique foundational role in the establishment of the church,[8] which Paul describes as "the household of God, built on the foundation of the apostles and prophets, Christ Jesus himself being the cornerstone" (Eph. 2:20). By identifying the apostles and prophets with the foundation-laying stage of the church, Paul indicated that those offices were limited to the earliest stages of church history.

In keeping with their foundational role, the apostles and the prophets declared the revelation of God's Word (Eph. 3:5; cf. Acts 11:28; 21:10–11) and confirmed their message with miraculous signs (2 Cor. 12:12; cf. Acts 8:6–7; Heb. 2:3–4). All subsequent generations of the church have been built on the revelatory foundation laid by the apostles and prophets in the writing of the New Testament (cf. 2 Pet. 1:19–21). The other groups—evangelists and pastor-teachers—have continued to build on that foundation by fervently proclaiming the gospel of grace and faithfully preaching the Word of truth (cf. 2 Tim. 4:1–5).

Apostles

The Greek word *apostolos*, translated "apostle," means "sent one" and applies to an ambassador, representative, or messenger. The term is sometimes used in the New Testament in a general sense to refer to the messengers of local churches (2 Cor. 8:23; Phil. 2:25). However, the primary New Testament use of the title applies to "apostles of Jesus Christ" (e.g., Gal. 1:1; 1 Pet. 1:1; Jude 17), those specific men whom Jesus personally selected to be his authorized representatives. That limited group included the Twelve (Matthias replacing Judas Iscariot, cf. Acts 1:26) and Paul, who was commissioned by Christ to be an apostle to the Gentiles (Gal. 1:15–17; cf. 1 Cor. 15:7–9; 2 Cor. 11:5).

The apostles of Jesus Christ met three basic qualifications. First, they were chosen directly by the Lord Jesus (Mark 3:14; Luke 6:13; Acts 1:2, 24; Gal. 1:1). Second, they were able to perform the signs of an apostle, being authenticated by miraculous "signs and wonders and mighty works" (2 Cor. 12:12; cf. Matt. 10:1–2; Acts 1:5–8; 2:43; 4:33; 5:12; Heb. 2:3–4). Third, with their own eyes they were witnesses of the resurrected Christ (Acts 1:21–25; 10:39–41; 1 Cor. 9:1; 15:7–8). Paul explicitly states that he was the last person to have met this third qualification (1 Cor. 15:8–9). This indicates that there have been no genuine apostles since Paul.

The New Testament apostles were Christ's authoritative revelatory agents; that is, he would continue to reveal his truth to them through the Holy Spirit (John 14:26; 15:26–27; 16:12–15). The early church recognized the apostles' teaching as

8 For a discussion of the gift of apostleship in response to charismatic claims, see John MacArthur, *Strange Fire: The Danger of Offending the Holy Spirit with Counterfeit Worship* (Nashville: Thomas Nelson, 2013), 85–103. For a specific response to those who claim that Paul's statement in Eph. 4:11–13 implies that all five ministries listed there continue throughout church history, see *Strange Fire*, 100–2. For a survey of the church fathers' perspective on the uniqueness of apostleship, see *Strange Fire*, 96–99.

having Christ's very authority, and that teaching was accorded the same weight as the Old Testament Scriptures (cf. Acts 2:42; 1 Cor. 14:37; 1 Thess. 2:13; 2 Tim. 3:16–17; 2 Pet. 3:16).

Prophets

The word translated "prophet," from the Greek *prophētēs*, means "one who speaks in the place of" or "a spokesman." New Testament prophets, then, were spokesmen for God, though second in rank to the apostles (1 Cor. 12:28). As in the Old Testament, prophets in the early church were primarily distinguished by their reception and delivery of new revelation from God (Acts 11:27–28), though sometimes they expounded on previously revealed truth (cf. Acts 13:1).

There was a constant threat of false prophets (Matt. 7:15; Acts 20:29–31; Jude 3–4). Accordingly, the prophet's message was to be tested against previously revealed truth (1 Cor. 14:29; 1 Thess. 5:20–22), and its genuineness was determined by its doctrinal accuracy (Deut. 13:1–5; Acts 20:29–30; 2 Pet. 2:1). Moreover, true prophets were characterized by both moral purity (Matt. 7:15–17; 2 Pet. 2:2–3; cf. Jer. 23:14–16) and revelatory accuracy (Deut. 18:20–22; Ezek. 13:3–9).[9]

Like the apostles, prophets were given to lay the revelatory foundation for the church (Eph. 2:20), and when the canon of New Testament revelation was complete, the prophetic office was no longer necessary (cf. Rev. 22:18–19). However, the *proclamation* of the prophetic word (2 Pet. 1:19–21) continues through the faithful preaching of Scripture, and in the future, after the church age ends, God will again raise up prophets to accomplish his revelatory purposes (cf. Rev. 11:3).

Evangelists

All believers are commanded to preach the gospel (Matt. 28:18–20; Acts 1:8), but some are especially gifted as evangelists. Apart from Ephesians 4:11, the term "evangelist" occurs only twice in the New Testament—Acts 21:8 of Philip (cf. Acts 8:4–40), and Timothy is instructed to "do the work of an evangelist" (2 Tim. 4:5). However, the Greek noun *euangelion* ("good news" or "gospel") is used more than seventy-five times, and the cognate verb *euangelizō* ("to declare the good news") occurs more than fifty times.

Evangelists are uniquely gifted by God at reaching lost sinners with the saving truth of the gospel. Their ministry is one that every church ought to prioritize—both by encouraging evangelism in the local community and by supporting missionary work around the world.

9 For a longer discussion regarding the gift of prophecy in response to modern charismatic claims, see MacArthur, *Strange Fire*, 105–32.

Pastor-Teachers

In Ephesians 4:11, the Greek word *poimēn* can be translated as either "pastor" or "shepherd." It describes the leadership, protection, and care that pastors exhibit toward the members of their flock. The Lord Jesus is the great Shepherd (Heb. 13:20–21; 1 Pet. 2:25); those whom he has given to the church as pastors are to be his undershepherds (1 Pet. 5:2). Their primary function is to feed the sheep (cf. John 21:15–17), a responsibility that they accomplish through teaching the Word (cf. 2 Tim. 3:16–17; 1 Pet. 2:2–3). Teaching may be identified as a distinct ministry (1 Cor. 12:28); however, the combination of "shepherds and teachers" in Ephesians 4:11 describes two facets of a single office of pastoral leadership (see "shepherds" in Acts 20:28; 1 Pet. 5:2; and "teachers" in 1 Tim. 3:2; 5:17).

Like the apostles, pastors ought to devote themselves primarily "to prayer and to the ministry of the word" (Acts 6:4). The diligent pastor-teacher is a "good servant of Christ Jesus" (1 Tim. 4:6), being approved as "a worker who has no need to be ashamed, rightly handling the word of truth" (2 Tim. 2:15; cf. 4:2), and struggling in prayer on behalf of his people (cf. Col. 4:12). Though structure and administration have their place, true power in the church comes through prayer and the ministry of the Word.

The New Testament uses two other terms to denote the office of the pastor. The first is "bishop" (Gk. *episkopos*, "overseer" or "guardian"), which occurs five times in the New Testament (Acts 20:28; Phil. 1:1; 1 Tim. 3:2; Titus 1:7; 1 Pet. 2:25). In secular Greek, the term designated a delegate appointed by the emperor to provide leadership and political oversight to a municipality. Similarly, in the church, bishops operate under the authority of Jesus as they lead in the church, albeit through humble service rather than authoritarian control (Mark 10:42–43). The spiritual overseer is responsible for both feeding (1 Tim. 3:2) and protecting the flock (Acts 20:28) under his charge.

The other term is "elder" (Gk. *presbyteros*), which speaks to the seasoned spiritual maturity of those who lead in the church. In the New Testament, *presbyteros* can be used in a generic sense to refer to people of advanced age (Acts 2:17; cf. 1 Tim. 5:2). It can also refer to the first-century leaders of Israel (Matt. 15:2; 27:3, 41; Mark 7:3, 5; Luke 22:52; Acts 4:8). But in an ecclesiological context, the title designates a specific office of spiritual leadership within the church (e.g., Acts 11:30; 14:23; 15:2, 4, 6, 22; 16:4; 20:17; 21:18).

The New Testament concept of the office of elder is primarily drawn from Old Testament Judaism (cf. Ex. 12:21; 19:7; Num. 11:16; Deut. 27:1; 1 Sam. 11:3; 16:4). The elders of Israel were mature men who exhibited strong moral convictions, being characterized by truth, integrity, courage, the fear of the Lord, wisdom, and discernment (Ex. 18:21–22; cf. Num. 11:16–17; Deut. 1:13–17).

That the early church was led by elders is clearly demonstrated throughout the New Testament. The Jerusalem church had elders (Acts 11:29–30); Paul appointed elders in the churches he planted (Acts 14:23; 20:17); the churches to whom Peter addressed his epistles were similarly led by elders (1 Pet. 5:1–2). The book of Revelation further indicates that twenty-four elders will represent the redeemed in eternity future (e.g., Rev. 4:4, 10; 5:5–6, 8, 11, 14; 7:11).

Textual evidence indicates that all three New Testament terms ("pastor," "bishop," and "elder") refer to the same office of church leadership. A comparison of 1 Timothy 3:1–7 and Titus 1:6–9 demonstrates that the qualifications for a bishop and an elder are the same, suggesting that the two offices are identical. In Titus 1:5–7, Paul even uses both titles to refer to the same person. All three terms are found together in 1 Peter 5:1–2: "the elders (plural of *presbyteros*)," are to "shepherd (Gk. *poimainō*) the flock," by "exercising oversight (Gk. *episkopeō*)." In Acts 20, after assembling the elders (plural of *presbyteros*, 20:17) of Ephesus, Paul called them "overseers [plural of *episkopos*]" and charged them "to care for [*poimainō*] the church of God" (20:28).

Each term has a unique emphasis: "elder" emphasizes a man's maturity and personal character; "bishop" speaks to his leadership role as protector of the flock; and "pastor" emphasizes his sincere care for the people whom he serves. Because some of these titles (such as *bishop* and even *pastor*) have taken on unbiblical connotations, the title *elder* may be preferable as the basic title for this office.

ELDERS

Scripture teaches that God has given elders to each local congregation in order to oversee and lead his people. The office of elder (pastor-teacher) entails a responsibility that must not be taken lightly (cf. Luke 12:48; cf. James 3:1)

Responsibilities

The responsibilities of an *episkopos* include to "care for God's church" (1 Tim. 3:5) and to provide leadership and give oversight to local church affairs—"to rule" (1 Tim. 5:17). The term translated "rule" (Gk. *proistēmi*) is applied to elders several times throughout the New Testament (Rom. 12:8; 1 Thess. 5:12; 1 Tim. 3:4–5, 12; 5:17). This responsibility of oversight is entrusted to elders by Christ himself, signifying that there is no earthly authority in the local church higher than theirs.

Yet their authority is not coerced by force or intimidation; rather, it is an authority built on precept and example to which the church gladly submits (cf. Heb. 13:17). The elders lead the local church, but the congregation—the flock—does not belong to them. The members of the church constitute the "flock of God" (1 Pet. 5:2), which he bought (Acts 20:28) and for which the elders serve as caretakers and stewards. Spiritual authority, unlike worldly leadership, is characterized by Christlike humility and a desire to serve (Mark 10:43–45).

The responsibility of preaching and teaching lies with the elders (1 Tim. 5:17), so elders must be "able to teach" (1 Tim. 3:2). They must instruct in sound doctrine and refute error and falsehood (Titus 1:9), through the careful exposition of the Scriptures (1 Tim. 4:13; 2 Tim. 2:15; cf. Neh. 8:8). This is the primary means by which the flock is spiritually fed and nourished (1 Pet. 2:2; cf. Ps. 1:2–3; Heb. 5:12–13). Preaching the Word teaches, reproves, and equips the flock (2 Tim. 3:16–17).

Beyond teaching, elders are also responsible to determine church government and structure (cf. Acts 15:22), ordain other elders (1 Tim. 4:14), set an example for the sheep to follow (1 Pet. 5:1–3; Heb. 13:7), protect the flock from doctrinal error (Acts 20:28–30), and pray for the members of the church (James 5:14).

Qualifications

Paul delineates the qualifications for elders in 1 Timothy 3:1–7 and Titus 1:6–9. In both places, the overarching standard for an elder is that he must be "above reproach," meaning that he is a man of impeccable spiritual and moral character. Simply put, these qualities demand that elders must be men whose lives are characteristically free from any corruption or stain that might bring reproach on the gospel.

In every sphere of life—marriage, family, community, and church—the elder must be above reproach. He must be "the husband of one wife" (1 Tim. 3:2)—literally translated, "a one-woman man." This obviously prohibits polygamy, but the meaning is that an elder must be a man of moral integrity and total sexual fidelity as a husband—fully devoted to the one wife whom God has given him. If unmarried, his life must be an example of moral purity, free from fornication or a reputation for flirtatious behavior.

An elder must be "sober-minded" and "self-controlled" (1 Tim. 3:2)—characterized by wisdom and maturity, exhibiting temperance and moderation. He must conduct himself in a "respectable" manner (1 Tim. 3:2) as a representative of Christ's church. He is to be "hospitable" toward others— welcoming and friendly to those in the church as well as to those who do not know him (1 Tim. 3:2). The word "hospitable" speaks of "the love of strangers."

In 1 Timothy 3:3, Paul lists the qualities that must be absent from the life of an elder: "not a drunkard, not violent but gentle, not quarrelsome, not a lover of money." As a servant of Christ, an elder must not be controlled by sinful addictions (e.g., drunkenness, Eph. 5:18), reckless passions (e.g., anger and belligerence, Eph. 4:26–27), or financial ambitions (e.g., the love of money, 1 Tim. 6:9–10).

In 1 Timothy 3:4 Paul writes that an elder "must manage his own household well, with all dignity keeping his children submissive." An elder must demonstrate irreproachable behavior in his home, in front of those who know him most intimately. Skillful management of his family demonstrates his ability to shepherd the church (1 Tim. 3:5).

These high standards demand that an elder should not be a recent convert (1 Tim. 3:6). The personal and spiritual maturity required of an elder takes years to develop, and there must be adequate time for others to observe his life and affirm his qualifications. As Paul warned Timothy, those who are too quickly elevated to the position of elder are susceptible to the sin of pride.

An elder must also have an excellent reputation with those outside the church (1 Tim. 3:7).

In addition to the qualifications mentioned in 1 Timothy 3, in Titus 1:6–9 Paul explains that an elder's *children* should be "believers and not open to the charge of debauchery or insubordination" (Titus 1:6). Because the behavior of an elder's children reflects on his spiritual leadership in the home, they must not be characterized by rebellion.

"As God's steward," an elder must not be "arrogant," "quick-tempered," "a drunkard," "violent," or "greedy for gain" (Titus 1:7). Conversely, he must be "hospitable, a lover of good, self-controlled, upright, holy, and disciplined" (Titus 1:8). Added to that, he ought to be a skillful student of God's Word, being "able to give instruction in sound doctrine" while also rebuking "those who contradict it" (Titus 1:9).

The New Testament makes no provision for and does not permit women to hold the office of pastor or teacher (cf. Acts 13:1; 1 Cor. 12:28; Eph. 4:11); only men may serve as elders and pastors. As Paul directs in 1 Timothy 2:12, "I do not permit (Gk. *epitrepō*) a woman to teach or to exercise authority over a man; rather, she is to remain quiet." The verb "to teach" (or "to be a teacher") indicates that women are not to hold teaching positions over men in the church. That stipulation does not reflect a first-century cultural bias or Pauline prejudice. Rather, it is grounded in both the created order and the events of the fall (cf. 1 Tim. 2:13–14). This would not preclude a woman from teaching in other appropriate contexts, such as teaching other women (Titus 2:3–4) or teaching children (2 Tim. 1:5; 3:14–15). The Bible clearly indicates that women are spiritual equals with men and that the ministry of women is essential to the body of Christ.

Ordination

In the New Testament, elders were uniquely set apart for their office. The Greek word *kathistēmi*, meaning "to ordain," was normally used to describe the appointment of elders and signifies a divine calling and setting aside to spiritual leadership that is officially recognized by the church.

In 1 Timothy 4:14 Paul refers to the practice of laying on of hands by the elders. This practice finds its roots in the Old Testament sacrificial system. In the Old Testament, the laying on of hands indicated identification with the one on whom hands were placed (as in the case of the sacrifices, see Lev. 1:4; 3:2–13; 4:4–33; 8:14, 18, 22; 16:21), and it also symbolized a transference of authority (Num. 27:18–23; Deut. 34:9). It was also used to indicate a blessing conveyed from one party to another (Gen. 48:13–20; 2 Kings 13:16; Job 9:33; Ps. 139:5). Since these solemn purposes are also reflected in New Testament ordination of elders, this act must not be performed rashly (cf. 1 Tim. 5:22). Men being considered for ordination must be adequately tested by the recognized leaders of the church (cf. Acts 14:23; 1 Tim. 4:14; Titus 1:5) in order to demonstrate that they are qualified to serve in pastoral ministry.

Acts 6:2–6 does not teach that it is the congregation's responsibility to select and approve new elders. In that instance the seven men who were chosen are not called elders. They were chosen to serve tables, not to lead the church.[10] Furthermore, the congregation brought these men to the apostles for approval, not vice versa. The apostles initiated the process (Acts 6:3) and were the ones who ultimately appointed these men to minister (Acts 6:6).

The first qualification for an elder is a God-given desire in the heart of the individual being consider for eldership (1 Tim. 3:1). Potential elders should not be coerced or manipulated into pursuing the office, since serving in that capacity begins with a humble and heartfelt willingness to lead (cf. 1 Pet. 5:2)

Before the ordination can be completed, the elders must prayerfully seek the Lord's wisdom (cf. James 1:5) and his will with regard to the appointment (cf. Acts 13:2; 14:23). Appointing elders in an attitude of prayer rightly recognizes that God is ultimately the One who gifts, calls, and commissions men to spiritual leadership.

Because it is the highest calling from God in the life of a local church, spiritual leadership must not be taken lightly or sought superficially (cf. Acts 20:28).

Support

The New Testament indicates that it is appropriate for elders to be compensated financially by the church for their ministry labors. Paul articulates this principle when he writes, "Let the elders who rule well be considered worthy of double honor, especially those who labor in preaching and teaching. For the Scripture says, 'You shall not muzzle an ox when it treads out the grain' and, 'The laborer deserves his wages'" (1 Tim. 5:17–18). The word translated "honor" in 5:17 (from Gk. *timē*) refers to remuneration, as the biblical allusions in 5:18 make clear. Paul expands on this theme in 1 Corinthians 9:4–9.

Plurality

New Testament churches were governed by a plurality of elders in each local congregation. The word *presbyteros* regularly occurs in the plural when used in

10 See the section on "Acts 6 and Deacons," below.

the New Testament (e.g., Acts 11:30; 14:23; 15:2; 20:17; Titus 1:5; James 5:14). The few exceptions occur when a biblical author applies the term to himself (e.g., 1 Pet. 5:1; 2 John 1; 3 John 1) or when an individual elder is being singled out (1 Tim. 5:19). Paul addresses the believers in Philippi by greeting "all the saints in Christ Jesus who are at Philippi, with the overseers [plural of *episkopos*] and deacons" (Phil. 1:1). Significantly, the New Testament never mentions a one-pastor congregation.[11]

A church governed by a plurality of godly elders enjoys all the divinely intended benefits, including their combined knowledge, wisdom, and experience. This provides a wealth of counsel for shepherding the flock (Prov. 11:14; 15:22) and also safeguards the congregation from any self-serving preferences of a single individual.

Church Government

Elders are shepherds of the flock, leading by giving direction and by personal example, and feeding and protecting the flock by teaching God's Word. They are under the authority of Christ, the Chief Shepherd, and are answerable to him (1 Pet. 5:2–4). After Christ, they represent the highest level of spiritual authority within the local church. Consequently, each local assembly ought to be governed by its own elders (cf. Titus 1:5), without coercion from external hierarchies. As God-ordained leaders of the church, the elders ought to determine matters of policy, membership, and discipline as they prayerfully look for guidance from the Scriptures (cf. Acts 15:19–31; 20:28; 1 Cor. 5:4–7, 13; 1 Pet. 5:1–4). Churches are free to cooperate with other churches but should do so at the discretion of the elders in keeping with biblical principles.

While democratic political values often prompt modern churchgoers to be suspicious of elder rule, the clear New Testament paradigm for spiritual leadership within the church calls for qualified, godly elders to take the primary responsibility for serving and leading God's people.

Historically, the various forms of church government include the episcopal, presbyterian, and congregational forms.[12] The episcopal form places primary leadership responsibility with the *episkopos*, or "bishop" (e.g., Methodism, Anglicanism, and Roman Catholicism) and usually involves multiple levels of hierarchy (e.g., priests, bishops, archbishops). However, this system creates a distinction

11 Some appeal to Revelation 1–3 to support an only-one-pastor model, arguing that "the angels [lit., "messengers"] of the seven churches" (1:20) refer to the singular pastors of each church. However, given the New Testament pattern, which clearly depicts a plurality of godly leaders in every local congregation (cf. Acts 14:23; Titus 1:5), it is likely that these messengers were key leaders who represented a group of elders in each church.

12 For a more detailed discussion of these forms of church government, see the helpful survey in Millard J. Erickson, *Christian Theology*, 2nd ed. (Grand Rapids, MI: Baker, 2001), 1080–93.

between the *episkopos* ("bishop") and the *presbyteros* ("elder")—a distinction not found in the New Testament. Furthermore, this form of church government is especially vulnerable to corruption due to its hierarchical structure.[13]

The presbyterian form of church government focuses on the role of the *presbyteros*, or "elder," noting that the terms "bishop" and "elder" are interchangeable in the New Testament (cf. 1 Tim. 3:1–2; Titus 1:7) (e.g., Presbyterian and Reformed denominations). This emphasis on elder rule is clearly affirmed in the New Testament (1 Thess. 5:12; Heb. 13:17). However, the extrabiblical hierarchical structures historically associated with Presbyterianism (e.g., local church sessions, regional presbyteries, synods, general assemblies) are not found in the New Testament.

Congregational forms of church government, such as those of Baptists and Congregationalists, emphasize the individual autonomy of each local congregation. While congregationalism rightly rejects ecclesiastical hierarchy, it usually insists on a democratic approach to leadership in which all church members (not just the elders) are involved in church decision making. However, this does not reflect the New Testament pattern of local church oversight by a plurality of godly elders, as discussed above.

Authority

On account of both their position of leadership and their responsibility for the flock, elders ought to be treated with great respect (cf. 1 Thess. 5:12–13), and the congregation is to submit to the leadership of the elders (cf. Heb. 13:17). Church members are to esteem their leaders and are instructed to follow their godly example (Heb. 13:7; cf. 1 Cor. 4:16; 11:1).

Though elders are to be respected, they are not above God's law. Credible accusations of sin against an elder should not be ignored or treated lightly (cf. 1 Tim. 5:19–21). When elders sin, they are subject to the same process of church discipline as any other member of the church (cf. Matt. 18:15–17). When a church willfully ignores sin in the lives of its leaders, its testimony before the watching world suffers and the purity of the people is negatively affected. A church's disobedience in this regard will invite the chastising judgment of God, rather than his blessing (cf. Heb. 12:3–11; Rev. 2:20–23; 3:19).

DEACONS

Office and Qualifications

Paul's language in 1 Timothy 3:8–13 indicates that deacons occupy a recognized office in the church, just as the elders do. As the elders lead the church, they are assisted in their ministry by the deacons. However, in defining the office of dea-

13 Cf. William Webster, *The Church of Rome at the Bar of History* (Carlisle, PA: Banner of Truth, 1997); E. R. Chamberlin, *The Bad Popes* (Stroud, UK: Sutton, 2003).

con, the New Testament puts more weight on a person's moral integrity, spiritual maturity, and doctrinal purity than on the functions of the office. Scripture reveals more about the deacons' spiritual qualifications than it does about their duties.

The Greek words *diakonos* ("servant"), *diakonia* ("service"), and *diakoneō* ("to serve") are all used to describe the ministry of a deacon. Initially, this word group may have specifically applied to serving food and waiting tables (cf. Luke 4:39; 10:40; 17:8; 22:27; John 2:5, 9; 12:2; Acts 6:2), but it came to include any service or ministry that might be performed to meet the needs of other people (cf. John 12:26; Rom. 13:3–4). These words were also used to describe spiritual service to the Lord on the part of a believer, including acts of obedience or acts of service on behalf of the church (cf. Acts 20:19; Rom. 12:6–7; 15:25; 1 Cor. 12:5; 16:15; 2 Cor. 4:1; 8:3–4; 9:1; Rev. 2:19).

Deacons must be "dignified," honorable in behavior and respectable in reputation. They must be "not double-tongued," that is, they must be consistent and truthful in their speech. They must not be "addicted to much wine" but be known for being sober-minded and Spirit-filled (1 Tim. 3:8; cf. Eph. 5:18). A deacon must not be "greedy for dishonest gain" or motivated by the love of money (1 Tim. 6:9–10), especially since his service in the church might involve handling funds.

As Paul explains, "They must hold the mystery of the faith with a clear conscience" (1 Tim. 3:9), that is, they must not only embrace sound doctrine ("the mystery of the faith") but must also apply it consistently in their actions, which is why their consciences are clear. They should "be tested first" and so "prove themselves blameless" (1 Tim. 3:10). As elders are to be above reproach, so also deacons must demonstrate a consistent pattern of life that is irreproachable.

As with elders, deacons must "be the husband of one wife" 1 Tim. 3:12). (See above under "Elders: Qualifications.") As with elders, deacons must manage "their children and their own households well" (3:12). By leading his family well, the deacon demonstrates that he is also capable of serving in key roles of responsibility within the church (cf. 3:5). (See above under "Elders: Qualifications.")

The primary difference between deacons and elders is that elders must possess the ability to teach (1 Tim. 3:2). Nonetheless, deacons contribute to the teaching ministry of the elders by assisting them with other tasks, thereby freeing up the elders for the ministry of the Word.

Deacons care for the flock under the oversight of the elders by organizing and executing administrative tasks and other service-oriented ministries. The deacon's role is one of selfless service on behalf of others—a role that Christ himself modeled perfectly (Phil. 2:3–7). The reward for such service does not consist of temporal riches or worldly fame; rather, it is measured in terms of the eternal blessings that await those who faithfully serve their heavenly Master (1 Tim. 3:13; cf. Matt. 25:21, 23).

Deaconesses

First Timothy 3:11 indicates that the office of deacon was available not only to men but also to women (i.e., deaconesses). Some interpret this verse as referring to the wives of deacons, but such is unlikely. First, the possessive pronoun "their" or the article "the" that some Bible versions add before the word "women" or "wives" is not in the original, and the grammar suggests that the women addressed in 3:11 are relationally distinct from the men addressed in the previous verses (cf. the marginal notes in the ESV, NASB, NIV, and HCSB).

Also, the description of Phoebe in Romans 16:1 provides a likely example of a woman who served as a deaconess. Paul refers to her as "our sister Phoebe, a servant [a form of *diakonos*] of the church at Cenchreae." Apparently, Phoebe served on her own (with no mention of her husband as a deacon) in some recognized capacity—likely as a deaconess—within her local congregation.

Acts 6 and Deacons

Many have understood Acts 6:1–6 to be a New Testament example of deacons. In that passage, Luke uses the Greek terms *diakonia* and *diakoneō*. However, the use of those terms is inconclusive in this context, since *diakonia* is also applied to the ministry of the apostles in 6:4. Furthermore, the New Testament never specifically refers to the seven men listed in Acts 6:5 as "deacons." Stephen and Philip are both mentioned later in Acts (6:8–15; 7:1–60; 8:5–12, 26–40) but neither are called deacons. The situation in Acts 6:1–6 seems to be a specific dilemma in the early church, with these seven men being selected to resolve a one-time crisis (rather than being appointed to a permanent office).[14] Accordingly, the terms *diakonia* and *diakoneō* in Acts 6 should be interpreted in the general sense of "service" and "to serve."

While the seven men in Acts 6 cannot be classified as deacons in an official sense, they do offer an example for the office of deacon in important ways. First, these men assisted the leaders so that they could remain focused on their primary spiritual responsibilities of teaching and prayer (cf. Acts 6:4). Second, their spiritual character anticipated Paul's list of qualifications in 1 Timothy 3:8–13 (cf. Acts 6:3). Third, they provided practical care (such as organizing and implementing the distribution of food, resolving conflict, addressing the grievances of those who had been neglected, and providing physical care with sensitivity to the spiritual state of the individuals to whom they ministered).

14 The fact that the men chosen in Acts 6 are not mentioned (along with the elders) in Acts 11:29–30 further supports the conclusion that their role was temporary.

Biblical Dynamics of Church Life

One of the most defining depictions of the early church is found in Acts 2:41–47. As Luke describes the Jerusalem church, he delineates five marks of that faithful church that characterized their devotion.

DEVOTED TO CHRIST

On the day of Pentecost (Acts 2:14–40) three thousand people (Acts 2:41) believed in Christ, were baptized, and were incorporated into the church. They demonstrated the genuineness of their profession of faith in their continual devotion to Christ. In Acts 2:42, the Greek verb translated "devoted" carries the idea of steadfast dedication and persevering affection. In the face of ridicule, rejection, and persecution, these believers exhibited the abiding commitment to Christ that characterizes genuine Christians (John 15:1–4; cf. Matt. 13:3–9, 21; 1 John 2:19), showing themselves to truly be his disciples (John 8:31).

Churches that are courageously devoted to the Lord Jesus will be characterized by purity in both life and doctrine (cf. 1 Tim. 4:16), often causing the world to resist or avoid them (cf. Acts 5:13–14). Their priority will be to honor Christ, the Head of the church, by equipping their members both to do the work of the ministry (Eph. 4:12) and to evangelize the lost as they go about their daily lives (Matt. 28:19). The New Testament commends churches that demonstrate a Christ-centered commitment to both moral and doctrinal purity—as Paul commended the Thessalonians (cf. 1 Thess. 1:2–10).

DEVOTED TO SCRIPTURE

Acts 2:42 says the Jerusalem believers "devoted themselves to the apostles' teaching." The content of that instruction included expositions of the Old Testament Scriptures (Acts 6:4; cf. Luke 24:44–49), teachings from the life and ministry of Jesus (John 14:26; 1 Cor. 11:23–26), and new revelation given by the Holy Spirit to the apostles (John 16:12–15).

The New Testament emphasizes the importance of reading and teaching the Scriptures in the church (1 Tim. 4:13), charging pastors to preach the Word faithfully and without compromise (cf. 2 Tim. 4:1–2) and charging the members of the congregation to edify one another with Scripture (cf. Col. 3:16). Those leaders who faithfully proclaim what Scripture teaches firmly establish their congregations in the truth (cf. Ps. 1:1–3; 1 John 2:12–14).

DEVOTED TO ONE ANOTHER

The members of the early church were also devoted to "the fellowship" (Acts 2:42). They were distinguished by devotion and commitment to their fellow members of the body of Christ. The term "fellowship" (Gk. *koinōnia*) refers to "sharing" or "partnership." Every believer is in permanent fellowship with the Lord Jesus Christ through faith in him (John 17:21; 1 Cor. 1:9). As a result, believers are also in fellowship with one another (1 John 1:3). They demonstrate that fellowship through a commitment to serve fellow believers and encourage them to love and good deeds (cf. Heb. 10:24–25).

DEVOTED TO THE LORD'S TABLE

The first church was also devoted "to the breaking of bread," a reference to the celebration of the Lord's Supper (Acts 2:42). Jesus himself instituted this ordinance (cf. Matt. 26:26–29), which symbolizes the believer's union with Christ (cf. Rom. 6:5) and the unity that believers share with one another (cf. Eph. 4:5; 1 Cor. 10:16–17).

Celebrating the Lord's Table also causes believers to examine their hearts, confessing and repenting of any known sin. In that way, it operates as a purifying influence in the church, as believers reflect on the cross and forsake their sin. Those who participate in the Lord's Supper in an unworthy manner invite the Lord's chastising judgment (1 Cor. 11:27–32).

DEVOTED TO PRAYER

Finally, Acts 2:42 explains that the early church was also devoted to "the prayers." Recognizing the necessity of divine wisdom and assistance (cf. John 14:13–14; James 1:5), these believers were characterized by a relentless commitment to corporate prayer (cf. Acts 1:14, 24; 4:24–31). That same priority ought to mark the church today. Congregations that fail to commune with the Lord through prayer will inevitably be characterized by spiritual weakness and apathy. By contrast, the New Testament repeatedly calls believers to pray fervently and continually (Luke 18:1; Rom. 12:12; Eph. 6:18; Col. 4:2; 1 Thess. 5:17).

RESULTS OF DEVOTION

The church of Acts 2:42 understood the vital importance of pursuing the right priorities. In Acts 2:43–47, Luke details the results that flowed out of the devotion exhibited by these believers. They experienced a sense of holy awe as they witnessed the miraculous signs being performed by the apostles (Acts 2:43). Their congregation was also characterized by sacrificial sharing and selfless generosity (Acts 2:44–45). Their eagerness to sell their belongings to meet the needs of others was a demonstration of the genuineness of their love for one another (Acts 4:34–36), but it was not a form of communism or communalism. The imperfect tense of the verbs "selling" and "distributing" indicates that these were ongoing actions, meaning that, in response to the Spirit's prompting, believers sold personal belongings as individual needs arose (cf. 1 Cor. 16:1–2). Acts 2:46 makes it clear that these believers retained ownership of their homes and that personal property was sold only on a voluntary basis (Acts 5:4; cf. 2 Cor. 8:13–14).

This early congregation also experienced supernatural joy (Acts 2:46). The generosity of their heartfelt love for one another produced an uncontainable gladness that erupted in praise to God (Acts 2:47) and impacted the unbelievers around them, who responded favorably to the irrefutable transformation and selfless virtues they observed in the lives of these believers (Acts 2:47).

Means of Grace within the Church[15]

Historically, the "means of grace"[16] are the instruments through which God's Spirit graciously grows believers in Christlikeness as he fortifies them in the faith and conforms them into the image of the Son (2 Cor. 3:17–18). The New Testament teaches that God also promotes the spiritual welfare of his people through the preaching of the Word, the right practice of the ordinances (baptism and the Lord's Supper), as well as other means—including prayer, worship, fellowship, and the process of church discipline.[17]

GOD'S WORD

The primary means the Spirit of God uses to grow believers in sanctification is his Word (1 Pet. 2:1–3 NASB; cf. John 17:17). When believers saturate their minds with the Word of God (cf. Col. 3:16), they come under the Spirit's control (cf. Rom. 8:14; Gal. 5:16–18; Eph. 5:18), and they produce the fruit of the Spirit (Gal. 5:22–23). The Scripture is a key part of the Spirit's armor against sin and temptation (Eph. 6:17; cf. Matt. 4:4, 7, 10).

It is essential for churches to prioritize the vital ministry of the Word—just as the apostles themselves did (Acts 6:4). This ministry is primarily accomplished through reading, preaching, and teaching the Scriptures (cf. 1 Tim. 4:13).

BAPTISM

The Lord Jesus gave the church two ordinances that they are to observe: baptism (Matt. 3:13–17; 28:19) and the celebration of the Lord's Supper (Luke 22:19–20). The word *baptize* (from Gk. *baptizō*) means "to immerse" or "to dip," and this ought to guide the church in the practice of this ordinance.

15 For further discussion concerning the means of grace as they relate to the believer's sanctification, see "The Character of Progressive Sanctification," in chap. 7, "Salvation" (p. 346).

16 "Means of grace" should not be confused with the "sacraments" of Roman Catholicism. For a fuller treatment of this point see Wayne Grudem, *Systematic Theology: An Introduction to Biblical Doctrine* (Grand Rapids, MI: Zondervan, 1994), 951–52.

17 For a similar list of the "means of grace," see Grudem, *Systematic Theology*, 951.

Baptism of the Holy Spirit

The New Testament teaches that all believers are immersed into Christ Jesus at the moment of conversion (Rom. 6:3; cf. Matt. 3:11). They are baptized by Christ with his Holy Spirit. Through this Spirit baptism (which is entirely God's work), believers are united with Christ (1 Cor. 6:17; 2 Cor. 5:17; Gal. 3:27) and placed into his body, the church (1 Cor. 12:13).

Spirit baptism occurs only once, at the moment of salvation, and should not be sought as a secondary, post-conversion experience. Some look to the book of Acts to defend their view that believers ought to seek a baptism of the Holy Spirit after conversion. However,

> Scripture contains no command, suggestion, or method for believers to seek or receive the baptism of the Spirit. You do not seek or ask for that which you already possess. . . . [The] special transitional events [in Acts, of those waiting to receive Spirit baptism] did not represent the norm, as our present text makes clear, but were given to indicate to all that the Body was one (Acts 11:15–17).[18]

Baptism a Symbol for Believers

Water baptism is intended to symbolize that internal reality of salvation. A new believer is to be baptized in water as a public testimony to their faith in and solidarity with the Lord Jesus. It is the outward, post-conversion demonstration of an inward reality that has already occurred at conversion.

Baptism is the first step of obedience for believers after they have embraced the Lord Jesus in saving faith. Though not salvific, baptism is commanded by Christ himself (Matt. 28:19).

The proper mode of baptism is by immersion, as indicated by the Greek word *baptizō*. Immersion also serves as a symbol of one's burial and resurrection, signifying the spiritual reality that believers have died to sin and risen with Christ (cf. Rom. 6:4, 10).

In Scripture, only believers are said to be baptized[19] since baptism requires that repentance and faith precede the external symbol (cf. Acts 2:38). According to Colossians 2:12, those who have been baptized into Christ (a spiritual reality represented by water baptism) have been "raised with him through faith." First Peter 3:21 explains that baptism symbolizes "an appeal to God for a good conscience."

18 John MacArthur, *1 Corinthians*, MNTC (Chicago: Moody Press, 1984), comment on 1 Cor. 12:13.

19 Arguments for infant baptism from the "household" passages in Acts 10:34–48; 11:14; 16:11–15; and 1 Cor. 1:4–16 are unconvincing. Infants and children are not mentioned in these verses, and it is clear that in each case the recipients of baptism first heard the gospel and believed.

None of these realities can be exhibited by an infant.[20] Hence, the practice of infant baptism (paedobaptism) should be rejected. Believer's baptism (credobaptism) was the prevailing practice of the early church until at least the third century.[21]

Baptism and Salvation

Water baptism is not a means of salvation, but a symbol of the believer's union with Christ and of Spirit baptism. The thief on the cross provides an example of one who was saved without being baptized (Luke 23:40–43). Similarly, Cornelius was clearly saved and received the Holy Spirit before being baptized (Acts 10:44–48). Water baptism is an external demonstration of what has already occurred in the heart through the regenerating power of the Holy Spirit.

In spite of Scripture's clarity regarding what is necessary for salvation (Acts 16:30–31), some mistakenly insist that the symbol of water baptism is actually the means of salvation rather than an outward demonstration of it (a view known as "baptismal regeneration"). By confusing the symbol of water baptism with the reality of God's grace in salvation, they eliminate the reality by adding works to the gospel (cf. Rom. 11:6).

However, baptism is closely associated with salvation (cf. Eph. 4:5). In Acts, those who believed were baptized immediately (Acts 2:41; 8:38; 9:18; 10:48; 18:8; 19:1–5), indicating that it should closely follow a genuine profession of faith.

Believers are to be baptized "in the name of the Father and of the Son and of the Holy Spirit" (Matt. 28:19), not as a sacramental formula but rather as a comprehensive acknowledgment of the union believers have with the triune God through faith in Christ.

THE LORD'S TABLE

A second ordinance that must be observed by the church is the Lord's Table (or the Lord's Supper). Unlike baptism, which is observed once following conversion, the Lord's Supper is to be celebrated repeatedly throughout the Christian life.

Background and Practice

On the night before his death, the Lord Jesus celebrated a final Passover meal with his disciples and instituted what came to be known as the Lord's Supper, or Communion (Matt. 26:26–29).

The observance of Communion was practiced by the church from its inception on the day of Pentecost (Acts 2:42). The early church also developed congregational meals that came to be known as love feasts (Jude 12), which were

20 For further explanation of these and similar texts, see the concise response to paedobaptism in John Piper, *Brothers, We Are Not Professionals*, expanded ed. (Nashville: B&H, 2013), 154–62.

21 For a detailed discussion of this point, see Everett Ferguson, *Baptism in the Early Church: History, Theology, and Liturgy in the First Five Centuries* (Grand Rapids, MI: Eerdmans, 2009).

associated with the Lord's Supper. These meals were designed to foster fellowship and mutual care among the members of the church. But some used these meals as an opportunity to show partiality and engage in drunkenness (1 Cor. 11:18, 21; cf. 2 Pet. 2:13). When they connected such behavior to the Lord's Supper, they desecrated the holy ordinance (cf. 1 Cor. 11:27–32).

Though believers ought to pursue holiness at all times (1 Pet. 1:15–17), the celebration of the Lord's Supper is an occasion when they ought to carefully examine their hearts, confessing and repenting from any known sin before the Lord. Those who participate in Communion without repenting of known sin profane the celebration and invite the chastisement of God (cf. 1 Cor. 11:23–26).

Views on the Meaning of Communion

Jesus's repeated instruction, "Do this in remembrance of me" (Luke 22:19; 1 Cor. 11:24–25), indicates that the celebration of the Lord's Supper is not optional. It should be observed routinely, and prolonged failure to do so constitutes a sin. Jesus instituted his Supper as a perpetual memorial for his followers so that they might repeatedly reflect on the eternal significance of his death. When believers celebrate the Lord's Supper, they commune with the risen Christ, who indwells them and is spiritually present with his people (1 Cor. 10:16).

The bread and cup are symbols, chosen by the Lord himself to signify and memorialize his atoning death. To celebrate Communion is not to offer a new sacrifice; rather, it is to rejoice in the once-for-all sacrifice of the Lord Jesus (cf. Rom. 6:10; Heb. 9:26–28; 1 Pet. 3:18).

There are four major views of the Lord's Table. The Roman Catholic view (transubstantiation) purports that the substance of the elements is transformed into the physical body and blood of Christ at the moment of the priest's blessing; hence the act is regarded as an actual sacrifice. However, this view fails to recognize the symbolic significance of Christ's statements "This is my body" and "This is my blood" (Matt. 26:26–28). When Jesus said things like "I am the bread of life" (John 6:35), "I am the light of the world" (John 8:12), "I am the door" (John 10:9), "I am the good shepherd" (John 10:11), and "I am the vine" (John 15:1), his hearers would have understood these words to be metaphorical expressions to illustrate the truth of his person and mission in profound ways. They are not to be understood in woodenly literalistic terms. So too with his words "This is my body" and "This is my blood." Also, the notion of Christ's death on the cross as a repeated or ongoing sacrifice undermines the reality that it was a once-for-all sacrifice (Rom. 6:10; Heb. 9:28; 10:10; 1 Pet. 3:18), fully completed at Calvary (John 19:30).[22]

22 For more on this point, see the section in chap. 7 titled, "The Sufficiency of the Atonement" (p. 274).

Though Martin Luther rejected the Roman Catholic notion of transubstantiation, he nonetheless maintained that Christ's body and blood are really present "in, with, and under" the Communion elements. This view is called consubstantiation or real presence. Luther's insistence on the "real presence" of Christ continued to ignore the symbolic nature of Jesus's statements.

Other Reformers such as Ulrich Zwingli and John Calvin distanced themselves from the Roman Catholic position further than Luther did. For Zwingli, the Lord's Table was primarily a memorial celebration that commemorated the work of Christ on the cross, as indicted by his words "Do this in *remembrance* of me" (1 Cor. 11:24–25). Zwingli's position influenced the Reformed tradition and was adopted by many Anabaptist groups. John Calvin taught that, although Christ is not physically present in the celebration of Communion, he is nonetheless spiritually present. However, his views did not necessarily exclude those of Zwingli. Accordingly, when Calvin met with Heinrich Bullinger (Zwingli's successor in Zurich) in 1549, the two agreed that their views regarding the nature of Communion were generally compatible.

While it is not wrong to speak of the Lord Jesus being spiritually present with his people when they celebrate Communion, since he is spiritually present with believers all the time (Matt. 28:20; Heb. 13:5), to speak of his *spiritual presence* at the Lord's Supper seems rather vague, and, if understood mystically, is unhelpful.

The Lord's Table is best understood as a memorial celebration intended to commemorate Jesus's substitutionary sacrifice (symbolized by the elements of the bread and the cup); to remind believers of the historical truths of the gospel, including Christ's incarnation, death, resurrection, and ascension; to prompt believers to repent of any known sin and to cause them to rejoice in their redemption from sin and in their saving union with Christ; to motivate them to continue walking in loving obedience to the Lord; and finally to rekindle their hope in his imminent return (cf. 1 Cor. 11:26; Matt, 26:29; Mark 14:25).

PRAYER[23]

In 1 Thessalonians 5:17, Paul instructed the church in Thessalonica to "pray without ceasing." That imperative designates the heart attitude that ought to characterize every congregation. The command "pray" (cf. Matt. 6:5–6; Mark 11:24; Luke 5:16; 11:1–2; Acts 10:9; Rom. 8:26; 1 Cor. 14:13–15; Eph. 6:18; Col. 1:9; 2 Thess. 3:1; James 5:13–14, 16) includes all facets of prayer: dependence,

23 This section is adapted from John MacArthur, *1 and 2 Thessalonians*, MNTC (Chicago: Moody Press, 2002), 186–88. Used by permission of Moody Publishers.

adoration, confession, intercession, thanksgiving, and supplication. The phrase "without ceasing" refers to a constant way of life that is characterized by a prayerful attitude, not an endless string of utterances (cf. Matt. 6:7).

Jesus exemplified fervent prayer (Matt. 14:23; 26:38–46; Mark 1:35; 6:46; Luke 9:18, 28–29; 22:41, 44; John 6:15; 8:1–2; 17:1–26) and he also taught his disciples how to pray (Matt. 6:5–14; Luke 11:2–4). He illustrated the importance of persistent prayer in his parables (Luke 11:5–10; 18:1–8).

This heartfelt commitment to prayer was exemplified by the early church (Acts 2:42; cf. 1:14; 4:23–31; 12:11–16), including the apostles, who prioritized it alongside the ministry of the word (Acts 6:4). Paul's ministry was similarly characterized by a constant attitude of prayerfulness (cf. Rom. 12:12; Eph. 6:18–19; Phil. 4:6; Col. 4:2; 2 Thess. 3:1; 1 Tim. 2:8).

WORSHIP

Worship is the theme of salvation history, the supreme purpose for which believers were redeemed (John 4:23), the occupation with which they will be eternally enthralled (Rev. 22:3–4; cf. 19:1–6), and vital for the life of the church. To worship the Lord is to ascribe to him the honor, glory, adoration, praise, reverence, and devotion that is due him, both for his greatness and for his goodness. As the sovereign Creator of the universe, the triune God alone—Father, Son, and Holy Spirit—is worthy of worship (cf. Isa. 42:8; 48:11; Matt. 4:10; Rev. 14:7).

True worship must begin in the heart and mind of the worshiper. Elaborate services, ornate buildings, eloquent prayers, or beautiful music may be outward expressions of worship, but God accepts only that which flows from sincere devotion to him. Church worship is more than a music program. Music is important, but it is only one avenue through which worship can be expressed. Worship should include prayer, expressions of praise and thanksgiving (Heb. 13:15), serving others for the sake of Christ (Heb. 13:16; cf. Phil. 4:18), and especially listening to the reading and preaching of his word. Contributing financially to the church through giving is also an expression of worship when done from a heart of joy (cf. 2 Cor. 9:6–15).

For believers, the supreme act of worship is to offer all of themselves as a living sacrifice to the Lord (cf. Matt. 22:37; cf. Rom. 12:1–2). Worship, then, is a way of thinking and living for God's honor and glory.

While worship must be passionate, it must always be grounded in truth (John 4:23–24; cf. Phil. 3:3). Many in the church today confuse emotionalism for worship. But genuine worship engages the mind; it does not bypass it (cf. 1 Cor. 14:15, 19). Moreover, God-honoring expressions of worship are characterized by decency and orderliness (1 Cor. 14:40).

FELLOWSHIP

The word *fellowship* comes from the Greek term *koinōnia*, meaning "partnership" or "sharing." Because believers are in fellowship with the Lord Jesus, they are also in fellowship with one another (1 John 1:3; cf. 1 Cor. 6:17). The practice of fellowship (i.e., what believers do) is premised on their position of fellowship in Christ (i.e., who believers are in him). Because they are united to the Lord Jesus in faith, they are united to one another in love (cf. John 13:35; 17:21).

The practice of fellowship consists of sacrificial service toward other members of the body of Christ (Phil. 2:1–4; cf. Acts 4:32–37). It is this kind of unity, commonality, and togetherness that ought to characterize the fellowship in every church (Rom. 12:16). Expressions of fellowship include discipleship (Matt. 28:19–20; 2 Tim. 2:2), mutual accountability (Gal. 6:1–2; Heb. 10:24–25), and joyful service (1 Cor. 15:58; Eph. 4:12; Rev. 22:12). The "one another" commands of the New Testament further elaborate on how fellowship should be expressed within the congregation (cf. Rom. 12:10, 16; 13:8; 15:5, 7, 14; 16:16; 1 Cor. 12:25; Gal. 5:13, 26; 6:2; Eph. 4:2, 32; 5:19; Phil. 2:3; Col. 3:9, 13, 16; 1 Thess. 3:12; 4:9, 18; 5:11, 13, 15; 2 Thess. 1:3; Heb. 3:13; 10:24–25; James 5:16; 1 Pet. 1:22; 4:8–10; 5:5; 1 John 3:11, 23; 4:7, 11–12; 2 John 5).

CHURCH DISCIPLINE

The practice of church discipline ought to be motivated by a positive, loving desire both to preserve the purity of the church (2 Cor. 7:1; cf. Acts 5:11; 1 Cor. 5:1–13; 2 Thess. 3:6–15; 1 Tim. 1:19–20; Titus 1:10–16) and to restore sinning brothers and sisters to the fellowship (cf. Luke 15:3–8; Jude 23). Church discipline should always be motivated by a longing to see wandering sheep repent, return, and be restored (cf. Gal. 6:1).

Matthew 18:15–17 delineates a four-step process for church discipline, for dealing with sin among church members. First, believers are to address sin on an individual level, approaching the offending party with a spirit of gentleness and humility. If the sinning brother responds to that private confrontation in repentance, the church discipline process comes to an end. He is forgiven and restored (Matt. 18:15). But if he refuses to repent, the process moves to a second step, in which one or two more believers join in confronting the sinning brother. These witnesses (cf. Num. 35:30; Deut. 17:6; 19:15; John 8:17; 2 Cor. 13:1; 1 Tim. 5:19; Heb. 10:28) primarily confirm that the sin was committed, and they also observe how the offending party responds after being confronted a second time (Matt. 18:16).

Should he still refuse to repent after being given adequate time, the process moves to a third step. In light of the sinning brother's persistent hard-heartedness, the witnesses are to bring the matter to the church (Matt. 18:17) by notifying the elders, who in turn communicate it to the congregation. The purpose of alerting the church is twofold: to remind other members of the seriousness of sin (cf. 1 Tim. 5:20) and to encourage them to confront the sinning brother in the hopes that he will repent and be restored.

If the confronted brother still refuses to repent, the final step of church discipline is to formally separate and to ostracize him from the fellowship. The unrepentant person is no longer to be treated as a brother but as "a Gentile and a tax-collector" (Matt. 18:17)—meaning as an outsider to whom the benefits and blessings of church membership are no longer extended. The motivation is not to punish the person but to see him yet come to his senses and repent (cf. 2 Thess. 3:11–15). Consequently, the only contact with such individuals should be for the purpose of admonishing them and calling them to repentance. In the early church, believers were not even to share a meal with those who persisted in unrepented sin (1 Cor. 5:11; cf. 2 Thess. 3:6, 14). Putting them out of the church protects the purity of the remaining members (1 Cor. 5:6) and safeguards the congregation's testimony in the eyes of the world.

The authority to practice church discipline in this manner comes from the Lord Jesus himself (see Matt. 18:18–20). The phrases "bound in heaven" and "loosed in heaven" were rabbinical expressions that spoke, respectively, of actions either forbidden or permitted in light of God's truth. In this context, the Lord's meaning is clear. When the church follows the biblical procedure for church discipline, its verdict stands in harmony with God's revealed will.

UNITY AND PURITY

The New Testament emphasis on fellowship underscores the biblical call to pursue love and spiritual unity in the church. At the same time, the Lord's instructions for church discipline in Matthew 18:15–20 remind believers that he desires his church to be pure, both in doctrine and in practice. Both of these qualities, unity and purity, must be maintained as believers consider how to relate to other professing Christians.

On the one hand, the New Testament repeatedly calls believers to live in harmony with one another (Rom. 12:16; 15:5; Col. 3:14). They are to "have unity of mind" (1 Pet. 3:8) as they eagerly seek "to maintain the unity of the Spirit in the bond of peace" (Eph. 4:3). Those who cause divisions in the church are to be confronted (cf. Rom. 16:17; 1 Cor. 1:10), and disciplined if they do not repent (Titus 3:10–11; cf. James 3:14–18).

On the other hand, the New Testament also instructs believers to guard the truth (1 Tim. 6:20; 2 Tim. 1:14), to contend earnestly for the purity of the faith (Jude 3), and to watch their life and doctrine closely (1 Tim. 4:16). Scripture repeatedly warns Christians to be on the alert against sin (Eph. 6:10–18; 1 Pet. 5:8;

1 John 2:15–17) and error (2 Tim. 3:1–9; 2 Pet. 2:1–2; 1 John 4:1–3). They are not to associate with immoral people (1 Cor. 5:9; Eph. 5:11; 2 Thess. 3:6, 14) or those who propagate error (2 John 10; cf. Gal. 1:8–9; Titus 3:10). In fact, the New Testament reserves its harshest condemnations for false teachers who would seek to undermine sound doctrine and promote immoral behavior (cf. 2 Pet. 2:1–3). Such purveyors of error are variously condemned as "ravenous wolves" (Matt. 7:15; Acts 20:29), "dogs" who return to their own vomit (2 Pet. 2:22; cf. Phil. 3:2), "blots and blemishes" (2 Pet. 2:13), "accursed children" (2 Pet. 2:14), "slaves of corruption" (2 Pet. 2:19), pigs that return "to wallow in the mire" (2 Pet. 2:22), "unreasoning animals" (Jude 10; cf. 2 Pet. 2:12), "hidden reefs" (Jude 12), "waterless clouds" (Jude 12; cf. 2 Pet. 2:17), "fruitless trees" (Jude 12), "wild waves of the sea" that "[cast] up the foam of their own shame" (Jude 13), and "loud-mouthed boasters" (Jude 16).

The unity described in Scripture is not a superficial unity that turns a blind eye to fundamental doctrinal or moral issues. Rather, true unity is grounded in a shared commitment to the lordship of Christ and the truth of his gospel. The New Testament rejects any so-called unity that dilutes doctrinal or moral purity. When believers separate from apostates and false teachers, they are not being divisive; they are following a divine mandate—as Paul explained to the Corinthians (cf. 2 Cor. 6:14–18).

Church Membership[24]

THE DEFINITION

To become a member of a church is to formally commit oneself to an identifiable local body of believers who have joined together for specific, divinely ordained purposes, such as receiving instruction from God's Word (1 Tim. 4:13; 2 Tim. 4:2), serving and edifying one another through the proper use of spiritual gifts (Rom. 12:3–8; 1 Cor. 12:4–31; 1 Pet. 4:10–11), participating in the ordinances (Luke 22:19; Acts 2:38–42), and proclaiming the gospel to those who are lost (Matt. 28:18–20). When one becomes a member of a church, he submits himself to the care and authority of the biblically qualified elders whom God has placed in that assembly and invites their oversight into his life.

THE BIBLICAL BASIS

Although Scripture does not contain an explicit command to formally become a member of a local church, the biblical foundation for church membership

24 This section is adapted from Grace Community Church, "Church Membership: A Grace Community Church Distinctive" (Sun Valley, CA: Grace Community Church, 2002). Used by permission of Grace Community Church.

may be discerned from (1) the example of the early church, (2) the existence of church government, (3) the exercise of church discipline, and (4) the exhortation to mutual edification.

The Example of the Early Church

In the early church, coming to Christ meant coming to the church. The idea of experiencing salvation without belonging to a local church is foreign to the New Testament. When individuals repented and believed in Christ, they were baptized, brought into the church (Acts 2:41, 47; 5:14; 16:5), and engaged in the activities of the church (cf. Acts 2:42). (See the "Means of Grace," above.)

Many of the epistles of the New Testament were written to churches or to the leaders of churches. The assumption of these epistles was that believers would be committed to a local assembly. The New Testament also bears evidence that, just as there was a list of widows eligible for financial support (1 Tim. 5:9), there may also have been broader lists of all members of given local churches—lists that grew ever longer as more people came to faith (cf. Acts 2:41, 47; 5:14; 16:5). Apparently, when a believer moved to another city, his church often wrote a letter of commendation to his new church (Acts 18:27; Rom. 16:1; Col. 4:10; cf. 2 Cor. 3:1–2). Such letters would be impossible to write if these believers were not known by and accountable to their spiritual leaders. The letters would also be superfluous if believers were not to be formally received as belonging to their new church.

Much of the terminology found in Acts fits only with the concept of formal church membership. Phrases such as "the whole congregation" (Acts 6:5 NASB), "the church in Jerusalem" (Acts 8:1), "the disciples" in Jerusalem (Acts 9:26), "in every church" (Acts 14:23), "the whole church" (Acts 15:22), and "the elders of the church" in Ephesus (Acts 20:17) all suggest recognizable church membership with well-defined boundaries (see also 1 Cor. 5:4; 14:23; Heb. 10:25), because unless one knows who the members of the church are, one cannot say whether the "whole church" is present.

The Existence of Church Government

The New Testament displays a consistent pattern of a plurality of elders overseeing each local body of believers. (See above, "Elders: Church Government.") The specific duties given to these elders presuppose a clearly defined group of church members under their care.

The Exercise of Church Discipline

As noted above, Matthew 18:15–17 outlines how the church is to seek the restoration of a believer who has fallen into sin—a process known as church discipline.[25] The exercise of church discipline according to Matthew 18 and other passages

25 For more, see "Church Discipline" (p. 415).

(1 Cor. 5:1–13; 1 Tim. 5:20; Titus 3:10–11) presupposes that the elders of a church know who their members are and that these members can be formally removed from fellowship.

The Exhortation to Mutual Edification

Scripture exhorts all believers to edify the other members by practicing the "one another" commands of the New Testament (e.g., Heb. 10:24–25) and exercising their spiritual gifts (Rom. 12:6–8; 1 Cor. 12:4–7; 1 Pet. 4:10–11). Mutual edification can take place only in the context of the corporate body of Christ. Exhortations to this kind of ministry presuppose that believers have committed themselves to other believers in a specific local assembly. Church membership is simply the formal way to make that commitment.

The Admonition to Submit to Leadership

Believers are commanded, "Obey your leaders and submit to them, for they are keeping watch over your souls, as those who will have to give an account. Let them do this with joy and not with groaning, for that would be of no advantage to you" (Heb. 13:17). Such overseers "have charge over you in the Lord" (1 Thess. 5:12, NASB). The requirement for the sheep to submit to their shepherds, as well as the requirement that the shepherds be accountable before the Lord for their sheep, requires formal membership, where the mutual commitment between shepherd and sheep is made known to one another.

Spiritual Gifts within the Church

As in the first century (see 1 Corinthians 12–14[26]) so in the church today, few areas of doctrine are more controversial or confused than spiritual gifts (Gk. *charismata*, or "gifts of grace"). Nevertheless, spiritual gifts play a vital role in the body of Christ.

Not only has Christ endowed his church with gifted men to equip the saints (Eph. 4:11–12), but his Spirit also bestows all believers with spiritual abilities (1 Cor. 12:4, 6–11) and they are all obligated to exercise their giftedness in ministry to others to build up one another in the church (Rom. 12:5–8; 1 Cor. 12:4–31; 1 Pet. 4:10–11). The triune God is the source of these gifts (1 Cor. 12:4–6): they are given by the "same Spirit," the "same Lord," and the "same God."

The primary Greek word associated with spiritual gifts is *charisma*, meaning "gift of grace." It is almost always used in the New Testament to designate a gift that has been freely bestowed by God, including the gift of salvation (Rom. 5:15–16;

26 For a cessationist interpretation of 1 Corinthians 12–14, see Robert L. Thomas, *Understanding Spiritual Gifts: A Verse-by-Verse Study of 1 Corinthians 12–14*, 2nd ed. (Grand Rapids, MI: Kregel, 1999). See also MacArthur, *1 Corinthians.*

6:23), the undeserved blessings of God (Rom. 1:11; 11:29), and divine enablements for ministry (Rom. 12:6; 1 Pet. 4:10).

Another important Greek term, *pneumatikos* ("pertaining to the Spirit"; 1 Cor. 12:1), means "spirituals" or "spiritualities," that is, spiritual characteristics, under spiritual control.

As a human body would not function properly if every member had the same function (cf. 1 Cor. 12:7–27), so the Holy Spirit endows believers with a variety of gifts so that as each member of the body of Christ exercises his or her gift, the entire body works together productively.

Spiritual gifts are not signs of prestige or privilege; they are given to enable believers to serve with a spirit of selflessness (Phil. 2:2–4) and humility (Rom. 12:3). The purpose of spiritual gifts is not self-edification but the edification of others (1 Pet. 4:10; cf. Eph. 4:11–12). Paul explicitly states that they are given "for the common good" (1 Cor. 12:7); they are not for a believer's private use.[27]

To use one's gift to edify oneself clearly runs contrary to Paul's entire point in 1 Corinthians 12–14, where he repeatedly emphasizes the priority of love for others as essential to the proper exercise of spiritual gifts (1 Cor. 12:7–10; 13:1–7; 14:12, 26). As Paul's words in 1 Corinthians 13:1–3 demonstrate, the loveless exercise of any gift (no matter how elevated or extreme) nullifies its spiritual value.

CATEGORIZING GIFTS

The New Testament provides several lists of spiritual gifts (Rom. 12:6–8; 1 Cor. 12:8–10, 28–30; cf. 1 Cor. 13:1–3, 8–9; Eph. 4:11; 1 Pet. 4:10–11). The apostle Peter says that each believer has received "a gift" (1 Pet. 4:10), but such a single divine enablement can be a combination of spiritual abilities, such as those listed in Romans 12 and 1 Corinthians 12. Peter also divides them into the general categories of speaking gifts and serving gifts (1 Pet. 4:11).

The best way to discover one's spiritual giftedness is by engaging in ministry according to one's God-given desires, opportunities to serve, and the response of those served. As believers minister to one another, their areas of giftedness gradually become apparent both to them and to others.

In a broad sense, the gifts might be categorized under two major headings: the temporary, miraculous gifts, and the permanent, ministering gifts. The miraculous gifts include the apostolic sign gifts (Heb. 2:3–4; cf. 2 Cor. 12:12) and the revelatory gifts, through which God gave new revelation to his church. These gifts were

27 Some might object by pointing to 1 Cor. 14:4, where Paul wrote, "The one who speaks in a tongue builds up himself, but the one who prophesies builds up the church." But that verse does not validate self-edification as a legitimate end in itself. If it did, it would run contrary to Paul's instruction throughout the entirety of chapters 12–14. Rather, it laments self-edification as a misuse of spiritual gifts.

limited to the apostolic age of the church (see discussion below). The ministering gifts, including both speaking gifts and serving gifts (1 Pet. 4:10–11), continue to be bestowed by the Holy Spirit in his church for the purpose of edification, growth, and witness.

Miraculous Gifts

At critical times throughout redemption history, God authenticated his messengers by empowering them to perform miraculous signs—for instance Moses (cf. Ex. 4:3–4, 30; 7:10, 12; 17:5–6; Num. 16:46–50), Joshua (cf. Josh. 10:12–14), and Elijah and Elisha (1 Kings 17:9–24; 18:41–45; 2 Kings 1:10–12; 2:8, 14; 4:1–7, 18–41; 5:1–19; 6:6, 17).

In the New Testament, the ministry of Jesus Christ was also confirmed by miracles and healings (John 2:11, 23; 3:2; 4:54; 6:2, 14; 7:31; 10:25, 37–38; 12:37; 20:30; cf. Acts 2:22). The signs and wonders Jesus did proved that he was who he claimed to be.

Jesus's disciples were given his power to heal and cast out demons (Matt. 10:1, 8; Mark 6:12–13). After his ascension, the apostles continued to exhibit that supernatural power (Mark 16:20; Acts 2:43; 4:30; 5:12; 6:8; 8:6, 13; 14:3; 15:12). The message they proclaimed was validated through the signs and wonders they performed.

The birth of the church was also marked by miraculous signs—including the ability of the disciples to speak fluently in human foreign languages that they had never learned (Acts 2:4–11; cf. 10:46 and 11:17). That supernatural ability served as a sign to unbelievers (and especially unbelieving Israel) that the gospel is true (1 Cor. 14:22; cf. Isa. 28:11) and that its truth is to be proclaimed throughout the entire world (cf. Matt. 28:18–20; Acts 1:8). Others, such as Stephen and Philip, exhibited the ability to perform miracles and healings (Acts 6:8; 8:5–7), publicly confirming the legitimacy of their evangelistic ministries. Such extraordinary gifts were necessary to validate that the church was a true work of God and to authenticate the apostles as his chosen messengers (cf. Rom. 15:19; 2 Cor. 12:12; Heb. 2:3–4). As those who received divine revelation through the Holy Spirit (John 14:26; 16:12–15; cf. 1 Thess. 2:13; 2 Pet. 3:15–16), the apostles and prophets were laying the doctrinal foundation for the church (Eph. 2:20; cf. Acts 2:42). Once the apostolic age ended and the New Testament canon was complete, the gifts uniquely associated with the offices of apostle and prophet were no longer needed and therefore they passed away.

The Temporary Nature of Miraculous Gifts[28]

Cessationism is the view that the sign gifts (e.g., the performing of miracles, gifts of healing, speaking in tongues) and the revelatory gifts (i.e., the reception and

28 This section is adapted from MacArthur's comments in an interview with Tim Challies, "John MacArthur Answers His Critics," *Challies.com: Informing the Reforming* (blog), November 4, 2013, http://www.challies.com/interviews/john-macarthur-answers-his-critics. Used by permission of

proclamation of new revelation from God) passed away when the foundation stage of the church ended. Miraculous gifts will not return until the tribulation period, after the church has been raptured and during the ministry of the two witnesses (cf. Rev. 11:3–11). In contrast to cessationism, the *charismatic* or *continuationist* position asserts that the miraculous and revelatory gifts are still in operation today.

One approach to defending the cessationist position begins with recognizing that there are no apostles in the church today[29]—a fact ubiquitously affirmed throughout church history and acknowledged by many modern noncessationists. No one today can meet the qualifications necessary for apostleship (which include seeing the risen Christ with one's own physical eyes; cf. Acts 1:22; 9:1–9). Paul explicitly states that the resurrected Jesus appeared "last of all" to him (1 Cor. 15:8). Hence, there were no apostles after Paul.

In Ephesians 2:20 Paul says the "foundation" of the church is "the foundation of the apostles and prophets," with Jesus Christ being the cornerstone. Once a foundation is laid, that phase of the construction ceases. The "foundation" of the church is the teaching of the apostles (found in the New Testament Scriptures) and the ministry of those New Testament prophets. The work of those "gifts to the church" (cf. Eph. 4:11) has ceased. The apostolic age came to its end when John, the last surviving apostle, died. Significantly, John was also the last canonical prophet (cf. Rev. 1:3; 22:18–19), with the book of Revelation completing the New Testament Scriptures. Consequently, the revelatory role of New Testament prophets, like that of the apostles, was fulfilled, and the gifts associated with that role were no longer needed. In the all-sufficient Scriptures, God's truth is self-attesting and self-evident, as the illuminating power of the Holy Spirit confirms (Heb. 4:12).

The cessationist position is further confirmed by comparing modern "charismatic gifts" with the realities described in the New Testament. Though charismatics use biblical terminology to describe their experiences, nothing about modern "miraculous gifts" matches the biblical reality.

For example, God's Word explicitly says that true prophets must adhere to a standard of 100 percent accuracy (Deut. 18:20–22), and nothing in the New Testament exempts them from that standard. But modern "prophetic revelation" has been shown to be fallible and full of errors time and time again.

Furthermore, the book of Acts depicts the gift of tongues as producing real human languages (Acts 2:6–11), and nothing in 1 Corinthians necessitates that

---

Tim Challies. See also the section in chap. 5 titled, "The Cessation of Revelatory and Confirmatory Gifts" (p. 213).

29 For example, this is the approach taken by Samuel E. Waldron, *To Be Continued? Are the Miraculous Gifts for Today?* (Merrick, NY: Calvary Press, 2005). See also Thomas R. Edgar, *Satisfied by the Promise of the Spirit* (Grand Rapids, MI: Kregel, 1996), 52–88; MacArthur, *Strange Fire*, 85–103.

they be redefined as something else. But modern "tongues" consists of unintelligible speech that does not conform to any human language.

The New Testament further describes the miraculous healings of Jesus and the apostles (including the healing of organic diseases like paralysis, blindness, and leprosy) as being immediate, complete, and undeniable (e.g., Mark 1:42; 10:52). But modern "gifts of healing" do not come close to replicating the miracles performed by Jesus and the apostles.

Incredibly, many continuationist scholars acknowledge this discontinuity, arguing for a lesser quality or lower category of gifts in which to place these modern charismatic expressions. Such admissions, however, provide a tacit acknowledgment that the true sign gifts (as depicted in Scripture) have not continued.[30]

Ministering Gifts

The Holy Spirit continues to endow his *permanent, ministering gifts* to believers for the edification of the church (1 Pet. 4:10–11). These include both speaking gifts, to proclaim the truth of Scripture through preaching, teaching, encouraging, exhorting; and serving gifts, to minister to others in the church through acts like helping, giving, administrating, and showing mercy.

SURVEYING THE LISTS OF GIFTS

Combining the lists of gifts in Romans 12:6–8 and 1 Corinthians 12:8–10 and 12:28–30 produces the "master list" of representative spiritual gifts.

Apostleship

The Greek term *apostolos* refers to an ambassador, an emissary, or someone sent on a mission. Though it is sometimes used in a general sense to designate "apostles of the churches" (2 Cor. 8:23 [ESV mg.]; cf. Phil. 2:25), it is primarily used to refer to a specific group of "apostles of Jesus Christ." (See the qualifications of an apostle, above.)

The apostles of Jesus Christ had three primary responsibilities. First, they were used by the Lord to lay the doctrinal foundation of the church (Eph. 2:20). Second, they were appointed to receive, preach, and write divine revelation (cf. Acts 2:42; 6:4; Eph. 3:5). Third, they were called to confirm that divine Word through "signs and wonders and mighty works" (2 Cor. 12:12; cf. Heb. 2:3–4).

30 Some commentators appeal to 1 Cor. 13:10 to support their position either for or against cessationism. But doing so stretches the point of that text beyond what Paul intended. While the meaning of the Greek word translated "perfect" (*teleion*) has been widely debated by commentators, "of the possible interpretations, the believer's entrance into the Lord's presence best fits Paul's use of the 'perfect' in 1 Corinthians 13:10" (see MacArthur, *Strange Fire*, 148–49; cf. Edgar, *Satisfied by the Promise of the Spirit*, 246).

The New Testament identifies apostleship as both an office and a gift. Ephesians 4:11 refers to apostles (along with prophets, evangelists, pastor-teachers) as gifts given by Jesus Christ to the church, and 1 Corinthians 12 includes "apostles" in the list of charismatic gifts delineated in that chapter (1 Cor. 12:4–5, 28–31).

Working of Miracles

Among the signs that validated the ministry of the apostles was the "working of miracles" (1 Cor. 12:10, 28–29). A *miracle* might be broadly defined as an extraordinary work of God in which he works *super*naturally so that the result cannot be explained by any natural cause. The working of miracles was a gift that involved human agency. The working of miracles validated those human agents as spokesmen for God (cf. Acts 2:22; 14:3; 2 Cor. 12:12; Heb. 2:3–4). The New Testament does not record any of the apostles performing miracles related to nature, but they did exhibit power (Gk. *dynamis*) over demons, disease, and death (cf. Acts 9:41–42; 20:7–12).

Gifts of Healing

If the working of miracles relates to divinely granted power (Gk. *dynamis*) over demons, the term "gifts of healing" (1 Cor. 12:9, 28) refers to supernatural power over disease. Miraculous healing was displayed in the ministries of Christ (Matt. 8:16–17), the apostles (Matt. 10:1), the Seventy-Two (Luke 10:1, 9), and some apostolic associates (Acts 8:5–7). The New Testament record of the healings performed by these individuals demonstrates that they were immediate, undeniable, and always complete[31] (cf. Matt. 8:2–3; 9:1–8; 20:29–34; 21:14; Mark 1:42; 8:22–26; 10:52; Luke 17:11–21; John 5:1–9; Acts 3:8; 14:8–18).

Miraculous healings served to authenticate God's messenger (cf. John 10:38; Acts 2:22; Rom. 15:18–19; 2 Cor. 12:12; Heb. 2:3–4), not merely to restore the sick to physical health. Though believers no longer possess such supernatural abilities, they do have the right to ask God to heal them, knowing that he hears and answers the prayers of his people (James 5:13–16; cf. Luke 18:1–6; 1 John 5:14–15).

Speaking in and Interpreting Tongues[32]

The Greek word for "tongues" (*glōssa*) is best translated "languages." The exercise of this gift is most clearly seen on the day of Pentecost (cf. Acts 2:4–11). There the apostles, along with some of the 120 who were gathered in the upper room

31 This is in contrast to the dubious claims of modern "faith healers." See MacArthur, *Strange Fire*, 155–76. See also Richard Mayhue, *The Healing Promise: Is It Always God's Will to Heal?* (Fearn, Ross-Shire, Scotland: Mentor, 1997).

32 This section is adapted from Nathan A. Busenitz, "Are Tongues Real Foreign Languages? A Response to Four Continuationist Arguments," *MSJ* 25.2 (2014): 63–84. Used by permission of *MSJ*.

(Acts 1:15), began speaking fluently in foreign languages and dialects that they did not know.

Some recent commentators have attempted to distinguish the gift of languages depicted in Acts 2 (actual foreign languages) from the gift of languages described in 1 Corinthians 12–14, in an effort to make room for the unintelligible utterances that characterize modern *glossolalia* (or tongues speech). However, the exegetical evidence indicates that the tongues speech depicted in 1 Corinthians consisted of the same basic phenomenon as that found in Acts 2. In both places, the genuine gift of tongues resulted in the supernatural ability to speak human foreign languages.[33]

Prophecy and Preaching

In both 1 Corinthians 12:28 and Ephesians 4:11, Paul lists "prophets" immediately after "apostles." Like apostleship, prophecy encompassed both an office and a gift. Because they were given divine revelation, the New Testament prophets assisted the apostles in laying the doctrinal foundation of the church (Eph. 2:20).

As with prophets in the Old Testament, New Testament prophets were held to the highest standards of revelatory accuracy (cf. Deut. 18:20–22; Ezek. 13:3–9), doctrinal purity (cf. Deut. 13:1–5; 2 Pet. 2:1), and moral integrity (cf. Jer. 23:14–16; 2 Pet. 2:2–3).[34] This was especially important because of the continual threat that false prophets posed to the early church (cf. Matt. 7:15; 24:11; 2 Tim. 4:3–4; 2 Pet. 2:1–3; 1 John 4:1; Jude 4), which explains why prophecies needed to be tested for doctrinal orthodoxy (cf. 1 Cor. 14:29; 1 Thess. 5:20–22; 1 John 4:1–6). According to Romans 12:6, the content of prophecy was to be measured against "our faith" (or literally, "the faith"), meaning that it was to be evaluated against the body of Christian truth that God the Holy Spirit had previously revealed (cf. 1 Tim. 3:9; 4:1, 6; Jude 3, 20).

Words of Wisdom and Knowledge

Little detail is given about the "utterance of wisdom" and the "utterance of knowledge" (1 Cor. 12:8), but clearly they involved an individual receiving and declaring

33 Paul's mention of the "tongues of angels" in 1 Cor. 13:1 is a hyperbolic expression, a point made clear in light of the other extreme examples he gives in verses 2–3. The apostle's point is that if someone were to speak in human foreign languages (the "tongues of men") or even in the languages of angels (a hypothetical scenario designed to make a rhetorical point), it would still be meaningless if love were absent. See MacArthur, *Strange Fire*, 133–54.

34 Regarding New Testament prophets, it is important to recognize that "the New Testament uses identical terminology to describe both Old and New Testament prophets. In the book of Acts, Old Testament prophets are mentioned in Acts 2:16; 3:24–25; 10:43; 13:27, 40; 15:15; 24:14; 26:22, 27; and 28:23. References to New Testament prophets are interspersed using the same vocabulary without any distinction, comment, or caveat (cf. Acts 2:17–18; 7:37; 11:27–28; 13:1; 15:32; 21:9–11)" (MacArthur, *Strange Fire*, 119).

revelation from God. It seems that those who were given a "word of wisdom" were able to rightly understand divinely revealed truth and articulate the proper application of it for everyday life (cf. Matt. 13:54; Mark 6:2; Acts 6:10; James 1:5; 3:17; 2 Pet. 3:15). Those who communicated a "word of knowledge" provided insight into the profound truths of God's Word (cf. Eph. 3:3; Col. 1:26; 2:2).

Any revelatory aspect associated with these gifts ceased with the completion of the New Testament canon and the end of the apostolic age.

Distinguishing between Spirits

With this gift, God divinely enables someone to discern true from false statements made by people deceptively claiming that their words were prophetic revelations from God (1 Cor. 12:10). The exercise of this gift is illustrated by both Peter, when he recognized the spiritual duplicity of Ananias (Acts 5:3), and Paul, who perceived that a slave girl was possessed by an evil spirit (Acts 16:16–18). This represents the temporary, miraculous aspect of the gift.

Teaching

Another group that Paul identifies in 1 Corinthians 12:28 is that of "teachers" (cf. Rom. 12:7; Eph. 4:11). Like apostleship and prophecy, teaching can refer to both an office and a gift. The gift of teaching involves the Spirit-endowed ability to interpret and articulate the truth of God's Word clearly and accurately so that others can understand and learn (cf. Acts 18:24–25; 2 Tim. 2:2). Although this gift is a necessary qualification for elders (1 Tim. 3:2; Titus 1:9; cf. 1 Tim. 4:16), it is not reserved exclusively for pastors. (See above on "Elders: Qualifications.")

Paul charged Timothy, "What you have heard from me in the presence of many witnesses entrust to faithful men, who will be able to teach others also" (2 Tim. 2:2). Faithful church leaders are those who rightly divide the Word of God (2 Tim. 2:15) and impart its truth to the congregation. Many laypeople are also given this enablement to provide sound instruction throughout the fellowship of the church.

Exhortation

The Greek words *parakaleō* ("exhorts") and *paraklēsis* ("exhortation") in Romans 12:8 are both compounds of *para* ("alongside") and *kaleō* ("to call"). These same words are joined together to constitute the title *paraklētos* ("paraclete," "advocate," "comforter," "helper"), used in reference to both the Lord Jesus (1 John 2:1) and the Holy Spirit (John 14:16, 26; 15:26; 16:7). The gift of exhortation, then, involves coming alongside fellow believers to help and encourage them in the way of godliness (cf. Heb. 10:24–25). As Paul told the Thessalonians, "We urge you, brothers, admonish the idle, encourage the fainthearted, help the weak, be patient with them all" (1 Thess. 5:14; cf. 2 Cor. 1:3–5; 2 Tim. 3:16–17; 4:2).

Service and Helping

The gift of "service" (Rom. 12:7) and the gift of "helping" (1 Cor. 12:28) are virtually synonymous. "Service" is derived from the same Greek word translated "deacon" (*diakonia*). It is a broad term that can refer to any kind of practical assistance or help (cf. Acts 20:35). "Helping" (from Gk. *antilēmpsis*) is a similarly broad term, referring to any kind of service or assistance rendered on behalf of others. Often these acts of service involve completing mundane and unglamorous tasks. Yet they are essential to the life and ongoing effectiveness of the church.

Leading and Administrating

Those with the gift of leading (Rom. 12:8) or "administrating" (1 Cor. 12:28) are responsible to guide the congregation, both spiritually and in everyday decision making. The phrase "the one who leads" translates the participial form of the Greek term *proistēmi* ("to stand before"). It is used in the New Testament to describe headship in both the home (1 Tim. 3:4–5, 12) and the church (1 Tim. 5:17). "Administrating" is from the Greek word *kybernēsis*, meaning "to guide." Acts 27:11 and Revelation 18:17 use that same term to refer to a pilot who steers a ship. This illustrates how gifted leaders help others navigate through life and ministry by guiding them with wisdom and good counsel (cf. Prov. 12:5; Ezek. 27:8, where the same Greek term is used in the Septuagint). Though this gift is not limited to a particular office, the gift of leadership in the church clearly belongs to the pastors and elders whom God has ordained to shepherd the flock.

Giving

In Romans 12:8, Paul describes the gift of giving with these words: "the one who contributes, in generosity." The Greek word translated "contributes" is a form of the verb *metadidōmi*, which could also be rendered "gives" or "shares." It speaks of sacrificial generosity in giving for the sake of meeting another's needs (cf. 2 Cor. 8:2–5). Although every believer is called to share and to give (Eph. 4:28; cf. Luke 3:11), those with the gift of giving are particularly equipped with the strong desire and eagerness to contribute sacrificially to others. Consequently, they experience the full measure of knowing that "God loves a cheerful giver" (2 Cor. 9:7).

The term "generosity" comes from the Greek word *haplotēs* and speaks of a sincere liberality. Such giving is fueled not by an ulterior motive (cf. Acts 5:1–11) but out of genuine love for others and, ultimately, for the Lord.

Showing Mercy

The list of gifts in Romans 12 concludes with these words: "the one who does acts of mercy, with cheerfulness" (12:8). The Greek verb *eleeō* ("does acts of mercy") conveys both an attitude of sympathy toward those who are hurting and an ability to comfort and encourage them effectively.

Faith

The gift of faith, delineated by Paul in 1 Corinthians 12:9, refers to an extraordinary ability to trust God in the face of difficulty and hardship. The "faith" of which Paul speaks is not saving faith but rather unwavering confidence in the power and promises of God. Those with the gift of faith are characterized by persistent prayer, confident in knowing that God hears the pleas of his people (cf. James 5:16–18).

Spiritual Discernment

The "ability to distinguish between spirits" (1 Cor. 12:10) refers to the permanent gift of spiritual discernment—the Spirit-empowered capacity to identify forms of doctrinal error and religious deception (cf. 1 John 4:1). As "the father of lies" (John 8:44), Satan continually seeks to counterfeit the true work of God by disguising himself as "an angel of light" (2 Cor. 11:14) and enabling false teachers, who dispense the "teachings of demons" (1 Tim. 4:1).

Evangelism

The office or gift of evangelist, referenced third in Ephesians 4:11, involves the divine enablement to explain, exhort, and apply the gospel to non-Christians. Paul employed the Greek verb *euangelizō* ("to preach the gospel") twenty-one times in his letters. He urged Timothy to "do the work of an evangelist" (2 Tim. 4:5) both in general and at Ephesus in particular (cf. Philip of Caesarea in Acts 21:8). Thus, the evangelist appears to be primarily a church planter whose duty it is to establish new churches through gospel preaching.

Shepherding and Teaching

This office or gift, referenced fourth in Ephesians 4:11, involves the divine enablement to pastor by leading, feeding, protecting, and otherwise caring for believers in local churches. (See the entire discussion on "Elders," above.)

A Foretaste of Heaven

In concluding a discussion on the church, it is fitting to remember that the church provides believers with a foretaste of heaven. Though imperfect, the church represents the one place where the activities of heaven are reflected on earth.

The church resembles heaven in a number of important ways. In the church, God's people desire to submit to his moral will as expressed in his Word (Matt. 6:10). They seek to obey him out of their love and devotion to him (John 14:15; 1 John 2:3). In heaven, believers will serve him perfectly (Rev. 22:3–5), and that future hope motivates their pursuit of holiness in this life (1 John 3:2–3).

In the church, believers offer continual adoration to God as a sacrifice of praise (Heb. 13:15). Such expressions of worship characterize the life of heaven (see Revelation 4:8–11).

For all eternity, believers will exalt the Lord Jesus for his work of redemption (Rev. 5:11–14; cf. Phil. 2:9–11). The worship that echoes through the halls of Christ-exalting churches here on earth will continue to reverberate without end throughout the halls of heaven.

In the church, though its members are not yet perfected, one begins to glimpse the holiness and purity that characterizes heaven. The absolute holiness of heaven is underscored in Revelation 21:8 and 22:14–15, which explain that the eternal glory of the new earth will be free from immorality, idolatry, and any form of impurity. The church reflects this holiness when its members walk in righteousness (Eph. 4:1; Phil. 1:27; Col. 1:10; 1 Pet. 1:16; cf. Ps. 15:2) and when they are faithful to discipline those who persist in unrepented sin (Matt. 18:15–20; 1 Cor. 5:13).

In the church, God's people also enjoy rich fellowship with one another. That fellowship is a foretaste of the perfect communion they will one day share with all the saints and with their Savior, the Lord Jesus (cf. 1 John 1:3; 3:2). When believers gather in the church, they are reminded that they are citizens of heaven (Phil. 3:20–21) and that this world is not their home (cf. 1 John 2:15–17). They are part of the fellowship of the saints, belonging to "the assembly of the firstborn who are enrolled in heaven" (Heb. 12:23).

Submission to God's will, Christ-centered worship, the pursuit of holiness, and fellowship with other believers—these are just some of the ways in which the church on earth foreshadows the glories of heaven. Such anticipations should cause believers to grow both in their love for the church and in their longing for heaven. As the apostle Paul explained to the Corinthians, "For now we see in a mirror dimly, but then face to face. Now I know in part; then I shall know fully, even as I have been fully known" (1 Cor. 13:12). In light of that kind of heavenly perspective, what a joy it is for believers to be part of the company of the redeemed, eagerly "waiting for our blessed hope, the appearing of the glory of our great God and Savior Jesus Christ, who gave himself for us to redeem us from all lawlessness and to purify for himself a people for his own possession who are zealous for good works" (Titus 2:13–14).

Questions:

1. What is the biblical definition of "the church?" And what is Christ's design for the church?
2. How does the "church" relate to the "kingdom?"
3. What do the terms "visible church" and "invisible church" mean? What do the terms "universal church" and "local church" mean?
4. What distinguishes the nation of Israel from the New Testament church?
5. What are the purposes of the church?
6. What are the New Testament terms (offices) for "authority" in the church?

7. What are the responsibilities and qualifications of an elder? And a deacon?
8. What are the various (historical) forms of church government, and what does the "plurality of elders" indicate relative to church government?
9. What are the "biblical dynamics" of church life?
10. What is the biblical teaching on baptism? And the Lord's Table?
11. What is the importance of prayer, worship, and fellowship in the life of the church?
12. What is church discipline, and why is it important? Why are unity and purity important for the life and testimony of the church?
13. What is the biblical basis of church membership, and why is it important?
14. What does the New Testament teach about spiritual gifts? (categories and functions)
15. What are the biblical proofs for cessationism?

10

THE FUTURE

Eschatology

THEOLOGIES OFTEN CURTAIL THE discussion of future events, especially as they relate to Old Testament promises for national Israel. However, end-time events serve as the culmination of God's redemptive purposes and should not be minimized. Eschatology concerns the events to come that are associated with the final "restoration of all things" (Acts 3:21 NASB).

Introduction to Eschatology

ESCHATOLOGY DEFINED

The term *eschatology* comes from the Greek word *eschatos*, which means "last," "end," or "final." In Christian doctrine, eschatology is the study of the end times and the events associated with the return of Jesus, including the tribulation, resurrections, judgments, and the kingdom.

Two categories of eschatology exist—personal and cosmic. Personal eschatology addresses the future destiny of the individual and deals with matters such as death, the intermediate state, resurrection, judgment, and where a person will reside eternally. Cosmic or prophetic eschatology addresses broader issues such as the biblical covenants, the rapture, the tribulation period, the second coming of Jesus, the millennium, and the eternal state.

ESCHATOLOGICAL MODELS

There are two models or overall approaches for understanding and describing God's eschatological purposes—the spiritual vision model and the new creation model.

Spiritual Vision Model

The spiritual vision model involves a stark dualism that elevates "spiritual" realities (perceived as the highest ideals and good) over the material (perceived as bad, inferior, or evil). This model adopts the worldview of the Greek philosopher Plato (ca. 428–348 BC), who taught the superiority of the spiritual over the material. A number of philosophies and religious systems stem from his views. For instance Gnosticism, which was a form of Platonism and disparaged the goodness of the material world, was a major threat to the early church.

While most early Christians were neither Platonists nor Gnostics, Plato's ideas often infiltrated the early church. Origen (ca. AD 184–ca 254) came close to denying bodily resurrection. The influential theologian Augustine (AD 354–430) believed that the idea of an earthly kingdom of Jesus was carnal and opted for the view that the kingdom of God is a spiritual entity, the church. His spiritual view of God's kingdom, as explained in his work *The City of God*, came to be known as *amillennialism*. These two influential theologians downplayed the physical aspects of Bible prophecy and elevated the spiritual. The Roman Catholic Church of the Middle Ages, which embraced Augustine's amillennial perspective, also operated according to overspiritualized assumptions about God's kingdom. The unbiblical mixture of Plato's ideas with Christianity has been called "Christoplatonism."[1]

This model has had a long history and has impacted Christian theology in significant ways. It is evident when people think their eternal destiny is a bodiless existence in the sky or sitting on a cloud all day with nothing to do. Spiritual-vision-model thinking can be spotted in beliefs that physical, land, and national promises to Israel in the Old Testament must be fulfilled spiritually in the church or be absorbed into the person of Christ.

New Creation Model

The new creation model, on the other hand, affirms the goodness of all of God's creation, including its material elements (cf. Col. 1:16). The new creation model understands that creation is composed of both spiritual and material realities, and that both of these realities matter to God. Both were negatively affected by sin and the fall of man, and both will eventually be restored by God (cf. Acts 3:21 NASB). A new creation approach does not deny the importance of spiritual truths and realities; it affirms them. But it opposes efforts to spiritualize physical realities or treat them as inferior. Spiritual and physical blessings come together.

Passages like Isaiah 11; 25; 65; 66; Romans 8; and Revelation 21 affirm that God's future plans involve material realities. When discussing the glories of the coming new earth, God declares, "Behold, I am making all things new" (Rev.

1 Randy C. Alcorn, *Heaven* (Wheaton, IL: Tyndale, 2004), 475.

21:5). The final destiny of God's people is not an ethereal spiritual presence in the sky but a tangible existence on a new earth.

The new creation model also affirms the continuing importance of both individuals and national entities. God pursues the salvation of individual human beings, and he also judges and blesses nations as national entities. The Abrahamic covenant reveals that God's purposes extend to involve blessing all nations (Gen. 12:3; 22:18). Nations with their kings even exist on the new earth (Rev. 21:24, 26).

The Bible also teaches that God will use Israel as a means of blessing the nations (Gen. 12:2–3). Israel was the vessel through whom Jesus the Messiah came and is the center of the Messiah's kingdom, in which Israel will lead in both service and function (Isa. 2:2–4; Acts 3:25; Rom. 11:11–12, 15).

The new creation model also connects eschatology ("last things") and protology ("first things"). If one grasps God's original purposes for man and the creation, then one is in a better position to grasp what is still to come. God created a tangible world in six days and then deemed it all "very good" (Gen. 1:31); thus there is no essential dualism in which spirit is viewed as inherently superior to the physical.

That God's kingdom purposes are related to this earth is seen in the commands given to Adam in Genesis 1:26–28, where Adam is told to "have dominion over," "subdue," and "fill" the earth. God created the world and then designated man as a mediator to rule over it for God's glory. Adam failed this command and did not fulfill God's intent for mankind. Man was therefore subjected to death, and the ground was cursed and subjected to futility (Gen. 3:17–19; Rom. 8:20). Today, humanity is characterized by sin, and the creation works against man. But God's plan is to restore and regenerate this earth (Matt. 19:28; Acts 3:21).

ESCHATOLOGY AND BIBLE INTERPRETATION

Using correct interpretative principles is critical for understanding Bible prophecy and eschatology. The "grammatical-historical" method of Bible interpretation seeks to understand the original, intended meaning of the Bible writers, including in its prophetic sections, in the way that the original readers would have understood it. It views Bible texts as having a single meaning, not multiple, hidden, or allegorical meanings. Most Bible-believing Christians use grammatical-historical interpretation for most passages of Scripture. However, there is a long history of unwarranted abandonment of grammatical-historical interpretation when it comes to eschatological sections. A spiritual approach to prophecy has often led to beliefs that the church is the new Israel or that land promises in the Old Testament are only about spiritual blessings for the church.

Abandoning grammatical-historical interpretation leads to discarding what the Bible says about the coming millennial kingdom of Jesus. Even those who deny a future earthly kingdom of Jesus admit that a literal approach to Old Testament prophecy must lead to a coming, literal, earthly kingdom. For instance, O. T. Allis conceded that "the Old Testament prophecies if literally interpreted cannot be regarded as having been fulfilled or as being capable of fulfillment in this present age."[2] And Floyd E. Hamilton acknowledged, "Now we must frankly admit that a literal interpretation of the Old Testament prophecies gives us just such a picture of an earthly reign of the Messiah as the premillennialist pictures."[3]

The grammatical-historical approach to interpretation fits with normal means of communication. It also has support from the fact that many prophecies concerning Jesus's first coming were fulfilled in a normal, literal sense (cf. Isa. 7:14; Mic. 5:2; Isaiah 53). This method must be applied to prophecies of Jesus's second coming.

ESCHATOLOGY AND JESUS CHRIST

Jesus is the ultimate King and the center of God's kingdom program. Yet Christians are often confused about Jesus's role in fulfilling Old Testament promises. Some incorrectly believe that promises concerning Israel and Israel's land in the Old Testament are fulfilled or absorbed into Jesus in such a way that one should not expect a future literal fulfillment of these matters. They suggest that Jesus is the ultimate or true Israelite who replaced Israel, thus no theological significance exists for the nation of Israel anymore. It is true that Jesus is the focal point of God's purposes, and through him all promises, prophecies, and covenants will be fulfilled; however, this occurs through the literal fulfillment of what was promised.

When addressing the misperception that he was doing away with the Hebrew Scriptures, Jesus said,

> Do not think that I have come to abolish the Law or the Prophets; I have not come to abolish them but to fulfill them. For truly, I say to you, until heaven and earth pass away, not an iota, not a dot, will pass from the Law until all is accomplished. (Matt. 5:17–18)

When Jesus referred to "the Law or the Prophets," he meant the Hebrew Scriptures as a whole, including its prophecies—"all" that was foretold in the Old Testament had to be "accomplished." Jesus expected a literal fulfillment of Old Testament prophecies (see Matt. 24:15 plus Dan. 9:27; Matt. 24:30 plus Isa. 3:10). Repeatedly, Jesus viewed the details of Old Testament prophecies as needing to be fulfilled just as the Old Testament stated.

2 O. T. Allis, *Prophecy and the Church: An Examination of the Claim of Dispensationalists That the Christian Church Is a Mystery Parenthesis Which Interrupts the Fulfilment to Israel of the Kingdom Prophecies of the Old Testament* (1945; repr., Nutley, NJ: Presbyterian & Reformed, 1977), 238.

3 Floyd E. Hamilton, *The Basis of the Millennial Faith* (Grand Rapids, MI: Eerdmans, 1942), 38.

Like Jesus, the New Testament writers also viewed Old Testament prophecies as requiring exact fulfillment after Jesus's first coming. Both Paul and Peter said that the "day of the Lord" still needed to occur (1 Thess. 5:2; 2 Pet. 3:10). Paul expected a coming Antichrist figure, a "man of lawlessness," who would enter the Jewish temple exalting himself and declaring himself to be God (2 Thess. 2:3–4 plus Dan. 9:27). Paul also declared a coming salvation for the nation of Israel in connection with new covenant promises for the nation (Rom. 11:26–27). The New Testament does not transcend or alter the Old Testament prophetic expectation but sees the Old Testament prophecies as needing to be fulfilled over the course of the two comings of Jesus.

The Old Testament predicted a Messiah who would reign over a worldwide kingdom (Zech. 14:9) but would also suffer for the sins of his people (Isaiah 53). Yet there was little in the Old Testament to indicate two comings of this Messiah. The truth of two distinct arrivals of the Messiah was revealed in the New Testament.

Both John the Baptist and Jesus proclaimed that Jesus was the King and that the kingdom of heaven was near (Matt. 3:2; 4:17). Jesus's healings, exorcisms, words, and natural miracles verified this claim. But Jesus experienced opposition from the people of Israel. The cities were not believing in him (Matt. 11:20–24), and Israel's religious leaders committed blasphemy by saying that Jesus was working with Satan (Matt. 12:22–32).

As the Gospels unfold, it becomes clearer that two comings of Jesus will be necessary (cf. the parable in Luke 19:11–27). Understanding the two comings of Jesus is important for grasping the fulfillment of Bible prophecy. The fact that there are two comings means that the fulfillment of prophecies related to him also occurs in stages. Some prophecies were fulfilled with Jesus's first coming, while others await his return.

Comprehending eschatology involves discerning which details of prophecy were fulfilled with Jesus's first coming and which await his second coming. If one sees too much fulfillment with Jesus's first coming, one will miss significant matters that still need to occur at Jesus's return. On the other hand, if one places too much significance on the second coming of Jesus, one could miss significant fulfillment that occurred with Jesus's first advent.

Personal Eschatology

What happens when one dies? The answer to this question is related to personal eschatology. Since the Bible teaches about the important destinies for both unbelievers and believers, this part looks at personal eschatology from the standpoint of these two groups.

DEATH

The Bible speaks of three types of death. First, *physical death* involves the cessation of bodily life (cf. James 2:26; Eccles. 12:7)—the separation of the soul from the body (2 Cor. 5:1–4).

Second, *spiritual death* involves separation from God. A person can be physically alive yet spiritually dead. In fact, all people are conceived and born into a state of spiritual alienation from God (Ps. 51:5; Eph. 2:1)

Third, *eternal death* is punishment and separation from God for eternity. This happens to those who physically die while spiritually dead. The unrepentant will experience eternal, conscious banishment from God's presence to bless (2 Thess. 1:9). The lake of fire is their destiny (Rev. 21:8).

Scripture teaches other important truths about death. First, sin is the cause of death (Rom. 5:12).

Second, death is real, not an illusion as some cults and quasi-Christian sects teach. There is an actual separation of the body from the soul.

Third, death is unnatural. God did not create man to die, and death was not an original part of the creation (Genesis 1–2). Death is an intrusion in God's universe, an enemy that needs to be conquered. Death will not be present in the new heaven and new earth (Revelation 21–22; esp. 21:4). Paul thus declared, "The last enemy to be destroyed is death" (1 Cor. 15:26). The apostle John likewise revealed that "death" will be "thrown into the lake of fire" (Rev. 20:14). Death is headed for defeat because of Jesus (cf. 1 Cor. 15:54–57).

Fourth, death is not a transfer from existence to nonexistence but a transition from one state of existence to another. Believers will transition to the intermediate heaven where God, the resurrected Jesus, angels, and previously deceased believers reside (Rev. 6:9–11). The nonbeliever will transition to Hades, a temporary place of punishment for the wicked (Luke 16:19–31).

Death and the Unbeliever

For the unbeliever, death not only brings an end to one's physical life; it also takes a person into direct accountability with God (Heb. 9:27). Jesus warned that people should fear God, "who can destroy both soul and body in hell" (Matt. 10:28).

All people, including nonbelievers, experience God's common grace in blessings such as food, air, sunshine, and relationships. Yet Paul also warns of rejecting God's kindness: "But because of your stubbornness and unrepentant heart you are storing up wrath for yourself in the day of wrath and revelation of the righteous judgment of God" (Rom. 2:5 NASB). Experiencing God's blessings without giving him honor increases wrath for a person. Those who die in unbelief will experience eternal death with no chance of reprieve or escape. There is no postmortem second chance.

Death and the Believer

Death is a result of sin, but the Christian is forgiven of all sins (Rom. 8:1). Therefore, death is not a punishment for the Christian like it is for the nonbeliever. Instead, physical death occurs because we live in a fallen world still awaiting the restoration of all things (Acts 3:21). The process of decay and death reminds Christians of their frailty and total reliance on God.

While on the road to physical death, the Christian does not have to fear death, for Christ has conquered it (Rev. 1:18). In fact, Paul viewed the options of continuing his present ministry on earth or departing to be with Christ as a difficult choice (cf. Phil. 1:22–24). Paul knew God wanted him to remain on earth and serve others, yet he desired to be present with Christ in heaven (cf. 2 Cor. 5:8).

THE INTERMEDIATE STATE

The intermediate state refers to the conscious existence of people between physical death and the resurrection of the body.

The Intermediate State of the Unbeliever

The intermediate state of unbelievers involves conscious torment in a place called *Hades*, from the Greek term for the abode of the dead.[4] In the Septuagint, it was used to translate the Hebrew word *sheol*, which referred to the realm of the dead in general, without necessarily distinguishing between righteous and unrighteous souls. But in the New Testament, *Hades* refers to the place of the wicked prior to the final judgment in the lake of fire (Rev. 20:13). *Hades*, therefore, serves to describe a temporary place of conscious torment for the wicked (cf. Luke 16:19–31).

The Intermediate State of the Believer

The intermediate destiny of the believer involves a conscious, peaceful existence in heaven with Jesus between physical death and the resurrection of the body. The believer's soul is translated immediately to the presence of Jesus in heaven upon physical death (2 Cor. 5:8; Phil. 1:22–24; Acts 7:59; Luke 23:43). Paul said that being with the Lord Jesus in this state is "far better" (Phil. 1:23) than physical life in a fallen world (2 Cor. 5:8). Yet he also stated that the intermediate condition is comparable to being "naked" (2 Cor. 5:3), that is, disembodied. It is the glorification of the resurrected body for which Paul longs most (2 Cor. 5:1–2). For the Christian, resurrection is better than the intermediate state, which is better than life in this fallen world.

Revelation 6:9–11 reveals several truths about the intermediate state of believers. The people in view in this passage are those "who had been slain for the word

4 This paragraph is adapted from John MacArthur, ed., *The MacArthur Study Bible: English Standard Version* (Wheaton, IL: Crossway, 2010), 1510. Used by permission of Thomas Nelson/HarperCollins Christian Publishing.

of God and for the witness they had borne" (6:9). First, these saints in heaven have keen self-awareness and knowledge of others and of world circumstances—these saints long for justice on the earth, a justice that will come with the return of Jesus and the saints in Revelation 19:11–21. Second, they are mindful of the distinction between heaven and earth. Third, heaven is not their final destiny. Fourth, the martyred saints in heaven appear to have some body-like form. They can be seen by John (Rev. 6:9), they can speak and be heard (6:10), and they can appear to wear clothing (6:11a).

RESURRECTION

God created human beings as a complex unity of body and soul. In this age, physical death results in the separation of a person's body from his or her soul. But this state does not last forever. Everyone is destined for a resurrection of the body fitted for his or her eternal destiny.

Resurrection of the Believer

Believers in God are destined for the resurrection of the body (Job 19:25–26). Job knew his "skin" would be "destroyed" (physical death) but that this was not the end. His "Redeemer" would stand on the earth, and in the end Job would, in his "flesh," "see God." Physical resurrection is real and occurs because of the Redeemer.

In 1 Corinthians 15:35–49, Paul discussed the nature of the resurrection body of believers. He asked, "How are the dead raised?" and "With what kind of body do they come?" (15:35). He contrasted our flawed mortal ("natural") bodies with our glorified ("spiritual") bodies of the coming age (15:44). Glorified bodies will be imperishable (15:42), will not be tainted with the shame of sin, and will be powerful (15:43). Jesus is the prototype of glorified bodies, while our natural bodies take after Adam (15:45–46).

Jesus had a tangible, physical existence when he rose from the dead, and so too will Jesus's followers. After all, Jesus is the "firstfruits" of those who die in him (1 Cor. 15:20). Glorified bodies are required to enter God's eternal kingdom (1 Cor. 15:50).

Resurrection involves the body coming to life and reuniting with the soul. When discussing the rapture of the church in 1 Thessalonians 4:13–18, Paul said, "God will bring with him those who have fallen asleep" (1 Thess. 4:14), referring to the souls of deceased Christians in heaven. At the rapture, God will bring the souls of departed Christians and join them with their resurrected bodies (1 Thess. 4:16).

Resurrection of the Unbeliever

Daniel 12:2 says that the unsaved "awake" to "shame and everlasting contempt." Daniel 12:2 and John 5:28–29 indicate that when they come out of the grave, unbelievers will experience a tangible bodily resurrection.

Just as believers will receive a body to live on the new earth (Rev. 21:1–22:5), which is a real place, nonbelievers will receive a body fit to experience the lake of fire, which also is an actual place (Rev. 20:15; Isa. 66:22–24).

The resurrected unbelievers will have a miserable existence in hell: eternal conscious torment with no rest.

HELL

The Bible presents the eternal reality of hell, a place of fiery torment for the unrepentant that lasts forever. The majority of references to hell in the Bible come from Jesus's own mouth (e.g., Matt. 5:22; 10:28; 23:33).

The Greek term translated "hell" in the above passages is *gehenna*, which occurs twelve times in the New Testament and relates to the Valley of Hinnom on the south and east sides of Jerusalem. In this place, children were sacrificed in fire to the god Molech (2 Kings 23:10; Jer. 7:31–32). This *gehenna* was a real place used to symbolize the future place of punishment for the wicked. These references show that hell is real. Hell is not merely a "state of mind" or unending torment in some sort of spiritual existence. The language used cannot be attributed to metaphor alone.

Hell is associated with three everlasting negative consequences: (1) punishment, (2) destruction, and (3) banishment. Not one of these concepts explains all of what hell is, but together they offer a multidimensional understanding of why hell is so terrible. First, the wicked are punished and receive retribution for their deeds (Luke 12:47–48). Second, hell involves destruction (2 Thess. 1:9), which entails the concepts of ruin and waste. Third, hell includes banishment from God's eternal kingdom (Rev. 22:14–15).

HEAVEN[5]

The term "heaven" appears approximately six hundred times in the Bible. The Hebrew term often translated "heaven" (*shamayim*) literally means "the heights." The Greek term (*ouranos*) refers to that which is raised up or lofty. The Bible uses these terms to refer to three different places—the atmospheric heaven, the planetary heaven, and the third heaven.

The atmospheric, or first, heaven is the sky or troposphere—the region of the breathable atmosphere that covers the earth (Gen. 7:11–12; Ps. 147:8; Acts 14:17).

The planetary, or second, heaven is where the sun, moon, planets, and stars exist. This understanding of heaven is referred to in Genesis 1:14–17. The planetary or stellar heaven serves several purposes. The lights in this heaven separate

5 This section is adapted from John MacArthur, *The Glory of Heaven: The Truth about Heaven, Angels, and Eternal Life* (Wheaton, IL: Crossway, 1996), 55–56. Used by permission of Crossway, a publishing ministry of Good News Publishers, Wheaton, IL.

day and night and exist for signs and seasons. The feasts of Israel would later be tied to the planetary heaven (Num. 10:10; 28:14). The planetary heaven also reveals the glory of God (Ps. 19:1–4).

The third heaven is the dwelling place of God, the holy angels, and deceased saints. Paul referred to this third heaven in 2 Corinthians 12:2–4. God the Father is the center of the third heaven (Matt. 6:9; Rev. 4:2). The resurrected Jesus is also in the third heaven (Acts 1:11; 7:56). Deceased brothers and sisters in Christ are also in the third heaven (Heb. 12:23). As glorious as the present third heaven is, it is not the final domain of God and his saints, for we await a new creation (2 Pet. 3:13).

Cosmic Eschatology

THE KINGDOM OF GOD[6]

While the Bible includes many important themes, the kingdom of God should be considered the grand, overarching theme of Scripture, encompassing all the other major themes.

Kingdom in the Old Testament

God's kingdom program started when the King of the universe created the world in six days (Genesis 1). The King is God; his kingdom is the earth. Man, created as God's image bearer on the sixth day, was tasked with a kingdom command—fill, rule, and subdue the earth for God's glory (Gen. 1:26–28). The psalmist referred to that high and lofty role in Psalm 8:3–9, which reaffirmed man's right "to rule over the works of God's hands." But Adam sinned against God and failed in his kingdom command (Genesis 3). Adam's failure will be overcome by the Messiah, the "Son of Man," who will fulfill mankind's role as the human race's only perfect representative (cf. Heb. 2:5–14). He will rule over the earth and will succeed as the *last* Adam, in the realm where the first Adam failed (cf. 1 Cor. 15:20–28, 45).

A kingdom of God on earth was established with the deliverance of the Israelites from Egypt, the giving of the Mosaic covenant, and the possession of the land of Canaan. Eventually, Israel received monarchs in the form of Saul, David (through whom the Davidic covenant was given; 2 Sam. 7:12–16), and Solomon. After Solomon, Israel was divided into two kingdoms, with both headed toward

6 This section is adapted from Richard L. Mayhue, "The Kingdom of God: An Introduction," *MSJ* 23.2 (2012): 167–71; William D. Barrick, "The Kingdom of God in the Old Testament," *MSJ* 23.2 (2012): 173–92; F. David Farnell, "The Kingdom of God in the New Testament," *MSJ* 23.2 (2012): 193–208. All used by permission of *MSJ*. For a more comprehensive study of this topic, see these three articles and the following articles from the same journal issue (*MSJ* 23.2 [2012]): Keith Essex, "The Mediatorial Kingdom and Salvation," 209–23; Michael J. Vlach, "The Kingdom of God and the Millennium," 225–54; Nathan Busenitz, "The Kingdom of God and the Eternal State," 255–74; Dennis M. Swanson, "Bibliography of Works on the Kingdom of God," 275–81.

captivity and dispersion. The ten tribes of the northern kingdom, Israel, were conquered by Assyria in 722 BC, and Judah was conquered by Babylon and the temple destroyed in 586 BC.

Israel's prophets rebuked both Israel's leaders and the people for turning from God and breaking the Mosaic covenant. Yet they also foretold of a kingdom under the Messiah—a restoration of the Davidic kingdom—in the latter days (Isa. 2:2–4). This kingdom would bring blessings for the nations under Israel's king (cf. Amos 9:11–12). The restored kingdom would have spiritual requirements, since faith and a willing heart to serve God were necessary to enter it, yet this kingdom would include physical and material prosperity for Israel and the nations. Only the Messiah could bring the needed spiritual and national deliverance.

Kingdom in the New Testament

At the beginning of the New Testament era, there was great anticipation concerning the Messiah and the kingdom of God. The angel Gabriel informed Mary that she would have a Son who would be great and would sit on the throne of his father David (Luke 1:32–33).

The expectation of the promised Davidic King was fulfilled in Jesus—a descendant of David (cf. Matt. 1:1). Both Jesus and his forerunner, John the Baptist, proclaimed the same message: "Repent, for the kingdom of heaven is at hand" (Matt. 3:2; 4:17). The kingdom they preached was the same as the kingdom proclaimed by the Old Testament prophets, namely, an earthly kingdom under the Messiah, with a restored Israel and blessings for the nations (Matt. 19:28). Repentance was the condition for entering this kingdom.

Jesus's teaching (cf. Matthew 5–7; 13) and his miracles were evidence of his messianic mission and his credentials as King. His miracles in nature, physical healings, exorcisms, and raising of the dead fulfilled Old Testament prophecy and showed that the kingdom had come upon the people (Isaiah 35; Matt. 11:2–5; 12:28). Yet the people of Israel did not repent. The cities of Israel rejected the kingdom message (Matt. 11:20–24), and the leaders committed blasphemy against the Holy Spirit by attributing Jesus's miracles to the power of Satan (Matt. 12:22–32). This rejection by Israel of her Messiah would bring judgment on Israel in the form of the AD 70 destruction of Jerusalem (Matt. 23:37–39; Luke 19:41–44). Jesus began to speak of the kingdom as coming in the future, after his return to heaven (Luke 19:11) and after the events of the tribulation period (Luke 21:31). And he spoke of the "secrets of the kingdom of heaven" in the form of parables (Matthew 13).

In the latter part of Jesus's ministry, his message focused mostly on his coming sacrificial death (Matt. 16:21). Yet he still predicted the kingdom's coming. In Matthew 19:28 Jesus foretold of sitting on the glorious Davidic throne and of his disciples ruling with him over a restored and united national Israel at the time of cosmic renewal, which is clearly future.

With his death, resurrection, and ascension, Jesus has been exalted as Messiah to the right hand of God the Father, where Jesus possesses all authority in heaven and on earth (Matt. 28:18; Eph. 1:20–22). Yet the actual exercise of his kingdom authority on earth awaits the future (Heb. 10:12–13; cf. Ps. 110:1–2).

The New Testament Epistles reveal that salvific benefits of the kingdom apply to believers in this church age. Christians experience the new covenant spiritual blessings of a new heart and the indwelling Holy Spirit (2 Cor. 3:6). They are positionally transferred into the kingdom of God's Son (Col. 1:13) and experience kingdom righteousness in their lives (Rom. 14:17). Yet the earthly kingdom *reign* of Jesus and his saints is presented as future (2 Tim. 2:12).

In the book of Revelation, Jesus is presented as "the ruler of kings on earth" (Rev. 1:5), a rule that will be actualized with his second coming to earth and his reign as described in Revelation 19:11–20:6. With his return to earth, Jesus will rule the nations (19:11–15). He will destroy his enemies and establish his millennial reign on the earth (19:17–20:6).

FUTURISTIC PREMILLENNIALISM

Futuristic premillennialism is based on three main beliefs. First, it accords with the consistent application of the grammatical-historical method of interpretation to all areas of the Bible, including its prophetic and eschatological passages. Second, it maintains the biblical distinction between Israel and the church and understands that the Bible does not confuse the two. Third, it recognizes that Scripture presents a coming fulfillment of Daniel's seventieth week that is a seven-year period of tribulation and that comes before Jesus's earthly millennial kingdom (Dan. 9:27).

ISRAEL AND THE CHURCH

Understanding eschatology requires knowing how God works through both Israel and the church.

Israel

The first purpose of Israel—to be a vehicle for the Savior and Messiah—has been fulfilled. Jesus, the ultimate Israelite (Isa. 49:3; Gal. 4:4–5) and offspring of Abraham (Gal. 3:16), arrived, bringing forgiveness and salvation to all who believe in him, regardless of nationality. Yet Israel's role in leading and serving other nations awaits fulfillment (Isa. 2:2–4). The picture of Israel that the prophets offered as a prominent nation in an earthly reign of the Messiah is yet future (see Isaiah 60). Matthew 19:28 indicates that Jesus expected a coming time of cosmic renewal, and Acts 1:3, 6 indicates the disciples were still expecting a coming kingdom, as they asked, "Lord, will you at this time restore the kingdom to Israel?" In his response, Jesus assumed the correctness of their belief in a restoration of the kingdom to Israel but told them that the timing of this event was known only by the Father (Acts 1:7).

Paul declared a future salvation of Israel when he stated, "All Israel will be saved" (Rom. 11:26). This salvation of Israel will bring even greater blessings for the world (Rom. 11:12, 15; cf. Isaiah 11; 65:17–25). God has not rejected his people (Rom. 11:1, 28–29).

Israel is currently experiencing a temporary hardening (Rom. 11:25) and facing the consequences for rejecting the Messiah. Jesus declared that Israel missed its time of "visitation," and in so doing they experienced the judgment of the destruction of Jerusalem in AD 70 and are currently experiencing the "times of the Gentiles" (Luke 19:41–44; 21:20–24). In this age, there is a remnant of believing Jews (Rom. 11:5), whom Paul calls the "Israel of God" (Gal. 6:16). This elect and faithful remnant serves as a reminder of a coming salvation of "all Israel" (Rom. 11:26–27). Zechariah foretold that a day is coming when God will "pour out" a "spirit of grace" on the people of Israel so that they will "look on . . . him whom they have pierced" and "they shall mourn for him" (Zech. 12:10). God will fulfill all promises and biblical covenants with Israel, just as he said, because God is impeccably true to his name and his promises to the patriarchs of Israel (Deut. 7:6–9).

The Church

The church was not explicitly predicted in the Old Testament, but it is a major phase of God's kingdom program and is connected to the covenants of promise (i.e., the Abrahamic, Davidic, and new covenants). The greater, ultimate Son of David (Jesus) arrived, bringing salvation to all who believe in him. In Galatians 3, Paul stated that Gentile Christians are connected to the Abrahamic promises of Genesis 12:3 and 22:18, which declared that God's blessings would one day go to Gentiles. Members of the church are spiritual sons of Abraham and are related to the Abrahamic covenant (Gal. 3:7–9, 29). Jesus's death brought an inauguration of the new covenant, and those who trust in Jesus benefit from the new covenant. This includes the new covenant promise of the indwelling Holy Spirit, who enables Christians to obey God as they should (Acts 2:4, 17; Rom. 8:3–4). Christians are also proclaimers of this covenant (2 Cor. 3:6; cf. Heb. 8:8–13). And Jew-Gentile spiritual unity under Israel's Messiah is already occurring (Acts 15:14–18; Eph. 2:11–22; 3:6).

The church has a Great Commission (Matt. 28:19–20). It is called to take the gospel and the message of the kingdom to the nations. Those who believe in Jesus become "sons of the kingdom" (Matt. 13:38) and are to evidence kingdom righteousness in their lives (Matthew 5–7).

In this age the church faces persecution from Satan and those who do his bidding. Nevertheless, the church operates in this present evil age with the promise of reward (Gal. 1:4). Endurance in this age will lead to a kingdom reign in the future (cf. 2 Tim. 2:12; Rev. 2:26–27; 3:21).

Yet the church is not the final phase of God's kingdom program before the eternal state. Much still needs to be fulfilled, including an international reign of the Messiah on and over the earth. Israel has not yet been saved and restored as a nation. The nations as national entities are not serving God (Isa. 19:24–25), nor are they experiencing international harmony and the removal of war (Isa. 2:2–4). The renewal of the planet (Matt. 19:28; Rom. 8:19–23) and harmony in the animal kingdom (Isa. 11:6–9) must still happen. Satan still actively deceives the world and persecutes the saints of God (Revelation 12–13). Creation as a whole still works against man as it remains under the curse (Gen. 3:17). Humanity, while still required to rule the earth for God (Ps. 8:6), is not yet ruling the earth in a successful way for the glory of God (Gen. 1:26–28; Heb. 2:5–8). These conditions do not fit the kingdom characteristics predicted by the prophets. There must be a successful reign of Jesus the Messiah and his saints on this earth before Jesus hands the kingdom over to the Father and the eternal state begins (1 Cor. 15:24–28). While Christians celebrate many spiritual blessings already, there is still much more to come.

RESURRECTION ORDER

Based on Biblical data, five conclusions can be offered concerning the order of resurrections:

1. The Bible speaks of the resurrection of the redeemed as "the first resurrection" (Rev. 20:5), the "resurrection of life" (John 5:29), "eternal life" (Rom. 2:7), or "everlasting life" (Dan. 12:2).
2. This "first resurrection" of the redeemed occurs in three phases: (a) Christ the firstfruits (1 Cor. 15:23); (b) church saints (1 Cor. 15:23, 50–58; 1 Thess. 4:13–18); (c) Old Testament saints (Ezek. 37:12–14; Dan. 12:2) and tribulation saints (Rev. 20:4).
3. The Bible does not use the term "second resurrection" but refers to the resurrection of the unredeemed as "a resurrection of judgment" (John 5:29) or "the second death" (Rev. 20:6, 14; 21:8).
4. The Bible gives no warrant to conclude that only one general resurrection of the righteous will occur at the end.
5. Thus, there are four recognized times of resurrection in Scripture: (a) Christ's resurrection (1 Cor. 15:23); (b) church saints' resurrection (1 Cor. 15:23, 50–58; 1 Thess. 4:13–18); (c) the resurrection of Old Testament saints (Ezek. 37:12–14; Dan. 12:2) and tribulation saints (Rev. 20:4); and (d) the resurrection of the unredeemed of all time (Rev. 20:5).

FUTURE JUDGMENTS

The Bible clearly teaches that all people will face a judgment day before God, when his judgment will be all that matters. A day of reckoning is coming when all will stand before the Creator to account for every thought and deed.

The Judgment Seat of Christ

All Christians are headed for a day of judgment before Jesus Christ. Scripture explicitly mentions the judgment seat of Christ in two places—Romans 14:10 and 2 Corinthians 5:10. In both cases, the Greek word for "judgment" is *bēma*. In ancient times, a *bēma* was a raised platform or step used in athletic or political arenas. Rulers or judges would ascend the *bēma* to render decisions in legal cases (see Matt. 27:19; John 19:13).

Scripture reveals several truths about the judgment seat of Christ. First, Jesus is the Judge who presides over this *bēma* judgment (2 Cor. 5:10; John 5:22).

Second, the subjects of this judgment are Christians (Rom. 14:10; 1 Cor. 3:11–15).

This judgment results in rewards for what a Christian has done with his or her life—for deeds good or bad (2 Cor. 5:10). The "good" refers to those works done in the power of the Holy Spirit that bring glory to God. The "bad" refers to worthless deeds that do not bring God honor, works done in the flesh (Gal. 5:19–21). Paul explains this in 1 Corinthians 3:12–15. Good works will lead to a reward (1 Cor. 3:14), but bad works will be burned up in the fire—they are linked with suffering "loss" (1 Cor. 3:15). This loss is not loss of salvation, for "he himself will be saved" (1 Cor. 3:15); nor is it punishment for sin, for Jesus has atoned for our sins (Rom. 8:1). It is the "loss" of the rewards the Christian could have received had he been more faithful, obedient, and diligent. Still, the Christian's appearance before Jesus is a joyous event. (1 Cor. 1:7–8).

The *bēma* of Jesus also has corporate implications for the church. The resurrected and rewarded church will return victoriously with Jesus at his second coming to earth (Rev. 19:14) and will be granted the right to share in Jesus's Davidic reign and to rule the nations with him (Rev. 3:21; cf. 2:26–27).

Judgment of Israel

Jesus will return to earth and set up his kingdom (Zech. 14:4, 9), yet since only those who are redeemed can enter the kingdom (John 3:3), there must be judgments to determine who will enter. One of these judgments involves Jews living at the time of Jesus's return (see Ezekiel 20:33–38).

This coming judgment of Israel will be a mighty act of God. With "wrath poured out," God will "be king" over Israel (Ezek. 20:33). He will gather Jews from the "countries" where they were scattered (Ezek. 20:34). The setting for this judgment scene will be "the wilderness of the peoples," and it will be an actual face-to-face meeting that parallels God's meeting with Israel in the wilderness of Egypt (Ezek. 20:35–36). Israel will pass under the Lord's kingly and shepherd-like rod to enter the "bond of the covenant" (Ezek. 20:37). This refers not to the Mosaic covenant but to national Israel's entrance into the blessings of the new covenant. Paul speaks of this in Romans 11:26–27, where the salvation of "all Israel" is linked with the new covenant passages of Isaiah 59:20–21 and Jeremiah 31:31–34. The new covenant was inaugurated with Jesus's death (Luke 22:20), and some of its spiritual blessings are experienced in this present age, but Israel will come into the covenant as Jesus establishes his kingdom on earth. Yet not all Israelites will enter this kingdom (Ezek. 20:38a). Even for Israel, spiritual birth is the prerequisite for entering the kingdom of God. The wicked will not enter the kingdom (Ezek. 20:38b).

Judgment of the Nations

The return of Jesus to earth also results in a judgment of living Gentiles. Two passages directly address this: Joel 3:1–16 and Matthew 25:31–46.

The context in Joel 2 and 3 is the day-of-the-Lord judgments which involve the salvation and blessing of Israel. At this "time" when God restores Israel, he will "gather all the nations" and judge them on behalf of Israel. The Gentile nations will be judged for scattering the Jewish people and dividing up Israel's land, as well as for other atrocities (Joel 3:2b–3). The place of this judgment is specific: "the Valley of Jehoshaphat." From there God will "judge all the surrounding nations" (Joel 3:12). In sum, Joel 3 reveals that God will judge the nations that harmed Israel.

Matthew 25:31–46 also describes a general judgment of Gentile nations. This judgment of Gentiles is often referred to as *the sheep-goat judgment* since believers are likened to "sheep" and the wicked to "goats" (vv. 31–32). The purpose of this judgment is to determine who is qualified to enter Jesus's earthly kingdom (righteous sheep) and who is not (wicked goats). The "sheep" enter the earthly kingdom of Jesus in their mortal bodies, while the "goats" are executed and enter eternal fire (vv. 41, 46).

The basis of this judgment is how the Gentile peoples treated others. Those who treated "the least of these" (Matt. 25:40, 45) does not indicate that salvation is based on works but rather makes clear that works accurately reveal character (see Rom. 2:5–11).

Judgment of Satan and Demons

Revelation 12:7–13 tells of a tribulational judgment when Satan and his demons will be thrown from heaven to earth. This will happen around the midpoint of Daniel's seventieth week (Dan. 9:27) since this event is linked with the period called "a time, and times, and half a time" (Rev. 12:14), which is three and one-half years. From this point onward, Satan will no longer have access to heaven and will not be able to accuse believers of sin in the presence of God (Rev. 12:10–11).

Satan is currently active, opposing God's plans, deceiving the nations, and persecuting the saints of God. But Revelation 20:1–3 chronicles a coming millennial judgment, after Jesus's return to earth (Rev. 19:11–21), when Satan will be seized, bound, and thrown into a pit, probably with all the demons with him. This pit is not the lake of fire but a spiritual prison that will completely remove Satan's access to the earth and his ability to deceive.

The final judgment of Satan and the demons will take place in the eternal judgment after the millennium (Rev. 20:7–10). At that time, Satan and all demons (Matt. 25:41; 2 Pet. 2:4; Jude 6) will join the Antichrist and the False Prophet in the lake of fire (Rev. 20:10). This is the final judgment of Satan and his demons, when they will forever be removed from opposing God's kingdom and his people.

The Great White Throne Judgment

All unbelievers are ultimately destined for the great white throne judgment—described in Revelation 20:11–15. This final sentencing of the lost is the most serious, sobering, and tragic passage in the Bible. This is the last courtroom scene in history.

This great white throne judgment takes place after the thousand-year reign of Christ and his saints (Rev. 20:4–7). The One present on the throne is none other than God Almighty (Rev. 4:2–11), which must certainly refer to Jesus, since all judgment has been granted to him (John 5:22, 26–27).

The purpose of this judgment is to declare who will be sent to the lake of fire (Rev. 20:15), which is also referred to as "the second death" (Rev. 20:6). The subjects of the great white throne judgment are unbelievers, whose bodies are raised from "Death and Hades" for this judgment (Rev. 20:13).

The basis of the great white throne judgment is works (Rev. 20:13), and the evidence for this judgment is contained in books that reveal the character and deeds of every person. A book identified as "the book of life" is opened (Rev. 20:15). This book lists those who have been saved by Jesus. The book of life is a testimony against the unsaved, whose names are not in it. These are "thrown into the lake of fire," which is the final destiny of the lost.

COVENANTS[7]

Covenants are central to God's plans and constitute the vehicles through which God's kingdom purposes unfold. A covenant is a formal agreement or treaty between two parties, with obligations and regulations. The majority of covenants in the Bible (1) are unconditional or non-nullifiable in that once the covenant is ratified, the covenant must be fulfilled; and (2) are referred to as everlasting. The unconditional covenants include the Noahic, Abrahamic, priestly,

7 For a more detailed discussion of covenants, consult the articles in *MSJ* 10.2 (1999): 173–280.

Davidic, and new covenants. The one conditional and temporary covenant is the Mosaic covenant.

Some theologians assert that the biblical covenants should be understood in terms of theologically derived covenants. Covenant theology affirms three such covenants: (1) the covenant of works, (2) the covenant of grace, and (3) the covenant of redemption. While there may be certain truths associated with these theological covenants (election and predestination), these are not actual covenants found in the Bible.

Unlike covenant theology, futuristic premillennialism asserts that God's covenant plans should be anchored in a proper understanding of the biblical covenants and how they unfold in salvation history. Introducing theological covenants is not necessary, since God's covenant program can be understood through the biblical covenants.

The Noahic Covenant

The first occurrence of the word "covenant" (*berit*) is found in a post-fall context in Genesis 6:18, where God says to Noah, "But I will establish my covenant with you." Thus, the first biblical covenant is the Noahic covenant, which is also called an "everlasting covenant" in Genesis 9:16.

Several developments stem from the Noahic covenant: (1) it guarantees stability of nature (Gen. 8:22); (2) Noah is told to multiply and fill the earth (Gen. 9:1, 7), a reissuing of the command first given to Adam (Gen. 1:28); (3) God causes animals, birds, and fish to fear man (Gen. 9:2); (4) animals become food for man just like the plants were at creation (Gen. 9:3–4); (5) it affirms the dignity of man as God's image bearer even after the fall of mankind and makes provision for capital punishment as the punishment for those who murder an image bearer of God (Gen. 9:6); (6) God promises never to destroy the world by water again (Gen. 9:15).

The Noahic covenant is an unconditional and eternal covenant still in effect today. Man continues to experience stability of nature for the outworking of God's purposes and of man's relationship to other people and to animals.

The Abrahamic Covenant

The Noahic covenant is the initial platform for God's purposes, yet the Abrahamic covenant details how God plans to save people and restore all things. This restoration will occur through three great promises: (1) land for Abraham, (2) a great number of descendants of Abraham, and (3) universal blessings for the nations.

This Abrahamic covenant is also the basis for the other covenants that God will institute. The initial and foundational promises of the Abrahamic covenant are found in Genesis 12:1–3. Several promises are contained here. First, God promises to make Abraham a "great nation." Second, God promises Abraham that he will be blessed, and his name will be made great. Third, Abraham will be a blessing for others. Fourth, God will treat others based on how they treat Abraham, whether for blessing or for curse. Fifth, Abraham and the nation to come from him will be a blessing to "all the families of the earth." Thus, Abraham and Israel will be used by God as a means for bringing blessings to Gentiles.

Genesis 12:6–7 promises land to Abraham's descendants, and Genesis 13:14–17 promises this land to them "forever." The specific dimensions of the land promise are given by God in Genesis 15:18–21: it will extend from the river of Egypt to the river Euphrates (Gen. 15:18).

Kings will come from Abraham (Gen. 17:6), in anticipation of the coming Davidic covenant, which highlights the importance of the kingly line in God's program (2 Sam. 7:12–16).

In Matthew 1:1, Jesus is declared "the son of Abraham." Mary stated that God was bringing help to "his servant Israel, in remembrance of his mercy, as he spoke to our fathers, to Abraham and to his offspring forever" (Luke 1:54–55). As he was "filled with the Holy Spirit," John the Baptist's father, Zechariah, prophesied that God was remembering "his holy covenant, the oath that he swore to our father Abraham, to grant us that we, being delivered from the hand of our enemies, might serve him without fear" (Luke 1:67, 72–74). Both Mary and Zechariah expressed hope that God would save Israel and deliver Israel from her enemies. These truths concerning national salvation and deliverance for the nation of Israel do not need to be spiritualized as referring to the church today. Instead, they will be fulfilled by Jesus at his second coming (see Zechariah 14; Rom. 11:26).

The Mosaic Covenant

The Mosaic covenant is the law God gave Israel through Moses to govern the life and conduct of Israel in the Promised Land of Canaan (Ex. 19:5–6).

This covenant was bilateral, conditional, and nullifiable, being contingent on Israel's obedience to God. Adherence to the Mosaic covenant was the means through which Israel could stay connected to the blessings of the Abrahamic covenant. Keeping the Mosaic covenant out of love to God would lead to spiritual and material prosperity, but disobedience would result in judgment, including removal from the land and dispersion throughout the nations (Deuteronomy 28–29).

The Mosaic covenant was a gracious covenant. It was not a means of salvation but the God-intended way for Israel to show its love and commitment to God. Though Israel promised to obey (Ex. 24:1–8), the biblical record demonstrates that they disobeyed God and faced curses for breaking the covenant. In addition to continually violating the law, Israel perverted the law in two main ways. First, many Jews wrongly twisted the covenant to become a means of works-righteousness salvation (Rom. 9:30–32). Second, many emphasized the external rituals of the covenant at the expense of the heart of love (Mic. 6:6–8).

The Mosaic covenant was holy, righteous, and good (Rom. 7:12). So the problem arising with the covenant was within the hearts of people, not in the covenant itself. The Mosaic covenant also revealed the people's sinfulness (cf. Rom. 3:20). Since Israel failed and broke the Mosaic covenant, God promised that it would be superseded by a better, new covenant as revealed in Jeremiah 31:31–32.

The end of the Mosaic covenant as a rule of life occurred with the death of Jesus, because he fulfilled the demands of the covenant and established the new covenant with his blood (Luke 22:20). Paul explained, "For Christ is the end of the law for righteousness to everyone who believes" (Rom. 10:4). Paul also said that Christ became our peace "by abolishing the law of commandments expressed in ordinances" (Eph. 2:14–15). The writer of Hebrews similarly stated, "In speaking of a new covenant, he makes the first one [the Mosaic covenant] obsolete. And what is becoming obsolete and growing old is ready to vanish away" (Heb. 8:13).

Since the Mosaic covenant was given to Israel alone (Ex. 19:3; 34:27), and since Christ brought an end to the covenant with his death (Eph. 2:14–15), Christians are not under the Mosaic covenant and its laws (cf. Rom. 6:14). That Christians are not under the Mosaic law does not mean they are free to sin. They are joined to Christ and are under the new covenant.

Nevertheless, this is not to say that the Mosaic covenant is not relevant today. The Mosaic covenant reveals unchanging attributes of and truths about God's character, which is the basis of his required principles for life. Paul sometimes quotes Mosaic legislation as wisdom for right living (Eph. 6:1–2). Plus, God's moral commands in the Old Testament show great continuity with what God expects from believers in this age.

The Priestly Covenant[8]

With the priestly covenant of Numbers 25, God promised a perpetual priesthood in the line of Phinehas that would continue all the way through the existence of the Lord's earthly millennial temple (Num. 25:10–13 NASB). This covenant given to Phinehas also included his descendants (Num. 25:13). God promised Phinehas and his offspring a perpetual priesthood, highlighting its enduring nature. The genealogical line of Phinehas will continue into the millennial kingdom through Zadok (1 Chron. 6:50–53). Ezekiel indicates that the only priests who will be permitted to minister in the millennial temple will be those of the line of Zadok (Ezek. 44:15; 48:11). Non-Zadokian priests will be prohibited from the priestly office because of past idolatrous activity (Ezek. 44:10).

8 This section is adapted from Irvin A. Busenitz, "Introduction to the Biblical Covenants: The Noahic Covenant and the Priestly Covenant," *MSJ* 10.2 (1999): 173–89. Used by permission of *MSJ*.

The perpetual nature of the priestly covenant suggests that it stands as a separate covenant and not as part of the Mosaic covenant, which is temporary. First, the terminology employed is similar to the covenants made with Noah, Abraham, David, and the new covenant. Second, that it remains when the Mosaic covenant was rendered obsolete speaks even louder for its standing as a separate covenant. The Mosaic covenant was abrogated by the new covenant, but the promise given to Phinehas continues into the millennium. Third, the language of Jeremiah 33:20–21 places its permanence alongside the Davidic covenant, contending that it remains in force as long as the cycle of day and night remains.

The Davidic Covenant

The Davidic covenant is the next unconditional covenant of promise, in which God promised the perpetuity of David's descendants on the throne in Israel. While several passages reveal truths concerning this covenant, the heart of the Davidic covenant is found in 2 Samuel 7:12–16. This passage outlines several provisions in the Davidic covenant. David's name will be made great (7:9). A home will be provided for Israel (7:10). Israel will be given undisturbed rest from all enemies (7:10–11). A house or dynasty in the line of David will endure (7:11). A coming son will establish this kingdom (7:12). Solomon will build the temple (7:13). Solomon's kingdom will be established forever (7:13). God will be a father to Solomon, and when Solomon disobeys, God will not take the kingdom from him as he did with Saul (7:14–15). David's dynasty and kingdom will endure forever, and the throne of David will be established forever (7:16).

In 2 Samuel 7:18–29, David offers a prayer of gratitude to the Lord. This covenant God is making with him is "instruction for mankind" (7:19). The word for "instruction" is *torah* ("law"), and the phrase could be rendered "law for mankind." This means the Davidic covenant will positively impact Gentiles, and it reaffirms the promise of the Abrahamic covenant that God's blessings will include Gentiles (see Gen. 12:3; 22:18). The Davidic covenant also pushes God's covenant plans forward by focusing on the royal descendants who are coming from the broader category of Abraham's national descendants via Isaac and Jacob.

As the New Testament era arrives, Jesus is manifested as the ultimate Son of David. The Gospels begin, "The book of the genealogy of Jesus Christ, the son of David" (Matt. 1:1). Jesus was recognized as the Son of David throughout his earthly ministry (see Matt. 9:27; 15:22; 21:15). The early church believed that the crucified and risen Jesus was the fulfillment of the promised seed of David and that because of this, he had to be resurrected from the dead (see Acts 2:30–36; 13:34–37). In Revelation, John identified Jesus as "the one who has the key of David" (Rev. 3:7), and Jesus referred to himself as both "the root and the descendant of David" (Rev. 22:16).

The Davidic covenant contains promises that were fulfilled with Jesus's first coming, while other promises await fulfillment at his second coming. Jesus's manifestation as King in the line of David is a first-coming fulfillment. Those who believe in him are positionally transferred to the kingdom (Col. 1:13). The spreading of messianic salvation to Gentiles is also a fulfillment of the Davidic covenant (Acts 15:14–18). But Jesus's ultimate assumption of the throne of David and his kingdom reign await his second coming in glory (Matt. 25:31), when the earth will be renewed, and he and the apostles will rule over a united and restored nation of Israel (Matt. 19:28).

The New Covenant

The Abrahamic covenant promised Abraham many descendants and a great nation that would come from him. He and this nation would mediate blessings to the world (Gen. 12:2–3). Then the Davidic covenant promised a kingly line from David that would rule Israel (2 Sam. 7:12–16) and ultimately the earth (Zech. 14:9; Matt. 25:31–34). But the hearts of the people still needed to be changed. What good would descendants, land, and a king be without people who loved God and desired to obey him? This is where the new covenant is significant. The new covenant is an unconditional and eternal covenant whereby God enables and empowers his people to serve him willingly and to remain in his blessings. The foundational passage that describes this covenant is Jeremiah 31:31–34.

The Mosaic covenant was a conditional and nullifiable covenant that Israel constantly broke. God was faithful to the covenant, but Israel was not. The substance of the new covenant was that God would put his law within his people and "write it on their hearts" (Jer. 31:33). They would be God's people and would wholeheartedly obey his law. They no longer needed to be compelled by an external threat. Obedience would be internal, and all who participated in this covenant would know God and obey him.

A new heart is the center of the new covenant. While the Mosaic law was "holy," "righteous," and "good" (Rom. 7:12), it did not enable people to obey. But the new covenant enables God's people to lovingly serve him. Ezekiel 36:26–27 includes the indwelling Holy Spirit as part of this covenant, whose redemptive features became effective in AD 30. As God places the Holy Spirit within his people, God will cause them to "walk" in his "statutes" and "obey" his "rules."

Various new covenant passages reveal both spiritual and physical blessings (Deut. 30:1–6; Ezek. 16:53–63). A new heart, the indwelling Holy Spirit, and forgiveness of sins are the spiritual blessings at the center of the covenant. Yet there also are national and material blessings, such as a united and restored Israel in the Land of Promise, the rebuilding of Jerusalem, and material prosperity for Israel (Isa. 61:8; Jer. 32:41; Ezek. 34:25–27). The spiritual, physical, and national promises are all important, and all need to be fulfilled.

The new covenant is based unconditionally on the "I will" of God (Jer. 31:31–34; Ezek. 16:60–62). Also, on multiple occasions the covenant is called eternal (Isa. 24:5; 61:8; Jer. 31:36, 40; 32:40; 50:5; Ezek. 37:26). It is as certain as it is everlasting.

The New Testament presents Jesus as the Son of David who is the Mediator of the new covenant and the One who brings new covenant blessings. John the Baptist declared that the Messiah "will baptize you with the Holy Spirit and fire" (Matt. 3:11). Since the ministry of the Holy Spirit was closely linked with the new covenant, John declared that Jesus was the One who would bring the new covenant to believers. At the Last Supper Jesus explicitly linked his death with the new covenant: "This cup that is poured out for you is the new covenant in my blood" (Luke 22:20; 1 Cor. 11:25).

The new covenant is in effect in this church age. Those who trust in Jesus the Messiah are indwelt with the Holy Spirit and participate in the full promises of the new covenant. Those who proclaim the gospel in this age are presenting the new covenant. Paul said that God "has made us sufficient to be ministers of a new covenant, not of the letter but of the Spirit" (2 Cor. 3:6). Quoting the new covenant passage of Jeremiah 31:31–34 in Hebrews 8:8–12, the writer of Hebrews explains that the new covenant is superior to the old covenant, which is becoming "obsolete" (Heb. 8:13). Hebrews 9:15 and 12:24 both affirm that Jesus is "the mediator of a new covenant." Yet while spiritual blessings of the new covenant are in effect for the church, national and physical promises of the new covenant regarding Israel still need to be fulfilled. The Lord thus declared, "Behold, the days are coming" (Jer. 31:27, 31, 38) when Israel will receive the salvation promised in the new covenant. This will occur when Jesus returns.

MILLENNIAL VIEWS

The ongoing debate about the millennium centers on the meaning of the "thousand years" mentioned six times in Revelation 20:1–7. In spite of the clarity of the text, a long-running debate has transpired concerning how to understand the thousand years. Three primary views have emerged: amillennialism, postmillennialism, and premillennialism.

Amillennialism

Amillennialism asserts that the millennium of Revelation 20 is being fulfilled spiritually in this present age between the two comings of Jesus and has nothing to do with an actual thousand years. Some amillennialists believe that the millennium is being fulfilled as Jesus and perfected saints presently rule from heaven. Others believe that the kingdom reign involves the church on earth or the rule of God over the lives of believers. Some combine these two ideas.

Postmillennialism

Postmillennialism also claims that the millennium of Revelation 20 (which is not viewed to mean "one thousand") occurs between the two comings of Jesus. Through the reign of Jesus from heaven and the Holy Spirit–blessed gospel, the kingdom of God will start small but will increasingly grow, spread, and become the dominant influence in the world. Not only will most people be saved, but also all areas of society will be transformed. The world will experience a golden era of peace, prosperity, and blessing. After a long period of a largely Christianized world, this millennial kingdom will then lead to the return of Jesus from heaven. At that time, Jesus will resurrect and judge all humanity, including both the righteous and the wicked.

Premillennialism

Premillennialism follows the clear sequential chronology of John's apocalypse and asserts that the kingdom of Revelation 20:1–7 occurs on earth after the second coming of Jesus described in Revelation 19:11–21 but before the eternal state of Revelation 21:1–22:5. The reason this view is called premillennialism is because Jesus returns before (*pre-*) the millennium. The millennium, therefore, is future and earthly. Most premillennialists believe that this intermediate kingdom between the present age and the eternal state (Rev. 21:1–22:5) lasts for a literal "thousand years." What unites all premillennialists is the belief that there will be a kingdom of Jesus on earth with his saints after this present age but before the eternal state.

Premillennialism also teaches that a thousand years separate the first and second resurrections of Revelation 20:4–5. Revelation 20:4 states that martyrs for Christ "came to life and reigned with Christ for a thousand years," but 20:5 then declares, "The rest of the dead did not come to life until the thousand years were ended." Premillennialism holds that these two resurrections are bodily resurrections from the dead that are separated by a thousand-year period. The order is (1) a bodily resurrection of the saints; (2) a thousand-year period; and (3) a bodily resurrection of the lost.

Biblical Support for Premillennialism. There is strong biblical support for premillennialism. First, it offers the clearest understanding of Revelation 19:11–21:8, which includes a sequence of events with a recurring chronological time marker—*kai eidon* (Gk. "then I saw," in Rev. 19:11, 17, 19; 20:1, 4, 11, 12; 21:1). These markers indicate a progression of events beginning with a tribulation period and followed by the second coming of Jesus, a thousand-year reign of Jesus, and finally, the eternal state.

Second, the binding of Satan described in Revelation 20:1–3 must be a future reality and not a present one.[9] The language of 20:1–3 indicates a dramatic incarceration of the person Satan in a specific location—the Abyss. Much more than a curtailing of Satan's deceptive activities, this is the incarceration of Satan himself. The binding of Satan is not occurring today (2 Cor. 4:4; 1 Pet. 5:8; 1 John 5:19). Revelation 12:9 states that before Jesus returns, Satan will be actively deceiving the nations with much success: "And the great dragon was thrown down, that ancient serpent, who is called the devil and Satan, the deceiver of the whole world."

Third, the reign of the saints mentioned in Revelation 20:4 best fits with a future kingdom reign after Jesus's second coming. This passage says that the martyred saints "came to life," which refers to physical resurrection. These saints first appeared in Revelation 6:9–11 as those who were killed for their testimony for Jesus. Coming to life means the resurrection of the body for these faithful saints, and since physical resurrection has not yet occurred, "came to life" in Revelation 20:4 must refer to resurrection after the return of Jesus. Also, Revelation 5:10 affirms the coming reign of the saints on earth—"they shall reign on the earth." However, the experience of the church in this present age is persecution, not reigning (Revelation 2–3). Reigning is held out as a motivation for those who endure until Jesus returns (Rev. 2:26–27).

Fourth, several Old Testament passages point to an intermediate kingdom that is far better than this present age but not yet perfect like the final eternal state. For example, Isaiah 65:17–25 predicts a time of incomparable prosperity, peace, and harmony of creation, yet a time when the possibility of death remains (65:20). The reason why Isaiah 65:20 points toward a coming earthly kingdom is that the conditions described here do not fit this present age, when life spans are around eighty years. Nor do they fit the coming eternal state, when sin will not exist and no one will die. But they do fit an intermediate kingdom like that described in Revelation 20.

Zechariah 14:16–19 also depicts conditions consistent with a future millennial kingdom. This passage describes a period when the nations will be required to go up to Jerusalem. Those who do not, like Egypt, will face the prospect of "no rain," "plague," and "punishment." Such conditions fit neither this present age nor the coming eternal state. Yet the conditions described in Zechariah 14 fit well with an intermediate earthly kingdom.

A fifth reason for premillennialism is that this view best fits the Bible's redemptive storyline. God created the first Adam to rule from and over the earth. Adam failed, but Christians now look to the last Adam (1 Cor. 15:45) to succeed where

9 This paragraph is adapted from Michael J. Vlach, "The Kingdom of God and the Millennium," *MSJ* 23.2 (2012): 246–49. Used by permission of *MSJ*.

the first Adam failed. Adam was to rule from the earth and over the earth (Gen. 1:26–28), and according to the premillennialism scenario Jesus the second Adam will successfully rule from earth, over the earth, with an extended reign that is recognized by all. Those who belong to Jesus are also destined for a kingdom reign on the earth. Persecution on earth is the norm for the saints in this age, but a time is coming when the saints will rule in the realm where they are currently persecuted (Dan. 7:26–27; Rev. 2:26–27; 5:10).

DANIEL'S "SEVENTY WEEKS" PROPHECY

The prophecy of the "seventy weeks" in Daniel 9:24–27 is one of the most important prophetic passages in the Bible. Several New Testament prophetic passages rely heavily on its contents (Matt. 24:15; 2 Thessalonians 2; Revelation 11–13). Jesus, Paul, and John all refer to this section of Daniel.

Defining the "Seventy Weeks"

Jeremiah had prophesied that Jerusalem's desolation at the hands of the Babylonians would end after seventy years (Dan. 9:2; cf. Jer. 25:12; 29:10). Israel failed to observe a Sabbath rest for the land (cf. Leviticus 25) seventy times. The seventy-year Babylonian captivity was God's way of giving the land the rest he wanted it to have. As Daniel contemplated Jeremiah's prophecy, and prayed on behalf of his sinful people, Israel (Dan. 9:3–19), the angel Gabriel came to Daniel and relayed a vision concerning Israel's future.

The "seventy weeks" of Daniel 9:24 is at the heart of this prophecy and concerns Daniel's "people"—Israel and the "holy city"—Jerusalem (cf. Dan. 9:2). To interpret Israel and Jerusalem as anything else does injustice to the context.

In Hebrew, "seventy weeks" literally means "seventy sevens." Seventy sevens (or seventy times seven) equals 490. The context indicates that this is 490 years. Since Sabbath-year violations were the reason for Israel's expulsion and the ensuing seventy-year Babylonian captivity, a period of 490 days or 490 months would be far too short for the fulfillment of the six predictions in Daniel 9:24.

This 490-year period of Daniel 9:24 will yield six results: it will (1) "finish the transgression," (2) "put an end to sin," (3) "atone for iniquity," (4) "bring in everlasting righteousness," (5) "seal both vision and prophecy" (NASB), and (6) "anoint the most holy place" (NASB). The first three effects focus on defeating sin in Israel. The final three focus on positive developments regarding the kingdom—the bringing in of righteousness with Messiah's kingdom, fulfillment of all prophecies in Scripture, and anointing the temple in Jerusalem. The basis for the first three was accomplished with Jesus's first coming and death, although their application to Israel as a nation is still future. The final three await fulfillment at the second coming of Jesus, because everlasting righteousness has not yet been brought in, all prophecies in Scripture have not yet been fulfilled, and the temple in Jerusalem has not been anointed. However, these will occur when Jesus establishes his millennial kingdom.

The seventy weeks (490 years) begin with "the going out of the word to restore and build Jerusalem" (Dan. 9:25). This restoration was likely fulfilled in ca 445 BC when King Artaxerxes decreed that the Jews could return and rebuild Jerusalem (Neh. 2:1–8). Next, the "seven weeks" or forty-nine years can refer to the closing of Nehemiah's career in the rebuilding of "squares and moat," as well as to the end of the ministry of Malachi and the close of the Old Testament. After these forty-nine years, another "sixty-two" weeks or 434 years (sixty-two times seven) is added to the timeline. Put together, this 483-year period following Artaxerxes's decree in ca 445 BC culminates in Jesus's entry into Jerusalem in March AD 30.

Daniel 9:26 declares that "after" sixty-two weeks, which is really sixty-nine weeks (seven plus sixty-two), the "anointed one shall be cut off and shall have nothing." Days after entering Jerusalem, Jesus is crucified. That the Messiah "has nothing" is shocking. The Messiah of Israel comes, is killed, and dies with nothing. No kingdom and no everlasting righteousness occur. The rest of 9:26 describes other events "after" the first sixty-nine weeks: "And the people of the prince who is to come shall destroy the city and the sanctuary. Its end shall come with a flood, and to the end there shall be war. Desolations are decreed." This statement predicts the destruction of Jerusalem and the Jewish temple with the Roman invasion of Jerusalem in AD 70 (Luke 21:20–24).

The "people" in Daniel 9:26 refers to the Romans, since they were the ones who destroyed Jerusalem in AD 70. From this "people" a "prince who is to come" will someday arrive. This is the evil Antichrist figure who will arise sometime after the destruction of the city and the sanctuary. That this is an evil person and not Jesus the Messiah is affirmed by the descriptions in Daniel 9:27, in which he commits an abominable act in the temple and is destroyed for his desolations. Also, he will make a covenant with the people of Israel for one week (seven years), something Jesus never did. So the context points to the evil Antichrist figure, who is also identified as the "little . . . horn" in Daniel 7:8 and the willful king of Daniel 11:36. The statements "There shall be war" and "Desolations are decreed" (Dan. 9:26) reveal that Jerusalem's trials and woes will continue even after the destruction of Jerusalem. That has certainly been the case, as Israel's tumultuous history since AD 70 shows. Jesus himself predicted that the "times of the Gentiles" would continue even after the destruction of Jerusalem in AD 70 (Luke 21:24).

Daniel 9:27 goes on to say that the evil prince from the Romans "shall make a strong covenant with many for one week." The "many" refers to the people of Israel, and the "one week" is a seven-year period. Just as the first sixty-nine weeks were literal, so too must the last week of seven years be literal. To make the final week anything other than a seven-year period is to violate the context. That this covenant is future from our standpoint is verified by the fact that no seven-year covenant between a leader from the Roman Empire and the Jewish people has ever happened in history.

At "half of the week" (three and one-half years), this leader breaks the covenant with Israel. He "shall put an end to sacrifice and offering." In other words, he halts the Jewish worship system. This happens "on the wing of abominations" by the "one who makes desolate." This desolator sets up an abomination in an area of the temple. Jesus picks up this wording when he states, "So when you see the abomination of desolation spoken of by the prophet Daniel, standing in the holy place . . ." (Matt. 24:15).

Yet this desolator is headed for destruction. He does his "abominations" only "until the decreed end is poured out on the desolator" (Dan. 9:27). God's wrath will be visited on this evil prince. Paul draws on Daniel 9:27 when he refers to a coming "man of lawlessness" (2 Thess. 2:3) whom Jesus will slay with his own coming (2 Thess. 2:8).

Gap between the Sixty-Ninth and Seventieth Weeks

Many interpreters agree that the sixty-nine weeks (483 years of 360 days each) of Daniel's prophecy were fulfilled with Jesus's first coming and his death around AD 30. But some disagree about whether the final week of years, a seven-year period, was fulfilled immediately after the first sixty-nine weeks expired or whether there is a gap of time between the end of the sixty-ninth weeks and the beginning of the seventieth week. In other words, did Daniel's seventieth week expire in the late 30s—that is, in the seven years following the end of the sixty-ninth week, around AD 30—or will Daniel's seventieth week be fulfilled in the future? The correct view is the latter.

The evidence for a gap between the sixty-ninth and seventieth weeks is strong. The following reasons explain why there is a gap.

1. *A gap exists between the first and second comings of Jesus.* An obvious and significant gap of time exists between the first coming and second coming of Jesus. Several prophecies about Jesus are best understood in the light of this gap. For example, Zechariah 9:9 predicted that the Messiah would come to Jerusalem lowly on a donkey. This was fulfilled with Jesus's triumphal entry into Jerusalem (Matt. 21:1–8). But Zechariah 9:10 also declared a worldwide reign of the Messiah on the earth—this verse will be fulfilled with Jesus's second coming. It certainly did not immediately follow his entry into Jerusalem on a donkey in the first century. Gaps of time in prophetic passages such as Zechariah 9:9–10 indicate that a gap could be present in Daniel 9:24–27. Such is to be expected with two comings of Jesus.

2. *Daniel 9:26 states that the Messiah will be cut off "after" the sixty-nine weeks.* Daniel's use of the word "after" reveals a gap. According to Daniel 9:26, the Messiah

is not cut off at the "end" of the sixty-nine weeks or at the "beginning" of the seventieth week. Instead, he is cut off "after" the sixty-nine weeks.

3. *The destruction of Jerusalem predicted in Daniel 9:26 occurred decades after the culmination of the sixty-ninth week.* Daniel 9:26 states that "after the sixty-two weeks," the coming prince "will destroy the city and the sanctuary." This is a reference to Jerusalem and the temple, and this destruction took place in AD 70. With no gap, the seventieth week would have expired in the AD 30s. But Jerusalem and the temple were destroyed nearly four decades after the end of the sixty-ninth week, and therefore a gap between the sixty-ninth week and seventieth week is necessary to include the AD 70 destruction.

4. *The six predictions of Daniel 9:24 have not yet all been fulfilled.* In Daniel 9:24 (NASB), Daniel mentions six important predictions that will result from the seventy-weeks decree: (1) "to finish the transgression," (2) "to make an end of sin," (3) "to make atonement for iniquity," (4) "to bring in everlasting righteousness," (5) "to seal up vision and prophecy," and (6) "to anoint the most holy place." If one holds that the seventy weeks expired in the first century, then all six predictions should have been completely fulfilled in the 30s. But (as noted above) they were not. Since several predictions of Daniel 9:24 have yet to occur, these must be fulfilled in the future.

5. *What is described for the seventieth week of Daniel 9:27 has not yet been fulfilled.* The lack of fulfillment of Daniel 9:27 at this point in history is evidence that Daniel's seventieth week will be fulfilled at a future time. A coming evil prince from the Roman Empire has not made a seven-year covenant with the Jewish people. No violation of a seven-year covenant after three and one-half years has occurred. No Antichrist figure has committed abominations in the temple. Nor has the one doing this been destroyed. These events were not completed in the AD 30s and thus await future fulfillment.

6. *Jesus refers to the abomination of desolation of Daniel 9:27 as future after his first coming.* In Matthew 24–25, Jesus predicted events to come. With Matthew 24:15, Jesus made reference to "the abomination of desolation spoken of by the prophet Daniel." This is the same event predicted in Daniel 9:27: "On the wing of abominations shall come one who makes desolate." This event, though, was future from Jesus's standpoint and was not fulfilled in the 30s.

7. *In the AD 50s Paul spoke of the events of Daniel 9:27 as future.* In 2 Thessalonians 2, Paul writes about a "man of lawlessness" being revealed who enters a temple and declares himself to be God (2 Thess. 2:3–4). He also speaks of this wicked man as facing the wrath of the Lord Jesus, who slays him at his return (2 Thess. 2:8). Paul relies on Daniel 9:27 to establish that there will be a coming abomination of desolation by a wicked person and that this person will be

destroyed by God. That Paul is predicting these events in the 50s shows that these events are future from his standpoint and were not fulfilled in the 30s.

8. *Revelation places the time frame of Daniel 9:27 in the future.* Daniel 9:27 tells of a seven-year period in which a coming prince will make a covenant with the "many" for one week (seven years). But in the middle of this week, at the three-and-one-half-year mark, he will break this covenant. Writing in the AD 90s, the apostle John referred on multiple occasions to a coming three-and-one-half-year period (see Rev. 11:2; 12:6; 13:5). This parallels Daniel 9:27 and the association of an evil figure with a three-and-one-half-year period. In sum, since John refers to the time frame and events of Daniel 9:27 as needing to be fulfilled in the future, this shows that the events of this period must be future.

EVENTS TO COME

Several prophetic events await future fulfillment. These include the rapture, the tribulation period, the coming of the Antichrist, the day of the Lord, the second coming of Jesus, the millennium, Satan's final revolt, and the eternal state.

The Rapture[10]

The rapture is one of the most recognizable events of eschatology. The English word *rapture* comes from the Latin term *raptura*, which in Latin Bibles translates the Greek word *harpazō*. This Greek word means "to suddenly remove" or "to snatch away." The New Testament uses it in reference to stealing or plundering (Matt. 11:12; 12:29; 13:19; John 10:12, 28, 29) and removing (John 6:15; Acts 8:39; 23:10; Jude 23). A third use focuses on being caught up to heaven, as is seen in Paul's third-heaven experience (2 Cor. 12:2–4) and Christ's ascension (Rev. 12:5). *Harpazō* also describes God's sudden taking of the church from earth to heaven as the first part of Christ's second coming (1 Thess. 4:17). While not employing *harpazō*, 1 Corinthians 15:51–52 refers to the same eschatological event as 1 Thessalonians 4:16–17 when it refers to the sudden change that will be experienced by believers when they are "raised imperishable." Scripture points to an eschatological rapture, even though neither of these foundational texts contains any explicit time indicators.

Views on the Timing of the Rapture. The passages cited above mention a snatching away and transforming of Christians, but they do not state when this event occurs. However, it seems best to understand that the church will be raptured before Daniel's seventieth week. Since the entire period of tribulation is the "wrath of God," the church must be rescued prior to the tribulation to fulfill

10 This section is adapted from Richard L. Mayhue, "Why a Pretribulational Rapture?," *MSJ* 13.2 (2002): 241–53. Used by permission of *MSJ*.

God's promise that the church will escape the wrath of God (1 Thess. 1:9–10; Rev. 3:10). The pretribulational rapture functions as a rescue mission by which Jesus delivers his church from the divine wrath of the tribulation.

Evidence for Pretribulationism. There are several reasons to accept pretribulationism as the correct view for the timing of the rapture. First, Jesus declares that the church will be removed prior to "the hour of trial that is coming" on the entire earth (Rev. 3:10) and Jesus promises a reward for "patient endurance." Thus, the rapture is a future promise or reward to the church for enduring patiently during present sufferings. The church that endures the trials of this present age will be kept from the special hour of testing for the people of the earth.

Second, the church goes unmentioned in Revelation 6–18. The common New Testament term for "church" is *ekklēsia*. It is used nineteen times in Revelation 1–3 in relation to the historical church of the first century. However, "church" appears only once more in Revelation, in the epilogue of the book (Rev. 22:16). Nowhere in Revelation 6–18 is the "church" mentioned. A pretribulational rapture best explains the total absence of the "church" on earth during the events of Revelation 6–18.

Third, the rapture is rendered inconsequential if the church goes through the tribulation. If God miraculously preserves the church through the tribulation, why have a rapture at all? If it is to avoid the wrath of God at Armageddon, then why would God not continue to protect the saints on earth (as postulated by posttribulationism) as he protected the church in the events leading up to Armageddon or as God protected Israel from the plagues in Egypt (Ex. 8:22; 9:4, 26; 10:23; 11:7)?

Fourth, the Epistles contain no preparatory warnings of an impending tribulation for church-age believers. God's instructions to the church in the Epistles contain a variety of warnings, but believers are not warned to prepare for entering and enduring the tribulation. The New Testament admonishes believers to endure amid present tribulation (1 Thess. 2:13–14; 2 Thess. 1:4) but gives no instruction for enduring the global and catastrophic tribulation described in Revelation 6–18. Only a pretribulational rapture satisfactorily explains this lack of instruction for the church.

Fifth, in 1 Thessalonians 4:13–18 Paul is consoling the Thessalonians who had lost loved ones in death. But if the church was destined to go through the tribulation then we would expect the Thessalonians to be rejoicing that their loved ones are home with the Lord and will not endure the horrors of the tribulation. But instead, we discover that the Thessalonians are actually grieving because they fear their loved ones will miss the rapture. Only a pretribulational rapture accounts for this grief. Also, we would expect the Thessalonians to be grieving over their own impending trial rather than over their loved ones who escaped it. But we find no indication of any impending tribulation.

Sixth, the close parallels between John 14:1–3 and 1 Thessalonians 4:13–18, two texts referring to Christ's second coming, fit with a pretribulational rapture:

1. The promise of presence with Christ:
   "Where I am, there you may be also." (John 14:3 NASB)
   "So we shall always be with the Lord." (1 Thess. 4:17 NASB)
2. The promise of comfort:
   "Do not let your heart be troubled." (John 14:1 NASB)
   "Therefore comfort one another with these words." (1 Thess. 4:18 NASB)

Jesus instructed the disciples that he was going to his Father's house (heaven) to prepare a place for them. He promised them that he would return and receive them so that they could be with him wherever he was (John 14:1–3). The phrase "where I am," while implying continued presence in general, here means presence in heaven in particular (cf. John 7:34).

Seventh, events at Christ's return to earth after the tribulation differ from the rapture. If one compares what happens at the rapture in 1 Thessalonians 4:13–18 and 1 Corinthians 15:50–58 with what happens in the final events of Christ's second coming in Matthew 24–25, at least eight significant contrasts or differences can be observed, which demand that the rapture and Christ's second coming occur at different times:

1. At the rapture, Christ comes in the air and returns to heaven (1 Thess. 4:17), while at the final event of the second coming, Christ comes to earth to dwell and reign (Matt. 25:31–32).
2. At the rapture, Christ gathers his own (1 Thess. 4:16–17), while at the second coming, angels gather the elect (Matt. 24:31).
3. At the rapture, Christ comes to reward (1 Thess. 4:17), while at the second coming, Christ comes to judge (Matt. 25:31–46).
4. At the rapture, resurrection is prominent in Jesus's coming (1 Thess. 4:15–16), while at the second coming, no resurrection is mentioned with Christ's descent.
5. At the rapture, *believers* depart from the earth (1 Thess. 4:15–17), while at the second coming, *unbelievers* are taken away from the earth (Matt. 24:37–41).
6. At the rapture, *unbelievers* remain on the earth (implied), while at the second coming, *believers* remain on the earth (Matt. 25:34).
7. At the rapture, there is no mention of Christ's kingdom on earth, while at the second coming, Christ's kingdom on earth is established (Matt. 25:31, 34).

8. At the rapture, believers will receive glorified bodies (cf. 1 Cor. 15:51–57), while at the second coming, no one who is alive receives glorified bodies.

The Tribulation Period

Jesus promised his followers that they would experience tribulation in the world (John 16:33). This has indeed happened, as many Christians have suffered and died for the cause of Christ. Yet Jesus also predicted a "great tribulation, such as has not been from the beginning of the world until now, no, and never will be" (Matt. 24:21). This unique time is called the tribulation or tribulation period, (see Matt. 24:9, 21). The tribulation is a seven-year period of divine judgments before the return of Jesus Christ and the establishment of his kingdom on earth. This is based on the future seventieth week of Daniel, which is seven years in length (Dan. 9:27).

The Bible reveals more about the coming tribulation than any other prophetic event still to come (see Deut. 4:30; Isa. 34:8; Jer. 30:7; Zeph. 1:15). Matthew 24–25 (along with Mark 13; Luke 21) and Revelation 6–19 offer the most detailed New Testament information concerning the tribulation period. Jesus speaks of "birth pains" such as wars, rumors of wars, famines, and earthquakes in various places (Matt. 24:4–8). Persecution of Jesus's followers will be intense (Matt. 24:9). Apostasy and betrayal will occur (Matt. 24:10). Many false prophets will arise (Matt. 24:11), and lawlessness will increase (Matt. 24:12). Yet amid this terrible period, the gospel of the kingdom will be proclaimed to the whole world (Matt. 24:14), and both Jews and Gentiles will be saved (Rev. 7:4–9).

Strategic to this period is the fulfillment of the "abomination of desolation," which occurs at the midpoint of the tribulation, or at the three-and-one-half-year mark. First spoken of by Daniel (Dan. 9:27), this describes the Antichrist's breaking of his covenant with Israel in which he tries to stop the Jewish worship system in the temple. Paul notes that this "man of lawlessness" enters the temple declaring himself to be God (2 Thess. 2:3–4). This event launches a severe persecution in Israel, which is why Jesus warns the residents of Judea to flee with no thought of returning for any item (Matt. 24:16–20). The end of this period brings cosmic signs (Matt. 24:29). Jesus returns to earth in power and glory (Matt. 24:30) and gathers his elect (Matt. 24:31). The return of Jesus in glory with his angels leads to a judgment of nations to see who will enter his kingdom (Matt. 25:31–46).

Revelation 6–19 details the judgments—of the seals, trumpets, and bowls—which are predominantly sequential and escalating. They are from God against an unbelieving world and the kingdom of the Antichrist. Since Jesus is the One who opens the seal judgments, all subsequent judgments are the wrath of God and Jesus (Rev. 6:1). The six seals include (1) the arrival of Antichrist, (2) war, (3) famine, (4) death, (5) martyrdom, and (6) earthquake (Rev. 6:2–12). These correspond closely with the conditions of "birth pains" found in Matthew 24:4–7.

Next, the seventh seal brings the second wave of judgments—the seven trumpets:

1. First trumpet: One-third of the earth, trees, and grass are burned up (Rev. 8:7).
2. Second trumpet: One-third of the sea creatures die, and the ships are destroyed (8:8–9).
3. Third trumpet: One-third of the waters are polluted, and many die (8:10–11).
4. Fourth trumpet: One-third of the sun, moon, and stars are darkened (8:12).
5. Fifth trumpet: Locusts/demons are released to torment people (9:1–11).
6. Sixth trumpet: Four bound demons are released to kill one-third of humanity (9:13–19).
7. Seventh trumpet: Christ's kingdom reign is proclaimed (11:15–18).

The final cluster of judgments are the bowl judgments. These come later in the tribulation period in rapid succession and are extremely severe:

1. First bowl: Painful sores come on people (Rev. 16:2).
2. Second bowl: The sea becomes like blood, and everything in the sea dies (16:3).
3. Third bowl: The rivers and springs of water are turned to blood (16:4–7).
4. Fourth bowl: The sun scorches people with fire and heat (16:8–9).
5. Fifth bowl: Darkness and intense pain afflict humanity (16:10–11).
6. Sixth bowl: The Euphrates River is dried up to prepare the way for kings from the East (16:12–16).
7. Seventh bowl: Severe earthquakes split the great city into three parts, cities fall, and severe hail drops from heaven (16:17–21).

The purpose of the tribulation is twofold. First, God will use the tribulation to save Israel. This involves the completion of the purposes of Daniel 9:24. Jeremiah 30:7 says that this will be "a time of distress for Jacob [Israel]," yet Israel "shall be saved from it." Israel enters the tribulation making a covenant with the Antichrist but ends this period by calling on her Messiah.

Second, God will use the tribulation to judge the unbelieving world (Rev. 3:10). Isaiah 24 describes this as a time of global judgment in which "the Lord will empty the earth and make it desolate" and "will twist its surface and scatter its inhabitants" (Isa. 24:1). This is because of man's sinfulness (Isa. 24:5). Thus, the tribulation is a time of intense global wrath from God on a sinful, rebellious world.

The Antichrist

The Bible predicts a coming Antichrist, a representative of Satan who is the embodiment of evil. John refers to a specific Antichrist to come, yet he also mentions "antichrists" that have already arrived (1 John 2:18). These are not *the* Antichrist, but they function in the spirit of antichrist, opposing who Jesus is and what he stands for. We can expect many who possess the antichrist spirit while knowing that a personal Antichrist is also still coming.

The prefix *anti-* can mean "against" or "instead of." So the coming Antichrist is a counterfeit to the Messiah, yet he is also against Jesus by opposing Jesus and his saints.

Daniel offers the most detailed Old Testament information about the Antichrist. This evil person is the blasphemous political ruler, the "little . . . horn" who speaks great and boastful words and wages war against the saints of God (Dan. 7:8, 21). He is the wicked "prince" who arises from the Romans (Dan. 9:26). This prince makes a covenant with the Jewish people for seven years but breaks this covenant at the midpoint, stopping the Jewish sacrificial system and desolating the temple (Dan. 9:27). In Daniel 11:36–45, he is the willful king who exalts himself, speaks against God, rejects any rival gods, and trusts in his military might.

The apostle Paul refers to the Antichrist as the "man of lawlessness" (2 Thess. 2:3). Relying on Daniel 9:26–27 and 11:36–45, Paul reveals that this evil man arrives in connection with the day of the Lord (2 Thess. 2:1–2). This person "opposes and exalts himself against every so-called god or object of worship, so that he takes his seat in the temple of God, proclaiming himself to be God" (2 Thess. 2:4; this act is associated with the desolation of the temple that Daniel 9:27 predicted; cf. Matt. 24:15). This horrible event of desolation leads to intense persecution in Judea (Matt. 24:16–22).

The most detailed discussion of the Antichrist was revealed to the apostle John and recorded in Revelation 13. John refers to this individual as a "beast." This beast comes from the nations and is empowered by Satan (Rev. 13:1–2). He recovers from a mortal wound with some kind of resurrection that causes the world to marvel at him (Rev. 13:3). He blasphemes God (Rev. 13:5–6), wages war on the saints, and exercises authority over the earth (Rev. 13:7–8). He attempts to establish a permanent kingdom on earth for Satan.

Debate exists as to whether the Antichrist will be a Jew or a Gentile. Since he is the prince who comes from the people who destroyed Jerusalem and the temple in AD 70 (Dan. 9:26), he must come from the Roman Empire, for the Romans were the ones who destroyed Jerusalem and the temple. Also, Daniel's prediction concerning Antiochus IV Epiphanes (215–164 BC) in Daniel 8:9–14, 23–25 supports the view that the Antichrist will be a Gentile. Antiochus was a Syrian who desecrated the Jewish temple around 167 BC by instituting Zeus worship in Jerusalem and having a pig slaughtered in the temple. This desolating act seems to prefigure what the Antichrist of Daniel 9:27 will do. Since Antiochus was a Gentile, the Antichrist will probably be a Gentile as well.

While a frightening and powerful figure, the Antichrist has a brief career and is destroyed. Paul says that Jesus "will kill [the man of lawlessness] with the breath of his mouth and bring [him] to nothing by the appearance of his coming" (2 Thess. 2:8). Daniel says that a "decreed end is poured out on the desolator" (Dan. 9:27) and that "he shall come to his end, with none to help him" (Dan. 11:45). This "beast" is thrown into the lake of fire at Jesus's return, where his fate is sealed forever (Rev. 19:20).

The Day of the Lord[11]

The biblical phrase "the day of the Lord" is a key term in understanding God's revelation about the future. The New Testament writers' use of "the day of the Lord" rested on their understanding of the Old Testament prophets. The prophets used it when speaking of both near-historical events and far-future eschatological events involving God's wrath. The New Testament writers picked up on the eschatological use and applied "the day of the Lord" both to the judgment that will climax the tribulation period and to the judgment that will usher in the new earth.

The Old Testament prophets use the phrase in reference to both near-historical fulfillment and far-future eschatological events. The prophet Joel (1:15) refers to a historical day of the Lord involving a severe locust plague within Israel, yet the day of the Lord in Joel 2 and 3 refers to a future day of the Lord in which Israel is restored and blessed and the Gentile nations are judged. The near fulfillment (Joel 1:15) prefigures the far fulfillment (Joel 3:14). The historical day of the Lord serves as a harbinger for a greater day of the Lord to come.

The New Testament writers use the phrase in this eschatological sense. They apply it to the two periods of the day of the Lord that are yet to be fulfilled on earth: (1) the judgment that climaxes the tribulation period (2 Thess. 2:2; Revelation 16–18) and (2) the consummating judgment of this earth after the millennium that ushers in the new earth (2 Pet. 3:10–13; Rev. 20:7–21:1).

In sum, the day of the Lord: involves judgment only, not judgment and blessing; occurs twice in God's prophetic plan, not once; occurs at the end of the tribulation period, not throughout its duration; occurs again at the end of the millennium, not throughout its duration; as defined here, does not necessarily prove pretribulationism, but it certainly and easily allows for it; supports futuristic premillennialism.

The Second Coming of Jesus

The focal point of prophesied events still to come is the second coming of Jesus Christ. While specific language of "second coming" is rare in Scripture, the con-

11 This section is adapted from Richard L. Mayhue, "The Bible's Watchword: Day of the Lord," *MSJ* 22.1 (2011): 65–88. Used by permission of *MSJ*. For a fuller discussion of the topic, see the article.

cept is well established (Matt. 25:31; John 14:3; Acts 1:11). Belief in the return of Jesus is an indispensable doctrine of orthodox Christianity. The New Testament declares the necessity of a second coming of Jesus (Heb. 9:28). The second coming of Jesus will put an end to the present age and to Daniel's seventieth week, which features a Satan-inspired global reign of the Antichrist. The second coming is also the starting point for the millennial reign of Jesus on the earth. The return of Jesus functions as an important transition point from this present evil age to the righteous kingdom of Jesus.

The second coming is detailed in several New Testament sections. Jesus discussed his return to earth in his Olivet Discourse (Matthew 24–25; Mark 13; Luke 21). His disciples asked him, "What will be the sign of your coming?" (Matt. 24:3). Jesus detailed several events but then declared, "Immediately after the tribulation of those days," the tribes of the earth "will see the Son of Man coming on the clouds of heaven with power and great glory" (Matt. 24:29–30; cf. Luke 21:27; Acts 1:9–11). Peter referred to the second coming and kingdom in Acts 3:19–21:

> Repent therefore, and turn back, that your sins may be blotted out, that times of refreshing may come from the presence of the Lord, and that he may send the Christ appointed for you, Jesus, whom heaven must receive until the time for restoring all the things about which God spoke by the mouth of his holy prophets long ago.

This passage reveals the necessity of a future sending of Christ and the restoration of all things that is connected with the message of the "holy prophets," who are the Old Testament prophets. Thus, while many Old Testament passages apply to the second coming of Jesus, the doctrine of a second coming is primarily a matter of New Testament revelation.

The Millennium

The millennium is the coming thousand-year reign of Jesus and his saints on the earth after this present age and before the eternal state. It occurs soon after Daniel's seventieth week and the return of Jesus, and it is the time when mankind, through the last Adam, Jesus, fulfills the mandate to rule and subdue the earth successfully on God's behalf (Gen. 1:26–28). Jesus the Messiah also fulfills the promise that an ultimate Son of David will rule from David's throne over Israel (Luke 1:32–33) and the entire earth (Zech. 14:9). Jesus's enemies who opposed him during the tribulation are defeated (Rev. 19:20–21). Satan is bound (Rev. 20:1–3). Deceased Old Testament saints and martyrs from the tribulation period come to life and reign with Christ (Dan. 12:2; Rev. 20:4). Jesus rules and shares his kingdom reign with the church of the current age, which remained faithful during persecution (Rev. 2:26–27; 3:21; 5:10). The millennial kingdom is a time of creation renewal, prosperity, righteousness, peace, and international harmony on the earth (Matt. 19:28; Isa. 2:2–4; 11; 65:17–25). It is also the period when all covenant promises, both spiritual and physical, come to complete fulfillment for both Israel and the nations. Israel is saved and restored, and she fulfills her role of leadership and service to the nations, functioning out of the capital city of Jerusalem (Isa. 2:2–4). Nations, who have also become the people of God, experience spiritual and physical blessings alongside Israel (Isa. 19:16–25; 27:6). While the eternal state will certainly exhibit these characteristics perfectly, these matters need to first be fulfilled under the mediatorial rulership of man with the ultimate man, Jesus. When the last Adam completes his mission, then Jesus will hand the kingdom over to God the Father, and the eternal kingdom of the Father will begin (1 Cor. 15:24–28).

The millennium must also come for a Christ-centered reason: There must be a sustained, recognized, and visible reign of Jesus in the realm (the earth) where Jesus experienced rejection at his first coming. At his first coming, Jesus came unto his own, but they did not receive him (John 1:11). He was rejected and killed. The Jesus who stood bound before men at his passion will return in glory on the clouds of heaven to reign over the earth (Matt. 26:63–66). The millennial kingdom spotlights the recognition of Jesus as King. He will reign in glory for an extended period before he hands his kingdom over to the Father in triumph and the eternal state begins (1 Cor. 15:24–28). This is also the time when the saints of God are vindicated and reigning in the realm where they experienced persecution from Satan and the world (Rev. 6:9–11; 20:4).

While conditions in the millennial kingdom are dramatically better than this present age, they have not reached the perfection of the coming eternal state. For example, infant mortality is nonexistent and life spans are greatly expanded, but the possibility of death still exists. A person who dies at the age of one hundred will be thought accursed (Isa. 65:20). Also, unlike today or the coming eternal state, the millennium features nations who serve God yet have inhabitants who are still capable of sinning and receiving punishment (Zech. 14:16–19).

Satan's Final Revolt

At the end of the millennium, Satan is released from his incarceration in the Abyss and leads an intentional revolt against the holy city of Jerusalem. Those involved in this rebellion are immediately destroyed with fire from heaven, and Satan is sent to the lake of fire forever (Rev. 20:7–10).

This rebellion highlights two important truths. First, the presence of unbelievers in the millennium while Satan is bound in the Abyss shows that man's primary problem is a wicked heart, whether Satan is present or not. Even under ideal conditions, with Jesus physically present on the earth, some choose to rebel in sin. Second, the rebellion offers a display of God's power against evil before the great white throne judgment takes place (Rev. 20:11–15) and the eternal state begins (Rev. 21:1–22:5). This is a dramatic display of kingdom power over the final rebellion against God in human history.

The Eternal State

The new heaven and new earth are the final destiny of redeemed humanity. The millennium is past. The great white throne judgment has occurred. Satan and all unbelievers have been cast into the lake of fire forever. A glorious destiny awaits God's saints when they will live on a new earth with direct access to God, who will then live among them. This is what John the apostle explains: "Then I saw a new heaven and a new earth, for the first heaven and the first earth had passed away" (Rev. 21:1).

This "new heaven" and "new earth" language occurs three other times in the Bible: Isaiah 65:17; Isaiah 66:22; and 2 Peter 3:13. The latter reference reveals that this new heaven and new earth are what believers are ultimately anticipating: "But according to his promise we are waiting for new heavens and a new earth in which righteousness dwells" (2 Pet. 3:13). So the believer's ultimate hope and destination is not the current heaven but the new earth.

The most extended discussion of the new heaven and new earth, often called the eternal state, is found in Revelation 21:1–22:5. John's language indicates that the "new heaven" and "new earth" have similarities with and differences from the present heaven and earth. Even though it is "new," there is still a heaven (or sky) and an earth where people will dwell. Yet it is contrasted with the present heaven and earth in that the older heaven and earth have "passed away."

The New Earth: Entirely New or Restored? Will this new heaven and new earth be entirely new, or will it be a restoration and renewal of the present planet? The biblical language describing the destruction of the old order argues in favor of a completely new planet, because the old has been put out of existence. John writes that the first heaven and earth "passed away" (Rev. 21:1). Then there is the strong wording of fiery destruction in 2 Peter 3 (see v. 7, vv. 10–12).

Also, Jesus said, "Heaven and earth will pass away, but my words will not pass away" (Matt. 24:35). Psalm 102 declares that the earth and the heavens "will perish" and will "wear out like a garment" (Ps. 102:25–26). Isaiah 24:20 states, "The earth staggers like a drunken man; it sways like a hut; . . . and it falls, and will not rise again." In his first epistle, John writes, "The world is passing away" (1 John 2:17).

On the other hand, arguments for the renewal of this earth include the following. First, Paul teaches that the creation is longing for glorification, not annihilation (Rom. 8:19) and that the creation was subjected to futility but "in hope" (Rom. 8:20–21). This picture portrays the creation as anticipating glorification, not annihilation.

Second, the creation's anticipation for glorification is linked with the glorification of God's people (Rom. 8:23). A parallel exists. Believers are not annihilated but are resurrected. If the destiny of the earth parallels that of believing mankind, then the creation that exists now will also exist in the future, albeit in a glorified form. Just as creation suffered when man fell because of sin, so too the creation will be restored when God's people are given glorified bodies.

Third, the Bible uses renewal language to describe the earth. Jesus predicted a coming "regeneration" of the cosmos (Matt. 19:28 NASB). Peter foretold a coming restoration of all things (Acts 3:21). This terminology indicates that the universe is heading for a renewal in which the marred earth is fixed and made better than ever. A renewal view asserts that God, not Satan, achieves the final victory over God's "very good" creation (Gen. 1:31).

Those who hold a renewal view reason that the destruction language of 2 Peter 3 does not mean annihilation. The same passage speaks of the world being destroyed by water at the time of Noah (2 Pet. 3:6), but the world was not annihilated with the flood. Also, the best rendering of 2 Peter 3:10 is not that the earth is "burned up," but that "the earth . . . will be exposed." The idea is that of being "found" or "manifested," much like metal that goes through a refiner's fire is not annihilated but purified (Mal. 3:2–3).

Life on the New Earth. The new earth will be a tangible place where believers will dwell in actual physical bodies. God made man as a complex unity of body and soul to live in a physical environment, and man's destiny on the new earth will include residing on a physical planet.

Altogether, there are ten features that make the new earth new and highlight the glory of the coming eternal state. John summarizes the "newness" in Revelation 21:1–22:5: new heaven and earth (21:1); new Jerusalem (21:2, 9–21); new people of God (21:3); new compassion (21:4); new order (21:5–8); new temple (21:22); new light (21:23); new population (21:24–27); new life (22:1–2); new glory (22:3–5).

The Bible speaks of a new Jerusalem that will be the capital city of the new earth (Rev. 21:2), a real city where God will dwell among his people (v. 3). It will have "a great, high wall, with twelve gates" (v. 12). Its features and dimensions ought to be understood literally (vv. 16–17). Other features are clearly figurative (the city is "pure gold, like clear glass," v. 18; the foundations "were adorned with every kind of jewel," v. 19), but this does not detract from the real nature of this city.

No temple exists in the new Jerusalem. Both God the Father and Jesus function as its temple (Rev. 21:22). Since the glory of God illumines the city, no need exists for the light of the sun or moon to shine on it (21:23). The nations and kings of the earth will be drawn to the city because of its light and "will bring their glory into it" (21:24, 26). The presence of nations and world leaders shows that literal nations exist on the new earth and that activity takes place outside the new Jerusalem. While there is one people of God in regard to salvation, the presence of nations reveals ethnic and national diversity on the new earth. The best cultural contributions of these nations are brought to the new Jerusalem. These nations act in complete harmony, as the leaves of the tree of life, which appears for the first time since the fall of man in Genesis 3, function "for the healing of the nations" (Rev. 22:2). Access to the city is always open, as "its gates will never be shut" and no night will ever exist there (21:25). From the throne of God and Jesus the Lamb flows the "river of the water of life" (22:1). The tree of life bears "twelve kinds of fruit, yielding its fruit each month" (Rev. 22:2). The mention of "each month" indicates that time exists on the new earth.

The best part is the presence of God and the Lamb, who are on the throne (Rev. 21:3; 22:3). God's servants will worship him and "will see his face" with eternal, unbroken fellowship (22:3–4). The final depiction of the new Jerusalem reveals that the saints "will reign forever and ever" (22:5). Genesis 1:26–28 revealed that God created man to rule and subdue the earth, and the last verse describing the new earth explains that God's people will be reigning. Then there will be no deception of Satan (Genesis 3) and no potential for sin. Everyone here has been washed in the blood of the Lamb and will serve the Creator willingly. The wicked will never enter this city (Rev. 21:27), and the story ends well for the people of God.

This present fallen world will not exist forever. Sin, the curse, and death will be forever removed (Rev. 22:3). Man will be fully restored in his previously marred relationships with God, people, and creation. This picture expresses the ultimate hope of eschatology. This is the actual, thrilling conclusion to a really great story. So our heartfelt response to the end of the story that we eagerly anticipate and vigorously strive for should be that of the apostle John, "Come, Lord Jesus!" (Rev. 22:20).

Questions:

1. What is the definition of eschatology, and what are the two overall models of eschatology?
2. Why is the use of correct interpretive principles important for the study of biblical eschatology?
3. What was Jesus's view of eschatology?
4. What is personal eschatology, and how is that different for the believer and the unbeliever?
5. What does the Bible teach about the intermediate state? And the resurrection of believers and unbelievers?
6. What does the Bible teach about hell? And heaven?

7. What does the Bible teach about the overarching theme of the kingdom of God?
8. What are the major distinctives of futuristic premillennialism?
9. What are the future judgments?
10. What are the biblical covenants, and why is a correct understanding of them important for eschatology?
11. What are the major views regarding the millennium, and why should one consider premillennialism to be the correct view?
12. What are the important features of Daniel's prophecy of the seventy weeks?
13. What are the eschatological events to come, and what is the order of those events?

GENERAL INDEX

SCRIPTURE INDEX

1 Corinthians

Galatians